THE BIG BOOK OF ENGLISH VERBS

Mark Lester, Ph.D. | **Daniel Franklin** | **Terry Yokota, M.A.**

New York Chicago San Francisco Lisbon London Madrid Mexico City
Milan New Delhi San Juan Seoul Singapore Sydney Toronto

With profound gratitude to our parents,
who taught us language and taught us to love it

Beulah and Roy Lester
Agnes and Clyde Franklin
Ruby and George Yokota

1 2 3 4 5 6 7 8 9 0   QPD/QPD   0 9

ISBN   978-0-07-160288-4 (book and CD set)
MHID   0-07-160288-7 (book and CD set)

ISBN   978-0-07-160290-7 (book)
MHID   0-07-160290-9 (book)

Interior design by Village Bookworks, Inc.

CD-ROM for Windows

To install: Insert the CD-ROM into your CD-ROM drive. The CD-ROM will start automatically.
If it does not, double-click on MY COMPUTER; find and open your CD-ROM disk drive,
then double-click on the install.exe icon. The CD-ROM includes audio instructions to guide
you in using this program effectively.

CD-ROM for Mac

To install: Insert the CD-ROM into your CD-ROM drive. A window will open with the contents
of the CD. Drag the program icon to your Applications folder. For easy access, create an alias
of the program on your desktop or your dock.

Minimum System Requirements:

Computer: Windows 2000, XP, Vista / Mac OS X 10.3.9, 10.4.x, 10.5.x
Pentium II, AMD K6-2, or better / Power PC (G3 recommended) or better; any Intel processor
256 MB RAM
14″ color monitor
8× or better CD-ROM
Sound card
Installation: Necessary free hard-drive space: 300 MB
Settings: 800 × 600 screen resolution
256 (8-bit) colors (minimum)
Thousands (24- or 32-bit) of colors (preferred)

Call 800-722-4726 if the CD-ROM is missing from this book.
For technical support go to http://www.mhprofessional.com/support/technical/contact.php

McGraw-Hill books are available at special quantity discounts to use as premiums and sales
promotions, or for use in corporate training programs. To contact a representative please
e-mail us at bulksales@mcgraw-hill.com.

This book is printed on acid-free paper.

Contents

Preface

The Big Book of English Verbs provides more information on the most important verbs in the English language than any other book ever written. It contains basic conjugations and comprehensive usage patterns for 152 irregular verbs (all the irregular verbs that you will probably encounter), plus 403 of the most commonly used regular verbs: **555** verbs in all, with more than **14,000** example sentences.

No other book provides these unique features:

A complete listing of the complements for each verb

Verb complements are grammatical structures that verbs use to make correct, meaningful sentences. English has 18 basic complements, plus dozens of combinations of these. For instance, the verb *help,* when it means "assist, support," may use two complements together: an object and an infinitive. The infinitive, however, must be in its base form, that is, used without the *to* that normally accompanies an infinitive.

OBJECT + *BASE-FORM INFINITIVE*   We helped **the staff** *answer the phones*.

Most English learners, even advanced ones, make the mistake of using *to* with the infinitive, because that is the more common complement. *The Big Book of English Verbs* is the only book that provides the correct complement in a useful format.

A listing of the important phrasal verb constructions for each verb

Phrasal verbs are idiomatic combinations of verbs plus adverbs or prepositions. For example, the phrasal verb *go off* can mean "to explode," even though nothing in the meaning of *go* or *off* would lead you to expect this meaning.

Moreover, there are important grammatical differences between phrasal verbs that consist of a verb + an adverb (separable phrasal verbs) and those that consist of a verb + a preposition (inseparable phrasal verbs). If the second element in a phrasal verb is an adverb, the adverb can (and in some cases MUST) be placed after the object. If the second element is a preposition, however, it can NEVER be moved away from the verb. *The Big Book of English Verbs* not only gives the meaning of every phrasal verb, but also indicates which combinations are separable and which are inseparable.

We've also included a CD-ROM, which contains self-assessment tests on verb tenses, verb complements, and phrasal verbs, as well as five sets of exercises featuring verb use issues that are difficult for English learners.

We are pleased to provide the keys that unlock the English verb system for English learners worldwide.

Mark Lester
Daniel Franklin
Terry Yokota

The English Verb

VERB FORMS AND TENSE USAGE

The Six Basic Verb Forms

Six basic verb forms are used to create the entire tense system of English: base form, present, past, infinitive, present participle, and past participle. These forms are illustrated in the following chart by the regular verb *walk* and the irregular verb *fly*.

BASE FORM	walk	fly
PRESENT	walk | walks	fly | flies
PAST	walked	flew
INFINITIVE	to walk	to fly
PRESENT PARTICIPLE	walking	flying
PAST PARTICIPLE	walked	flown

See "Guide to Conjugations" on page 10.

Base Form

The base form of a verb is its form in a dictionary entry. For example, if you looked up *sang*, the dictionary would refer you to the base form *sing*.

The base form is also the source (or base) for the present (with a few exceptions), infinitive, and present participle of the verb, whether the verb is regular or irregular.

The base form is used as a verb in three ways.

(1) It follows certain helping verbs, the most important being the **modal auxiliary verbs**, or **modals** for short: *can/could, may/might, will/would, shall/should*, and *must*. (Modal verbs themselves have no base form, infinitive, present participle, or past participle; they have only present and past forms.) Note the base form of the verb *be* in the following sentences.

> I may **be** a little late.
> He will **be** in New York all week.
> You must **be** more careful.

Other verbs followed by the base form of a verb include *dare* (with *not*), *need* (with *not*), and *help*.

> We need not **be** silent on the issue.

(2) The base form is used in imperatives (commands).

> **Be** good!
> **Come** here, please.
> Oh, **stop** it!

(3) Less commonly, the base form is used as a complement of certain verbs.

> OBJECT + BASE-FORM INFINITIVE   We made **them** *be* quiet.
> My parents helped **me** *be* a success.

A base-form infinitive is an infinitive minus the *to*. If an infinitive including the word *to* were substituted for the base-form infinitive in the first example above, the resulting sentence would be ungrammatical.

> ✗ We made **them** *to be* quiet.

1

Present

With the sole exception of the verb *be*, the present form of all verbs is derived directly from the base form. The main difference between the present and base forms is that the third-person singular present form adds **-s** or **-es** to the base form of the verb; all other present forms are identical to the base form.

The base form of *be* is different from all of its present tense forms.

	SINGULAR	PLURAL
FIRST PERSON	I **am**	we **are**
SECOND PERSON	you **are**	you **are**
THIRD PERSON	he/she/it **is**	they **are**

Both the pronunciation and the spelling of the third-person singular present ending are predictable. If the base form ends in a sibilant sound (*s, z, x, sh, ch, tch,* or *j* (as in *judge*)), the ending is pronounced as a separate syllable rhyming with *buzz*. The ending is spelled *-es,* unless the base form already ends in *-e,* in which case only *-s* is added.

BASE FORM	THIRD-PERSON SINGULAR PRESENT FORM
cross	cross**es**
place	place**s**
buzz	buzz**es**
fix	fix**es**
wish	wish**es**
attach	attach**es**
budge	budge**s**

If the base form ends in a voiceless consonant sound other than a sibilant, the ending is pronounced /s/ and is spelled *-es.* (The voiceless consonants are usually spelled with a *p, t, ck, k, f,* or *gh* (when pronounced /f/).

help	help**s**
collect	collect**s**
back	back**s**
park	park**s**
scoff	scoff**s**
laugh	laugh**s**

If the base form ends in a voiced consonant other than a sibilant or in a pronounced vowel (as opposed to a silent final *-e*), the ending is pronounced /z/ and is spelled *-s.*

absorb	absorb**s**
forbid	forbid**s**
dig	dig**s**
love	love**s**
swim	swim**s**
join	join**s**
feel	feel**s**
pay	pay**s**
agree	agree**s**
cry	cri**es**
owe	owe**s**
argue	argue**s**

Note that if the base form ends in *-y* without a preceding vowel, the *-y* changes to *-ie* before the *-s* ending (see *cry* above).

A few verbs have irregular third-person singular present forms.

be	**is**
have	**has**

Two verbs have irregular pronunciations in the third-person singular present form.

do	**does** (rhymes with *buzz*)
say	**says** (rhymes with *fez*)

Past

There are two types of past forms: regular and irregular.

Regular verbs form the past tense by adding *-ed* to the base form (or simply *-d* if the base form already ends in *-e*).

BASE FORM	REGULAR PAST FORM
open	open**ed**
need	need**ed**
move	move**d**
place	place**d**

The regular past ending has three different, but completely predictable, pronunciations. If the base form ends in a /t/ or /d/ sound, the *-ed* is pronounced as a separate syllable rhyming with *bud*.

BASE FORM	PAST FORM PRONOUNCED AS A SEPARATE SYLLABLE
adopt	adopt**ed**
vote	vot**ed**
decide	decid**ed**
depend	depend**ed**

If the base form ends in a voiceless consonant sound other than /t/, the *-ed* is pronounced /t/. The final voiceless consonants are usually spelled with a *p, ck, k, s, sh, ch, tch, x, f,* or *gh* (when pronounced /f/).

BASE FORM	PAST FORM PRONOUNCED AS /t/
tap	tapp**ed**
attack	attack**ed**
miss	miss**ed**
wish	wish**ed**
match	match**ed**
mix	mix**ed**
cough	cough**ed**

Note that if the base form ends in a single consonant preceded by a stressed short vowel, the consonant is usually doubled to form the past: *permit ~ permitted, stop ~ stopped*.

If the base form ends in a pronounced vowel or in a voiced consonant sound other than /d/, the *-ed* is pronounced /d/. The voiced consonants are usually spelled with a *b, g, z, j, m, n, l,* or *r*.

BASE FORM	PAST FORM PRONOUNCED AS /d/
tie	tie**d**
enjoy	enjoy**ed**
judge	judge**d**
kill	kill**ed**
care	care**d**

Note that if the base form ends in *-y* without a preceding vowel, the *-y* changes to *-ie* before the *-d* ending (*cry ~ cried*). Also note the spellings of the past forms of *lay* and *pay*: *laid* and *paid*, respectively.

The past forms of irregular verbs reflect older patterns of forming the past tense. These patterns have merged to such an extent that it is not practical to learn the past forms of irregular verbs on the basis of their historical patterns. Similarities exist, however, in how some irregular verbs form the past tense.

VOWEL CHANGE	ring	**rang**	sing	**sang**
VOWEL CHANGE + -d	sell	**sold**	tell	**told**
NO CHANGE	bet	**bet**	put	**put**	rid	**rid**

Following are the past forms of the ten most common verbs in English, all irregular.

BASE FORM	PAST FORM
be	**was	were**
have	**had**
do	**did**
say	**said** (rhymes with *fed*)
make	**made**
go	**went**
take	**took**
come	**came**
see	**saw**
know	**knew**

Infinitive

The infinitive of a verb consists of *to* + its base form. There are no exceptions—even the verb *be* is regular: *to be*.

BASE FORM	INFINITIVE
walk	**to walk**
fly	**to fly**
be	**to be**
do	**to do**

Infinitives are used as complements of certain verbs.

> I would like **to meet** your friend.
> They invited us **to stay** for dinner.

Present Participle

The present participle is formed by adding *-ing* to the base form.

BASE FORM	PRESENT PARTICIPLE
walk	walk**ing**
fly	fly**ing**
be	be**ing**
do	do**ing**

Note that if a verb ends in a single consonant preceded by a stressed short vowel, the consonant is usually doubled: *bet ~ betting, dig ~ digging, drop ~ dropping, refer ~ referring, rid ~ ridding.* If a verb ends in silent *-e*, the *-e* is dropped before the *-ing* ending: *observe ~ observing, rule ~ ruling, write ~ writing.*

The present participle is used in two ways. By far the more common is after a form of the verb *be* in the progressive tenses.

> The kids were **walking** to the beach.
> I am **flying** to Chicago tomorrow.

Less common is the present participle's use as a complement of certain verbs.

> I hate **doing** the dishes every night.
> I saw Holly **talking** to Christopher.

Past Participle

There are two types of past participles: regular and irregular.

Regular past participles are formed in exactly the same way as the regular past, that is, by adding -ed to the base form. To distinguish the two forms, remember that the past form can occur by itself, but the past participle almost always occurs after a form of *be* or *have*.

Like irregular past forms, irregular past participle forms are unpredictable. There is one generalization, however, we can make about them. In older periods of English, most irregular past participles ended in -*en*. Today, about one third of irregular past participles still retain this -*en* ending. Thus, if an irregular verb form has an -*en* (or -*n*) ending, we know it is a past participle.

BASE FORM	PAST PARTICIPLE
choose	chos**en**
eat	eat**en**
fly	flo**wn**
see	see**n**
speak	spok**en**

Past participles are used in three ways in English.
(1) They are used in the perfect tenses after the helping verb *have*.

> They have **flown** in from Pittsburgh for the wedding.
> We had **walked** over to meet some friends.
> He will have **raised** $200.

(2) Past participles are used in passive sentences after the helping verb *be*.

> Motorists are being **stopped** at the border.
> Her play was **seen** by thousands of people.

(3) Much less common is the past participle's use as a complement of certain verbs.

> We need the car **taken** to the garage for an oil change.

Tense Formation and Usage

The term **tense** can have several different meanings, but we use **tense** to refer to any of the nine different verb constructions that result when the three logical time divisions (present, past, and future) are integrated with the three aspect categories of verbs (simple, perfect, and progressive—*simple* here means that it is not perfect or progressive). These nine tenses are illustrated in the following chart, with first-person singular forms of *walk* and *fly*.

	SIMPLE	PERFECT	PROGRESSIVE
PRESENT	I walk	I have walked	I am walking
	I fly	I have flown	I am flying
PAST	I walked	I had walked	I was walking
	I flew	I had flown	I was flying
FUTURE	I will walk	I will have walked	I will be walking
	I will fly	I will have flown	I will be flying

The Three Simple Tenses

PRESENT TENSE

The most confusing feature of the present tense for English learners is that the simple present tense does not actually signify present time. Its three main uses are the following: (1) making factual statements and generalizations, (2) describing habitual actions, and (3) describing predictable future events or actions.

(1) The simple present tense is used to state objective facts that are not restricted by time.

A mile **is** 5,280 feet.
The Mississippi River **drains** the center of the North American continent.

Similarly, the simple present tense is used to state facts that are true for the foreseeable future.

We **live** on Elm Street.

This sentence means, "We have not always lived on Elm Street, and at some point in the future, we may move. Nevertheless, it is our current intention to remain living on Elm Street indefinitely." Contrast this sentence with the following one, which uses the present progressive tense.

We **are living** on Elm Street.

This sentence means, "We are only living on Elm Street temporarily, and we expect to move eventually."

The simple present tense is also used to make generalizations that are considered valid for the foreseeable future.

I **hate** spinach.
Smoking **causes** cancer.

(2) The simple present tense is used to describe habitual actions.

Bob **checks** his e-mail first thing in the morning.

This sentence describes what Bob normally does first thing in the morning. It does not mean that Bob is checking his e-mail now, at this very moment. The sentence would still be valid if Bob were on vacation and hadn't checked his e-mail in a week.

(3) The simple present tense is often used for near-future events or actions that one expects to happen.

Our flight **leaves** at nine.
I **return** home on Sunday.

Note that the simple present tense is not used for uncertain future events. For example, it is not used to describe future weather.

✗ It **rains** tomorrow.

PAST TENSE

The simple past tense describes an event or action that was completed before the present moment in time; that is, the event or action has already taken place. The past tense can refer to a single point in past time.

We **moved** into our house on September 5, 1980.

The past tense can also refer to a span of time in the past, as long as it was completed before the present.

Janet **worked** in sales for nearly ten years.

This sentence means that Janet is no longer working in sales at this time.

In addition, the simple past tense has inherited one of the functions of the subjunctive from older periods of English: indicating that the speaker is talking hypothetically or even contrary to fact. This hypothetical use of the past tense does NOT indicate past time. Its most common use is in IF-CLAUSES.

If I **were** you, I **would** be sure that I **was** finished on time.

The use of *were* rather than the expected *was* survives from an old subjunctive form. Notice also that the other two verbs in the sentence are in the past tense, even though the sentence does not refer to past time.

FUTURE TENSE

The simple future tense consists of the helping verb *will* followed by the base form of the main verb.

> I **will take** a taxi to the airport.
> They **will be** disappointed if you don't see them.

The helping verb *will* is one of the nine modal auxiliary verbs: *can/could, may/might, will/ would, shall/should,* and *must.* Although *will* is used to form the future tense, any of the other eight modals can refer to future time.

> I **can take** a cab to the airport.
> I **could take** a cab to the airport.
> I **may take** a cab to the airport.
> I **must take** a cab to the airport.

Each of the nine modals has its own range of meanings, allowing English speakers to make a number of subtly different statements about the possibility, certainty, desirability, or necessity of a future action.

The Three Perfect Tenses

The three perfect tenses consist of a form of the helping verb *have* followed by the past participle of the main verb. The present tense form of *have* is used for the present perfect, the past tense form for the past perfect, and the future tense form for the future perfect.

PRESENT PERFECT TENSE

The present perfect tense consists of *have* or *has* followed by the past participle of the main verb. This tense is used to describe an action that began in the past and has continued up to the present time, with the implication that it will continue into the future. The best way to understand the present perfect tense is to compare it to the past tense.

> PAST TENSE John **lived** in Los Angeles for five years.
> PRESENT PERFECT TENSE John **has lived** in Los Angeles for five years.

According to the past tense sentence, John no longer lives in Los Angeles; he has moved. According to the present perfect tense sentence, John still lives in Los Angeles and is expected to continue living there into the foreseeable future.

PAST PERFECT TENSE

The past perfect tense consists of *had* followed by the past participle of the main verb. The most common use of this tense is to emphasize that an event in the past was completed before a more recent event took place.

> My parents **had left** for the airport before my plane landed.

This sentence describes two past-time events. The first event is the parents' leaving for the airport, and the second event is the plane landing. The use of the past perfect tense makes it clear that the first event was completed before the second one occurred. Note that the events can also be stated in reverse order.

> Before my plane landed, my parents **had left** for the airport.

FUTURE PERFECT TENSE

The future perfect tense consists of *will have* followed by the past participle of the main verb. This tense, which is rarely used, describes a future action or event that must be completed BEFORE a second future action, event, or time. The following sentence uses the future perfect tense to describe an event completed before a second event.

> The game **will have started** before we get to the stadium.

Note that the two events can also be stated in reverse order.

> Before we get to the stadium, the game **will have started**.

The following sentence uses the future perfect tense to describe an action completed before a specific time in the future.

> They **will have finished** by noon.

The Three Progressive Tenses

The progressive tenses consist of a form of the helping verb *be* followed by the present participle of the main verb. The present progressive uses the present tense of *be*, the past progressive uses the past tense of *be*, and the future progressive uses the future tense of *be*.

The progressive tenses are used to describe an action in progress (hence the name **progressive**) at some present, past, or future time.

PRESENT PROGRESSIVE TENSE

The present progressive tense consists of *am, are,* or *is* followed by the present participle of the main verb. This tense can describe an action at the precise moment that the sentence is spoken.

> Turn the TV down! I **am talking** on the phone.

The present progressive tense can also refer to a span of time that includes the present.

> Global warming **is causing** climate change.

In addition, the tense is often used to describe future plans or events.

> We **are going** to Paris this June.
> Hurry, the taxi **is coming** in 10 minutes.

PAST PROGRESSIVE TENSE

The past progressive tense consists of *was* or *were* followed by the present participle of the main verb. This tense refers to an action that took place at or during some time in the past, whether it occurred at a specific moment or during a span of time in the past.

> I **was working** at my desk by 9 o'clock.
> During the game, he **was talking** on his cell phone.

The time in the past can be defined by another event.

> We **were working** in the garden when we heard the news.

The past progressive tense can also be used in an adverbial clause.

> We heard the news while we **were working** in the garden.

FUTURE PROGRESSIVE TENSE

The future progressive tense consists of *will be* followed by the present participle of the main verb. This tense describes an activity that will occur at some time in the future, whether it will occur at a specific moment or, more commonly, during a span of time in the future.

> Their plane **will be landing** at 6:35.
> During the school year, I **will be living** on campus.

Often, the future time is defined by a present tense adverbial clause.

> We **will be staying** in a motel while they remodel the kitchen.

The Intensive Tenses

The so-called intensive tenses consist of a form of the helping verb *do* followed by the base form of the main verb. The present intensive tense is formed with *do* or *does,* and the past intensive tense is formed with *did.* There is no future intensive tense, nor is the intensive used in the progressive tenses.

The intensive tenses are used in three ways.

(1) They emphasize the fact that the action of the verb is or was actually performed.

> She **does like** going to the opera.
> I **did arrive** on time.

(2) The intensive tenses are used with *not* to form the negative of the simple present and past tenses.

> They **do** not **go** to the library anymore.
> We **did** not **see** Larry at the mall.

(3) The intensive tenses are used to ask simple yes/no questions.

> **Does** the teacher **color** her hair?
> **Did** all the children **finish** the assignment?

The Passive Voice

In traditional grammar, verbs have **voice**. Voice is determined by whether the subject is the performer of the action of the verb (**active voice**) or the receiver of the action (**passive voice**). Compare the following sentences.

> ACTIVE VOICE   The dog **bit** the man.
> PASSIVE VOICE   The man **was bitten** by the dog.

In the active voice sentence, the subject (the dog) performs the action of biting. In the passive voice sentence, the subject (the man) does not perform the action of biting; instead, he is the receiver of the action. The *by* phrase is not necessary and is, in fact, usually not used.

The passive voice is easily recognized, because it uses a form of the helping verb *be* immediately followed by the past participle form of the main verb—a combination found only in passive voice sentences.

> PRESENT TENSE PASSIVE   Our flight **is canceled**.
> PAST TENSE PASSIVE   Our flight **was canceled**.
> FUTURE TENSE PASSIVE   Our flight **will be canceled**.

The progressive tenses may be used in the passive voice, although the future progressive tense usually sounds awkward.

> PRESENT PROGRESSIVE TENSE PASSIVE   Our car **is being washed**.
> PAST PROGRESSIVE TENSE PASSIVE   Our car **was being washed**.
> FUTURE PROGRESSIVE TENSE PASSIVE   *?* Our car **will be being washed**.

The passive voice has two primary uses.

(1) It is used to switch attention from the subject of an active voice sentence to another part of the sentence (usually, but not always, the direct object).

> ACTIVE VOICE   **The authors** sent the manuscript to Marisa.
> PASSIVE VOICE   **The manuscript** was sent to Marisa.
> PASSIVE VOICE   **Marisa** was sent the manuscript.

(2) The passive voice is used when the performer of the verb's action is not known.

> This beer was brewed in St. Louis, Missouri.
> The car was stolen yesterday afternoon.

Text continues on page 12.

GUIDE TO CONJUGATIONS

①   ②
433   **send**   send | sends · sent · have sent   ④ ☑ IRREGULAR
                                                    ③

⑤ **PRESENT**

I send	we send
you send	you send
he/she/it sends	they send

⑦ • *The firm sends letters by registered mail.*

⑥ **PRESENT PROGRESSIVE**

I am sending	we are sending
you are sending	you are sending
he/she/it is sending	they are sending

• *I am sending you an e-mail.*

PAST

I sent	we sent
you sent	you sent
he/she/it sent	they sent

• *They sent us a nice note.*

PAST PROGRESSIVE

I was sending	we were sending
you were sending	you were sending
he/she/it was sending	they were sending

• *They were sending their children to a private school.*

⑧ **PRESENT PERFECT** ... have | has sent
PAST PERFECT ... had sent

FUTURE ... will send
FUTURE PROGRESSIVE ... will be sending
FUTURE PERFECT ... will have sent

⑨ **PAST PASSIVE**

I was sent	we were sent
you were sent	you were sent
he/she/it was sent	they were sent

• *The letter was sent to the wrong address.*

1 This is the verb number.

2 This is the base form of the verb. If this were a Top 40 Verb, there would be an additional page for Complements, Phrasal Verbs, and Expressions, and both pages would have a Top 40 Verb icon at the bottom.

3 These are the principal parts of the verb: present | third-person singular present · past · past perfect (containing the past participle).

4 This indicates whether a verb forms its past and past participle regularly. Some verbs, like *shine* (No. 443), have both regular and irregular forms.

5 Five tense paradigms are shown in the table format familiar to most English learners, where row and column represent verb person and number, respectively. These five tenses were chosen because they are the most frequently used.

6 Some verbs are never used in the progressive tenses, like *belong* (No. 58); others are rarely used in these tenses, like *prefer* (No. 353). For these verbs, the progressive forms are not given. We only show forms that an English learner might be expected to use in ordinary conversation or writing.

7 An example sentence is supplied for each tense shown.

8 The forms for these five tenses are displayed in single lines with no pronouns. Thus, all nine simple, progressive, and perfect tenses in the active voice are shown (see pages 5–9), plus the most frequently used passive tense.

9 Some verbs are never used in the passive voice, like *amount* (No. 25); no forms are given for these. Other verbs cannot have a personal subject in the passive voice, like *achieve* (No. 8); only *it* and *they* forms are given for these. Some writers, of course, may use these personal passive forms in highly figurative or poetic senses. However, because an English learner might be led to use these forms incorrectly, we do not show them.

Some verbs are only used in the passive voice when they are part of a phrasal verb, like *dream* (No. 163). Because this is a valid use of the passive, all forms are shown for these verbs.

GUIDE TO COMPLEMENTS AND PHRASAL VERBS

1 This meaning of *pour* requires no complement.

2 The blank line indicates that this meaning of *pour* requires a complement. Either the single complement OBJECT or the double complement INDIRECT OBJECT + DIRECT OBJECT may be used.

3 The object in the example sentence is bold.

4 One element in a double complement is italicized to distinguish the two complements. The INDIRECT OBJECT + DIRECT OBJECT construction may have a *for* PARAPHRASE, as shown below.

5 The direct object is bold, and the indirect object is bold italic (corresponding to the italic in the complement name).

6 An example sentence in the passive voice uses bold italic to indicate the second element of a double complement.

7 This use of *pour* as a phrasal verb requires no complement. Several phrasal verb particles are possible in this construction.

8 This use of *pour* as a phrasal verb requires a complement. The SEP on the blank line indicates that the phrasal verb is separable (see page 15).

9 This use of *pour* as a phrasal verb requires a complement. The blank line without SEP indicates that the phrasal verb is inseparable (see page 15).

Complement types are not identified in the Phrasal Verbs section, since virtually every complement of a phrasal verb functions as an object of the verb, whether it is an OBJECT, REFLEXIVE PRONOUN, or PRESENT PARTICIPLE. Bold and bold italic are not used in examples sentences in the Phrasal Verbs section.

The Expressions section (not shown here) includes a blank line for a required complement.

(COMPLEMENTS)

① **pour** *fall/flow steadily* [OF A LIQUID]
It has been pouring all night.
The milk was pouring down the baby's chin.

pour ___②___ *fill a glass/cup with* [a liquid], *serve* [a liquid] ③
OBJECT
Please pour **the wine**, will you?
Don't pour **the coffee** until the guests arrive.

④ INDIRECT OBJECT + DIRECT OBJECT
We poured *the children* **some lemonade**. ⑤
The hostess poured *everyone* **a glass of wine**.

for PARAPHRASE
We poured **some lemonade** *for the children*.
The hostess poured **a glass of wine** *for everyone*.

pour ___ *dispense* [a liquid]
OBJECT + ADVERB OF PLACE
I poured **the marinade** *over the meat*.
He poured **the water** *down the drain*.
She carefully poured **the medicine** *into the dispenser*.

⑥ PASSIVE
The unused olive oil was poured *back into the bottle*.

(PHRASAL VERBS)

⑦ **pour back/down/forth/in/out/through/** etc. *flow in a specified direction*
The levee collapsed, and the floodwater poured in.

⑧ **pour** ___SEP___ **away/back/in/out/**etc. *cause to flow in a specified direction*
Pour the milk back into the jug.

⑨ **pour into / out of** ___ *enter/exit in large numbers*
Fans poured into the stadium.

pour [oneself] into ___ *become very involved in*
After being laid off, he poured himself into finding a new job.

pour ___SEP___ **out** *discard* [a liquid]
The milk is past its expiration date; we need to pour it out.

VERB COMPLEMENTS

We use the term **complement** as a collective word for all the different grammatical structures required by verbs to make a grammatical sentence. **Complement** is much broader than the term **transitive**. In traditional grammar, a transitive verb must be followed by a direct or indirect object. The term **complement**, however, includes not only objects, but predicate adjectives, predicate nouns, several types of infinitives and clauses, and several types of adverbs. A verb may require one complement or more than one complement to make a grammatical sentence. Many intransitive verbs require no complement at all, for example, the intransitive verb *cried* in *John cried*.

The verb *put* with the sense "place, set" takes the double complement OBJECT + ADVERB OF PLACE, illustrated by the following sentence.

> I put **my keys** *on the dresser*.

If either complement is deleted, the sentence is ungrammatical.

> ✗ I put *on the dresser*.
> ✗ I put **my keys**.

When you use the verb *put* to mean "place, set," you must put SOMETHING (an object) SOMEWHERE (an adverb of place).

Most English verbs may be used with more than one type of complement. The choice of complement type is determined by the particular meaning of a verb. If the meaning of the verb changes, the complement type(s) may change too, and vice versa: If the complement type changes, the verb's meaning often changes.

To illustrate the interconnection between verb meaning and complement type, consider the complements for the verb *argue*.

argue *disagree, quarrel*	They argue all the time.
argue _____ *debate*	
OBJECT	The justices argued **the issue**.
argue _____ *assert, try to prove by giving reasons*	
OBJECT	Vince argued **his case** before the judge.
THAT-CLAUSE	Vince argued **that he was innocent**.

There are as many entries for a verb as there are distinct meanings, three in the case of *argue*. Each entry has its own group of complements that can be used with that particular meaning, including the possibility of no complement, as in the first entry for *argue*.

If a verb is followed by a blank line (_____), the verb with that particular meaning requires an actual complement to make the sentence grammatical. The types of complements that the meaning requires are given in small capital letters as subentries. For example, the third meaning of *argue* (*assert, try to prove by giving reasons*) can take either of two different complements: an OBJECT or a THAT-CLAUSE (a noun clause beginning with *that*). To the right of the complement type are one or more sentences illustrating use of the complement. The words of the sentence that correspond to the complement are in bold. Using the third entry for *argue*, **his case** is an example of an OBJECT complement and **that he was innocent** is an example of a THAT-CLAUSE complement. (See "Guide to Complements and Phrasal Verbs" on the previous page.)

If a verb is NOT followed by a blank line, it is **intransitive**, that is, it does not require an actual complement to make the sentence grammatical. In this book, the intransitive meanings of a verb are listed before the meanings that require actual complements. In the example of *argue*, the fact that the first meaning (*disagree, quarrel*) is not followed by a blank line means that the verb with this particular meaning is intransitive. In the example sentence *They argue all the time*, the adverbial expression *all the time* is not obligatory; the sentence would still be grammatical if we deleted it.

They argue.

Most of the complement types in this book will be familiar to you, but some may require further explanation. Following is a list of special terms that you will encounter in the description of complements.

THAT-CLAUSE This is a noun clause beginning with *that*.

> I thought **that dinner was good, but a little too heavy**.

BASE-FORM THAT-CLAUSE The verb in the THAT-CLAUSE is in its uninflected base form and does not need to agree with the subject. For example, *be* in the following THAT-CLAUSE does not agree with its subject *defendant*.

> The court ordered **that the defendant be kept in jail**.

PRESENT PARTICIPLE This term includes both present participles and gerunds (present participles modified by a possessive noun or pronoun).

> I hated **leaving so early**. (PRESENT PARTICIPLE)
> I hated **John's leaving so early**. (GERUND)

WH-CLAUSE This is a noun clause beginning with a *wh*-word (*who, whom, whose, what, which, when, where, why,* and *how* (which does not actually begin with *wh*)), as well as compounds of these words (*whoever, whomever, whatever,* etc.).

> Did you hear **who won the game?**
> We will grow **what sells the best**.
> They will hire **whoever is the most qualified**.

WH-INFINITIVE This is a noun clause beginning with a *wh*-word followed by an infinitive.

> Raymond asked him **what to do next**.
> I told them **where to go**.

Complement Types

This book uses 18 basic, or single-element, complement types, which appear in bold in the example sentences. Many of these basic complement types can be combined and used together. If two complements are used, one complement (usually the first) is in bold and the other in bold italic.

Single Grammatical Element Complements

ADVERB OF TIME	The presentation will last **fifty minutes**.
ADVERB OF PLACE	He always stays **in town** during the week.
ADVERB OF PLACE TO/FROM	The refugees fled **into the woods**.
ADVERB OF MANNER	The children behaved **badly**.
OBJECT	I hurt **my elbow**.
*for/in/of/to/*etc. OBJECT	Haste always results **in confusion**. The bill amounted **to $137.50**.
REFLEXIVE PRONOUN	I flung **myself** into jazz.
PREDICATE NOUN	Her father was **a famous artist**.
PREDICATE ADJECTIVE	The moon was **bright**.
INFINITIVE	We would like **to meet your friends**.
THAT-CLAUSE	We soon discovered **that we had made a mistake**.
BASE-FORM THAT-CLAUSE	The doctor recommended **that Mr. Smith be kept overnight for observation**.

WH-CLAUSE	We will soon know **who will get the job.**
	We will soon know **where the new office will be.**
WH-INFINITIVE	The teacher explained **where to get the information.**
	The teacher explained **how to do it.**
IF-CLAUSE	He asked **if we were ready.**
PRESENT PARTICIPLE	I hate **(our) leaving in the middle of a meeting.**
PAST PARTICIPLE	We felt **overwhelmed by the experience.**
DIRECT QUOTATION	**"Good morning,"** she said. **"We're glad you're here."**

Multiple Grammatical Element Complements

Fifteen multiple element complements are commonly used.

OBJECT + ADVERB OF PLACE	We left **the children** *at home.*
OBJECT + ADVERB OF PLACE TO/FROM	He drove **us** *to the station.*
	A policeman directed **the traffic** *onto a side street.*
INDIRECT OBJECT + DIRECT OBJECT	The driver gave *us* **directions.**
	He did *us* **a big favor.**
to PARAPHRASE	The driver gave **directions** *to us.*
for PARAPHRASE	He did **a big favor** *for us.*
OBJECT + PREDICATE NOUN	They called **the idea** *a stroke of genius.*
OBJECT + PREDICATE ADJECTIVE	They called **the idea** *silly.*
OBJECT + INFINITIVE	They invited **us** *to stay for dinner.*
OBJECT + BASE-FORM INFINITIVE	We helped **them** *answer the phones.*
OBJECT + THAT-CLAUSE	He persuaded **the jury** *that his client was innocent.*
OBJECT + BASE-FORM THAT-CLAUSE	He urged **John** *that he reconsider his decision.*
OBJECT + WH-CLAUSE	I told **my friends** *what they should expect.*
OBJECT + WH-INFINITIVE	I told **my friends** *what to expect.*
OBJECT + PRESENT PARTICIPLE	I hate **him** *complaining about everything.*
OBJECT + PAST PARTICIPLE	We need **the filter** *changed in our furnace.*

Other combinations may be used by certain verbs. Note that OBJECT is divided into INDIRECT OBJECT and DIRECT OBJECT complements for certain verbs, like *give* and *do* above.

PHRASAL VERBS

A **phrasal verb** is a verb + particle combination that has a meaning different from the combined meanings of the verb and particle (an adverb or preposition). For example, the verb *pick* means "choose, select" or "pluck, remove; gather, harvest." When combined with *up,* it can have at least a dozen different meanings. Four of the meanings for *pick up* are given here with example sentences.

increase, improve	Business has **picked up** since Christmas.
stop for and take along	Would you **pick** us **up** at seven?
learn easily	I **picked up** Italian over the summer.
make tidy	You must **pick up** your room before going out to play.

None of the ordinary meanings of *pick* and *up* indicate that these words used together would have the meanings above. That is why we call phrasal verbs **idiomatic.**

English abounds with phrasal verbs. In fact, there are many more phrasal verbs in English than nonphrasal verbs. Because they are idiomatic, phrasal verbs can be difficult for English learners.

Not all verb + particle combinations are phrasal verbs. In some cases, the particle is used as a preposition that doesn't change the basic meaning of the verb. *Arrange for* is an example.

arrange _____ *plan, cause something to happen*
   (*for*) OBJECT   They will arrange **(for) a celebration**.
   for OBJECT + INFINITIVE   He arranged **for John *to visit them in Chicago***.

In the first sentence above, *for* is optional. In the second sentence, *for* is obligatory, but it doesn't change the meaning of *arrange*. For this reason, *arrange for* is not considered a phrasal verb, and it is included in the Complements section instead.

Some verbs must always be used with a particular preposition; for example, *amount* is always used with *to*.

amount _____ *add up*
   to OBJECT   The bill amounted **to $137.50**.
   to WH-CLAUSE   It amounted **to however much you could afford**.

Since *amount* must always be used with *to*, *amount to* is included in the Complements section.

Separable and Inseparable Phrasal Verbs

Many phrasal verbs take no object.

settle down *establish a home*   Our son eventually settled down in south St. Louis.
swim off *swim in the opposite*   After we fed the dolphins, they swam off.
direction

For these phrasal verbs, the particle must be placed immediately after the verb.

Most phrasal verbs, however, take an object. For some of these, the particle can be placed after the object—away from the verb—and for others, the particle must be placed after the verb. There are no simple rules for determining whether the particle is placed after the verb or after the object.

Generally, if the particle is considered a preposition, it must be placed after the verb; this type of phrasal verb is called **inseparable**. However, if the particle is considered an adverb, it can, and sometimes MUST, be placed after the object; this type of phrasal verb is called **separable**. Most phrasal verbs are separable.

INSEPARABLE PHRASAL VERB   My brother **depended on** his car. ("rely on")
SEPARABLE PHRASAL VERB   My brother **turned on** his car. ("switch on")

In the first example, *on* is considered a preposition, and therefore it cannot be placed after the object *his car*.

    ✗ My brother **depended** his car **on**.

In the second example, *on* is considered an adverb, and therefore it can be placed after the object *his car*.

    My brother **turned** his car **on**.

For separable phrasal verbs, the particle can be placed after the verb or after the object. There is an important exception, however: If the object is a pronoun, the particle MUST be placed after the object.

    My brother **turned** it **on**.
    ✗ My brother **turned on** it.

You can test whether a phrasal verb is separable or inseparable by using a pronoun as its object: If the particle MUST be placed after the pronoun object, the phrasal verb is separable; otherwise, it is inseparable.

Note that if the object of a separable phrasal verb is a long noun phrase, it is better to place the particle after the verb.

Don't **throw away** the lamp that I spent four hours fixing.
? Don't **throw** the lamp that I spent four hours fixing **away**.

You can often determine whether a phrasal verb is separable by knowing whether the particle is considered an adverb or a preposition. In the preceding examples, *on* is used both as a preposition (*depend on*) and as an adverb (*turn on*). However, some particles are almost always used as prepositions; these generally form inseparable phrasal verbs.

across	into
after	of
against	to
at	upon
between	with
for	

The club **leaped at** Kyle's offer.
✗ The club **leaped** Kyle's offer **at**.

Acid was **eating into** the countertop.
✗ Acid was **eating** the countertop **into**.

Some particles are almost always used as adverbs; these particles generally form separable phrasal verbs.

ahead	forth
aside	in
away	off
back	out
down	up

She **poured off** a little sauce before cooking.
She **poured** a little sauce **off** before cooking.
She **poured** it **off**.

A young attorney **drew up** my will.
A young attorney **drew** my will **up**.
A young attorney **drew** it **up**.

Other particles are separable with some verbs and inseparable with others.

about	on
along	over
around	through
behind	under
by	

See the examples with *depend on* and *turn on* on the previous page.

To indicate a separable phrasal verb, a blank line with SEP is used for the complement (object).

figure __SEP__ **out** *solve, determine*   Tim figured the crossword puzzle out in six minutes.
Tim figured out the crossword puzzle in six minutes.
Tim figured it out in six minutes.

An inseparable phrasal verb is indicated by a blank line (without SEP) after the particle.

figure on _____ *plan/count/depend on*   Let's figure on going to a movie after dinner.

A phrasal verb may have more than one particle. If there are two or more particles, the last particle is almost always a preposition with its own object.

beat _____ **back to** *return to [a place]*   My sister beat her friend back to the station.
sooner than

For phrasal verbs like this, the object is placed between the verb and its particle(s). In the sentence above, the object of the verb (*her friend*) is placed between *beat* and *back*, and the object of the preposition (*the station*) is placed after the preposition.

The Most Common Phrasal Particles

Following is a list, with examples, of the particles most commonly used in phrasal verbs.

across
come across _____ *find by accident*   She **came across** her high school yearbook.

after
keep after _____ *nag, harass*   Mom **keeps after** us about our homework.

along
pass _SEP_ **along** *transfer [a price change]*   The store **passed along** the price increase to its customers.

around
get around _____ *avoid*   He **got around** the problem by installing new software.

aside
lay _SEP_ **aside** *save*   She **laid aside** $100 a month for her son's college education.

at
leap at _____ *accept eagerly*   The class **leaped at** Hilary's offer to bake a cake.

away
pack _SEP_ **away** *store*   Gene and Jan **packed** the baby clothes **away**.

back
cut _SEP_ **back** *shorten*   We must **cut** the shrubs **back** after they flower.

behind
fall behind (on _____ **)** *lag behind*   They **were falling behind on** the rent.

between
come between _____ *cause trouble between*   We can't let a silly quarrel **come between** us.

down
knock _SEP_ **down** *demolish*   Workers **knocked** the vacant building **down**.

for
go for _____ *be attracted by*   She **goes for** men with beards.

forth
put _SEP_ **forth** *propose, suggest*   Johanna **put forth** her plan to save the black-footed ferret.

in
hold _SEP_ **in** *suppress*   The candidate is good at **holding** his emotions **in**.

in on
move in on _____ *get closer to*   The FBI **is moving in on** the counterfeiter.

into
marry into _____ *become a member of by marrying someone who is a member*   Diana **married into** royalty.

of

complain of _____ *report the symptoms of*

Rosemarie **complains of** arthritis and backache.

off

run _SEP_ off *print, make copies of*

I **ran** several extra sets **off** for you.

on

improve on _____ *make something better than*

How could you **improve on** Post-it notes?

out

hand _SEP_ out *distribute*

She **handed out** the schedule to reporters.

out of

change out of _____ *replace [one set of clothing with another]*

I'm all sweaty—I have to **change out of** these running clothes.

over

make _SEP_ over *change the appearance of*

The programmer **made over** his cubicle with movie posters.

through

carry _SEP_ through *accomplish*

She is determined to **carry through** her vision of a drug-free America.

to

look to _____ *depend on*

Students **look to** their teachers for help.

under

fall under _____ *be influenced/controlled by*

The princess **fell under** the power of the wicked queen.

up

mark _SEP_ up *raise the price of*

The art dealer **marks** paintings **up** 200%.

up on

catch _____ up on *bring up-to-date about*

The assistant will **catch** the actor **up on** the news.

upon

hit upon _____ *discover*

She **hit upon** the idea of extending Medicare to people 55 and over.

with

live with _____ *endure, put up with*

He **lived with** a limp for the rest of his life.

Note the double particles *in on, out of,* and *up on* in the list above.

Verbs of Motion

Verbs of motion typically form many phrasal verbs with particles considered to be adverbs. This is listed as the first entry in the Phrasal Verbs section.

pull away/back/down/in/out/over/up/etc. *move in a specified direction*

The van **pulled away** slowly.
We're lost. Let's **pull over** and look at a map.

pull _SEP_ along/aside/away/over/under/up/etc. *cause to move in a specified direction*

Can you **pull** the kids **away** from the TV?
Sam **pulled up** a chair and sat down.

EXPRESSIONS

An Expressions section is included on verb pages where space permits. The entries are common idiomatic set phrases that are useful to the English learner.

555
ENGLISH VERBS

Conjugations
Complements
Phrasal Verbs
Expressions

TOP 40 VERBS

The following forty verbs have been selected because of their semantic and syntactic richness, both in their basic meanings and complements and in their phrasal verbs. A full page of example sentences provides guidance on correct usage and immediately precedes or follows the conjugation/complements page.

	Verb no.
be	52
bear	53
blow	66
break	68
bring	69
call	75
carry	77
catch	79
come	95
cut	128
do	161
feel	201
find	206
get	226
give	227
go	228
have	239
hold	246
keep	273
lay	282
leave	287
look	300
make	304
move	316
pass	337
play	345
pull	370
put	374
read	381
run	421
see	428
set	436
show	446
slip	455
stand	470
strike	484
take	505
throw	515
turn	524
work	551

PRESENT

I abandon	we abandon
you abandon	you abandon
he/she/it abandons	they abandon

• *He often abandons failing projects.*

PRESENT PROGRESSIVE

I am abandoning	we are abandoning
you are abandoning	you are abandoning
he/she/it is abandoning	they are abandoning

• *We are abandoning our original plan.*

PAST

I abandoned	we abandoned
you abandoned	you abandoned
he/she/it abandoned	they abandoned

• *She abandoned any hope of succeeding.*

PAST PROGRESSIVE

I was abandoning	we were abandoning
you were abandoning	you were abandoning
he/she/it was abandoning	they were abandoning

• *They were abandoning the search.*

PRESENT PERFECT ... have | has abandoned
PAST PERFECT ... had abandoned

FUTURE ... will abandon
FUTURE PROGRESSIVE ... will be abandoning
FUTURE PERFECT ... will have abandoned

PAST PASSIVE

I was abandoned	we were abandoned
you were abandoned	you were abandoned
he/she/it was abandoned	they were abandoned

• *That mine was abandoned years ago.*

COMPLEMENTS

abandon _____ *give up completely*
  OBJECT (+ *to* OBJECT)

The soldiers have abandoned **their attack.**
Our neighbors abandoned **the cats *to the snowstorm.***

  WH-CLAUSE

We abandoned **what we were trying to do.**

  PRESENT PARTICIPLE

They abandoned **trying to put out the fire.**

abandon _____ *stop using, leave behind*
  OBJECT

The captain is abandoning **the sinking ship.**
The villagers abandoned **their flooded houses.**
The immigrants will eventually abandon **their native language.**

abandon _____ *give [oneself] over completely*
  REFLEXIVE PRONOUN + *to* OBJECT

John abandoned **himself *to his work.***

  REFLEXIVE PRONOUN + *to* WH-CLAUSE

She abandoned **herself *to what she had always wanted to do.***

  REFLEXIVE PRONOUN +
    to PRESENT PARTICIPLE

They abandoned **themselves *to eating everything in the refrigerator.***

PRESENT

I absorb	we absorb
you absorb	you absorb
he/she/it absorbs	they absorb

• *Sand absorbs water rapidly.*

PRESENT PROGRESSIVE

I am absorbing	we are absorbing
you are absorbing	you are absorbing
he/she/it is absorbing	they are absorbing

• *We are absorbing the new information.*

PAST

I absorbed	we absorbed
you absorbed	you absorbed
he/she/it absorbed	they absorbed

• *We absorbed severe financial losses.*

PAST PROGRESSIVE

I was absorbing	we were absorbing
you were absorbing	you were absorbing
he/she/it was absorbing	they were absorbing

• *I was absorbing the bad news.*

PRESENT PERFECT   ... have | has absorbed
PAST PERFECT   ... had absorbed

FUTURE   ... will absorb
FUTURE PROGRESSIVE   ... will be absorbing
FUTURE PERFECT   ... will have absorbed

PAST PASSIVE

I was absorbed	we were absorbed
you were absorbed	you were absorbed
he/she/it was absorbed	they were absorbed

• *The gas was absorbed by charcoal.*

COMPLEMENTS

absorb _____ *take in and make a part of oneself*

OBJECT

The paper towels absorbed **the spilled milk**.
Plants absorb **nourishment** through their roots.
China has always absorbed **its invaders**.
An acoustic ceiling will absorb **most of the sound**.
The largest union absorbed **two others** into its organization.

PASSIVE   Alcohol is absorbed into the bloodstream quickly.

WH-CLAUSE

We absorbed **what we needed to pass the course**.
They absorbed **whatever they were taught**.

absorb _____ *assume, take on*

OBJECT   We will absorb **all the losses**.

WH-CLAUSE   The company will absorb **whatever costs are incurred**.

PHRASAL VERBS

absorb in/into _____ *pass through*   Does lead absorb directly into
          the skin?

EXPRESSIONS

absorbed *engaged entirely*   Our professor is absorbed in thought—
          don't disturb her.

2a accceptonal (handwritten)

PRESENT

I accept	we accept
you accept	you accept
he/she/it accepts	they accept

• *I accept your generous offer.*

PAST

I accepted	we accepted
you accepted	you accepted
he/she/it accepted	they accepted

• *The court accepted our argument.*

PRESENT PERFECT ... have | has accepted
PAST PERFECT   ... had accepted

PRESENT PROGRESSIVE

I am accepting	we are accepting
you are accepting	you are accepting
he/she/it is accepting	they are accepting

• *Jane is accepting the award for all of us.*

PAST PROGRESSIVE

I was accepting	we were accepting
you were accepting	you were accepting
he/she/it was accepting	they were accepting

• *They were accepting all valid receipts.*

FUTURE   ... will accept
FUTURE PROGRESSIVE ... will be accepting
FUTURE PERFECT   ... will have accepted

PAST PASSIVE

I was accepted	we were accepted
you were accepted	you were accepted
he/she/it was accepted	they were accepted

• *The gifts were accepted gratefully by the hosts.*

(**COMPLEMENTS**)

accept _____ *receive willingly*

OBJECT | They accepted **the peace offering.**
She accepted **my apology.**
We should accept **the newspaper's offer of free publicity.**

accept _____ *take as payment*

OBJECT | The grocery store doesn't accept **personal checks.**

accept _____ *agree to, believe to be valid/true*

OBJECT | Everyone accepted **the dimensions of the problem.**
Why won't she accept **my explanation?**

OBJECT + *as* PREDICATE NOUN | The board accepted **Tim** *as their spokesperson.*
They will accept **Cleveland** *as the regional headquarters.*

PASSIVE | Cleveland was accepted *as the regional headquarters.*

OBJECT + *as* PREDICATE ADJECTIVE | Should we accept **the company's offer** *as final?*
Experts accept **the document** *as authentic.*

PASSIVE | The document was accepted *as authentic.*

THAT-CLAUSE | I accepted **that the situation was quite unusual.**

WH-CLAUSE | Everyone has accepted **what needs to be done.**

PRESENT PARTICIPLE | He will accept **Richard's naming his own successor.**

(**EXPRESSIONS**)

acceptable damage *damage that is tolerable* | Fewer than 20 flooded homes is acceptable damage.

acceptable loss(es) *loss(es) that is/are tolerable* | There is no acceptable loss of life in such a disaster.
The president believes 4,000 combat deaths to be in the range of acceptable losses.

dotrzymać (towarzystwa)

4 accompany

accompany | accompanies ·
accompanied · have accompanied

☑ REGULAR

Bezokolicznik

PRESENT *(czas teraźniejszy)*

I accompany   we accompany
you accompany   you accompany
he/she/it accompanies they accompany

• *The dog accompanies us everywhere.*

PRESENT PROGRESSIVE *czas teraźniejszy*

I am accompanying   we are accompanying
you are accompanying   you are accompanying
he/she/it is accompanying they are accompanying

• *Jane is accompanying us as far as Mexico City.*

PAST *(przeszły)*

I accompanied   we accompanied
you accompanied   you accompanied
he/she/it accompanied they accompanied

• *My parents accompanied us on the trip.*

PAST PROGRESSIVE

I was accompanying   we were accompanying
you were accompanying   you were accompanying
he/she/it was accompanying they were accompanying

• *I was accompanying them around the site.*

PRESENT PERFECT ... have | has accompanied
PAST PERFECT   ... had accompanied

FUTURE   ... will accompany *– czas przyszły*
FUTURE PROGRESSIVE   ... will be accompanying
FUTURE PERFECT   ... will have accompanied

PAST PASSIVE

I was accompanied   we were accompanied
you were accompanied   you were accompanied
he/she/it was accompanied they were accompanied

• *The CEO was accompanied by the board.*

COMPLEMENTS

accompany _____ *go with as a companion*

   OBJECT   Robert accompanied **the reporter.**

   PASSIVE   All children must be accompanied by an adult.

   OBJECT + ADVERB OF PLACE TO/FROM   We accompanied **them** *to the showroom.*
They will accompany **you** *back from the restaurant.*
Hermione will be accompanying **Harry Potter** *on his next
   adventure.*

accompany _____ *be associated/included with*

   OBJECT   Color photographs accompany **the text.**
In the South, gravy often accompanies **biscuits.**
A glass of wine accompanied **each course.**

accompany _____ *play an instrument in support of the musical performance of*

   OBJECT   Jan will accompany **the singers** on the piano.

PRESENT

I accomplish	we accomplish
you accomplish	you accomplish
he/she/it accomplishes	they accomplish

• *She accomplishes what she needs to.*

PRESENT PROGRESSIVE

I am accomplishing	we are accomplishing
you are accomplishing	you are accomplishing
he/she/it is accomplishing	they are accomplishing

• *I am accomplishing a lot here.*

PAST

I accomplished	we accomplished
you accomplished	you accomplished
he/she/it accomplished	they accomplished

• *I accomplished everything I set out to do.*

PAST PROGRESSIVE

I was accomplishing	we were accomplishing
you were accomplishing	you were accomplishing
he/she/it was accomplishing	they were accomplishing

• *We were accomplishing our goals.*

PRESENT PERFECT   ... have | has accomplished
PAST PERFECT   ... had accomplished

FUTURE   ... will accomplish
FUTURE PROGRESSIVE   ... will be accomplishing
FUTURE PERFECT   ... will have accomplished

PAST PASSIVE

—	—
—	—
it was accomplished	they were accomplished

• *Our goal was accomplished by hard work.*

COMPLEMENTS

accomplish _____ *finish, complete successfully*

OBJECT	I will accomplish **my goal**.
	We accomplished **a lot** today.
	We will accomplish **our task** soon.
WH-CLAUSE	They accomplished **what they set out to do**.
	We will accomplish **whatever we promised to do**.

EXPRESSIONS

accomplished *skillful, expert*   Peter is an accomplished pianist.
Jessica is quite accomplished on the harpsichord.

PRESENT

I account	we account
you account	you account
he/she/it accounts	they account

• *That accounts for everything!*

PRESENT PROGRESSIVE

Account is rarely used in the progressive tenses.

PAST

I accounted	we accounted
you accounted	you accounted
he/she/it accounted	they accounted

• *Poor sales accounted for our losses.*

PAST PROGRESSIVE

Account is rarely used in the progressive tenses.

PRESENT PERFECT ... have | has accounted
PAST PERFECT ... had accounted

FUTURE ... will account
FUTURE PROGRESSIVE —
FUTURE PERFECT ... will have accounted

PAST PASSIVE

I was accounted	we were accounted
you were accounted	you were accounted
he/she/it was accounted	they were accounted

• *All the keys were accounted for.*

───────────────────────────────────(COMPLEMENTS)───

account _____ *consider*

OBJECT + (to be) PREDICATE NOUN	I accounted **myself *(to be) an honest person.***
	I accounted **Alex *(to be) a good friend.***
PASSIVE	Alex was accounted *(to be) a good friend.*
OBJECT + (to be) PREDICATE ADJECTIVE	I accounted **myself *(to be) lucky.***
	I accounted **Jan *(to be) reliable.***
PASSIVE	Jan was accounted *(to be) reliable.*

───────────────────────────────────(PHRASAL VERBS)───

account for _____ *explain*

We still can't account for what
 happened to the money.
Can you account for their missing the train?

account for _____ *make sure of the whereabouts of*

I had accounted for all the office computers.

account for _____ *be the sole/primary factor for*

Albert Pujols accounted for all the Cardinals' runs.
Cars and trucks account for 18% of Germany's exports.
The recession accounted for our doing so badly recently.

───────────────────────────────────(EXPRESSIONS)───

take _____ **into account** *take into consideration*

Have you taken increased gas
 prices into account?
We took into account that most people are undecided.

PRESENT

I accuse	we accuse
you accuse	you accuse
he/she/it accuses	they accuse

• *He often accuses us of carelessness.*

PRESENT PROGRESSIVE

I am accusing	we are accusing
you are accusing	you are accusing
he/she/it is accusing	they are accusing

• *They are accusing him of being negligent.*

PAST

I accused	we accused
you accused	you accused
he/she/it accused	they accused

• *The manager accused George at first.*

PAST PROGRESSIVE

I was accusing	we were accusing
you were accusing	you were accusing
he/she/it was accusing	they were accusing

• *The editor was accusing him of plagiarism.*

PRESENT PERFECT ... have | has accused
PAST PERFECT   ... had accused

FUTURE   ... will accuse
FUTURE PROGRESSIVE ... will be accusing
FUTURE PERFECT   ... will have accused

PAST PASSIVE

I was accused	we were accused
you were accused	you were accused
he/she/it was accused	they were accused

• *I was never accused of anything.*

───────────────────────────────(COMPLEMENTS)───

accuse _____ *charge with [a fault/offense]*

OBJECT	The inspector accused **Frank.**
	I am not accusing **anyone.**
OBJECT + *of* OBJECT	He accused **Frank** *of the crime.*
	They accused **the company** *of fraud.*
PASSIVE	The company was accused *of fraud.*
OBJECT + *of* PRESENT PARTICIPLE	He accused **Frank** *of doing it.*
	They accused **the company** *of committing fraud.*
PASSIVE	The company was accused *of committing fraud.*

───────────────────────────────(EXPRESSIONS)───

the accused *the defendant(s) in a criminal case*

The accused has a long list of prior arrests.

PRESENT

I achieve	we achieve
you achieve	you achieve
he/she/it achieves	they achieve

• *He usually achieves his goals.*

PRESENT PROGRESSIVE

I am achieving	we are achieving
you are achieving	you are achieving
he/she/it is achieving	they are achieving

• *We are achieving a high level of success.*

PAST

I achieved	we achieved
you achieved	you achieved
he/she/it achieved	they achieved

• *They achieved a fine record of safety.*

PAST PROGRESSIVE

I was achieving	we were achieving
you were achieving	you were achieving
he/she/it was achieving	they were achieving

• *They were achieving record sales.*

PRESENT PERFECT ... have | has achieved
PAST PERFECT ... had achieved

FUTURE ... will achieve
FUTURE PROGRESSIVE ... will be achieving
FUTURE PERFECT ... will have achieved

PAST PASSIVE

—	—
—	—
it was achieved	they were achieved

• *Our goals were gradually achieved.*

COMPLEMENTS

achieve _____ attain, accomplish

OBJECT   We achieved **the results we had hoped for.**
I have achieved **a high level of proficiency in French.**
The company has achieved **a 10% increase in production.**
The band achieved **overnight fame.**
We will be achieving **a lot** this year.

WH-CLAUSE   She achieved **what she set out to do.**
They always achieve **whatever they say they will.**

EXPRESSIONS

achiever *one who attains success*   Polly was a dreamer; Molly was
an achiever.

PRESENT

I acquire	we acquire
you acquire	you acquire
he/she/it acquires	they acquire

• *I acquire a few extra pounds every winter.*

PRESENT PROGRESSIVE

I am acquiring	we are acquiring
you are acquiring	you are acquiring
he/she/it is acquiring	they are acquiring

• *They are acquiring an excellent reputation.*

PAST

I acquired	we acquired
you acquired	you acquired
he/she/it acquired	they acquired

• *The band acquired a loyal following.*

PAST PROGRESSIVE

I was acquiring	we were acquiring
you were acquiring	you were acquiring
he/she/it was acquiring	they were acquiring

• *She was acquiring a first-class education there.*

PRESENT PERFECT … have | has acquired
PAST PERFECT … had acquired

FUTURE … will acquire
FUTURE PROGRESSIVE … will be acquiring
FUTURE PERFECT … will have acquired

PAST PASSIVE

I was acquired	we were acquired
you were acquired	you were acquired
he/she/it was acquired	they were acquired

• *Success was acquired one step at a time.*

COMPLEMENTS

acquire _____ *get, obtain*
  OBJECT

Students must acquire **proficiency in math.**
Pets help children acquire **immunity to allergies.**

acquire _____ *take possession of*
  OBJECT

I acquired **100 shares of ABC Corporation.**
The company will acquire **a new store in Brooklyn.**
The museum acquired **an Albrecht Dürer watercolor.**
  PASSIVE   He was acquired in a trade with the White Sox.
  WH-CLAUSE   I acquired **what I wanted** over the Internet.
They acquired **whatever resources they needed.**

EXPRESSIONS

acquire a taste for _____ *develop an appreciation for*

She will never acquire a taste for
  coffee.
They acquired a taste for visiting exotic islands.

acquired taste *appreciation developed after repeated experience*

Beer is an acquired taste, like coffee and tea.

PRESENT

I act · we act
you act · you act
he/she/it acts · they act
 • John always acts as if he were the boss.

PAST

I acted · we acted
you acted · you acted
he/she/it acted · they acted
 • They acted properly.

PRESENT PERFECT … have | has acted
PAST PERFECT … had acted

PRESENT PROGRESSIVE

I am acting · we are acting
you are acting · you are acting
he/she/it is acting · they are acting
 • The kids are acting pretty silly.

PAST PROGRESSIVE

I was acting · we were acting
you were acting · you were acting
he/she/it was acting · they were acting
 • They were acting under my orders.

FUTURE … will act
FUTURE PROGRESSIVE … will be acting
FUTURE PERFECT … will have acted

PAST PASSIVE

— · —
— · —
it was acted · they were acted
 • The role was acted by Jason Jones.

COMPLEMENTS

act *do something* — Think before you act.
We must act now to stop global warming.

act *have an effect* — The sedative acted quickly.

act ____ *behave*
ADVERB OF MANNER — He acted **foolishly**.
He acted **like a fool**.
They acted **like they didn't have a care in the world**.
Politicians always act **in their own interests**.

act ____ *behave like, pretend to be*
PREDICATE NOUN — Please act **your age**!
He acted **the fool**.
PREDICATE ADJECTIVE — He acted **dumb**.
She acted **embarrassed**.

act ____ *play the role of*
OBJECT — Martin always acts **the expert on international trade**.
Colin acted **the part of a visiting Englishman** in the play.
PASSIVE — The part of a visiting Englishman was acted by Colin.

PHRASAL VERBS

act as ____ *perform the duty/function of* — She acted as club president for three years.

act for ____ *represent the interests of* — The realtor is acting for the homeowner.

act on ____ *take action on* — The police acted on the anonymous tip.

act out *misbehave* — Randy has been acting out in the classroom.

act SEP **out** *put into action* — He's acting out his frustration.
She acted out her dream of being a ballerina.

act up *misbehave* — The children were acting up at the school picnic.

act up *malfunction* — My computer is acting up.

act up *become troublesome* — Grandpa's arthritis is acting up again.

PRESENT

I add	we add
you add	you add
he/she/it adds	they add

• *We add sales tax to every purchase.*

PRESENT PROGRESSIVE

I am adding	we are adding
you are adding	you are adding
he/she/it is adding	they are adding

• *We are adding a new feature to the program.*

PAST

I added	we added
you added	you added
he/she/it added	they added

• *Poor weather added weeks to the job.*

PAST PROGRESSIVE

I was adding	we were adding
you were adding	you were adding
he/she/it was adding	they were adding

• *I was adding onto the garage.*

PRESENT PERFECT ... have | has added
PAST PERFECT ... had added

FUTURE ... will add
FUTURE PROGRESSIVE ... will be adding
FUTURE PERFECT ... will have added

PAST PASSIVE

I was added	we were added
you were added	you were added
he/she/it was added	they were added

• *The dock was added on over the winter.*

COMPLEMENTS

add *perform addition*
     The second grader adds very well.

add ____ *make an addition*
  TO OBJECT
     We added **to our retirement fund.**

add ____ *combine to form a sum*
  OBJECT
     I added **the long column of numbers.**

add ____ *join so as to increase the size or quantity of something*
  OBJECT (+ to/into/onto OBJECT)
     I added **too much water.**
     The lawyer added **another clause** *to the agreement.*
     We will add **$1,000** *to our retirement fund.*
     Add **a cup of milk** *to the dry ingredients.*
     Add **the egg whites** *into the mixture.*
     Our neighbors added **a second floor** *onto their garage.*
  WH-CLAUSE
     They added **whatever supplies they needed.**

add ____ *create as an improvement*
  OBJECT
     Framed photos add **a nice touch** to your office.

add ____ *say further*
  OBJECT
     The speaker added **a quote from Mark Twain.**
  THAT-CLAUSE
     Bob added **that he fully supported the plan.**
  DIRECT QUOTATION
     Bob added, **"I fully support the plan."**

PHRASAL VERBS

add on *build an addition*
     Unless we add on, we won't
     have enough space.

add _SEP_ on *build [an addition] to an existing structure*
     Let's add on a deck.

add _SEP_ together *combine to form a sum*
     Add together these three numbers.
     If I add these CDs together with those, I'll have quite
     a collection.

add up *make sense*
     These figures of yours don't add up.
     His story about ghosts just doesn't add up.

add up to ____ *amount to*
     Four quarters or two halves—it adds up to the same thing.
     Coupons and advertised specials add up to big savings.

I address   we address
you address   you address
he/she/it addresses   they address

• *He addresses current issues in his talks.*

I am addressing   we are addressing
you are addressing   you are addressing
he/she/it is addressing   they are addressing

• *I am addressing envelopes right now.*

I addressed   we addressed
you addressed   you addressed
he/she/it addressed   they addressed

• *We addressed this problem last summer.*

I was addressing   we were addressing
you were addressing   you were addressing
he/she/it was addressing   they were addressing

• *He was addressing some visitors.*

... have | has addressed
... had addressed

... will address
... will be addressing
... will have addressed

I was addressed   we were addressed
you were addressed   you were addressed
he/she/it was addressed   they were addressed

• *This concern was addressed in the proposal.*

NOTE: The verb *address* is always stressed on the second syllable.
The noun *address* is usually stressed on the first syllable when it refers to a location.

───(COMPLEMENTS)───

address _____ *speak to*

OBJECT   He addressed **the waiting crowd.**

address _____ *speak to, using a title or in a particular manner*

OBJECT + *as* OBJECT   You should address **the queen** *as "Your Majesty."*
                                          The politicians addressed **each other** *as equals.*

address _____ *speak about, discuss*

OBJECT   Senator Blather addressed **the farm bill.**

WH-CLAUSE   They addressed **what they should do next.**
                                          He addressed **how they could solve the problem.**

PRESENT PARTICIPLE   He addressed **his voting on the issue.**

address _____ *direct [one's words]*

OBJECT + *to* OBJECT   Address **your remarks** *to me,* please.

OBJECT + *to* WH-CLAUSE   You may address **your complaints** *to whoever will listen.*

address _____ *direct one's attention/efforts to*

REFLEXIVE PRONOUN + *to* OBJECT   The CEO will address **himself** *to workplace safety*
                                              problems.

address _____ *write directions for delivery on*

OBJECT   They addressed **all the envelopes and packages.**

PRESENT

I adjust	we adjust
you adjust	you adjust
he/she/it adjusts	they adjust

- *She adjusts well to new situations.*

PRESENT PROGRESSIVE

I am adjusting	we are adjusting
you are adjusting	you are adjusting
he/she/it is adjusting	they are adjusting

- *I am adjusting the children's seat belts.*

PAST

I adjusted	we adjusted
you adjusted	you adjusted
he/she/it adjusted	they adjusted

- *We adjusted our budget plans.*

PAST PROGRESSIVE

I was adjusting	we were adjusting
you were adjusting	you were adjusting
he/she/it was adjusting	they were adjusting

- *They were constantly adjusting the thermostat.*

PRESENT PERFECT   ... have | has adjusted
PAST PERFECT   ... had adjusted

FUTURE   ... will adjust
FUTURE PROGRESSIVE   ... will be adjusting
FUTURE PERFECT   ... will have adjusted

PAST PASSIVE

—	—
—	—
it was adjusted	they were adjusted

- *The data were adjusted for inflation.*

COMPLEMENTS

adjust *adapt, conform*

He adjusts easily in strange
   surroundings.
The cougar adjusted well in captivity.
The monitor adjusts in height from 3 to 12 inches.

adjust ____ *adapt, conform*
  to OBJECT

He didn't adjust well **to early morning classes.**
I will eventually adjust **to the change in schedule.**

adjust ____ *improve, make correct*
  OBJECT

We adjusted **the projections for future income.**
Pat needs to adjust **his attitude.**
I adjusted **the car seat and the rearview mirror.**

  PASSIVE

The car seat and the rearview mirror were adjusted.

  WH-CLAUSE

I adjusted **what we had previously forecast.**
They adjusted **how they had previously measured
  growth.**

EXPRESSIONS

adjustable rate mortgage *a mortgage whose
interest rate is periodically adjusted*

If you plan to keep your home
  for less than five years, get an adjustable
  rate mortgage.

PRESENT

I admit	we admit
you admit	you admit
he/she/it admits	they admit

• *Harry admits doing it.*

PRESENT PROGRESSIVE

I am admitting	we are admitting
you are admitting	you are admitting
he/she/it is admitting	they are admitting

• *Brad is finally admitting his mistake.*

PAST

I admitted	we admitted
you admitted	you admitted
he/she/it admitted	they admitted

• *He admitted that he was wrong.*

PAST PROGRESSIVE

I was admitting	we were admitting
you were admitting	you were admitting
he/she/it was admitting	they were admitting

• *They were admitting more international students.*

PRESENT PERFECT ... have | has admitted
PAST PERFECT ... had admitted

FUTURE ... will admit
FUTURE PROGRESSIVE ... will be admitting
FUTURE PERFECT ... will have admitted

PAST PASSIVE

I was admitted	we were admitted
you were admitted	you were admitted
he/she/it was admitted	they were admitted

• *John was admitted to graduate school.*

(**COMPLEMENTS**)

admit _____ *acknowledge as true*

(to) OBJECT — Allen admitted **(to) the mistake.**
Allen admitted **the mistake** to the teacher.

OBJECT + *to be* PREDICATE ADJECTIVE — Rodney admits **his claims** *to be false.*

THAT-CLAUSE — They admitted **that they had goofed.**

(to) PRESENT PARTICIPLE — Sam admits **(to) his taking the money.**
Sam admits **(to) taking the money.**
Zack admits **(to) being inconsiderate sometimes.**

admit _____ *permit*

of OBJECT — The poem admits **of two different interpretations.**

admit _____ *permit to enter*

OBJECT — The guards admitted **us.**
The school only admits **in-state applicants.**
One ticket admits **four adults.**

OBJECT + to/into OBJECT — UCLA admitted **Lou** *to its MBA program.*
The judge admitted **the videotape** *into evidence.*
The manager admitted **us** *into the secure area.*

admit _____ *have space/seating for*

OBJECT — The concert hall admits **750 people.**

admit _____ *accept [into a hospital as a patient]*

OBJECT — The hospital admitted **17 new patients** yesterday.

PASSIVE — I was admitted to the hospital for surgery.

PRESENT

I adopt	we adopt
you adopt	you adopt
he/she/it adopts	they adopt

• *The actor adopts the lifestyle of a monk.*

PRESENT PROGRESSIVE

I am adopting	we are adopting
you are adopting	you are adopting
he/she/it is adopting	they are adopting

• *They are adopting a child in July.*

PAST

I adopted	we adopted
you adopted	you adopted
he/she/it adopted	they adopted

• *The company adopted a new logo.*

PAST PROGRESSIVE

I was adopting	we were adopting
you were adopting	you were adopting
he/she/it was adopting	they were adopting

• *They were adopting an aggressive attitude.*

PRESENT PERFECT ... have | has adopted
PAST PERFECT   ... had adopted

FUTURE   ... will adopt
FUTURE PROGRESSIVE ... will be adopting
FUTURE PERFECT   ... will have adopted

PAST PASSIVE

I was adopted	we were adopted
you were adopted	you were adopted
he/she/it was adopted	they were adopted

• *The messaging system was adopted recently.*

(COMPLEMENTS)

NOTE: *Adopt* is often confused with *adapt*, which means "to modify/adjust."
Compare the following sentences.
   We adopted the plan. (*took and used*)
   We adapted the plan to fit within the budget. (*adjusted*)

adopt *legally take another person's child*   Our neighbors hope to adopt.
as one's own

adopt ____ *legally take [another person's child] as one's own*
   OBJECT   They have adopted **three children.**

adopt ____ *take and use [ideas, suggestions] as one's own*
   OBJECT   We have adopted **your approach to the problem.**
                                 They will adopt **the format that you developed.**
                                 Plato adopted **Socrates' philosophy** as his own.
   WH-CLAUSE   The company will adopt **whichever plan the committee
                                    recommends.**

adopt ____ *take and follow [a course of action]*
   OBJECT   After his setback, John adopted **a very different tone.**

adopt ____ *approve, accept*
   OBJECT   The committee adopted **the amendment.**
                                 Professor Jones adopted **the book** as the required text.
   WH-CLAUSE   The Senate adopted **what the subcommittee
                                    recommended.**

PRESENT

I advance	we advance
you advance	you advance
he/she/it advances	they advance

• *He advances the interests of his company.*

PRESENT PROGRESSIVE

I am advancing	we are advancing
you are advancing	you are advancing
he/she/it is advancing	they are advancing

• *They are advancing the date of the meeting.*

PAST

I advanced	we advanced
you advanced	you advanced
he/she/it advanced	they advanced

• *I advanced equal opportunity hiring.*

PAST PROGRESSIVE

I was advancing	we were advancing
you were advancing	you were advancing
he/she/it was advancing	they were advancing

• *We were advancing all along the front.*

PRESENT PERFECT … have | has advanced
PAST PERFECT … had advanced

FUTURE … will advance
FUTURE PROGRESSIVE … will be advancing
FUTURE PERFECT … will have advanced

PAST PASSIVE

I was advanced	we were advanced
you were advanced	you were advanced
he/she/it was advanced	they were advanced

• *The timetable was advanced by two weeks.*

COMPLEMENTS

advance *move forward in space/time/ value/status*

The army is advancing on the town from the southeast.
The hours were steadily advancing.
The euro advanced against the dollar on the news of a slower economy.
Ray slowly advanced from rank to rank.

advance _____ *bring forward in space/time*
OBJECT

The Seahawks advanced **the football** six yards on first down.
The general advanced **the infantry**.
I advanced **the time of the meeting**.

advance _____ *advocate, propose*
OBJECT
WH-CLAUSE

George is always advancing **his own causes**.
He advances **whatever will do him the most good**.

advance _____ *give a promotion to*
OBJECT
WH-CLAUSE

We advanced **Alice** from clerk to assistant manager.
They will advance **whoever they think is most qualified**.

advance _____ *loan, pay ahead of time*
INDIRECT OBJECT + DIRECT OBJECT
to PARAPHRASE
PASSIVE

I advanced *him* **a week's salary**.
I advanced **a week's salary** *to him*.
He was advanced a week's salary.

EXPRESSIONS

advanced *higher-level*

The professor assigned an advanced text in astronomy.

advanced *far along in time*

My cousin was diagnosed with an advanced stage of cancer.
Ruth took up knitting at an advanced age.

advanced *progressive*

The politician's advanced ideas met a lot of resistance.

advanced degree *a university degree higher than a bachelor's*

Sam decided to pursue an advanced degree at Eastern State University.

PRESENT

I advertise	we advertise
you advertise	you advertise
he/she/it advertises	they advertise

• *The company advertises only on the Web.*

PRESENT PROGRESSIVE

I am advertising	we are advertising
you are advertising	you are advertising
he/she/it is advertising	they are advertising

• *They are advertising several new jobs.*

PAST

I advertised	we advertised
you advertised	you advertised
he/she/it advertised	they advertised

• *They advertised frequently in the* Times.

PAST PROGRESSIVE

I was advertising	we were advertising
you were advertising	you were advertising
he/she/it was advertising	they were advertising

• *We were advertising the product on TV.*

PRESENT PERFECT ... have | has advertised
PAST PERFECT ... had advertised

FUTURE ... will advertise
FUTURE PROGRESSIVE ... will be advertising
FUTURE PERFECT ... will have advertised

PAST PASSIVE

I was advertised	we were advertised
you were advertised	you were advertised
he/she/it was advertised	they were advertised

• *The job opening was widely advertised.*

(**COMPLEMENTS**)

advertise *solicit business in the media*
They advertise in the New York metropolitan area.

advertise _____ *solicit applicants in the media*
  for OBJECT
The church advertised **for a new administrator.**

advertise _____ *publicize/promote [a product/service]*
  OBJECT
We usually advertise **new products** heavily.
Chris doesn't advertise **his lawnmowing business.**
  WH-CLAUSE
We only advertise **whatever we need to sell quickly.**

advertise _____ *make publicly known*
  OBJECT
Their announcement just advertised **their failures.**
We advertised **the rollout of the new models** nationally.
  OBJECT + *as* PREDICATE NOUN
Donald advertised **himself** *as an expert.*
They advertised **the school** *as the only totally green institution on the East Coast.*
  PASSIVE
I was advertised *as the youngest competitor in the meet.*
  OBJECT + *as* PREDICATE ADJECTIVE
Willie advertised **himself** *as fluent in Russian.*
  THAT-CLAUSE
They advertised **that they were an equal opportunity employer.**
The negotiators advertised **that they were open to new proposals.**
  PRESENT PARTICIPLE
The company advertised **their opening a new plant in China.**

(**EXPRESSIONS**)

as advertised *according to published claims*
This spyware performs as advertised.
The job was not quite as advertised.

<table>
<tr><td colspan="2">

PRESENT

I advise · · · · · · · · we advise
you advise · · · · · · · you advise
he/she/it advises · · · they advise

</td><td colspan="2">

PRESENT PROGRESSIVE

I am advising · · · · · · · · · · · we are advising
you are advising · · · · · · · · · you are advising
he/she/it is advising · · · · · · they are advising

</td></tr>
</table>

PRESENT

I advise — we advise
you advise — you advise
he/she/it advises — they advise

• *The consultant advises us to reduce costs.*

PRESENT PROGRESSIVE

I am advising — we are advising
you are advising — you are advising
he/she/it is advising — they are advising

• *The TV is advising us to stay off the roads.*

PAST

I advised — we advised
you advised — you advised
he/she/it advised — they advised

• *John advised us against renewing.*

PAST PROGRESSIVE

I was advising — we were advising
you were advising — you were advising
he/she/it was advising — they were advising

• *I was advising my clients to sell.*

PRESENT PERFECT ... have | has advised
PAST PERFECT ... had advised

FUTURE ... will advise
FUTURE PROGRESSIVE ... will be advising
FUTURE PERFECT ... will have advised

PAST PASSIVE

I was advised — we were advised
you were advised — you were advised
he/she/it was advised — they were advised

• *We were advised to be very cautious.*

NOTE: The verb *advise* is spelled with an *s*, pronounced /z/.
The related noun *advice* is spelled with a *c*, pronounced /s/.

COMPLEMENTS

advise *counsel*

This expert only advises on economic matters.

advise ____ *counsel*

OBJECT

I advise **caution.**
The company advises **large corporations.**

OBJECT + *about/on* OBJECT

The art department can advise **you** *about website design.*
Rebecca will advise **Raymond** *on which computer to buy.*

OBJECT + *against* PRESENT PARTICIPLE

The accountant advised **me** *against taking out a loan.*

OBJECT + INFINITIVE

The doctor advised **me** *to get X-rays of my elbow.*

PASSIVE

The company was advised *to diversify its product lines.*

BASE-FORM THAT-CLAUSE

We advise **that you be careful driving in this weather.**

advise ____ *warn, suggest*

OBJECT + THAT-CLAUSE

He advised **us** *that we might need to sell the stock.*

advise ____ *notify about*

OBJECT + *of* OBJECT

The judge advised **them** *of their rights.*
The director advised **them** *of the consequences of being late.*

PRESENT

I affect	we affect
you affect	you affect
he/she/it affects	they affect

• *John affects an interest in opera.*

PRESENT PROGRESSIVE

I am affecting	we are affecting
you are affecting	you are affecting
he/she/it is affecting	they are affecting

• *The bad weather is affecting sales.*

PAST

I affected	we affected
you affected	you affected
he/she/it affected	they affected

• *The loss affected us greatly.*

PAST PROGRESSIVE

I was affecting	we were affecting
you were affecting	you were affecting
he/she/it was affecting	they were affecting

• *The recession was affecting everyone.*

PRESENT PERFECT ... have | has affected
PAST PERFECT ... had affected

FUTURE ... will affect
FUTURE PROGRESSIVE ... will be affecting
FUTURE PERFECT ... will have affected

PAST PASSIVE

I was affected	we were affected
you were affected	you were affected
he/she/it was affected	they were affected

• *Everyone was affected by the tragedy.*

NOTE: The verb *affect* is often confused with the noun *effect*. (They are usually pronounced the same way.) Visualize the two *e*'s in the expression *the effect*: The word *the* is never used before the verb *affect*.

───(**COMPLEMENTS**)───

affect _____ *have an effect on*

OBJECT	John affected **everyone he met** for the better.
	Exercise affects **both blood pressure and pulse.**
WH-CLAUSE	It really affected **what we could do.**
	Exercise affects **how well your brain functions.**
PRESENT PARTICIPLE	The cutbacks affected **our doing the job properly.**

affect _____ *put on a false/pretentious show of*

OBJECT	Cal was affecting **an upper-class British accent.**
	Dick affected **an air of superiority.**
WH-CLAUSE	He affected **whatever was fashionable at the moment.**
PRESENT PARTICIPLE	He affected **being a citizen of the world.**

PRESENT

I afford	we afford
you afford	you afford
he/she/it affords	they afford

• *It affords you a wonderful opportunity.*

PRESENT PROGRESSIVE

I am affording	we are affording
you are affording	you are affording
he/she/it is affording	they are affording

• *We are affording you one last chance.*

PAST

I afforded	we afforded
you afforded	you afforded
he/she/it afforded	they afforded

• *The vacation afforded us time to read.*

PAST PROGRESSIVE

I was affording	we were affording
you were affording	you were affording
he/she/it was affording	they were affording

• *The salesperson was affording me a good deal.*

PRESENT PERFECT ... have | has afforded
PAST PERFECT ... had afforded

FUTURE ... will afford
FUTURE PROGRESSIVE ... will be affording
FUTURE PERFECT ... will have afforded

PAST PASSIVE

I was afforded	we were afforded
you were afforded	you were afforded
he/she/it was afforded	they were afforded

• *No opportunity to congregate was afforded the protesters.*

COMPLEMENTS

afford _____ *have enough money for*
  OBJECT
  WH-CLAUSE

They can afford **a new car.**
We couldn't afford **what they were asking.**

afford _____ *bear without serious risk*
  OBJECT
  INFINITIVE
  PRESENT PARTICIPLE

We can afford **patience in the negotiations.**
I can't afford **to make the same mistake again.**
We can't afford **his making the same mistake again.**

afford _____ *spare*
  OBJECT

We can only afford **half an hour** for lunch.

afford _____ *provide*
  OBJECT

The porch afforded **a wonderful view of the valley.**
The sun affords **warmth and life.**

  INDIRECT OBJECT + DIRECT OBJECT
   for PARAPHRASE

It afforded *me* **a wonderful opportunity.**
It afforded **a wonderful opportunity** *for me.*

EXPRESSIONS

affordable housing *dwelling units whose total cost is within the means of a particular group of people*

Affordable housing is essential to the health of a community.

PRESENT

I agree	we agree
you agree	you agree
he/she/it agrees	they agree

- *She agrees that we should do it.*

PAST

I agreed	we agreed
you agreed	you agreed
he/she/it agreed	they agreed

- *We agreed to a new contract.*

PRESENT PERFECT   ... have | has agreed
PAST PERFECT   ... had agreed

PRESENT PROGRESSIVE

I am agreeing	we are agreeing
you are agreeing	you are agreeing
he/she/it is agreeing	they are agreeing

- *You are always agreeing with them!*

PAST PROGRESSIVE

I was agreeing	we were agreeing
you were agreeing	you were agreeing
he/she/it was agreeing	they were agreeing

- *They were agreeing with each other.*

FUTURE   ... will agree
FUTURE PROGRESSIVE   ... will be agreeing
FUTURE PERFECT   ... will have agreed

PAST PASSIVE

—	—
—	—
it was agreed	they were agreed

- *The plan was finally agreed to.*

COMPLEMENTS

agree *come to an understanding, be in accord*	The two sides finally agreed.
	We agree in our choice for president.
	Our tastes in music agree.
agree _____ *be in accord, consent*	
on/upon OBJECT	They agreed **on the solution to the problem.**
PASSIVE	The price was agreed upon at the last minute.
to OBJECT	They agreed **to the plan.**
with OBJECT (+ *on/upon* OBJECT)	I'm sorry, but I don't agree **with you.**
	They agree **with us** *on all important points*.
INFINITIVE	They agreed **to cooperate on the project.**
THAT-CLAUSE	I agree **that we should go ahead.**
about WH-CLAUSE	They agreed **about what they should do.**
to WH-CLAUSE	They agreed **to what the board had recommended.**

PHRASAL VERBS

agree with _____ *be healthful for, be acceptable to*	Garlic doesn't agree with me.
	The dry climate agrees with us.
agree with _____ *be compatible with*	Your shirt doesn't agree with your slacks.
	Your copy doesn't agree with the original manuscript.
agree with _____ *correspond in grammatical features*	The verb must agree with the subject in person and number.

EXPRESSIONS

agree to disagree *conclude that the parties to a discussion don't concur about something*	We've argued for two hours; let's just agree to disagree.

PRESENT

I aim	we aim
you aim	you aim
he/she/it aims	they aim

• *Our staff aims to please the customer.*

PRESENT PROGRESSIVE

I am aiming	we are aiming
you are aiming	you are aiming
he/she/it is aiming	they are aiming

• *We are aiming at setting a new record.*

PAST

I aimed	we aimed
you aimed	you aimed
he/she/it aimed	they aimed

• *We aimed to be the best in the field.*

PAST PROGRESSIVE

I was aiming	we were aiming
you were aiming	you were aiming
he/she/it was aiming	they were aiming

• *I was aiming for a new personal best.*

PRESENT PERFECT ... have | has aimed
PAST PERFECT ... had aimed

FUTURE ... will aim
FUTURE PROGRESSIVE ... will be aiming
FUTURE PERFECT ... will have aimed

PAST PASSIVE

—	—
—	—
it was aimed	they were aimed

• *The gun was aimed right at my head.*

COMPLEMENTS

aim _____ direct/point [something at a target]

OBJECT + ADVERB OF PLACE TO/FROM

The boxer aimed **his punch** *at his opponent's head.*
I aimed **the car** *away from oncoming traffic.*
He aimed **the boat** *back toward the dock.*
The sheriff aimed **his pistol** *at Black Bart.*
We aimed **all our efforts** *at the new goal.*

aim _____ aspire, have as a goal

for OBJECT

I was aiming **for a position on the team.**
Now that she's turned 90, she's aiming **for 100.**

INFINITIVE

I aimed **to do my best.**
They are aiming **to finish by 5 o'clock.**

at PRESENT PARTICIPLE

I aimed **at doing my best.**
They aimed **at finishing by 5 o'clock.**
As a young girl, I aimed **at playing Juliet on stage.**

EXPRESSIONS

aim for the sky *set one's goals very high*

If you aim for the sky, you'll land in a tree. If you aim for a tree, you'll land on the ground.

PRESENT

I allow	we allow
you allow	you allow
he/she/it allows	they allow

- *He allows extra time when it rains.*

PAST

I allowed	we allowed
you allowed	you allowed
he/she/it allowed	they allowed

- *The board allowed the project to proceed.*

PRESENT PERFECT ... have | has allowed
PAST PERFECT ... had allowed

PRESENT PROGRESSIVE

I am allowing	we are allowing
you are allowing	you are allowing
he/she/it is allowing	they are allowing

- *They are allowing us to board the aircraft.*

PAST PROGRESSIVE

I was allowing	we were allowing
you were allowing	you were allowing
he/she/it was allowing	they were allowing

- *We were allowing for some delays.*

FUTURE ... will allow
FUTURE PROGRESSIVE ... will be allowing
FUTURE PERFECT ... will have allowed

PAST PASSIVE

I was allowed	we were allowed
you were allowed	you were allowed
he/she/it was allowed	they were allowed

- *Pets weren't allowed in the hotel.*

COMPLEMENTS

allow _____ *permit*

OBJECT	They allow **left turns onto one-way streets**.
PASSIVE	Smoking is not allowed in restaurants.
OBJECT + INFINITIVE	He allowed **us** *to start early*.
OBJECT + WH-CLAUSE	They allowed **them** *what they had requested*.
INDIRECT OBJECT + DIRECT OBJECT	They allowed *Bob* **some extra time**.
for PARAPHRASE	They allowed **some extra time** *for Bob*.
of OBJECT	This note allows **of interpretation**.

allow _____ *schedule*

OBJECT	You must allow **plenty of time to get there**.

allow _____ *admit, concede*

OBJECT	They allowed **his claim for $50 in damages**.
THAT-CLAUSE	They allowed **that we were right after all**.

PHRASAL VERBS

allow (_____) for *make provision for, allocate for*
We must allow for traffic delays.
Allow $20 for taxes and fees.

allow _____ **in/into** *permit to enter*
They don't allow dogs in their home.

allow _SEP_ **up** *permit to rise*
They pushed him down and wouldn't allow him up.

EXPRESSIONS

Allow me. *Please let me help you.*
Lucas opened the door, stepped back, and said, "Allow me."

PRESENT

I alter	we alter
you alter	you alter
he/she/it alters	they alter

• *He alters meeting times without notice.*

PRESENT PROGRESSIVE

I am altering	we are altering
you are altering	you are altering
he/she/it is altering	they are altering

• *I'm altering the beginning of the report.*

PAST

I altered	we altered
you altered	you altered
he/she/it altered	they altered

• *I never altered any data.*

PAST PROGRESSIVE

I was altering	we were altering
you were altering	you were altering
he/she/it was altering	they were altering

• *They were altering the dress when I walked in.*

PRESENT PERFECT ... have | has altered
PAST PERFECT ... had altered

FUTURE ... will alter
FUTURE PROGRESSIVE ... will be altering
FUTURE PERFECT ... will have altered

PAST PASSIVE

I was altered	we were altered
you were altered	you were altered
he/she/it was altered	they were altered

• *His itinerary was altered at the last minute.*

COMPLEMENTS

alter *become different*

The situation has altered recently.
Jack had altered greatly over the years.
His expression altered.

alter _____ *change*

OBJECT

I altered **my exercise routine.**
The store altered **the pants** for me.
We must alter **our plans.**

WH-CLAUSE

They altered **what they were originally doing.**
We altered **how we should approach the problem.**

PRESENT		PRESENT PROGRESSIVE	
I amount	we amount	I am amounting	we are amounting
you amount	you amount	you are amounting	you are amounting
he/she/it amounts	they amount	he/she/it is amounting	they are amounting

- *It amounts to very little.*

- *The sales aren't amounting to much.*

PAST		PAST PROGRESSIVE	
I amounted	we amounted	I was amounting	we were amounting
you amounted	you amounted	you were amounting	you were amounting
he/she/it amounted	they amounted	he/she/it was amounting	they were amounting

- *The dividends never amounted to much.*

- *It wasn't amounting to anything.*

PRESENT PERFECT	... have | has amounted
PAST PERFECT	... had amounted

FUTURE	... will amount
FUTURE PROGRESSIVE	... will be amounting
FUTURE PERFECT	... will have amounted

PAST PASSIVE

    Amount is never used in the passive voice.

(COMPLEMENTS)

NOTE: The verb *amount* is always used with *to*.

amount _____ add up

  to OBJECT
    The bill amounted **to $137.50.**
    The closing costs amounted **to a small fortune.**
    The bill amounted **to less than I thought it would be.**
    It amounted **to little.**
    The insurance amounted **to more than it was worth.**

  to WH-CLAUSE
    The rental amounts **to whatever the contract calls for.**
    It amounted **to however much you could afford.**

amount _____ be equivalent

  to OBJECT
    His actions amounted **to treason.**
    The decision amounted **to a huge defeat.**
    Being laid off or being fired—it amounts **to the same thing.**

  to WH-CLAUSE
    It amounted **to what I would consider a failure.**

  to PRESENT PARTICIPLE
    The case against him amounts **to his being in the wrong place at the wrong time.**

(EXPRESSIONS)

amount to something *become very good/important*

We hope that Garrett amounts to something someday.

PRESENT

I announce	we announce
you announce	you announce
he/she/it announces	they announce

• *She usually announces the winners.*

PRESENT PROGRESSIVE

I am announcing	we are announcing
you are announcing	you are announcing
he/she/it is announcing	they are announcing

• *We are announcing the new CEO soon.*

PAST

I announced	we announced
you announced	you announced
he/she/it announced	they announced

• *They announced the lineup this morning.*

PAST PROGRESSIVE

I was announcing	we were announcing
you were announcing	you were announcing
he/she/it was announcing	they were announcing

• *He was announcing the finalists.*

PRESENT PERFECT ... have | has announced
PAST PERFECT ... had announced

FUTURE ... will announce
FUTURE PROGRESSIVE ... will be announcing
FUTURE PERFECT ... will have announced

PAST PASSIVE

I was announced	we were announced
you were announced	you were announced
he/she/it was announced	they were announced

• *The winner was announced afterward.*

COMPLEMENTS

announce _____ *make publicly known*

OBJECT	They just announced **the winner.**
OBJECT + AS PREDICATE NOUN	The judges announced **her** *as the winner.*
OBJECT + INFINITIVE	CNN announced **her** *to be the winner.*
to OBJECT + THAT-CLAUSE	We announced **to the press** *that the company was going public.*
THAT-CLAUSE	Sam announced **that he was getting married.**
WH-CLAUSE	He announced **what the prize would be.**
	The teacher is announcing **how the test will be scored.**
PRESENT PARTICIPLE	I will announce **Jane's winning the contest.**

announce _____ *give notice of the arrival of, foretell*

OBJECT	The emcee announced **the bride and groom.**
	The hostess announced **dinner.**
	Shorter days announce **the coming of winter.**

announce _____ *act as a broadcast announcer of*

OBJECT	I used to announce **baseball games.**

PHRASAL VERBS

announce for _____ *declare one's candidacy for*
Three candidates have already announced for Congress.

announce for _____ *declare one's support for*
He told reporters, "Today I'm announcing for Lynn Davis, our next senator."

PRESENT

I answer	we answer
you answer	you answer
he/she/it answers	they answer

• *An intern answers customer inquiries.*

PRESENT PROGRESSIVE

I am answering	we are answering
you are answering	you are answering
he/she/it is answering	they are answering

• *Rob is answering the reporters' questions.*

PAST

I answered	we answered
you answered	you answered
he/she/it answered	they answered

• *I finally answered all my e-mails.*

PAST PROGRESSIVE

I was answering	we were answering
you were answering	you were answering
he/she/it was answering	they were answering

• *The entire staff was answering the phones.*

PRESENT PERFECT … have | has answered
PAST PERFECT   … had answered

FUTURE   … will answer
FUTURE PROGRESSIVE … will be answering
FUTURE PERFECT   … will have answered

PAST PASSIVE

I was answered	we were answered
you were answered	you were answered
he/she/it was answered	they were answered

• *All my questions were answered by the candidate.*

(**COMPLEMENTS**)

answer *speak/write in reply*	He answered in a friendly manner.
answer *act in response*	The visiting team quickly answered with a three-pointer.
answer _____ *speak/write in reply*	
OBJECT	I answered **the question** as best I could.
	He will answer **his critics** in an op-ed article.
THAT-CLAUSE	I answered **that I hadn't decided yet.**
DIRECT QUOTATION	I answered, **"I haven't decided yet."**
answer _____ *speak/write in rebuttal*	
OBJECT	The defendant answered **all of the prosecutor's accusations.**
answer _____ *act in response to*	
OBJECT	The country answered **the president's call to arms.**
answer _____ *fulfill*	
OBJECT	The microwave answers **our need for fast food.**

(**PHRASAL VERBS**)

answer _SEP_ **back** *reply to, usually rudely*	Ben's mother became angry when he answered her back.
answer for _____ *be accountable for*	Teenagers must answer for their behavior.
answer to _____ *be subordinate to*	I answer to the deputy prime minister.
answer to _____ *match, correspond to*	My neighbor answers to the suspect's description.

PRESENT

I appear	we appear
you appear	you appear
he/she/it appears	they appear

• *It appears that you are right after all.*

PRESENT PROGRESSIVE

I am appearing	we are appearing
you are appearing	you are appearing
he/she/it is appearing	they are appearing

• *She is appearing in three performances.*

PAST

I appeared	we appeared
you appeared	you appeared
he/she/it appeared	they appeared

• *The ghost appeared to Jayne once before.*

PAST PROGRESSIVE

I was appearing	we were appearing
you were appearing	you were appearing
he/she/it was appearing	they were appearing

• *The reporter was appearing at every meeting.*

PRESENT PERFECT ... have | has appeared
PAST PERFECT ... had appeared

FUTURE ... will appear
FUTURE PROGRESSIVE ... will be appearing
FUTURE PERFECT ... will have appeared

PAST PASSIVE

Appear is never used in the passive voice.

COMPLEMENTS

appear *come into sight/existence*	The sun appeared on the horizon. Hamlet's father's ghost appears before him. The ghost only appears in the first and third acts. Dinosaurs first appeared in the Triassic period.
appear *come before the public*	The candidates will appear together on TV this Sunday. *Harper's* magazine appears monthly.
appear *go before an official body*	I must appear in traffic court on Tuesday.
appear _____ *seem*	
to be + ADVERB OF TIME	Our train appears **to be on time.**
to be + ADVERB OF PLACE	Our train appears **to be on Track 9.**
(to be) PREDICATE NOUN	Jack appeared **(to be) a complete fool.**
(to be) PREDICATE ADJECTIVE	Jack appears **(to be) angry.**
it + *appear* + THAT-CLAUSE	It appeared **that we made a mistake.** It appears **that it is going to rain this afternoon.**
there + *appear* + to be PREDICATE NOUN	There appears **to be a mistake on my bill.** There appeared **to have been an error.**
appear _____ *go [before an official body]* *before* OBJECT	I have to appear **before Judge Perry** next week.

PHRASAL VERBS

appear as _____ *play the role of*	Jennifer Ehle appeared as Miss Elizabeth Bennet in the BBC's 1995 production of *Pride and Prejudice.*
appear at _____ *perform at*	Cellist Yo-Yo Ma will appear at Carnegie Hall.
appear for _____ *represent [someone who is absent]*	Barry appeared for Matt at the council meeting.
appear in _____ *perform in*	Sean Connery appeared in seven James Bond movies.

EXPRESSIONS

appear out of nowhere *come into sight suddenly and without warning*	The two robbers appeared out of nowhere and demanded our wallets. A car appeared out of nowhere and struck a pedestrian.

PRESENT

I apply	we apply
you apply	you apply
he/she/it applies	they apply

• *She applies logic to solve all her problems.*

PRESENT PROGRESSIVE

I am applying	we are applying
you are applying	you are applying
he/she/it is applying	they are applying

• *I am applying to half a dozen schools.*

PAST

I applied	we applied
you applied	you applied
he/she/it applied	they applied

• *Tony really applied himself to his work.*

PAST PROGRESSIVE

I was applying	we were applying
you were applying	you were applying
he/she/it was applying	they were applying

• *He was applying glue to the broken chair leg.*

PRESENT PERFECT ... have | has applied
PAST PERFECT   ... had applied

FUTURE   ... will apply
FUTURE PROGRESSIVE ... will be applying
FUTURE PERFECT   ... will have applied

PAST PASSIVE

—	—
—	—
it was applied	they were applied

• *The grant was first applied for back in 2006.*

───────────────────────────(**COMPLEMENTS**)───

apply *be pertinent/relevant*	The usual conditions apply.
apply *request admission*	He applied last fall.
apply —— *have to do with* to OBJECT	This law applies **to all citizens**.
apply —— *put into action, put to some practical use* OBJECT	I applied **the brakes**. They must apply **the rule of law**.
OBJECT + to OBJECT	We applied **the money** *to the mortgage*.
OBJECT + to WH-CLAUSE	We applied **the money** *to whichever bill was the most urgent*.
WH-CLAUSE	He applied **what he had learned**.
WH-CLAUSE + to OBJECT	We applied **what we had saved** *to the mortgage*.
WH-CLAUSE + to WH-CLAUSE	We applied **what we had saved** *to whatever needed paying first*.
apply —— *request admission* to OBJECT	He applied **to UCLA** last fall.
to WH-CLAUSE	I will apply **to whatever schools give full scholarships**.
apply —— *request formally* for OBJECT	I have applied **for a tax exemption**. I am applying **for the bookkeeping job**. I will apply **for whatever grants are available**.
apply —— *spread (on)* OBJECT	Apply **two coats of varnish**.

───────────────────────────(**PHRASAL VERBS**)───

apply [oneself] to —— *devote oneself to*	Let's apply ourselves to our English studies.

───────────────────────────(**EXPRESSIONS**)───

apply within *request [something] inside*	Job seekers should apply within.

PRESENT

I appoint	we appoint
you appoint	you appoint
he/she/it appoints	they appoint

• *He only appoints people he knows.*

PRESENT PROGRESSIVE

I am appointing	we are appointing
you are appointing	you are appointing
he/she/it is appointing	they are appointing

• *They are appointing several new judges to the court.*

PAST

I appointed	we appointed
you appointed	you appointed
he/she/it appointed	they appointed

• *Tanya appointed me to fill the position.*

PAST PROGRESSIVE

I was appointing	we were appointing
you were appointing	you were appointing
he/she/it was appointing	they were appointing

• *She was appointing new members to the committee.*

PRESENT PERFECT ... have | has appointed
PAST PERFECT ... had appointed

FUTURE ... will appoint
FUTURE PROGRESSIVE ... will be appointing
FUTURE PERFECT ... will have appointed

PAST PASSIVE

I was appointed	we were appointed
you were appointed	you were appointed
he/she/it was appointed	they were appointed

• *I was appointed to the commission.*

COMPLEMENTS

appoint _____ *designate for an office/position*

OBJECT + (*as*) PREDICATE NOUN	He appointed **her** *(as) attorney general*.
	They have appointed **me** *(as) secretary*.
OBJECT + (*to be*) PREDICATE NOUN	He appointed **her** *(to be) attorney general*.
	They have appointed **me** *(to be) secretary*.
OBJECT (+ *to* OBJECT)	The president appoints **all cabinet heads**.
	He appointed **himself**.
	She appointed **six policemen** *to the task force*.
OBJECT + INFINITIVE	She appointed **me** *to serve out the term*.
	The court appointed **Jason** *to serve as executor of the estate*.

EXPRESSIONS

appointed *nicely furnished*

The condo is spacious and beautifully appointed.
The bedrooms are small but stylishly appointed.

PRESENT

I approach	we approach
you approach	you approach
he/she/it approaches	they approach

• *He never approaches strangers.*

PRESENT PROGRESSIVE

I am approaching	we are approaching
you are approaching	you are approaching
he/she/it is approaching	they are approaching

• *The train is approaching the station.*

PAST

I approached	we approached
you approached	you approached
he/she/it approached	they approached

• *The boat never approached the bay.*

PAST PROGRESSIVE

I was approaching	we were approaching
you were approaching	you were approaching
he/she/it was approaching	they were approaching

• *He was approaching middle age.*

PRESENT PERFECT	... have	has approached
PAST PERFECT	... had approached

FUTURE	... will approach
FUTURE PROGRESSIVE	... will be approaching
FUTURE PERFECT	... will have approached

PAST PASSIVE

I was approached	we were approached
you were approached	you were approached
he/she/it was approached	they were approached

• *I was approached several times by major universities.*

(**COMPLEMENTS**)

approach *come near(er)*

Take cover. A storm is approaching.
It is getting lighter—dawn must be approaching.

approach _____ *come near(er) to*
OBJECT

The train is approaching **the station**.
The robber had approached **his victim** twice before.
We are approaching **our project deadline**.

approach _____ *make a proposal to*
OBJECT

Larry approached **a group of venture capitalists**
about investing.

WH-CLAUSE

He will approach **whoever he thinks will listen to him**.

approach _____ *be almost the same as*
OBJECT

His philosophical ideas approach **mysticism**.
Senator Blather's speech approaches **slander**.
Bobby's golf swing approaches **perfection**.

WH-CLAUSE

This shade of red approaches **what we want**.

approach _____ *begin to deal with, begin to work on*
OBJECT + ADVERB OF MANNER

Let's approach **the subject** *with an open mind*.
Our class is approaching **the project** *with enthusiasm*.

approve   approve | approves · approved · have approved   ☑ REGULAR

PRESENT

I approve	we approve
you approve	you approve
he/she/it approves	they approve

• *He approves of your approach.*

PAST

I approved	we approved
you approved	you approved
he/she/it approved	they approved

• *They approved your recommendation.*

PRESENT PERFECT … have | has approved
PAST PERFECT … had approved

PRESENT PROGRESSIVE

I am approving	we are approving
you are approving	you are approving
he/she/it is approving	they are approving

• *I am approving your loan.*

PAST PROGRESSIVE

I was approving	we were approving
you were approving	you were approving
he/she/it was approving	they were approving

• *They were approving most applications.*

FUTURE … will approve
FUTURE PROGRESSIVE … will be approving
FUTURE PERFECT … will have approved

PAST PASSIVE

I was approved	we were approved
you were approved	you were approved
he/she/it was approved	they were approved

• *The plan was approved unanimously.*

COMPLEMENTS

approve _____ *accept as satisfactory*

OBJECT — I can't approve **such careless work.**
Both of us approved **our son's choice.**

WH-CLAUSE — He won't approve **what he doesn't like.**
They will approve **whatever course of action you decide on.**

PRESENT PARTICIPLE — We can't approve **adding 15 more employees to the payroll.**
I couldn't approve **their taking such a risk.**

approve _____ *take a favorable view*

of OBJECT — They approved **of his actions.**

of WH-CLAUSE — You can't approve **of what they were doing.**

of PRESENT PARTICIPLE — I don't approve **of their acting that way.**

approve _____ *give consent to*

OBJECT — The Senate finally approved **the treaty.**
My boss has approved **my application for a transfer.**

WH-CLAUSE — They will approve **whomever we recommend.**

PRESENT PARTICIPLE — Will voters approve **taking bids from private firms?**
The CEO approved **our taking them to court.**

PRESENT

I argue	we argue
you argue	you argue
he/she/it argues	they argue

• *John argues about everything.*

PRESENT PROGRESSIVE

I am arguing	we are arguing
you are arguing	you are arguing
he/she/it is arguing	they are arguing

• *We are arguing over nothing.*

PAST

I argued	we argued
you argued	you argued
he/she/it argued	they argued

• *I argued against the proposal.*

PAST PROGRESSIVE

I was arguing	we were arguing
you were arguing	you were arguing
he/she/it was arguing	they were arguing

• *Our cousins were arguing again.*

PRESENT PERFECT ... have | has argued
PAST PERFECT ... had argued

FUTURE ... will argue
FUTURE PROGRESSIVE ... will be arguing
FUTURE PERFECT ... will have argued

PAST PASSIVE

—	—
—	—
it was argued	they were argued

• *The case was argued by Margaret White.*

(**COMPLEMENTS**)

argue *disagree, quarrel*	They argue all the time.
argue _____ *debate*	
OBJECT	The justices argued **the issue**.
argue _____ *assert, try to prove by giving reasons*	
OBJECT	Vince argued **his case** before the judge.
THAT-CLAUSE	Vince argued **that he was innocent**.

(**PHRASAL VERBS**)

argue about/over _____ *quarrel about*	They argued about what they should do. We argued about their going to Chicago. They have always argued over money. We argued over going to Chicago.
argue back *quarrel in rebuttal*	They argued back every time I told them to do something.
argue SEP **down** *defeat in a debate/discussion*	She argued the manager down every time. He argued the proposal down at the meeting.
argue for/against _____ *give reasons in favor of / against*	He had argued for the proposal. She argued for accepting the bid. I argued against what they had proposed. She argued against their accepting the bid.
argue _____ **into** *persuade to do*	I argued him into going with us.
argue _____ **out** *settle by full discussion*	Let's argue this out when we have more time.
argue _____ **out of** *dissuade [someone] from*	I argued him out of his silly plan. I argued him out of going ahead with his plan.
argue with _____ *quarrel with, challenge*	I don't want to argue with Audrey anymore. Face it, you can't argue with the facts.

I arise	we arise
you arise	you arise
he/she/it arises	they arise

• *He arises every morning at the same time.*

PRESENT PROGRESSIVE

I am arising	we are arising
you are arising	you are arising
he/she/it is arising	they are arising

• *George is slowly arising from the sofa.*

PAST

I arose	we arose
you arose	you arose
he/she/it arose	they arose

• *I always arose before seven on school days.*

PAST PROGRESSIVE

I was arising	we were arising
you were arising	you were arising
he/she/it was arising	they were arising

• *He was just arising when the phone rang.*

PRESENT PERFECT ... have | has arisen
PAST PERFECT   ... had arisen

FUTURE   ... will arise
FUTURE PROGRESSIVE ... will be arising
FUTURE PERFECT   ... will have arisen

PAST PASSIVE

Arise is never used in the passive voice.

(**COMPLEMENTS**)

NOTE: The verb *arise* is interchangeable with *rise* in most meanings and uses. See verb No. 418.

arise *get out of bed*

I usually arise around six.
Nobody arises early on weekends.

arise *stand/spring up, move upward*

The audience always arises when the president enters the room.
Rebecca arose from the sofa gracefully.
The dolphins arose from the water.
A cloud of dust arose from the ruins.
He arose out of inner-city poverty to become mayor.

arise *come into being*

The rumor arose when Rob had to appear in court.
A new controversy about ethanol has arisen since the meeting.

arise _____ *originate*
ADVERB OF PLACE TO/FROM

The spring arises **behind our house**.
These glaciers arise **in the Alps**.
Birds arose **from small specialized dinosaurs**.
Prejudice arises **from ignorance and unfamiliarity**.

PRESENT

I arm	we arm
you arm	you arm
he/she/it arms	they arm

• *We arm ourselves against violent crime.*

PAST

I armed	we armed
you armed	you armed
he/she/it armed	they armed

• *They armed the civilian defense force.*

PRESENT PERFECT	... have | has armed
PAST PERFECT	... had armed

PRESENT PROGRESSIVE

I am arming	we are arming
you are arming	you are arming
he/she/it is arming	they are arming

• *We are arming ourselves as best we can.*

PAST PROGRESSIVE

I was arming	we were arming
you were arming	you were arming
he/she/it was arming	they were arming

• *They were arming the National Guard.*

FUTURE	... will arm
FUTURE PROGRESSIVE	... will be arming
FUTURE PERFECT	... will have armed

PAST PASSIVE

I was armed	we were armed
you were armed	you were armed
he/she/it was armed	they were armed

• *The submarine was armed with acoustic torpedoes.*

COMPLEMENTS

arm _____ *equip with weapons*

OBJECT	The police armed **the guards**.
PASSIVE	Be careful—the hijacker is armed.
	The solders were all armed with rifles.
WH-CLAUSE	They armed **whoever was capable of firing weapons**.
	We will arm **whatever force we can scrape together**.

arm _____ *prepare for use, activate*

OBJECT	The sailors armed **the torpedoes**.
	We have armed **the alarm system**.

PHRASAL VERBS

arm _____ **with** *furnish [someone] with [weapons, some kind of protection]*

I armed myself with a flashlight
    and extra batteries.
I armed myself with a stiff drink.
The courts armed citizens with the right of habeas corpus.

EXPRESSIONS

armed to the teeth *very heavily armed*   Captain Jack Sparrow was armed
    to the teeth.

PRESENT

I arrange	we arrange
you arrange	you arrange
he/she/it arranges	they arrange

• *Susan arranges everybody's schedule.*

PRESENT PROGRESSIVE

I am arranging	we are arranging
you are arranging	you are arranging
he/she/it is arranging	they are arranging

• *I am arranging some appointments for you.*

PAST

I arranged	we arranged
you arranged	you arranged
he/she/it arranged	they arranged

• *They arranged to see you yesterday.*

PAST PROGRESSIVE

I was arranging	we were arranging
you were arranging	you were arranging
he/she/it was arranging	they were arranging

• *They were arranging the final details.*

PRESENT PERFECT … have | has arranged
PAST PERFECT … had arranged

FUTURE … will arrange
FUTURE PROGRESSIVE … will be arranging
FUTURE PERFECT … will have arranged

PAST PASSIVE

—	—
—	—
it was arranged	they were arranged

• *A meeting was arranged by the secretary.*

(**COMPLEMENTS**)

arrange _____ *put in a certain order*

OBJECT — I arranged **the books** in alphabetical order.
We arranged **the flowers** for the reception.

arrange _____ *plan, cause something to happen*

OBJECT — They arranged **the conference on China.**
(*for*) OBJECT — They will arrange **(for) a celebration.**
for OBJECT + INFINITIVE — He arranged **for John** *to visit them in Chicago.*
(*it*) *for* OBJECT + INFINITIVE — I arranged **(it) for him** *to tour the plant in Japan.*
INFINITIVE — He arranged **to visit them in Chicago.**
WH-CLAUSE — He arranged **what you had asked for.**
She will arrange **whatever they need.**
(*for*) PRESENT PARTICIPLE — Frank arranged **(for) my interviewing them.**

arrange _____ *adapt a musical composition for other voices or instruments*

OBJECT — He arranged **a Bach fugue** for a modern orchestra.

PRESENT

I arrive	we arrive
you arrive	you arrive
he/she/it arrives	they arrive

- *Our guests arrive on Tuesday.*

PRESENT PROGRESSIVE

I am arriving	we are arriving
you are arriving	you are arriving
he/she/it is arriving	they are arriving

- *We are arriving soon.*

PAST

I arrived	we arrived
you arrived	you arrived
he/she/it arrived	they arrived

- *She arrived at her destination late.*

PAST PROGRESSIVE

I was arriving	we were arriving
you were arriving	you were arriving
he/she/it was arriving	they were arriving

- *The speaker was finally arriving at his conclusion.*

PRESENT PERFECT ... have | has arrived
PAST PERFECT ... had arrived

FUTURE ... will arrive
FUTURE PROGRESSIVE ... will be arriving
FUTURE PERFECT ... will have arrived

PAST PASSIVE

—	—
—	—
it was arrived	they were arrived

- *An agreement was arrived at.*

COMPLEMENTS

arrive *reach a destination*	We will arrive before dark. They arrived there just minutes ago.
arrive *make an appearance*	The guests have arrived in their car. The train has just arrived from Chicago.
arrive *come finally*	The moment has arrived to turn words into action.
arrive *achieve success/fame*	George has really arrived.
arrive _____ *reach by traveling* at OBJECT	 The train arrived **at the station** early.

PHRASAL VERBS

arrive at _____ *reach by effort/thought*	We arrived at an agreement. We will arrive at whatever agreement is possible.

EXPRESSIONS

arrive at the scene (of _____ **)** *reach the location of*	The cops arrived at the scene of the burglary.
arrive in force *reach a location in full strength*	Winter arrived in force yesterday. The National Guard arrived in force to quell the riot.
arrive in the (very) nick of time *reach a location just in time*	The doctor arrived in the nick of time to save the child.

PRESENT

I ask	we ask
you ask	you ask
he/she/it asks	they ask

• *He always asks for tea for breakfast.*

PRESENT PROGRESSIVE

I am asking	we are asking
you are asking	you are asking
he/she/it is asking	they are asking

• *They are asking about tonight's menu.*

PAST

I asked	we asked
you asked	you asked
he/she/it asked	they asked

• *You already asked me that.*

PAST PROGRESSIVE

I was asking	we were asking
you were asking	you were asking
he/she/it was asking	they were asking

• *I was asking for a second opinion.*

PRESENT PERFECT ... have | has asked
PAST PERFECT ... had asked

FUTURE ... will ask
FUTURE PROGRESSIVE ... will be asking
FUTURE PERFECT ... will have asked

PAST PASSIVE

I was asked	we were asked
you were asked	you were asked
he/she/it was asked	they were asked

• *I was asked to say a few words.*

(**COMPLEMENTS**)

ask _____ *inquire about*

OBJECT	The detective asked **his whereabouts last night**.
INDIRECT OBJECT + DIRECT OBJECT	They are asking *everyone* **the same question**.
of PARAPHRASE	They are asking **the same question** *of everyone*.
(OBJECT +) *if* CLAUSE	The pilot asked **if everyone was on board**.
	He asked *us* **if we were ready**.
(OBJECT +) WH-CLAUSE	The waiter asked **which of us was vegetarian**.
	He asked *us* **who was coming**.

ask _____ *request*

(OBJECT +) *for* OBJECT	She is asking **for help from her brother**.
	I will ask *the boss* **for a raise** tomorrow morning.
OBJECT + INFINITIVE	I have asked **them** *to go home early today*.
(OBJECT +) WH-INFINITIVE	We should ask **how to turn the lights on**.
	Raymond asked *him* **what to do next**.
INFINITIVE	She had asked **to see the manager**.
BASE-FORM THAT-CLAUSE	She asked **that he reschedule the meeting**.

ask _____ *invite*

OBJECT + *to* OBJECT	The U.N. asked **China** *to the conference*.
	I asked **Mary** *to the party*.

(**PHRASAL VERBS**)

ask after _____ *inquire about someone's health/well-being*	She asked after my mother.
ask around *request information from different sources*	She asked around about the missing necklace.
ask _____ **back** *invite again to one's home*	We will never ask the Smiths back.
ask _____ **down/over/up** *invite to one's home*	We asked Jim and Lara down for the weekend.
	Let's ask Bill and Fran over Friday night.
ask _____ **in/into** *invite inside*	Please ask the applicant in.
	They asked us into the house.
ask _____ **of** *request/demand from*	You'll have to ask that of your supervisor.
ask _____ **out** *invite on a date*	I'd like to ask Gretchen out to dinner.

PRESENT

I assist	we assist
you assist	you assist
he/she/it assists	they assist

• *He assists the vet with large animals.*

PRESENT PROGRESSIVE

I am assisting	we are assisting
you are assisting	you are assisting
he/she/it is assisting	they are assisting

• *He is assisting Bob right now.*

PAST

I assisted	we assisted
you assisted	you assisted
he/she/it assisted	they assisted

• *She assisted at four operations yesterday.*

PAST PROGRESSIVE

I was assisting	we were assisting
you were assisting	you were assisting
he/she/it was assisting	they were assisting

• *They were assisting us onto the bus.*

PRESENT PERFECT ... have | has assisted
PAST PERFECT   ... had assisted

FUTURE   ... will assist
FUTURE PROGRESSIVE ... will be assisting
FUTURE PERFECT   ... will have assisted

PAST PASSIVE

I was assisted	we were assisted
you were assisted	you were assisted
he/she/it was assisted	they were assisted

• *I was assisted by Mrs. Laurent.*

COMPLEMENTS

assist *help out*

I am assisting at the information desk.
They will assist wherever they are needed.

assist _____ *provide support/aid to*

OBJECT

The new coach assists **the junior basketball team.**
He assists **the drivers** when they unload the trucks.

OBJECT + *with* OBJECT

OBJECT + (*in*) PRESENT PARTICIPLE

OBJECT + (*with*) PRESENT PARTICIPLE

The makeup artist assisted **the actor *with his costume.***
They assisted **him *(in) painting the deck.***
Emily will assist **Matt *(with) tying down the kayak.***

EXPRESSIONS

assisted living *housing and care for senior citizens who need limited assistance in day-to-day living*

Assisted living is the perfect solution
  for your dad.

40 (**associate**) associate | associates ·
associated · have associated
☑ REGULAR

PRESENT	
I associate	we associate
you associate	you associate
he/she/it associates	they associate

· *He associates with some strange people.*

PAST	
I associated	we associated
you associated	you associated
he/she/it associated	they associated

· *I always associated Greece with sunshine.*

PRESENT PERFECT	... have | has associated
PAST PERFECT	... had associated

PRESENT PROGRESSIVE	
I am associating	we are associating
you are associating	you are associating
he/she/it is associating	they are associating

· *They are associating with the wrong people.*

PAST PROGRESSIVE	
I was associating	we were associating
you were associating	you were associating
he/she/it was associating	they were associating

· *I was mistakenly associating Jack with Ernest.*

FUTURE	... will associate
FUTURE PROGRESSIVE	... will be associating
FUTURE PERFECT	... will have associated

PAST PASSIVE	
I was associated	we were associated
you were associated	you were associated
he/she/it was associated	they were associated

· *Stratford was always associated with Shakespeare.*

──────────────────────────────(**COMPLEMENTS**)──────

NOTE: The verb *associate* is always used with *with*.

associate _____ *be friendly, spend time*

with OBJECT

He only associates **with other lawyers.**
Donald is associating **with drug users and gang members.**

with WH-CLAUSE

I will associate **with whomever I want to.**

associate _____ *form an alliance*

(REFLEXIVE PRONOUN +) with OBJECT

They are associating **with a new advertising agency.**
They are associating *themselves* **with a new advertising
agency.**

associate _____ *make a connection between*

OBJECT + with OBJECT

We associate **robins** *with spring.*
Everyone associates **pineapple** *with Hawaii.*

PASSIVE

President Theodore Roosevelt was associated *with the
conservation movement in the United States.*
The swelling was associated *with chills and fever.*

be associated _____ *be caused by* [USED ONLY IN THE PASSIVE]

with OBJECT

Memory loss is associated with vitamin B-12 deficiency.

PRESENT

I assume	we assume
you assume	you assume
he/she/it assumes	they assume

· *He always assumes that he is right.*

PRESENT PROGRESSIVE

I am assuming	we are assuming
you are assuming	you are assuming
he/she/it is assuming	they are assuming

· *I am assuming the worst.*

PAST

I assumed	we assumed
you assumed	you assumed
he/she/it assumed	they assumed

· *They assumed a lot of responsibility.*

PAST PROGRESSIVE

I was assuming	we were assuming
you were assuming	you were assuming
he/she/it was assuming	they were assuming

· *He was assuming a high interest rate.*

PRESENT PERFECT ... have | has assumed
PAST PERFECT ... had assumed

FUTURE ... will assume
FUTURE PROGRESSIVE ... will be assuming
FUTURE PERFECT ... will have assumed

PAST PASSIVE

I was assumed	we were assumed
you were assumed	you were assumed
he/she/it was assumed	they were assumed

· *The problem was assumed to be under control.*

COMPLEMENTS

assume ____ *take [responsibility for]*

OBJECT

He assumed **responsibility** for the mortgage.
The new captain assumed **control of the ship**.
She will assume **her new husband's debt**.

assume ____ *pretend to have*

OBJECT

He assumed **an air of total confidence**.
They assumed **a level of knowledge he did not have**.

assume ____ *suppose [something] to be true, take for granted*

OBJECT

We assumed **the worst**.
You're assuming **too much**.

OBJECT + *to be* ADVERB OF TIME   We assumed **the plane** *to be on time*.
OBJECT + *to be* PREDICATE NOUN   We assumed **the plane** *to be a jet*.
OBJECT + *to be* PREDICATE ADJECTIVE   We assumed **the plane** *to be ready*.
THAT-CLAUSE   We assumed **that the worst had happened**.

EXPRESSIONS

assumed name *an adopted name, often to deceive others*

The holding company transacts business
    under several assumed names.
Samuel Clemens wrote under the assumed name
    of Mark Twain.
She uses an assumed name when she posts a comment
    to a blog.

PRESENT

I assure	we assure
you assure	you assure
he/she/it assures	they assure

• *He assures us that it will be done on time.*

PRESENT PROGRESSIVE

I am assuring	we are assuring
you are assuring	you are assuring
he/she/it is assuring	they are assuring

• *They are assuring us that it will be okay.*

PAST

I assured	we assured
you assured	you assured
he/she/it assured	they assured

• *The inspection assured 100% compliance.*

PAST PROGRESSIVE

I was assuring	we were assuring
you were assuring	you were assuring
he/she/it was assuring	they were assuring

• *We were assuring complete satisfaction.*

PRESENT PERFECT ... have | has assured
PAST PERFECT ... had assured

FUTURE ... will assure
FUTURE PROGRESSIVE ... will be assuring
FUTURE PERFECT ... will have assured

PAST PASSIVE

I was assured	we were assured
you were assured	you were assured
he/she/it was assured	they were assured

• *I was assured that it would be ready.*

──(**COMPLEMENTS**)──

assure ⎯⎯ *guarantee*

OBJECT

Double-checking assures **accuracy**.
Mutual interest assures **cooperation**.

assure ⎯⎯ *cause to feel sure, promise*

OBJECT + *of* OBJECT

I assured **him** *of our continuing support*.
They assured **us** *of his full recovery*.

OBJECT + THAT-CLAUSE

I assured **him** *that the plane was on time*.
He assured **us** *that he could do it*.
Sam assured **them** *that no one was watching*.
I looked in the rearview mirror to assure **myself**
    that I wasn't being followed.

──(**EXPRESSIONS**)──

(self-)assured *showing confidence*

It is important to act in a professional
    and (self-)assured manner.

PRESENT

I attach	we attach
you attach	you attach
he/she/it attaches	they attach

  • *He attaches himself to losing causes.*

PRESENT PROGRESSIVE

I am attaching	we are attaching
you are attaching	you are attaching
he/she/it is attaching	they are attaching

  • *We are attaching the memo.*

PAST

I attached	we attached
you attached	you attached
he/she/it attached	they attached

  • *I attached comments to the essay.*

PAST PROGRESSIVE

I was attaching	we were attaching
you were attaching	you were attaching
he/she/it was attaching	they were attaching

  • *They were attaching name tags to the bags.*

PRESENT PERFECT ... have | has attached
PAST PERFECT ... had attached

FUTURE ... will attach
FUTURE PROGRESSIVE ... will be attaching
FUTURE PERFECT ... will have attached

PAST PASSIVE

I was attached	we were attached
you were attached	you were attached
he/she/it was attached	they were attached

  • *She was attached to her family.*

─(**COMPLEMENTS**)─

attach ＿＿＿ *fasten*
  OBJECT (+ to OBJECT)

I attached **a self-addressed, stamped envelope.**
I attached **the new legs** *to the table.*
They attached **labels** *to all the packages.*

attach ＿＿＿ *form an emotional link*
  REFLEXIVE PRONOUN + to OBJECT

Children quickly attach **themselves** *to their caregivers.*
He attached **himself** *to the green movement.*

attach ＿＿＿ *attribute*
  OBJECT + to OBJECT
  OBJECT + to WH-CLAUSE

Politicians attach **a lot of importance** *to polling.*
They attached **great significance** *to what he said.*

attach ＿＿＿ *assign temporarily*
  OBJECT + to OBJECT
    PASSIVE

The captain attached **two platoons** *to Company B.*
The corporal was attached *to our platoon.*

attach ＿＿＿ *take by legal authority*
  OBJECT
    PASSIVE

The bank attached **the property.**
His salary was attached for nonpayment of child support.

─(**EXPRESSIONS**)─

be attached to ＿＿＿ *be fond of*

Greg was really attached to his dad.
Little Lisa has gotten attached to her blanket.

PRESENT

I attack	we attack
you attack	you attack
he/she/it attacks	they attack

• *A cobra attacks when it is surprised.*

PRESENT PROGRESSIVE

I am attacking	we are attacking
you are attacking	you are attacking
he/she/it is attacking	they are attacking

• *We are attacking with all our might.*

PAST

I attacked	we attacked
you attacked	you attacked
he/she/it attacked	they attacked

• *They attacked the enemy fleet.*

PAST PROGRESSIVE

I was attacking	we were attacking
you were attacking	you were attacking
he/she/it was attacking	they were attacking

• *They were attacking all of their opponents.*

PRESENT PERFECT ... have | has attacked
PAST PERFECT ... had attacked

FUTURE ... will attack
FUTURE PROGRESSIVE ... will be attacking
FUTURE PERFECT ... will have attacked

PAST PASSIVE

I was attacked	we were attacked
you were attacked	you were attacked
he/she/it was attacked	they were attacked

• *His ideas were attacked by his co-workers.*

───(COMPLEMENTS)───

attack *make an assault*

Mosquitoes attack at dusk.

attack _____ *assault physically/verbally*

OBJECT

The soldiers attacked **the guard post.**
Aphids were attacking **the roses.**
They bitterly attacked **the new plan.**

WH-CLAUSE

He attacks **whatever I propose to do.**

PRESENT PARTICIPLE

I attacked **John's doing nothing about the situation.**

attack _____ *begin to work on vigorously*

OBJECT

Our team will attack **the problem** with gusto.

WH-CLAUSE

They attacked **whatever problems we had to solve.**

───(EXPRESSIONS)───

attack in force *attack in full strength*

After massing troops for weeks,
the general attacked in force.

PRESENT

I attempt	we attempt
you attempt	you attempt
he/she/it attempts	they attempt

· *Jim always attempts to do too much.*

PRESENT PROGRESSIVE

I am attempting	we are attempting
you are attempting	you are attempting
he/she/it is attempting	they are attempting

· *I am attempting to do something new.*

PAST

I attempted	we attempted
you attempted	you attempted
he/she/it attempted	they attempted

· *They attempted everything without success.*

PAST PROGRESSIVE

I was attempting	we were attempting
you were attempting	you were attempting
he/she/it was attempting	they were attempting

· *They were attempting to do too much.*

PRESENT PERFECT ... have | has attempted
PAST PERFECT ... had attempted

FUTURE ... will attempt
FUTURE PROGRESSIVE ... will be attempting
FUTURE PERFECT ... will have attempted

PAST PASSIVE

—	—
—	—
it was attempted	they were attempted

· *A prison break was attempted several times.*

─(**COMPLEMENTS**)─

attempt ──── *try to do/accomplish*

OBJECT	They attempted **the impossible.**
	The climbers attempted **the north side.**
	Let's attempt **the crossword puzzle** and see how far we get.
INFINITIVE	They will attempt **to finish the job on time.**
	He will attempt **to run the Boston Marathon.**
WH-CLAUSE	We attempted **what had never been done before.**
	I attempted **whatever was asked of me.**

PRESENT

I attend	we attend
you attend	you attend
he/she/it attends	they attend

 • *She attends City College.*

PRESENT PROGRESSIVE

I am attending	we are attending
you are attending	you are attending
he/she/it is attending	they are attending

 • *Dr. Maret is attending to the new patients.*

PAST

I attended	we attended
you attended	you attended
he/she/it attended	they attended

 • *I attended to the situation promptly.*

PAST PROGRESSIVE

I was attending	we were attending
you were attending	you were attending
he/she/it was attending	they were attending

 • *I was attending high school at the time.*

PRESENT PERFECT ... have | has attended
PAST PERFECT ... had attended

FUTURE ... will attend
FUTURE PROGRESSIVE ... will be attending
FUTURE PERFECT ... will have attended

PAST PASSIVE

I was attended	we were attended
you were attended	you were attended
he/she/it was attended	they were attended

 • *The problem was attended to.*

COMPLEMENTS

attend *be present at a meeting/program*	I hope we can attend.
	Will both parents be able to attend?
attend _____ *be present at [a meeting, program]*	
OBJECT	I attended **all those PowerPoint presentations.**
	They always attend **their children's recitals.**
	Everyone has attended **the required safety class.**
attend _____ *be present as an enrollee at [a school, program]*	
OBJECT	She attended **the University of Denver.**
	We attended **the American Red Cross CPR classes.**
WH-CLAUSE	Bart will attend **whatever college he can get into.**
attend _____ *assist, care for*	
OBJECT	She attended **old Mrs. Moore.**
	This department attends only **emergency patients.**
attend _____ *take care of, apply oneself*	
to OBJECT	Attend **to your own problems** first.
	Is anyone attending **to you?**
	I'll attend **to that** as soon as I can.
to WH-CLAUSE	I will attend **to whoever needs care.**
	They attend **to whatever has to be done.**
to PRESENT PARTICIPLE	Please attend **to finishing your job.**
	I attended **to filling out the paperwork.**
attend _____ *pay attention*	
to OBJECT	Children should attend **to the teacher's presentation.**
attend _____ *accompany as a result*	
OBJECT	Enthusiastic applause attended **the candidate's speech.**
PASSIVE	The candidate's speech was attended by enthusiastic applause.

PRESENT

I attract	we attract
you attract	you attract
he/she/it attracts	they attract

• *John always attracts a crowd.*

PRESENT PROGRESSIVE

I am attracting	we are attracting
you are attracting	you are attracting
he/she/it is attracting	they are attracting

• *The teens are attracting unwanted attention.*

PAST

I attracted	we attracted
you attracted	you attracted
he/she/it attracted	they attracted

• *The sale attracted a lot of attention.*

PAST PROGRESSIVE

I was attracting	we were attracting
you were attracting	you were attracting
he/she/it was attracting	they were attracting

• *We were attracting new investors.*

PRESENT PERFECT ... have | has attracted
PAST PERFECT   ... had attracted

FUTURE   ... will attract
FUTURE PROGRESSIVE ... will be attracting
FUTURE PERFECT   ... will have attracted

PAST PASSIVE

I was attracted	we were attracted
you were attracted	you were attracted
he/she/it was attracted	they were attracted

• *I was attracted by the bright lights.*

COMPLEMENTS

attract _____ *cause to come nearer*

OBJECT

Magnets attract **iron filings.**
The flowers are attracting **a lot of bees.**
Her presentations always attract **a large audience.**

to OBJECT [USED ONLY IN THE PASSIVE]

I was really attracted to Jack.
People are attracted to his philosophy.
Everyone is attracted to effortless diet programs.

WH-CLAUSE

His crazy schemes attract **whoever wants to get rich quick.**

attract _____ *arouse by appeal to interest/emotion*

OBJECT

Their ideas attract **a great deal of attention.**
Advertising attracts **interest in the product.**

PRESENT

I avoid	we avoid
you avoid	you avoid
he/she/it avoids	they avoid

• *Nathan avoids crowds.*

PAST

I avoided	we avoided
you avoided	you avoided
he/she/it avoided	they avoided

• *We avoided the morning rush.*

PRESENT PERFECT ... have | has avoided
PAST PERFECT ... had avoided

PRESENT PROGRESSIVE

I am avoiding	we are avoiding
you are avoiding	you are avoiding
he/she/it is avoiding	they are avoiding

• *She is avoiding me.*

PAST PROGRESSIVE

I was avoiding	we were avoiding
you were avoiding	you were avoiding
he/she/it was avoiding	they were avoiding

• *They were avoiding the topic.*

FUTURE ... will avoid
FUTURE PROGRESSIVE ... will be avoiding
FUTURE PERFECT ... will have avoided

PAST PASSIVE

I was avoided	we were avoided
you were avoided	you were avoided
he/she/it was avoided	they were avoided

• *The problem was avoided by careful planning.*

COMPLEMENTS

avoid _____ *keep away from*

OBJECT

I am avoiding **my boss.**
Everyone avoids **crowds** during flu season.
You are just avoiding **the problem.**

WH-CLAUSE
A politician avoids **whatever gets voters upset.**

avoid _____ *refrain from*

PRESENT PARTICIPLE

I avoid **overeating at holidays.**
He avoids **flying through Chicago.**
He is avoiding **finishing his thesis.**
I avoided **making a big mistake.**

EXPRESSIONS

avoid _____ **like the plague** *stay away from completely*

He is obnoxious, and everyone
avoids him like the plague.

☑	REGULAR	awake | awakes · awaked · have awaked	
☑	IRREGULAR	awake | awakes · awoke · have awoken	**awake(n)** 49
☑	REGULAR	awaken | awakens · awakened · have awakened	

PRESENT

I awake	we awake
you awake	you awake
he/she/it awakes	they awake

• *He awakes every morning at seven.*

PRESENT PROGRESSIVE

I am awaking	we are awaking
you are awaking	you are awaking
he/she/it is awaking	they are awaking

• *He is awaking to the danger.*

PAST

I awoke	we awoke
you awoke	you awoke
he/she/it awoke	they awoke

• *It awoke bad memories for me.*

PAST PROGRESSIVE

I was awaking	we were awaking
you were awaking	you were awaking
he/she/it was awaking	they were awaking

• *They were awaking to a hot morning.*

PRESENT PERFECT ... have | has awoken
PAST PERFECT ... had awoken

FUTURE ... will awake
FUTURE PROGRESSIVE ... will be awaking
FUTURE PERFECT ... will have awoken

PAST PASSIVE

I was awoken	we were awoken
you were awoken	you were awoken
he/she/it was awoken	they were awoken

• *We were awoken by the storm.*

─────────────(COMPLEMENTS)─────────────

NOTE: *Awake* and *awaken* have the same meanings and uses. They are similar to *wake/waken* (verb No. 536), with this difference: *Wake* is used with *up* (*Jane woke up at 7 o'clock*), but *awake, awaken,* and *waken* are not.

awake *quit sleeping*	The children awoke early.
awake *become aroused*	The crowd's anger suddenly awoke.
	Excitement awoke in everyone.
awake _____ *arouse from sleeping*	
OBJECT	The storm awoke **the children** early.
	He will awake **everybody in the house** with his snoring.
WH-CLAUSE	The commotion awoke **whoever was still asleep.**
awake _____ *stir up*	
OBJECT	The crisis has awoken **memories of the 1960s.**
	Sam awoke **Stella's interest in China.**
WH-CLAUSE	It awoke **what had been long forgotten.**
	I awoke **whatever concern he had felt.**

─────────────(PHRASAL VERBS)─────────────

awake from _____ *wake up out of*	Ned awoke from a sound sleep.
awake to _____ *wake up to*	Patsy awoke to the aroma of freshly brewed coffee.
	The corporal awoke to the sound and fury of battle.
awake to _____ *become aware of*	She awoke to the possibilities that technology offered.
	Dad awoke to the reality of the moment.

PRESENT

I back	we back
you back	you back
he/she/it backs	they back

- *He always backs into parking places.*

PAST

I backed	we backed
you backed	you backed
he/she/it backed	they backed

- *I backed the car out of the garage.*

PRESENT PERFECT ... have | has backed
PAST PERFECT ... had backed

PRESENT PROGRESSIVE

I am backing	we are backing
you are backing	you are backing
he/she/it is backing	they are backing

- *He is backing the desk against the wall.*

PAST PROGRESSIVE

I was backing	we were backing
you were backing	you were backing
he/she/it was backing	they were backing

- *The newspapers were backing the incumbent.*

FUTURE ... will back
FUTURE PROGRESSIVE ... will be backing
FUTURE PERFECT ... will have backed

PAST PASSIVE

I was backed	we were backed
you were backed	you were backed
he/she/it was backed	they were backed

- *The candidate was backed by her party.*

COMPLEMENTS

back *go backward*	The car backed into the street.
back _____ *cause something to go backward*	
OBJECT + ADVERB OF PLACE TO/FROM	Back **the riding mower** *off the driveway.*
	Can you back **the car** *into this narrow parking space*?
back _____ *support*	
OBJECT	I will back **your proposal.**
	We are backing **John** for the Senate.
	They back **the product** with a one-year warranty.
PASSIVE	The product is backed with a one-year warranty.
WH-CLAUSE	I will back **whatever proposal you make.**
PRESENT PARTICIPLE	He backs **John's running for the Senate.**
back _____ *put [something] on the back of*	
OBJECT + with OBJECT	The mill backs **the carpet** *with nonslip rubber.*
back _____ *bet on*	
OBJECT	I'm backing **Sky's Limit** in the third race.

PHRASAL VERBS

back away/down/in/out/up/etc. *go backward in a specified direction*	Jeff backed down the ladder slowly. We backed up when we saw the snarling dog.
back SEP away/down/in/out/up/etc. *cause to go backward in a specified direction*	Back the car away from the curb. The carpenter backed the screw out.
back away/down/off (from _____) *withdraw (from [a position, commitment])*	The supervisors backed away from the original proposal. The president backed down from a fight with the Senate.
back onto _____ *have one's back facing*	The hotel backs onto a lovely park.
back out (of _____) *withdraw (from [a commitment, contest])*	The contractor backed out of the deal. She backed out of the track meet because of a sore ankle.
back up *accumulate in a clogged state*	The sewer backed up again. The traffic was backed up for three miles.
back SEP up *support*	I'll back you up when you go to court. Studies back up the recommendation for more exercise.
back SEP up *make a copy of* [COMPUTER]	Be sure to back up your files tonight. Tom backs his files up twice a day.

I base	we base
you base	you base
he/she/it bases	they base

• *He bases his plans on economic models.*

I am basing	we are basing
you are basing	you are basing
he/she/it is basing	they are basing

• *We are basing everything on the election outcome.*

I based	we based
you based	you based
he/she/it based	they based

• *They based their tactics on polling data.*

I was basing	we were basing
you were basing	you were basing
he/she/it was basing	they were basing

• *I was basing it on what I knew at the time.*

PRESENT PERFECT ... have | has based
PAST PERFECT ... had based

FUTURE ... will base
FUTURE PROGRESSIVE ... will be basing
FUTURE PERFECT ... will have based

I was based	we were based
you were based	you were based
he/she/it was based	they were based

• *His decisions were based on misinformation.*

―――(COMPLEMENTS)―――

base _____ establish [a decision/course of action/opinion]

OBJECT + *on* OBJECT

I based **my decision** *on your recommendation.*
We based **our plan** *on the information we had.*
They based **their love** *on mutual respect.*

PASSIVE

Their love was based *on mutual respect.*

OBJECT + *on* WH-CLAUSE

I based **my decision** *on what you recommended to me.*
We based **it** *on what information we had.*

WH-CLAUSE + *on* OBJECT

I based **what I decided to do** *on your recommendation.*
We based **what we did** *on your information.*

WH-CLAUSE + *on* WH-CLAUSE

I based **what I did** *on what you told me to do.*
We based **what we did** *on what information we had.*

base _____ locate the headquarters of

OBJECT + ADVERB OF PLACE

The board based **the new company** *in Albuquerque.*

base _____ station [MILITARY]

OBJECT + ADVERB OF PLACE

The army based **three regiments** *in Spain.*

PASSIVE

Three regiments were based *in Spain.*

NOTE: Many of the following phrasal verbs are used informally.

be down be depressed	I asked her why she was down.
be down on _____ be angry with	Why are you always down on your brother?
be down with _____ be sick due to	Ellery is down with the flu.
be for _____ support	I was for Robert in the last election. I am for renovating the building, not demolishing it.
be in be in one's home/office	The doctor is in.
be in be in fashion	Ruffles are in, pleats are out.
be in on _____ share in	Four seniors were in on the prank.
be into _____ be interested/involved in	Katrina was into gymnastics in a big way.
be off not be at work	The workers will be off for the next three days.
be off not be operating	The lights were off in the auditorium.
be off be less	Sales are off for the third month in a row.
be off be wrong	These estimates are off by 50%.
be off not be taking place	Tomorrow's meeting is off.
be on be operating	The television is on.
be on be in effect	I hope Saturday's party is still on.
be onto _____ be aware of	Oscar is onto your tricks.
be onto _____ be about to discover	The detective was onto something.
be out not be inside	You can lock the doors after everyone is out. The family was out for a stroll along the river.
be out be made public	The news is out that Alison broke her engagement.
be out be out of fashion	Sitcoms are out, documentaries are in.
be out be asleep/unconscious	He went to bed and was out within two minutes.
be out not be permitted	You can eat apples, but chocolate is out.
be out and about travel around	Philip is out and about with his friends.
be out of _____ no longer possess	We're out of coffee—would you like tea?
be out (with _____**)** be absent (due to [an illness])	Half of the third graders are out with the flu.
be out (with _____**)** be unable to play/work (due to [an injury, illness])	He was out for two weeks with a bruised elbow.
be over be finished	The baseball game is finally over.
be through (with _____**)** be finished (with [something])	We were through with our homework by 7 o'clock.
be up be finished	Turn in the exam—your time is up.
be up be more/greater	Food prices are up seven percent.
be up be risen, be put up	We'll leave for Kentucky once the sun is up. The for sale sign has been up for six months.
be up and about/around be out of bed and moving around	I had a cold, but I was up and about on the third day.
be up for _____ be a candidate for	Samantha is up for class president. George is up for re-election.

be up for _____ be available for	The neighbor's house is up for sale again.
be up for _____ be ready and willing for	Are you up for a game of cards?
be up for _____ be on trial for [a crime]	Tori is up for armed robbery.
be up on _____ be knowledgeable about	Veronica is up on all the latest CD releases.
be up to _____ be able to	Are you up to cleaning your room today?

PRESENT

I am	we are
you are	you are
he/she/it is	they are

• *William is here.*

PRESENT PROGRESSIVE

I am being	we are being
you are being	you are being
he/she/it is being	they are being

• *You are being very difficult.*

PAST

I was	we were
you were	you were
he/she/it was	they were

• *He was the manager for eight years.*

PAST PROGRESSIVE

I was being	we were being
you were being	you were being
he/she/it was being	they were being

• *They were only being helpful.*

PRESENT PERFECT … have | has been
PAST PERFECT … had been

FUTURE … will be
FUTURE PROGRESSIVE … will be being
FUTURE PERFECT … will have been

PAST PASSIVE

Be is never used in the passive voice.

COMPLEMENTS

NOTE: *Be* is also used as a helping verb
• to form the progressive tenses
  be + PRESENT PARTICIPLE   They were driving down the wrong street.
• to form the passive voice
  be + PAST PARTICIPLE   You will be arrested if you drive drunk.

be *exist*   "I think, therefore I am." [RENÉ DESCARTES]
            Oh, let it be.

be ____ *exist*
  there + *be* + PREDICATE NOUN   There was **a policeman** on the corner.

be ____ *have the identity, a property, or a characteristic of*

ADVERB OF TIME	The meeting is **at ten.**
	My birthday is **in September.**
	The time is **now.**
ADVERB OF PLACE	The principal is **out of the office.**
	My parents have never been **to Singapore.**
PREDICATE NOUN	Greg is **a bachelor.**
	It is **a streetcar.**
	It is **I**, Mother. [FORMAL] / It's **me**, Mom. [INFORMAL]
PREDICATE ADJECTIVE	Everett is **handsome and rich.**
	The school is **excellent.**

be ____ *must*

INFINITIVE	You are **to report to the office.**
	Gary is **to be ready at seven.**

PHRASAL VERBS

NOTE: Many of the following phrasal verbs are used informally.

be against ____ *oppose*   The group is against gun control.

be along *arrive* [USED ONLY IN THE   Fred will be along any minute now.
  FUTURE TENSE]

be around *exist*   Dinosaurs were around for 150 million years.

be around ____ *be located*   The keys are around here somewhere.

be away *be absent*   The sales clerk is away for a moment.

be behind *lag*   He's behind in his studies.

be down *not be operating*   The server is down, and I can't get my files.

bear _____ *give birth to*	
OBJECT	She bore **a son** in 1982.
	Lois has borne **three children**.
PASSIVE	Three children have been born to Lois.
bear _____ *have as a characteristic*	
OBJECT	Rory bears **a scar** on his left arm.
	Sasha bears **a strong resemblance** to her mother.
bear _____ *have as an identification*	
OBJECT	All three wills bore **Uncle Leland's signature**.
bear _____ *behave*	
REFLEXIVE PRONOUN + ADVERB OF MANNER	He's bearing **himself** *with dignity*.
bear _____ *take care of, pay for*	
OBJECT	My parents bore **all the expenses of my college education**.
bear _____ *call for, require*	
OBJECT	The committee bears **watching**.

─────────────────────────────────── **PHRASAL VERBS** ───

bear down *try hard*	If you bear down, you'll get an "A" in the course.
bear down on _____ *press down on*	Bear down on the pen—you're making four copies.
bear off _____ *turn off*	Bear off the gravel road when you see a large barn.
bear on _____ *have to do with*	These observations don't bear on the matter at all.
bear _SEP_ **out** *prove right*	The testimony will bear this out.
bear up *survive, endure*	Lila bore up well in spite of the criticism.
	The bridge couldn't bear up under such heavy traffic.
bear with _____ *be patient with*	Please bear with us while we discuss the matter.

─────────────────────────────────────── **EXPRESSIONS** ───

bear arms *possess a weapon*	A citizen may bear arms to protect himself.
bear fruit *yield satisfactory results*	The discussions will hopefully bear fruit soon.
bear _____ **in mind** *consider, remember*	Our representatives should bear in mind that their decisions affect millions of people.
bear [one's] cross *endure one's troubles*	The cancer took its toll, but Nick bore his cross bravely.
bear the brunt of _____ *endure the worst part of*	The walnut trees bore the brunt of the storm.
grin and bear it *endure an unpleasant surprise with good humor*	We got laid off, and all we can do is grin and bear it.

PRESENT

I bear	we bear
you bear	you bear
he/she/it bears	they bear

• *Alice bears a lot of responsibility for this.*

PRESENT PROGRESSIVE

I am bearing	we are bearing
you are bearing	you are bearing
he/she/it is bearing	they are bearing

• *They are bearing up well.*

PAST

I bore	we bore
you bore	you bore
he/she/it bore	they bore

• *The monk bore his suffering in silence.*

PAST PROGRESSIVE

I was bearing	we were bearing
you were bearing	you were bearing
he/she/it was bearing	they were bearing

• *We were bearing a heavy load.*

PRESENT PERFECT ... have | has borne
PAST PERFECT   ... had borne

FUTURE   ... will bear
FUTURE PROGRESSIVE   ... will be bearing
FUTURE PERFECT   ... will have borne

PAST PASSIVE

I was borne/born	we were borne/born
you were borne/born	you were borne/born
he/she/it was borne/born	they were borne/born

• *The charges were borne out in today's testimony.*
• *I was born in Richland.*

NOTE: *Born* is the past participle in the sense "give birth to" in the passive voice. *Borne* is used in all other senses.

───────────────────────────────(COMPLEMENTS)───

bear *produce fruit*	In Ecuador, apple trees bear twice a year.
bear _____ *produce* OBJECT	These apple trees won't bear **fruit** for three years.
bear _____ *go* ADVERB OF PLACE TO/FROM	This road bears **to the left**. Bear **right** at the next stoplight.
bear _____ *carry* OBJECT	"Beware of Greeks who bear **gifts**." [VERGIL]
bear _____ *carry/move along* OBJECT	A strong current bore **the ship** out to sea.
bear _____ *support* OBJECT	The pillars bear **the weight of the roof**.
bear _____ *be accountable for* OBJECT	The engineers bear **a heavy responsibility for the disaster**.
bear _____ *endure* OBJECT	He can't bear **the pain**. He will bear **a substantial financial loss**.
for OBJECT + INFINITIVE	I can't bear **for you** *to leave so soon*.
INFINITIVE	I can't bear **to hear such a sad story**.
(it) THAT-CLAUSE	I can't bear **(it)** *that you have to leave so soon*.
PRESENT PARTICIPLE	I can't bear **hearing such a sad story**.
bear _____ *carry in one's mind* OBJECT	He bears **a real grudge** against them. I bear **no hard feelings** toward them.
INDIRECT OBJECT + DIRECT OBJECT *against* PARAPHRASE	I bear *him* no malice. I bear **no malice** *against him*.

PRESENT

I beat	we beat
you beat	you beat
he/she/it beats	they beat

• *In the long run, you never beat the odds.*

PRESENT PROGRESSIVE

I am beating	we are beating
you are beating	you are beating
he/she/it is beating	they are beating

• *I am beating some eggs.*

PAST

I beat	we beat
you beat	you beat
he/she/it beat	they beat

• *He beat the rugs outside.*

PAST PROGRESSIVE

I was beating	we were beating
you were beating	you were beating
he/she/it was beating	they were beating

• *He was beating back a nasty infection.*

PRESENT PERFECT ... have | has beaten
PAST PERFECT ... had beaten

FUTURE ... will beat
FUTURE PROGRESSIVE ... will be beating
FUTURE PERFECT ... will have beaten

PAST PASSIVE

I was beaten	we were beaten
you were beaten	you were beaten
he/she/it was beaten	they were beaten

• *The record was beaten by three of the swimmers.*

COMPLEMENTS

beat *pulsate, throb*

My pulse was beating rapidly.
The drums were beating again.

beat _____ *strike repeatedly*
OBJECT

I beat **the drum** in time to the music.
The jockeys beat **their horses** in the final lap.
The blacksmith beat **the iron** into swords.
The sergeant beat **the recruits** into submission.

beat _____ *mix by stirring*
OBJECT

Beat **the batter** with a wooden spoon.

beat _____ *defeat, win*
OBJECT

The Phillies have beaten **the Red Sox**.
You beat **the record** easily.

beat _____ *be better than*
OBJECT
WH-CLAUSE
PRESENT PARTICIPLE

Good home cooking always beats **restaurant food**.
Your idea beats **what I was trying to do**.
Nothing beats **having lots of money in your wallet**.
That beats **my trying to do it myself**.

beat _____ *confuse, puzzle*
OBJECT + WH-CLAUSE

It beats **me *how anyone can understand these instructions***.

beat _____ *flap*
OBJECT

A hummingbird beats **its wings** up to 70 times per second.

PHRASAL VERBS

beat _____ back/down/up/in/out/etc.
arrive at a specified location sooner than

My sister beat me back to the station.
They raced to the top of the hill, and Ben beat the others up.

beat _SEP_ back *drive back*

Our platoon beat back the enemy's attack.

beat _SEP_ down *cause to collapse*

The warriors beat the doors down with clubs.

beat down (on _____ **)** *fall (on)*

A driving rain beat down on the stadium crowd.
A blazing sun beat down on the spectators.

beat _SEP_ off *drive away*

She beat the would-be robbers off with pepper spray.

beat _SEP_ up *attack savagely*

Gang members beat the man up and took his car.

PRESENT		PRESENT PROGRESSIVE	
I become	we become	I am becoming	we are becoming
you become	you become	you are becoming	you are becoming
he/she/it becomes	they become	he/she/it is becoming	they are becoming

• *Jackson becomes cross when he's hungry.*   • *The kids are becoming tired.*

PAST		PAST PROGRESSIVE	
I became	we became	I was becoming	we were becoming
you became	you became	you were becoming	you were becoming
he/she/it became	they became	he/she/it was becoming	they were becoming

• *The situation became a real mess.*   • *His old jokes were becoming quite tiresome.*

PRESENT PERFECT ... have | has become

PAST PERFECT ... had become

FUTURE ... will become

FUTURE PROGRESSIVE ... will be becoming

FUTURE PERFECT ... will have become

PAST PASSIVE

Become is never used in the passive voice.

COMPLEMENTS

become ＿＿＿ *grow/come to be*

PREDICATE NOUN   The recording became **a huge success.**
Alice became **chair of the department.**

PREDICATE ADJECTIVE   Robert became **quite friendly.**
The weather became **stormy.**

WH-CLAUSE   It became **what we feared the most.**
He will become **whoever he needs to be.**

become ＿＿＿ *enhance the appearance of, look good on*

OBJECT   Moonlight becomes **her.**
His sneering attitude really doesn't become **him.**

PHRASAL VERBS

become of ＿＿＿ *happen to*   Whatever became of your plan to
start your own business?
I don't know what has become of Mary.

EXPRESSIONS

be becoming on ＿＿＿ *look good on*   This shade of blue is very becoming on you.

becoming *attractive*   Your dress is very becoming.
That is a most becoming dress you are wearing.

becoming *suitable to*   She gave a eulogy becoming the occasion of her father's funeral.

PRESENT

I begin	we begin
you begin	you begin
he/she/it begins	they begin

• *He always begins breakfast with coffee.*

PRESENT PROGRESSIVE

I am beginning	we are beginning
you are beginning	you are beginning
he/she/it is beginning	they are beginning

• *It is beginning to rain.*

PAST

I began	we began
you began	you began
he/she/it began	they began

• *I began to feel uneasy.*

PAST PROGRESSIVE

I was beginning	we were beginning
you were beginning	you were beginning
he/she/it was beginning	they were beginning

• *We were beginning to get worried.*

PRESENT PERFECT ... have | has begun
PAST PERFECT ... had begun

FUTURE ... will begin
FUTURE PROGRESSIVE ... will be beginning
FUTURE PERFECT ... will have begun

PAST PASSIVE

— —
— —
it was begun   they were begun

• *Therapy was begun immediately.*

COMPLEMENTS

begin *start*	His meetings never begin on time.
	Meetings always begin with the reading of the minutes.
	The trouble began when Mack called Thack a fool.
	When does the parade begin?
begin ____ *start [an activity, event, process]*	
OBJECT	The chairperson began **the meeting** promptly at 2 o'clock.
	He began **the discussion** with a joke.
INFINITIVE	I began **to fall asleep** during the long lecture.
	The orchestra began **to play**.
WH-CLAUSE	We only began **what absolutely had to be finished**.
	They began **whatever they needed to do**.
PRESENT PARTICIPLE	I began **falling asleep** during the long lecture.
	The orchestra began **playing**.

PHRASAL VERBS

begin by/with ____ *start a sequence/ process with*	The new owners began by firing all the managers.
	Career planning begins with assessing your strengths.
begin ____ **by/with** *start [a process, event] by [doing something first]*	Let's begin the meeting with a big thank-you to the organizers.
	The song begins with a reference to fields of strawberries.

EXPRESSIONS

beginner *one who is starting to learn something*	He's a beginner when it comes to woodworking.
beginner's luck *luck of an inexperienced person*	Winning my very first case was just beginner's luck.
to begin with *first of all*	To begin with, there were no eyewitnesses.

PRESENT

I believe	we believe
you believe	you believe
he/she/it believes	they believe

- *I believe that you are right.*

PRESENT PROGRESSIVE

Believe is rarely used in the progressive tenses.

PAST

I believed	we believed
you believed	you believed
he/she/it believed	they believed

- *I believed her side of the story.*

PAST PROGRESSIVE

Believe is rarely used in the progressive tenses.

PRESENT PERFECT … have | has believed
PAST PERFECT … had believed

FUTURE … will believe
FUTURE PROGRESSIVE —
FUTURE PERFECT … will have believed

PAST PASSIVE

I was believed	we were believed
you were believed	you were believed
he/she/it was believed	they were believed

- *His story was believed by everyone.*

COMPLEMENTS

believe *have religious faith*

Do you believe?
They have believed for years.

believe _____ *accept as true/real/truthful*

OBJECT

The police believe **George's story.**
They believe **George.**

WH-CLAUSE

We believe **what they have told us.**

believe _____ *have an opinion, guess*

OBJECT + *(to be)* PREDICATE NOUN

I believed **him** *(to be) a complete fool.*
We believe **the project** *(to be) a done deal.*

OBJECT + *(to be)* PREDICATE ADJECTIVE

I believed **the proposal** *(to be) dead.*
We believed **the will** *(to be) valid.*

OBJECT + INFINITIVE

We believe **her** *to be dead.*
They believe **the recession** *to have run its course.*

THAT-CLAUSE

I believe **that it is going to rain.**
We believe **that the dollar will strengthen.**

WH-CLAUSE

You won't believe **whom we met.**

PHRASAL VERBS

believe in _____ *accept the existence of*

They believe in ghosts.

believe in _____ *be convinced of the merits of*

I believe in hard work.
We believe in exercise.
We believe in exercising every day.
They believe in doing their best.

EXPRESSIONS

believe it of _____ *accept as true a statement about*

Vera stole the money? I can't
  believe it of her.

believe it or not *it may be unlikely, but it's true*

Believe it or not, Margaret won the spelling bee.

believe you me! *take my word for it!*

I'm going to sue those scoundrels, believe you me!

not believe [one's] ears/eyes *not trust what one has heard/seen*

He used lots of profanity—I couldn't believe my ears.
When I got the electric bill, I couldn't believe my eyes.

PRESENT

I belong	we belong
you belong	you belong
he/she/it belongs	they belong

• *All these CDs belong to me.*

PRESENT PROGRESSIVE

Belong is never used in the progressive tenses.

PAST

I belonged	we belonged
you belonged	you belonged
he/she/it belonged	they belonged

• *The house belonged to my family once.*

PAST PROGRESSIVE

Belong is never used in the progressive tenses.

PRESENT PERFECT ... have | has belonged
PAST PERFECT ... had belonged

FUTURE ... will belong
FUTURE PROGRESSIVE —
FUTURE PERFECT ... will have belonged

PAST PASSIVE

Belong is never used in the passive voice.

──────────────(**COMPLEMENTS**)──────

belong _____ *be properly placed*
  ADVERB OF PLACE

The lamp belongs **here.**
The recycle bin belongs **under the stairs.**
The Dreyfus documents belong **under the letter "D."**

belong _____ *be suitable [in an occupation/activity]*
  ADVERB OF PLACE

Tim belongs **in engineering.**
Ralph belongs **at the FBI.**

──────────────(**PHRASAL VERBS**)──────

belong to _____ *be the property of*

The book belongs to Alice.
That dog belongs to me.

belong to _____ *be a member of*

We have belonged to a book club for 19 years.
They belong to the Republican Party.

belong to _____ *be a part/component of*

Those wheels belong to the lawn mower.
Guam belongs to the United States.
Tomatoes belong to the nightshade family.

PRESENT

I bend	we bend
you bend	you bend
he/she/it bends	they bend

• *He always bends the rules.*

PRESENT PROGRESSIVE

I am bending	we are bending
you are bending	you are bending
he/she/it is bending	they are bending

• *He is bending over backward to help you.*

PAST

I bent	we bent
you bent	you bent
he/she/it bent	they bent

• *I bent my fishhook.*

PAST PROGRESSIVE

I was bending	we were bending
you were bending	you were bending
he/she/it was bending	they were bending

• *The kids were bending clay into shapes.*

PRESENT PERFECT ... have | has bent
PAST PERFECT ... had bent

FUTURE ... will bend
FUTURE PROGRESSIVE ... will be bending
FUTURE PERFECT ... will have bent

PAST PASSIVE

I was bent	we were bent
you were bent	you were bent
he/she/it was bent	they were bent

• *The minister's head was bent in sorrow.*

COMPLEMENTS

bend *become curved/crooked*	The road bends to the right. The trees bent in the wind.
bend *stoop, dip*	I bent to pick up the cat's water bowl. The rod bent under the heavy load.
bend *distort*	His smile bent into an ugly leer.
bend _____ *cause to curve, change the shape of* OBJECT	The archers bent **their bows**. The wind was bending **the trees**. I bent **the wire** into a hook. The magnets bend **the beam of electrons**. The rocks bend **the stream** to the far bank.
bend _____ *distort, cheat* OBJECT	The storm bent **the windmill** out of shape. Politicians bend **the rules** to suit themselves. They bent **the truth** in the run-up to war.

PHRASAL VERBS

bend backward/down/forward/etc. *lean in a specified direction*	Brad bent backward to dodge the ball. She bent down to pet the dog. The girl bent forward to get a better look.
bend SEP **back/down/over/up**/etc. *change the shape of in a specified direction*	Norvel bent the pins back into place. Adrian bent the corner of the page over.
bend over *lean down at the waist*	The class bent over to touch their toes.
bend over backward *do more than required*	The store bends over backward to please its customers.
bend to _____ *concentrate on*	After a break, Jasper bent to his studies.
bend to _____ *give in to*	He bent to the will of the voters and endorsed the plan.
bend _____ **to** *cause to give in*	Cleopatra bent Antony to her will.
be bent on _____ *be determined [to do]*	Helen was bent on going to law school.

EXPRESSIONS

bend [someone's] ear *talk excessively to*	The stranger bent my ear for 45 minutes.

PRESENT

I bet	we bet
you bet	you bet
he/she/it bets	they bet

• *Floyd always bets on the Yankees.*

PAST

I bet	we bet
you bet	you bet
he/she/it bet	they bet

• *She bet $20 on Breezy Summit to win.*

PRESENT PERFECT ... have | has bet
PAST PERFECT ... had bet

PRESENT PROGRESSIVE

I am betting	we are betting
you are betting	you are betting
he/she/it is betting	they are betting

• *I'm betting that you are right.*

PAST PROGRESSIVE

I was betting	we were betting
you were betting	you were betting
he/she/it was betting	they were betting

• *They were all betting that he would win.*

FUTURE ... will bet
FUTURE PROGRESSIVE ... will be betting
FUTURE PERFECT ... will have bet

PAST PASSIVE

—	—
—	—
it was bet	they were bet

• *A fortune was bet by professional gamblers.*

COMPLEMENTS

bet *make a wager*

I never bet.
They are always betting.

bet ____ *place as a wager*

OBJECT

Jason bet **a fortune**.
They are betting **a lot of money**.

OBJECT + THAT-CLAUSE

We bet **five dollars** *that you can't eat the entire cake.*

WH-CLAUSE

They will bet **whatever they can afford to lose**.

bet ____ *wager [something] with [someone]*

OBJECT + OBJECT

I bet **Floyd** *10 dollars.*
He bet **me** *dinner at a nice restaurant.*

OBJECT + THAT-CLAUSE

We bet **Robert** *that his team would finish last.*
I bet **you** *that you can't do it.*

bet ____ *assert [that something will/won't happen]*

THAT-CLAUSE

The company bet **that consumers would like the new design**.
Marisa bet **that the Dodgers wouldn't win**.

PHRASAL VERBS

bet on ____ *place a wager on [a contestant]*

I'm betting on the gray stallion.
I'm betting on St. Louis for the convention site.
I'm betting on St. Louis to be the convention site.

EXPRESSIONS

You bet! *Certainly!* [INFORMAL]

"Can you help me move this sofa?"
"You bet!"

PRESENT

I bid	we bid
you bid	you bid
he/she/it bids	they bid

• *He always bids the limit.*

PRESENT PROGRESSIVE

I am bidding	we are bidding
you are bidding	you are bidding
he/she/it is bidding	they are bidding

• *We are bidding on a vacation condo.*

PAST

I bade/bid	we bade/bid
you bade/bid	you bade/bid
he/she/it bade/bid	they bade/bid

• *I bid $200 for the painting.*

PAST PROGRESSIVE

I was bidding	we were bidding
you were bidding	you were bidding
he/she/it was bidding	they were bidding

• *They were bidding more than they could afford.*

PRESENT PERFECT ... have | has bidden/bid
PAST PERFECT ... had bidden/bid

FUTURE ... will bid
FUTURE PROGRESSIVE ... will be bidding
FUTURE PERFECT ... will have bidden/bid

PAST PASSIVE

I was bidden/bid	we were bidden/bid
you were bidden/bid	you were bidden/bid
he/she/it was bidden/bid	they were bidden/bid

• *Twenty-five dollars was just bid.*

COMPLEMENTS

bid *offer to pay a particular price*

I never bid at auctions.
John will bid when it comes on the market.

bid _____ *offer [a price] for*
OBJECT (+ *for* OBJECT)

When bidding began on the dollhouse, Dave bid **$200**.
He bid **$25** *for the rocking chair*.

on OBJECT

We are bidding **on a first edition of Jane Austen's** *Emma*.

WH-CLAUSE

They will bid **whatever is necessary**.

NOTE: Only *bid* (not *bade* or *bidden*) is used as the past form in the sense "offer as a price."

bid _____ *declare one's intention to take [tricks in a card game]*
OBJECT

I bid **two spades**.

NOTE: Only *bid* (not *bade* or *bidden*) is used as the past form in the sense "declare one's intention to take."

bid _____ *tell [a greeting]*
INDIRECT OBJECT + DIRECT OBJECT
to PARAPHRASE

We bade *them* farewell.
We bade **farewell** *to them*.

bid _____ *urge/ask*
OBJECT + INFINITIVE

The butler bid **the guests** *to enter*.
He bid **them** *to be careful*.

PASSIVE

The guests were bidden *to enter*.

PHRASAL VERBS

bid SEP **out** *offer [work] for bids from outside contractors*

The army bid out the construction
  of four new barracks.
The ad agency bids out the production of TV commercials.

bid SEP **up** *raise [an auction price] by offering more and more money*

Luana bid the price up on the antique lamp.

EXPRESSIONS

outbid _____ *offer more than*

Laura outbid four other people for the rug.

underbid _____ *offer to do something for less than*

The new firm underbid the others by $5,000.

PRESENT

I bind	we bind
you bind	you bind
he/she/it binds	they bind

• *Duct tape binds the parts together.*

PRESENT PROGRESSIVE

I am binding	we are binding
you are binding	you are binding
he/she/it is binding	they are binding

• *We are binding the reports with staples and tape.*

PAST

I bound	we bound
you bound	you bound
he/she/it bound	they bound

• *I bound the essays before shelving them.*

PAST PROGRESSIVE

I was binding	we were binding
you were binding	you were binding
he/she/it was binding	they were binding

• *The gears were binding against each other.*

PRESENT PERFECT ... have | has bound
PAST PERFECT   ... had bound

FUTURE   ... will bind
FUTURE PROGRESSIVE   ... will be binding
FUTURE PERFECT   ... will have bound

PAST PASSIVE

I was bound	we were bound
you were bound	you were bound
he/she/it was bound	they were bound

• *They were bound by their promises.*

COMPLEMENTS

bind *stick, become stuck*	The pulley was binding.
bind *be uncomfortably tight*	This dress is binding.

NOTE: The verb *bind*, when it takes an object, is often used with *together*.

bind _____ *wrap, cover, bandage*
    OBJECT

We bound **the package** with tape.
The printer bound **the books** in red leather.
The doctor bound **my ankle**.

bind _____ *fasten together*
    OBJECT

The secretary bound **the pages** with a clip.

bind _____ *cause to stick together*
    OBJECT

The glue binds **the fibers** together.
The enzyme binds **the calcium ions**.

bind _____ *put an edge/border on*
    OBJECT

He bound **the rug** with cotton tape to keep the edges
   from raveling.

bind _____ *legally/morally obligate*
    OBJECT

My promise binds **me**.
His father's will binds **the use of the property**.

bind _____ *cause to have an emotional attachment*
    OBJECT

Duty and honor bound **the company of soldiers** together.

PHRASAL VERBS

bind _SEP_ **off** *cast off* [KNITTING]	Be sure to bind off the scarf loosely.
bind _SEP_ **over** *hold on bail*	The judge will bind the suspect over for trial.
bind _SEP_ **up** *tie up*	The medics bound up the soldiers' wounds.
	The old issues were bound up with twine.

EXPRESSIONS

be bound to _____ *be certain to*
[*do something*]

It's bound to snow this afternoon.
Erin is bound to be a great lawyer someday.
East Junior High is bound to win the math contest.

PRESENT			PRESENT PROGRESSIVE	
I bite	we bite		I am biting	we are biting
you bite	you bite		you are biting	you are biting
he/she/it bites	they bite		he/she/it is biting	they are biting

• Be careful—the dog bites.

• The fish are biting this afternoon.

PAST			PAST PROGRESSIVE	
I bit	we bit		I was biting	we were biting
you bit	you bit		you were biting	you were biting
he/she/it bit	they bit		he/she/it was biting	they were biting

• He looks like he bit into a sour lemon.

• They were biting off more than they could chew.

PRESENT PERFECT ... have | has bitten
PAST PERFECT ... had bitten

FUTURE ... will bite
FUTURE PROGRESSIVE ... will be biting
FUTURE PERFECT ... will have bitten

PAST PASSIVE	
I was bitten	we were bitten
you were bitten	you were bitten
he/she/it was bitten	they were bitten

• I was bitten by dozens of mosquitoes last night.

COMPLEMENTS

bite *cut with the teeth*	Does your dog bite?
bite *sting*	The mosquitoes are biting tonight.
	Ouch, that ointment bites.
bite *be annoying/objectionable*	His criticisms really bite!
bite *take the bait, be tricked/cheated*	The fish are biting in Big Moose Lake.
	Do you think the customers will bite?
bite _____ *seize/wound with the teeth*	
OBJECT	I just bit **my tongue**.
	The neighbor's dog bit **Thomas**.
WH-CLAUSE	The puppy was biting **whatever it could reach**.

PHRASAL VERBS

bite into _____ *sink one's teeth into*	Sammy bit into the orange and got juice all over his face.
bite (into) _____ *hurt in a stinging way*	The icy wind was biting into my face.
bite _SEP_ **off** *remove with the teeth*	Susan bit off only a morsel.
bite on _____ *chew on*	Wade bit on his lip as he decided what to do.
bite on _____ *be tricked by*	Did Dennis bite on your latest ruse?

EXPRESSIONS

be bitten by the _____ **bug** *be obsessed with*	Jayne was bitten by the tennis bug: She spent $400 on a racket.
bite off more than [one] can chew *undertake more than one can handle*	By opening five stores last year, the owners bit off more than they could chew.
bite [one's] tongue *hold back from saying something offensive*	Sheila had to bite her tongue to keep from calling her boyfriend a stupid idiot.
bite [someone's] head off *speak very angrily to someone*	I broke the copier, and my boss bit my head off.
bite the bullet *be brave in a painful situation*	I bit the bullet and attended my ex-girlfriend's wedding.
bite the dust *die, be defeated*	How old was the cowboy when he bit the dust?
	My first laptop finally bit the dust.

PRESENT

I bleed	we bleed
you bleed	you bleed
he/she/it bleeds	they bleed

• *His nose bleeds at high altitudes.*

PRESENT PROGRESSIVE

I am bleeding	we are bleeding
you are bleeding	you are bleeding
he/she/it is bleeding	they are bleeding

• *I'm bleeding onto my shirt.*

PAST

I bled	we bled
you bled	you bled
he/she/it bled	they bled

• *His wound bled for quite some time.*

PAST PROGRESSIVE

I was bleeding	we were bleeding
you were bleeding	you were bleeding
he/she/it was bleeding	they were bleeding

• *The company was bleeding money.*

PRESENT PERFECT … have | has bled
PAST PERFECT … had bled

FUTURE … will bleed
FUTURE PROGRESSIVE … will be bleeding
FUTURE PERFECT … will have bled

PAST PASSIVE

I was bled	we were bled
you were bled	you were bled
he/she/it was bled	they were bled

• *He was bled dry by the blackmailers.*

COMPLEMENTS

bleed *lose blood*	Her hands and knees were bleeding.
bleed *seep, ooze*	The cut plants bled onto the rug. The newsprint is bleeding onto my hands.
bleed *lose money*	The automobile industry is bleeding at an unsustainable rate.
bleed *feel sympathy*	My heart bleeds for the widow. Her heart bleeds at her neighbor's misfortune.
bleed _____ *draw blood/fluid from* OBJECT	Doctors used to bleed **their patients** regularly. The mechanic bled **the brake line**.
bleed _____ *extort money from over time* OBJECT	Blackmailers bleed **their victims** of all their money.
bleed _____ *lose rapidly* OBJECT	Newspapers are bleeding **money** at an amazing rate.

PHRASAL VERBS

bleed off _____ *be printed so the image goes off the edge of [a page, sheet]*	The photo of the wolf bleeds off the page.
bleed off _____ *remove the contents of*	Irene bled off the air compressor.
bleed through _____ *show through [a layer]*	The dark blue is bleeding through the coat of white paint.

EXPRESSIONS

bleed _____ **dry/white** *drain of resources*	Legal fees will bleed you dry. The rock star's entourage bled him white.
bleed money *lose money rapidly*	The entire industry is bleeding money.
bleed to death *die from loss of blood*	If the doctors can't stop the bleeding, the boy will bleed to death.
bleeding heart *one who is exceptionally sympathetic toward the underprivileged*	George is a bleeding heart for the homeless.

PRESENT		PRESENT PROGRESSIVE	
I blend	we blend	I am blending	we are blending
you blend	you blend	you are blending	you are blending
he/she/it blends	they blend	he/she/it is blending	they are blending

  • *The repainted section blends in well.*   • *We are blending red and white to make pink.*

PAST		PAST PROGRESSIVE	
I blended	we blended	I was blending	we were blending
you blended	you blended	you were blending	you were blending
he/she/it blended	they blended	he/she/it was blending	they were blending

  • *The two families blended perfectly.*   • *They were blending in as best they could.*

PRESENT PERFECT	... have	has blended	FUTURE	... will blend
PAST PERFECT	... had blended	FUTURE PROGRESSIVE	... will be blending
		FUTURE PERFECT	... will have blended

PAST PASSIVE

—   —

—   —

it was blended   they were blended

  • *Their voices were blended in song.*

COMPLEMENTS

NOTE: The verb *blend* is often used with *together.*

blend *mingle socially*   The participants blended nicely with each other.
He never blends well in a crowd.

blend *go well together*   Her odd clothing choices actually blended rather well.
The food and wine blended beautifully.

blend _____ *mix together*
OBJECT   Blend **the sugar and butter** until smooth.
We deliberately blended **the freshmen and seniors** together.
Blend **the ingredients** together and pour the batter into
an 8-inch square baking pan.

PHRASAL VERBS

blend in (with _____ **)** *mix well (with)*   Darin doesn't blend in with his co-workers.
The gray color blends in with the concrete sidewalk.

EXPRESSIONS

blended family *family that includes*   The blended family will soon be the
children of a previous marriage of one   most common type of family unit in the country.
or both spouses

PHRASAL VERBS

blow away/off/out/etc. *be carried by a current of air in a specified direction* — Janet's hat blew off.

blow _SEP_ **away** *defeat soundly* — The visitors blew the home team away.

blow _SEP_ **away** *affect intensely* — This new poem of yours blows me away.

blow _SEP_ **away** *kill with a gun* — The gangsters blew the guard away.

blow down *collapse due to a strong current of air* — The shed blew down in the storm.

blow _SEP_ **down** *cause to collapse due to a strong current of air* — The storm blew the shed down.

blow in / (into _____) *arrive unexpectedly (at)* — Well, look who just blew in! / Three strangers blew into town on Saturday night.

blow _SEP_ **off** *ignore, choose not to deal with* — Lanny blew off the assignment. / Ramona blew off her friends and left town.

blow out *be extinguished* — The candle blew out because of the open windows.

blow out *burst suddenly* — The tire blew out, sounding like a gunshot.

blow _SEP_ **out** *extinguish with a gust of air* — Blow the candle out and go to sleep.

blow _SEP_ **out** *damage severely* — Chuck blew out his knee in the first game.

blow _SEP_ **out** *defeat soundly* — The Cougars blew the Tigers out in an exhibition game.

blow [oneself] out *subside* — The guests left after the storm blew itself out.

blow over *subside* — The storm blew over almost as quickly as it arrived. / This crisis will blow over soon.

blow up *arrive with wind* — A storm blew up out of the southwest.

blow up *explode* — The truck blew up on contact with a mine.

blow up *lose one's temper* — The teacher will blow up if you don't be quiet.

blow _SEP_ **up** *fill with air* — The clown blew up 20 balloons.

blow _SEP_ **up** *cause to explode* — The soldiers blew the headquarters up with mortars.

blow _SEP_ **up** *enlarge* — Let's blow the map up to 400%.

EXPRESSIONS

blow a fuse/gasket *become extremely angry* — Natalie blew a fuse when her secretary lost the files.

blow off (some) steam *release a pent-up emotion* — The players went to a bar to blow off some steam.

blow [one's] cool *lose one's composure* — I know you're frustrated, but don't blow your cool.

blow [someone's] mind *affect intensely* — The revelation really blows my mind.

blow [one's] (own) horn *praise oneself* — Rebecca is talented, but she never blows her own horn.

blow [one's] top/stack *speak/act very angrily* — The candidate blew his top at the nosy reporter.

blow _____ out of the water *destroy completely* — The new motorcycle will blow its competition out of the water.

blow [someone] a kiss *indicate a kiss by pantomime* — Renni blew him a kiss from the platform.

blow the whistle (on _____) *report wrongdoing to authorities (about)* — A secretary blew the whistle on the accountant.

blow _____ to bits/pieces/smithereens *blow completely apart* — A single mortar round blew the police station to pieces.

PRESENT

I blow	we blow
you blow	you blow
he/she/it blows	they blow

• *The wind always blows in the wintertime.*

PRESENT PROGRESSIVE

I am blowing	we are blowing
you are blowing	you are blowing
he/she/it is blowing	they are blowing

• *The wind is blowing my hair.*

PAST

I blew	we blew
you blew	you blew
he/she/it blew	they blew

• *He blew up all the balloons himself.*

PAST PROGRESSIVE

I was blowing	we were blowing
you were blowing	you were blowing
he/she/it was blowing	they were blowing

• *The fans were blowing the gas out of the chamber.*

PRESENT PERFECT ... have | has blown
PAST PERFECT   ... had blown

FUTURE   ... will blow
FUTURE PROGRESSIVE ... will be blowing
FUTURE PERFECT   ... will have blown

PAST PASSIVE

I was blown	we were blown
you were blown	you were blown
he/she/it was blown	they were blown

• *The boat was blown off course.*

───────────────────────────────(**COMPLEMENTS**)───

blow *move with force*	The wind was blowing softly.
blow *force air out*	The fans were blowing at low speed.
blow *produce a sound by having air forced through it*	The horns were all blowing.
blow *explode, erupt*	The volcano blew with a huge roar.
blow *abruptly fail*	The tire blew when we were going 55 miles an hour.
	The fuse blew when I turned on the iron.

blow _____ *move/carry away with a current of air*
OBJECT + ADVERB OF PLACE TO/FROM
The fans were blowing **the stale air** *outside*.
The wind was blowing **dirt** *in my eyes*.
The breeze blew **the boat** *onto the rocks*.

blow _____ *force air at/into/through, fill with air*
OBJECT
John blew **his nose**.
The kids were blowing **bubbles** all afternoon.
OBJECT + PREDICATE ADJECTIVE
Compressed air blew **the pipes** *clear*.
She blew **her hair** *dry*.

blow _____ *produce a sound by forcing air through*
OBJECT
The jazzman blew **the trumpet** with all his might.
The referee blew **his whistle** before the ball was thrown.

blow _____ *cause to explode*
OBJECT + PREDICATE ADJECTIVE
He blew **the safe** *open*.

blow _____ *botch, fail to keep*
OBJECT
I blew **the exam**.
The actors blew **their lines** repeatedly.
The Giants blew **a 14-point lead**.

blow _____ *waste [money]*
OBJECT
Zack blew **his money** on gambling.

blow _____ *leave hurriedly*
OBJECT
I'm bored—let's blow **this joint**.

PRESENT

I bother	we bother
you bother	you bother
he/she/it bothers	they bother

• *He rarely bothers to answer his phone.*

PRESENT PROGRESSIVE

I am bothering	we are bothering
you are bothering	you are bothering
he/she/it is bothering	they are bothering

• *The loud music isn't bothering me.*

PAST

I bothered	we bothered
you bothered	you bothered
he/she/it bothered	they bothered

• *He never bothered my family.*

PAST PROGRESSIVE

I was bothering	we were bothering
you were bothering	you were bothering
he/she/it was bothering	they were bothering

• *The dog was bothering the children.*

PRESENT PERFECT ... have | has bothered
PAST PERFECT ... had bothered

FUTURE ... will bother
FUTURE PROGRESSIVE ... will be bothering
FUTURE PERFECT ... will have bothered

PAST PASSIVE

I was bothered	we were bothered
you were bothered	you were bothered
he/she/it was bothered	they were bothered

• *I was bothered by what he said.*

―――――――(**COMPLEMENTS**)―――

bother _____ *annoy, pester*

OBJECT

His negative attitude really bothers **me**.
Paul's little sister is always bothering **him**.

bother _____ *cause pain/anxiety/concern for*

OBJECT

My knee is bothering **me**.
His proposal bothers **all of us**.
This analysis bothers **me**.

bother _____ *make an effort*

INFINITIVE

He never bothers **to knock**.
He won't bother **to do the job correctly**.
Will they bother **to reply**?

NOTE: In conversation, the infinitive is often understood: "Don't bother (to get it). I'll get it."

―――――――(**PHRASAL VERBS**)―――

bother about/with _____ *concern*
oneself with

Don't bother about the misspellings—
    the computer will fix them.
Dixie never bothers with details.

bother _____ **about/with** *annoy with*

Don't bother yourself about the missing money—
    I'll replace it.
Charlene was always bothering Otto with jokes
    she had read.

―――――――(**EXPRESSIONS**)―――

bother [one's] (pretty little) head
about/with _____ *worry about*

Don't bother your pretty little head
    about the cost of the dress.

PRESENT	
I break	we break
you break	you break
he/she/it breaks	they break

• *He never breaks his word.*

PRESENT PROGRESSIVE	
I am breaking	we are breaking
you are breaking	you are breaking
he/she/it is breaking	they are breaking

• *We are breaking for lunch now.*

PAST	
I broke	we broke
you broke	you broke
he/she/it broke	they broke

• *They broke every single agreement.*

PAST PROGRESSIVE	
I was breaking	we were breaking
you were breaking	you were breaking
he/she/it was breaking	they were breaking

• *The company was just breaking even.*

PRESENT PERFECT	... have	has broken
PAST PERFECT	... had broken

FUTURE	... will break
FUTURE PROGRESSIVE	... will be breaking
FUTURE PERFECT	... will have broken

PAST PASSIVE	
I was broken	we were broken
you were broken	you were broken
he/she/it was broken	they were broken

• *The window was already broken.*

COMPLEMENTS

break *fragment, shatter*	The delicate cup broke into pieces. The waves were breaking close to the shore.
break *fail in strength/resolve/control/ usability*	His health broke. His voice broke with emotion. The criminals broke under questioning. The replacement parts broke too.
break *begin/appear suddenly*	When the storm broke, I was on my bicycle. Dawn is breaking.
break *become publicly known*	The news broke this morning.
break *end suddenly*	Jasmine's fever broke last night.
break *become clear*	I hope the weather breaks soon.
break ⎯⎯ *fracture, render inoperable* OBJECT	He broke **his left wrist.** They broke **my cell phone.**
break ⎯⎯ *violate [a rule, agreement]* OBJECT	They broke **the rules.** We broke **our promise to them.**
break ⎯⎯ *exceed, surpass* OBJECT	He was arrested because he broke **the speed limit.** They broke **the old record** by four seconds.
break ⎯⎯ *make publicly known* OBJECT	The reporters broke **the news** this morning.
break ⎯⎯ *disrupt, make ineffective* OBJECT	The soldiers broke **formation.** The noise broke **my concentration.** She broke **the spell.**
break ⎯⎯ *stop, interrupt* OBJECT PASSIVE	The net broke **the trapeze artist's fall.** Esther broke **the silence** with a scream. The deadlock was broken at 3 A.M.

break _____ *solve, figure out*	
OBJECT	The police broke **the case**.
	The scientists broke **the code**.
break _____ *give the equivalent of in smaller monetary units*	
OBJECT	Can you break **a twenty-dollar bill**?
break _____ *ruin financially*	
OBJECT	One more financial setback will break **the company**.
break _____ *tame, train to obey*	
OBJECT	The cowboys broke **the wild horses**.

(PHRASAL VERBS)

break away *leave suddenly*	Helene broke away from the rest of the sprinters.
break down *become inoperative/ineffective*	My car broke down at Sixth and Pine.
	Negotiations broke down after three days.
break down *become upset*	Seth broke down and cried at the news.
break down *give in*	Lonnie broke down and bought an MP3 player.
break SEP **down** *divide into [pieces]*	Let's break the sentence down into subject and predicate.
break for _____ *interrupt one's activities for*	Let's break for lunch at 12 o'clock.
break SEP **in** *train [an employee]*	Has Marilyn broken Mary in yet?
break SEP **in** *use [something] until it functions well*	I have to break in a new pair of shoes.
break into _____ *enter, usually by force*	Thieves broke into the pharmacy.
break into _____ *begin suddenly*	When she's really happy, Gretchen breaks into song.
break into _____ *become engaged in*	Bert broke into show business at the age of four.
break into / in on _____ *interrupt*	I'm sorry to break in on your conversation, but I must go.
break _____ **into** *divide [something] into [pieces]*	We should break the project into individual tasks.
break off *stop suddenly*	Aaron's voice broke off in mid-sentence.
break SEP **off** *discontinue*	The two nations have broken off diplomatic relations.
break out *develop*	Fire broke out in the kitchen area.
break out *be covered with*	Dave broke out in a sweat.
break out (of _____ **)** *escape (from)*	The prisoners broke out of jail in the early morning.
break up *fall apart, scatter*	The partnership broke up on amicable terms.
	The crowd broke up after the speech.
break up *laugh hard*	Every time I hear this monologue, I break up.
break up (with _____ **)** *end a romance (with)*	Have you heard? Alison broke up with Todd.
break SEP **up** *cause to laugh hard*	This monologue just breaks me up.
break SEP **up** *put an end to*	The FBI tried to break up the drug cartel.
	Two students broke the fight up.

(EXPRESSIONS)

break even *achieve a balance between income and expenses*	The firm broke even in 2008.
break the ice *overcome awkwardness/formality*	The president broke the ice with a couple of jokes.

PRESENT

I bring	we bring
you bring	you bring
he/she/it brings	they bring

• *April showers bring May flowers.*

PRESENT PROGRESSIVE

I am bringing	we are bringing
you are bringing	you are bringing
he/she/it is bringing	they are bringing

• *We are bringing the books with us.*

PAST

I brought	we brought
you brought	you brought
he/she/it brought	they brought

• *They brought us some good news.*

PAST PROGRESSIVE

I was bringing	we were bringing
you were bringing	you were bringing
he/she/it was bringing	they were bringing

• *They were bringing the dessert.*

PRESENT PERFECT ... have | has brought
PAST PERFECT ... had brought

FUTURE ... will bring
FUTURE PROGRESSIVE ... will be bringing
FUTURE PERFECT ... will have brought

PAST PASSIVE

I was brought	we were brought
you were brought	you were brought
he/she/it was brought	they were brought

• *This message was brought to you by our sponsor.*

(**COMPLEMENTS**)

NOTE: The verb *bring* generally indicates movement toward the speaker or toward the focus of attention; compare with *take* (verb No. 505).

bring _____ *carry, lead*

OBJECT (+ ADVERB OF PLACE TO/FROM)

Who will bring **dessert**?
Bring **the book** *here*, please.
I brought **the visitors** *to their hotel*.
The coupons really brought **a crowd** *to the store*.
You should bring **them** *back*.

INDIRECT OBJECT + DIRECT OBJECT

He brought *me* **my dinner**.
She brought *us* **the new account**.
The sale brought *them* **a small fortune**.

to PARAPHRASE

He brought **my dinner** *to me*.
She brought **the new account** *to us*.
The sale brought **a small fortune** *to them*.

OBJECT + WH-CLAUSE

She brought **us** *whatever she could*.

WH-CLAUSE (+ ADVERB OF PLACE TO/FROM)

Bring **whomever you want**.
Bring **whatever you can** *to the picnic*.

bring _____ *cause to be in a particular state/condition*

OBJECT + to OBJECT

I brought **the water** *to a boil*.
They brought **the meeting** *to a conclusion*.

bring _____ *bear as an attribute*

OBJECT

He brought **lots of experience** to the table.

bring _____ *result in*

OBJECT

The storm brought **ten inches of rain**.
The drug will bring **nearly immediate relief**.

bring _____ *cause*

OBJECT + INFINITIVE

What brought **you** *to apply to 13 colleges*?

bring _____ *sell for*

OBJECT

Our old used car brought **$350**.
The sale will bring **a lot of money**.

bring _____ *file in court*

OBJECT

He brought **charges** against the owners.

bring _SEP_ **about** *cause to happen*	How can we bring about change?
bring _SEP_ **along** *have [someone] come along*	Be sure to bring a friend along on the tour.
bring _SEP_ **around** *cause to regain consciousness*	The medic brought the injured man around.
bring _SEP_ **around** *persuade*	They brought Andy around on going to Cancun.
bring _SEP_ **away** *come away with [information]*	We bring valuable insights away from the meeting.
bring _SEP_ **back** *recall*	These photographs bring back lots of memories.
bring _____ **before** *cause to appear before [an authority]*	The guards brought the defendant before Judge Flynn.
bring _____ **before** *introduce for consideration by*	I brought the zoning issue before the city council.
bring _SEP_ **down** *cause to fall*	His own mistakes brought him down.
bring _SEP_ **forth** *give birth to, produce*	Amy expects to bring forth a healthy son. Reinforcements brought forth the historic victory.
bring _SEP_ **forth** *make known*	The accountant brought forth two good arguments.
bring _SEP_ **in** *produce, earn*	The subsidiary brought in $30 million last year.
bring _____ **in on** *include [someone] in [an activity]*	The president brought them in on the decision.
bring _SEP_ **off** *make happen, accomplish*	He brought off one of the biggest upsets in history.
bring _SEP_ **on** *cause to appear*	It's time to bring on the clowns.
bring _SEP_ **out** *cause to emerge*	A police siren will bring people out into the street.
bring _SEP_ **out** *publish, issue*	The novelist brings out a new book every two years.
bring _SEP_ **over** *persuade*	Alexandra brought Gil over to our side.
bring _____ **through** *help to endure*	My sister brought her husband through.
bring _____ **to** *cause to regain consciousness*	We brought Anne to before the medics arrived.
bring _SEP_ **together** *cause to gather*	We brought the class together for one last party.
bring _SEP_ **up** *mention*	Jackie brought up the idea of having more parties.
bring _SEP_ **up** *raise [a child]*	It's not easy to bring up twins. Camelia's parents brought her up to be nice.
bring _____ **up on** *provide in [someone's] childhood*	Mom brought us up on the Beatles.
bring _____ **up on / up-to-date on / up to speed on** *inform [someone] about*	Would you like to bring us up on the latest developments?

bring _____ **into play** *cause to be a factor*	The campaign is bringing Internet strategies into play.
bring _____ **into question** *cause to be doubted*	Reports have brought his character into question.
bring _____ **into service** *begin to use*	The company will bring 30 wind farms into service.
bring _____ **into view** *cause to be seen*	The viewfinder brought the mountain into view.
bring _____ **to a head** *cause to reach a crisis*	The theft brought the question of security to a head.
bring _____ **to an end / a close / a climax** *end*	My new book will bring the case to a close.
bring _____ **to life** *give vitality to*	The children want to bring the puppet to life.
bring _____ **to light** *reveal*	The journalist brought the corruption to light.
bring _____ **to mind** *recall*	The reunion brought to mind all the good times we had.
bring _____ **to [someone's] attention** *make aware of*	Citizens have brought the issue to our attention.
bring _____ **to terms** *force to agree*	Her persuasiveness brought the opposing sides to terms.

PRESENT

I broadcast	we broadcast
you broadcast	you broadcast
he/she/it broadcasts	they broadcast

· *He broadcasts all of their games.*

PRESENT PROGRESSIVE

I am broadcasting	we are broadcasting
you are broadcasting	you are broadcasting
he/she/it is broadcasting	they are broadcasting

· *They are broadcasting the debate live.*

PAST

I broadcast	we broadcast
you broadcast	you broadcast
he/she/it broadcast	they broadcast

· *The station broadcast the show for 50 years.*

PAST PROGRESSIVE

I was broadcasting	we were broadcasting
you were broadcasting	you were broadcasting
he/she/it was broadcasting	they were broadcasting

· *We were broadcasting from Los Angeles then.*

PRESENT PERFECT ... have | has broadcast
PAST PERFECT ... had broadcast

FUTURE   ... will broadcast
FUTURE PROGRESSIVE ... will be broadcasting
FUTURE PERFECT   ... will have broadcast

PAST PASSIVE

—	—
—	—
it was broadcast	they were broadcast

· *The news was broadcast in high definition.*

(**COMPLEMENTS**)

broadcast *transmit programming via radio/TV*	They broadcast in Latin America. They broadcast in Spanish. We broadcast on the FM dial in stereo. Shhh! They're broadcasting.
broadcast *participate in a broadcast program*	She broadcasts live from Rockefeller Center.
broadcast ____ *transmit via radio/TV* OBJECT	They broadcast **news about Asia.** We broadcast **college football games.**
broadcast ____ *communicate via radio/TV* OBJECT	The police broadcast **a description of the suspect.** The weather bureau broadcast **a storm warning for the region.**
THAT-CLAUSE	The networks broadcast **that Senator Blather was the likely winner.** The radio broadcast **that all the major downtown freeways were closed.**
WH-CLAUSE	The stations only broadcast **what they think the public wants to hear.**
broadcast ____ *make widely known* OBJECT	I'll broadcast **my marriage proposal** on the stadium scoreboard. Please don't broadcast **the rumor** to everyone you see.
THAT-CLAUSE	I model part-time. But I don't go broadcasting **that I do.**
WH-CLAUSE	Don't go broadcasting **why we split up.**

PRESENT

I build	we build
you build	you build
he/she/it builds	they build

• *He builds custom-made furniture.*

PRESENT PROGRESSIVE

I am building	we are building
you are building	you are building
he/she/it is building	they are building

• *They are building a new house.*

PAST

I built	we built
you built	you built
he/she/it built	they built

• *They just built a house near us.*

PAST PROGRESSIVE

I was building	we were building
you were building	you were building
he/she/it was building	they were building

• *They were building passenger cars on truck frames.*

PRESENT PERFECT ... have | has built
PAST PERFECT ... had built

FUTURE ... will build
FUTURE PROGRESSIVE ... will be building
FUTURE PERFECT ... will have built

PAST PASSIVE

—	—
—	—
it was built	they were built

• *Our house was built in 1996.*

COMPLEMENTS

build *increase in size/intensity*

The waves were building ever higher.
Our debt was building to scary levels.
Excitement is building over who will be elected.

build ____ *construct*

OBJECT

Tommy built **the wagon** out of parts he found in the garage.
We built **a deck** this summer.
They are building **a communications network**.
We have built **a good plan**.
The prosecutor built **a strong case** against the suspect.

INDIRECT OBJECT + DIRECT OBJECT

They built *us* **a two-car garage**.
We built *them* **a new investment package**.

for PARAPHRASE

They **built a two-car garage** *for us*.
We built **a new investment package** *for them*.

WH-CLAUSE

We can only build **what we can afford**.
They will build **whatever the marketplace wants**.

build ____ *increase*

OBJECT

The campaign built **support** by offering free T-shirts.
The company is building **their business** one store at a time.

PHRASAL VERBS

build ____ **in/into** *make [something] an integral part of*

We will build cabinets into the laundry room.
The programmers built security into the server software.

build ____ **on/onto** *construct [something] as an addition to*

We built a deck onto the house this summer.

build _SEP_ **up** *increase*

The politicians built up hope among poor people.
Steven is building up leg strength by running five miles a day.

build _SEP_ **up** *promote*

The agency built Eileen up as a pop singer.

EXPRESSIONS

build ____ **to order** *construct to individual specifications*

The woodworker builds bookcases to order.
Every computer is built to order.

PRESENT

I burn	we burn
you burn	you burn
he/she/it burns	they burn

• *He really burns me up.*

PRESENT PROGRESSIVE

I am burning	we are burning
you are burning	you are burning
he/she/it is burning	they are burning

• *She is burning loveletters from her ex-husband.*

PAST

I burned/burnt	we burned/burnt
you burned/burnt	you burned/burnt
he/she/it burned/burnt	they burned/burnt

• *We burned oak firewood last winter.*

PAST PROGRESSIVE

I was burning	we were burning
you were burning	you were burning
he/she/it was burning	they were burning

• *A light was burning in the window.*

PRESENT PERFECT ... have | has burned/burnt
PAST PERFECT ... had burned/burnt

FUTURE ... will burn
FUTURE PROGRESSIVE ... will be burning
FUTURE PERFECT ... will have burned/burnt

PAST PASSIVE

I was burned/burnt	we were burned/burnt
you were burned/burnt	you were burned/burnt
he/she/it was burned/burnt	they were burned/burnt

• *My hand was burned by the hot plate.*

COMPLEMENTS

burn *be on fire*	Get out—the building is burning! A small fire was burning in the fireplace.
burn *be destroyed by fire*	Our apartment building burned last night. The paper and kindling burned quickly.
burn *give off light*	Every lamp in the house was burning.
burn *be/feel hot/painful*	Her forehead was burning. My ears were burning from the cold.
burn *become sunburned*	With her fair complexion, she burns easily.
burn _____ *set fire to, destroy by fire* OBJECT	We burned **the trash** in the fireplace.
burn _____ *damage/injure by heat/fire* OBJECT	A spark burned **a hole** in my pants. I burned **my fingers**. I burned **myself** on the stove.
burn _____ *use as fuel/energy* OBJECT WH-CLAUSE	Most cars can burn **regular gas**. Soccer players burn **more calories** than golfers. We burned **whatever we could get our hands on**.
burn _____ *cause to feel hot* OBJECT	The salsa burned **my mouth**.
burn _____ *record data on* OBJECT	We burned **some new CDs**.
burn _____ *defeat, trick, cheat* OBJECT PASSIVE	The quarterback burned **the defense** on that play. I got burned by the dot-com crash in 2000. We were burned in the commodities market.

PHRASAL VERBS

burn down *burn smaller and smaller*	The candle burned down and went out.
burn _SEP_ **up** *make very angry*	That nasty remark really burns me up.

PRESENT

I burst	we burst
you burst	you burst
he/she/it bursts	they burst

• *He always bursts into tears.*

PAST

I burst	we burst
you burst	you burst
he/she/it burst	they burst

• *He burst all of our hopes.*

PRESENT PERFECT ... have | has burst
PAST PERFECT ... had burst

PRESENT PROGRESSIVE

I am bursting	we are bursting
you are bursting	you are bursting
he/she/it is bursting	they are bursting

• *I'm bursting to tell you what happened.*

PAST PROGRESSIVE

I was bursting	we were bursting
you were bursting	you were bursting
he/she/it was bursting	they were bursting

• *We were just bursting after Thanksgiving dinner.*

FUTURE ... will burst
FUTURE PROGRESSIVE ... will be bursting
FUTURE PERFECT ... will have burst

PAST PASSIVE

—	—
—	—
it was burst	they were burst

• *The dam was burst by the heavy rains.*

COMPLEMENTS

burst *break, rupture*	The balloons all burst. I was afraid that my eardrums would burst from the sudden pressure change.
burst *be filled to the breaking point*	The auditorium was bursting with students.
burst *explode*	The rocket burst above the spectators' heads. The bushes are just bursting with blossoms.
burst *give way to sudden emotion*	I felt like my heart would burst. I was bursting with pride.
burst _____ *cause to break/explode* OBJECT	The explosion burst **the windows**. The older kids burst **all the balloons**. The hurricane burst **the retaining walls**.
burst _____ *be very eager* *for* OBJECT + INFINITIVE	We are bursting **for him to tell us**. I am bursting **for Mary to see what we have done**.
INFINITIVE	I'm bursting **to know what happened**. The kids are bursting **to open their presents**.

PHRASAL VERBS

burst in on _____ *interrupt suddenly*	The secretary burst in on the private meeting.
burst in/into _____ *enter suddenly*	The children burst into the room.
burst onto _____ *emerge suddenly in a location*	The singer burst onto the stage.
burst out *explode outward*	When the glass burst out, I was cut by flying shards.
burst out _____ *begin suddenly [to do]*	We all burst out laughing at the joke.
burst (out) into _____ *begin [an activity] suddenly*	After the accident, Kathleen burst into tears. When I hear bongo drums, I burst out into song.
burst out of _____ *be too big for*	She was embarrassed to be bursting out of her dress.
burst out of _____ *leave quickly*	At midnight, the partygoers burst out of the hall.
burst through _____ *break through with force*	The troops burst through the enemy line.

PRESENT

I buy	we buy
you buy	you buy
he/she/it buys	they buy

• *He always buys locally.*

PRESENT PROGRESSIVE

I am buying	we are buying
you are buying	you are buying
he/she/it is buying	they are buying

• *We are buying a new TV.*

PAST

I bought	we bought
you bought	you bought
he/she/it bought	they bought

• *We bought a new car last week.*

PAST PROGRESSIVE

I was buying	we were buying
you were buying	you were buying
he/she/it was buying	they were buying

• *They were buying it on credit.*

PRESENT PERFECT ... have | has bought
PAST PERFECT ... had bought

FUTURE ... will buy
FUTURE PROGRESSIVE ... will be buying
FUTURE PERFECT ... will have bought

PAST PASSIVE

I was bought	we were bought
you were bought	you were bought
he/she/it was bought	they were bought

• *The house was bought in 1982.*

COMPLEMENTS

buy _____ *purchase*
     OBJECT

I bought **take-out** for dinner.
We will buy **500 shares of Apex Corporation**.
A dollar buys **less** than a euro does.

     INDIRECT OBJECT + DIRECT OBJECT

I bought *the kids* **some new toys**.
They bought *us* **dinner**.

     for PARAPHRASE

I bought **some new toys** *for the kids*.
They bought **dinner** *for us*.

     WH-CLAUSE

Mom buys **whichever brand is cheapest**.

buy _____ *accept, believe, agree to/with*
     OBJECT

They bought **our proposal**.
Will the students buy **the idea**?
I don't buy **that** at all.

PHRASAL VERBS

buy into _____ *purchase shares of*

Our investment club bought into
     the Triangle Corporation.

buy into _____ *agree with, believe in*

I don't buy into his money-making scheme.

buy _SEP_ **off** *bribe*

The candidate changed positions; lobbyists bought him off.

buy _SEP_ **out** *purchase all assets/interests of [a business]*

We bought out our competitors.

buy _SEP_ **up** *purchase all of*

We bought up every copy of the *Times* that had Tim's
     crossword puzzle in it.

EXPRESSIONS

buy _____ **for a song** *purchase cheaply*

She bought this new rocking chair for a song.

buy _____ **on credit/time** *purchase now and pay later for*

Can we buy this refrigerator on credit?

buy _____ **sight unseen** *purchase without looking at first*

My parents bought a condo in Florida sight unseen.

buy (some) time *delay an action/decision in hopes that a situation will improve*

The owner wants to buy some time while he considers
     all his options.

call around *telephone several people about something*

She called around to find out where her son was.

call back *telephone someone who telephoned earlier*

I hope that the doctor calls back soon.

call _____ back *telephone [someone who telephoned earlier]*

No message—I'll call her back later.

call for _____ *arrive to pick up*

Hello, Mrs. Smith. I'm calling for Emily.
Good morning, sir. I'm calling for the package.

call for _____ *demand, require*

The crowd is calling for the prisoner.
The protesters are calling for lower taxes.

call _____ forward *call to the front*

He called the student forward to receive an award.

call SEP off *cancel [an event]*

The organizers called off the concert.

call on _____ *make a brief visit to*

I will call on my grandmother tomorrow morning.

call on _____ *ask to speak*

The teacher called on Jamie for the answer.

call _____ on *challenge about*

The speaker told a lie, and Randy called him on it.

call out *shout*

Betty called out to Jody from across the street.

call SEP up *telephone*

Let's call Mom up and ask her to bake brownies.

call SEP up *recall*

This postcard calls up memories of the Depression.

call SEP up *summon to active military duty*

They called up 100 guardsmen in the first month.

call upon/on _____ *order, require*

The mayor called upon the citizens to remain calm.

call a spade a spade *speak frankly*

In her speeches, the candidate calls a spade a spade.

call a halt to _____ *stop*

The general called a halt to the bombing.

call (all) the shots *be in charge*

Everyone knows that his wife calls the shots.

call _____ by [a name] *address by [a particular name]*

The teacher calls us by our first names.

call in sick *telephone one's place of work to report that one is sick and cannot come to work*

I woke up with the flu and called in sick.

call _____ into question *cast doubt on*

The new data call our conclusions into question.

call it a day, call it quits *stop what one has been doing*

I'm worn out! Let's call it a day.

call _____ names *speak insultingly to*

Jimmy's classmates called him names.

call _____ on the carpet *reprimand*

Because Ira arrived late, the boss called him on the carpet.

call ([someone]'s) attention to _____ *cause to be noticed (by someone)*

Alyssa likes to call attention to herself.
May I call your attention to the latest report?

call [someone's] bluff *challenge a false claim by [someone]*

The teacher said he would quit, but the school board called his bluff.

on call *ready when summoned*

The resident doctor is on call 24/7.

PRESENT

I call	we call
you call	you call
he/she/it calls	they call

• *She always calls at dinnertime.*

PAST

I called	we called
you called	you called
he/she/it called	they called

• *I called the office twice.*

PRESENT PERFECT ... have | has called
PAST PERFECT   ... had called

PRESENT PROGRESSIVE

I am calling	we are calling
you are calling	you are calling
he/she/it is calling	they are calling

• *I'm calling everyone on the list.*

PAST PROGRESSIVE

I was calling	we were calling
you were calling	you were calling
he/she/it was calling	they were calling

• *We were just calling to say hello.*

FUTURE   ... will call
FUTURE PROGRESSIVE   ... will be calling
FUTURE PERFECT   ... will have called

PAST PASSIVE

I was called	we were called
you were called	you were called
he/she/it was called	they were called

• *The meeting was called for tomorrow.*

COMPLEMENTS

call *telephone*

Did he call?
Please call when you get a chance.

call *shout*

Someone was calling in the darkness.

call _____ *telephone*
    OBJECT

I called **my sister** last night.
Call **the doctor**!

call _____ *announce, read loudly*
    OBJECT

The teacher called **the roll**.
She called **the winning number**.

call _____ *address as, name, label*
    OBJECT + PREDICATE NOUN

They called **us** *their best friends*.
Let's call **the baby** *Linda*.
She called **him** *a fool*.

       PASSIVE
    OBJECT + PREDICATE ADJECTIVE

He was called *a fool* to his face.
She called **him** *foolish*.
They called **us** *lucky*.

call _____ *bring together people for*
    OBJECT

The chairman called **a meeting**.
The union called **a strike**.

call _____ *summon*
    INDIRECT OBJECT + DIRECT OBJECT
     for PARAPHRASE

She called *him* a taxi.
She called **a taxi** *for him*.

call _____ *stop*
    OBJECT

The umpire called **the game** because of rain.

call _____ *predict*
    OBJECT

William called **the election** for the TV
    network.

PRESENT

I care	we care
you care	you care
he/she/it cares	they care

• *She cares about her work.*

PRESENT PROGRESSIVE

I am caring	we are caring
you are caring	you are caring
he/she/it is caring	they are caring

• *One nurse is caring for the whole ward.*

PAST

I cared	we cared
you cared	you cared
he/she/it cared	they cared

• *I cared for them all week long.*

PAST PROGRESSIVE

I was caring	we were caring
you were caring	you were caring
he/she/it was caring	they were caring

• *He was caring for his disabled wife.*

PRESENT PERFECT ... have | has cared
PAST PERFECT ... had cared

FUTURE ... will care
FUTURE PROGRESSIVE ... will be caring
FUTURE PERFECT ... will have cared

PAST PASSIVE

I was cared	we were cared
you were cared	you were cared
he/she/it was cared	they were cared

• *The children were cared for by their grandparents.*

COMPLEMENTS

care *feel concern/interest*

I don't care.
They act like they don't care.

care _____ *feel concern/interest*

THAT-CLAUSE

I care **that we are going to be late.**
Don't you care **that we missed the train?**
They won't care **that we left early.**

WH-CLAUSE

He doesn't care **who will be there.**
I don't care **what people think.**
Do they care **how late we stay out?**

care _____ *like, choose, be inclined*

INFINITIVE

Would you care **to dance?**
I don't care **to do it.**
You wouldn't care **to say that again,** would you?

PHRASAL VERBS

care about _____ *cherish, value*

Joanne cares very much about
 her invalid sister.
Lori only cares about animals.

care for _____ *be responsible for, watch over*

A nurse cared for Mom after her stroke.
Hilary cared for Ashley's cats when she was gone.

care for _____ *like, want*

George doesn't care for broccoli.
Would you care for another cup of coffee?

EXPRESSIONS

care nothing about _____ *have no
interest in*

I care nothing about your CD
 collection.

care nothing for _____ *not like*

I care nothing for horror films.

could care less, couldn't care less
have no interest at all

She could care less about the prom.
She couldn't care less about the prom.

NOTE: These seemingly contradictory expressions mean the same thing.

PRESENT

I carry	we carry
you carry	you carry
he/she/it carries	they carry

• *He carries a heavy burden.*

PRESENT PROGRESSIVE

I am carrying	we are carrying
you are carrying	you are carrying
he/she/it is carrying	they are carrying

• *I'm already carrying too many credit hours.*

PAST

I carried	we carried
you carried	you carried
he/she/it carried	they carried

• *They carried their own weight.*

PAST PROGRESSIVE

I was carrying	we were carrying
you were carrying	you were carrying
he/she/it was carrying	they were carrying

• *Their voices were not carrying very far.*

PRESENT PERFECT ... have | has carried
PAST PERFECT   ... had carried

FUTURE   ... will carry
FUTURE PROGRESSIVE ... will be carrying
FUTURE PERFECT   ... will have carried

PAST PASSIVE

I was carried	we were carried
you were carried	you were carried
he/she/it was carried	they were carried

• *The kitten was carried to its mother.*

COMPLEMENTS

carry *reach over a distance, travel far*	Voices carry well over water.
	The balls didn't carry very far against the wind.
carry *win adoption*	The resolution carried unanimously.
carry _____ *transport, hold while moving* OBJECT	The fireman carried **the child** to safety. That pipe carries **water.**
carry _____ *bear, support* OBJECT	Those beams carry **the main load of the house.** The pillars carry **the weight of the arch.**
carry _____ *bear responsibility for* OBJECT	I am carrying **20 credit hours** this fall. We carry **150 people** on the payroll. The firm carries **five full-time and three part-time employees.**
carry _____ *have on one's person* OBJECT	Are you carrying **much cash**?
carry _____ *have space for* OBJECT	Our car only carries **four people.**
carry _____ *have for sale* OBJECT	Do you carry **straw hats**?
carry _____ *make available to the public* OBJECT	Most newspapers carry **a listing of TV programs.** Channel 28 is carrying **the game.**
carry _____ *win* OBJECT	Senator Blather has carried **Ohio.** They carried **the election.**
carry _____ *be pregnant with* OBJECT	She is carrying **her second child.**
carry _____ *sing on key* OBJECT	None of my brothers can carry **a tune.**

carry _____ *involve, imply*
  OBJECT
                        The crime carried **a sentence of 10 years in prison.**

carry _____ *transfer a figure from one column to the next* [MATHEMATICS]
  OBJECT
                        Add 6 and 7, write 3, and carry **the 1.**

carry _____ *sit/stand/walk in a particular way*
  REFLEXIVE PRONOUN
                        The First Lady carries **herself** with dignity.

(**PHRASAL VERBS**)

carry _SEP_ **along/around/in/out**/etc. | Be sure to carry along extra batteries.
transport / hold while moving in a specified | It's not easy to carry the baby around with you.
direction |

carry _SEP_ **away** *cause to lose emotional* | The speaker carried the audience away with
control | her forcefulness.

carry _____ **back** *remind of an earlier time* | This song carries me back to my childhood.

carry _____ **forward** *advance* [USUALLY | She was carried forward on a wave of popular support.
PASSIVE] |

carry _SEP_ **off** *kill* | The 1918 flu epidemic carried off 20 million people
| worldwide.
| Grandma was carried off by a heart attack.

carry on (_____) *continue* | Let's carry on as if nothing has happened.
| Darren carried on a long conversation with his teacher.
| We hope our children carry on the family business.

carry on (about _____) *behave in a silly* | Watch how those two boys carry on when their parents
manner, talk at length, make a fuss (about | are gone.
[someone/something]) | The comic carried on about his next-door neighbors.

carry on (with _____) *flirt, have a love affair* | Jamal and Brittany have been carrying on for six months.
(with [someone]) |

carry _SEP_ **out/through** *accomplish* | The biologist carried out a series of experiments.
| Will the candidate carry out his economic plan?
| She is determined to carry through her vision of
| a drug-free America.

carry over *continue (to a later time/location)* | Will their enthusiasm carry over to next week?
| Their great hitting should carry over into the postseason.
| The article carries over onto page 18.

carry _____ **through** *help survive* | These pills will carry you through the week.

(**EXPRESSIONS**)

be/get carried away *lose control of one's* | I got carried away and forgot what
emotions | I was doing.

carry (a lot of) weight (with _____) | Your opinion carries a lot of weight with my family.
be influential (with [someone]) |

carry it off *manage something successfully* | I hope they can carry it off at tomorrow's meeting.

carry [one's] own weight *do one's share* | We'll win first place if all the students carry their
| own weight.

        carry the ball | Volunteers carried the ball to get the candidate elected.
        be primarily responsible |

        carry the day *win* | The game was hard fought, but our team carried the day.

        carry-on *luggage allowed* | Passengers are limited to two carry-ons.
        to be taken aboard an
        aircraft

PRESENT

I cast	we cast
you cast	you cast
he/she/it casts	they cast

• *The statue casts a long shadow.*

PRESENT PROGRESSIVE

I am casting	we are casting
you are casting	you are casting
he/she/it is casting	they are casting

• *I am casting the play this week.*

PAST

I cast	we cast
you cast	you cast
he/she/it cast	they cast

• *He cast me in the role of the duke.*

PAST PROGRESSIVE

I was casting	we were casting
you were casting	you were casting
he/she/it was casting	they were casting

• *We were casting off by 6 A.M.*

PRESENT PERFECT ... have | has cast
PAST PERFECT   ... had cast

FUTURE   ... will cast
FUTURE PROGRESSIVE ... will be casting
FUTURE PERFECT   ... will have cast

PAST PASSIVE

I was cast	we were cast
you were cast	you were cast
he/she/it was cast	they were cast

• *The dice were cast.*

COMPLEMENTS

cast *throw a fishing line/net into the water*

He cast wherever he could see fish.

cast _____ *throw*
  OBJECT

The fishermen cast **their nets** off their boats.
I cast **a line** to the children in the boat.
The boys cast **stones** into the pond.

cast _____ *direct, focus*
  OBJECT + ADVERB OF PLACE

The fireplace cast **a cheerful light** *into the room.*
He cast **a quick glance** *at his audience.*
The moon cast **its light** *on the shimmering lake.*

cast _____ *convey*
  OBJECT + ADVERB OF PLACE

Recent events cast **doubt** *on our decision.*
His actions cast **suspicion** *on his motives.*

cast _____ *choose actors for*
  OBJECT

Roberta has already cast **the play.**

cast _____ *assign a role to*
  OBJECT + *as* OBJECT

We cast **him** *as the hero's father.*
Senator Blather cast **his opponent** *as a reckless spender.*

  OBJECT + *in* OBJECT

He cast **her** *in the leading role.*
Sally cast **Harry** *in the role of best friend.*

cast _____ *form by pouring liquid into a mold*
  OBJECT

The foundry casts **brass bells.**
We cast **wax candles** with the children.

cast _____ *deposit [a ballot, vote]*
  OBJECT

Samuel cast **his ballot** for the liberal candidate.

PHRASAL VERBS

cast _SEP_ **aside/away/off** *discard, throw away*

Lisa cast aside her winter clothes.
The boss cast off all his doubts about the new salesperson.

cast _SEP_ **back** *direct to the past*

The retired teacher cast his thoughts back to happier times.

cast off *push away from the dock*

The cruise ship cast off at 0900 hours.

cast _SEP_ **out** *expel*

The club cast Ollie out for failure to pay dues.

catch _____ *draw even with, overtake*
OBJECT

Their Gross Domestic Product is catching **Spain's**.
I tried to catch **him** on the last lap.

catch _____ *take/get quickly*
OBJECT

Norvel caught **a glimpse of himself** in the mirror.
I caught **sight of Cary** on the subway platform.
Try to catch **some sleep** before you leave.

catch _____ *attract and hold*
OBJECT

Lori's poster will catch **everybody's attention**.
The new employee caught **her eye**.

PHRASAL VERBS

catch _____ **from** *get [a disease] from
[someone/something]*

The whole class caught
the flu from Jimmy.

catch on *become popular*

The Beatles caught on after *The Ed Sullivan Show*.

catch on (to _____) *figure out, learn*

Dexter finally caught on to what Delia had meant.
Cal is new at the job, but he's catching on quickly.

catch [someone]'s eye *get [someone's] attention*

I caught her eye from across the room.

catch _SEP_ up in *interest/involve [someone] in*

Her husband caught her up in his latest scheme.
The crowd was caught up in all the excitement.

catch _____ up (on) *bring up-to-date about*

The assistant will catch the actor up on the news.

catch up on _____ / get caught up on _____
make oneself current about

I hope to catch up on my reading when I retire.
Tonight we can get caught up on our sleep.

catch up (to/with _____) *get even (with
[someone/something])*

Will supply ever catch up to demand?
The taxi caught up with the bus at Skinker Blvd.

EXPRESSIONS

be caught short *be without money when one
needs it*

Bill was caught short today
and couldn't pay for his lunch.

catch a whiff of _____ *smell*

I caught a whiff of sweet perfume.

catch _____ at it *discover [someone doing
something wrong]*

They were sneaking cookies, and Mother caught
them at it.

catch _____ dead *see at any time*
[USUALLY NEGATIVE]

You wouldn't catch me dead in that place.
I wouldn't be caught dead in that place.

catch _____ napping *surprise [someone who
is unprepared]*

The enemy caught our platoon napping.

catch _____ off balance/guard *surprise*

The question caught Senator Blather off balance.

catch (on) fire *become ignited*

The kindling finally caught fire.

catch [one's] breath *rest after intense activity*

I just ran four miles—let me catch my breath!

catch [one's] death of cold *become sick with
a severe cold*

Put on a sweater or you'll catch your death of cold.

catch _____ red-handed *discover [someone]
doing something wrong*

The police caught the thief red-handed.

catch _____ with [someone's]
pants down *discover [someone]
in an embarrassing situation*

They were taking bribes, and investigators caught
them with their pants down.

catch wind of _____ *hear about*

We just caught wind of the new energy proposal.

top
40
verb

PRESENT

I catch	we catch
you catch	you catch
he/she/it catches	they catch

• *The basin catches rainwater.*

PRESENT PROGRESSIVE

I am catching	we are catching
you are catching	you are catching
he/she/it is catching	they are catching

• *I am catching the last train.*

PAST

I caught	we caught
you caught	you caught
he/she/it caught	they caught

• *I caught a cold over the weekend.*

PAST PROGRESSIVE

I was catching	we were catching
you were catching	you were catching
he/she/it was catching	they were catching

• *The kids were catching minnows in the pond.*

PRESENT PERFECT ... have | has caught
PAST PERFECT ... had caught

FUTURE ... will catch
FUTURE PROGRESSIVE ... will be catching
FUTURE PERFECT ... will have caught

PAST PASSIVE

I was caught	we were caught
you were caught	you were caught
he/she/it was caught	they were caught

• *The burglar was finally caught by the police.*

COMPLEMENTS

catch *begin to burn/operate*	The leaves and twigs finally caught. The engine coughed twice and caught.
catch *become entangled*	My sleeve caught on a hook.
catch *act as a catcher* [BASEBALL]	Molina caught in all four games of the series.
catch _____ *capture, seize, trap, snag, entangle* OBJECT	They caught **the thief.** We caught **some trout** for dinner. The bushes caught **my jacket.**
PASSIVE	I was caught in traffic for 45 minutes. Basil was caught in a hailstorm.
catch _____ *grasp and hold onto (physically)* OBJECT	I caught **the ball.**
catch _____ *understand, comprehend* OBJECT	I caught **the joke.** Sorry, I didn't catch **your name.**
catch _____ *discover [someone doing something wrong]* OBJECT + PRESENT PARTICIPLE	I caught **them** *sleeping on the job.* We caught **the kids** *smoking in the garage.*
PASSIVE	Zack was caught *breaking into a car.*
catch _____ *board [a vehicle]* OBJECT	I have to catch **a plane.** I'll catch **a taxi** at the hotel.
catch _____ *become sick with* OBJECT	Everyone caught **a cold.**
catch _____ *go to see* OBJECT	We caught **the last performance of the night.**
catch _____ *watch, listen to* OBJECT	Did you catch **the game** on TV?
catch _____ *meet with* OBJECT	I'll catch **you** later. We will catch **him** at the meeting tomorrow.

PRESENT

I cause	we cause
you cause	you cause
he/she/it causes	they cause

• *He always causes trouble.*

PRESENT PROGRESSIVE

I am causing	we are causing
you are causing	you are causing
he/she/it is causing	they are causing

• *Their presence is causing difficulties.*

PAST

I caused	we caused
you caused	you caused
he/she/it caused	they caused

• *He caused problems on the last trip.*

PAST PROGRESSIVE

I was causing	we were causing
you were causing	you were causing
he/she/it was causing	they were causing

• *The situation was causing me to lose sleep.*

PRESENT PERFECT ... have | has caused
PAST PERFECT ... had caused

FUTURE ... will cause
FUTURE PROGRESSIVE ... will be causing
FUTURE PERFECT ... will have caused

PAST PASSIVE

—	—
—	—
it was caused	they were caused

• *The fire was caused by faulty wiring.*

COMPLEMENTS

cause _____ *make happen*

OBJECT

He caused **an accident**.
The short circuit caused **a fire**.

WH-CLAUSE

His carelessness caused **what happened**.
It must have caused **whatever went wrong**.

cause _____ *compel, force*

OBJECT + INFINITIVE

The scandal caused **him** *to resign*.
The rain caused **the river** *to flood*.

WH-CLAUSE + INFINITIVE

They caused **whoever came next** *to miss their turn*.
Hearing the fax tone caused **whoever it was** *to hang up*.

EXPRESSIONS

cause (a lot of) hard feelings *make people angry/upset*

Greta's remarriage caused a lot of hard feelings.

cause (some) eyebrows to raise *shock people*

Her short skirt caused some eyebrows to raise.

cause (some) tongues to wag *make people gossip*

His outrageous behavior at the reception caused tongues to wag.

PRESENT			PRESENT PROGRESSIVE	

PRESENT

I change	we change
you change	you change
he/she/it changes	they change

• *He changes sides whenever it suits him.*

PRESENT PROGRESSIVE

I am changing	we are changing
you are changing	you are changing
he/she/it is changing	they are changing

• *I'm changing Internet service providers.*

PAST

I changed	we changed
you changed	you changed
he/she/it changed	they changed

• *I changed my mind about the candidates.*

PAST PROGRESSIVE

I was changing	we were changing
you were changing	you were changing
he/she/it was changing	they were changing

• *The weather was changing rapidly.*

PRESENT PERFECT ... have | has changed
PAST PERFECT   ... had changed

FUTURE   ... will change
FUTURE PROGRESSIVE ... will be changing
FUTURE PERFECT   ... will have changed

PAST PASSIVE

I was changed	we were changed
you were changed	you were changed
he/she/it was changed	they were changed

• *The contract was changed by mutual consent.*

COMPLEMENTS

change *become different*	The weather changed overnight. The mood of the party changed abruptly.
change *put on different clothes*	Please change before dinner. We changed in the locker room at school.
change *trade places*	Will you change with me?

change _____ *make different, alter*

OBJECT	We changed **all of our plans.** He's always changing **his mind.**
WH-CLAUSE	I changed **what I was going to do.** We changed **where the meeting was going to be.**

change _____ *switch [one thing with another]*

OBJECT	Let's change **the subject.** We need to change **rooms.** The union has changed **its position.**
to OBJECT	We change **to daylight saving time** in the spring. The sleet changed **to snow** at noon.

change _____ *transfer [from one bus/plane/train to another]*

OBJECT	Passengers will change **trains** at Union Station. We change **planes** in Hong Kong.

change _____ *replace [old with new]*

OBJECT	We need to change **the sheets** today. It's your turn to change **the baby's diaper.**

change _____ *give the equivalent of in smaller monetary units*

OBJECT	Can you change **a twenty-dollar bill?**

PHRASAL VERBS

change back (in/into _____) *return to one's original form/state*	The werewolves changed back into humans at dawn.
change into _____ *put on [clothing]*	Feel free to change into something more comfortable.
change into _____ *transform oneself into*	The frog changed into a handsome prince.
change out of _____ *replace [one set of clothing with another]*	I'm all sweaty—I have to change out of these running clothes.

PRESENT

I charge	we charge
you charge	you charge
he/she/it charges	they charge

• *The psychiatrist charges by the hour.*

PRESENT PROGRESSIVE

I am charging	we are charging
you are charging	you are charging
he/she/it is charging	they are charging

• *I'm charging the suit to my credit card.*

PAST

I charged	we charged
you charged	you charged
he/she/it charged	they charged

• *I charged it to my business account.*

PAST PROGRESSIVE

I was charging	we were charging
you were charging	you were charging
he/she/it was charging	they were charging

• *They were charging him with reckless driving.*

PRESENT PERFECT   ... have | has charged
PAST PERFECT   ... had charged

FUTURE   ... will charge
FUTURE PROGRESSIVE   ... will be charging
FUTURE PERFECT   ... will have charged

PAST PASSIVE

I was charged	we were charged
you were charged	you were charged
he/she/it was charged	they were charged

• *The battery was charged two days ago.*

COMPLEMENTS

charge *rush, attack*	The crowd was charging forward.
charge *bill*	The store doesn't charge for gift wrapping.
charge _____ *rush at, attack*	
OBJECT	The soldiers suddenly charged **the enemy lines**.
charge _____ *set as a price, bill*	
OBJECT	He charges **45 dollars an hour** for design work.
	We must charge **enough** to cover our costs.
INDIRECT OBJECT + DIRECT OBJECT	He charged *us* $250 for the job.
	They charge *users* $20 an hour.
charge _____ *pay for by credit*	
OBJECT	I charged **all my purchases**.
	Will you pay cash or charge **it**?
WH-CLAUSE	I charged **what I had purchased**.
	They charged **whatever they could**.
charge _____ *power [an electric device]*	
OBJECT	I need to charge **my cell phone**.
	You must charge **your electric drill** every night.
charge _____ *claim, accuse*	
OBJECT	The police charged **the suspect**.
OBJECT + *with* OBJECT	They charged **him** *with foul play*.
PASSIVE	My classmate was charged *with petty theft*.
THAT-CLAUSE	The police charged **that he fled the scene of the crime**.
	He charged **that his opponent was incompetent**.
charge _____ *make responsible for*	
OBJECT + *with* OBJECT	The boss charged **Edmund** *with inventory control*.
charge _____ *excite*	
OBJECT	The violinist charged **the concert hall** with excitement.
charge _____ *attribute*	
OBJECT + *to* OBJECT	Kimberly charged **her election loss** *to bad publicity*.
charge _____ *give instructions to* [LEGAL]	
OBJECT	The circuit court judge charged **the jury**.

PRESENT

I check	we check
you check	you check
he/she/it checks	they check

• *He checks his e-mail all the time.*

PRESENT PROGRESSIVE

I am checking	we are checking
you are checking	you are checking
he/she/it is checking	they are checking

• *I'm checking on it now.*

PAST

I checked	we checked
you checked	you checked
he/she/it checked	they checked

• *We checked all the facts yesterday.*

PAST PROGRESSIVE

I was checking	we were checking
you were checking	you were checking
he/she/it was checking	they were checking

• *The police were checking his alibi.*

PRESENT PERFECT ... have | has checked
PAST PERFECT ... had checked

FUTURE ... will check
FUTURE PROGRESSIVE ... will be checking
FUTURE PERFECT ... will have checked

PAST PASSIVE

I was checked	we were checked
you were checked	you were checked
he/she/it was checked	they were checked

• *My bags were checked by the airline.*

(**COMPLEMENTS**)

check *agree point by point*   Jack's account checks with Jill's.

check _____ *examine in order to confirm/verify*

   OBJECT   We checked **all the information.**
             I checked **the ropes.**
   THAT-CLAUSE   He checked **that the luggage was securely tied down.**
   WH-CLAUSE   We checked **what they told us.**

check _____ *deposit/consign for temporary safekeeping*

   OBJECT   She checked **her coat** in the lobby.
             I need to check **two bags.**
   WH-CLAUSE   The hotel will check **whatever you need to leave here.**

check _____ *restrain, block, stop*

   OBJECT   The fallen branch checked **the flow of the little stream.**
             I had to check **the impulse to go too fast.**

(**PHRASAL VERBS**)

check back (with _____ **)** *inquire (of) again*	I'll check back with you later.
check in *register at a hotel/conference*	Let's check in before we go sightseeing.
check SEP **in** *record the return/receipt of*	Did Leon check the book in before it was due?
	The clerk checked the order in.
check into _____ *investigate*	The police will check into the suspect's past.
check into _____ *register at [a hotel, etc.]*	Brian and Allison checked into a hotel near Philadelphia.
check SEP **off** *mark as completed / accounted for*	Hal checked the last four items off.
	Someone needs to check off the people as they register.
check out *appear to be true*	The suspect's story checks out.
check out *settle one's bill [at a hotel, store]*	We need to check out by 10 A.M.
	The Andersons filled two grocery carts and checked out.
check SEP **out** *record the withdrawal of*	Tim checked out six books on astronomy.
check SEP **out/over** *examine, look at appraisingly*	Hey! Check out the guy in the tweed sweater!
	Check the apartment over before you sign the lease.
check (up) on _____ *evaluate*	Would you check up on Jody's performance?
	The nurse checked on the patient in Room 325.

PRESENT

I choose	we choose
you choose	you choose
he/she/it chooses	they choose

• *He always chooses to take Amtrak.*

PRESENT PROGRESSIVE

I am choosing	we are choosing
you are choosing	you are choosing
he/she/it is choosing	they are choosing

• *They are choosing someone right now.*

PAST

I chose	we chose
you chose	you chose
he/she/it chose	they chose

• *They chose a new president.*

PAST PROGRESSIVE

I was choosing	we were choosing
you were choosing	you were choosing
he/she/it was choosing	they were choosing

• *They were choosing a new secretary.*

PRESENT PERFECT ... have | has chosen
PAST PERFECT ... had chosen

FUTURE ... will choose
FUTURE PROGRESSIVE ... will be choosing
FUTURE PERFECT ... will have chosen

PAST PASSIVE

I was chosen	we were chosen
you were chosen	you were chosen
he/she/it was chosen	they were chosen

• *My candidate was chosen.*

COMPLEMENTS

choose *make a selection*

You need to choose.
They are still choosing.
You may choose between lemon and cherry Danish.

choose _____ *select, opt for, prefer*

OBJECT

Giuseppe chose **the toasted ravioli.**
The delegates chose **Senator Blather.**
The residents chose **pumpkin pie** over cheesecake.
The bride chose **satin** for her wedding dress.

INDIRECT OBJECT + DIRECT OBJECT

I chose *myself* **a new computer.**
My son chose *his mother* **a present.**

for PARAPHRASE

I chose **a new computer** *for myself.*
My son chose **a present** *for his mother.*

OBJECT + *as* PREDICATE NOUN

He chose **Ralph** *as his partner.*
They chose **Sue** *as captain.*

OBJECT + *for* PREDICATE NOUN

We will choose **Meg** *for treasurer.*
She chose **Sarah** *for her maid of honor.*

OBJECT + *to be* PREDICATE NOUN

They chose **him** *to be secretary.*

OBJECT + INFINITIVE

They chose **her** *to give the keynote address.*
He chose **Larry** *to be his best man.*
You should choose **Kay** *to design your book.*

INFINITIVE

We chose **to fly to Denver.**

WH-CLAUSE

He is choosing **what to take.**
We chose **where we would go on vacation.**

PRESENT PARTICIPLE

We chose **flying to Denver** over driving there.

EXPRESSIONS

choose (up) sides *form opposing teams by having captains alternately select players*

Once they chose up sides, they had to decide which team would bat first.

pick and choose *select carefully*

Shoppers can pick and choose from a wide variety of produce.

PRESENT		PRESENT PROGRESSIVE	
I cite	we cite	I am citing	we are citing
you cite	you cite	you are citing	you are citing
he/she/it cites	they cite	he/she/it is citing	they are citing

• *He always cites The New York Times.*   • *I'm citing all my sources.*

PAST		PAST PROGRESSIVE	
I cited	we cited	I was citing	we were citing
you cited	you cited	you were citing	you were citing
he/she/it cited	they cited	he/she/it was citing	they were citing

• *The police cited them several times.*   • *He was always citing obscure references.*

PRESENT PERFECT	... have | has cited
PAST PERFECT	... had cited

FUTURE	... will cite
FUTURE PROGRESSIVE	... will be citing
FUTURE PERFECT	... will have cited

PAST PASSIVE

I was cited	we were cited
you were cited	you were cited
he/she/it was cited	they were cited

• *He was cited for contempt.*

───────────────(COMPLEMENTS)───────────────

cite _____ *quote as an authority*

   OBJECT Always cite **your sources.**
             The lawyers cited **the Constitution.**

   WH-CLAUSE I cited **what I considered reliable sources.**
             He cited **whoever would help his cause.**

cite _____ *mention as support/proof*

   OBJECT The company cited **bad weather** for its decreased sales.

cite _____ *formally honor*

   OBJECT The general cited **the entire unit.**
             The committee cited **Jayne** for her volunteer work.

cite _____ *charge [with breaking the law]*

   OBJECT The policeman cited **Sam** for parking illegally.
             The judge cited **the entire group of belligerents.**

PRESENT

I claim	we claim
you claim	you claim
he/she/it claims	they claim

• *He claims that he was interfered with.*

PRESENT PROGRESSIVE

I am claiming	we are claiming
you are claiming	you are claiming
he/she/it is claiming	they are claiming

• *They are claiming that they didn't do anything.*

PAST

I claimed	we claimed
you claimed	you claimed
he/she/it claimed	they claimed

• *She claimed five victories in a row.*

PAST PROGRESSIVE

I was claiming	we were claiming
you were claiming	you were claiming
he/she/it was claiming	they were claiming

• *We were claiming compensation.*

PRESENT PERFECT ... have | has claimed
PAST PERFECT ... had claimed

FUTURE ... will claim
FUTURE PROGRESSIVE ... will be claiming
FUTURE PERFECT ... will have claimed

PAST PASSIVE

I was claimed	we were claimed
you were claimed	you were claimed
he/she/it was claimed	they were claimed

• *The title was claimed by his evil twin brother.*

──(COMPLEMENTS)──

claim _____ *assert as true*
   OBJECT — The company claimed **a spotless environmental record.**
   THAT-CLAUSE — He claimed **that his team would win.**
                 She claims **that polar bears are not endangered.**

claim _____ *profess*
   INFINITIVE — He claimed **to be the first one to climb to the top.**
               They claimed **to be the original owners.**

claim _____ *achieve, win*
   OBJECT — He claimed **three gold medals** at the meet.

claim _____ *destroy, kill*
   OBJECT — The fire claimed **four houses.**
               The accident claimed **three victims.**
               The tornado claimed **the lives of six residents.**

claim _____ *call for, require*
   OBJECT — The report claimed **my full attention.**
               The situation claimed **our utmost efforts.**

claim _____ *ask for, take as one's own/right*
   OBJECT — Has anyone claimed **the necklace in the lost and found**?
               The children claimed **their inheritance** immediately.
               Each tribe claims **the territory** for itself.

PRESENT

I clean	we clean
you clean	you clean
he/she/it cleans	they clean

- *The janitor cleans the offices every night.*

PRESENT PROGRESSIVE

I am cleaning	we are cleaning
you are cleaning	you are cleaning
he/she/it is cleaning	they are cleaning

- *I am cleaning the bathrooms this afternoon.*

PAST

I cleaned	we cleaned
you cleaned	you cleaned
he/she/it cleaned	they cleaned

- *I cleaned out my locker.*

PAST PROGRESSIVE

I was cleaning	we were cleaning
you were cleaning	you were cleaning
he/she/it was cleaning	they were cleaning

- *The kids were cleaning up their rooms.*

PRESENT PERFECT ... have | has cleaned
PAST PERFECT ... had cleaned

FUTURE ... will clean
FUTURE PROGRESSIVE ... will be cleaning
FUTURE PERFECT ... will have cleaned

PAST PASSIVE

I was cleaned	we were cleaned
you were cleaned	you were cleaned
he/she/it was cleaned	they were cleaned

- *The rugs were cleaned by a carpet specialist.*

(**COMPLEMENTS**)

clean *get rid of dirt/trash/impurities*
     The new brush cleans well.
     The boys clean rather carelessly.

clean _____ *rid [something] of dirt/trash/impurities*
     OBJECT
     I will clean **the oven**.
     We cleaned **the house** thoroughly.
     The nurse cleaned **the wound** with peroxide.
     We cleaned **the bathroom** before our guests arrived.
     They cleaned **the basement** in a single day.

     WH-CLAUSE
     He only cleaned **what was going to be sold**.
     They cleaned **whatever needed it**.

clean _____ *eat all the food on*
     OBJECT
     The kids need to clean **their plates**.

clean _____ *remove the innards of [fish, fowl]*
     OBJECT
     We cleaned **the fish**.

(**PHRASAL VERBS**)

clean _SEP_ **off** *get rid of, remove*
     Rory cleaned the graffiti off.

clean _SEP_ **out** *remove the occupants/ contents of*
     The ushers cleaned the auditorium out.
     She needs to clean out her desk.

clean _SEP_ **out** *deprive of money/ possessions* [INFORMAL]
     His roommates cleaned him out in a poker game.

clean **up** *make oneself presentable*
     It's time to clean up for the party.

clean **up** *make a lot of money*
     Langdon really cleaned up on the stock transactions.

clean _SEP_ **up** *rid [something] of dirt/trash*
     It took us two hours to clean up the living room.

clean _SEP_ **up** *rid [something] of corruption*
     The candidate promised he would clean up City Hall.

(**EXPRESSIONS**)

clean house *get rid of what is undesirable*
     When I'm president, I'm going
       to clean house: No one's job will be safe.

clean up [one's] act / clean [one's] act up
begin to behave better
     The boss gave Darrell one last chance to clean up his act.

PRESENT

I clear	we clear
you clear	you clear
he/she/it clears	they clear

• *He clears his throat before he speaks.*

PRESENT PROGRESSIVE

I am clearing	we are clearing
you are clearing	you are clearing
he/she/it is clearing	they are clearing

• *He is clearing the kitchen drain.*

PAST

I cleared	we cleared
you cleared	you cleared
he/she/it cleared	they cleared

• *The check cleared this morning.*

PAST PROGRESSIVE

I was clearing	we were clearing
you were clearing	you were clearing
he/she/it was clearing	they were clearing

• *We were clearing some brush in the backyard.*

PRESENT PERFECT ... have | has cleared
PAST PERFECT ... had cleared

FUTURE ... will clear
FUTURE PROGRESSIVE ... will be clearing
FUTURE PERFECT ... will have cleared

PAST PASSIVE

I was cleared	we were cleared
you were cleared	you were cleared
he/she/it was cleared	they were cleared

• *The channel was cleared by the Coast Guard.*

COMPLEMENTS

clear	*be credited to a bank account*	Your check will clear tomorrow.
clear	*become transparent*	The air in the shop cleared.
clear	*become free of clouds*	The sky cleared before sunset.
clear	*become free of objects/obstructions*	The drain finally cleared by itself.
clear _____ OBJECT	*make free of objects/obstructions*	I cleared **the driveway** after the storm. The boys will clear **the table**. The soldiers cleared **the mine field**.
clear _____ OBJECT	*remove*	Please clear **the snow** off the sidewalk.
clear _____ OBJECT	*pass over/under/by without touching*	The jumper cleared **the bar** at six feet six inches. The truck cleared **the overpass** by eight inches.
clear _____ OBJECT	*remove the occupants of*	The guards cleared **the hall** because of the bomb threat.
clear _____ OBJECT	*free from accusation/blame*	DNA evidence cleared **the suspect** of the crime.
clear _____ OBJECT	*be approved by*	The shipment cleared **customs**. We cleared **security** 40 minutes before departure.
clear _____ OBJECT	*make as a profit*	We cleared **$2000** in the sale.
clear _____ OBJECT	*submit for approval*	Be sure to clear **the budget** with me beforehand.

PHRASAL VERBS

clear out	*go away*	When do you think the crowd will clear out?
clear up	*become cured, disappear*	I hope my acne clears up before the party.
clear _SEP_ up	*cure, make disappear*	This ointment will clear up your heat rash.
clear _SEP_ up	*explain, solve*	The detective will clear up the mystery.

PRESENT

I climb	we climb
you climb	you climb
he/she/it climbs	they climb

• *He always climbs alone.*

PRESENT PROGRESSIVE

I am climbing	we are climbing
you are climbing	you are climbing
he/she/it is climbing	they are climbing

• *I'm climbing Mt. Hood this summer.*

PAST

I climbed	we climbed
you climbed	you climbed
he/she/it climbed	they climbed

• *The plane climbed to 30,000 feet.*

PAST PROGRESSIVE

I was climbing	we were climbing
you were climbing	you were climbing
he/she/it was climbing	they were climbing

• *Vines were climbing up the porch railing.*

PRESENT PERFECT ... have | has climbed
PAST PERFECT   ... had climbed

FUTURE   ... will climb
FUTURE PROGRESSIVE   ... will be climbing
FUTURE PERFECT   ... will have climbed

PAST PASSIVE

—	—
—	—
it was climbed	they were climbed

• *Mera Peak was first climbed in 1953.*

(**COMPLEMENTS**)

climb *go upward, rise*	The plane was climbing. Interest rates are climbing. His approval rate climbed steadily in September.
climb _____ *go upward on*	
OBJECT	The kids were climbing **the apple tree**. Can you climb **the stairs**?
WH-CLAUSE	He climbed **whatever he could get access to**.
climb _____ *grow up/over*	
OBJECT	Ivy was climbing **the walls of the cottage**.

(**PHRASAL VERBS**)

climb up/down/through/etc. *climb in a specified direction*	He climbed up two steps at a time. The fireman climbed down holding the kitten. Open the window and let me climb through.

(**EXPRESSIONS**)

climb all over _____ *reprimand, scold*	The boss climbed all over me for the missing reports.
climb on the bandwagon *join the popular* *side of an issue*	Once recycling became popular, everyone climbed on the bandwagon.
climb the wall(s) *be very anxious*	Before the verdict was returned, Tammy was climbing the walls.

PRESENT	
I cling	we cling
you cling	you cling
he/she/it clings	they cling

• *We cling to our beliefs as long as we can.*

PRESENT PROGRESSIVE	
I am clinging	we are clinging
you are clinging	you are clinging
he/she/it is clinging	they are clinging

• *He is clinging to life by a thread.*

PAST	
I clung	we clung
you clung	you clung
he/she/it clung	they clung

• *He clung to them throughout the ordeal.*

PAST PROGRESSIVE	
I was clinging	we were clinging
you were clinging	you were clinging
he/she/it was clinging	they were clinging

• *The passengers were clinging to the handrails.*

PRESENT PERFECT ... have | has clung
PAST PERFECT ... had clung

FUTURE ... will cling
FUTURE PROGRESSIVE ... will be clinging
FUTURE PERFECT ... will have clung

PAST PASSIVE

— —
— —
it was clung they were clung

• *The story was clung to desperately.*

──────────(COMPLEMENTS)──────────

NOTE: The verb *cling*, when not used with an object, is always followed by *together*.

cling *hold on tightly to each other*

The twins clung together under the umbrella.
The socks were clinging together when I removed them from the dryer.

cling ____ *adhere, hold on tightly*
to OBJECT

He clung **to the ledge** until he was rescued.
The climbers were clinging **to the rope**.
The girl clung **to her father's hand**.
The ivy was clinging **to the wall**.
The price stickers always cling **to the fruit**.
The molecules cling **to each other**.
The office was clinging **to outdated software**.

cling ____ *have a strong emotional attachment*
to OBJECT

Believers cling **to their faith**.
Elvis's fans always clung **to him** no matter what.

to WH-CLAUSE

They will cling **to whoever their prophet is**.
They clung **to whatever their leader told them**.

PRESENT

I close	we close
you close	you close
he/she/it closes	they close

  • *He closes his shop at six every day.*

PAST

I closed	we closed
you closed	you closed
he/she/it closed	they closed

  • *The auctioneer closed the bidding at $30.*

PRESENT PERFECT   ... have | has closed
PAST PERFECT   ... had closed

PRESENT PROGRESSIVE

I am closing	we are closing
you are closing	you are closing
he/she/it is closing	they are closing

  • *I'm closing the door now.*

PAST PROGRESSIVE

I was closing	we were closing
you were closing	you were closing
he/she/it was closing	they were closing

  • *We were closing in on the solution.*

FUTURE   ... will close
FUTURE PROGRESSIVE   ... will be closing
FUTURE PERFECT   ... will have closed

PAST PASSIVE

—	—
—	—
it was closed	they were closed

  • *The gates were closed at dusk.*

NOTE: The verb *close* is pronounced with a /z/, rhyming with *nose*.
The adjective *close* is pronounced with an /s/, rhyming with *dose*.

(COMPLEMENTS)

close *become shut*	The door closed slowly. Daisies close at sunset.
close *come to an end*	The play will close next week.
close *cease operation temporarily/permanently*	The store will close in 15 minutes. The plant will close next month.
close *end the day's business*	The markets closed lower today.
close _____ *shut, block* OBJECT	Please close **the windows**. They closed **the street** for repairs. We closed **the plant in Singapore**.
close _____ *bring to an end* OBJECT	She closed **her savings account**. Her solo closed **the performance**. He closed **the letter** with "XXOO." The college closed **registration** to out-of-state students.
close _____ *settle, come to terms on* OBJECT	We finally closed **the deal**.
close _____ *make [an electrical circuit] continuous* OBJECT	The lever closed **the circuit**.

(PHRASAL VERBS)

close _SEP_ **down/up** *shut/stop permanently/completely*	The health department closed the restaurant down last week.
close in (on _____**)** *draw near (to [someone/something]) to attack/arrest/overwhelm*	Our platoon closed in on the enemy's ammunition dump. The police are closing in on the killer. Mary's financial problems are closing in on her.
close _SEP_ **off** *block*	Construction crews closed the area off to tourists.
close _SEP_ **out** *sell cheaply in order to dispose of the stock of*	The department store is closing out its entire line of designer shoes.

PRESENT

I collect	we collect
you collect	you collect
he/she/it collects	they collect

• *He collects foreign stamps.*

PRESENT PROGRESSIVE

I am collecting	we are collecting
you are collecting	you are collecting
he/she/it is collecting	they are collecting

• *I am collecting for Special Olympics.*

PAST

I collected	we collected
you collected	you collected
he/she/it collected	they collected

• *I collected all the dirty dishes.*

PAST PROGRESSIVE

I was collecting	we were collecting
you were collecting	you were collecting
he/she/it was collecting	they were collecting

• *He was collecting a sizable pension.*

PRESENT PERFECT ... have | has collected
PAST PERFECT ... had collected

FUTURE ... will collect
FUTURE PROGRESSIVE ... will be collecting
FUTURE PERFECT ... will have collected

PAST PASSIVE

I was collected	we were collected
you were collected	you were collected
he/she/it was collected	they were collected

• *Taxes were collected by the local governments.*

COMPLEMENTS

collect _____ *accumulate, gather*
   ADVERB OF PLACE

Dust always collects **on the bookshelves.**
Rain collects **on the window ledges.**
A crowd was collecting **outside the station.**
The students collected **around the professor** after class.

collect _____ *gather as a hobby*
   OBJECT

He collects **books about the Civil War.**
They collect **classical LPs.**

   WH-CLAUSE

I collect **whatever World War Two items I can find.**

collect _____ *gather together, pick up*
   OBJECT

Please collect **the ballots.**
I collected **all the used paper plates and cups.**
They collect **the trash** on Tuesday.
Dark clothes really collect **lint.**

   WH-CLAUSE

He collects **whatever refuse gets left behind.**

collect _____ *call for and receive [money, contributions]*
   OBJECT

The IRS collects **taxes** quarterly.
We are collecting **canned goods** for the food bank.

collect _____ *seek and bring back*
   OBJECT

The kids were collecting **eggs** in the barn.
I will collect **the passengers** at the station.

collect _____ *regain control of [one's thoughts, emotions]*
   OBJECT

He took a minute to collect **himself.**
I need to collect **my thoughts** before speaking.

PHRASAL VERBS

collect on _____ *take as payment on*

His agency collects on overdue accounts.

EXPRESSIONS

cool, calm, and collected *relaxed and*
self-assured

My opponent ranted and raved, and
   I just sat there cool, calm, and collected.

PRESENT

I color	we color
you color	you color
he/she/it colors	they color

- *He always colors his skies dark gray.*

PRESENT PROGRESSIVE

I am coloring	we are coloring
you are coloring	you are coloring
he/she/it is coloring	they are coloring

- *I'm coloring it yellow.*

PAST

I colored	we colored
you colored	you colored
he/she/it colored	they colored

- *She colored in all the background.*

PAST PROGRESSIVE

I was coloring	we were coloring
you were coloring	you were coloring
he/she/it was coloring	they were coloring

- *The kids were coloring in their workbooks.*

PRESENT PERFECT ... have | has colored
PAST PERFECT ... had colored

FUTURE   ... will color
FUTURE PROGRESSIVE   ... will be coloring
FUTURE PERFECT   ... will have colored

PAST PASSIVE

I was colored	we were colored
you were colored	you were colored
he/she/it was colored	they were colored

- *His story was colored by personal experience.*

(COMPLEMENTS)

color *engage in coloring*	He always colors outside the lines.
color *blush*	The little girl colored as she talked.

color _____ *apply color to, change the color of*

OBJECT	Do you want to color **the cards**?
	She is coloring **her hair** now.
	The kids love to color **Easter eggs**.
OBJECT + PREDICATE ADJECTIVE	We colored the **porch ceiling** *light blue*.
	I colored **my egg** *purple*.
WH-CLAUSE	We colored **whatever we could reach**.

color _____ *influence, affect, distort*

OBJECT	His unhappy childhood colored **his adult life**.
	Your hostile attitude colored **the judge's decision**.
	The years since the accident have colored **the facts**.
WH-CLAUSE	The criticism colored **what he did later**.
	His controversial topics colored **how his audience viewed his paintings**.

(PHRASAL VERBS)

color <u>SEP</u> **in** *fill in the outline of [something] with color*	Why don't you color in the man's coat?

PRESENT

I combine	we combine
you combine	you combine
he/she/it combines	they combine

• *Oxygen combines with most elements.*

PRESENT PROGRESSIVE

I am combining	we are combining
you are combining	you are combining
he/she/it is combining	they are combining

• *We are combining our forces.*

PAST

I combined	we combined
you combined	you combined
he/she/it combined	they combined

• *I combined the first two ingredients.*

PAST PROGRESSIVE

I was combining	we were combining
you were combining	you were combining
he/she/it was combining	they were combining

• *They were combining red and white to make pink.*

PRESENT PERFECT ... have | has combined
PAST PERFECT ... had combined

FUTURE ... will combine
FUTURE PROGRESSIVE ... will be combining
FUTURE PERFECT ... will have combined

PAST PASSIVE

I was combined	we were combined
you were combined	you were combined
he/she/it was combined	they were combined

• *The two proposals were combined into a single plan.*

NOTE: The verb *combine* is stressed on the second syllable, like *refine*.
The noun *combine* is stressed on the first syllable.

COMPLEMENTS

combine *mix, act together*

The two gases readily combine.
Iron and oxygen combine to form rust.
The chocolate and peanut butter combined nicely.

combine *merge*

The two armies combined to produce a powerful force.
The liberal and moderate members combined to form a new party.

NOTE: *Combine* is often used with *and* or *with*.

combine _____ *join [two or more elements] together*

OBJECT

The recipe combines **several ingredients**.
The recipe combines **peppers and tomatoes**.
The recipe combines **peppers with tomatoes**.

combine _____ *possess in combination*

OBJECT

He combines **many good qualities**.
He combines **speed and strength**.
He combines **speed with strength**.

PRESENT

I come	we come
you come	you come
he/she/it comes	they come

• *He comes here on weekends.*

PRESENT PROGRESSIVE

I am coming	we are coming
you are coming	you are coming
he/she/it is coming	they are coming

• *I'm coming as fast as I can.*

PAST

I came	we came
you came	you came
he/she/it came	they came

• *They came to see you.*

PAST PROGRESSIVE

I was coming	we were coming
you were coming	you were coming
he/she/it was coming	they were coming

• *The ships were just coming into view.*

PRESENT PERFECT ... have | has come
PAST PERFECT ... had come

FUTURE ... will come
FUTURE PROGRESSIVE ... will be coming
FUTURE PERFECT ... will have come

PAST PASSIVE

Come is never used in the passive voice.

── (COMPLEMENTS) ──

come *move toward the speaker*	Please come here. Don't come too close—I have a cold.
come *fare, get along*	How's Harry coming in his new job?
come ____ *arrive/appear in space/time*	
ADVERB OF TIME	The deadline has come **all too soon**.
ADVERB OF PLACE TO/FROM	The car came **over the hill** at 60 miles an hour.
(+ ADVERB OF TIME)	The class came **to the chapter on ancient Rome**. They come **home** *once a week*.
come ____ *extend, reach*	
ADVERB OF PLACE TO/FROM	Her skirt comes **below her knees**. His property comes **as far as this fence**.
come ____ *originate*	
ADVERB OF PLACE TO/FROM	Doris comes **from a large family**. Most malware comes **from China**.
come ____ *be available*	
ADVERB OF MANNER	The new model comes **in three colors**. The DVD player comes **ready to use**. The computer comes **without a keyboard**.
come ____ *reach a state/conclusion*	
to OBJECT	The two sides came **to an understanding**. Barney came **to his senses** at last.
INFINITIVE	I came **to like him** after all. We came **to enjoy walking to school**. The time has come **to say good-bye**.
come ____ *arrive in a particular condition*	
PREDICATE ADJECTIVE	He came **ready to work**. They came **eager for the show to begin**.
come ____ *become*	
PREDICATE ADJECTIVE	The steering wheel came **loose** and he lost control of the car. Stella's dream of becoming an astronaut came **true**.

come away/forward/in/out/up/etc. *approach in a specified direction*	Marcy came up from the basement. Melinda came in through the back door.
come about *happen*	How did the agreement come about?
come across/upon _____ *find/meet by accident*	She came across her high school yearbook.
come along *appear*	We'll ask the first person who comes along.
come along *make progress*	The project is coming along fairly well.
come (along) with _____ *accompany*	Jayne may come along with us to the grocery. These instructions came with the new monitor.
come around *recover*	He was knocked unconscious, but he soon came around.
come around (to _____**)** *agree finally (to)*	He eventually came around to my point of view.
come at _____ *attack*	Rudy came at the burglar with his fists flying.
come back *be popular again*	Smaller cars are coming back.
come between _____ *cause trouble between*	We can't let a silly quarrel come between us.
come down *decrease* [OF PRICES]	Gasoline prices are coming down.
come down *be demolished*	The historic inn will come down for urban renewal.
come down *be handed down by tradition*	Western philosophy came down to us from the Greeks.
come down to _____ *be a matter of*	The debate comes down to money.
come down with _____ *become sick with*	A third of my classmates came down with a cold.
come from _____ *be caused by*	John's problems come from his lack of control.
come in *become available, arrive*	The election results are coming in now. The new encyclopedias will come in tomorrow.
come in _____ *finish a contest*	Carrie came in second in the 100-meter dash.
come of _____ *result from*	Nothing came of my complaint to the board.
come off _____ *become separated from*	A fender came off my bike today.
come off *happen*	The dinner party came off just as we expected.
come on *be illuminated*	The streetlights come on at dusk.
come on *begin to be broadcast*	When does *Countdown* come on tonight?
come out *be made public*	The facts came out at the afternoon meeting.
come out *declare oneself*	Senator Blather came out in favor of wind farms.
come out *turn out, end up, do*	Everything came out fine in the end.
come (out) to _____ *amount to*	Your repair bill comes out to $227.46. All of Ellery's efforts came to nothing.
come out with _____ *introduce [a product]*	The company came out with three new workstations.
come through _____ *survive*	Randall came through the ordeal of boot camp.
come to *regain consciousness*	Gertie came to before the medics arrived.
come to _____ *be a matter of*	When it comes to idioms, we are the experts.
come up *increase* [OF PRICES]	Stock prices have come up over the past week.
come up *appear for consideration*	The issue comes up every few months. Did the issue of slavery come up in history class?

come up against _____ *encounter, confront*	The activists came up against a lot of opposition.
come up for _____ *be in line for*	These antique lamps don't come up for sale very often. The position comes up for election every four years.
come up with _____ *find, produce*	Alicia came up with two quarters for the parking meter. Has the detective come up with a motive yet?

PRESENT

I command   we command
you command   you command
he/she/it commands   they command

• *I command the Third Infantry Division.*

PRESENT PROGRESSIVE

I am commanding   we are commanding
you are commanding   you are commanding
he/she/it is commanding   they are commanding

• *They are commanding us to leave.*

PAST

I commanded   we commanded
you commanded   you commanded
he/she/it commanded   they commanded

• *He commanded them to stop.*

PAST PROGRESSIVE

I was commanding   we were commanding
you were commanding   you were commanding
he/she/it was commanding   they were commanding

• *He was commanding three regiments at the time.*

PRESENT PERFECT   ... have | has commanded
PAST PERFECT   ... had commanded

FUTURE   ... will command
FUTURE PROGRESSIVE   ... will be commanding
FUTURE PERFECT   ... will have commanded

PAST PASSIVE

I was commanded   we were commanded
you were commanded   you were commanded
he/she/it was commanded   they were commanded

• *The ships were commanded to return to port.*

(COMPLEMENTS)

command *be in authority*

General Brown is commanding.
You have commanded with great effectiveness.

command _____ *have control of*
    OBJECT

She commands **a large fortune.**
He commands **a Navy battle group.**
They no longer command **many resources.**

command _____ *order*
    OBJECT + INFINITIVE

The teacher commanded **the class *to be silent.***
The sergeant commanded **his men *to attack.***
She commanded **the dog *to sit.***

    PASSIVE

The dog was commanded ***to sit.***

command _____ *demand/receive as one's due*
    OBJECT

The law firm commands **huge fees.**
The professor commands **a great deal of respect.**
Their leader commanded **instant obedience.**

command _____ *dominate, overlook*
    OBJECT

The guns command **the entrance to the port.**
The fortress commands **the entire valley.**

PRESENT

I commit	we commit
you commit	you commit
he/she/it commits	they commit

• *He commits himself to do too much.*

PRESENT PROGRESSIVE

I am committing	we are committing
you are committing	you are committing
he/she/it is committing	they are committing

• *I'm committing myself to this project.*

PAST

I committed	we committed
you committed	you committed
he/she/it committed	they committed

• *They committed the suicide attacks.*

PAST PROGRESSIVE

I was committing	we were committing
you were committing	you were committing
he/she/it was committing	they were committing

• *The witness was committing perjury.*

PRESENT PERFECT ... have | has committed
PAST PERFECT ... had committed

FUTURE ... will commit
FUTURE PROGRESSIVE ... will be committing
FUTURE PERFECT ... will have committed

PAST PASSIVE

I was committed	we were committed
you were committed	you were committed
he/she/it was committed	they were committed

• *A crime was committed in my neighborhood.*

COMPLEMENTS

commit _____ *obligate, devote*

OBJECT + *to* OBJECT

He committed **the reserves *to the attack*.**
We must commit **more resources *to the problem*.**
John committed **himself *to public service*.**

PASSIVE

More resources were committed ***to the project*.**

OBJECT + INFINITIVE

Our group is committing **itself *to buy toys for needy children*.**
They committed **a tenth of their income *to fund homeless shelters*.**

commit _____ *place in a prison / mental institution*

OBJECT

The court committed **Harry** for three years.
The state cannot commit **people** without a hearing.

commit _____ *reveal one's views/plans*

REFLEXIVE PRONOUN

The senator never committed **himself**.
You shouldn't commit **yourself** too early.

commit _____ *perform [an illegal/wrong action]*

OBJECT

They had committed **a crime**.
The accountant had committed **forgery**.
He was committing **bigamy**.

commit _____ *set apart [for a particular purpose]*

OBJECT + *to* OBJECT

Tasha commits **much of her time *to volunteer work*.**

commit _____ *refer for consideration*

OBJECT + *to* OBJECT

They committed **the bill *to the Foreign Relations Committee*.**

EXPRESSIONS

commit _____ **to memory** *memorize*

Telford committed the entire poem to memory.

PRESENT

I compare	we compare
you compare	you compare
he/she/it compares	they compare

• *They always compare themselves to us.*

PRESENT PROGRESSIVE

I am comparing	we are comparing
you are comparing	you are comparing
he/she/it is comparing	they are comparing

• *We are comparing results.*

PAST

I compared	we compared
you compared	you compared
he/she/it compared	they compared

• *I compared the questionnaires.*

PAST PROGRESSIVE

I was comparing	we were comparing
you were comparing	you were comparing
he/she/it was comparing	they were comparing

• *He was comparing apples and oranges.*

PRESENT PERFECT   ... have | has compared
PAST PERFECT   ... had compared

FUTURE   ... will compare
FUTURE PROGRESSIVE   ... will be comparing
FUTURE PERFECT   ... will have compared

PAST PASSIVE

I was compared	we were compared
you were compared	you were compared
he/she/it was compared	they were compared

• *The drugs were compared with each other.*

COMPLEMENTS

compare *be evaluated against others*	The new phone compares pretty well.
	The trainees compare favorably.
compare *be equal/alike*	Nothing compares with you.
	He can't compare with the others.
	The two novels don't really compare.
compare ____ *examine in order to find similarities and differences in*	
OBJECT + to/and/with OBJECT	She compared **the carnivores** *to herbivores*.
	I compared **this year's results** *and last year's*.
	He compared **Christian** *and Enlightenment* **ideas of marriage**.
	We compared **job losses** *with job creation*.
WH-CLAUSE + to/and/with WH-CLAUSE	I compared **what we had gained** *to what we had lost*.
	We will compare **how much you made** *and how much everybody else made*.
	They compared **how the Jets played** *with how the Giants played*.
compare ____ *consider as alike*	
OBJECT + to OBJECT	"Shall I compare **thee** *to a summer's day*?" [SHAKESPEARE]
	The author compares **the United States** *to imperial Rome*.

EXPRESSIONS

compare notes on ____ *share observations about*	The students compared notes on their teachers.

PRESENT

I complain	we complain
you complain	you complain
he/she/it complains	they complain

• *Jerry always complains about the food.*

PRESENT PROGRESSIVE

I am complaining	we are complaining
you are complaining	you are complaining
he/she/it is complaining	they are complaining

• *I'm complaining to the boss.*

PAST

I complained	we complained
you complained	you complained
he/she/it complained	they complained

• *I complained until I was blue in the face.*

PAST PROGRESSIVE

I was complaining	we were complaining
you were complaining	you were complaining
he/she/it was complaining	they were complaining

• *They were complaining about their long hours.*

PRESENT PERFECT ... have | has complained
PAST PERFECT ... had complained

FUTURE ... will complain
FUTURE PROGRESSIVE ... will be complaining
FUTURE PERFECT ... will have complained

PAST PASSIVE

I was complained	we were complained
you were complained	you were complained
he/she/it was complained	they were complained

• *The phone service was complained about.*

COMPLEMENTS

complain *express dissatisfaction/annoyance*

He is always complaining.
The children were complaining loudly.
The old chair complained when I sat down in it.

complain _____ *express dissatisfaction/annoyance*

to OBJECT (+ *about* OBJECT)

He complained **to the customer service representative**.
We complained **to the manager** *about the terrible service*.

(*to* OBJECT +) THAT-CLAUSE

The kids complained **that there was nothing to do**.
She complained *to me* **that the meeting had started an hour late**.
I complained *to anyone who would listen* **that our air conditioning wasn't working**.

about OBJECT

I complained **about my job assignment**.
Everyone complains **about the weather**.
We complained **about the terrible service**.

about WH-CLAUSE

He complained **about what he had been promised**.
They complained **about how much they were being paid**.

complain _____ *make a formal accusation*

to OBJECT

I complained **to the police**.
The prosecutor complained **to the judge**.

PASSIVE

The judge was complained to.

(*to* OBJECT +) THAT-CLAUSE

The prosecutor complained **that the defense witness was not answering his questions**.
The defense attorney complained *to the judge* **that the prosecution witness had perjured himself**.

PHRASAL VERBS

complain of _____ *report the symptoms of*

Rosemarie complains of arthritis and backache.

PRESENT

I complete   we complete
you complete   you complete
he/she/it completes   they complete
  • *He always completes what he starts.*

PRESENT PROGRESSIVE

I am completing   we are completing
you are completing   you are completing
he/she/it is completing   they are completing
  • *I'm just completing the inventory now.*

PAST

I completed   we completed
you completed   you completed
he/she/it completed   they completed
  • *I completed the form in 10 minutes.*

PAST PROGRESSIVE

I was completing   we were completing
you were completing   you were completing
he/she/it was completing   they were completing
  • *We were completing the agenda when you called.*

PRESENT PERFECT   ... have | has completed
PAST PERFECT   ... had completed

FUTURE   ... will complete
FUTURE PROGRESSIVE   ... will be completing
FUTURE PERFECT   ... will have completed

PAST PASSIVE

—   —
—   —
it was completed   they were completed
  • *The job was completed by the entire team.*

COMPLEMENTS

complete _____ *finish*
     OBJECT   The painters completed **the living room.**
                 The orchestra completed **the piece** with a flourish.

     WH-CLAUSE   You must complete **what you begin.**
                 They will complete **whatever needs to be done.**

     PRESENT PARTICIPLE   They will complete **sanding the floors** today.
                 I have completed **sending out all the invitations.**

complete _____ *mark the end of*
     OBJECT   This number completes **our program** tonight.
                 The film completes **his epic trilogy.**

complete _____ *make whole*
     OBJECT   A plaid vest completes **the outfit.**
                 This shipment completes **your order.**

PRESENT

I conceive	we conceive
you conceive	you conceive
he/she/it conceives	they conceive

• *He conceives a quite different approach.*

PRESENT PROGRESSIVE

I am conceiving	we are conceiving
you are conceiving	you are conceiving
he/she/it is conceiving	they are conceiving

• *We are conceiving an ambitious marketing plan.*

PAST

I conceived	we conceived
you conceived	you conceived
he/she/it conceived	they conceived

• *They conceived their third child.*

PAST PROGRESSIVE

I was conceiving	we were conceiving
you were conceiving	you were conceiving
he/she/it was conceiving	they were conceiving

• *During the war, women were conceiving less.*

PRESENT PERFECT ... have | has conceived
PAST PERFECT ... had conceived

FUTURE ... will conceive
FUTURE PROGRESSIVE ... will be conceiving
FUTURE PERFECT ... will have conceived

PAST PASSIVE

I was conceived	we were conceived
you were conceived	you were conceived
he/she/it was conceived	they were conceived

• *The project was conceived by the CEO.*

───(**COMPLEMENTS**)───

conceive *become pregnant*

She hopes to conceive soon.
Jane has finally conceived after two years of trying.

conceive _____ *become pregnant with*
  OBJECT

Jane has conceived **a child.**
She has conceived **twins.**

conceive _____ *understand*
  OBJECT

Ray cannot conceive **their reasoning.**
I can't conceive **the appeal of his approach.**

  WH-CLAUSE
  WH-INFINITIVE

I can't conceive **what the problem is.**
We can easily conceive **how to improve the situation.**

conceive _____ *think of, imagine*
  (*of*) OBJECT

I conceived **(of) the idea** this morning.
They conceived **(of) a whole new approach to the problem.**

  (*of*) OBJECT + *as* OBJECT

They couldn't conceive **(of)** me *as a college professor.*
I can conceive **(of) this abandoned church** *as a microbrewery.*

conceive _____ *consider*
  OBJECT + INFINITIVE

They conceived **Jackson** *to be at fault.*
I conceived **it** *to be a hopeless situation.*

conceive _____ *believe*
  THAT-CLAUSE

I can conceive **that he might be right.**
He can't conceive **that they did it intentionally.**

PRESENT

I concentrate	we concentrate
you concentrate	you concentrate
he/she/it concentrates	they concentrate

· *He only concentrates on one thing at a time.*

PRESENT PROGRESSIVE

I am concentrating	we are concentrating
you are concentrating	you are concentrating
he/she/it is concentrating	they are concentrating

· *I am concentrating on the problem.*

PAST

I concentrated	we concentrated
you concentrated	you concentrated
he/she/it concentrated	they concentrated

· *We concentrated the solution of cells.*

PAST PROGRESSIVE

I was concentrating	we were concentrating
you were concentrating	you were concentrating
he/she/it was concentrating	they were concentrating

· *They were concentrating all their efforts on it.*

PRESENT PERFECT ... have | has concentrated
PAST PERFECT ... had concentrated

FUTURE ... will concentrate
FUTURE PROGRESSIVE ... will be concentrating
FUTURE PERFECT ... will have concentrated

PAST PASSIVE

I was concentrated	we were concentrated
you were concentrated	you were concentrated
he/she/it was concentrated	they were concentrated

· *Wealth was concentrated in only a few hands.*

—————————————————————————————————(**COMPLEMENTS**)———

concentrate *draw together, become denser*

Dust always seems to concentrate in the corners.
Birds concentrate before they migrate in the fall.
Mercury concentrates higher up the food chain.
Fluid is concentrating in the lungs.

concentrate _____ *bring together in a single body*

OBJECT

The general concentrated **his forces** in the capital.
We will concentrate **our IT services** in Chicago.
The government has concentrated **more and more power** in the executive branch.

concentrate _____ *make denser/thicker*

OBJECT

We concentrated **the solution** in a beaker.
They concentrate **the sugar syrup** into a semisolid mass.

concentrate _____ *focus [one's thoughts/efforts]*

OBJECT + on OBJECT

You must concentrate **your thinking** *on the problem at hand.*
We concentrated **our efforts** *on new product development.*

OBJECT + on PRESENT PARTICIPLE

I concentrated **my energy** *on solving the problem.*

on OBJECT

Holmes was concentrating **on the puzzle** when Watson walked in.

on PRESENT PARTICIPLE

The boys were concentrating **on getting the lawn mower running.**

concern concern | concerns · concerned · have concerned ☑ REGULAR

PRESENT

I concern	we concern
you concern	you concern
he/she/it concerns	they concern

• *He only concerns himself with philosophy.*

PRESENT PROGRESSIVE

I am concerning	we are concerning
you are concerning	you are concerning
he/she/it is concerning	they are concerning

• *I am concerning myself with developing alternatives.*

PAST

I concerned	we concerned
you concerned	you concerned
he/she/it concerned	they concerned

• *They concerned themselves in these issues.*

PAST PROGRESSIVE

I was concerning	we were concerning
you were concerning	you were concerning
he/she/it was concerning	they were concerning

• *We were concerning ourselves with homeless people.*

PRESENT PERFECT ... have | has concerned
PAST PERFECT ... had concerned

FUTURE ... will concern
FUTURE PROGRESSIVE ... will be concerning
FUTURE PERFECT ... will have concerned

PAST PASSIVE

I was concerned	we were concerned
you were concerned	you were concerned
he/she/it was concerned	they were concerned

• *We were concerned by the test results.*

COMPLEMENTS

concern _____ *be about*

OBJECT

The movie concerns **the cold war.**
The memo concerns **next year's budget.**

WH-CLAUSE

The speech concerns **what we should do next year.**
The report concerns **where we should locate the
  new plant.**

concern _____ *be important to, involve*

OBJECT

This discussion concerns **you.**
The election concerns **everyone.**

concern _____ *make anxious*

OBJECT

Her poor health concerns **us all.**
Don't let the grammatical errors concern **you.**

concern _____ *concentrate on*

REFLEXIVE PRONOUN + *in/with* OBJECT

The king concerns **himself** *in the welfare of his subjects.*
His daughter concerns **herself** *with every aspect
  of the business.*

EXPRESSIONS

be concerned about/for _____
be worried/anxious about

We were concerned about Dad's health.
The pilot was concerned for the passengers' safety.

PRESENT

I conclude	we conclude
you conclude	you conclude
he/she/it concludes	they conclude

• *My run always concludes with stretching.*

PRESENT PROGRESSIVE

I am concluding	we are concluding
you are concluding	you are concluding
he/she/it is concluding	they are concluding

• *I am concluding with an appeal for support.*

PAST

I concluded	we concluded
you concluded	you concluded
he/she/it concluded	they concluded

• *I concluded that we should switch plans.*

PAST PROGRESSIVE

I was concluding	we were concluding
you were concluding	you were concluding
he/she/it was concluding	they were concluding

• *The team was concluding its final home series.*

PRESENT PERFECT ... have | has concluded
PAST PERFECT ... had concluded

FUTURE ... will conclude
FUTURE PROGRESSIVE ... will be concluding
FUTURE PERFECT ... will have concluded

PAST PASSIVE

—	—
—	—
it was concluded	they were concluded

• *The session was concluded at 9:30.*

COMPLEMENTS

conclude _____ *come to an end*

ADVERB OF TIME	I am concluding promptly **at noon.**
	The series concludes **Tuesday.**
ADVERB OF MANNER	The seminar will conclude **with a party at the professor's home.**

conclude _____ *bring to an end*

OBJECT	An argument concluded **the roundtable discussion.**
	Scheduling next week's meeting concluded **the meeting for this week.**
	The president concluded **his speech** with a call for unity.
WH-CLAUSE	We concluded **what we had planned to cover.**
	They concluded **whatever discussion they were having.**

conclude _____ *decide on the basis of reason/evidence*

THAT-CLAUSE	I concluded **that we should not go ahead.**
	We concluded **that their offer was acceptable.**
	They concluded **that they could wait three more days.**

conclude _____ *settle, arrange*

| OBJECT | We finally concluded **the sale.** |

PRESENT

I conduct	we conduct
you conduct	you conduct
he/she/it conducts	they conduct

• *Water conducts electricity.*

PRESENT PROGRESSIVE

I am conducting	we are conducting
you are conducting	you are conducting
he/she/it is conducting	they are conducting

• *The drain is conducting the water away.*

PAST

I conducted	we conducted
you conducted	you conducted
he/she/it conducted	they conducted

• *He conducted many of the sessions.*

PAST PROGRESSIVE

I was conducting	we were conducting
you were conducting	you were conducting
he/she/it was conducting	they were conducting

• *We were conducting an experiment.*

PRESENT PERFECT ... have | has conducted
PAST PERFECT ... had conducted

FUTURE ... will conduct
FUTURE PROGRESSIVE ... will be conducting
FUTURE PERFECT ... will have conducted

PAST PASSIVE

I was conducted	we were conducted
you were conducted	you were conducted
he/she/it was conducted	they were conducted

• *The class was conducted by a visiting professor.*

NOTE: The verb *conduct* is stressed on the second syllable.
The noun *conduct* is stressed on the first syllable.

(**COMPLEMENTS**)

conduct *lead a musical group*

He conducts with flair.
She conducts all over the world.

conduct *transmit electricity/heat/ light/sound*

Wood conducts very poorly.
Metal usually conducts well.

conduct _____ *lead, direct*
OBJECT

Slatkin conducted **the symphony orchestra** for 17 years.
Who will conduct **the Medieval Latin class?**

conduct _____ *manage, carry out*
OBJECT

They conducted **the whole operation.**
The detectives conducted **an investigation.**
The EPA conducted **the removal of the contaminated soil.**

conduct _____ *guide, convey*
OBJECT + ADVERB OF PLACE TO/FROM

The guide conducted **the tourists** *back to the bus.*
These pipes conduct **water** *to the tank.*

conduct _____ *transmit*
OBJECT

Copper conducts **electricity** very well.
The heat sink conducts **heat** away from the CPU.
The optical fiber conducts **light** from a laser.
Cold air conducts **sound** more slowly than warm air.

conduct _____ *behave*
REFLEXIVE PRONOUN

He conducted **himself** admirably.
They conducted **themselves** quite well.

PRESENT

I confirm · we confirm
you confirm · you confirm
he/she/it confirms · they confirm

• *They confirm each nominee separately.*

PRESENT PROGRESSIVE

I am confirming · we are confirming
you are confirming · you are confirming
he/she/it is confirming · they are confirming

• *Her secretary is confirming the reservation.*

PAST

I confirmed · we confirmed
you confirmed · you confirmed
he/she/it confirmed · they confirmed

• *She confirmed the rumor.*

PAST PROGRESSIVE

I was confirming · we were confirming
you were confirming · you were confirming
he/she/it was confirming · they were confirming

• *The police were confirming his story.*

PRESENT PERFECT   ... have | has confirmed
PAST PERFECT   ... had confirmed

FUTURE   ... will confirm
FUTURE PROGRESSIVE   ... will be confirming
FUTURE PERFECT   ... will have confirmed

PAST PASSIVE

I was confirmed · we were confirmed
you were confirmed · you were confirmed
he/she/it was confirmed · they were confirmed

• *The information was confirmed by two sources.*

───(**COMPLEMENTS**)───

confirm _____ *formally approve, ratify*

OBJECT
The board will confirm **my nomination** soon.
The Senate must confirm **all cabinet appointees.**

PASSIVE
All cabinet appointees must be confirmed by the Senate.

OBJECT + *as* PREDICATE NOUN
The panel confirmed **her** *as acting chair.*
They are confirming **him** *as company treasurer.*

PASSIVE
He was confirmed *as secretary of state.*

confirm _____ *prove to be true, verify*

OBJECT
The new research confirms **the original findings.**
Can anyone confirm **these rumors?**
The police are trying to confirm **his alibi.**

OBJECT + *to be* PREDICATE NOUN
The coroner confirmed **the death** *to be an accident.*

OBJECT + *to be* PREDICATE ADJECTIVE
The judge confirmed **the election** *to be valid.*
I can't confirm **the statement** *to be either true or false.*

THAT-CLAUSE
I confirmed **that the meeting was still on.**
Can we confirm **that the government has fallen?**
The X-rays confirmed **that the bone was cracked.**

WH-CLAUSE
It only confirmed **what we had expected.**
The candidate confirmed **what had been leaked to the press.**
The report confirmed **why the accident had happened.**

confirm _____ *strengthen*

OBJECT
The setback only confirmed **our resolve to succeed.**
The project's failure confirmed **our doubts about it.**
Her win confirmed **our confidence in her ability.**

confront

confront | confronts ·
confronted · have confronted

PRESENT

I confront	we confront
you confront	you confront
he/she/it confronts	they confront

• *He never confronts his opponents.*

PRESENT PROGRESSIVE

I am confronting	we are confronting
you are confronting	you are confronting
he/she/it is confronting	they are confronting

• *I'm confronting my fear of flying.*

PAST

I confronted	we confronted
you confronted	you confronted
he/she/it confronted	they confronted

• *I confronted my worst fears.*

PAST PROGRESSIVE

I was confronting	we were confronting
you were confronting	you were confronting
he/she/it was confronting	they were confronting

• *We were confronting them at every turn.*

PRESENT PERFECT ... have | has confronted
PAST PERFECT ... had confronted

FUTURE ... will confront
FUTURE PROGRESSIVE ... will be confronting
FUTURE PERFECT ... will have confronted

PAST PASSIVE

I was confronted	we were confronted
you were confronted	you were confronted
he/she/it was confronted	they were confronted

• *I was confronted with a terrible choice.*

──────────────────────────────────(**COMPLEMENTS**)──────

confront _____ *oppose, challenge*

OBJECT

The ships confronted **each other** with guns blazing.
We confronted **their absurd claims.**
Marcos confronted **the pollsters** about their shoddy
techniques.

WH-CLAUSE

They confronted **whomever the defense tried to use
as an expert witness.**

confront _____ *meet face to face*

OBJECT

You must confront **your problems.**
He confronted **his children's bad behavior.**

WH-CLAUSE

I confronted **what I most feared.**
He confronted **why he kept gaining weight.**

confront _____ *bring face to face*

OBJECT + *with* OBJECT

Nate confronted **the pundits** *with lots of statistics.*
Police confronted **the suspect** *with his partner's confession.*

PASSIVE

The suspect was confronted *with his partner's confession.*

PRESENT

I confuse	we confuse
you confuse	you confuse
he/she/it confuses	they confuse

• *He always confuses his audiences.*

PRESENT PROGRESSIVE

I am confusing	we are confusing
you are confusing	you are confusing
he/she/it is confusing	they are confusing

• *I'm sorry, I'm only confusing you more.*

PAST

I confused	we confused
you confused	you confused
he/she/it confused	they confused

• *You confused me with your new proposal.*

PAST PROGRESSIVE

I was confusing	we were confusing
you were confusing	you were confusing
he/she/it was confusing	they were confusing

• *We were confusing each other.*

PRESENT PERFECT ... have | has confused
PAST PERFECT   ... had confused

FUTURE   ... will confuse
FUTURE PROGRESSIVE ... will be confusing
FUTURE PERFECT   ... will have confused

PAST PASSIVE

I was confused	we were confused
you were confused	you were confused
he/she/it was confused	they were confused

• *I was confused by what he said.*

(**COMPLEMENTS**)

confuse ____ *perplex, bewilder*

OBJECT

Stop! You're confusing **us**.
The governor's speech totally confused **her audience**.
Bonnie confused **me** with her weird behavior.

WH-CLAUSE

The sign in the window will confuse **whoever walks by**.

confuse ____ *make unclear, make a mess of*

OBJECT

You're trying to confuse **the issue**.

WH-CLAUSE

Her amendments confused **what I was proposing**.
The discussion confused **what was being recommended**.

confuse ____ *fail to distinguish between*

OBJECT + *with/and* OBJECT

I'm sorry. I confused **you** *with your sister*.
He confuses **money** *with wealth*.
You are confusing **Alice** *and Mary*.

PRESENT		PRESENT PROGRESSIVE	
I connect	we connect	I am connecting	we are connecting
you connect	you connect	you are connecting	you are connecting
he/she/it connects	they connect	he/she/it is connecting	they are connecting

- *He always connects with his audiences.*

- *I'm connecting you now.*

PAST		PAST PROGRESSIVE	
I connected	we connected	I was connecting	we were connecting
you connected	you connected	you were connecting	you were connecting
he/she/it connected	they connected	he/she/it was connecting	they were connecting

- *I connected the two wires.*

- *We were connecting to a flight in Detroit.*

PRESENT PERFECT	... have | has connected
PAST PERFECT	... had connected

FUTURE	... will connect
FUTURE PROGRESSIVE	... will be connecting
FUTURE PERFECT	... will have connected

PAST PASSIVE	
I was connected	we were connected
you were connected	you were connected
he/she/it was connected	they were connected

- *Finally, I was connected to the Internet.*

COMPLEMENTS

connect *be joined/linked*

Our two hotel rooms connected.
Most computer peripherals easily connect.
The proposals all connect with each other.
Your flights connect in Chicago.

connect *link to the Internet*

Are you connected?
I'll connect once I'm in my hotel room.
I'm not connected when I travel.

connect *establish rapport*

Fortunately, our families connected well.
Harry and Sally really connected.
The speaker failed to connect with the audience.

connect *hit a baseball* [INFORMAL]

Albert connected for a three-run homer.

connect _____ *join together, unite*

OBJECT

A skyway connected **the two towers.**
We connected **the people requesting information.**

OBJECT + *with* OBJECT

Would you please connect **me** *with the customer service
  department*?

connect _____ *associate, consider related*

OBJECT

I finally connected **their names.**
We connected **all the pieces of the puzzle.**
The detective connected **all the clues.**

OBJECT + *with* OBJECT

Did you connect **Bing's silence** *with Frank's arrival*?

connect _____ *link physically*

OBJECT (+ *into/to* OBJECT)

We can connect **the server** now.
Connect **the monitor** *into the surge protector*.
The nurse connected **her** *to a heart monitor*.
How can I connect **my computer** *to the Internet*?

PASSIVE

Can my computer be connected *to the Internet*?

PHRASAL VERBS

connect up with _____ *meet with*

I hope to connect up with my cousins
  in Atlanta.

PRESENT

I consider	we consider
you consider	you consider
he/she/it considers	they consider

• *He considers John a good friend.*

PRESENT PROGRESSIVE

I am considering	we are considering
you are considering	you are considering
he/she/it is considering	they are considering

• *I'm considering quitting my job.*

PAST

I considered	we considered
you considered	you considered
he/she/it considered	they considered

• *I considered all the options.*

PAST PROGRESSIVE

I was considering	we were considering
you were considering	you were considering
he/she/it was considering	they were considering

• *We were considering what we should do.*

PRESENT PERFECT … have | has considered
PAST PERFECT … had considered

FUTURE … will consider
FUTURE PROGRESSIVE … will be considering
FUTURE PERFECT … will have considered

PAST PASSIVE

I was considered	we were considered
you were considered	you were considered
he/she/it was considered	they were considered

• *Every possibility was considered.*

(COMPLEMENTS)

consider *think carefully*

Stop and consider before you do something you will regret.
Take a moment to consider.

consider _____ *think about before making a decision / taking action, contemplate*

OBJECT

The judge considered **the defendant's motion for acquittal.**
You must consider **your options.**
He should consider **the family's reaction.**
They considered **him** for the job.
He considered **himself** in the mirror.
They considered **the appalling scene** in front of them.

WH-CLAUSE

I considered **what my next move should be.**
We considered **how much it would cost.**

WH-INFINITIVE

The boys considered **what to charge for the lemonade.**
The teacher considered **how to make the students behave.**

PRESENT PARTICIPLE

I considered **taking out a new loan.**
We considered **moving to Colorado.**

consider _____ *regard as*

OBJECT + (to be) PREDICATE NOUN

We considered **the movie** *(to be) a great success.*
They considered **Allen** *(to be) a natural leader.*

PASSIVE

The movie was considered *(to be) a great success.*

OBJECT + (to be) PREDICATE ADJECTIVE

They considered **the plan** *(to be) badly flawed.*
Everyone considered **George** *(to be) strange.*

PASSIVE

The plan was considered *(to be) badly flawed.*
George was considered *(to be) strange.*

consider _____ *take into account*

OBJECT

Grandpa is fairly active, considering **his age.**
In sentencing, the judge considered **the defendant's history of abuse.**

consider _____ *treat kindly/attentively*

OBJECT

The students should consider **the teacher's feelings.**

PRESENT

I consist · we consist
you consist · you consist
he/she/it consists · they consist

• *His breakfast consists of a sweet roll.*

PRESENT PROGRESSIVE

Consist is rarely used in the progressive tenses.

PAST

I consisted · we consisted
you consisted · you consisted
he/she/it consisted · they consisted

• *The plan consisted of wishful thinking.*

PAST PROGRESSIVE

Consist is rarely used in the progressive tenses.

PRESENT PERFECT ... have | has consisted
PAST PERFECT ... had consisted

FUTURE ... will consist
FUTURE PROGRESSIVE —
FUTURE PERFECT ... will have consisted

PAST PASSIVE

Consist is never used in the passive voice.

─(**COMPLEMENTS**)─

NOTE: The verb *consist* is always used with *of* or *in*.

consist _____ *be made up*
   of OBJECT

The book consists **of three parts.**
The city consists **of ten districts.**
The plan mainly consists **of a series of budget recommendations.**
I consist **of ten trillion cells organized into tissue and organs.**
We consist **of eight distribution centers and 200 retail outlets**
   worldwide.

consist _____ *have a basis*
   in OBJECT

The beauty of the plan consists **in its simplicity.**
A citizen's rights consist **in individual responsibility.**
The prosecutor's reputation consists **in always being honest.**

PRESENT

I constitute — we constitute
you constitute — you constitute
he/she/it constitutes — they constitute

• *His actions constitute fraud.*

PRESENT PROGRESSIVE

I am constituting — we are constituting
you are constituting — you are constituting
he/she/it is constituting — they are constituting

• *The legislature is constituting new campaign laws.*

PAST

I constituted — we constituted
you constituted — you constituted
he/she/it constituted — they constituted

• *We constituted a new policy last month.*

PAST PROGRESSIVE

I was constituting — we were constituting
you were constituting — you were constituting
he/she/it was constituting — they were constituting

• *We were constituting a new criminal code.*

PRESENT PERFECT ... have | has constituted
PAST PERFECT ... had constituted

FUTURE ... will constitute
FUTURE PROGRESSIVE ... will be constituting
FUTURE PERFECT ... will have constituted

PAST PASSIVE

— —
— —
it was constituted — they were constituted

• *The court was constituted in 1982.*

COMPLEMENTS

constitute _____ *establish legally*

OBJECT

The law duly constitutes **a new division** within the department.
The board constituted **a review process.**

constitute _____ *make up, be the equivalent of*

OBJECT

Sixteen ounces constitutes **an American pint.**
Eight board members constitute **a quorum.**
What he did constitutes **treason.**
Any illegal action constitutes **a crime.**

WH-CLAUSE

That area constitutes **what I would call a slum.**
His words constitute **what could be called slander.**

PRESENT

I construct	we construct
you construct	you construct
he/she/it constructs	they construct

• *He constructs architectural models.*

PRESENT PROGRESSIVE

I am constructing	we are constructing
you are constructing	you are constructing
he/she/it is constructing	they are constructing

• *I am constructing a shed in our backyard.*

PAST

I constructed	we constructed
you constructed	you constructed
he/she/it constructed	they constructed

• *They constructed a clever argument.*

PAST PROGRESSIVE

I was constructing	we were constructing
you were constructing	you were constructing
he/she/it was constructing	they were constructing

• *They were constructing a new piece of equipment.*

PRESENT PERFECT ... have | has constructed
PAST PERFECT   ... had constructed

FUTURE   ... will construct
FUTURE PROGRESSIVE ... will be constructing
FUTURE PERFECT   ... will have constructed

PAST PASSIVE

—	—
—	—
it was constructed	they were constructed

• *Our house was constructed in 1888.*

COMPLEMENTS

construct _____ *build physically*

OBJECT	I constructed **a birdhouse** when I was in seventh grade.
	The engineers constructed **a new transformer**.
WH-CLAUSE	We will only construct **what we can guarantee**.
	They will construct **whatever the customer asks for**.

construct _____ *create by arranging ideas*

OBJECT	They constructed **an elaborate theory**.
	He constructed **intricate plots** for all his movies.
	I constructed **a convincing case against the development**.

PRESENT

I consult	we consult
you consult	you consult
he/she/it consults	they consult

• *She consults with me on a regular basis.*

PRESENT PROGRESSIVE

I am consulting	we are consulting
you are consulting	you are consulting
he/she/it is consulting	they are consulting

• *I'm consulting at Mercy Hospital all week.*

PAST

I consulted	we consulted
you consulted	you consulted
he/she/it consulted	they consulted

• *I consulted a specialist.*

PAST PROGRESSIVE

I was consulting	we were consulting
you were consulting	you were consulting
he/she/it was consulting	they were consulting

• *Our company was consulting in the Middle East.*

PRESENT PERFECT ... have | has consulted
PAST PERFECT ... had consulted

FUTURE ... will consult
FUTURE PROGRESSIVE ... will be consulting
FUTURE PERFECT ... will have consulted

PAST PASSIVE

I was consulted	we were consulted
you were consulted	you were consulted
he/she/it was consulted	they were consulted

• *All the usual experts were consulted.*

COMPLEMENTS

consult *provide professional advice*	I consult for the state of New Jersey.
	Dr. Smith consults in all the area hospitals.
consult *confer*	Good practitioners consult frequently.
consult _____ *seek advice/information from*	
OBJECT	We consulted **every doctor in town**.
	I consulted **the dictionary**.
	You must consult **your own conscience**.
WH-CLAUSE	I will consult **whoever can offer the best advice**.
	He will consult **whichever specialist his doctor recommends**.
consult _____ *confer*	
(*with*) OBJECT	I will consult **(with) my colleagues** about your recommendation.
	We must consult **(with) the president** before we make a decision.

PRESENT

I contain	we contain
you contain	you contain
he/she/it contains	they contain

• *The book contains a lot of new data.*

PRESENT PROGRESSIVE

I am containing	we are containing
you are containing	you are containing
he/she/it is containing	they are containing

• *The levee is barely containing the floodwater.*

PAST

I contained	we contained
you contained	you contained
he/she/it contained	they contained

• *He barely contained himself.*

PAST PROGRESSIVE

I was containing	we were containing
you were containing	you were containing
he/she/it was containing	they were containing

• *We were containing the leaks with duct tape.*

PRESENT PERFECT ... have | has contained
PAST PERFECT ... had contained

FUTURE ... will contain
FUTURE PROGRESSIVE ... will be containing
FUTURE PERFECT ... will have contained

PAST PASSIVE

I was contained	we were contained
you were contained	you were contained
he/she/it was contained	they were contained

• *The epidemic was finally contained.*

(COMPLEMENTS)

contain _____ hold, include

OBJECT

This beaker contains **hydrochloric acid**.
The legislation contains **some surprises**.
The movie contains **some pretty amusing scenes**.
The book contained **a reference to Darwin**.

WH-CLAUSE

His speeches contain **what you would expect from a conservative**.
The fall fashion show contained **whatever was hot at the moment**.

contain _____ hold back, restrain

OBJECT

The police contained **the rioters**.
The firewalls contained **the spread of the blaze**.
I couldn't contain **myself** from laughing.
Please contain **your dogs**.
Their policy was to contain **communism**.

PRESENT		PRESENT PROGRESSIVE	
I continue	we continue	I am continuing	we are continuing
you continue	you continue	you are continuing	you are continuing
he/she/it continues	they continue	he/she/it is continuing	they are continuing

 • *The schedule continues as originally set.* • *I'm continuing on to Paris.*

PAST		PAST PROGRESSIVE	
I continued	we continued	I was continuing	we were continuing
you continued	you continued	you were continuing	you were continuing
he/she/it continued	they continued	he/she/it was continuing	they were continuing

 • *He continued to oppose the plan.* • *They were continuing to look very puzzled.*

PRESENT PERFECT	... have | has continued
PAST PERFECT	... had continued

FUTURE	... will continue
FUTURE PROGRESSIVE	... will be continuing
FUTURE PERFECT	... will have continued

PAST PASSIVE

— —

— —

it was continued they were continued

 • *The trial was continued by the judge.*

COMPLEMENTS

continue *persist, last, stay*	The rain continued all afternoon. Our New Year's Eve tradition continues unbroken. The play continues until next Sunday. We will continue here for a while longer. The treasurer will continue in office for six months.
continue *resume [after an interruption]*	We will continue after lunch. The session continues at four.
continue *extend*	The highway continues all the way to Springfield.
continue _____ *extend, persist in* OBJECT	They continued **their discussion** during dinner. They continued **the presentation** despite the interruptions.
INFINITIVE	I will continue **to support the plan**. He continued **to snore loudly**.
PRESENT PARTICIPLE	I will continue **supporting the plan**. He continued **snoring loudly**.
continue _____ *postpone formally* OBJECT	The defendant's lawyer asked to continue **the deposition**. The judge continued **the trial** until January 15.
PASSIVE	The trial was continued until January 15 by the judge.
continue _____ *keep on [doing]* (*with*) OBJECT	May I continue (**with**) **my piano playing** while you read the newspaper? Please continue (**with**) **the rest of the tutorial**.

contribute contribute | contributes ·
contributed · have contributed ☑ REGULAR

PRESENT
I contribute   we contribute
you contribute   you contribute
he/she/it contributes   they contribute
• *He always contributes to appeals.*

PRESENT PROGRESSIVE
I am contributing   we are contributing
you are contributing   you are contributing
he/she/it is contributing   they are contributing
• *I'm already contributing to that charity.*

PAST
I contributed   we contributed
you contributed   you contributed
he/she/it contributed   they contributed
• *I contributed twenty-five dollars.*

PAST PROGRESSIVE
I was contributing   we were contributing
you were contributing   you were contributing
he/she/it was contributing   they were contributing
• *We were contributing what we could afford.*

PRESENT PERFECT ... have | has contributed
PAST PERFECT   ... had contributed

FUTURE   ... will contribute
FUTURE PROGRESSIVE ... will be contributing
FUTURE PERFECT   ... will have contributed

PAST PASSIVE
—   —
—   —
it was contributed   they were contributed
• *The money was contributed by an anonymous donor.*

COMPLEMENTS

contribute *give along with others, donate*
We all contribute in our own ways.
I'm sorry, but I can't contribute any longer.

contribute _____ *help to bring about*
to OBJECT
She really contributed **to our success.**
The employees have contributed **to our reputation.**

contribute _____ *give along with others, donate*
OBJECT
I usually contribute **a hundred dollars.**
They contributed **a great deal of time.**

to OBJECT
I contributed **to Senator Blather's campaign.**
I always contribute **to the Boy Scouts.**

OBJECT + to OBJECT
I contributed **ten dollars** *to the office collection.*
They will contribute **something** *to the fund drive.*

WH-CLAUSE
I contribute **what I can.**
We will contribute **whatever we can afford.**

to WH-CLAUSE
We contribute **to whoever is most in need.**
People contribute **to whatever causes they feel
    most strongly about.**

contribute _____ *provide for publication*
OBJECT
She regularly contributes **feature stories.**
I contribute **local news items.**

PRESENT

I control   we control
you control   you control
he/she/it controls   they control
 • *She controls a large number of shares.*

PRESENT PROGRESSIVE

I am controlling   we are controlling
you are controlling   you are controlling
he/she/it is controlling   they are controlling
 • *I'm controlling for all the variables.*

PAST

I controlled   we controlled
you controlled   you controlled
he/she/it controlled   they controlled
 • *I controlled for gender and age.*

PAST PROGRESSIVE

I was controlling   we were controlling
you were controlling   you were controlling
he/she/it was controlling   they were controlling
 • *We were controlling the infection.*

PRESENT PERFECT   ... have | has controlled
PAST PERFECT   ... had controlled

FUTURE   ... will control
FUTURE PROGRESSIVE   ... will be controlling
FUTURE PERFECT   ... will have controlled

PAST PASSIVE

I was controlled   we were controlled
you were controlled   you were controlled
he/she/it was controlled   they were controlled
 • *The robot was controlled by a computer.*

(COMPLEMENTS)

control _____ regulate, direct, have power over

OBJECT

This lever controls **the speed.**
The hormone controls **the level of calcium in the blood.**
He controls **the entire operation.**
The president controls **Supreme Court nominations.**

WH-CLAUSE

The dictator controls **what citizens say and do.**
They control **whoever reports to this office.**
He controls **whatever resources they still have.**

control _____ hold back, restrain

OBJECT

Brandy doesn't control **her temper** very well.
The new owner couldn't control **the dog.**

control _____ prevent the spread of

OBJECT

Health workers controlled **the smallpox epidemic**
   by quarantine and vaccination.
The herbicide controls **leaf mold.**

(PHRASAL VERBS)

control for _____ *test for [variables]*
in a scientific experiment

You must control for nutrition and
   lifestyle.

PRESENT

I convince	we convince
you convince	you convince
he/she/it convinces	they convince

• *He always convinces his audiences.*

PRESENT PROGRESSIVE

I am convincing	we are convincing
you are convincing	you are convincing
he/she/it is convincing	they are convincing

• *I'm convincing the panelists with fancy charts.*

PAST

I convinced	we convinced
you convinced	you convinced
he/she/it convinced	they convinced

• *She convinced me to read the book.*

PAST PROGRESSIVE

I was convincing	we were convincing
you were convincing	you were convincing
he/she/it was convincing	they were convincing

• *He was convincing them to invest.*

PRESENT PERFECT   ... have | has convinced
PAST PERFECT   ... had convinced

FUTURE   ... will convince
FUTURE PROGRESSIVE   ... will be convincing
FUTURE PERFECT   ... will have convinced

PAST PASSIVE

I was convinced	we were convinced
you were convinced	you were convinced
he/she/it was convinced	they were convinced

• *I was convinced by the critic's argument.*

───(**COMPLEMENTS**)───

convince _____ *persuade*

OBJECT	He even convinces **himself.**
	His job is to convince **the jury.**
	I finally convinced **my boss.**
OBJECT + *of* OBJECT	They convinced **the mayor** *of the need for a new sewer plant.*
	You can't convince **the owner** *of the importance of decent wages.*
	They convinced **themselves** *of the righteousness of their cause.*
OBJECT + INFINITIVE	I convinced **him** *to do something about the situation.*
	We convinced **them** *to leave.*
	The failure convinced **us** *to change course.*
OBJECT + THAT-CLAUSE	He convinced **us** *that we should reconsider the project.*
	We convinced **them** *that they were wrong.*
	His behavior convinces **us** *that he is crazy.*
	She convinced **herself** *that she would win the lottery.*
WH-CLAUSE	He convinces **whomever he talks to.**
	They will convince **whomever they need to.**

───(**EXPRESSIONS**)───

convincing *believable*	The spy wore a convincing disguise.
	"The dog ate my homework" is not a convincing excuse.

PRESENT

I cook	we cook
you cook	you cook
he/she/it cooks	they cook

· *He cooks over 60 meals a day.*

PRESENT PROGRESSIVE

I am cooking	we are cooking
you are cooking	you are cooking
he/she/it is cooking	they are cooking

· *I'm cooking some pasta for lunch.*

PAST

I cooked	we cooked
you cooked	you cooked
he/she/it cooked	they cooked

· *I cooked for years before my marriage.*

PAST PROGRESSIVE

I was cooking	we were cooking
you were cooking	you were cooking
he/she/it was cooking	they were cooking

· *They were cooking on their gas grill.*

PRESENT PERFECT ... have | has cooked
PAST PERFECT ... had cooked

FUTURE ... will cook
FUTURE PROGRESSIVE ... will be cooking
FUTURE PERFECT ... will have cooked

PAST PASSIVE

I was cooked	we were cooked
you were cooked	you were cooked
he/she/it was cooked	they were cooked

· *Dinner was cooked by Donna.*

(**COMPLEMENTS**)

cook *prepare food by heating*	My father is cooking tonight. You have to cook every day.
cook *undergo the process of food preparation*	Dinner is cooking right now. The oatmeal is cooking at too high a temperature.
cook *happen* [INFORMAL]	What's cooking in technology stocks today? "What's cooking?" "Nothing."
cook *perform very well* [INFORMAL]	That band really cooks.
cook _____ *prepare [food] by heating*	
OBJECT	I cook **Chinese and Italian food**. They cooked **steaks** for everyone.
WH-CLAUSE	Cook only **what you can eat**. Anita will cook **whatever you would like**.
cook _____ *cause to be overheated*	
OBJECT	The sun really cooked **us** this afternoon.
PASSIVE	We were really cooked out there.
cook _____ *falsify* [INFORMAL]	
OBJECT	Did the analysts cook **the data**?

(**PHRASAL VERBS**)

cook out *prepare food out of doors*	We cook out almost every night in the summer.
cook _SEP_ **up** *prepare a batch of [food] by heating*	We'll cook up some spaghetti for our guests.
cook _SEP_ **up** *devise, plan*	Lenny and Mike cooked up a scheme to raise money for their new business. Let's cook up an excuse for skipping the exam.

(**EXPRESSIONS**)

cook [someone's] goose *cause damage to [someone]*	Sending obscene e-mails from work really cooked Paul's goose.
cook the books *falsify financial records*	The department had cooked the books for years.
cook _____ **to perfection** *cook perfectly*	My 13-year-old son cooked the lasagna to perfection.
cook up a storm *prepare a lot of food*	On Saturdays, Dad always cooked up a storm.

I cost   we cost
you cost   you cost
he/she/it costs   they cost
  • *The scarves cost more than 50 dollars.*

I am costing   we are costing
you are costing   you are costing
he/she/it is costing they are costing
  • *The delay is costing us a fortune.*

I cost   we cost
you cost   you cost
he/she/it cost   they cost
  • *That mistake cost us dearly.*

I was costing   we were costing
you were costing   you were costing
he/she/it was costing they were costing
  • *You were costing the company a lot of money.*

... have | has cost
... had cost

... will cost
... will be costing
... will have cost

  Cost is rarely used in the passive voice.

COMPLEMENTS

cost *be expensive*

Going to college really costs.
Hybrid cars cost, but so does gasoline.
Lack of training costs dearly.
Cheap mattresses cost in the long run.

cost _____ *have a price of*
  OBJECT

The new house cost **half a million dollars.**
My books cost **$200 a semester.**

cost _____ *cause the loss of*
  OBJECT

Starvation costs **25,000 lives** a day.
It cost **my job.**
It cost **his self-respect.**

  INDIRECT OBJECT + DIRECT OBJECT

The battle cost *the army* **a lot of good soldiers.**
The accident cost *me* **a fortune.**
The mistake cost *us* **the contract.**

cost _____ *cause suffering/loss to*
  OBJECT

My hesitation certainly cost **me.**

PHRASAL VERBS

cost _SEP_ **out** *estimate, set a value on/for*

I will cost the entire project out.
We were costing out the Johnston contract.

EXPRESSIONS

cost a fortune *be very expensive*

It would cost a fortune to move
  that printing press.

cost a pretty penny *be very expensive*

I'll bet that car cost a pretty penny.

cost an arm and a leg *be very expensive*

This watch cost me an arm and a leg.

PRESENT		PRESENT PROGRESSIVE	
I count	we count	I am counting	we are counting
you count	you count	you are counting	you are counting
he/she/it counts	they count	he/she/it is counting	they are counting

  · *Neatness counts.*   · *I'm counting to ten.*

PAST		PAST PROGRESSIVE	
I counted	we counted	I was counting	we were counting
you counted	you counted	you were counting	you were counting
he/she/it counted	they counted	he/she/it was counting	they were counting

  · *I counted a dozen trucks in two minutes.*   · *We were counting all the birds on the wire.*

PRESENT PERFECT	... have | has counted
PAST PERFECT	... had counted

FUTURE	... will count
FUTURE PROGRESSIVE	... will be counting
FUTURE PERFECT	... will have counted

PAST PASSIVE

I was counted	we were counted
you were counted	you were counted
he/she/it was counted	they were counted

  · *Some people were counted twice.*

(COMPLEMENTS)

count *name numbers in a sequence*
> I counted by fives.
> Saxton counted from 2 to 100 by twos.
> She counted out loud.

count *be valuable/significant*
> Her opinions count.
> Their efforts didn't really count.
> Loyalty really counts with the president.

count _____ *add to get a total, tally*
   OBJECT
> He counted **the crew members** in a loud voice.
> We must count **all the phone jacks in the office.**
> I had the musicians count **the beats.**

count _____ *consider, regard*
   OBJECT
> I count **David** among my best friends.
> Don't count **his youth** against him.

   OBJECT + *as* PREDICATE NOUN
> She counted **them** *as her best friends.*
> I counted **Jimmy** *as a neutral observer.*

   OBJECT + *as* PREDICATE ADJECTIVE
> Sarah counted **the neighbors** *as very friendly.*
> He counted **the voters** *as uncommitted.*

   OBJECT + *(to be)* PREDICATE NOUN
> I counted **Felipe** *(to be) a real friend.*
> John counted **his father** *(to be) a genuine hero.*

   OBJECT + *(to be)* PREDICATE ADJECTIVE
> I counted **the survivors** *(to be) lucky.*
> He always counted **his daughter** *(to be) fortunate in love.*

count _____ *take into account*
   OBJECT
> Did you count **Ovid** in your list of poets?
> There are seven sisters, counting **Agnes.**

(PHRASAL VERBS)

count for _____ *have a value of*
> A touchdown counts for six points.
> Experience counts for something.

count _____ **in** *include*
> "Who wants to play soccer?" "Count me in."

count on _____ *depend on*
> I counted on Mom and Dad to pay for my college education.

count _____ **out** *exclude, disregard*
> "Who wants to shovel the snow?" "Count me out."
> Tanya wasn't interested, so we counted her out.

PRESENT

I cover	we cover
you cover	you cover
he/she/it covers	they cover

- *His area covers northern California.*

PRESENT PROGRESSIVE

I am covering	we are covering
you are covering	you are covering
he/she/it is covering	they are covering

- *I'm covering for a friend.*

PAST

I covered	we covered
you covered	you covered
he/she/it covered	they covered

- *She covered many important stories.*

PAST PROGRESSIVE

I was covering	we were covering
you were covering	you were covering
he/she/it was covering	they were covering

- *We were covering the furniture with plastic.*

PRESENT PERFECT ... have | has covered
PAST PERFECT ... had covered

FUTURE ... will cover
FUTURE PROGRESSIVE ... will be covering
FUTURE PERFECT ... will have covered

PAST PASSIVE

I was covered	we were covered
you were covered	you were covered
he/she/it was covered	they were covered

- *His back was covered in red spots.*

COMPLEMENTS

cover _____ *place/spread something over*
OBJECT

I covered **the pan** with aluminum foil.
We covered **the floors** before we started painting.

cover _____ *spread over [a surface]*
OBJECT

Snow covered **the fields**.
Water covered **the road** for miles.
Lakes cover **the whole region**.

cover _____ *lay over, conceal*
OBJECT

The towel covered **my bare legs**.
A scarf covered **her face**.

cover _____ *deal with, discuss*
OBJECT

That about covers **everything**.
We will cover **the budget** in today's meeting.

cover _____ *be responsible for*
OBJECT

My job covers **retail sales**.
We will cover **any damage that results**.
The department only covers **incorporated areas of the city**.

cover _____ *have sufficient funds for*
OBJECT

Your balance doesn't cover **this check**.
Can you cover **the restaurant bill**?

cover _____ *protect from harm/loss, insure*
OBJECT

Does the insurance cover **your husband** too?
The policy even covers **cosmetic surgery**.

cover _____ *report news about*
OBJECT

The television stations covered **the traffic accident**.

cover _____ *travel [a certain distance]*
OBJECT

We covered **15 miles** today.

PHRASAL VERBS

cover for _____ *be a replacement for*   Hilary covered for Candi when she was sick.
cover _SEP_ **up** *hide*   The politicians tried to cover up the scandal.
cover up for _____ *make excuses for*   Rich was always covering up for his cubicle mate.

PRESENT

I create	we create
you create	you create
he/she/it creates	they create

- *Prosperity creates new markets.*

PRESENT PROGRESSIVE

I am creating	we are creating
you are creating	you are creating
he/she/it is creating	they are creating

- *I am creating a new ad.*

PAST

I created	we created
you created	you created
he/she/it created	they created

- *She created a masterpiece.*

PAST PROGRESSIVE

I was creating	we were creating
you were creating	you were creating
he/she/it was creating	they were creating

- *They were creating a whole new marketing plan.*

PRESENT PERFECT ... have | has created
PAST PERFECT ... had created

FUTURE ... will create
FUTURE PROGRESSIVE ... will be creating
FUTURE PERFECT ... will have created

PAST PASSIVE

I was created	we were created
you were created	you were created
he/she/it was created	they were created

- *Seventy new jobs were created this month.*

(COMPLEMENTS)

create _____ bring into being, produce, cause

    OBJECT
The cyclotron created **new elements.**
Computer technology has created **thousands of new jobs.**
The artist created **a limited edition of silkscreen prints.**
The kids created **a terrible mess in the kitchen.**
Their behavior created **a huge scandal.**
Scarcity creates **shortages.**

    WH-CLAUSE
They created **what can only be called a disaster.**
We will create **whatever you need.**

create _____ design

    OBJECT
Her assistants created **a new line of clothing.**

(EXPRESSIONS)

create a scene *cause a public disturbance*
Tom created a scene when his fiancée kissed her ex-boyfriend.

create a stink about/over _____
complain strongly about
My wife created a stink about our guests' untidy habits.

PRESENT

I creep	we creep
you creep	you creep
he/she/it creeps	they creep

• *Time creeps by when you're bored.*

PRESENT PROGRESSIVE

I am creeping	we are creeping
you are creeping	you are creeping
he/she/it is creeping	they are creeping

• *The fog is creeping into the hollow.*

PAST

I crept	we crept
you crept	you crept
he/she/it crept	they crept

• *Old age crept up on us.*

PAST PROGRESSIVE

I was creeping	we were creeping
you were creeping	you were creeping
he/she/it was creeping	they were creeping

• *The soldiers were creeping past the guards.*

PRESENT PERFECT ... have | has crept
PAST PERFECT ... had crept

FUTURE ... will creep
FUTURE PROGRESSIVE ... will be creeping
FUTURE PERFECT ... will have crept

PAST PASSIVE

Creep is never used in the passive voice.

(COMPLEMENTS)

creep *move along close to the ground*	Bob crept away from his pursuers. The lion crept toward the antelope.
creep *move cautiously/stealthily*	We crept down the stairs. I crept into the kids' room, trying not to wake them.
creep *grow along a surface*	Weeds were creeping into the flower beds.
creep *shiver from fear/dread*	The scream made my flesh creep.
creep ___ *advance slowly* ADVERB OF PLACE TO/FROM	Daylight crept **in through the windows**. Water from the clogged drain crept **across the floor**.
creep ___ *appear gradually* ADVERB OF PLACE TO/FROM	A sense of urgency crept **through the crowd**.

(PHRASAL VERBS)

creep by *pass slowly*	The years crept by when Lawrence was in prison.
creep in/into ___ *enter inconspicuously*	A note of resentment crept into his voice. Negativity crept into his later writing.
creep up on ___ *advance slowly and* *imperceptibly toward*	The cat crept up on the mouse.

(EXPRESSIONS)

creep out of the woodwork *appear after* *being gone for a long time*	Well, look who's crept out of the woodwork—it's Percy!

PRESENT

I cross	we cross
you cross	you cross
he/she/it crosses	they cross

• *The trails cross in that valley.*

PRESENT PROGRESSIVE

I am crossing	we are crossing
you are crossing	you are crossing
he/she/it is crossing	they are crossing

• *We are crossing the Atlantic now.*

PAST

I crossed	we crossed
you crossed	you crossed
he/she/it crossed	they crossed

• *He crossed his legs and began to whistle.*

PAST PROGRESSIVE

I was crossing	we were crossing
you were crossing	you were crossing
he/she/it was crossing	they were crossing

• *He was crossing the street.*

PRESENT PERFECT ... have | has crossed
PAST PERFECT ... had crossed

FUTURE ... will cross
FUTURE PROGRESSIVE ... will be crossing
FUTURE PERFECT ... will have crossed

PAST PASSIVE

I was crossed	we were crossed
you were crossed	you were crossed
he/she/it was crossed	they were crossed

• *His name was crossed out.*

COMPLEMENTS

cross *intersect*	Parallel lines never cross. Eventually Highways 120 and 337 cross.
cross *go past each other in opposite directions*	We must have crossed on the highway. Our letters must have crossed in the mail.
cross _____ *extend across/over* OBJECT	The road crosses **the river** at Glenwood. I-94 crosses **the entire width of North Dakota**.
cross _____ *go across/over* OBJECT	We crossed **the Mississippi** at Hannibal. I finally crossed **the finish line**. Blacks crossed **the color line** after World War II.
cross _____ *place crosswise one over the other* OBJECT	He crossed **his arms**. I crossed **my fingers** for luck.
cross _____ *mix [breeds of plants or animals]* OBJECT (+ *with* OBJECT)	The gardener crossed **two varieties of daylilies**. If you cross **a donkey** *with a horse*, you get a mule.
cross _____ *combine elements of* OBJECT + *with* OBJECT	The movie crosses **horror** *with mystery*.
cross _____ *draw a line across* OBJECT	Dot your i's and cross **your t's**.
cross _____ *obstruct, betray* OBJECT	Never cross **your boss**. You deliberately crossed **me**!

PHRASAL VERBS

cross _SEP_ **off** *draw a line through, eliminate [from a list]*	Don't cross my name off the list of volunteers. Don't cross me off the list of volunteers.
cross _SEP_ **out** *draw a line through the name of [on a list]*	You can cross the first three items out.
cross _SEP_ **up** *confuse, deceive*	They crossed us up by going home early.

PRESENT

I cry	we cry
you cry	you cry
he/she/it cries	they cry

• *The baby always cries when he is hungry.*

PRESENT PROGRESSIVE

I am crying	we are crying
you are crying	you are crying
he/she/it is crying	they are crying

• *I'm crying because I am upset.*

PAST

I cried	we cried
you cried	you cried
he/she/it cried	they cried

• *I cried my eyes out.*

PAST PROGRESSIVE

I was crying	we were crying
you were crying	you were crying
he/she/it was crying	they were crying

• *They were crying about nothing.*

PRESENT PERFECT ... have | has cried
PAST PERFECT ... had cried

FUTURE ... will cry
FUTURE PROGRESSIVE ... will be crying
FUTURE PERFECT ... will have cried

PAST PASSIVE

—	—
—	—
it was cried	they were cried

• *The alarm was cried out up and down the street.*

⟨ **COMPLEMENTS** ⟩

cry *sob, weep*	All the children were crying.
	Please don't cry.
cry *shout, call loudly*	The news vendors were crying as loudly as they could.
	The frightened animals were all crying.
cry _____ *utter loudly*	
OBJECT	I cried **a warning** to them.
	The soldier cried **a challenge** as I came closer.
THAT-CLAUSE	He cried **that he had been robbed.**
	A sailor cried **that he could see land.**
DIRECT QUOTATION	The wounded man cried, **"Help! Help!"**

⟨ **PHRASAL VERBS** ⟩

cry out *scream, shout*	The victim cried out in pain.
cry <u>SEP</u> **out** *shout*	Penfeld cried out a warning to the people passing by.
cry out for _____ *demand/require* [an immediate solution]	This economic recession cries out for government intervention.
cry over _____ *weep because of*	She's still crying over losing her job.

⟨ **EXPRESSIONS** ⟩

cry in [one's] beer *be sorry for oneself*	After he lost the election, Jack spent several days crying in his beer.
cry on [someone's] shoulder *tell one's problems to [someone] to be comforted*	My parakeet died. Can I cry on your shoulder? Her boyfriend left, and she needed a shoulder to cry on.
cry [one's] eyes out *weep inconsolably*	When Ed broke off the engagement, she cried her eyes out.
cry [oneself] to sleep *weep until one falls asleep*	After watching the movie, Cynthia cried herself to sleep. Bruno cried himself to sleep every night.
cry over spilled milk *regret something that cannot be undone*	Life is too short; don't cry over spilled milk.
cry wolf *give a false alarm*	Billy Joe cried wolf once too often, and no one believed him after that.

PRESENT			PRESENT PROGRESSIVE	
I cut	we cut		I am cutting	we are cutting
you cut	you cut		you are cutting	you are cutting
he/she/it cuts	they cut		he/she/it is cutting	they are cutting

   • *He cuts the lawn every weekend.*   • *I'm cutting class today.*

PAST			PAST PROGRESSIVE	
I cut	we cut		I was cutting	we were cutting
you cut	you cut		you were cutting	you were cutting
he/she/it cut	they cut		he/she/it was cutting	they were cutting

   • *I cut myself shaving.*   • *We were cutting the staff by ten percent.*

PRESENT PERFECT	... have | has cut		FUTURE	... will cut
PAST PERFECT	... had cut		FUTURE PROGRESSIVE	... will be cutting
			FUTURE PERFECT	... will have cut

PAST PASSIVE	
I was cut	we were cut
you were cut	you were cut
he/she/it was cut	they were cut

   • *Our budget was cut substantially.*

                                             (COMPLEMENTS)

cut *hurt someone's feelings*

His criticisms really cut.
He really knows how to cut.

cut _____ *make an incision, separate*
   ADVERB OF MANNER

A sharp knife cuts **safely**.
His ax cuts **like a razor**.

cut _____ *undergo an incision/separation*
   ADVERB OF MANNER

The dried wood cuts **easily**.

cut _____ *penetrate with a sharp object*
   OBJECT

Jill cut **her finger** on a knife.

cut _____ *sever, separate into pieces (slice, mow, pare, trim, dig, etc.)*
   OBJECT

I cut **the cake**.
My husband cut **the grass** this morning.
I need to cut **my fingernails**.
The new barber cut **my hair**.
The backhoe cut **a trench** for a new waterline.

cut _____ *make by chopping/hacking*
   OBJECT

We cut **a path** through the dense woods.

cut _____ *reduce the size/number of*
   OBJECT

They will cut **my hours** after Christmas.
We have to cut **the budget**.
The authors had to cut **the manuscript** by a third.

cut _____ *remove [from a group]*
   OBJECT

The coach cut **three players** from the squad.
The director cut **five scenes** from the movie.

cut _____ *change direction suddenly*
   ADVERB OF PLACE TO/FROM

Cut **to the right** just before the railroad tracks.

cut _____ *go directly, take a shortcut*
   ADVERB OF PLACE TO/FROM

We can cut **across Mr. Applegate's property**.
The highway cuts **through a national park**.
The seniors cut **to the front of the line**.

cut _____ *dilute*
   OBJECT

That bartender cuts **whiskey** with tap water.

top 40 verb

cut _____ *break, stop*	The storm cut **the telephone lines**.
OBJECT	Please cut **all the noise**.
	He cut **the engine**.
cut _____ *skip without permission*	
OBJECT	We cut **class** to watch the inauguration.
cut _____ *record*	
OBJECT	She is cutting **a new album**.
cut _____ *fill out and issue*	
OBJECT	The secretary cut **a check for $50.23**.
cut _____ *handle* [USUALLY NEGATIVE]	
OBJECT	I can't cut **the 45-minute drive to work** anymore.
PRESENT PARTICIPLE	Tom can't cut **being a police officer** anymore.

------------------------------(**PHRASAL VERBS**)

cut across _____ *transcend*	The president's economic proposal cuts across party lines.
cut back *reverse direction*	The receiver cut back to the middle of the field.
cut _SEP_ **back** *shorten*	We must cut back the shrubs after they flower.
cut back (on) _____ *reduce*	The department cut back spending in April.
cut _SEP_ **down** *chop/saw and cause to fall*	Our neighbors cut two elm trees down.
cut down (on) _____ *reduce*	The doctor told Ed to cut down on caffeine.
cut in *begin operating*	We pulled the crank six times before the motor cut in.
cut in *interrupt*	The reporter cut in before I finished my first sentence.
cut in *move into a line out of turn*	The motorist cut in just before his lane ended.
cut _SEP_ **in** *mix in*	Cut in the shortening with a pastry blender.
cut in on _____ *interrupt*	The actress cut in on the director.
cut _SEP_ **off** *interrupt*	The protester cut me off in mid-sentence.
cut _SEP_ **off** *move suddenly in front of, block*	A driver cut me off at the curve. The policeman cut the robbers off at the bridge.
cut _SEP_ **off** *shorten*	Gerry cut off the knotty end of the board.
cut _SEP_ **off** *shut off*	When his car overheated, the driver cut off the engine.
cut off/out *stop suddenly, shut off*	The water heater cuts off at 120 degrees.
cut out *go away quickly*	This party is boring; let's cut out.
cut _SEP_ **out** *eliminate*	I will cut out afternoon snacks for two weeks.
cut up *joke, clown, behave wildly*	Ken always cuts up when the teacher leaves the room.
cut _SEP_ **up** *separate into sections with a sharp object*	Cut the mushrooms up, and then we'll add them to the sauce.

------------------------------(**EXPRESSIONS**)

cut _____ **down to size** *humiliate*	His opponent cut him down to size.
cut _____ **some slack** *make an allowance for*	He wasn't feeling well, so the boss cut him some slack.
cut _____ **to the quick/bone** *badly hurt the feelings of*	Your nasty remarks cut me to the quick.
cut [one's] teeth on _____ *learn/do as a beginner*	The journalist cut her teeth on writing obituaries.
cut _SEP_ **short** *stop suddenly*	The president cut the press conference short.

PRESENT

I dance	we dance
you dance	you dance
he/she/it dances	they dance

• *He dances with the Royal Ballet.*

PRESENT PROGRESSIVE

I am dancing	we are dancing
you are dancing	you are dancing
he/she/it is dancing	they are dancing

• *Look at me! I'm dancing.*

PAST

I danced	we danced
you danced	you danced
he/she/it danced	they danced

• *He danced with both Lizzy and Jane.*

PAST PROGRESSIVE

I was dancing	we were dancing
you were dancing	you were dancing
he/she/it was dancing	they were dancing

• *We were dancing on air after winning the award.*

PRESENT PERFECT	... have	has danced
PAST PERFECT	... had danced

FUTURE	... will dance
FUTURE PROGRESSIVE	... will be dancing
FUTURE PERFECT	... will have danced

PAST PASSIVE

—	—
—	—
it was danced	they were danced

• *Swan Lake was first danced in 1877.*

COMPLEMENTS

dance *move the body and legs rhythmically, usually to music*	I dance every chance I get. She dances really well. Can you dance?
dance *bob up and down in a lively manner*	The rain was dancing on the pavement. The kids were dancing with excitement. The furniture danced across the floor during the earthquake.
dance _____ *perform as a dancer* OBJECT	I have danced **that role** many times. Can you dance **the tango**? The company will dance ***Romeo and Juliet*** this season.
dance _____ *cause to dance* OBJECT	The groom danced **his mother-in-law** across the ballroom.

EXPRESSIONS

be dancing on air *be very happy*	Since her promotion, Deborah has been dancing on air.
dance to _____ *respond to [music] by dancing* [OFTEN FIGURATIVE]	We love to dance to the pop music of the 1980s. European leaders refused to dance to the president's tune.

PRESENT

I dare	we dare
you dare	you dare
he/she/it dares	they dare

• *He dares to boast about it?*

PRESENT PROGRESSIVE

I am daring	we are daring
you are daring	you are daring
he/she/it is daring	they are daring

• *I'm daring you to enter without knocking.*

PAST

I dared	we dared
you dared	you dared
he/she/it dared	they dared

• *They dared to risk it.*

PAST PROGRESSIVE

I was daring	we were daring
you were daring	you were daring
he/she/it was daring	they were daring

• *We were daring the wrath of our families.*

PRESENT PERFECT ... have | has dared
PAST PERFECT ... had dared

FUTURE ... will dare
FUTURE PROGRESSIVE ... will be daring
FUTURE PERFECT ... will have dared

PAST PASSIVE

I was dared	we were dared
you were dared	you were dared
he/she/it was dared	they were dared

• *Sam was dared to do it by the other kids.*

(COMPLEMENTS)

dare *be brave enough*

Try the durian roll if you dare.

dare _____ *challenge to do something bold*

OBJECT

Ralph dared **his sister**.
They have all dared **me**.

OBJECT + INFINITIVE

I dared **him** *to stop me*.
He dared **us** *to cross the stream on a log*.

dare _____ *be bold/brave enough*

INFINITIVE

Would you dare **to be different**?
I didn't dare **to ask her out**.

BASE-FORM INFINITIVE

He dared not **fail his team**.
He dared not **be late for the meeting**.

PRESENT PARTICIPLE

I wouldn't dare **asking her out**.
He didn't dare **making the trip alone**.

dare _____ *face boldly/bravely, defy*

OBJECT

He dared **public criticism** throughout his career.
The captain dared **the roaring waves**.

PRESENT

I deal	we deal
you deal	you deal
he/she/it deals	they deal

• *He deals in antique furniture.*

PRESENT PROGRESSIVE

I am dealing	we are dealing
you are dealing	you are dealing
he/she/it is dealing	they are dealing

• *I'm dealing this hand.*

PAST

I dealt	we dealt
you dealt	you dealt
he/she/it dealt	they dealt

• *I dealt myself a bad hand.*

PAST PROGRESSIVE

I was dealing	we were dealing
you were dealing	you were dealing
he/she/it was dealing	they were dealing

• *They were dealing illegal drugs.*

PRESENT PERFECT ... have | has dealt
PAST PERFECT ... had dealt

FUTURE ... will deal
FUTURE PROGRESSIVE ... will be dealing
FUTURE PERFECT ... will have dealt

PAST PASSIVE

I was dealt	we were dealt
you were dealt	you were dealt
he/she/it was dealt	they were dealt

• *Justice was dealt to everyone.*

COMPLEMENTS

deal *distribute cards in a game*	Who's dealing? I will deal as soon as everyone sits down.
deal *engage in bargaining/negotiation*	The union will never deal. He only deals if the price is right.
deal ＿＿＿ *distribute [cards]* 　　OBJECT	I will deal **five cards** to each player. He deals **the cards** until none are left.
INDIRECT OBJECT + DIRECT OBJECT	You dealt *me* **an awful hand**. He dealt *her* **three aces**.
to PARAPHRASE	You dealt **a bad hand** *to me*. He dealt **three aces** *to her*.
deal ＿＿＿ *sell [illegal drugs]* 　　OBJECT	He deals **marijuana** to teenagers. The gang deals **stolen prescription drugs**.
deal ＿＿＿ *deliver, administer* 　　INDIRECT OBJECT + DIRECT OBJECT	Spike dealt *the intruder* **a blow to the head**. Fate dealt *him* **a terrible blow**. Life has dealt *them* **some bad times**.
to PARAPHRASE	Fate dealt **a terrible blow** *to him*. Life has dealt **some bad times** *to them*.

PHRASAL VERBS

deal in ＿＿＿ *buy and sell*	The real estate broker deals only 　in commercial properties.
deal ⎯SEP⎯ **in** *allow to take part*	Maurice has free time; let's deal him in.
deal ⎯SEP⎯ **out** *distribute piece by piece*	Agnes dealt the cards out three at a time.
deal with ＿＿＿ *behave toward, treat* *in a particular way*	The coach dealt fairly with his players.
deal with ＿＿＿ *handle, take care of*	The board agreed to deal with financial matters later.
deal with ＿＿＿ *have to do with, concern*	The article deals with early French-American customs.
deal with ＿＿＿ *try to accept/reconcile*	Meg dealt with three deaths in her family last year.

PRESENT		PRESENT PROGRESSIVE	
I decide	we decide	I am deciding	we are deciding
you decide	you decide	you are deciding	you are deciding
he/she/it decides	they decide	he/she/it is deciding	they are deciding

· *He always decides at the last minute.*   · *I'm deciding what to wear.*

PAST		PAST PROGRESSIVE	
I decided	we decided	I was deciding	we were deciding
you decided	you decided	you were deciding	you were deciding
he/she/it decided	they decided	he/she/it was deciding	they were deciding

· *I finally decided to eat out.*   · *We were deciding what to have for dinner.*

PRESENT PERFECT ... have | has decided
PAST PERFECT ... had decided

FUTURE ... will decide
FUTURE PROGRESSIVE ... will be deciding
FUTURE PERFECT ... will have decided

PAST PASSIVE

— —

— —

it was decided   they were decided

· *The election was decided by 342 votes.*

COMPLEMENTS

decide *make a choice/judgment*	You decide.
	Have you decided yet?
	Tamara couldn't decide between Joseph and Milton.

decide _____ *make a final choice/judgment about*

OBJECT	The court decided **the issue.**
	The election will decide **the matter.**
PASSIVE	The case was decided by a 5–4 vote.
in favor of OBJECT	The jury decided **in favor of the defendant.**
WH-CLAUSE	I can't decide **what we should do.**
	We decided **when we had to leave.**
	The boss will decide **how the employees will dress.**
WH-INFINITIVE	I can't decide **what to do.**
	We decided **when to leave.**
	The aldermen will decide **how to vote.**

decide _____ *choose*

ON OBJECT	I've decided **on a yellow cake with chocolate frosting.**
	The museum owner decided **on the painting by Picasso.**
	The judge decided **on leniency** for the young defendant.
INFINITIVE	We decided **to stay at home.**
	Charles decided **to take the offer.**

decide _____ *conclude*

THAT-CLAUSE	We decided **that we are going to sell the house.**
	Albert has decided **that he will major in English.**

decide _____ *determine the outcome of*

OBJECT	A goal in overtime decided **the game.**
	The voters in Ohio will decide **the election.**
	His key testimony decided **the trial.**

EXPRESSIONS

decided *unquestionable, definite*   The taller man had a decided advantage.

PRESENT

I declare	we declare
you declare	you declare
he/she/it declares	they declare

• *Jason declares that he will enter the race.*

PRESENT PROGRESSIVE

I am declaring	we are declaring
you are declaring	you are declaring
he/she/it is declaring	they are declaring

• *I am declaring all my income.*

PAST

I declared	we declared
you declared	you declared
he/she/it declared	they declared

• *The company declared a dividend.*

PAST PROGRESSIVE

I was declaring	we were declaring
you were declaring	you were declaring
he/she/it was declaring	they were declaring

• *We were just declaring how nice your garden looks.*

PRESENT PERFECT ... have | has declared
PAST PERFECT ... had declared

FUTURE ... will declare
FUTURE PROGRESSIVE ... will be declaring
FUTURE PERFECT ... will have declared

PAST PASSIVE

I was declared	we were declared
you were declared	you were declared
he/she/it was declared	they were declared

• *War was declared in 1939.*

COMPLEMENTS

declare *announce one's intention to run* [for office]	Jackson declared for sheriff today.
	When will the senator declare for re-election?
declare ___ *state formally/publicly/officially, proclaim*	
OBJECT	The president declared **war** on poverty.
	The company declared **victory** in its patent suit.
	The accused declares **his innocence**.
	The company had to declare **bankruptcy** today.
	The governor declared **a day of mourning**.
OBJECT + (to be) PREDICATE NOUN	Ralph declared **John *(to be) the best friend he ever had.***
	The paper declared **the senator *(to be) a credit to the nation.***
OBJECT + (to be) PREDICATE ADJECTIVE	The court declared **Uncle Henry *(to be) incompetent.***
	The lawyer declared **his client *(to be) innocent.***
THAT-CLAUSE	The author declared **that she would donate her royalties to charity**.
	The chairperson declared **that the meeting was in session**.
WH-CLAUSE	My father loudly declared **what a lucky man his son-in-law was**.
	The guests all declared **how tall Sally was getting**.
DIRECT QUOTATION	**"We are in a recession,"** George declared.
declare ___ *make a complete statement of [goods one is bringing into / sending out of the country]*	
OBJECT	We declared **the bottles of wine we bought in Italy**.

defend defend | defends · defended · have defended ☑ REGULAR

I defend	we defend
you defend	you defend
he/she/it defends	they defend

• *We defend your right to free speech.*

PRESENT PROGRESSIVE

I am defending	we are defending
you are defending	you are defending
he/she/it is defending	they are defending

• *I'm defending two juveniles accused of burglary.*

PAST

I defended	we defended
you defended	you defended
he/she/it defended	they defended

• *He defended some pretty odd clients.*

PAST PROGRESSIVE

I was defending	we were defending
you were defending	you were defending
he/she/it was defending	they were defending

• *They were defending the whole coastline.*

PRESENT PERFECT ... have | has defended
PAST PERFECT ... had defended

FUTURE ... will defend
FUTURE PROGRESSIVE ... will be defending
FUTURE PERFECT ... will have defended

PAST PASSIVE

I was defended	we were defended
you were defended	you were defended
he/she/it was defended	they were defended

• *The fort was strongly defended.*

 (**COMPLEMENTS**)

defend *engage in defense, play the role of defender*

I am defending.
Their team defends well against the run.

defend _____ *protect from attack/danger/criticism/challenge*

OBJECT

The soldiers defended **the village** against armed attack.
Stanford is defending **the north goal.**
Huxley defended **Darwin's ideas.**
The press vigorously defends **the right of free speech.**

WH-CLAUSE

You must defend **what you hold dear.**
Alice defended **what she had written.**
The elite units defended **wherever the threat was the greatest.**

defend _____ *act as attorney for*

OBJECT

Clarence Darrow defended **John Scopes.**

defend _____ *uphold the validity of [an academic thesis]*

OBJECT

Ruth is defending **her M.A. thesis** at noon.

defend _____ *seek to retain [a title, position]*

OBJECT

The Giants are defending **their title.**
He will defend **his championship** this fall.
I have to defend **my job** at every board meeting.

defend _____ *make an excuse for, justify*

OBJECT

How do you defend **your outrageous behavior at the party?**

PRESENT

I define	we define
you define	you define
he/she/it defines	they define

• *His work defines what is stylish.*

PRESENT PROGRESSIVE

I am defining	we are defining
you are defining	you are defining
he/she/it is defining	they are defining

• *I'm defining it as a total failure.*

PAST

I defined	we defined
you defined	you defined
he/she/it defined	they defined

• *The military defined lines of authority.*

PAST PROGRESSIVE

I was defining	we were defining
you were defining	you were defining
he/she/it was defining	they were defining

• *The surveyors were defining the property lines.*

PRESENT PERFECT ... have | has defined
PAST PERFECT ... had defined

FUTURE ... will define
FUTURE PROGRESSIVE ... will be defining
FUTURE PERFECT ... will have defined

PAST PASSIVE

I was defined	we were defined
you were defined	you were defined
he/she/it was defined	they were defined

• *The concept was defined by the ancient Greeks.*

(COMPLEMENTS)

define _____ *state the meaning of*

OBJECT

Who can define **justice**?
The coach tried to define **the offside rule.**

OBJECT + *as* OBJECT

I defined **justice** *as a sense of fair play.*
The dictionary defines **"persnickety"** *as "fussy about small details."*

define _____ *describe in detail, make clear*

OBJECT

Please define **the duties of the secretary.**
The candidates tried to define **the important campaign issues.**
The advertisement defined **the new features of the operating system.**

WH-CLAUSE

Can you define **what a barouche is?**
I defined **what duty means to me.**

define _____ *characterize*

OBJECT

People define **themselves** by their choices.
Politicians always try to define **their opponents.**

OBJECT + *as* OBJECT

The president defined **Simpson's behavior** *as outrageous and uncalled-for.*
Language defines **us** *as human.*

define _____ *mark/fix the limits/outline of*

OBJECT

The row of trees defines **our property line.**
Rivers often define **state boundaries.**

WH-CLAUSE

The speed of light defines **how fast things can move.**
Usury laws define **how much interest can be charged on a loan.**

PRESENT

I deliver	we deliver
you deliver	you deliver
he/she/it delivers	they deliver

• *The company only delivers on weekdays.*

PRESENT PROGRESSIVE

I am delivering	we are delivering
you are delivering	you are delivering
he/she/it is delivering	they are delivering

• *I'm delivering the speech tonight.*

PAST

I delivered	we delivered
you delivered	you delivered
he/she/it delivered	they delivered

• *Someone just delivered the pizza.*

PAST PROGRESSIVE

I was delivering	we were delivering
you were delivering	you were delivering
he/she/it was delivering	they were delivering

• *They were delivering furniture yesterday.*

PRESENT PERFECT ... have | has delivered
PAST PERFECT ... had delivered

FUTURE ... will deliver
FUTURE PROGRESSIVE ... will be delivering
FUTURE PERFECT ... will have delivered

PAST PASSIVE

I was delivered	we were delivered
you were delivered	you were delivered
he/she/it was delivered	they were delivered

• *The package was delivered this morning.*

(**COMPLEMENTS**)

deliver *engage in delivery*

Do you deliver?
The deli only delivers in the neighborhood.

deliver *fulfill promises/expectations*

He always delivers when he is most needed.
No matter how sick he is, a good player always delivers.

deliver *give birth*

The mother in Room 313 delivered yesterday.

deliver ⎯⎯ *transport [to the proper person or location]*

OBJECT

Did they deliver **my package**?
They delivered **the wrong thing** again!

WH-CLAUSE

We can only deliver **what has been prepaid**.
They will deliver **whatever you need to ship**.

deliver ⎯⎯ *provide [something desirable]*

OBJECT

My group can deliver **the votes**.
The new hybrid delivers **great mileage**.

deliver ⎯⎯ *hand over, surrender*

OBJECT (+ to OBJECT)

The suspect delivered **the stolen goods**.
The guard delivered **the prisoners** *to the county jail*.

deliver ⎯⎯ *set free, rescue*

OBJECT + *from* OBJECT

Please deliver **us** *from our enemies*.
My aunt and uncle delivered **me** *from an unhappy childhood*.

deliver ⎯⎯ *speak/sing in a performance*

OBJECT

The senator delivered **his speech** in Chicago.
She delivered **her song** in a clear, ringing voice.

deliver ⎯⎯ *give birth to*

OBJECT

Andrea delivered **a baby girl** this morning.

deliver ⎯⎯ *help in giving birth to*

OBJECT

The nurse delivered **the twin girls**.

(**EXPRESSIONS**)

deliver a blow *strike [someone/ something] in a certain way* [OFTEN FIGURATIVE]

The policeman delivered a blow that broke
  the hoodlum's jaw.
The candidate delivered a blow that undermined
  his opponent's argument.

PRESENT

I demand	we demand
you demand	you demand
he/she/it demands	they demand

• *He demands to see a lawyer.*

PRESENT PROGRESSIVE

I am demanding	we are demanding
you are demanding	you are demanding
he/she/it is demanding	they are demanding

• *I'm demanding that they be punished.*

PAST

I demanded	we demanded
you demanded	you demanded
he/she/it demanded	they demanded

• *She demanded a refund.*

PAST PROGRESSIVE

I was demanding	we were demanding
you were demanding	you were demanding
he/she/it was demanding	they were demanding

• *They were demanding equal rights.*

PRESENT PERFECT	... have | has demanded
PAST PERFECT	... had demanded

FUTURE	... will demand
FUTURE PROGRESSIVE	... will be demanding
FUTURE PERFECT	... will have demanded

PAST PASSIVE

—	—
—	—
it was demanded	they were demanded

• *An apology was demanded.*

$\overline{}$ COMPLEMENTS

demand _____ *call for forcefully, often as a right or with authority*

OBJECT	The customer demanded **a refund.**
	I demanded **an apology.**
	The crowd demanded **justice.**
	The boss demanded **too much** of his employees.
	The robber demanded **money** from the bank teller.
INFINITIVE	I demand **to be heard.**
	The owner demanded **to be paid for the damages.**
BASE-FORM THAT-CLAUSE	The senator demanded **that he be given equal time.**
	The chair demanded **that the meeting be called to order.**
	We demand **that we be permitted to leave.**
WH-CLAUSE	I'm only demanding **what is owed to me.**
	The robber demanded **whatever valuables we had.**

demand _____ *require, need*

OBJECT	This job demands **strong attention to detail.**

EXPRESSIONS

demanding *requiring much attention/ effort/time*	This secretarial job is very demanding.
	One cannot please the most demanding customers.

demonstrate demonstrate | demonstrates · demonstrated · have demonstrated ☑ REGULAR

PRESENT

I demonstrate · we demonstrate
you demonstrate · you demonstrate
he/she/it demonstrates · they demonstrate

 • *He always demonstrates a desire to help.*

PRESENT PROGRESSIVE

I am demonstrating · we are demonstrating
you are demonstrating · you are demonstrating
he/she/it is demonstrating · they are demonstrating

 • *The union is demonstrating against the company.*

PAST

I demonstrated · we demonstrated
you demonstrated · you demonstrated
he/she/it demonstrated · they demonstrated

 • *They demonstrated their trustworthiness.*

PAST PROGRESSIVE

I was demonstrating · we were demonstrating
you were demonstrating · you were demonstrating
he/she/it was demonstrating · they were demonstrating

 • *We were demonstrating for equal rights.*

PRESENT PERFECT ... have | has demonstrated
PAST PERFECT ... had demonstrated

FUTURE ... will demonstrate
FUTURE PROGRESSIVE ... will be demonstrating
FUTURE PERFECT ... will have demonstrated

PAST PASSIVE

— · —
— · —
it was demonstrated · they were demonstrated

 • *The procedure was demonstrated to the other doctors.*

COMPLEMENTS

demonstrate *illustrate a process/ procedure*

Professor, will you demonstrate?
I will demonstrate to the audience.

demonstrate *participate in a public display of opinion*

The students seem to demonstrate every week against
 the university's involvement in war research.
The workers are demonstrating for higher wages.

demonstrate _____ *show clearly, illustrate, explain, prove [with examples, experiments]*

OBJECT

Dr. Brown demonstrated **the procedure.**
The girls demonstrated **their science project.**
The salespeople demonstrated **the computers** to the customers.

WH-CLAUSE

I will demonstrate **what I had in mind.**
The expert demonstrated **why the validity of the photograph
 was in question.**
The police demonstrated **how the accident had happened.**

WH-INFINITIVE

He demonstrated **what to do in case of fire.**
The nurse demonstrated **how to put on a bandage.**

PRESENT

I deny	we deny
you deny	you deny
he/she/it denies	they deny

• *He totally denies doing anything wrong.*

PRESENT PROGRESSIVE

I am denying	we are denying
you are denying	you are denying
he/she/it is denying	they are denying

• *The suspect is denying everything.*

PAST

I denied	we denied
you denied	you denied
he/she/it denied	they denied

• *They denied him a visa.*

PAST PROGRESSIVE

I was denying	we were denying
you were denying	you were denying
he/she/it was denying	they were denying

• *He was denying them the right of free speech.*

PRESENT PERFECT ... have | has denied
PAST PERFECT ... had denied

FUTURE ... will deny
FUTURE PROGRESSIVE ... will be denying
FUTURE PERFECT ... will have denied

PAST PASSIVE

I was denied	we were denied
you were denied	you were denied
he/she/it was denied	they were denied

• *The story was denied by the senator.*

COMPLEMENTS

deny ⎯⎯ *declare to be false*

OBJECT

He denies **any claim that he was involved.**
I deny **the allegation.**

WH-CLAUSE

We totally deny **what the prosecution has alleged.**
I deny **whatever they have said about me.**

deny ⎯⎯ *refuse to believe*

OBJECT

Some groups deny **the theory of evolution.**
The police denied **Mike's story.**

deny ⎯⎯ *refuse to admit/acknowledge*

OBJECT

He denied **any responsibility for the accident.**
I denied **Jerry's crazy accusations.**

THAT-CLAUSE

We denied **that we were even at the party.**
Drivers always deny **that they were speeding.**

PRESENT PARTICIPLE

The kids denied **breaking the window.**
The salesman denied **promising a 90-day warranty on the car.**

deny ⎯⎯ *reject, refuse to grant*

OBJECT

The governor denied **the petition.**
The CEO denied **my request for a meeting.**

INDIRECT OBJECT + DIRECT OBJECT

Would you deny *a hungry child* **food**?

to PARAPHRASE

Would you deny **food** *to a hungry child*?

PRESENT

I depend	we depend
you depend	you depend
he/she/it depends	they depend

• *John depends on his staff.*

PRESENT PROGRESSIVE

I am depending	we are depending
you are depending	you are depending
he/she/it is depending	they are depending

• *I'm depending on you.*

PAST

I depended	we depended
you depended	you depended
he/she/it depended	they depended

• *I depended on outside consultants.*

PAST PROGRESSIVE

I was depending	we were depending
you were depending	you were depending
he/she/it was depending	they were depending

• *We were depending on getting a larger budget.*

PRESENT PERFECT ... have | has depended
PAST PERFECT ... had depended

FUTURE ... will depend
FUTURE PROGRESSIVE ... will be depending
FUTURE PERFECT ... will have depended

PAST PASSIVE

I was depended	we were depended
you were depended	you were depended
he/she/it was depended	they were depended

• *His advice was greatly depended on.*

(**COMPLEMENTS**)

NOTE: The verb *depend* is usually used with *on*. However, *on* is optional with WH-CLAUSE complements, especially in conversation.

depend *be contingent on something*   "Will you go to the party?" "That depends."

depend _____ *be based/contingent on, be determined by*

on OBJECT

Plant life depends **on water and oxygen.**
Our department depends **on government grants.**
Where we go on vacation depends **on the value of the dollar.**
Crowd size depends **on the weather and available parking.**

(on) WH-CLAUSE

My job depends **(on) who wins the election.**
It depends **(on) what you mean.**
The price depends **(on) where you want to go.**
It depends **(on) how much it costs.**

depend _____ *rely on, trust*

on OBJECT

You can depend **on me.**
Stella depended **on the kindness of strangers.**
We are going to win. Depend **on it!**

on OBJECT + INFINITIVE

I depended **on him** *to give us good advice.*
They depended **on the shelter** *to protect them from the storm.*
People depend too much **on milk** *to provide their calcium.*

on PRESENT PARTICIPLE

The village depends **on getting safe drinking water from their wells.**
They are depending **on your getting them home.**
My parents depend **on my helping them with their computer problems.**

PRESENT

I derive	we derive
you derive	you derive
he/she/it derives	they derive

• *He derives his income from investments.*

PRESENT PROGRESSIVE

I am deriving	we are deriving
you are deriving	you are deriving
he/she/it is deriving	they are deriving

• *He is not deriving much satisfaction from it.*

PAST

I derived	we derived
you derived	you derived
he/she/it derived	they derived

• *I derived a solution within five minutes.*

PAST PROGRESSIVE

I was deriving	we were deriving
you were deriving	you were deriving
he/she/it was deriving	they were deriving

• *They were deriving ethanol from corn.*

PRESENT PERFECT ... have | has derived
PAST PERFECT ... had derived

FUTURE ... will derive
FUTURE PROGRESSIVE ... will be deriving
FUTURE PERFECT ... will have derived

PAST PASSIVE

—	—
—	—
it was derived	they were derived

• *The compound was derived in our labs.*

COMPLEMENTS

derive _____ *originate*
   from OBJECT

My optimism derives **from the robust economy.**
"Duke" derives **from the Latin word "dux."**
Western philosophy derives **from the ancient Greeks**.

derive _____ *get, obtain*
   OBJECT (+ *from* OBJECT)

We derive **the chemical** organically.
We derive **gas** *from coal.*
He derives **his information** *from the foreign press.*
I derive **much satisfaction** *from my work.*
Popular culture derives **many expressions** *from sports.*

    PASSIVE
  WH-CLAUSE (+ *from* OBJECT)

Many English words are derived *from the Vikings.*
We derive **what we need** synthetically.
They derive **whatever energy they need** *from water power*.

derive _____ *arrive at by reasoning*
   OBJECT

She derived **that equation** from the definitions given in class.
They derived **a completely different conclusion.**
Holmes derived **the killer's identity** through reasoning alone.

PRESENT

I describe	we describe
you describe	you describe
he/she/it describes	they describe

- *Melville accurately describes whaling.*

PAST

I described	we described
you described	you described
he/she/it described	they described

- *She described what he looks like.*

PRESENT PERFECT ... have | has described
PAST PERFECT ... had described

PRESENT PROGRESSIVE

I am describing	we are describing
you are describing	you are describing
he/she/it is describing	they are describing

- *I'm not describing it very well, I'm afraid.*

PAST PROGRESSIVE

I was describing	we were describing
you were describing	you were describing
he/she/it was describing	they were describing

- *The students were describing their summer vacations.*

FUTURE ... will describe
FUTURE PROGRESSIVE ... will be describing
FUTURE PERFECT ... will have described

PAST PASSIVE

I was described	we were described
you were described	you were described
he/she/it was described	they were described

- *The pre-war situation was described in the last lecture.*

(**COMPLEMENTS**)

describe _____ *portray, represent, explain*

OBJECT	Can you describe **your attacker**?
	Please describe **your living room** to me.
	His articles describe **the consequences of global warming**.
	The dance describes **the nature of conflict**.
OBJECT + *as* OBJECT	He described **the operation** *as a complete success*.
	The press described **the verdict** *as a travesty of justice*.
PASSIVE	The verdict was described *as a travesty of justice*.
WH-CLAUSE	The book describes **what you should do to protect yourself from inflation**.
	The presentation described **how we can improve our job skills**.
WH-INFINITIVE	The guide described **what to look for**.
	The article described **how to make money in real estate**.
PRESENT PARTICIPLE	He described **living in London during the war**.
	The doctor described **having a heart attack**.

describe _____ *trace the outline of*

OBJECT	He described **a circle** with a compass.
	Figure skaters must describe **elaborate shapes on the ice**.

PRESENT

I deserve	we deserve
you deserve	you deserve
he/she/it deserves	they deserve

• *He deserves a medal.*

PRESENT PROGRESSIVE

Deserve is rarely used in the progressive tenses.

PAST

I deserved	we deserved
you deserved	you deserved
he/she/it deserved	they deserved

• *He deserved everything he got.*

PAST PROGRESSIVE

Deserve is rarely used in the progressive tenses.

PRESENT PERFECT ... have | has deserved
PAST PERFECT ... had deserved

FUTURE ... will deserve
FUTURE PROGRESSIVE —
FUTURE PERFECT ... will have deserved

PAST PASSIVE

—   —
—   —
it was deserved   they were deserved

• *Marion's reward was well deserved.*

―(COMPLEMENTS)―

deserve _____ *be worthy of, should get*

OBJECT	They deserve **a second chance.**
	She certainly deserves **our admiration.**
	This problem deserves **our full attention.**
	The term paper deserves **an "A."**
INFINITIVE	He didn't deserve **to be treated that way.**
	I deserve **to be heard.**
	Her restaurant deserves **to have three stars.**
WH-CLAUSE	He deserves **what he has coming to him.**
	They really deserve **whatever tips they earn.**
	People usually deserve **whatever reputation they have.**
PRESENT PARTICIPLE	He didn't deserve **being treated that way.**
	I didn't deserve **being ignored.**
	No restaurant deserves **losing its license that way.**

―(EXPRESSIONS)―

deserve credit for _____ *should be recognized for*

Rebecca deserves credit for keeping the construction project on schedule.

deserve blame for _____ *should be held responsible for*

Congress deserves much of the blame for the financial crisis.

be deserving of _____ *be worthy of* [*praise, help*]

Zack is deserving of the award.
Mrs. Nichols is deserving of energy assistance.

PRESENT

I design	we design
you design	you design
he/she/it designs	they design

• *She designs dresses in Milan.*

PRESENT PROGRESSIVE

I am designing	we are designing
you are designing	you are designing
he/she/it is designing	they are designing

• *I'm designing something new.*

PAST

I designed	we designed
you designed	you designed
he/she/it designed	they designed

• *I designed a wonderful waterfall.*

PAST PROGRESSIVE

I was designing	we were designing
you were designing	you were designing
he/she/it was designing	they were designing

• *Our team was designing accounting software.*

PRESENT PERFECT ... have | has designed
PAST PERFECT ... had designed

FUTURE ... will design
FUTURE PROGRESSIVE ... will be designing
FUTURE PERFECT ... will have designed

PAST PASSIVE

—	—
—	—
it was designed	they were designed

• *The school was designed by architect William B. Ittner.*

COMPLEMENTS

design _____ *conceive and develop (plans for)*

OBJECT
He designed **the new mall.**
They design **artwork for CD covers.**
My boss designed **a perfect scheme for betting on horse races.**

WH-CLAUSE
We only design **what we can build in six months.**
They will design **whatever you need.**
They will design **whatever kind of advertising campaign the company wants.**

design _____ *conceive and develop [for a specific purpose]*

OBJECT + *as* OBJECT
The firm designed **the external drive** *as a USB device.*
The publisher designed **the book** *as an aid to language learners.*
He designed **his blog** *as an alternative to the mainstream media.*

OBJECT + *to be* OBJECT
The firm designed **the external drive** *to be a USB device.*
The publisher designed **the book** *to be an aid to language learners.*
He designed **his blog** *to be an alternative to the mainstream media.*

OBJECT + INFINITIVE
I designed **a new device** *to record messages.*
We design **cars** *to go faster and faster.*
Nate designed **a statistical model** *to predict elections better.*
We designed **the operating system** *to be more robust.*

EXPRESSIONS

be designed for _____
be intended for

This bread machine was not designed for daily use.

PRESENT

I desire	we desire
you desire	you desire
he/she/it desires	they desire

• *He desires to be introduced.*

PAST

I desired	we desired
you desired	you desired
he/she/it desired	they desired

• *We desired too much too soon.*

PRESENT PERFECT ... have | has desired
PAST PERFECT   ... had desired

PRESENT PROGRESSIVE

Desire is rarely used in the progressive tenses.

PAST PROGRESSIVE

Desire is rarely used in the progressive tenses.

FUTURE   ... will desire
FUTURE PROGRESSIVE   —
FUTURE PERFECT   ... will have desired

PAST PASSIVE

I was desired	we were desired
you were desired	you were desired
he/she/it was desired	they were desired

• *An immediate response was desired.*

──────(**COMPLEMENTS**)──────

desire _____ *wish for, request*

OBJECT	We all desire **a good job with benefits.**
	The kids desired **more computer time.**
	The world desires **peace.**
(*for*) OBJECT + INFINITIVE	The company desired (**for**) **the CEO** *to be a member of the board.*
	We desired (**for**) **the party** *to be a complete surprise.*
INFINITIVE	He desires **to see them one last time.**
	Ingrid desired **to be left alone.**
	The manager desired **to be kept informed.**
WH-CLAUSE	We all seem to desire **what we can't get.**
	The kids all desire **whatever they see on TV.**

PRESENT

I destroy	we destroy
you destroy	you destroy
he/she/it destroys	they destroy

• *A tornado destroys everything in its path.*

PRESENT PROGRESSIVE

I am destroying	we are destroying
you are destroying	you are destroying
he/she/it is destroying	they are destroying

• *I'm destroying my old bank statements.*

PAST

I destroyed	we destroyed
you destroyed	you destroyed
he/she/it destroyed	they destroyed

• *They destroyed all the records.*

PAST PROGRESSIVE

I was destroying	we were destroying
you were destroying	you were destroying
he/she/it was destroying	they were destroying

• *Forest roads were destroying the stream beds.*

PRESENT PERFECT ... have | has destroyed
PAST PERFECT ... had destroyed

FUTURE ... will destroy
FUTURE PROGRESSIVE ... will be destroying
FUTURE PERFECT ... will have destroyed

PAST PASSIVE

I was destroyed	we were destroyed
you were destroyed	you were destroyed
he/she/it was destroyed	they were destroyed

• *The army was destroyed.*

———(**COMPLEMENTS**)———

destroy _____ *ruin, demolish, crush*

OBJECT
The storm destroyed **the old barn.**
The noise from the TV destroyed **my concentration.**
Their stupid argument totally destroyed **our dinner party.**

WH-CLAUSE
Critics destroy **what they don't understand.**
The advancing army destroyed **whatever was in its path.**

destroy _____ *kill [an animal]*

OBJECT
The vet had to destroy **the injured horse.**

PASSIVE
Abandoned pets are often destroyed.

PRESENT

I detail	we detail
you detail	you detail
he/she/it details	they detail

• *He details even the smallest expenses.*

PAST

I detailed	we detailed
you detailed	you detailed
he/she/it detailed	they detailed

• *He detailed the recruits to the mess hall.*

PRESENT PERFECT ... have | has detailed

PAST PERFECT ... had detailed

PRESENT PROGRESSIVE

I am detailing	we are detailing
you are detailing	you are detailing
he/she/it is detailing	they are detailing

• *I'm detailing everything you need to know.*

PAST PROGRESSIVE

I was detailing	we were detailing
you were detailing	you were detailing
he/she/it was detailing	they were detailing

• *We were detailing all of the recommendations.*

FUTURE ... will detail

FUTURE PROGRESSIVE ... will be detailing

FUTURE PERFECT ... will have detailed

PAST PASSIVE

I was detailed	we were detailed
you were detailed	you were detailed
he/she/it was detailed	they were detailed

• *His complaints were detailed in the company log.*

─────(COMPLEMENTS)─────

detail _____ *report/list even the smallest things about*

OBJECT	Please detail **the events that led to the accident.**
	You must detail **all of your expenses.**
	I detailed **everything that had happened since I arrived.**
WH-CLAUSE	I detailed **what happened that night.**
	You should detail **how often the operating system failed.**
	In my diary, I detailed **wherever we stopped on our trip.**

detail _____ *assign [to/for a task]*

OBJECT	The captain detailed **the men** for guard duty.
PASSIVE	We were detailed to another unit.

detail _____ *wash, wax, and restore to pristine condition [a vehicle]*

OBJECT	Some car washes will also detail **your car.**
	Owners often detail **their antique cars** to an incredible degree.

determine

PRESENT		PRESENT PROGRESSIVE	
I determine	we determine	I am determining	we are determining
you determine	you determine	you are determining	you are determining
he/she/it determines	they determine	he/she/it is determining	they are determining

• *Economic conditions determine the result.*   • *We are still determining what is the best thing to do.*

PAST		PAST PROGRESSIVE	
I determined	we determined	I was determining	we were determining
you determined	you determined	you were determining	you were determining
he/she/it determined	they determined	he/she/it was determining	they were determining

• *We determined to continue the expansion.*   • *I was determining where I could have lost my wallet.*

PRESENT PERFECT … have | has determined   **FUTURE** … will determine
PAST PERFECT … had determined   **FUTURE PROGRESSIVE** … will be determining
          FUTURE PERFECT … will have determined

PAST PASSIVE	
I was determined	we were determined
you were determined	you were determined
he/she/it was determined	they were determined

• *Our policies were determined by pure self-interest.*

COMPLEMENTS

determine _____ *decide, figure out*

OBJECT	The board determines **all company policies.**
	You must first determine **the area of the floor to be painted.**
INFINITIVE	They determined **to try again.**
	George determined **to mind his own business** in the future.
THAT-CLAUSE	We determined **that we should go ahead.**
	The jury determined **that the defendant was innocent.**
WH-CLAUSE	I haven't determined **what I should major in.**
	We still couldn't determine **why the experiment failed.**
WH-INFINITIVE	I never determined **what to do.**
	Have you determined **where to stay** yet?

determine _____ *be the cause of, control*

OBJECT	Our team's superior physical condition determined **the outcome of the game.**
	National interest always determines **national policy.**
WH-CLAUSE	In war, luck often determines **who will live and who will die.**

EXPRESSIONS

be determined *be resolved, have one's mind set*   My spouse is determined to get a Ph.D.
          The owner was determined to turn a profit last year.

determine the root of a problem *figure out the causes of a problem*   You must determine the root of a problem before you can solve it.

PRESENT

I develop	we develop
you develop	you develop
he/she/it develops	they develop

• *Prostate cancer usually develops slowly.*

PRESENT PROGRESSIVE

I am developing	we are developing
you are developing	you are developing
he/she/it is developing	they are developing

• *He is developing the land north of the freeway.*

PAST

I developed	we developed
you developed	you developed
he/she/it developed	they developed

• *They developed an interesting proposal.*

PAST PROGRESSIVE

I was developing	we were developing
you were developing	you were developing
he/she/it was developing	they were developing

• *The patient was developing resistance to the drug.*

PRESENT PERFECT ... have | has developed
PAST PERFECT ... had developed

FUTURE ... will develop
FUTURE PROGRESSIVE ... will be developing
FUTURE PERFECT ... will have developed

PAST PASSIVE

—	—
—	—
it was developed	they were developed

• *The new software was developed by our division.*

COMPLEMENTS

develop *grow and mature*	A human develops from a single fertilized egg.
	Infants develop at an amazing rate.
	Nicole is developing into a fine golfer.
	Our reunion plans are developing nicely.
develop *come into being gradually*	The situation is developing as we expected.
develop ____ *turn out, happen*	
it + *develop* + THAT-CLAUSE	It developed **that three senators were also involved in the scandal.**
develop ____ *elaborate*	
OBJECT	He needs to develop **his ideas** further.
	Mozart develops **two new themes** in the second movement.
develop ____ *utilize, exploit*	
OBJECT	The company is developing **its land in Idaho.**
	We must develop **our advantage in skilled labor.**
WH-CLAUSE	You can only develop **what resources you have.**
develop ____ *promote the growth of, expand*	
OBJECT	Only exercise can develop **muscles.**
	The warm weather is developing **the wheat** rapidly.
	He developed **his tiny restaurant** into a national chain.
develop ____ *acquire gradually*	
OBJECT	I have developed **an interest in opera.**
develop ____ *bring into being and evolve*	
OBJECT	The company leads the industry in developing **new products.**
	We develop **video games** for the entertainment industry.
	Arnold is developing **a new television show.**
PASSIVE	The website was developed by our engineers and designers.
WH-CLAUSE	The company only develops **what it can sell.**
	Our team will develop **whatever plug-ins you want.**
develop ____ *get [a disease]*	
OBJECT	Annie developed **a rash** on her arms and legs.
	Bart developed **measles** at summer camp.

PRESENT

I devote	we devote
you devote	you devote
he/she/it devotes	they devote

• *He devotes his weekends to restoring cars.*

PRESENT PROGRESSIVE

I am devoting	we are devoting
you are devoting	you are devoting
he/she/it is devoting	they are devoting

• *I'm devoting a lot of time to it.*

PAST

I devoted	we devoted
you devoted	you devoted
he/she/it devoted	they devoted

• *I devoted 10% of my tax refund to charity.*

PAST PROGRESSIVE

I was devoting	we were devoting
you were devoting	you were devoting
he/she/it was devoting	they were devoting

• *We were devoting our resources to staff development.*

PRESENT PERFECT ... have | has devoted
PAST PERFECT   ... had devoted

FUTURE   ... will devote
FUTURE PROGRESSIVE   ... will be devoting
FUTURE PERFECT   ... will have devoted

PAST PASSIVE

I was devoted	we were devoted
you were devoted	you were devoted
he/she/it was devoted	they were devoted

• *The fund was devoted to wildlife preservation.*

― **COMPLEMENTS** ―

devote _____ *commit, apply [to a specific purpose]*

OBJECT + *to* OBJECT	I devote **my free time** *to charity work.*
	Our company devotes **itself** *to research.*
	We devote **ourselves** *to our children.*
	I devoted **fully half of the basement** *to a print shop.*
OBJECT + *to* WH-CLAUSE	We devote **our resources** *to whoever needs them the most.*
	They devote **their restoration efforts** *to whatever buildings are most at risk.*
OBJECT + *to* PRESENT PARTICIPLE	Sally devotes **her time** *to saving the environment.*
WH-CLAUSE + *to* OBJECT	They devote **whatever they can afford** *to their church.*
WH-CLAUSE + *to* WH-CLAUSE	I devote **what I can** *to what needs doing.*
WH-CLAUSE + *to* PRESENT PARTICIPLE	We devote **whatever profits we make** *to building a stronger community.*

devote _____ *consecrate*

| OBJECT + *to* OBJECT | The Romans devoted **their greatest temple** *to Jupiter.* |
| PASSIVE | The greatest Roman temple was devoted *to Jupiter.* |

― **EXPRESSIONS** ―

devoted *loyal, dedicated*   Amber was a truly devoted daughter.

PRESENT		PRESENT PROGRESSIVE	
I die	we die	I am dying	we are dying
you die	you die	you are dying	you are dying
he/she/it dies	they die	he/she/it is dying	they are dying

  • *The engine dies whenever I brake.*   • *The tomato plants are dying.*

PAST		PAST PROGRESSIVE	
I died	we died	I was dying	we were dying
you died	you died	you were dying	you were dying
he/she/it died	they died	he/she/it was dying	they were dying

  • *The rumors finally died.*   • *We were dying of thirst.*

PRESENT PERFECT	... have | has died
PAST PERFECT	... had died

FUTURE	... will die
FUTURE PROGRESSIVE	... will be dying
FUTURE PERFECT	... will have died

PAST PASSIVE

  Die is never used in the passive voice.

(COMPLEMENTS)

die *stop living*	His aunt died of cancer.
	In *Hamlet*, nearly everyone dies at the end.
	My grandfather died before I was born.
	The criminal was sentenced to die by hanging.
	"It is sweet and fitting to die for one's country." [HORACE]
die *stop functioning*	My iPod just died.
	The chain saw kept dying.
die *go out of existence*	The committee dies at the end of the session.
	My anger died when I learned what had really happened.
	The storm finally died during the night.
die *fail, lose force*	All of his early plays died after a few performances.
	The bill died before it came to a vote.
	The crowd's laughter slowly died.
die *suffer greatly, agonize* [FIGURATIVE]	I'm dying here in all this heat.
die ＿＿ *suffer greatly, agonize* [FIGURATIVE]	
of OBJECT	My mother was dying **of curiosity**.
	Our son was dying **of boredom** at Grandma's house.
die ＿＿ *desire greatly* [FIGURATIVE]	
for OBJECT	The kids were dying **for ice cream**.
	That chocolate cake is to die **for**!
INFINITIVE	I'm dying **to find out what happened**.
	The kids are dying **to open their presents**.
	Thelma is dying **to see Louise**.

(PHRASAL VERBS)

die away/down/out *disappear gradually*	The echo of her footsteps died away.
	The wind died down after midnight.
	The noise from the bar finally died down.
	The fire will eventually die out.
die back *die from the tips toward the roots, become dormant* [OF PLANTS]	Perennials die back in the fall or winter.
die off/out *become extinct, die one by one until all are gone*	Mammals thrived after the dinosaurs died off.
	When did the Neanderthals die out?
die on ＿＿ *stop functioning while being operated by*	My cell phone died on me again.

PRESENT		PRESENT PROGRESSIVE	
I dig	we dig	I am digging	we are digging
you dig	you dig	you are digging	you are digging
he/she/it digs	they dig	he/she/it is digging	they are digging

• *He really digs in at suppertime.*   • *I'm digging as fast as I can.*

PAST		PAST PROGRESSIVE	
I dug	we dug	I was digging	we were digging
you dug	you dug	you were digging	you were digging
he/she/it dug	they dug	he/she/it was digging	they were digging

• *They dug up a lot of information.*   • *The kids were digging in the backyard.*

PRESENT PERFECT ... have | has dug
PAST PERFECT ... had dug

FUTURE ... will dig
FUTURE PROGRESSIVE ... will be digging
FUTURE PERFECT ... will have dug

PAST PASSIVE

— —

— —

it was dug   they were dug

• *The foundation was dug last week.*

COMPLEMENTS

dig *turn up / remove soil by hand, tool, or machine*	I have been digging all afternoon. We will dig tomorrow.
dig *search [for something]*	Nicole dug in her suitcase for the shampoo. I am digging everywhere I can think of. The accountants are really digging.
dig _____ *create [a hole] by removing soil* OBJECT	The road crew was digging **a trench**. The dog dug **a hole** in our front lawn. They have dug **the foundation**.
dig _____ *remove from the soil* OBJECT	The farmer dug **potatoes** in the field. Miners can dig **coal** from the slopes.
dig _____ *notice, understand, like* [INFORMAL] OBJECT	Did you dig **that crazy shirt**? I couldn't dig **all that technical talk**. Kids don't dig **classical music**.
WH-CLAUSE	Did you dig **what he was saying**? I can't dig **what the teacher is saying**. Did you dig **who was in that movie**?

PHRASAL VERBS

dig at _____ *criticize*	He's always digging at me for my conservatism.
dig down/deep *be generous*	We all must dig down to feed the poor.
dig in *start to work intensively*	There were 23 court cases to study, and the lawyers dug in.
dig in *start eating*	Supper's on the table. Dig in!
dig into _____ *investigate thoroughly*	The detectives dug into the suspect's background.
dig into _____ *start eating*	The workmen dug into the stew and biscuits.
dig SEP **out** *uncover by digging*	Tim dug his car out with a snow shovel.
dig SEP **out** *obtain by searching*	Let's dig out the family photo albums.
dig SEP **up** *uncover by digging*	We dug 23 arrowheads up in one afternoon.
dig SEP **up** *obtain by searching*	Reporters dug up a lot of information about the mayor.

PRESENT

I direct	we direct
you direct	you direct
he/she/it directs	they direct

• *He directs the emergency response team.*

PRESENT PROGRESSIVE

I am directing	we are directing
you are directing	you are directing
he/she/it is directing	they are directing

• *He is directing a play.*

PAST

I directed	we directed
you directed	you directed
he/she/it directed	they directed

• *She directed a number of movies.*

PAST PROGRESSIVE

I was directing	we were directing
you were directing	you were directing
he/she/it was directing	they were directing

• *The police were directing traffic on Elm Street.*

PRESENT PERFECT ... have | has directed
PAST PERFECT   ... had directed

FUTURE   ... will direct
FUTURE PROGRESSIVE ... will be directing
FUTURE PERFECT   ... will have directed

PAST PASSIVE

I was directed	we were directed
you were directed	you were directed
he/she/it was directed	they were directed

• *The archaeological dig was directed by Dr. Brown.*

(**COMPLEMENTS**)

direct *lead people in a performance*

Henry Smith will be directing.
He has never directed before.

direct ⎯⎯ *be in charge of, manage*

OBJECT

I am directing **the new project**.
She will direct **the program**.
He will direct **all fund-raising activities**.
She is directing **the installation of the new piece
  of sculpture**.

direct ⎯⎯ *supervise performers in [an artistic production]*

OBJECT

He directed **one of the Harry Potter films**.
The brothers have directed **a number of movies**.
I have directed **four Broadway plays**.

direct ⎯⎯ *point/channel to a specified person/place*

OBJECT + ADVERB OF PLACE TO/FROM

The signs directed **us** *down a side street*.
The ships directed **their guns** *on the fort*.
Direct **your questions** *to my press secretary*.
The tourists directed **their attention** *to the statue of Venus*.
We directed **the floodwater** *away from the house*.

PASSIVE

Our attention was directed *to the inscription on the monument*.

direct ⎯⎯ *order*

OBJECT + INFINITIVE

The judge directed **the jury** *to ignore the last statement*.
The police directed **him** *to put up his hands*.

PASSIVE

He was directed *to put up his hands*.

disappear | disappears ·
disappeared · have disappeared

☑ REGULAR

PRESENT

I disappear	we disappear
you disappear	you disappear
he/she/it disappears	they disappear

• *He disappears right after dinner.*

PRESENT PROGRESSIVE

I am disappearing	we are disappearing
you are disappearing	you are disappearing
he/she/it is disappearing	they are disappearing

• *Wild mushrooms are disappearing from the forests.*

PAST

I disappeared	we disappeared
you disappeared	you disappeared
he/she/it disappeared	they disappeared

• *The money disappeared last night.*

PAST PROGRESSIVE

I was disappearing	we were disappearing
you were disappearing	you were disappearing
he/she/it was disappearing	they were disappearing

• *The T-shirts were disappearing fast.*

PRESENT PERFECT ... have | has disappeared
PAST PERFECT ... had disappeared

FUTURE ... will disappear
FUTURE PROGRESSIVE ... will be disappearing
FUTURE PERFECT ... will have disappeared

PAST PASSIVE

Disappear is rarely used in the passive voice.

COMPLEMENTS

disappear *vanish from view*

The mountains disappeared in the fog.
Alice stared as the Cheshire cat disappeared.
The man disappeared around the corner.
The suspects disappeared into the crowd.

disappear *go out of existence*

The fog disappeared as the sun rose.
Many species of frogs have disappeared over the last decade.
All of the investors' money has just disappeared.
When the ship passed us by, our last hope disappeared.

PRESENT

I discover	we discover
you discover	you discover
he/she/it discovers	they discover

• *Holmes always discovers the murderer.*

PRESENT PROGRESSIVE

I am discovering	we are discovering
you are discovering	you are discovering
he/she/it is discovering	they are discovering

• *I'm discovering how much I need to learn.*

PAST

I discovered	we discovered
you discovered	you discovered
he/she/it discovered	they discovered

• *I discovered an important letter.*

PAST PROGRESSIVE

I was discovering	we were discovering
you were discovering	you were discovering
he/she/it was discovering	they were discovering

• *We were discovering something new every day.*

PRESENT PERFECT ... have | has discovered
PAST PERFECT ... had discovered

FUTURE ... will discover
FUTURE PROGRESSIVE ... will be discovering
FUTURE PERFECT ... will have discovered

PAST PASSIVE

I was discovered	we were discovered
you were discovered	you were discovered
he/she/it was discovered	they were discovered

• *The spy's identity was never discovered.*

COMPLEMENTS

discover _____ *be the first to see / learn about*

OBJECT
William Hershel discovered **Uranus** in 1781.
Marie and Pierre Curie discovered **radium** in 1902.
Francis Crick and James Watson discovered **the structure of DNA** on the basis of research by Rosalind Franklin.
Edwin Hubble discovered **the first direct evidence that the universe is expanding.**

discover _____ *see / become aware of for the first time*

OBJECT
We discovered **a new problem with the design.**
I finally discovered **a solution.**
They discovered **a leak in the water line.**

OBJECT + INFINITIVE
The doctor discovered **George** *to be diabetic.*
We discovered **him** *to be encouraged by recent events.*

PASSIVE
He was discovered *to be sleeping on the job.*

OBJECT + PRESENT PARTICIPLE
The police discovered **him** *breaking into a car.*
We discovered **a squirrel** *gnawing a hole in our roof.*

PASSIVE
He was discovered *sleeping on the job.*

OBJECT + PAST PARTICIPLE
She discovered **her mother** *exhausted from the trip.*
We discovered **him** *encouraged by recent events.*
We discovered **Frank** *embittered by what had happened.*

THAT-CLAUSE
We discovered **that we were in real trouble.**
I discovered **that the battery was dead.**
We discovered **that he was encouraged by recent events.**

WH-CLAUSE
Jasper discovered **what had gone wrong.**
We discovered **where we could park without getting a ticket.**
They discovered **why the company was losing so much money.**
We discovered **why he was encouraged by recent events.**

WH-INFINITIVE
I quickly discovered **what not to do.**
We discovered **where to get good pizza.**
The kids discovered **how to turn on the TV.**

discover _____ *reveal, make known*

OBJECT
Our investigation discovered **several instances of contamination.**

OBJECT + INFINITIVE
The investigation discovered **the patrolman** *to be taking bribes.*

PRESENT

I discuss	we discuss
you discuss	you discuss
he/she/it discusses	they discuss

• *He discusses politics on the radio.*

PRESENT PROGRESSIVE

I am discussing	we are discussing
you are discussing	you are discussing
he/she/it is discussing	they are discussing

• *I'm discussing the proposal with my group.*

PAST

I discussed	we discussed
you discussed	you discussed
he/she/it discussed	they discussed

• *We discussed this problem yesterday.*

PAST PROGRESSIVE

I was discussing	we were discussing
you were discussing	you were discussing
he/she/it was discussing	they were discussing

• *We were discussing him when you came in.*

PRESENT PERFECT ... have | has discussed
PAST PERFECT ... had discussed

FUTURE ... will discuss
FUTURE PROGRESSIVE ... will be discussing
FUTURE PERFECT ... will have discussed

PAST PASSIVE

I was discussed	we were discussed
you were discussed	you were discussed
he/she/it was discussed	they were discussed

• *The plans were thoroughly discussed at the meeting.*

—(**COMPLEMENTS**)—

discuss _____ *talk about, consider in writing/speech*

OBJECT	We were discussing **the latest rumor**.
	They discussed **Tim's behavior at the party**.
	The board discussed **a possible merger**.
	Last week we discussed **the causes of World War I**.
	The article discusses **Albert Einstein's theory of relativity**.
	The Gettysburg Address discussed **the principles of human equality**.
WH-CLAUSE	The committee discussed **who would receive bonuses this year**.
	They discussed **what they had seen on Oprah**.
	The book discusses **how electricity is generated by wind turbines**.
	We discussed **how much we were all paying for gas**.
WH-INFINITIVE	The lawyers discussed **whom to bill**.
	They discussed **where to go on vacation**.
	My report discusses **how to save electricity**.
	My wife and I discussed **how much to pay the babysitter**.

PRESENT

I display	we display
you display	you display
he/she/it displays	they display

• *He displays his work at art fairs.*

PRESENT PROGRESSIVE

I am displaying	we are displaying
you are displaying	you are displaying
he/she/it is displaying	they are displaying

• *I'm displaying my lawn sculptures this weekend.*

PAST

I displayed	we displayed
you displayed	you displayed
he/she/it displayed	they displayed

• *She displayed fine motor skills.*

PAST PROGRESSIVE

I was displaying	we were displaying
you were displaying	you were displaying
he/she/it was displaying	they were displaying

• *The soldiers were displaying great bravery.*

PRESENT PERFECT ... have | has displayed
PAST PERFECT ... had displayed

FUTURE ... will display
FUTURE PROGRESSIVE ... will be displaying
FUTURE PERFECT ... will have displayed

PAST PASSIVE

I was displayed	we were displayed
you were displayed	you were displayed
he/she/it was displayed	they were displayed

• *His paintings were displayed at a museum in New York.*

COMPLEMENTS

display *exhibit artwork*	I am displaying in Miami this fall. Will you be able to display soon? Have you ever displayed in a gallery?
display *engage in a breeding ritual*	Most birds display during mating season. Many male mammals display both to attract females and to discourage male rivals.
display ___ *exhibit, place into view*	
OBJECT	They display **the flag** on every holiday. Merchants displayed **their wares** in booths. Mary Ann displayed **her new winter coat**. Their son proudly displayed **his missing tooth**.
WH-CLAUSE	They displayed **what they had to sell**. The shops displayed **whatever goods they had left after the flood**.
display ___ *demonstrate, reveal*	
OBJECT	The unit displayed **great courage under fire**. His behavior displayed **great consideration for others**. The senator's proposal displayed **a total disregard for his constituents**.
WH-CLAUSE	They displayed **what they were made of**. The inventor displayed **how his device worked**.
display ___ *show off*	
OBJECT	Richard likes to display **his knowledge of Latin**. He is always displaying **his erudition**.
WH-CLAUSE	They display **how rich they are**. He displays **how much everything costs**.

PRESENT

I distinguish | we distinguish
you distinguish | you distinguish
he/she/it distinguishes | they distinguish

- *She distinguishes two types of tumors.*

PRESENT PROGRESSIVE

I am distinguishing | we are distinguishing
you are distinguishing | you are distinguishing
he/she/it is distinguishing | they are distinguishing

- *The student is distinguishing himself from the others.*

PAST

I distinguished | we distinguished
you distinguished | you distinguished
he/she/it distinguished | they distinguished

- *He distinguished himself in linguistics.*

PAST PROGRESSIVE

I was distinguishing | we were distinguishing
you were distinguishing | you were distinguishing
he/she/it was distinguishing | they were distinguishing

- *They were distinguishing ant species by their DNA.*

PRESENT PERFECT ... have | has distinguished
PAST PERFECT ... had distinguished

FUTURE ... will distinguish
FUTURE PROGRESSIVE ... will be distinguishing
FUTURE PERFECT ... will have distinguished

PAST PASSIVE

I was distinguished | we were distinguished
you were distinguished | you were distinguished
he/she/it was distinguished | they were distinguished

- *Her research was distinguished by its originality.*

COMPLEMENTS

distinguish _____ *notice as different, tell apart*

OBJECT	We need to distinguish **the difference.**
	Can you distinguish **the twins?**
OBJECT + *and* OBJECT	Any farmer can distinguish **wheat** *and barley.*
OBJECT + *from* OBJECT	All morality distinguishes **right** *from wrong.*
WH-CLAUSE + *from* WH-CLAUSE	You must distinguish **what people say** *from what they actually do.*
	We distinguish **what we want** *from what we need.*

distinguish _____ *make special, set apart*

| OBJECT | Teamwork and camaraderie distinguish **the Cardinals.** |
| OBJECT + *from* OBJECT | His enthusiasm distinguishes **him** *from his co-workers.* |

distinguish _____ *recognize*

OBJECT	It is always easy to distinguish **Beethoven's music.**
	Everybody can distinguish **the skyline of Manhattan.**
PASSIVE	His paintings are easily distinguished.

distinguish _____ *make [oneself] famous*

| REFLEXIVE PRONOUN | My neighbor distinguished **himself** in the field of molecular biology. |
| REFLEXIVE PRONOUN + *as* PREDICATE NOUN | Grace distinguished **herself** *as a pioneer in pediatric health care.* |

EXPRESSIONS

distinguished *famous, outstanding* | We heard the distinguished cellist Yo-Yo Ma play.

PRESENT

I dive	we dive
you dive	you dive
he/she/it dives	they dive

• *The market dives after bad economic news.*

PRESENT PROGRESSIVE

I am diving	we are diving
you are diving	you are diving
he/she/it is diving	they are diving

• *I'm diving into the bond market.*

PAST

I dived/dove	we dived/dove
you dived/dove	you dived/dove
he/she/it dived/dove	they dived/dove

• *I never dived from the highest board.*

PAST PROGRESSIVE

I was diving	we were diving
you were diving	you were diving
he/she/it was diving	they were diving

• *We were diving for lobsters.*

PRESENT PERFECT ... have | has dived
PAST PERFECT   ... had dived

FUTURE   ... will dive
FUTURE PROGRESSIVE ... will be diving
FUTURE PERFECT   ... will have dived

PAST PASSIVE

Dive is never used in the passive voice.

─────────────────────────────────(COMPLEMENTS)───

dive *plunge into water headfirst*	She dived into the pool.
	I dived from the 10-meter board.
	I dove with my eyes closed.
	Michael has been diving since he was four years old.
dive *go/swim underwater*	The submarine dove to 75 meters.
	The ducks were diving in the pond.
	The whale dove as soon as the boat approached.
	We were diving in wet suits.
dive *fall sharply and quickly*	The plane dived under the clouds.
	The temperature dives at nightfall.
	The market dived on the news.
dive _____ *plunge quickly, lunge*	
for OBJECT	The soldiers dove **for cover**.
	The shortstop dove **for the ball**.

─────────────────────────────────(PHRASAL VERBS)───

dive in *start doing something energetically*	We put the craft materials on the table and told the kids to dive right in.
dive into _____ *start doing energetically*	Becky dove into the new design project.
	New arrivals are diving right into the discussion.

PRESENT

I divide	we divide
you divide	you divide
he/she/it divides	they divide

• *He divides his clients into two groups.*

PRESENT PROGRESSIVE

I am dividing	we are dividing
you are dividing	you are dividing
he/she/it is dividing	they are dividing

• *I'm dividing the room into two sections.*

PAST

I divided	we divided
you divided	you divided
he/she/it divided	they divided

• *I divided the assignment into three parts.*

PAST PROGRESSIVE

I was dividing	we were dividing
you were dividing	you were dividing
he/she/it was dividing	they were dividing

• *The cells were dividing rapidly.*

PRESENT PERFECT ... have | has divided
PAST PERFECT ... had divided

FUTURE ... will divide
FUTURE PROGRESSIVE ... will be dividing
FUTURE PERFECT ... will have divided

PAST PASSIVE

I was divided	we were divided
you were divided	you were divided
he/she/it was divided	they were divided

• *The money was divided evenly.*

COMPLEMENTS

divide *replicate*	Bacteria divide rapidly in a favorable environment. Cancer cells divide more frequently than normal cells.
divide *branch out, become separated*	The branches are dividing close to the trunk of the tree. Voters usually divide along party lines.

divide _____ *separate [into parts/groups]*

OBJECT	A stone fence divides **the farmers' fields** from each other.
OBJECT + *into* OBJECT	Researchers divided **the participants** *into three groups*. The Civil War divides **American history** *into two distinct periods*.
PASSIVE	All Gaul is divided *into three parts*.

divide _____ *separate into opposing sides*

OBJECT	The issue divided **the country**.

divide _____ *distribute, portion out*

OBJECT	Ruby divided **her daylilies**.
OBJECT + *between/among* OBJECT	Grandmother divides **her time** *between reading and working crossword puzzles*. We will divide **the cookies** *among us*.
PASSIVE	The estate was divided *among the heirs*.
WH-CLAUSE	We will divide **whatever we get** equally. They divided **what they had earned**.

divide _____ *separate arithmetically [into equal parts]*

OBJECT	Please divide **84** by 6. Can you divide **356** into 4 equal shares?

PHRASAL VERBS

divide up *separate*	The class should divide up into three teams.
divide _SEP_ **up** *apportion*	The four brothers divided the acreage up among themselves.

EXPRESSIONS

divide and conquer / divide and rule *cause a group of people to fight each other, then defeat them all*	The boss knows how to divide and conquer his managers.

PRESENT		**PRESENT PROGRESSIVE**	
I do	we do	I am doing	we are doing
you do	you do	you are doing	you are doing
he/she/it does	they do	he/she/it is doing	they are doing

   • *He always does his best.*   • *I'm doing what I can.*

PAST		**PAST PROGRESSIVE**	
I did	we did	I was doing	we were doing
you did	you did	you were doing	you were doing
he/she/it did	they did	he/she/it was doing	they were doing

   • *I did everything you asked.*   • *We were doing just fine until we had an accident.*

PRESENT PERFECT … have | has done   **FUTURE**   … will do
PAST PERFECT   … had done   **FUTURE PROGRESSIVE** … will be doing
                                      FUTURE PERFECT   … will have done

PAST PASSIVE	
I was done	we were done
you were done	you were done
he/she/it was done	they were done

   • *The job was done in record time.*

(**COMPLEMENTS**)

NOTE: *Do* is also used with the base form of a verb
• to ask questions in the simple present and past tenses
    Do you want some candy?
• to form negative statements with *not* in the simple present and past tenses
    I do not think we will win.
• to emphasize what one is saying
    I do wish Mary would attend.

do *manage, get along*   "How is your son doing in school?" "He's doing well, thanks."

do *be adequate/right*   A couple of hours will do.
                            Ten dollars will do.
                            Your blue suit will do for the party.

do _____ *perform, finish working on*
    OBJECT   I did **some errands** after lunch.
                            I was just doing **my job**.
                            We always do **the crossword puzzle** together.
                            The kids should do **their homework** soon.
    WH-CLAUSE   I did **what needed to be done**.
                            We will do **whatever job we are assigned**.

do _____ *perform [for someone's benefit]*
    INDIRECT OBJECT + DIRECT OBJECT   Do *me* a favor.
                            He did *them* **a good deed**.
                            They did *the company* **a real service**.
      for PARAPHRASE   Do **a favor** *for me*.
                            He did **a good deed** *for them*.
                            They did **a real service** *for the company*.

do _____ *prepare, clean, decorate, arrange*
    OBJECT   We did **the table** before the guests came.
                            I did **a nice roast** for dinner.
                            I did **the dishes** afterwards.
                            My husband does **the laundry**.
                            We did **the living room** in pale blue.
                            She does **my hair**.

do _____ *travel [a distance] / visit [a place] / spend [time]*
    OBJECT

Hikers can do **20 miles a day**.
His car can do **100 miles an hour**.
We will do **several museums** this afternoon.
I did **three years** in the Navy.

do _____ *be right/proper* [USUALLY NEGATIVE]
    INFINITIVE

It won't do **to be late for the meeting**.
It doesn't do **to get all upset about it**.
It will never do **to come in over budget**.

do _____ *cause, have as an effect*
    OBJECT
    INDIRECT OBJECT + DIRECT OBJECT

The wind did **a lot of damage**.
A nap will do *you* **some good**.

do _____ *create, produce, play a role in*
    OBJECT

The author is doing **a biography of Abraham Lincoln**.
The artist is doing **portraits of famous people**.
The actress did **three movies** last year.

PHRASAL VERBS

do away with _____ *eliminate*

I did away with my landline phone at home.
The company did away with employee bonuses.

do away with _____ *murder*

He did away with three wives before he was caught.

do SEP **in** *make very tired*

Driving for three hours does me in.

do SEP **in** *cause the death/failure of, kill*

Pneumonia finally did him in.
The mob tried to do in the entire police force.
The politician was done in by greed.

do [someone] out of _____ *prevent [someone] from getting*

The con artist did investors out of their life's savings.

do SEP **over** *repeat*

I misspelled a word and had to do the sign over.

do SEP **over** *decorate differently*

The couple did over the living room last summer.

do SEP **up** *wrap [a package]*

Would you do up this gift for me?

do SEP **up** *fasten [clothing]*

She did up her son's coat.

do SEP **up** *decorate, dress up*

We will do up the office for the boss's birthday.
Anya really did herself up for the party.

do without _____ *get along without*

We can't do without your help.

EXPRESSIONS

could do with _____ *want, need*

I could do with some ice cream
    right now.

do a job/number on _____ *damage, harm*

The kids really did a job on our furniture.
The committee did a number on his budget proposal.

do _____ **dirty** *treat poorly*

The team did him dirty by trading him to the Lions.

do _____ **for a living** *earn money on which to live by doing*

"What does she do for a living?" "She does web
    design."

do the trick *be exactly what is needed*

Lowering interest rates does the trick every time.
This pocketknife will do the trick.

do well to _____ *be lucky in doing*

Nancy does well to give a speech without crying.
Gordon did well to escape the fire uninjured.

have to do with _____ *concern, be about*

What does my zip code have to do with my car
    insurance?
The problem has something to do with the cable
    service.

top 40 verb

PRESENT

I draw	we draw
you draw	you draw
he/she/it draws	they draw

• *He draws a grim picture of the economy.*

PRESENT PROGRESSIVE

I am drawing	we are drawing
you are drawing	you are drawing
he/she/it is drawing	they are drawing

• *The play is drawing well.*

PAST

I drew	we drew
you drew	you drew
he/she/it drew	they drew

• *Her presentation drew a large audience.*

PAST PROGRESSIVE

I was drawing	we were drawing
you were drawing	you were drawing
he/she/it was drawing	they were drawing

• *We were drawing up a new will.*

PRESENT PERFECT ... have | has drawn
PAST PERFECT ... had drawn

FUTURE ... will draw
FUTURE PROGRESSIVE ... will be drawing
FUTURE PERFECT ... will have drawn

PAST PASSIVE

I was drawn	we were drawn
you were drawn	you were drawn
he/she/it was drawn	they were drawn

• *The sketches were drawn by Leonardo da Vinci.*

(COMPLEMENTS)

draw *create a picture*	She draws beautifully. Art students must draw every day.
draw *attract an audience*	Costume dramas rarely draw well.
draw *show a handgun*	Policemen are trained to draw and aim but hold their fire.
draw _____ *create [a picture]* OBJECT	The children drew **pictures of their families**. The architects have drawn **a floor plan**.
INDIRECT OBJECT + DIRECT OBJECT	The children drew *them* pictures. The economist drew *us* a scary picture of the future.
for PARAPHRASE	The children drew **pictures** *for them*. The economists **drew a scary picture of the future** *for us*.
draw _____ *create a picture of* OBJECT	The artist drew **the Taj Mahal**. I'd like to draw **Queen Victoria without her crown**.
draw _____ *drag, pull, extract* OBJECT	The teacher drew **the children** away from the window. I drew **the curtains** across the windows. The archers drew **their bows**. The nurse needs to draw **a blood sample**. He drew **the winning number**.
draw _____ *move steadily* ADVERB OF PLACE TO/FROM	The robber drew **closer to his victim**. My business day was drawing **to a close**.
draw _____ *attract* OBJECT	Water always draws **mosquitoes**. He usually draws **a big crowd**.
draw _____ *form* OBJECT	Voters must draw **their own conclusions** from the debate.

(PHRASAL VERBS)

draw _SEP_ **up** *write, formulate*	A young attorney drew up my will. Our family drew up an evacuation plan.

dream dream | dreams · dreamed · have dreamed
dream | dreams · dreamt · have dreamt

☑ REGULAR
☑ IRREGULAR

PRESENT

I dream	we dream
you dream	you dream
he/she/it dreams	they dream

• *He dreams of getting rich.*

PRESENT PROGRESSIVE

I am dreaming	we are dreaming
you are dreaming	you are dreaming
he/she/it is dreaming	they are dreaming

• *If I'm dreaming, don't wake me up.*

PAST

I dreamed	we dreamed
you dreamed	you dreamed
he/she/it dreamed	they dreamed

• *I dreamed that I ate a giant marshmallow.*

PAST PROGRESSIVE

I was dreaming	we were dreaming
you were dreaming	you were dreaming
he/she/it was dreaming	they were dreaming

• *I was dreaming that I was late to work.*

PRESENT PERFECT ... have | has dreamed
PAST PERFECT ... had dreamed

FUTURE ... will dream
FUTURE PROGRESSIVE ... will be dreaming
FUTURE PERFECT ... will have dreamed

PAST PASSIVE

I was dreamed	we were dreamed
you were dreamed	you were dreamed
he/she/it was dreamed	they were dreamed

• *It was never even dreamed of 50 years ago.*

COMPLEMENTS

dream *have thoughts and images while one sleeps*

I think I was dreaming.
We can all dream, can't we?
I must have been dreaming.

dream *pass time idly*

Sorry, I was just dreaming.

dream _____ *have [thoughts and images] while one sleeps*

about OBJECT

Last night I dreamed **about my grandmother.**
Do rabbits dream **about carrots?**
She dreamt **about Cassie and Pookie.**
I never dream **about my childhood.**

THAT-CLAUSE

I dreamed **that I had gotten lost in the woods.**
Cinderella dreamt **that she had met her prince.**

about PRESENT PARTICIPLE

I dreamt **about losing my job.**
He dreamed **about their moving back home.**

dream _____ *imagine, wish*

of OBJECT

We all dream **of a better future for our children.**
Everyone dreams **of world peace.**

THAT-CLAUSE

Everyone dreams **that they will be rich and famous.**
People always dream **that tomorrow will be better than today.**

of PRESENT PARTICIPLE

Cubs fans could only dream **of winning the World Series.**
Actors always dream **of getting the big break.**

dream _____ *consider possible/proper* [ALWAYS NEGATIVE]

of PRESENT PARTICIPLE

We wouldn't dream **of going to the party without you.**
He would never dream **of eating meat.**

PHRASAL VERBS

dream _SEP_ **away** *spend [time] idly*

Let's sit on the riverbank and dream
away the day.

dream _SEP_ **up** *invent, concoct*

Our board dreamed up a plan to avoid bankruptcy.
My brother and I dream up all kinds of wacky ideas.

PRESENT

I dress	we dress
you dress	you dress
he/she/it dresses	they dress

• *She dresses very stylishly.*

PRESENT PROGRESSIVE

I am dressing	we are dressing
you are dressing	you are dressing
he/she/it is dressing	they are dressing

• *Just a minute, I'm dressing.*

PAST

I dressed	we dressed
you dressed	you dressed
he/she/it dressed	they dressed

• *I dressed the children in hats and coats.*

PAST PROGRESSIVE

I was dressing	we were dressing
you were dressing	you were dressing
he/she/it was dressing	they were dressing

• *We were dressing up for the party.*

PRESENT PERFECT ... have | has dressed
PAST PERFECT   ... had dressed

FUTURE   ... will dress
FUTURE PROGRESSIVE   ... will be dressing
FUTURE PERFECT   ... will have dressed

PAST PASSIVE

I was dressed	we were dressed
you were dressed	you were dressed
he/she/it was dressed	they were dressed

• *The salad was dressed before we served it.*

COMPLEMENTS

dress *put on / wear clothes*

I had to dress at my friend's house.
We dressed as quickly as we could.
We need to dress carefully for the reception.
You must learn to dress for success.

dress _____ *put [clothes] on [someone]*

OBJECT

You need to dress **the children** before breakfast.
I dressed **them** in their snow jackets.
We dressed **ourselves** in our Sunday best.

PASSIVE

The babies were dressed by their grandmother.

dress _____ *provide with clothes*

OBJECT

It is expensive to dress **a family**.
We need to feed and dress **all the refugees**.

dress _____ *decorate*

OBJECT

The committee will dress **the speaker's platform**.
We always dress **the church** for Easter.

dress _____ *apply medicine and bandages to [a wound]*

OBJECT

The corpsmen dressed **all the open wounds**.
I dressed **Harry's scraped knee**.

PASSIVE

All the open wounds were dressed by the corpsmen.

dress _____ *prepare [food] for cooking/serving*

OBJECT

Carl dressed **the deer that he had shot**.
I will dress **the salad** at the table.

dress _____ *arrange [hair]*

OBJECT

She dresses **my hair** for me.
I need to dress **Alice's hair** before she leaves.

PHRASAL VERBS

dress down *wear casual clothes*   On Casual Friday, we all dress down.
dress up *wear formal clothes*   We have to dress up for the gala opening.
dress up *wear a costume*   My daughter is dressing up as Princess Leia for Halloween.
dress _SEP_ **up** *put formal clothes on*   We have to dress the children up for the birthday party.
dress _SEP_ **up** *put a costume on*   We dressed our daughter up as Princess Leia.

PRESENT

I drink	we drink
you drink	you drink
he/she/it drinks	they drink

• *John drinks white wine.*

PRESENT PROGRESSIVE

I am drinking	we are drinking
you are drinking	you are drinking
he/she/it is drinking	they are drinking

• *I'm only drinking green tea these days.*

PAST

I drank	we drank
you drank	you drank
he/she/it drank	they drank

• *I drank two cups of coffee.*

PAST PROGRESSIVE

I was drinking	we were drinking
you were drinking	you were drinking
he/she/it was drinking	they were drinking

• *They were drinking in the hotel bar.*

PRESENT PERFECT ... have | has drunk
PAST PERFECT ... had drunk

FUTURE ... will drink
FUTURE PROGRESSIVE ... will be drinking
FUTURE PERFECT ... will have drunk

PAST PASSIVE

—	—
—	—
it was drunk	they were drunk

• *Orange juice was always drunk at breakfast.*

COMPLEMENTS

drink *take a liquid in one's mouth and swallow it*	Is the patient able to drink? He is drinking without any trouble now. Don't try to drink too soon.
drink *consume alcoholic beverages*	Jack is drinking again. They never drink. We drink only on special occasions.
drink _____ *consume [a liquid]*	
OBJECT	I like to drink **sparkling water.** He only drinks **imported beer.** Their kids never drink **soda pop.**
WH-CLAUSE	We will drink **what is already open.** I'll drink **whatever is on tap.**

drink _____ *cause [oneself] to be in a particular state as a result of excessive alcohol consumption*

REFLEXIVE PRONOUN + *into* OBJECT	He drank **himself *into oblivion.*** The college students drank **themselves *into a stupor.***
REFLEXIVE PRONOUN + *to* OBJECT	One of my neighbors drank **himself *to death.***
REFLEXIVE PRONOUN + PREDICATE ADJECTIVE	He drank **himself *stupid.*** They drank **themselves *blind.*** I drank **myself *senseless.***

PHRASAL VERBS

drink _SEP_ **away** *consume alcohol to relieve oneself of*	The lonely widower drank his troubles away.
drink _SEP_ **down** *swallow [a liquid] completely*	Mother told me to drink the syrup down in one gulp.
drink _SEP_ **in** *absorb with the mind/senses*	He drinks in knowledge like a sponge. The tourists drank in the mountain scenery. We drank in the sights and sounds of New Year's Eve.
drink to _____ *make a toast to*	Let's drink to the couple's health and happiness. I'll drink to that!
Drink up! *Start/keep drinking!*	There's more wine in the cellar. Drink up!
drink _SEP_ **up** *consume all of [a liquid]*	My teenage sons drank up all the milk.

PRESENT		PRESENT PROGRESSIVE	
I drive	we drive	I am driving	we are driving
you drive	you drive	you are driving	you are driving
he/she/it drives	they drive	he/she/it is driving	they are driving

  • *He drives a blue Toyota.*   • *I'm driving home this afternoon.*

PAST		PAST PROGRESSIVE	
I drove	we drove	I was driving	we were driving
you drove	you drove	you were driving	you were driving
he/she/it drove	they drove	he/she/it was driving	they were driving

  • *I drove the kids to school.*   • *We were driving to Seattle.*

PRESENT PERFECT ... have | has driven
PAST PERFECT ... had driven

FUTURE ... will drive
FUTURE PROGRESSIVE ... will be driving
FUTURE PERFECT ... will have driven

PAST PASSIVE	
I was driven	we were driven
you were driven	you were driven
he/she/it was driven	they were driven

  • *The decision was driven by the need to be more cost effective.*

COMPLEMENTS

drive *operate a vehicle*
Who can drive?
My grandmother never drives at night.

drive *move with great force/speed*
The rain was driving across the road.
The army drove forward relentlessly.

drive ____ *operate [a vehicle (equipped with)]*
  OBJECT
He is driving **an old pickup truck.**
We drove **a rented convertible** in Hawaii.
Who can drive **a stick shift?**

drive ____ *cause to go [to a specific place]*
  OBJECT + ADVERB OF PLACE TO/FROM
I drove **the car** *into the garage.*
Can you drive **me** *home?*
The waves drove **the boat** *onto the rocks.*
The farmers were driving **their sheep** *to pasture.*

drive ____ *press forcefully*
  OBJECT
The company drives **its sales force** hard.
The jockeys drove **their horses** as hard as they could.

drive ____ *force into a specific condition/behavior*
  OBJECT + to OBJECT
Reading Dr. King's speeches drove **him** *to a life of service.*
  OBJECT + PREDICATE ADJECTIVE
You are driving **me** *crazy.*
His behavior drove **his parents** *mad.*
  OBJECT + INFINITIVE
The bad reviews drove **the author** *to completely revise the play.*
Famine drove **the peasants** *to revolt.*

drive ____ *shape, propel*
  OBJECT
National interest always drives **foreign policy.**
Opposition to slavery drove **public opinion in the North.**
Oil prices now drive **the value of the dollar.**

PHRASAL VERBS

drive _SEP_ **down** *cause to decrease*   Foreclosures are driving down home prices.

drive _SEP_ **up** *cause to increase*   Limiting oil production will drive prices up.

drive ____ **on** *cause to move forward to success*   It is the memory of my mother that drives me on.

PRESENT

I drop	we drop
you drop	you drop
he/she/it drops	they drop

• *He always drops by at the wrong time.*

PRESENT PROGRESSIVE

I am dropping	we are dropping
you are dropping	you are dropping
he/she/it is dropping	they are dropping

• *I'm dropping a package off for you.*

PAST

I dropped	we dropped
you dropped	you dropped
he/she/it dropped	they dropped

• *Our team dropped three games in a row.*

PAST PROGRESSIVE

I was dropping	we were dropping
you were dropping	you were dropping
he/she/it was dropping	they were dropping

• *The kids were dropping coins in the fountain.*

PRESENT PERFECT ... have | has dropped
PAST PERFECT ... had dropped

FUTURE ... will drop
FUTURE PROGRESSIVE ... will be dropping
FUTURE PERFECT ... will have dropped

PAST PASSIVE

I was dropped	we were dropped
you were dropped	you were dropped
he/she/it was dropped	they were dropped

• *The plan was dropped for lack of support.*

COMPLEMENTS

drop *fall*
The ginkgo leaves dropped in a single day.
Our spirits dropped when we heard the news.

drop *fall / lie down due to exhaustion*
She worked so hard in the yard that she just dropped.

drop *decrease*
The temperature dropped last night.
Production of new cars has dropped significantly.

drop _____ *let fall*
OBJECT
I dropped **the letter** into the mailbox.
Startled by the sudden noise, I dropped **my glass**.

drop _____ *lower*
OBJECT
The actor dropped **his voice** at the end of every line.

drop _____ *abandon, give up on*
OBJECT
The union dropped **its lawsuit against the company**.
I had to drop **the course**.

WH-CLAUSE
Drop **what you are doing** and help me.

drop _____ *omit*
OBJECT
Jackie always drops **the "g" in "doing."**
He dropped **these names** from the membership list.

drop _____ *lose*
OBJECT
Our team dropped **another close game** last night.
Sara has dropped **15 pounds** this year.

drop _____ *say/send casually*
OBJECT
He drops **hints that you need to pay attention to**.

INDIRECT OBJECT + DIRECT OBJECT
She dropped *her mother* **a brief note**.

to PARAPHRASE
She dropped **a brief note** *to her mother*.

drop _____ *end a relationship with* [INFORMAL]
OBJECT
After six months of dating, Gwen dropped **Ben**.

PHRASAL VERBS

drop by/in (on _____ **)** *make an informal/ unexpected visit (to [someone])*
Drop by anytime!
We dropped in on Grandpa yesterday.

drop _SEP_ **off** *take to a specific place and leave*
Please drop me off at the mall.

PRESENT		PRESENT PROGRESSIVE	
I dry	we dry	I am drying	we are drying
you dry	you dry	you are drying	you are drying
he/she/it dries	they dry	he/she/it is drying	they are drying

    • *This paint dries in four hours.*   • *I'm drying the laundry.*

PAST		PAST PROGRESSIVE	
I dried	we dried	I was drying	we were drying
you dried	you dried	you were drying	you were drying
he/she/it dried	they dried	he/she/it was drying	they were drying

    • *I dried off the table so we could eat.*   • *We were drying the rugs after the flood.*

| PRESENT PERFECT | ... have | has dried |
| PAST PERFECT | ... had dried |

FUTURE	... will dry
FUTURE PROGRESSIVE	... will be drying
FUTURE PERFECT	... will have dried

PAST PASSIVE

I was dried	we were dried
you were dried	you were dried
he/she/it was dried	they were dried

    • *The sample was dried by evaporation.*

COMPLEMENTS

dry *become moisture-free*

The herbs were drying in the sun.
My new shirt dries in just a couple of hours.
My hair will never dry in this humidity.

dry _____ *remove all the moisture from*

OBJECT

Can you dry **the children** when they get out of the pool?
This wind dries **my skin** terribly.
I waved the documents in the air to dry **the ink on the signatures**.

PASSIVE

The children were dried when they got out of the pool.

PHRASAL VERBS

dry off *make oneself dry*

I dry off before stepping out of the shower.

dry SEP **off** *make dry*

Linda dried the kids off before they ran into the house.
Dry yourself off before you come into the kitchen.
Dry off the table before you stack books on it.

dry out *undergo withdrawal from alcohol/drugs*

Luke dried out at Hope Center.

dry SEP **out** *cause [someone] to become sober*

The police dried him out before releasing him from jail.

dry up *become completely dry*

The farmer's well dried up in November.

dry up *disappear*

Our source for Italian soda has dried up.

dry SEP **up** *cut off the supply of*

The weak housing market has dried up opportunities for construction managers.

PRESENT

I eat	we eat
you eat	you eat
he/she/it eats	they eat

• He only eats cereal for breakfast.

PRESENT PROGRESSIVE

I am eating	we are eating
you are eating	you are eating
he/she/it is eating	they are eating

• We are eating out tonight.

PAST

I ate	we ate
you ate	you ate
he/she/it ate	they ate

• I ate breakfast early this morning.

PAST PROGRESSIVE

I was eating	we were eating
you were eating	you were eating
he/she/it was eating	they were eating

• I was eating lunch when I got the news.

PRESENT PERFECT ... have | has eaten
PAST PERFECT ... had eaten

FUTURE ... will eat
FUTURE PROGRESSIVE ... will be eating
FUTURE PERFECT ... will have eaten

PAST PASSIVE

—	—
—	—
it was eaten	they were eaten

• Only a third of the cat food was eaten.

─────────────────────────── **COMPLEMENTS** ───

eat take food in one's mouth and swallow it

The children usually eat around noon.
I eat too much when I get stressed.
I'll call you back, we're eating now.
Let's eat!

eat _____ consume [food]

OBJECT

The kids love to eat **pizza**.
My wife will never eat **liver**.

WH-CLAUSE

Can we eat **what was left over from last night**?
The dog eats **whatever the children drop on the floor**.

eat _____ bear the expense of

OBJECT

We will have to eat **the cost overrun**.
They are just going to eat **the overhead costs**.
You will have to eat **the rest of the contract**.

eat _____ make as if by eating

OBJECT

The paint remover ate **a hole** in my glove.

─────────────────────────── **PHRASAL VERBS** ───

eat (at) _____ bother, annoy

His criticisms have been eating at me all day.

eat at / away at / into _____ wear away, corrode

Rust was eating away at the exterior of my car.
Acid was eating into the countertop.

eat in have a meal at home

The weather is awful. Let's eat in.

eat out have a meal in a restaurant

I don't feel like cooking. Let's eat out.

Eat up! Start/keep eating!

Dinner is getting cold. Eat up!

eat _SEP_ **up** bite all over

Mosquitoes are eating the campers up.

eat _SEP_ **up** use up, consume, waste

The boss's lavish lifestyle ate up the company's profit.

eat _SEP_ **up** enjoy greatly

The singer told awful jokes, but the audience ate it up.

eat _SEP_ **up** believe [something]

My aunt ate up everything she read in the tabloids.

─────────────────────────── **EXPRESSIONS** ───

eat _____ **out of house and home**
consume all the food in [someone's] home

Our three sons are eating us out of
house and home.

PRESENT

I eliminate	we eliminate
you eliminate	you eliminate
he/she/it eliminates	they eliminate

• *The evidence eliminates all the suspects.*

PRESENT PROGRESSIVE

I am eliminating	we are eliminating
you are eliminating	you are eliminating
he/she/it is eliminating	they are eliminating

• *I'm eliminating all saturated fat from my diet.*

PAST

I eliminated	we eliminated
you eliminated	you eliminated
he/she/it eliminated	they eliminated

• *We eliminated two sales positions.*

PAST PROGRESSIVE

I was eliminating	we were eliminating
you were eliminating	you were eliminating
he/she/it was eliminating	they were eliminating

• *They were eliminating all low-performing stores.*

PRESENT PERFECT ... have | has eliminated
PAST PERFECT ... had eliminated

FUTURE ... will eliminate
FUTURE PROGRESSIVE ... will be eliminating
FUTURE PERFECT ... will have eliminated

PAST PASSIVE

I was eliminated	we were eliminated
you were eliminated	you were eliminated
he/she/it was eliminated	they were eliminated

• *My team was eliminated in the first round.*

COMPLEMENTS

eliminate *expel bodily waste*
You need to eliminate on a regular basis.
Some desert rats never eliminate.

eliminate _____ *put an end to, eradicate*
OBJECT — President Johnson tried to eliminate **poverty in America**.
She wanted to eliminate **bribery as a political way of life**.

eliminate _____ *remove from competition*
OBJECT — We have eliminated **all of the candidates**.
The Cardinals eliminated **the Panthers** in the semifinal round.

eliminate _____ *remove from consideration*
OBJECT — The board eliminated **the option of bankruptcy**.
Detectives have eliminated **two of the suspects**.
WH-CLAUSE — The police eliminated **whoever was not at the crime scene**.
The designer eliminated **whatever was distracting**.

eliminate _____ *get rid of, dispose of*
OBJECT — We have tried to eliminate **all unnecessary expenses**.
They've eliminated **any trace of having been there**.
WH-CLAUSE — We eliminated **what we didn't need to carry with us**.
They eliminated **whichever flights were nonstop**.

PRESENT

I emerge	we emerge
you emerge	you emerge
he/she/it emerges	they emerge

• *A great leader often emerges in a crisis.*

PAST

I emerged	we emerged
you emerged	you emerged
he/she/it emerged	they emerged

• *A new problem emerged the next day.*

PRESENT PROGRESSIVE

I am emerging	we are emerging
you are emerging	you are emerging
he/she/it is emerging	they are emerging

• *A pattern is emerging from the data.*

PAST PROGRESSIVE

I was emerging	we were emerging
you were emerging	you were emerging
he/she/it was emerging	they were emerging

• *We were finally emerging from the fog.*

PRESENT PERFECT ... have | has emerged
PAST PERFECT ... had emerged

FUTURE ... will emerge
FUTURE PROGRESSIVE ... will be emerging
FUTURE PERFECT ... will have emerged

PAST PASSIVE

Emerge is never used in the passive voice.

(**COMPLEMENTS**)

emerge *appear, come into view*	A plane emerged from the clouds.
	A dark shape suddenly emerged from the mist.
	A school of fish emerged from the shadow of the dock.
	The manager finally emerged from his office just before 5 o'clock.
emerge *come into existence*	Most mammal lines emerged before the dinosaurs became extinct.
emerge *become known*	Yet another problem with the program emerged today.
	New allegations are emerging almost daily.
	The extent of his injuries only emerged when the doctors saw the X-rays.
	Jones has emerged as a first-rate player.
emerge _____ *finish a contest/event in a specific condition/state*	
PREDICATE ADJECTIVE	The Democrats emerged **victorious** in the elections.
	Rick emerged **unhurt** from the collision.

PRESENT

I emphasize	we emphasize
you emphasize	you emphasize
he/she/it emphasizes	they emphasize

• *He always emphasizes safety.*

PRESENT PROGRESSIVE

I am emphasizing	we are emphasizing
you are emphasizing	you are emphasizing
he/she/it is emphasizing	they are emphasizing

• *He is emphasizing the need for donors.*

PAST

I emphasized	we emphasized
you emphasized	you emphasized
he/she/it emphasized	they emphasized

• *My first boss emphasized punctuality.*

PAST PROGRESSIVE

I was emphasizing	we were emphasizing
you were emphasizing	you were emphasizing
he/she/it was emphasizing	they were emphasizing

• *We were emphasizing our reduced prices.*

PRESENT PERFECT ... have | has emphasized
PAST PERFECT ... had emphasized

FUTURE ... will emphasize
FUTURE PROGRESSIVE ... will be emphasizing
FUTURE PERFECT ... will have emphasized

PAST PASSIVE

—	—
—	—
it was emphasized	they were emphasized

• *Accuracy was emphasized over speed.*

COMPLEMENTS

emphasize _____ *place special importance on, stress*

OBJECT	The real estate agent emphasized **the remodeled kitchen.**
	Emphasize **the second syllable in the verb "record."**
	The guide emphasized **the importance of wearing a life vest at all times.**
THAT-CLAUSE	The pilot emphasized **that we should have our seat belts fastened while we are seated.**
	Let me emphasize **that we need to hurry.**
	I can't emphasize enough **that the key to success is higher education.**
WH-CLAUSE	He emphasized **what we had to watch out for.**
	They emphasized **why everyone should vote.**
	The teacher emphasized **how we could improve our test scores.**
WH-INFINITIVE	The fireman emphasized **what to do in case of fire.**
	I emphasized **where to go for help.**
	The teacher emphasized **how to improve our test scores.**

PRESENT

I employ	we employ
you employ	you employ
he/she/it employs	they employ

• *The company employs over 500 workers.*

PRESENT PROGRESSIVE

I am employing	we are employing
you are employing	you are employing
he/she/it is employing	they are employing

• *I'm employing all of our resources.*

PAST

I employed	we employed
you employed	you employed
he/she/it employed	they employed

• *We employed a new secretary last week.*

PAST PROGRESSIVE

I was employing	we were employing
you were employing	you were employing
he/she/it was employing	they were employing

• *They were only employing college graduates.*

PRESENT PERFECT ... have | has employed
PAST PERFECT ... had employed

FUTURE ... will employ
FUTURE PROGRESSIVE ... will be employing
FUTURE PERFECT ... will have employed

PAST PASSIVE

I was employed	we were employed
you were employed	you were employed
he/she/it was employed	they were employed

• *I was first employed in 2002.*

COMPLEMENTS

employ *hire workers*

Are they employing?
The company might be employing.
They are not employing now.

employ _____ *hire*

OBJECT

They just employed **a new driver**.
We haven't employed **anyone** for that position yet.

PASSIVE

She was only employed yesterday.

OBJECT + *as* PREDICATE NOUN

The corporation employed **Kathryn** *as sales manager.*

employ _____ *have working for oneself*

OBJECT

The company employs **15,000 people** in 23 countries.
Our firm employs **three full-time accountants**.

PASSIVE

John has been employed here for 20 years.
Evelyn has been employed as a legal secretary for 13 years.
Helen is employed in customer service.

employ _____ *make use of*

OBJECT

You must employ **all of your talents**.
I employed **my newly acquired C++ programming skills**.
General Gage had to employ **his last reserve unit**.

WH-CLAUSE

The sergeant employed **whomever the captain sent him**.
We will employ **whatever manpower we have**.
I employed **whatever tools were at hand**.

employ _____ *use for a particular purpose*

OBJECT + INFINITIVE

I employed **an air compressor** *to clean the keyboards.*
They employed **me** *to fill in for Harry.*
She employed the **shop vac** *to clean the leaves off the deck.*
We employed **a lawn service** *to mow the grass.*

PRESENT

I enable	we enable
you enable	you enable
he/she/it enables	they enable

 • *This code enables the alarm system.*

PRESENT PROGRESSIVE

I am enabling	we are enabling
you are enabling	you are enabling
he/she/it is enabling	they are enabling

 • *The grant is enabling me to finish graduate school.*

PAST

I enabled	we enabled
you enabled	you enabled
he/she/it enabled	they enabled

 • *The Internet enabled me to work at home.*

PAST PROGRESSIVE

I was enabling	we were enabling
you were enabling	you were enabling
he/she/it was enabling	they were enabling

 • *The technicians were enabling the device.*

PRESENT PERFECT ... have | has enabled
PAST PERFECT ... had enabled

FUTURE ... will enable
FUTURE PROGRESSIVE ... will be enabling
FUTURE PERFECT ... will have enabled

PAST PASSIVE

I was enabled	we were enabled
you were enabled	you were enabled
he/she/it was enabled	they were enabled

 • *The feature was enabled in the latest software release.*

(COMPLEMENTS)

enable _____ *make possible/feasible*

OBJECT   The law enabled **the creation of a new agency.**
          The bipartisan agreement enabled **passage of the bill.**
          Excellent planning enabled **the success of the program.**

enable _____ *make it possible for [someone/something to do]*

OBJECT + INFINITIVE   His help enabled **me** *to succeed.*
          Its success enables **the company** *to provide health benefits.*
          The tow truck enabled **us** *to get out of the snow bank.*
          The loan enabled **Susan** *to finish school.*

enable _____ *activate, cause to operate*

OBJECT   Batteries enable **the panel** if the electricity fails.
          You have to enable **the alarm** every night.
          A computer program enables **the entire plant.**

encounter

PRESENT

I encounter	we encounter
you encounter	you encounter
he/she/it encounters	they encounter

· *Our proposals always encounter resistance.*

PRESENT PROGRESSIVE

I am encountering	we are encountering
you are encountering	you are encountering
he/she/it is encountering	they are encountering

· *Our infantry is encountering counterattacks.*

PAST

I encountered	we encountered
you encountered	you encountered
he/she/it encountered	they encountered

· *I encountered an ugly scene at the mall.*

PAST PROGRESSIVE

I was encountering	we were encountering
you were encountering	you were encountering
he/she/it was encountering	they were encountering

· *The bill was encountering a lot of opposition.*

PRESENT PERFECT ... have | has encountered
PAST PERFECT ... had encountered

FUTURE ... will encounter
FUTURE PROGRESSIVE ... will be encountering
FUTURE PERFECT ... will have encountered

PAST PASSIVE

I was encountered	we were encountered
you were encountered	you were encountered
he/she/it was encountered	they were encountered

· *Strong winds were encountered by the boats.*

COMPLEMENTS

encounter _____ *meet/face, often by chance*

OBJECT

Harriet encountered **her opponent** at the grocery store.
Our little boat encountered **a terrible storm**.
You encounter **all sorts of people** at the zoo.

encounter _____ *experience, come up against*

OBJECT

The proposal has encountered **total indifference**.
Her idea will encounter **opposition**.
The shuttle program has encountered **one delay after another**.
We encountered **problems getting the interest rate we had hoped for**.
Our forces are only encountering **light resistance**.
The senator has encountered **some pretty hostile interviewers** lately.

PRESENT

I encourage	we encourage
you encourage	you encourage
he/she/it encourages	they encourage

• *He encourages everyone to finish school.*

PRESENT PROGRESSIVE

I am encouraging	we are encouraging
you are encouraging	you are encouraging
he/she/it is encouraging	they are encouraging

• *I am encouraging my co-workers to donate.*

PAST

I encouraged	we encouraged
you encouraged	you encouraged
he/she/it encouraged	they encouraged

• *They encouraged me to read a lot.*

PAST PROGRESSIVE

I was encouraging	we were encouraging
you were encouraging	you were encouraging
he/she/it was encouraging	they were encouraging

• *Our teachers were always encouraging us.*

PRESENT PERFECT ... have | has encouraged
PAST PERFECT ... had encouraged

FUTURE ... will encourage
FUTURE PROGRESSIVE ... will be encouraging
FUTURE PERFECT ... will have encouraged

PAST PASSIVE

I was encouraged	we were encouraged
you were encouraged	you were encouraged
he/she/it was encouraged	they were encouraged

• *We were encouraged to go ahead with our plan.*

COMPLEMENTS

encourage _____ *give hope/confidence to*
OBJECT

His sermons encouraged **the entire congregation**.
Her example encouraged **all of us**.
The crowd's applause encouraged **the shy third graders**.
We encouraged **Alex** in his baseball career.

encourage _____ *advise, urge*
OBJECT + INFINITIVE

Karen encouraged **us *to begin a reading program***.
My mom encouraged **me *to become a doctor***.

encourage _____ *promote*
OBJECT

The fertilizer encouraged **a new round of plant growth**.
Run-off fertilizer has greatly encouraged **algae growth** in the lakes.
The program was designed to encourage **greater fuel efficiency**.

encourage _____ *make likely to*
OBJECT + INFINITIVE

The tax cut encouraged **companies *to expand***.
The sight of cannon encouraged **the crowds *to disperse***.

PRESENT

I end	we end
you end	you end
he/she/it ends	they end

• *The play ends with a merry dance.*

PRESENT PROGRESSIVE

I am ending	we are ending
you are ending	you are ending
he/she/it is ending	they are ending

• *They are ending their relationship.*

PAST

I ended	we ended
you ended	you ended
he/she/it ended	they ended

• *The game ended before dinnertime.*

PAST PROGRESSIVE

I was ending	we were ending
you were ending	you were ending
he/she/it was ending	they were ending

• *The long stalemate was finally ending.*

PRESENT PERFECT ... have | has ended
PAST PERFECT ... had ended

FUTURE ... will end
FUTURE PROGRESSIVE ... will be ending
FUTURE PERFECT ... will have ended

PAST PASSIVE

—	—
—	—
it was ended	they were ended

• *The ugly scene was ended when Jim stormed out.*

COMPLEMENTS

end *stop, cease*	Will this night never end?
	The morning sessions end promptly at noon.
	The symphony ended on a triumphant chord.
	The game ended in a tie.
end _____ *finish, stop*	
OBJECT	Wilma ended **their engagement**.
	The sudden storm abruptly ended **our picnic**.
	Macbeth ends **the summer season**.
	The senator ended **his speech** with a promise to cut taxes.
	The vote ended **all hope of a compromise**.
WH-CLAUSE	You must end **what you begin**.
	They need to end **whatever mischief they are up to**.

PHRASAL VERBS

NOTE: The following six constructions with *up* mean
"be in [a condition/position/situation/location] at the end."

end up _____	Our neighbor was a gambler and ended up broke.
end up as _____	Uncle Austin ended up as a lieutenant.
end up at _____	We had an accident and ended up at the hospital.
	The scholar ended up at the University of Wyoming.
end up (by) _____	We were so tired, we ended up by sleeping at Ned's house.
	Jim ended up going to Memphis for the weekend.
end (up) in _____	The argument ended up in a fistfight.
end (up) with _____	The meeting ended with the treasurer's report.
	The movie ended up with the boy and girl getting married.

EXPRESSIONS

end it all *commit suicide*	The pain became so severe that he ended it all.
_____ to end all _____ *the best/greatest*	That was the cruise to end all cruises.
end up with the short end of the stick *get less than others*	In the divorce settlement, Sonny ended up with the short end of the stick.
	Bonnie ended up with the short end of the stick when the company handed out bonuses.

PRESENT

I engage	we engage
you engage	you engage
he/she/it engages	they engage

- *Danny's play totally engages the audience.*

PRESENT PROGRESSIVE

I am engaging	we are engaging
you are engaging	you are engaging
he/she/it is engaging	they are engaging

- *We're engaging an architect for the restoration.*

PAST

I engaged	we engaged
you engaged	you engaged
he/she/it engaged	they engaged

- *I engaged a lawyer yesterday.*

PAST PROGRESSIVE

I was engaging	we were engaging
you were engaging	you were engaging
he/she/it was engaging	they were engaging

- *The operation was engaging all of our resources.*

PRESENT PERFECT ... have | has engaged
PAST PERFECT ... had engaged

FUTURE ... will engage
FUTURE PROGRESSIVE ... will be engaging
FUTURE PERFECT ... will have engaged

PAST PASSIVE

I was engaged	we were engaged
you were engaged	you were engaged
he/she/it was engaged	they were engaged

- *The battle was engaged at 5:30 this morning.*

COMPLEMENTS

engage *start fighting*	The ships were engaging at long range.
	The opposing attorneys engaged as soon as the trial started.
	He never engages unless he has a decided advantage.
engage *fit/lock together, be in gear*	Are the gears engaged?
	The gears never did engage properly.
	The clutch engaged with a loud grinding noise.
be/get engaged *be pledged to marry* [USED ONLY IN THE PASSIVE]	Sally got engaged last night.
	They will not be engaged very long.
	Are they engaged?
	He has never been engaged before.
engage _____ *start fighting against*	The army engaged **the enemy** at 0500 hours.
engage _____ *hire, contract the services of*	
OBJECT (+ *for* OBJECT)	We will need to engage **a lawyer**.
	They engaged **a bus and a driver**.
	Six seniors engaged **a limousine** *for prom night*.
	We engaged **a contractor** *for our remodeling project*.
	They engaged **the band** *for the wedding*.
OBJECT + INFINITIVE	We engaged **Mr. Smith** *to evaluate the estate*.
	We engaged **a consultant** *to help us launch the new product*.
PASSIVE	Mr. Smith was engaged *to evaluate the estate*.
engage _____ *attract and hold, keep busy*	
OBJECT	That painting really engaged **my attention**.
	Computer games totally engage **my daughter's interest**.
	Gardening engages **all my spare time**.
PASSIVE	Stevie is completely engaged by her new job.

PHRASAL VERBS

engage in _____ *participate in*	Will Penelope engage in sports when she gets to college?
engage _____ **in** *cause to participate in*	Tamara engaged William in conversation.
	The boss engaged Mike in an exciting new project.

PRESENT

I enjoy	we enjoy
you enjoy	you enjoy
he/she/it enjoys	they enjoy

• *He enjoys gardening.*

PAST

I enjoyed	we enjoyed
you enjoyed	you enjoyed
he/she/it enjoyed	they enjoyed

• *I enjoyed meeting your friends.*

PRESENT PERFECT ... have | has enjoyed
PAST PERFECT   ... had enjoyed

PRESENT PROGRESSIVE

I am enjoying	we are enjoying
you are enjoying	you are enjoying
he/she/it is enjoying	they are enjoying

• *I'm enjoying myself at the beach.*

PAST PROGRESSIVE

I was enjoying	we were enjoying
you were enjoying	you were enjoying
he/she/it was enjoying	they were enjoying

• *We were enjoying a quiet evening at home.*

FUTURE   ... will enjoy
FUTURE PROGRESSIVE ... will be enjoying
FUTURE PERFECT   ... will have enjoyed

PAST PASSIVE

—	—
—	—
it was enjoyed	they were enjoyed

• *The picnic was enjoyed by everyone.*

───────────────(**COMPLEMENTS**)───────

enjoy _____ *get pleasure/satisfaction from*

     OBJECT

I really enjoyed **the movie.**
We have always enjoyed **their friendship.**
The kids really enjoy **picnics.**
Everyone enjoys **success.**

     PRESENT PARTICIPLE

I enjoy **living in London.**
No one enjoys **commuting such long distances.**
We always enjoy **seeing our high school classmates.**
We enjoy **visiting with Harry and Rosie** on their farm.
I enjoy **eating out once in awhile.**

enjoy _____ *have/experience [something good]*

     OBJECT

The book enjoyed **great success.**
My uncle didn't enjoy **very good health.**
The team doesn't enjoy **a lot of financial support.**

enjoy _____ *have fun*

     REFLEXIVE PRONOUN

I hope you enjoyed **yourself** at the picnic.

───────────────────(**EXPRESSIONS**)───────

enjoy the best of both worlds *benefit from two opportunities that usually exclude each other*

We enjoy the best of both worlds:
    living out in the country and having
    high-speed Internet service.

PRESENT

I enter	we enter
you enter	you enter
he/she/it enters	they enter

- *Our son enters kindergarten this year.*

PRESENT PROGRESSIVE

I am entering	we are entering
you are entering	you are entering
he/she/it is entering	they are entering

- *I'm entering the building now.*

PAST

I entered	we entered
you entered	you entered
he/she/it entered	they entered

- *We entered into a new agreement.*

PAST PROGRESSIVE

I was entering	we were entering
you were entering	you were entering
he/she/it was entering	they were entering

- *They were entering a new era in broadcasting.*

PRESENT PERFECT ... have | has entered
PAST PERFECT ... had entered

FUTURE ... will enter
FUTURE PROGRESSIVE ... will be entering
FUTURE PERFECT ... will have entered

PAST PASSIVE

—	—
—	—
it was entered	they were entered

- *All the new data was entered last night.*

COMPLEMENTS

enter *come in*	Please enter.
	I will enter as soon as I can.
	They will be entering in just a minute.
	Hamlet enters from stage left.
	Tourists enter through the east gate.

enter _____ *come/go into* OBJECT	Elvis has entered **the building**.
	The Allies entered **Paris** on August 19, 1944.
	We entered **the dark room** cautiously.
	They entered **the United States** at LaGuardia Airport.
	The bullet entered **his shoulder**.

enter _____ *participate/enroll in* OBJECT	I entered **the drawing**.
	Harry entered **the hotdog eating contest**.
	I will enter **the university** this fall.
	She will enter **the race for the open Senate seat**.

enter _____ *register/enter [data]* OBJECT	They entered **their names** for the drawing.
	Please enter **your names** on the guest list.
	I entered **all the data** in the proper fields.

enter _____ *make a new beginning in* OBJECT	The insects will soon enter **a new developmental stage**.
	I would be entering **a totally new career**.
	He decided to enter **politics**.
	Our sons are just entering **puberty**.

PHRASAL VERBS

enter into _____ *take part in, become* *a part of*	The president entered into a dialog with our enemies.
	Our firm entered into an agreement with the mayor's office.
enter [someone/something] in(to) _____ *cause [someone/something] to join / enroll in*	They will enter Jenny in the contest. I am entering a painting in the school's art fair.
enter (up)on _____ *begin*	Lucas entered on a career in accounting.

PRESENT

I entitle	we entitle
you entitle	you entitle
he/she/it entitles	they entitle

• *The law entitles me to a trial by my peers.*

PRESENT PROGRESSIVE

I am entitling	we are entitling
you are entitling	you are entitling
he/she/it is entitling	they are entitling

• *I am entitling the poem "Lost Rainbows."*

PAST

I entitled	we entitled
you entitled	you entitled
he/she/it entitled	they entitled

• *It entitled them to apply for citizenship.*

PAST PROGRESSIVE

I was entitling	we were entitling
you were entitling	you were entitling
he/she/it was entitling	they were entitling

• *He was entitling the book* Lost Memories.

PRESENT PERFECT   ... have | has entitled
PAST PERFECT   ... had entitled

FUTURE   ... will entitle
FUTURE PROGRESSIVE   ... will be entitling
FUTURE PERFECT   ... will have entitled

PAST PASSIVE

I was entitled	we were entitled
you were entitled	you were entitled
he/she/it was entitled	they were entitled

• *He was entitled to request payment.*

COMPLEMENTS

entitle _____ *give the right*

OBJECT + *to* OBJECT	The coupon entitles **you** *to a free pass.*
PASSIVE	The ranchers were entitled *to a water allotment.*
OBJECT + INFINITIVE	The law entitles **him** *to call his lawyer.*
	It entitles **the injured party** *to sue.*
	The laws in Texas entitle **people** *to carry concealed firearms.*
	What entitles **you** *to complain*?
PASSIVE	We are entitled *to attend three seminars of our choosing.*

entitle _____ *give a name to*

OBJECT + PREDICATE NOUN	They entitled **their last album** *Broken Dreams.*
	Coward entitled **his most famous play** *Blithe Spirit.*
PASSIVE	The book is entitled *Happy Days.*
	The CD is entitled *Mexico Sunset.*

PRESENT

I escape	we escape
you escape	you escape
he/she/it escapes	they escape

- *His name escapes me.*

PRESENT PROGRESSIVE

I am escaping	we are escaping
you are escaping	you are escaping
he/she/it is escaping	they are escaping

- *I'm escaping the staff meeting.*

PAST

I escaped	we escaped
you escaped	you escaped
he/she/it escaped	they escaped

- *Dillinger escaped from prison again.*

PAST PROGRESSIVE

I was escaping	we were escaping
you were escaping	you were escaping
he/she/it was escaping	they were escaping

- *The sheep were escaping through a hole in the fence.*

PRESENT PERFECT ... have | has escaped
PAST PERFECT ... had escaped

FUTURE ... will escape
FUTURE PROGRESSIVE ... will be escaping
FUTURE PERFECT ... will have escaped

PAST PASSIVE

—	—
—	—
it was escaped	they were escaped

- *The danger was narrowly escaped.*

COMPLEMENTS

escape *get free [from confinement/ restriction], leak*	My pet turtle escaped yesterday. The balloons escaped from the party tent. Three prisoners escaped from the county jail. Fortunately, all of the crew escaped. The news quickly escaped to the public. The gas was escaping at a dangerous rate.
escape ___ *break free [from confinement / an unpleasant or difficult situation/event]*	
(from) OBJECT	No one ever escaped (**from**) Alcatraz alive. Three convicts escaped (**from**) the county jail last night. He escaped (**from**) a life of drudgery. I escaped (**from**) Senator Blather's talk.
WH-CLAUSE	You can never escape who you are. I escaped whoever was following me. We escaped whatever task we would have been given.
escape ___ *come from unintentionally*	
OBJECT	A tiny smile escaped her.
escape ___ *avoid*	
PRESENT PARTICIPLE	I escaped having to do the dishes. We will escape working all night. The driver barely escaped running off the road. We escaped having to listen to his boasting. They escaped being punished for it.
escape ___ *be forgotten by*	
OBJECT	The nurse's name escapes me.

EXPRESSIONS

escape [someone's] notice *be unnoticed by someone*	Nothing escapes the boss's notice. The darkening sky escaped his notice.
escape the ax *avoid being eliminated*	Four co-workers were laid off, but I escaped the ax.

PRESENT

I establish	we establish
you establish	you establish
he/she/it establishes	they establish

• *It establishes an important precedent.*

PRESENT PROGRESSIVE

I am establishing	we are establishing
you are establishing	you are establishing
he/she/it is establishing	they are establishing

• *He is establishing a new nonprofit foundation.*

PAST

I established	we established
you established	you established
he/she/it established	they established

• *We established our case before the court.*

PAST PROGRESSIVE

I was establishing	we were establishing
you were establishing	you were establishing
he/she/it was establishing	they were establishing

• *We were establishing what actually happened here.*

PRESENT PERFECT ... have | has established
PAST PERFECT ... had established

FUTURE ... will establish
FUTURE PROGRESSIVE ... will be establishing
FUTURE PERFECT ... will have established

PAST PASSIVE

I was established	we were established
you were established	you were established
he/she/it was established	they were established

• *The company was established in 1983.*

◖ **COMPLEMENTS** ◗

establish ―――― *bring about, create*

OBJECT
The Constitution established **three separate branches of government.**
The legislature established **the commission.**
Uncle Henry established **a trust fund for his children.**
He originally established **the company** in Delaware.

PASSIVE
The United States was established in 1787.

establish ―――― *prove beyond doubt*

OBJECT
The evidence will establish **my client's innocence.**
Astronomers have established **the existence of a black hole at the center of our galaxy.**
The facts establish **the validity of his complaint.**
The police cannot establish **the identity of the victim.**

THAT-CLAUSE
We will establish **that the will is invalid.**
New research has established **that people have been in the New World for 20,000 years.**
The geologists established **that there was oil in the region.**

WH-CLAUSE
The police have established **who broke into the house.**
This report will establish **what we have been saying all along.**
We need to establish **when the accident occurred.**

establish ―――― *put on a firm basis*

OBJECT
We need to establish **a good working relationship** with them.
They managed to establish **a level of mutual trust.**
All couples want to establish **a solid relationship.**
He established **his son** in business.

establish ―――― *cause to be recognized/accepted*

OBJECT
The album established **her reputation.**

OBJECT + *as* PREDICATE NOUN
The album established **her reputation** *as a star.*
Edgar established **himself** *as an economic guru.*
It established **him** *as someone to be reckoned with.*
The upset established **our team** *as a legitimate contender.*

I estimate   we estimate
you estimate   you estimate
he/she/it estimates they estimate
  • *I estimate that the job will take a week.*

I am estimating   we are estimating
you are estimating   you are estimating
he/she/it is estimating they are estimating
  • *He is estimating that it will take 10 working days.*

I estimated   we estimated
you estimated   you estimated
he/she/it estimated they estimated
  • *They estimated the price at $250.*

I was estimating   we were estimating
you were estimating   you were estimating
he/she/it was estimating they were estimating
  • *We were estimating college expenses today.*

... have | has estimated
... had estimated

... will estimate
... will be estimating
... will have estimated

I was estimated   we were estimated
you were estimated   you were estimated
he/she/it was estimated they were estimated
  • *The cost was estimated to be over a million dollars.*

(**COMPLEMENTS**)

estimate _____ *make a general guess about the worth/extent/size of*

OBJECT	They will estimate **the entire estate.**
	The Coast Guard was trying to estimate **the extent of the flooding.**
	I estimated **the number of square feet in the house.**
	We estimated **the rough cost of the project.**
OBJECT + *at* OBJECT	He estimated **Kyle** *at six feet tall.*
	The police estimated **the crowd** *at two million people.*
OBJECT + INFINITIVE	We estimated **the cost** *to be around $25,000.*
	They estimated **the land** *to be about 5.5 acres.*
	I estimated **the driving time** *to be four hours.*
	The police estimated **the crowd** *to be two million people.*
THAT-CLAUSE	The engineer estimated **that the project would require four years to complete.**
	Our analysts estimate **that the Democratic candidate will win in a landslide victory.**

examine examine | examines · examined · have examined ☑ REGULAR

PRESENT

I examine	we examine
you examine	you examine
he/she/it examines	they examine

 • *The committee examines all candidates.*

PRESENT PROGRESSIVE

I am examining	we are examining
you are examining	you are examining
he/she/it is examining	they are examining

 • *The doctor is examining him now.*

PAST

I examined	we examined
you examined	you examined
he/she/it examined	they examined

 • *The police examined the crime scene.*

PAST PROGRESSIVE

I was examining	we were examining
you were examining	you were examining
he/she/it was examining	they were examining

 • *We were examining every alternative.*

PRESENT PERFECT ... have | has examined
PAST PERFECT ... had examined

FUTURE ... will examine
FUTURE PROGRESSIVE ... will be examining
FUTURE PERFECT ... will have examined

PAST PASSIVE

I was examined	we were examined
you were examined	you were examined
he/she/it was examined	they were examined

 • *The bridge supports were carefully examined.*

───(**COMPLEMENTS**)───

examine _____ *inspect, investigate, analyze*

  OBJECT
      The vet examined **the injured parrot.**
      The pilot examined **the plane** carefully.
      The police examined **the victim's car.**
      The lieutenant examined **every rifle.**
      The doctor will examine **her** for signs of malnutrition.
      The committee examined **the issue of drunk driving.**

  WH-CLAUSE
      We examined **what had fallen from the ceiling.**
      The police examined **where the car had gone off the road.**
      The accountant always examines **whatever charges we make.**

examine _____ *interrogate, question*

  OBJECT
      The committee examined **me** for nearly an hour.
      I examined **him** myself.
      The professor examined **us** on the causes of the Civil War.

  PASSIVE
      You will be examined at the end of the course.

I exercise   we exercise
you exercise   you exercise
he/she/it exercises   they exercise

• *He exercises every day.*

PAST

I exercised   we exercised
you exercised   you exercised
he/she/it exercised   they exercised

• *Mom always exercised good judgment.*

PRESENT PERFECT	... have | has exercised
PAST PERFECT	... had exercised

PRESENT PROGRESSIVE

I am exercising   we are exercising
you are exercising   you are exercising
he/she/it is exercising   they are exercising

• *I'm exercising as we talk.*

PAST PROGRESSIVE

I was exercising   we were exercising
you were exercising   you were exercising
he/she/it was exercising   they were exercising

• *They were exercising their constitutional right.*

FUTURE	... will exercise
FUTURE PROGRESSIVE	... will be exercising
FUTURE PERFECT	... will have exercised

PAST PASSIVE

—   —
—   —
it was exercised   they were exercised

• *The horses were exercised this morning.*

COMPLEMENTS

exercise *perform physical activities*
to make oneself healthier/stronger

I need to exercise more.
I was exercising when you called.
I can only exercise on weekends.

exercise _____ *use repeatedly to strengthen / to make more flexible*
  OBJECT

I need to exercise **my wrist**.
The doctor told me to exercise **my neck muscles**.
I exercise **my knees** by running up steps.

exercise _____ *train, give a physical workout to*
  OBJECT

You must exercise **the animals** every day.
The guards exercised **the prisoners**.
The trainers exercised **their horses** according to
  a rigid schedule.
The captain exercised the **oarsmen** regularly.

exercise _____ *put into use/action*
  OBJECT

He always exercises **extreme caution**.
He didn't exercise **very good judgment** this time.
They are cautious about exercising **too much control**.
The newspaper exercises **a great deal of power**.
I am only exercising **my constitutional rights**.

exercise _____ *get the attention of, cause alarm to*
  OBJECT

Crime always exercises **the media**.
Politicians know how to exercise **public opinion**.

  PASSIVE

The talk show hosts were really exercised about it.

PRESENT

I exist	we exist
you exist	you exist
he/she/it exists	they exist

• *Dragons only exist in fiction.*

PRESENT PROGRESSIVE

I am existing	we are existing
you are existing	you are existing
he/she/it is existing	they are existing

• *I am existing from day to day.*

PAST

I existed	we existed
you existed	you existed
he/she/it existed	they existed

• *The problem existed for years.*

PAST PROGRESSIVE

I was existing	we were existing
you were existing	you were existing
he/she/it was existing	they were existing

• *The kids were existing on peanut butter sandwiches.*

PRESENT PERFECT ... have | has existed
PAST PERFECT   ... had existed

FUTURE   ... will exist
FUTURE PROGRESSIVE   ... will be existing
FUTURE PERFECT   ... will have existed

PAST PASSIVE

Exist is never used in the passive voice.

―(**COMPLEMENTS**)―

exist *be real*	Dark matter actually exists in outer space. No matter what you say, the problem still exists. A golden age never existed. The problem only exists in his imagination.
exist *continue to live / to be active*	I can't exist without you. We cannot exist without food and water. The colony managed to exist for many more years. Racism has always existed in American politics. Hope exists even when things look bad.
exist *occur, be found*	Tigers don't exist in Africa.

PRESENT

I expand · · · · · · · · we expand
you expand · · · · · · you expand
he/she/it expands · · they expand

• *It expands if you need more space.*

PRESENT PROGRESSIVE

I am expanding · · · · · · · · we are expanding
you are expanding · · · · · · you are expanding
he/she/it is expanding · · · · they are expanding

• *We are expanding our market.*

PAST

I expanded · · · · · · · we expanded
you expanded · · · · · you expanded
he/she/it expanded · · they expanded

• *We expanded our operations in Asia.*

PAST PROGRESSIVE

I was expanding · · · · · · · · we were expanding
you were expanding · · · · · · you were expanding
he/she/it was expanding · · · they were expanding

• *The business was expanding rapidly.*

PRESENT PERFECT ... have | has expanded
PAST PERFECT ... had expanded

FUTURE ... will expand
FUTURE PROGRESSIVE ... will be expanding
FUTURE PERFECT ... will have expanded

PAST PASSIVE

— · · · · · · —
— · · · · · · —
it was expanded · · they were expanded

• *The plant was recently expanded.*

COMPLEMENTS

expand *enlarge, become bigger*

The umbrella expanded with a pop.
The table expands to seat eight people.
The foam expands and seals all the leaks.
Our business is expanding all the time.
His influence has expanded greatly.
The company is expanding into New England and Canada.
We are expanding into home appliances.

expand _____ *make bigger*

OBJECT

They have expanded **their empire**.
We needed to expand **the committee**.
You must expand **your thinking**.

PASSIVE

The army was rapidly expanded.

expand _____ *express in full*

OBJECT

The senator expanded **his remarks on immigration reform**.
The professor expanded **his ideas on economic recovery**.
Please expand **all abbreviations**.

PHRASAL VERBS

expand on _____ *give more details about*

The reporters asked Senator Blather to
expand on his statement about global warming.

PRESENT

I expect	we expect
you expect	you expect
he/she/it expects	they expect

- *He expects that his team will win.*

PRESENT PROGRESSIVE

I am expecting	we are expecting
you are expecting	you are expecting
he/she/it is expecting	they are expecting

- *She is expecting a baby in June.*

PAST

I expected	we expected
you expected	you expected
he/she/it expected	they expected

- *I never expected special treatment.*

PAST PROGRESSIVE

I was expecting	we were expecting
you were expecting	you were expecting
he/she/it was expecting	they were expecting

- *We were expecting them at any moment.*

PRESENT PERFECT ... have | has expected
PAST PERFECT ... had expected

FUTURE ... will expect
FUTURE PROGRESSIVE ... will be expecting
FUTURE PERFECT ... will have expected

PAST PASSIVE

I was expected	we were expected
you were expected	you were expected
he/she/it was expected	they were expected

- *The sad news was expected.*

COMPLEMENTS

expect *be pregnant / due for delivery*
[USED ONLY IN THE PROGRESSIVE TENSES]

Sally is expecting.
She is expecting in early September.

expect _____ *think that [something] will happen*

OBJECT
Roberta is expecting **twins**.
She is expecting **a phone call**.
We expect **high tide** around nine.
I had expected **better results**.
He expected **the worst**.

INFINITIVE
I expected **to win**.
The CEO expected **to close the deal today**.
They expect **to stay in Detroit overnight**.

THAT-CLAUSE
Everyone expected **that Senator Blather would lose**.
Who could have expected **that we could get so lost**?
John expected **that he and Susan would get married this fall**.

WH-CLAUSE
I never expected **what happened**.
They never expected **what was coming**.
Who could have expected **how much it would cost**?

expect _____ *think that [something] should happen*

OBJECT
The boy expected **a reward** for finding my wallet.
The principal expects **better behavior** from the students.

OBJECT + INFINITIVE
I expect **you** *to do your homework*.
The president expects **all citizens** *to do their share*.
The weatherman expects **it** *to rain tomorrow*.

INFINITIVE
We all expect **to be treated with respect**.

expect _____ *suppose, think*

THAT-CLAUSE
I expect **that you are right**.
I expect **that it is true**.
I expect **that you believed everything he told you**.

PHRASAL VERBS

expect [someone] for _____ *think that [someone] will attend [an event]*

The family expected you for lunch today.

I experience   we experience
you experience   you experience
he/she/it experiences   they experience

• *He experiences severe headaches.*

PAST

I experienced   we experienced
you experienced   you experienced
he/she/it experienced   they experienced

• *She experienced a few disappointments.*

PRESENT PERFECT   ... have | has experienced
PAST PERFECT   ... had experienced

PRESENT PROGRESSIVE

I am experiencing   we are experiencing
you are experiencing   you are experiencing
he/she/it is experiencing   they are experiencing

• *We are experiencing a brief technical delay.*

PAST PROGRESSIVE

I was experiencing   we were experiencing
you were experiencing   you were experiencing
he/she/it was experiencing   they were experiencing

• *I was experiencing a total meltdown.*

FUTURE   ... will experience
FUTURE PROGRESSIVE   ... will be experiencing
FUTURE PERFECT   ... will have experienced

PAST PASSIVE

—   —
—   —
it was experienced   they were experienced

• *Some setbacks were experienced during the project.*

COMPLEMENTS

experience _____ *undergo, encounter*

OBJECT   I have experienced **a few bad days.**
He experienced **many hardships** growing up.
I've experienced **good days and bad days.**
I had never experienced **such a disappointment** before.
The market is experiencing **some bad news.**
I can't imagine experiencing **such a thing.**

WH-CLAUSE   I have never experienced **what he has gone through.**
They will soon experience **what it is like.**
The island experienced **what a Category 5 hurricane could do.**

PRESENT

I explain	we explain
you explain	you explain
he/she/it explains	they explain

• *She explains things very well.*

PRESENT PROGRESSIVE

I am explaining	we are explaining
you are explaining	you are explaining
he/she/it is explaining	they are explaining

• *I'm explaining where they should go.*

PAST

I explained	we explained
you explained	you explained
he/she/it explained	they explained

• *I explained to the police what happened.*

PAST PROGRESSIVE

I was explaining	we were explaining
you were explaining	you were explaining
he/she/it was explaining	they were explaining

• *He was explaining that he missed his train.*

PRESENT PERFECT ... have | has explained
PAST PERFECT ... had explained

FUTURE ... will explain
FUTURE PROGRESSIVE ... will be explaining
FUTURE PERFECT ... will have explained

PAST PASSIVE

—	—
—	—
it was explained	they were explained

• *The mystery was explained later.*

COMPLEMENTS

explain *engage in giving reasons/ justifications*

They tried to explain.
I'm sorry, I can't explain.

explain _____ *give the cause of / reason for*

OBJECT (+ *to* OBJECT)

He explained **his mistake.**
The CEO explained **the secret of our success.**
The coach tried to explain **their defeat.**
The technician explained **the malfunction *to his boss.***

explain _____ *make clear, give details about*

OBJECT (+ *to* OBJECT)

He explained **his new approach.**
The economist explained **the complicated math behind his model.**
We need to explain **our proposal.**
The attorney explained **the law *to his client.***

THAT-CLAUSE

He explained **that he wasn't feeling well.**
They explained **that their flight had been delayed.**
Mary explained **that she had to make a call.**

WH-CLAUSE

Can you explain **what went wrong?**
I explained **what we needed to do.**
He explained **where we had made our mistake.**
I will explain **where we are going to meet.**
The administrator explained **why it was a really bad idea.**
The repairman explained **how we could have prevented the problem.**

WH-INFINITIVE

The manager explained **what to do in case of fire.**
I will explain **where to park your cars.**
The consultant explained **how to increase our sales.**

explain _____ *give a reason for one's behavior*

REFLEXIVE PRONOUN

The wine bottle is empty. Explain **yourself,** son.

PHRASAL VERBS

explain _SEP_ **away** *justify with credible reasons/excuses*

The student tried to explain away her absences.
Janice explained away her bruises as the result of clumsiness.

PRESENT

I expose	we expose
you expose	you expose
he/she/it exposes	they expose

- *He exposes himself to a lot of criticism.*

PRESENT PROGRESSIVE

I am exposing	we are exposing
you are exposing	you are exposing
he/she/it is exposing	they are exposing

- *I am exposing everything that happened there.*

PAST

I exposed	we exposed
you exposed	you exposed
he/she/it exposed	they exposed

- *The paper exposed the crooked politician.*

PAST PROGRESSIVE

I was exposing	we were exposing
you were exposing	you were exposing
he/she/it was exposing	they were exposing

- *He was exposing his family to unnecessary risk.*

PRESENT PERFECT ... have | has exposed
PAST PERFECT   ... had exposed

FUTURE   ... will expose
FUTURE PROGRESSIVE   ... will be exposing
FUTURE PERFECT   ... will have exposed

PAST PASSIVE

I was exposed	we were exposed
you were exposed	you were exposed
he/she/it was exposed	they were exposed

- *The children were exposed to measles.*

(**COMPLEMENTS**)

expose _____ *leave unprotected from*

OBJECT + to OBJECT	The company exposed **us *to toxic chemicals*.**
PASSIVE	The hikers were exposed ***to the thunderstorm*.**
	The troops were needlessly exposed ***to enemy fire*.**
	I was exposed ***to typhoid*** on my trip.

expose _____ *cause to be affected/influenced by*

OBJECT + to OBJECT	I exposed **my legs *to the warm sun*.**
	You should expose **your children *to good music*.**
	The photographer exposed **the film *to the light*.**
PASSIVE	In Berkeley, I was exposed ***to a wide variety of food*.**

expose _____ *display, make visible, reveal*

OBJECT	The suspect exposed **his gang tattoos.**
	I didn't want to expose **my total ignorance.**
	Who wants to expose **their mistakes** in public?
OBJECT + as PREDICATE NOUN	The journalist exposed **the governor *as a fraud*.**
WH-CLAUSE	The reporter exposed **who was involved in the scandal.**
	I will expose **what you have been doing.**
	I only exposed **what everyone already knew.**
PRESENT PARTICIPLE	Mike exposed **the mayor's taking a bribe.**

expose _____ *display one's genitals*

REFLEXIVE PRONOUN	He was arrested because he exposed **himself** in public.

expose _____ *subject oneself*

REFLEXIVE PRONOUN + to OBJECT	Public officials expose **themselves *to the risk of investigation*.**

PRESENT

I express	we express
you express	you express
he/she/it expresses	they express

• He expresses himself well.

PRESENT PROGRESSIVE

I am expressing	we are expressing
you are expressing	you are expressing
he/she/it is expressing	they are expressing

• He is expressing his disapproval very clearly.

PAST

I expressed	we expressed
you expressed	you expressed
he/she/it expressed	they expressed

• I expressed my ideas in a long essay.

PAST PROGRESSIVE

I was expressing	we were expressing
you were expressing	you were expressing
he/she/it was expressing	they were expressing

• The author was only expressing his personal opinion.

PRESENT PERFECT ... have | has expressed
PAST PERFECT ... had expressed

FUTURE ... will express
FUTURE PROGRESSIVE ... will be expressing
FUTURE PERFECT ... will have expressed

PAST PASSIVE

—	—
—	—
it was expressed	they were expressed

• My position was expressed before the meeting.

──────────(COMPLEMENTS)──────────

express _____ *state, convey*

OBJECT	I expressed **my sympathy.**
	The ballet expresses **the enthusiasm of youth.**
	I can't express **my feelings** in words.
	His face expressed **worry.**
WH-CLAUSE	He expressed exactly **what he meant.**
	I tried to express **how I felt.**
	She expressed **how much our visit meant to her.**
	His attitude expressed **how upset he was.**

express _____ *send [something] by rapid delivery*

OBJECT	I will express **the product** right away.
	Please express **this document.**
PASSIVE	The package was expressed overnight.
OBJECT + *to* OBJECT	I expressed **the manuscript** *to the editor* this morning.
	They just expressed **the package** *to Jason.*

express _____ *state/show one's thoughts/feelings*

REFLEXIVE PRONOUN + ADVERB OF MANNER	Delia expressed **herself** *poorly* at last night's meeting.
	Norman expresses **himself** *best in his artwork.*
	Bonnie expresses **herself** *through music.*

PRESENT

I extend	we extend
you extend	you extend
he/she/it extends	they extend

- *The lake extends 15 miles to the east.*

PRESENT PROGRESSIVE

I am extending	we are extending
you are extending	you are extending
he/she/it is extending	they are extending

- *We are extending our trip.*

PAST

I extended	we extended
you extended	you extended
he/she/it extended	they extended

- *They extended the offer to all employees.*

PAST PROGRESSIVE

I was extending	we were extending
you were extending	you were extending
he/she/it was extending	they were extending

- *They were extending their deck.*

PRESENT PERFECT ... have | has extended
PAST PERFECT ... had extended

FUTURE ... will extend
FUTURE PROGRESSIVE ... will be extending
FUTURE PERFECT ... will have extended

PAST PASSIVE

I was extended	we were extended
you were extended	you were extended
he/she/it was extended	they were extended

- *The deadline was extended to next Saturday.*

(**COMPLEMENTS**)

extend _____ *stretch, continue, include*

ADVERB OF TIME	The conference extends **through the weekend.**
	The battle extended **through the night.**
	The Ming Dynasty extended **from 1368 to 1644.**
ADVERB OF PLACE TO/FROM	The damage extended **for miles.**
	The city extends **all the way to the ocean.**
	His influence extends **throughout the state.**
	The Rocky Mountains extend **from Canada to New Mexico.**
	His business interests extend **to oil drilling and casinos.**

extend _____ *stretch, lengthen, enlarge, prolong*

OBJECT	He extended **both his arms** to catch the kitten.
	We are extending **the kitchen.**
	We need to extend **the dining room table.**
	Senator Blather extended **his control of the Appropriations Committee.**
	They are extending **the deadline** for applications.
	Regular oil changes extend **the life of a car.**
	We are extending **our vacation** by a couple of days.
	The company extended **itself** too far.

extend _____ *offer, give*

OBJECT + *to* OBJECT	The government will extend **emergency aid** *to the flood victims.*
	They will extend **additional credit** *to their customers.*
	We extend **best wishes** *to the participants.*
	The club extends **membership** *to all senior citizens.*

extend _____ *work very hard*

REFLEXIVE PRONOUN	Esther is extending **herself** too far by joining so many clubs.

PRESENT

I face	we face
you face	you face
he/she/it faces	they face

• *Our house faces a lovely park.*

PRESENT PROGRESSIVE

I am facing	we are facing
you are facing	you are facing
he/she/it is facing	they are facing

• *We are facing a serious problem.*

PAST

I faced	we faced
you faced	you faced
he/she/it faced	they faced

• *We faced overwhelming odds.*

PAST PROGRESSIVE

I was facing	we were facing
you were facing	you were facing
he/she/it was facing	they were facing

• *They were facing certain defeat.*

PRESENT PERFECT ... have | has faced
PAST PERFECT ... had faced

FUTURE ... will face
FUTURE PROGRESSIVE ... will be facing
FUTURE PERFECT ... will have faced

PAST PASSIVE

I was faced	we were faced
you were faced	you were faced
he/she/it was faced	they were faced

• *The apartment building was faced with brick.*

COMPLEMENTS

face _____ *turn / be oriented in a certain direction*

ADVERB OF PLACE TO/FROM

The porch faces **north.**
Our hotel room faced **toward the ocean.**
Birds face **into the wind** to retain body heat.
Her apartment faced **onto Main Street.**

face _____ *turn / be oriented toward*

OBJECT

Please face **the front of the hall.**
Our hotel room faced **the ocean.**
The armies faced **each other.**
The ships faced **the oncoming waves.**
The people on the beach all faced **the sun.**

face _____ *confront / deal with [something difficult/unpleasant]*

OBJECT

You must face **the facts!**
The market was facing **a big sell-off of assets.**
The Cubs face **their old rivals** this weekend.

PASSIVE

He was faced with financial ruin.

WH-CLAUSE

We were facing **what we feared the most.**
They will face **whatever problems come up.**
He must face **whatever punishment he is given.**

face _____ *cover the surface of*

OBJECT + *with* OBJECT

They faced **the walls** *with marble.*
We faced **our kitchen counter** *with blue slate.*

PASSIVE

The bathroom surfaces are faced *with white tile.*

PHRASAL VERBS

face away/forward/in/out/etc.
turn / be oriented in a specified direction

The actor faced away from the audience.
Stand in a straight line and face forward!
The statue in the foyer faces in.
The statue in the portico faces out.

face _____ **head-on** *confront directly*

Cindy faced her drug addiction head-on.

face up to _____ *confront directly, accept*

Greg finally faced up to his alcohol problem.
You have to face up to the fact that you can't climb stairs anymore.

PRESENT

I fail	we fail
you fail	you fail
he/she/it fails	they fail

• *He never fails to answer his e-mail.*

PRESENT PROGRESSIVE

I am failing	we are failing
you are failing	you are failing
he/she/it is failing	they are failing

• *He is failing to keep up with the assignments.*

PAST

I failed	we failed
you failed	you failed
he/she/it failed	they failed

• *The air conditioning failed again.*

PAST PROGRESSIVE

I was failing	we were failing
you were failing	you were failing
he/she/it was failing	they were failing

• *His health was failing.*

PRESENT PERFECT ... have | has failed
PAST PERFECT ... had failed

FUTURE ... will fail
FUTURE PROGRESSIVE ... will be failing
FUTURE PERFECT ... will have failed

PAST PASSIVE

I was failed	we were failed
you were failed	you were failed
he/she/it was failed	they were failed

• *The class was failed by half the students.*

COMPLEMENTS

fail *weaken, decline*	My grandmother's eyesight is failing. My strength was beginning to fail. The light was failing.
fail *be unsuccessful*	The surprise attack failed miserably. I'm afraid that John is failing this semester.
fail *stop working, break down*	The old compressor finally failed. Their marriage eventually failed. His heart failed at the end. Most start-up companies fail in their first year.
fail _____ *not earn a passing grade in/on* OBJECT	Bryan failed **algebra** last semester. I failed **the test** the first time I took it. Thirty percent of applicants fail **the bar exam**. You cannot fail **the orals**.
fail _____ *disappoint, be of no help to* OBJECT	He would never fail **the team**. Mary's friends failed **her**. My courage failed **me** at the end. He never failed **his duty**.
PASSIVE	I was failed by several of my office mates.
fail _____ *not [do something]* INFINITIVE	Don't fail **to lock the door** when you leave. I fail **to see the point**. The team failed **to score in the first half**. The new program can't fail **to save you money**. Did he fail **to understand the instructions**?

PRESENT

I fall	we fall
you fall	you fall
he/she/it falls	they fall

• *Night falls early this time of year.*

PRESENT PROGRESSIVE

I am falling	we are falling
you are falling	you are falling
he/she/it is falling	they are falling

• *Look out! It's falling.*

PAST

I fell	we fell
you fell	you fell
he/she/it fell	they fell

• *The market fell like a rock yesterday.*

PAST PROGRESSIVE

I was falling	we were falling
you were falling	you were falling
he/she/it was falling	they were falling

• *The snow was falling heavily.*

PRESENT PERFECT	... have	has fallen
PAST PERFECT	... had fallen

FUTURE	... will fall
FUTURE PROGRESSIVE	... will be falling
FUTURE PERFECT	... will have fallen

PAST PASSIVE

Fall is never used in the passive voice.

COMPLEMENTS

fall *drop downward*	I fell on the ice. He fell to his knees. In the next mile, the river falls 100 feet. The valley fell in front of him.
fall *become lower/weaker/less*	My temperature finally started falling. His voice always falls at the end of his sentences. Their expectations are falling. The wind usually falls at sunset. The market fell today. Our productivity fell last quarter.
fall *be wounded/killed in battle*	Fifty thousand soldiers fell at the Battle of Gettysburg.
fall ____ *pass [into a specific state/condition], become* PREDICATE ADJECTIVE	Dad falls **asleep** in front of the news. Ursula fell **sick** after eating potato salad at the picnic. The crowd fell **silent** as she approached the podium.

PHRASAL VERBS

fall away/back/down/in/off/out/etc. *fall in a specified direction*	The castle walls are falling down. My hat fell off when I stood up.
fall apart/through *fail, come to nothing*	Our party plans fell through at the last minute.
fall back *retreat*	The regiment fell back to the new fort.
fall back on ____ *turn back to for help*	The Dickersons fell back on their savings.
fall behind (on ____**)** *lag behind*	On the second lap, the American swimmers fell behind. The doctor fell further behind as the day went on. My roommates and I are falling behind on the rent.
fall for ____ *become strongly attracted to*	Patrick fell for Tammy on their first date.
fall for ____ *be deceived by*	We won't fall for the politician's lies anymore.
fall in with ____ *associate with*	Our son fell in with computer nerds at school.
fall off *decline, diminish*	Attendance at our church has fallen off dramatically.
fall on ____ *happen on*	Christmas falls on a Saturday this year. The meeting falls on my day off.
fall out (with ____**)** *quarrel (with [someone])*	Nick fell out with the project director.
fall under ____ *be influenced/controlled by*	The princess fell under the power of the wicked queen.
fall (up)on/to ____ *become the duty of*	Organization of the meeting fell to the secretary.

PRESENT

I favor	we favor
you favor	you favor
he/she/it favors	they favor

• *He favors conservative causes.*

PRESENT PROGRESSIVE

I am favoring	we are favoring
you are favoring	you are favoring
he/she/it is favoring	they are favoring

• *He is favoring his right knee.*

PAST

I favored	we favored
you favored	you favored
he/she/it favored	they favored

• *I favored none of the applicants.*

PAST PROGRESSIVE

I was favoring	we were favoring
you were favoring	you were favoring
he/she/it was favoring	they were favoring

• *They were favoring the front runner until recently.*

PRESENT PERFECT ... have | has favored
PAST PERFECT ... had favored

FUTURE ... will favor
FUTURE PROGRESSIVE ... will be favoring
FUTURE PERFECT ... will have favored

PAST PASSIVE

I was favored	we were favored
you were favored	you were favored
he/she/it was favored	they were favored

• *The Democrats were favored this year.*

―――――――――――――――――――――――――――――(**COMPLEMENTS**)――

favor _____ *prefer, like*

OBJECT   "Fortune favors **the brave**" is a famous Latin saying.
I generally favor **Chinese food**.
He never favors **one grandchild** over another.

WH-CLAUSE   Audiences always favor **what they are already familiar with**.
Politicians always favor **whatever is popular**.
I would favor **whichever restaurant we can get a reservation at**.

favor _____ *consider most likely to win*

OBJECT   The sports bloggers favor **the Giants**.
WH-CLAUSE   The odds will favor **whoever wins the primary**.

favor _____ *help, facilitate*

OBJECT   Lax security favored **the prisoners' escape**.
Sunshine favored **the first game of the baseball season**.

favor _____ *treat gently*

OBJECT   He favors **his sore ankle**.
The horse is favoring **his left front hoof**.

PASSIVE   Handicapped children have to be favored.

favor _____ *look like*

OBJECT   Both twins favor **their father**.

―――――――――――――――――――――――――――――(**EXPRESSIONS**)――

favor [someone] with _____ *give*
[something] to [someone]

The singer favored us with an encore.

PRESENT

I fear	we fear
you fear	you fear
he/she/it fears	they fear

* *Everyone fears public embarrassment.*

PRESENT PROGRESSIVE

Fear is rarely used in the progressive tenses.

PAST

I feared	we feared
you feared	you feared
he/she/it feared	they feared

* *I feared his violent temper.*

PAST PROGRESSIVE

Fear is rarely used in the progressive tenses.

PRESENT PERFECT ... have | has feared
PAST PERFECT ... had feared

FUTURE ... will fear
FUTURE PROGRESSIVE —
FUTURE PERFECT ... will have feared

PAST PASSIVE

I was feared	we were feared
you were feared	you were feared
he/she/it was feared	they were feared

* *A dawn attack was feared by the general.*

COMPLEMENTS

fear _____ *be afraid of, worry about*

OBJECT	"Fear no more **the heat o' the sun.**" [SHAKESPEARE]
	I fear **a recession coming.**
	The sailors feared **the dark skies to the west.**
	The citizens feared **another terrorist attack.**
	We have long feared **exactly this happening.**
	Hearing news of the fatal accident, Martha feared **the worst.**
INFINITIVE	I feared **to even open my eyes.**
	We feared **to make a sound.**
	I feared **to go out after dark.**
THAT-CLAUSE	I fear **that you are right.**
	We fear **that your flight may be cancelled.**
	The lawyers feared **that the judge would not allow their arguments.**
WH-CLAUSE	We all fear **what we do not know.**
	They fear **what will happen next.**
	I feared **what might go wrong with our plans.**
PRESENT PARTICIPLE	I feared even **opening my eyes.**
	We feared **making a sound.**
	I feared **going out after dark.**

PHRASAL VERBS

fear for _____ *worry about*

My brother is a coal miner, and I fear for his safety.
The hurricane was approaching, and we feared for our lives.

PRESENT

I feed	we feed
you feed	you feed
he/she/it feeds	they feed

· *He feeds the birds every day.*

PRESENT PROGRESSIVE

I am feeding	we are feeding
you are feeding	you are feeding
he/she/it is feeding	they are feeding

· *I'm feeding the documents into the shredder.*

PAST

I fed	we fed
you fed	you fed
he/she/it fed	they fed

· *I fed the cat two hours ago.*

PAST PROGRESSIVE

I was feeding	we were feeding
you were feeding	you were feeding
he/she/it was feeding	they were feeding

· *They were feeding us misinformation.*

PRESENT PERFECT ... have | has fed
PAST PERFECT ... had fed

FUTURE ... will feed
FUTURE PROGRESSIVE ... will be feeding
FUTURE PERFECT ... will have fed

PAST PASSIVE

I was fed	we were fed
you were fed	you were fed
he/she/it was fed	they were fed

· *The children were fed earlier.*

(**COMPLEMENTS**)

feed *eat*

How often do they feed?
The birds were feeding on our plum tree.
Lions only feed when they are hungry.

feed *supply [food/materials]*

The zookeepers feed every morning and evening.
Don't feed too fast, or the shredder will jam.

feed _____ *give food to, supply materials to*

OBJECT

We feed **the homeless** at a downtown shelter.
You should only feed **the goldfish** once a week.
Keep feeding **the boiler** until we have enough steam.

INDIRECT OBJECT + DIRECT OBJECT

Feed *me* **some more rope.**

to PARAPHRASE

Feed **some more rope** *to me.*

feed _____ *send [an electric current, a signal]*

OBJECT

The sensor feeds **a signal** to the computer.
The station feeds **the broadcast** to a satellite.

PASSIVE

The current is fed to the circuit breaker.

feed _____ *foster, support*

OBJECT

Resentment feeds **hostility.**
Rumors are feeding **the confusion.**
Music feeds **the soul.**

PASSIVE

The mind can only be fed by education.

feed _____ *supply*

INDIRECT OBJECT + DIRECT OBJECT

We fed *the chickens* **corn.**
The company fed *the press* **misleading information.**
The director fed *the actress* **her lines.**
This cable feeds *the factory* **its power.**

to PARAPHRASE

We fed **corn** *to the chickens.*
The company fed **misleading information** *to the press.*
The director fed **the actress's lines** *to her.*
This cable feeds **power** *to the factory.*

feed _____ *move/push [into/through an opening]*

OBJECT + ADVERB OF PLACE TO/FROM

The nurse fed **the breathing tube** *into the patient's windpipe.*
The tourist fed **quarters** *into the vending machine.*

feel _____ *be aware of, sense* [continued]

OBJECT + PRESENT PARTICIPLE

They felt the **boat** *getting under way*.
I felt **myself** *getting sick*.
The speaker felt **the audience** *losing interest*.

feel _____ *believe, think*

OBJECT + INFINITIVE

The coach felt **the team** *to be ready for the game*.
John felt **them** *to be completely mistaken*.
I always felt **myself** *to be a good sport*.

THAT-CLAUSE

I feel **that I am right about it**.
We feel **that we should go ahead as planned**.
Sam felt **that he deserved a bigger raise**.

feel _____ *experience, have grief/pity because of*

OBJECT

We felt **Grandma's death** keenly.

─────────────────────────────(**PHRASAL VERBS**)─

feel (about/around) for _____
seek by touching

I felt for the light switch.
She was feeling around in the dark for her glasses.

feel for _____ *sympathize with*

I really feel for the team that lost.

feel _SEP_ **out** *find out the views of*

Senator Blather felt out the voters about the tax increase.

─────────────────────────────(**EXPRESSIONS**)─

feel at home *feel comfortable/accepted*

My friends feel at home here.

feel _____ **in [one's] bones** *sense by intuition*

I feel it in my bones that he's going to hit a home run tonight.

feel like _____ *desire, want*

I feel like pizza for dinner.
I feel like drinking lemonade.

feel like _____ *seem to be*

This feels like real wood.
It feels like January, even though it's only September.

feel like / as if / as though _____
believe/sense that

I feel like it's going to rain.
We feel as if we're never going to pay off the mortgage.

feel like a million (bucks/dollars)
feel physically and mentally strong

An early-morning walk through the woods makes me feel like a million bucks.

feel like a new person *feel refreshed/ renewed*

After a shower and shave, the hobo felt like a new person.

feel like death warmed over *feel very sick*

The flu made him feel like death warmed over.

feel like [oneself] *perceive oneself to be in a normal state*

After having a cold for a week, I feel like myself again.

feel no pain *be drunk*

After drinking a six pack, Meredith is feeling no pain.

feel [one's] oats *be lively*

The salesman danced a jig around the office; he's feeling his oats since he landed that big contract.

feel out of place *feel awkward*

Gordon feels out of place at wine-and-cheese parties.

feel the pinch *have too little money*

My parents want to vacation in Spain, but they're feeling the pinch.

feel up to _____
perceive oneself to be capable of

Do you feel up to going shopping?

PRESENT

I feel	we feel
you feel	you feel
he/she/it feels	they feel

• *My arm feels just fine, thanks.*

PRESENT PROGRESSIVE

I am feeling	we are feeling
you are feeling	you are feeling
he/she/it is feeling	they are feeling

• *I'm feeling tired.*

PAST

I felt	we felt
you felt	you felt
he/she/it felt	they felt

• *They felt sorry for her.*

PAST PROGRESSIVE

I was feeling	we were feeling
you were feeling	you were feeling
he/she/it was feeling	they were feeling

• *We were feeling our way through the cave.*

PRESENT PERFECT ... have | has felt
PAST PERFECT ... had felt

FUTURE   ... will feel
FUTURE PROGRESSIVE   ... will be feeling
FUTURE PERFECT   ... will have felt

PAST PASSIVE

—	—
—	—
it was felt	they were felt

• *The loss was felt by everyone.*

(**COMPLEMENTS**)

feel _____ *perceive oneself to be*

   PREDICATE NOUN   Sally felt **a complete fool**.
                           I felt **a victim of circumstances**.

   PREDICATE ADJECTIVE   John felt **foolish**.
                           We all felt **sad at the news**.
                           The situation felt **all wrong**.
                           Are you feeling **better** today?
                           I don't feel **well**.

   PAST PARTICIPLE   The team felt **defeated** after losing their best pitcher.
                           We felt **overwhelmed** by the experience.

feel _____ *have an emotion/opinion*

   ADVERB OF MANNER   He felt **badly** about what had happened.
                           Robert always feels **strongly** about political issues.

feel _____ *seem*

   it + *feel* + PREDICATE ADJECTIVE +   It felt **good** *to go to class again*.
     INFINITIVE   It feels **weird** *to be in the presence of so many geeks*.

feel _____ *seem to the sense of touch*

   PREDICATE ADJECTIVE   The water feels **too cold**.

feel _____ *search by touch*

   ADVERB OF PLACE   I felt **everywhere**.
                           He felt **in his pockets** for the key.
                           She felt **under the cushions**.

feel _____ *seek by touching*

   OBJECT   The burglars felt **their way** along the corridor.

feel _____ *touch in order to examine*

   OBJECT   I felt **his swollen ankle**.
                           The detective felt **the suspect** for a gun.
                           She carefully felt **the dog's injured leg**.

feel _____ *be aware of, sense*

   OBJECT   They felt **the impact of the explosion**.
                           I felt **a rock in my shoe**.
                           Ron felt **a pang of jealousy**.

PRESENT

I fight	we fight
you fight	you fight
he/she/it fights	they fight

• *He always fights for the underdog.*

PRESENT PROGRESSIVE

I am fighting	we are fighting
you are fighting	you are fighting
he/she/it is fighting	they are fighting

• *I'm fighting a nasty cold.*

PAST

I fought	we fought
you fought	you fought
he/she/it fought	they fought

• *The senator fought against corruption.*

PAST PROGRESSIVE

I was fighting	we were fighting
you were fighting	you were fighting
he/she/it was fighting	they were fighting

• *They were fighting a rearguard action in the hills.*

PRESENT PERFECT ... have | has fought
PAST PERFECT ... had fought

FUTURE ... will fight
FUTURE PROGRESSIVE ... will be fighting
FUTURE PERFECT ... will have fought

PAST PASSIVE

I was fought	we were fought
you were fought	you were fought
he/she/it was fought	they were fought

• *The battle of Gettysburg was fought in July 1863.*

COMPLEMENTS

fight *engage in combat/argument*

It is useless to fight with City Hall.
The damaged ship will never fight again.
It is noble to fight for one's country.
The media was fighting for access to the court transcripts.
The twins are always fighting.
What married couple doesn't fight occasionally?
She was fighting against other committee members.

fight _____ *contend/struggle against, oppose*

OBJECT

The Spanish fought **Napoleon's armies** savagely.
I am fighting **a terrible sore throat**.
The company is fighting **the judge's ruling**.
We will fight **the takeover bid**.
The neighborhood fought **the new development**.
The minority party is fighting **Senator Blather's amendment**.

WH-CLAUSE

We have fought **what we considered to be wrong**.
They will fight **whomever we nominate**.
We will fight **whatever forces are arrayed against us**.

fight _____ *wage, be engaged in*

OBJECT

We are fighting **a war on poverty**.
He is fighting **the good fight**.
They fought **a running battle** for a week.

PHRASAL VERBS

fight back *retaliate*

She may lose the argument, but
 she'll find a way to fight back.

fight SEP **back** *resist, struggle against*

Ruth fought back her tears after hearing about his death.

fight SEP **off** *repel an attack by*

I'm trying to fight off a bout of the flu.
The platoon fought off a much larger force.

fight on *continue to fight*

Although surrounded, Colonel Travis's men fought on.

fight SEP **out** *settle by struggle*

The rival gangs fought it out with guns.
Beth and Seth fought out their differences in court.

fight over _____ *struggle to obtain*

The classmates fought over who would get the award.
Jayne and Eve fought over Humphrey.

PRESENT

I figure	we figure
you figure	you figure
he/she/it figures	they figure

• *He figures to win his first match.*

PRESENT PROGRESSIVE

I am figuring	we are figuring
you are figuring	you are figuring
he/she/it is figuring	they are figuring

• *I am figuring out how much to tip.*

PAST

I figured	we figured
you figured	you figured
he/she/it figured	they figured

• *They figured out the total cost.*

PAST PROGRESSIVE

I was figuring	we were figuring
you were figuring	you were figuring
he/she/it was figuring	they were figuring

• *We were figuring that the flight would be canceled.*

PRESENT PERFECT ... have | has figured
PAST PERFECT ... had figured

FUTURE ... will figure
FUTURE PROGRESSIVE ... will be figuring
FUTURE PERFECT ... will have figured

PAST PASSIVE

I was figured	we were figured
you were figured	you were figured
he/she/it was figured	they were figured

• *The problem was quickly figured out.*

COMPLEMENTS

figure *be just as expected*

It figures that Ryan would be the team captain.

figure _____ *calculate, estimate*
   OBJECT

We need to figure **the fixed costs.**
The garage figured **the cost of repairing the dent.**
How do you figure **the time we spent on it?**
I can't begin to figure **our losses.**

   WH-CLAUSE

Did you figure **what replacing the rug would cost?**

figure _____ *believe, expect*
   OBJECT + INFINITIVE

We figured **the company** *to be quite safe.*
The writers figure **the Cubs** *to win the pennant.*

    PASSIVE

The Cubs were figured *to win the pennant.*

   THAT-CLAUSE

We figured **that it was too late to call them.**
The salesman figured **that we wouldn't notice the difference.**
They figured **that there would be a delay.**
Why did he figure **that the wedding would be in Chicago?**

figure *appear likely*
   INFINITIVE

He figures **to be the odds-on favorite.**
They figure **to heat their house with firewood.**
He figures **to beat the odds.**

PHRASAL VERBS

figure _____ **into** [something]
include in [a calculation]

Did you figure office supplies into
  the expense total?

figure in/into _____ *be involved/*
important in

The butler figures prominently in the story.
The physical evidence figured into the defendant's conviction.

figure on _____ *plan/count/depend on*

Let's figure on going to a movie after dinner.
The contractor figured on five sheets of plywood being left over.

figure SEP **out** *understand*

The teacher couldn't figure Stephanie out at all.

figure SEP **out** *solve, determine*

Tim figured the crossword puzzle out in six minutes.
The police figured out who committed the crime.
I figured out what our rate of return would be.
We figured out how much gas we would need.

PRESENT

I file	we file
you file	you file
he/she/it files	they file

• *He files all the correspondence.*

PRESENT PROGRESSIVE

I am filing	we are filing
you are filing	you are filing
he/she/it is filing	they are filing

• *I'm filing all the reports chronologically.*

PAST

I filed	we filed
you filed	you filed
he/she/it filed	they filed

• *She filed for the open seat on the council.*

PAST PROGRESSIVE

I was filing	we were filing
you were filing	you were filing
he/she/it was filing	they were filing

• *She was filing her nails.*

PRESENT PERFECT … have | has filed
PAST PERFECT … had filed

FUTURE … will file
FUTURE PROGRESSIVE … will be filing
FUTURE PERFECT … will have filed

PAST PASSIVE

—	—
—	—
it was filed	they were filed

• *The will was filed with the county clerk.*

COMPLEMENTS

file *catalog and store something*

We filed all day Tuesday.
Jack and Hannah are filing in the back office.

file _____ *catalog and store*
  OBJECT

I filed **all the letters and memos.**
We filed **all the CDs** by artist.
Senator Blather had filed **all of his press releases.**
File **this report** under "Worker Safety."

file _____ *put into official records*
  OBJECT

She filed **divorce papers** this morning.
We have just filed **our mortgage.**
The sheriff filed **an eviction notice** on them.
I filed **a complaint** with the company.
They are going to file **charges.**
He filed **a claim** for his share of the estate.
File **this copy** with the county clerk's office.

file _____ *send [copy] to a newspaper*
  OBJECT

The freelance reporter filed **the story** just before midnight.

file _____ *march/walk in line*
  ADVERB OF PLACE TO/FROM

The children filed **out of the classroom** quietly.
We glumly filed **into the meeting room.**

file _____ *smooth with a tool*
  OBJECT

The actress filed **her nails** while she waited.

PHRASAL VERBS

file away at _____ *scrape with a tool* The jeweler was filing away at the burr.
file _SEP_ **away** *keep in memory* You may want to file the idea away for future use.
file _SEP_ **down** *smooth/reduce with a tool* The locksmith filed down the key.
file for _____ *begin a legal proceeding* Irene has filed for divorce.
file for _____ *register as an election candidate* My brother will file for alderman tomorrow.
file _____ **off [something]** *remove from [something] with a tool* The woodworker filed the edge off the drill bit.

PRESENT

I fill	we fill
you fill	you fill
he/she/it fills	they fill

- *The clinic fills quickly in the evening.*

PRESENT PROGRESSIVE

I am filling	we are filling
you are filling	you are filling
he/she/it is filling	they are filling

- *I am filling two vacant positions.*

PAST

I filled	we filled
you filled	you filled
he/she/it filled	they filled

- *We already filled the order.*

PAST PROGRESSIVE

I was filling	we were filling
you were filling	you were filling
he/she/it was filling	they were filling

- *The boats were filling their tanks at the dock.*

PRESENT PERFECT ... have | has filled
PAST PERFECT ... had filled

FUTURE ... will fill
FUTURE PROGRESSIVE ... will be filling
FUTURE PERFECT ... will have filled

PAST PASSIVE

I was filled	we were filled
you were filled	you were filled
he/she/it was filled	they were filled

- *The positions were filled almost immediately.*

COMPLEMENTS

fill *become full*	The sails were filling in the rising breeze.
	The pool was slowly filling.
	The stadium was quickly filling with noisy fans.
	Janet's eyes filled with tears.
fill _____ *put as much as possible into, make full* OBJECT	I filled **my coffee cup** again.
	I filled **the hole in the driveway** with gravel.
	Kay fills **his days** with handsetting type and printing.
fill _____ *occupy all of* OBJECT	The crowd completely filled **the small hall**.
fill _____ *spread throughout, pervade* OBJECT	Smoke from the forest fire filled **the air**.
	That stupid tune completely filled **my head**.
	The scandal filled **the evening news**.
fill _____ *supply what is requested* OBJECT	Can you fill **the order** by Friday?
	The pharmacist filled **my prescription** while I shopped.
PASSIVE	My prescription was filled while I shopped.
fill _____ *put someone into [a job/office]* OBJECT	We filled **the vacancy on the committee**.
	I'm sorry, we have already filled **the position**.

PHRASAL VERBS

fill in *become full, spread*	The sign-up sheet is filling in quickly.
	The new grass is filling in nicely.
fill _SEP_ **in** *give details to*	C.J. filled the reporters in about the president's meeting.
fill _SEP_ **in/out** *write information on*	Fill in the blank with the correct verb form.
	Applicants must fill out both sides of the form.
fill in for _____ *take the place of*	Can you fill in for me on Tuesday?
fill up *become completely full*	The hall is filling up for the concert.
	The kids are filling up on cookies and milk.
fill _SEP_ **up** *make completely full*	We're filling up the truck with cardboard to recycle.

find _____ *declare as a legal verdict*
   OBJECT + PREDICATE ADJECTIVE

The jury found **the defendant** *guilty*.

find _____ *obtain*
   OBJECT

You must find **time to study**.
Charlotte and Kathy found **an apartment** on
   Walnut Street.
Our product found **lots of buyers** among senior citizens.
Grandma finds **comfort** in her photo albums.

PHRASAL VERBS

find for _____ *decide in favor of*

The jury found for the defendant.

find out *learn the truth*

Your mother will find out.
I'll search the Internet and find out for you.

find _SEP_ **out** *learn*

I found out what makes Jason tick.
What did you find out about the boss's husband?

EXPRESSIONS

find a way around _____ *discover a way
to avoid [something]*

The computer engineer found
   a way around the error message.
My attorney found a way around the regulation.

find fault (with _____ **)** *discover something
wrong with [someone/something]*

My landlord finds fault with everyone.
The moderator found fault with both candidates'
   arguments.

find favor with _____ *win the approval of*

Vergil found favor with the emperor Augustus.

find it in [one's] heart / in [oneself] _____
have the courage/compassion

We found it in our hearts to beg forgiveness.
The voters found it in themselves to elect a black president.

find neither hide nor hair of _____
fail to detect any sign of

The detectives found neither hide nor hair of the suspect.

find [one's] bearings *determine where
one is*

After wandering in the woods for four hours, we found
   our bearings.

find [one's] tongue/voice *determine what
to say*

The candidate finally found her voice, but it was too late.

find [one's] way *discover the route*
find [oneself] *become aware of what
one wants to be/do in life*

We eventually found our way to the log cabin.
Melanie found herself in her sophomore year of college.

find out the hard way *discover something
by (usually unpleasant) experience*

Senator Blather found out the hard way how much
   voters oppose tax hikes.

find the/[one's] mark *discover a way to
win / defeat someone*

She found her mark midway through the second period
   and scored four goals after that.

PRESENT

I find	we find
you find	you find
he/she/it finds	they find

• *He finds his new job interesting.*

PRESENT PROGRESSIVE

I am finding	we are finding
you are finding	you are finding
he/she/it is finding	they are finding

• *I'm finding it hard to concentrate.*

PAST

I found	we found
you found	you found
he/she/it found	they found

• *We found a really great babysitter.*

PAST PROGRESSIVE

I was finding	we were finding
you were finding	you were finding
he/she/it was finding	they were finding

• *They were finding more support than expected.*

PRESENT PERFECT ... have | has found
PAST PERFECT   ... had found

FUTURE   ... will find
FUTURE PROGRESSIVE ... will be finding
FUTURE PERFECT   ... will have found

PAST PASSIVE

I was found	we were found
you were found	you were found
he/she/it was found	they were found

• *The murderer was never found.*

COMPLEMENTS

find _____ *discover, come upon by chance*

OBJECT	I finally found **my missing wallet.** The hikers found **a path back to camp.** Astronomers found **a new moon orbiting Jupiter.**
INDIRECT OBJECT + DIRECT OBJECT	I found *Jane* **a great birthday present.** We found *the kittens* **a nice home.**
for PARAPHRASE	I found **a great birthday present** *for Jane.* We found **a nice home** *for the kittens.*
OBJECT + INFINITIVE	I found **the new job** *to have its limitations.* Larry found **the restaurant** *to get a lot of repeat customers.*
OBJECT + PRESENT PARTICIPLE	I found **myself** *holding my breath.* They found **the kids** *playing in the backyard.* Harriet found **Jim** *working in the garage.*
OBJECT + PAST PARTICIPLE	I found **the dog** *covered with mud.* We found **our car** *damaged beyond repair.* I found **myself** *drained by the experience.*
THAT-CLAUSE	I found **that there was no simple solution.** We all find **that we get tired more easily as we get older.** Amy found **that she liked living in Montana.** I find **that the new job has its limitations.**
WH-CLAUSE	We found **what we had been looking for.** I never found **why the computer failed.** The police will find **whoever did this.**

find _____ *consider*

OBJECT + (*to be*) PREDICATE NOUN	I found **him** *(to be) a poor listener.* The teacher found **the class** *(to be) good students.* They found **the car** *(to be) a piece of junk.*
OBJECT + (*to be*) PREDICATE ADJECTIVE	I found **myself** *(to be) upset with him.* We found **him** *(to be) amused at it.* They found **the situation** *(to be) very satisfactory.*

top
40
verb

PRESENT

I finish	we finish
you finish	you finish
he/she/it finishes	they finish

• *I always finish my assignments on time.*

PRESENT PROGRESSIVE

I am finishing	we are finishing
you are finishing	you are finishing
he/she/it is finishing	they are finishing

• *We're just finishing now.*

PAST

I finished	we finished
you finished	you finished
he/she/it finished	they finished

• *I just finished reading the news.*

PAST PROGRESSIVE

I was finishing	we were finishing
you were finishing	you were finishing
he/she/it was finishing	they were finishing

• *He was finishing the dishes when the power went out.*

PRESENT PERFECT ... have | has finished
PAST PERFECT ... had finished

FUTURE ... will finish
FUTURE PROGRESSIVE ... will be finishing
FUTURE PERFECT ... will have finished

PAST PASSIVE

I was finished	we were finished
you were finished	you were finished
he/she/it was finished	they were finished

• *The job was finished on time and under budget.*

COMPLEMENTS

finish *complete an activity/event*
When will we finish?
The play finishes around 10:15.

finish *come to an end*
The boring meeting finished at 5 o'clock.

finish _____ *bring to an end, complete*
    OBJECT
We finished **dinner** around 9 o'clock.
Have the kids finished **their homework**?
We hope to finish **our house** before winter comes.

    WH-CLAUSE
You must finish **what you have begun**.
He will finish **whatever painting still needs to be done**.

    PRESENT PARTICIPLE
He has finished **writing the report**.
You can finish **watching your program** after dinner.
Have they finished **eating dinner** yet?

finish _____ *consume completely*
    OBJECT
The kids must finish **their soup** before they get dessert.

finish _____ *completely exhaust*
    OBJECT
The 5K run nearly finished **me**.

finish _____ *end a contest in a certain position*
    PREDICATE ADJECTIVE
Our team finished **third** at the Science Fair.

finish _____ *apply a final coat of varnish/paint to*
    OBJECT
We'll finish **the desk** with urethane varnish.

finish _____ *ruin*
    OBJECT
His thoughtless remark finished **his political career**.

PHRASAL VERBS

finish SEP **off/up** *consume completely*
We could finish off the last of the chocolate cake.
Finish up your spaghetti, kids.

finish with _____ *stop being involved / dealing with*
I am finished with local politicians.
She was finished with trying to please her neighbors.

finish with _____ *stop using*
I need the spatula when you finish with it.
I need the spatula when you're finished with it.

PRESENT		PRESENT PROGRESSIVE	
I fire	we fire	I am firing	we are firing
you fire	you fire	you are firing	you are firing
he/she/it fires	they fire	he/she/it is firing	they are firing

• *Press the starter until the engine fires.* • *I am not firing anybody.*

PAST		PAST PROGRESSIVE	
I fired	we fired	I was firing	we were firing
you fired	you fired	you were firing	you were firing
he/she/it fired	they fired	he/she/it was firing	they were firing

• *The company fired several executives.* • *They were firing automatic weapons.*

PRESENT PERFECT	... have | has fired
PAST PERFECT	... had fired

FUTURE	... will fire
FUTURE PROGRESSIVE	... will be firing
FUTURE PERFECT	... will have fired

PAST PASSIVE	
I was fired	we were fired
you were fired	you were fired
he/she/it was fired	they were fired

• *A gun was fired during the protest meeting.*

COMPLEMENTS

fire *begin to burn*	The dry grass quickly fired in the hot wind.
	The boiler was firing and steam was being produced.
fire *discharge* [OF A WEAPON]	A gun fired, causing the crowd to panic.
fire _____ *shoot, launch*	
OBJECT	Someone had fired **a gun** nearby.
	The pilot fired **his missiles** at the enemy trucks.
fire _____ *inspire, arouse*	
OBJECT	The poem fired **my imagination**.
	Her example fired **our lagging spirits**.
fire _____ *dismiss from a job/position*	
OBJECT	He fired **the whole department**.
	They can't fire **everyone**, can they?
PASSIVE	Three programmers were fired yesterday.
WH-CLAUSE	The candidate will fire **whoever leaked the memo to the press**.
	He can fire **whomever he wants to**.

PHRASAL VERBS

fire down/in/out/up/etc. *shoot in a specified direction*	The Confederates fired down from Lookout Mountain.
	The commando raced to the window and fired in.
fire away *shoot continuously*	The sailors were firing away at the enemy ship.
fire away *speak without hesitation*	"I have three questions." "Fire away!"
fire back (at _____**)** *shoot (at [someone who shot first])*	When the enemy opens fire, you can fire back.
	The policeman fired back at the robber.
fire SEP **off** *write and send quickly*	His assistant fired off 15 memos in one hour.
fire SEP **up** *fill with enthusiasm*	His speech fired up the crowd, and they were ready to go.
fire SEP **up** *begin to operate*	The engine fired up with a roar.
fire SEP **up** *cause to begin to operate*	My wife fired up her laptop and checked e-mail.
fire SEP **up** *cause to burn*	The crew fired up the boilers and the ship got under way.
	Gerry fired up the grill and barbecued pork steaks.

PRESENT

I fit	we fit
you fit	you fit
he/she/it fits	they fit

　• *The theory fits all the facts.*

PRESENT PROGRESSIVE

I am fitting	we are fitting
you are fitting	you are fitting
he/she/it is fitting	they are fitting

　• *I am fitting them in as best I can.*

PAST

I fit/fitted	we fit/fitted
you fit/fitted	you fit/fitted
he/she/it fit/fitted	they fit/fitted

　• *We fit eight people at the table before.*

PAST PROGRESSIVE

I was fitting	we were fitting
you were fitting	you were fitting
he/she/it was fitting	they were fitting

　• *We were fitting in very nicely, I thought.*

PRESENT PERFECT ... have | has fit/fitted
PAST PERFECT ... had fit/fitted

FUTURE ... will fit
FUTURE PROGRESSIVE ... will be fitting
FUTURE PERFECT ... will have fit/fitted

PAST PASSIVE

I was fit/fitted	we were fit/fitted
you were fit/fitted	you were fit/fitted
he/she/it was fit/fitted	they were fit/fitted

　• *He was fitted for a new suit.*

COMPLEMENTS

NOTE: For the following six meanings, *fit* is not used in the progressive tenses.

fit *be the right size and shape*	The sweater fits perfectly.
	Will the new rug fit in the living room?
fit *be accommodated*	How many students can fit in a phone booth?
	These bags won't fit in the dumpster.
fit _____ *be the right size and shape for* 　OBJECT	The new suit fits **me** perfectly.
	The old frame won't fit **the new picture**.
fit _____ *be appropriate/suitable for* 　OBJECT	Your hat fits **the rest of your outfit**.
	The class fits **my schedule** pretty well.
	The punishment must fit **the crime**.
fit _____ *accommodate* 　OBJECT	Can we fit **24 children** in the classroom?
fit _____ *manage to insert* 　OBJECT	We can fit **four skeins of yarn** in this box.

NOTE: For the following four meanings, *fit* may be used in the progressive tenses.

fit _____ *adjust to the right size and shape* 　OBJECT	You need to fit **the rug** to the room.
fit _____ *measure for the right size* 　OBJECT 　　PASSIVE	The tailor is fitting **Dad** for a new suit. Dad was fitted for a new suit.
fit _____ *make appropriate/suitable* 　OBJECT + *to* OBJECT	Does a songwriter fit **words** *to music* or **music** *to words*?
fit _____ *supply, equip* 　OBJECT + *with* OBJECT	The shipyard will fit **the boat** *with everything it needs*.

PHRASAL VERBS

fit in *be in accord/harmony*	Our new neighbors fit in just fine.
fit _SEP_ **in** *provide a place for*	The hostess will fit the two unexpected guests in.

PRESENT

I fix	we fix
you fix	you fix
he/she/it fixes	they fix

- *He fixes all of our computers.*

PRESENT PROGRESSIVE

I am fixing	we are fixing
you are fixing	you are fixing
he/she/it is fixing	they are fixing

- *I'm fixing the toaster now.*

PAST

I fixed	we fixed
you fixed	you fixed
he/she/it fixed	they fixed

- *We fixed the date for the meeting.*

PAST PROGRESSIVE

I was fixing	we were fixing
you were fixing	you were fixing
he/she/it was fixing	they were fixing

- *She was fixing lunch.*

PRESENT PERFECT ... have | has fixed
PAST PERFECT ... had fixed

FUTURE ... will fix
FUTURE PROGRESSIVE ... will be fixing
FUTURE PERFECT ... will have fixed

PAST PASSIVE

I was fixed	we were fixed
you were fixed	you were fixed
he/she/it was fixed	they were fixed

- *The location was fixed by GPS.*

COMPLEMENTS

fix _____ *repair, mend*
  OBJECT

Only the dealer can fix **your car**.
We will try to fix **our relationship**.

fix _____ *make stable*
  OBJECT

I fixed **the mailbox post** in concrete.
To prevent earthquake damage, fix **all bookcases** to the wall.

fix _____ *direct and hold, focus*
  OBJECT

I fixed **my eyes** on the blurry image.
We fixed **the telescope** on the distant image.
She fixed **me** with an icy stare.

fix _____ *determine, establish*
  OBJECT

The committee will fix **the blame** for this mess.
They will fix **the agenda for the hearing**.

  PASSIVE

The amount of damage cannot be fixed yet.

fix _____ *attach*
  OBJECT

The pharmacist fixed **a label** to the bottle.

fix _____ *put in order, adjust*
  OBJECT

We're late, and Joan is still fixing **her hair**.

fix _____ *prepare [food/drink]*
  OBJECT

I am fixing **lunch** now.
I will fix **a salad** for the picnic.

  INDIRECT OBJECT + DIRECT OBJECT

Can I fix *you* **a martini**?

    for PARAPHRASE

Can I fix **a martini** *for you*?

fix _____ *neuter [an animal]*
  OBJECT

Most cities have a program to fix **dogs and cats** for free.

  PASSIVE

Our cat has already been fixed.

fix _____ *illegally influence the outcome of a contest*
  OBJECT

The mob fixed **all the boxing matches**.

  PASSIVE

Elections have been fixed before.

fix _____ *get even with, punish*
  OBJECT

Bert stole all our turnips. We'll fix **him**!

PRESENT

I flee	we flee
you flee	you flee
he/she/it flees	they flee

• *Everyone flees from imminent danger.*

PRESENT PROGRESSIVE

I am fleeing	we are fleeing
you are fleeing	you are fleeing
he/she/it is fleeing	they are fleeing

• *They are fleeing as fast as they can.*

PAST

I fled	we fled
you fled	you fled
he/she/it fled	they fled

• *I never fled from a fight.*

PAST PROGRESSIVE

I was fleeing	we were fleeing
you were fleeing	you were fleeing
he/she/it was fleeing	they were fleeing

• *The animals were fleeing from the forest fire.*

PRESENT PERFECT ... have | has fled
PAST PERFECT ... had fled

FUTURE ... will flee
FUTURE PROGRESSIVE ... will be fleeing
FUTURE PERFECT ... will have fled

PAST PASSIVE

Flee is rarely used in the passive voice.

COMPLEMENTS

flee *move/run away from danger/ unpleasantness, escape*

The fish fled when my shadow fell across the pond.
The deer fled when they heard the shot.
The birds fled before the coming storm.
The refugees fled into the woods.
The soldiers were fleeing back into the trenches.
The reporters had fled to the press bar.
Civilians were fleeing from the rampaging soldiers.

flee *move away swiftly, vanish*

The moon fled behind the clouds.
The ghostly shape fled from view.
Our shadows fled before us.

flee _____ *run away from*
   (*from*) OBJECT

The survivors quickly fled **(from) the scene of the explosion**.
The reporters fled **(from) the room** when the senator began his lengthy speech.
The entire city fled **(from) the rapidly rising floodwaters**.
The animals fled **(from) the burning barn**.
I fled **(from) the noisy, overcrowded arena**.

PRESENT

I fling	we fling
you fling	you fling
he/she/it flings	they fling

• *She flings her hair back if she's angry.*

PRESENT PROGRESSIVE

I am flinging	we are flinging
you are flinging	you are flinging
he/she/it is flinging	they are flinging

• *The dog is flinging dirt everywhere.*

PAST

I flung	we flung
you flung	you flung
he/she/it flung	they flung

• *He flung his clothes all over room.*

PAST PROGRESSIVE

I was flinging	we were flinging
you were flinging	you were flinging
he/she/it was flinging	they were flinging

• *The kids were flinging toys out the car window.*

PRESENT PERFECT ... have | has flung
PAST PERFECT ... had flung

FUTURE ... will fling
FUTURE PROGRESSIVE ... will be flinging
FUTURE PERFECT ... will have flung

PAST PASSIVE

I was flung	we were flung
you were flung	you were flung
he/she/it was flung	they were flung

• *The protesters were flung into police vans.*

COMPLEMENTS

fling _____ *move suddenly, scatter*
ADVERB OF PLACE TO/FROM

Roberta flung **out of the room.**
The leaves were flinging **all over the lawn.**

fling _____ *throw recklessly*
OBJECT + ADVERB OF PLACE TO/FROM

The kids had flung **their books** *everywhere.*
I flung **myself** *onto the sofa.*
The rioters had flung **the furniture** *in every direction.*
The wind was flinging **my raked leaves** *all over the lawn.*

fling _____ *cast, throw*
OBJECT + ADVERB OF PLACE TO/FROM

He flung **a rope** *over a tree limb.*
The cadets will fling **their caps** *into the air.*
I flung **a blanket** *over the shivering children.*
The fisherman is flinging **his net** *into the pond.*
The guards flung **him** *into an empty cell.*
The reporter flung **his shoe** *at the president.*

fling _____ *devote oneself entirely to*
REFLEXIVE PRONOUN + *into* OBJECT

I flung **myself** *into jazz.*
We flung **ourselves** *into the social scene.*
Freshmen tend to fling **themselves** *into too many activities.*
Frank flung **himself** *into his work.*

PHRASAL VERBS

fling SEP **around/aside/away/down/
in/off/out/up/etc.** *throw in a specified
direction*

The burglar flung away his loot as
  soon as he saw the cop.
Bill opened the car door and flung his jacket in.

EXPRESSIONS

fling caution to the wind *take a serious
risk*

Harry flung caution to the wind and
  jumped into the lake with all his clothes on.

fling [one's] head back *tilt one's head
back suddenly*

Don flung his head back and laughed.

fling _____ **(up) in [someone's] face**
confront [someone] with

She flung his extramarital affairs up in his face.

PRESENT		PRESENT PROGRESSIVE	
I flow	we flow	I am flowing	we are flowing
you flow	you flow	you are flowing	you are flowing
he/she/it flows	they flow	he/she/it is flowing	they are flowing

• *The river flows south from here.* • *The water is flowing into the drain.*

PAST		PAST PROGRESSIVE	
I flowed	we flowed	I was flowing	we were flowing
you flowed	you flowed	you were flowing	you were flowing
he/she/it flowed	they flowed	he/she/it was flowing	they were flowing

• *The stream flowed into the lake.* • *Money was flowing into his campaign.*

PRESENT PERFECT	... have | has flowed
PAST PERFECT	... had flowed

FUTURE	... will flow
FUTURE PROGRESSIVE	... will be flowing
FUTURE PERFECT	... will have flowed

PAST PASSIVE

Flow is rarely used in the passive voice.

────────────────────────(**COMPLEMENTS**)───

flow *move freely*
The river eventually flows into the Mississippi.
The clogged drain was finally beginning to flow.
The stream was flowing over the little dam.
Cold air was flowing in through the open window.
The wine was flowing freely.
Money was flowing out of the company like water.
The guests flowed easily from one room to another.

flow *proceed smoothly*
Mozart wanted his music to "flow like oil."
The conversation flowed around the table.
The wonderful smell of baking flowed throughout the house.
Ideas flowed easily at the conference.

flow *hang loosely*
Legolas's long blond hair flowed across his shoulders and
 down his back.

flow _____ *come from as a source*
 from OBJECT
The spring flowed **from a crack in the rocks.**
Wealth flows **from trade.**
Blood was flowing **from the boxer's nose.**

────────────────────────(**PHRASAL VERBS**)───

flow away/in/out/etc. *flow*
in a specified direction
People flowed away from the mall at closing time.
The tide flowed in and out.

PRESENT			PRESENT PROGRESSIVE	
I fly	we fly		I am flying	we are flying
you fly	you fly		you are flying	you are flying
he/she/it flies	they fly		he/she/it is flying	they are flying

• *Cathy flies to New York once a month.*   • *I am flying back tonight.*

PAST			PAST PROGRESSIVE	
I flew	we flew		I was flying	we were flying
you flew	you flew		you were flying	you were flying
he/she/it flew	they flew		he/she/it was flying	they were flying

• *I never flew in such a small plane before.*   • *The kids were flying kites in the park.*

PRESENT PERFECT ... have | has flown
PAST PERFECT ... had flown

FUTURE ... will fly
FUTURE PROGRESSIVE ... will be flying
FUTURE PERFECT ... will have flown

PAST PASSIVE	
I was flown	we were flown
you were flown	you were flown
he/she/it was flown	they were flown

• *The flags were flown at half-mast.*

(**COMPLEMENTS**)

fly *move through the air*	My hat flew into the air. The birds flew around us, screeching and squawking. The plane was flying at 36,000 feet.
fly *travel by aircraft*	Amelia Earhart was the first woman to fly solo across the Atlantic. When are you flying to Paris? Whoever thought that we could fly to the moon?
fly *wave/float in the air*	Flags were flying in the breeze. His shirttail was flying in the wind as he ran down the hill.
fly *move/spread/go/pass quickly*	The wood chips flew as the chain saw bit into the log. The door flew open, and in walked Grandmother. Rumors were flying everywhere. I'm already late for the meeting; I have to fly. My, how time flies.
fly *win acceptance*	His proposal will never fly with the voters. "Do you think the plan will fly?" "I think it will fly."
fly _____ *pilot / travel in [an aircraft]* OBJECT	My grandfather flew **fighter planes** in World War II. I flew **United** to Chicago.

fly _____ *transport by aircraft*
    OBJECT
 	
    PASSIVE
	
	We flew **the children** to England, where they would be safe.
	They flew **the engine** back to the manufacturer.
	The replacement parts were flown from Sweden.

fly _____ *cause to move through the air* OBJECT	 Didn't you fly **paper airplanes** when you were a kid? We always fly **the flag** on Memorial Day.

(**PHRASAL VERBS**)

fly away/back/down/in/out/over/ **up**/etc. *fly in a specified direction*	The robin flew down from its nest. The planes flew over in formation.
fly by *go quickly past*	Did you see the wild geese fly by, heading home again? January really flew by.
fly off *come off suddenly*	The truck's wheel flew off and hit Kathy's car.

PRESENT

I follow	we follow
you follow	you follow
he/she/it follows	they follow

• *The students never follow my advice.*

PRESENT PROGRESSIVE

I am following	we are following
you are following	you are following
he/she/it is following	they are following

• *I'm not following what you mean.*

PAST

I followed	we followed
you followed	you followed
he/she/it followed	they followed

• *The press followed his every move.*

PAST PROGRESSIVE

I was following	we were following
you were following	you were following
he/she/it was following	they were following

• *We were following their directions.*

PRESENT PERFECT ... have | has followed
PAST PERFECT ... had followed

FUTURE ... will follow
FUTURE PROGRESSIVE ... will be following
FUTURE PERFECT ... will have followed

PAST PASSIVE

I was followed	we were followed
you were followed	you were followed
he/she/it was followed	they were followed

• *The meeting was followed by a reception.*

COMPLEMENTS

follow *come/go after/behind*

Go ahead. I will follow.
When winter comes, spring will follow.

follow *occur as a result*

After a major forest fire, extensive erosion always follows.
When there is no planning, disaster will follow.

follow _____ *come/go after/behind*
OBJECT

Night follows **day**.
We followed **the guide** to the waterfall.
Police followed **the suspects** to their home.

follow _____ *occur as a result of*
OBJECT

Success follows **hard work**.
A big celebration followed **her election victory**.

follow _____ *obey, be guided by*
OBJECT

I was only following **orders**.
You didn't follow **the manual**.

WH-CLAUSE

You must follow **what you believe**.
He will follow **whatever advice you give him**.

follow _____ *understand*
OBJECT

Go ahead. I'm following **you** so far.
We followed **his explanations** pretty well.

WH-CLAUSE

I followed **what he was saying**.

follow _____ *pay close attention to*
OBJECT

She follows **every move the teacher makes**.
I don't follow **college basketball**.
We have followed **Senator Blather's career** with interest.

follow _____ *move forward on*
OBJECT

Follow **Highway 155** for seven miles.

PHRASAL VERBS

follow _____ **down/in/out/up**/etc.
follow in a specified direction

The dog followed Zack down to the village.
The chairman followed me out and congratulated me.

follow through/up (on _____ **)** *check on,*
find out more about, complete [a task]

My secretary will follow through on the woman's request.
The police followed up on several leads.

PRESENT

I forbid	we forbid
you forbid	you forbid
he/she/it forbids	they forbid

• *The law forbids the sale of handguns.*

PRESENT PROGRESSIVE

I am forbidding	we are forbidding
you are forbidding	you are forbidding
he/she/it is forbidding	they are forbidding

• *Sally's mother is forbidding any more parties.*

PAST

I forbade	we forbade
you forbade	you forbade
he/she/it forbade	they forbade

• *The police forbade parking on the street.*

PAST PROGRESSIVE

I was forbidding	we were forbidding
you were forbidding	you were forbidding
he/she/it was forbidding	they were forbidding

• *The department was forbidding fishing in the area.*

PRESENT PERFECT ... have | has forbidden
PAST PERFECT ... had forbidden

FUTURE ... will forbid
FUTURE PROGRESSIVE ... will be forbidding
FUTURE PERFECT ... will have forbidden

PAST PASSIVE

I was forbidden	we were forbidden
you were forbidden	you were forbidden
he/she/it was forbidden	they were forbidden

• *The lawyers were forbidden to talk to the press.*

COMPLEMENTS

forbid _____ *prohibit, not allow*

OBJECT	The law forbids **the sale of alcohol to minors.**
	Most religions forbid **marriage between close relatives.**
	My parents forbid **books at the dinner table.**
	Lack of time forbids **further explanation.**
PASSIVE	Campfires are forbidden in this area.
OBJECT + INFINITIVE	I forbid **you *to talk to me like that*.**
	Some churches forbid **priests *to marry*.**
	Jane's mother forbade **her *to go to the party*.**
PASSIVE	I was forbidden *to take pictures there.*
PRESENT PARTICIPLE	The new law forbids **smoking in public places.**
	The rules of soccer forbid **tripping an opponent.**
	My mother forbids **watching TV before finishing homework.**
	Space forbids **covering all the issues.**
PASSIVE	Using a cell phone in class is strictly forbidden.

EXPRESSIONS

God/Heaven forbid! *I hope it will not happen.*

God forbid that Mark should fall asleep
    and have an accident.
"Your ex-boyfriend is coming to the party."
    "Heaven forbid!"

PRESENT

I force	we force
you force	you force
he/she/it forces	they force

- *His silliness always forces me to smile.*

PRESENT PROGRESSIVE

I am forcing	we are forcing
you are forcing	you are forcing
he/she/it is forcing	they are forcing

- *The wind is forcing the boat off course.*

PAST

I forced	we forced
you forced	you forced
he/she/it forced	they forced

- *We forced them to apologize.*

PAST PROGRESSIVE

I was forcing	we were forcing
you were forcing	you were forcing
he/she/it was forcing	they were forcing

- *I was forcing myself to stay awake.*

PRESENT PERFECT ... have | has forced
PAST PERFECT ... had forced

FUTURE ... will force
FUTURE PROGRESSIVE ... will be forcing
FUTURE PERFECT ... will have forced

PAST PASSIVE

I was forced	we were forced
you were forced	you were forced
he/she/it was forced	they were forced

- *The door was forced open.*

COMPLEMENTS

force _____ move/open/break using effort

OBJECT
My husband forced **the desk** through the doorway.
We forced **three more candles** into the box.
The soldiers forced **the door**.
I had to force **the lock on the desk**.
The president forced **the legislation** through Congress.

force _____ produce/cause/compel

OBJECT
I finally forced **a smile** from her mother.
The police forced **a confession** from the murderer.
The police forced **the assailant** to his knees.
The coach forced **a faster pace**.

OBJECT + INFINITIVE
I forced **him** *to admit his mistake*.
We forced **the window** *to stay open*.
The storm forced **us** *to turn back*.
My grades forced **me** *to study harder*.

PASSIVE
The army was forced *to retreat*.

force _____ cause

OBJECT
The fourth-quarter touchdown forced **overtime**.
His statement forced **a murmur throughout the audience**.
The defeat forced **a cease-fire between the armies**.
Heavy snow is forcing **delays** at the airport.

PHRASAL VERBS

force _____ **back/down/in/out/up/etc.**
cause to move in a specified direction
The farmer forced the cows back
  into the barn.
The bad economic news forced the stock market down.
Peggy forced the medicine down.
We forced our way in.

EXPRESSIONS

force [someone's] hand *cause [someone]*
to act prematurely/unwillingly
The journalist didn't want to reveal
  her sources, but the judge forced her hand.

PRESENT		PRESENT PROGRESSIVE	
I forget	we forget	I am forgetting	we are forgetting
you forget	you forget	you are forgetting	you are forgetting
he/she/it forgets	they forget	he/she/it is forgetting	they are forgetting

  • *He always forgets to put the milk away.*   • *I'm always forgetting something.*

PAST		PAST PROGRESSIVE	
I forgot	we forgot	I was forgetting	we were forgetting
you forgot	you forgot	you were forgetting	you were forgetting
he/she/it forgot	they forgot	he/she/it was forgetting	they were forgetting

  • *I forgot his first name.*   • *I was forgetting what I was about to do.*

PRESENT PERFECT   ... have | has forgotten   FUTURE   ... will forget
PAST PERFECT   ... had forgotten   FUTURE PROGRESSIVE   ... will be forgetting
                                       FUTURE PERFECT   ... will have forgotten

PAST PASSIVE	
I was forgotten	we were forgotten
you were forgotten	you were forgotten
he/she/it was forgotten	they were forgotten

  • *The incident certainly wasn't forgotten.*

COMPLEMENTS

forget *fail to remember*

    Don't forget!
    He never forgets.
    They won't forget, will they?

forget _____ *fail to remember*

  OBJECT   I forgot **his e-mail address.**
               You must never forget **your password.**
               Don't forget **the flowers.**

  INFINITIVE   I forgot **to water the plants.**
               Don't forget **to run the dishwasher.**
               The kids always forget **to hang their coats up.**

  THAT-CLAUSE   We forgot **that we were having dinner with the Smiths tonight.**
               I forgot **that the meeting had been canceled.**
               She forgot **that she had to pick up the cat at the vet.**

  WH-CLAUSE   I forgot **what I was about to say.**
               He forgot **where he had put his car keys.**
               I will never forget **where we stayed in Florida.**

  WH-INFINITIVE   The author forgot **where to put the quote marks.**
               I forget **how to change my password.**

  PRESENT PARTICIPLE   I can't forget **taking her to the hospital.**
               He won't soon forget **doing that.**
               Did he forget **running into a tree?**

forget _____ *leave behind*

  OBJECT   Darn it. I forgot **my briefcase.**
               Don't forget **your hat** when you leave.
               People always forget **things** when they get off the plane.

forget _____ *neglect, disregard*

  (about) OBJECT   Don't forget **(about) your friends** when you send holiday cards.
               Sam forgot **(about) the ice cream in the trunk.**

EXPRESSIONS

Forget it! *Disregard it.*   "Do I have to clean the bathroom?"
                              "Forget it! I'll do it myself."

forget [oneself] *lose one's temper*   Peter forgot himself and cursed in front of the principal.

PRESENT

I forgive	we forgive
you forgive	you forgive
he/she/it forgives	they forgive

• *He forgives anything his daughter does.*

PRESENT PROGRESSIVE

I am forgiving	we are forgiving
you are forgiving	you are forgiving
he/she/it is forgiving	they are forgiving

• *I'm forgiving part of their debt.*

PAST

I forgave	we forgave
you forgave	you forgave
he/she/it forgave	they forgave

• *I forgave him for forgetting my birthday.*

PAST PROGRESSIVE

I was forgiving	we were forgiving
you were forgiving	you were forgiving
he/she/it was forgiving	they were forgiving

• *They were always forgiving my mistakes.*

PRESENT PERFECT ... have | has forgiven
PAST PERFECT ... had forgiven

FUTURE ... will forgive
FUTURE PROGRESSIVE ... will be forgiving
FUTURE PERFECT ... will have forgiven

PAST PASSIVE

I was forgiven	we were forgiven
you were forgiven	you were forgiven
he/she/it was forgiven	they were forgiven

• *You were forgiven for making such a mistake.*

COMPLEMENTS

forgive *pardon*

He forgives readily.
She can forgive without being superior about it.
I can't forgive so easily.

forgive _____ *excuse, pardon, stop feeling angry/punitive about/toward*

OBJECT
I tried to forgive **his insensitive behavior.**
Some people never forgive **even the smallest slight.**

PASSIVE
My sister was always forgiven, no matter what she had done.

OBJECT + *for* OBJECT
I forgave **Don** *for his thoughtless remark.*
Please forgive **me** *for this interruption.*

OBJECT + *for* PRESENT PARTICIPLE
Will she forgive **him** *for forgetting their anniversary*?
Can you forgive **me** *for being so late*?
I'll never forgive **her** *for eating the last piece of cake.*

forgive _____ *cancel payment of [a debt]*

OBJECT
Many parents forgive **their children's loans.**
The bank may temporarily forgive **interest payments on house loans.**
Some schools will forgive **a percentage of student loans.**

EXPRESSIONS

Forgive and forget. [PROVERB]
Pardon an offense, and forget it ever happened.

You could punish him forever—or just forgive and forget.

PRESENT

I form	we form
you form	you form
he/she/it forms	they form

- *A river forms the state's eastern boundary.*

PRESENT PROGRESSIVE

I am forming	we are forming
you are forming	you are forming
he/she/it is forming	they are forming

- *The data is forming a pattern.*

PAST

I formed	we formed
you formed	you formed
he/she/it formed	they formed

- *They formed a new company.*

PAST PROGRESSIVE

I was forming	we were forming
you were forming	you were forming
he/she/it was forming	they were forming

- *Clouds were forming above the mountains.*

PRESENT PERFECT   ... have | has formed
PAST PERFECT   ... had formed

FUTURE   ... will form
FUTURE PROGRESSIVE ... will be forming
FUTURE PERFECT   ... will have formed

PAST PASSIVE

I was formed	we were formed
you were formed	you were formed
he/she/it was formed	they were formed

- *The soldiers were quickly formed into a line.*

──────────────── (COMPLEMENTS)────────

form *assume a definite shape/structure*	An idea slowly formed in my mind.
	Tornadoes were forming along the storm front.
	The soldiers quickly formed into battlelines.
	When you look at any game of chance, patterns form— real or not.
form _____ *give a definite shape/structure to*	
OBJECT + *into* OBJECT	Form **the dough** *into a small ball*.
	The captain formed **the men** *into an effective fighting force*.
	The workers formed **the mud** *into adobe bricks*.
form _____ *create*	
OBJECT	My buddies and I formed **a motorcycle club**.
	If you arrange the pieces in a certain way, they form **a picture**.
form _____ *make up, constitute*	
OBJECT	The first ten amendments form **the Bill of Rights**.
	Greek and Roman statues form **the core of the museum collection**.
	The "-ed" ending forms **the regular past tense in English**.
	These three stars form **Orion's belt**.
form _____ *develop*	
OBJECT	A good education forms **the mind**.
	As a child, I formed **good study habits**.

PRESENT	
I freeze	we freeze
you freeze	you freeze
he/she/it freezes	they freeze

• *It usually freezes by mid-October.*

PRESENT PROGRESSIVE	
I am freezing	we are freezing
you are freezing	you are freezing
he/she/it is freezing	they are freezing

• *I'm freezing out here.*

PAST	
I froze	we froze
you froze	you froze
he/she/it froze	they froze

• *The bank froze their assets.*

PAST PROGRESSIVE	
I was freezing	we were freezing
you were freezing	you were freezing
he/she/it was freezing	they were freezing

• *They were freezing raspberries from their garden.*

PRESENT PERFECT ... have | has frozen
PAST PERFECT ... had frozen

FUTURE ... will freeze
FUTURE PROGRESSIVE ... will be freezing
FUTURE PERFECT ... will have frozen

PAST PASSIVE	
I was frozen	we were frozen
you were frozen	you were frozen
he/she/it was frozen	they were frozen

• *The water pipes were all frozen.*

COMPLEMENTS

freeze *harden into ice, become solid due to cold*
The muddy roads would soon freeze.
The rivers all froze that dreadful winter.

freeze *become uncomfortably/ dangerously cold*
Put on a hat or your ears will freeze.
Turn up the heat; the room is freezing.
The mountain climbers nearly froze to death.

freeze *be at or below 32° Fahrenheit*
The weatherman says it will freeze tonight.

freeze *be preserved in a very cold place*
Girl Scout cookies freeze well.

freeze *become motionless*
The rabbits froze when they heard the hawk.
His face froze when he heard us coming.

freeze *be damaged/destroyed by frost*
My petunias all froze last night.

freeze _____ *cause (the contents of) to harden into ice or other solid*
OBJECT
We froze **a couple of trays of ice**.
The cold snap froze **our garden hoses**.

freeze _____ *chill, make uncomfortably/dangerously cold*
OBJECT
The wind was freezing **my fingers**.
The driving rain froze **the crowd watching the game**.

freeze _____ *preserve in a very cold place*
OBJECT
We can freeze **the leftover vegetable soup**.

freeze _____ *cause to become motionless*
OBJECT
The shout froze **everyone** in the store.
The peace agreement froze **the armies** in place.
The accident froze **traffic** for hours.

freeze _____ *fix at a certain level*
OBJECT
The Federal Reserve froze **the interest rate** today.

freeze _____ *prohibit, restrict*
OBJECT
The government froze **foreign assets** today.

PHRASAL VERBS

freeze over *become covered with ice*
The lake froze over, and we went ice skating.

freeze up *stop functioning*
I just freeze up when I have to talk to a group of people.
If there is a power surge, my computer completely freezes up.

PRESENT

I frighten	we frighten
you frighten	you frighten
he/she/it frightens	they frighten

• *That costume frightens me.*

PRESENT PROGRESSIVE

I am frightening	we are frightening
you are frightening	you are frightening
he/she/it is frightening	they are frightening

• *You are frightening the children.*

PAST

I frightened	we frightened
you frightened	you frightened
he/she/it frightened	they frightened

• *The storm frightened the animals.*

PAST PROGRESSIVE

I was frightening	we were frightening
you were frightening	you were frightening
he/she/it was frightening	they were frightening

• *He was frightening everyone with his strange talk.*

PRESENT PERFECT ... have | has frightened
PAST PERFECT ... had frightened

FUTURE ... will frighten
FUTURE PROGRESSIVE ... will be frightening
FUTURE PERFECT ... will have frightened

PAST PASSIVE

I was frightened	we were frightened
you were frightened	you were frightened
he/she/it was frightened	they were frightened

• *All of us were frightened by the earthquake.*

COMPLEMENTS

frighten *become scared*

Harry frightens easily.
Investors frighten at any unexpected bad news.
The horses will frighten if you do that.

frighten _____ *scare*
  OBJECT

Icy roads frighten **me**.
The rumors frightened **the whole city**.
His accident frightened **all of us**.
The CEO's strange actions frightened **the shareholders**.
"I don't know what effect these men will have upon the enemy, but, by God, they frighten **me**." [DUKE OF WELLINGTON]

  PASSIVE

We were frightened by what he said.

frighten _____ *force by scaring*
  OBJECT + into OBJECT
  OBJECT + into PRESENT PARTICIPLE

The police frightened **him** *into a confession*.
The police frightened **him** *into confessing*.
The weather forecast frightened **us** *into canceling our trip*.
The bad economic news frightened **me** *into selling my stock in the company*.

  PASSIVE

I was frightened *into cooperating with them*.

frighten _____ *prevent by scaring*
  OBJECT + out of PRESENT PARTICIPLE

The crime reports frightened **my neighbors** *out of going downtown*.

PHRASAL VERBS

frighten _SEP_ **away/off** *cause to go/stay away by scaring*

Our dog frightened the burglar away.
We were frightened off by the unruly Mardi Gras crowd.

EXPRESSIONS

frighten _____ **to death** *scare badly*

His costume frightened me to death.

PRESENT

I furnish	we furnish
you furnish	you furnish
he/she/it furnishes	they furnish

• *The hotel furnishes beach towels.*

PRESENT PROGRESSIVE

I am furnishing	we are furnishing
you are furnishing	you are furnishing
he/she/it is furnishing	they are furnishing

• *We are furnishing everything free of charge.*

PAST

I furnished	we furnished
you furnished	you furnished
he/she/it furnished	they furnished

• *They furnished the suite quite nicely.*

PAST PROGRESSIVE

I was furnishing	we were furnishing
you were furnishing	you were furnishing
he/she/it was furnishing	they were furnishing

• *They were furnishing information about the victims.*

PRESENT PERFECT ... have | has furnished
PAST PERFECT ... had furnished

FUTURE ... will furnish
FUTURE PROGRESSIVE ... will be furnishing
FUTURE PERFECT ... will have furnished

PAST PASSIVE

I was furnished	we were furnished
you were furnished	you were furnished
he/she/it was furnished	they were furnished

• *The stables were furnished with clean straw.*

── **COMPLEMENTS** ──

furnish ____ *provide, supply*

OBJECT
We furnished **everything they needed.**
Our company furnished **the computers and printers.**
The landscapers furnished **all the flowers and trees.**

PASSIVE
The table decorations were furnished by the host committee.

INDIRECT OBJECT + DIRECT OBJECT
The government furnished *him* **a new identity.**
The car rental agency furnished *us* **an SUV.**
He furnished *the police* **a solid alibi.**

for PARAPHRASE
The government furnished **a new identity** *for him.*
The car rental agency furnished **an SUV** *for us.*
He furnished **a solid alibi** *for the police.*

furnish ____ *provide furniture for*

OBJECT
They furnished **the room** with everything.
An interior decorator furnished **the model house.**

PASSIVE
The guest cottage is completely furnished.

PRESENT

I gain	we gain
you gain	you gain
he/she/it gains	they gain

• *My watch gains three minutes a day.*

PRESENT PROGRESSIVE

I am gaining	we are gaining
you are gaining	you are gaining
he/she/it is gaining	they are gaining

• *We are gaining on them.*

PAST

I gained	we gained
you gained	you gained
he/she/it gained	they gained

• *I gained six pounds over the holidays.*

PAST PROGRESSIVE

I was gaining	we were gaining
you were gaining	you were gaining
he/she/it was gaining	they were gaining

• *The baby was gaining weight normally.*

PRESENT PERFECT ... have | has gained
PAST PERFECT ... had gained

FUTURE ... will gain
FUTURE PROGRESSIVE ... will be gaining
FUTURE PERFECT ... will have gained

PAST PASSIVE

—	—
—	—
it was gained	they were gained

• *His fortune was gained in commodities trading.*

COMPLEMENTS

gain _____ *benefit*
    ADVERB OF MANNER

Barney will gain **politically** from redistricting.
Kenny gained **career-wise** from interning with an ad agency.
Peter gained **in maturity** by joining the Peace Corps.
Bertha gained **in wisdom and experience**.

gain _____ *increase*
    ADVERB OF MANNER

The market has gained **steadily** over the last week.
My art collection has gained **in value** every year.

    OBJECT

I can gain **weight** just by looking at a package of cookies.
The hurricane gained **strength** as it approached land.
The Dow gained **two percent** today.
The company needs to gain **market share**.

gain _____ *get as an increase/advantage*
    OBJECT

We will gain **half an hour** by taking the shortcut.
You gain **time** when you fly westward.
We can gain **six inches** by moving the cabinet over.
He gained **a few seconds** on us every time we circled the track.

gain _____ *acquire, earn, win*
    OBJECT

They gained **control of the company**.
She gained **friends** easily.
The attack gained **the high ground**.
We hope to gain **recognition** with lots of TV commercials.
His argument gained **a number of followers**.

    INDIRECT OBJECT + DIRECT OBJECT

His speech gained *him* **a large following**.
The treaty gained *us* **several important trade concessions**.
The deal gained *the company* **a lot of publicity**.

    for PARAPHRASE

His speech gained **a large following** *for him*.
The treaty gained **several important trade concessions** *for us*.
The deal gained **a lot of publicity** *for the company*.

PHRASAL VERBS

gain on _____ *catch up to*

The yellow car was gaining on us rapidly.

PRESENT

I gather	we gather
you gather	you gather
he/she/it gathers	they gather

• *I gather that there is a problem.*

PRESENT PROGRESSIVE

I am gathering	we are gathering
you are gathering	you are gathering
he/she/it is gathering	they are gathering

• *I am gathering them together now.*

PAST

I gathered	we gathered
you gathered	you gathered
he/she/it gathered	they gathered

• *The soldiers gathered their gear.*

PAST PROGRESSIVE

I was gathering	we were gathering
you were gathering	you were gathering
he/she/it was gathering	they were gathering

• *He was gathering wild mushrooms for restaurants.*

PRESENT PERFECT ... have | has gathered
PAST PERFECT ... had gathered

FUTURE ... will gather
FUTURE PROGRESSIVE ... will be gathering
FUTURE PERFECT ... will have gathered

PAST PASSIVE

I was gathered	we were gathered
you were gathered	you were gathered
he/she/it was gathered	they were gathered

• *The blanket was gathered about the baby.*

───────────────────────────────(**COMPLEMENTS**)───

gather *cluster, come together*

Clouds were gathering in the west.
A mob was gathering in front of the gate.
A worldwide economic crisis was gathering.
The hungry cows gathered along the fence.
At sunset the birds all gather in the trees.

gather _____ *collect, bring together*

OBJECT

She was out gathering **flowers**.
I gathered **the children** around me.
He tried to gather **his scattered thoughts**.
His collection of rare books was just gathering **dust
in the basement**.
I tried to gather **my courage**.

WH-CLAUSE

They gathered **what provisions they still had**.
The bus gathered **whoever wanted to go on the field trip**.
Rescuers gathered **whatever survivors they could find**.

gather _____ *gain gradually*

OBJECT

The truck gathered **speed** on the open highway.
The proposal had gathered **a lot of support**.

gather _____ *conclude*

THAT-CLAUSE

They gathered **that the young couple wanted to be left alone**.
We gathered **that the trip to London was off**.
I gather **that the meeting wasn't a great success**.

gather _____ *pull/fold together*

OBJECT

We gathered **our cloaks** about us tightly.
She gathered **her hair** into a tight bun.
I gathered **the cloth** and stitched it.
The sailors gathered **the sails**.

PRESENT

I get	we get
you get	you get
he/she/it gets	they get

• *He gets to sleep late on weekends.*

PRESENT PROGRESSIVE

I am getting	we are getting
you are getting	you are getting
he/she/it is getting	they are getting

• *I'm getting ready now.*

PAST

I got	we got
you got	you got
he/she/it got	they got

• *We got good feedback on the proposal.*

PAST PROGRESSIVE

I was getting	we were getting
you were getting	you were getting
he/she/it was getting	they were getting

• *The plan was getting a lot of criticism.*

PRESENT PERFECT ... have | has got/gotten
PAST PERFECT ... had got/gotten

FUTURE ... will get
FUTURE PROGRESSIVE ... will be getting
FUTURE PERFECT ... will have got/gotten

PAST PASSIVE

I was got/gotten	we were got/gotten
you were got/gotten	you were got/gotten
he/she/it was got/gotten	they were got/gotten

• *Permission was gotten from the authorities.*

COMPLEMENTS

NOTE: *Get* is also used as a helping verb to form the passive voice.

get + PAST PARTICIPLE

The burglar got caught by police.
I got injured playing football.
Bobby got sent to the principal's office.
We'll get married in October.

get _____ *receive, obtain*

  OBJECT

They got **permission** to leave early.
I got **a "B"** in Social Studies last quarter.
I got **a traffic ticket** last night.
The company got **an award for community service**.
I'm getting **a busy signal**.
We are getting **a new car**.

  PASSIVE

Permission to leave early was gotten.

get _____ *bring*

  INDIRECT OBJECT + DIRECT OBJECT

Get *me* **a coffee**, will you?
I will get *her* **a blanket**.

  for PARAPHRASE

Get **a coffee** *for me*, will you?
I will get **a blanket** *for her*.

get _____ *notice, understand*

  OBJECT

Did you get **that smirky look on his face**?
"Did you get **the joke**?" "Yes, I got **it**."

  WH-CLAUSE

I got **what he was trying to say**.
Did you get **how he avoided talking to us**?

get _____ *become*

  PREDICATE ADJECTIVE

He really got **angry** about it.
I got **sick** on the way back.
The dogs got **loose** and headed for the barn.

get _____ *begin, start*

  PRESENT PARTICIPLE

Let's get **going**.

get _____ *have the opportunity, receive permission*

  INFINITIVE

We will get **to meet them at the reception**.
The kids get **to stay up late tonight**.

get _____ *cause/persuade [to do/be]*

OBJECT + PREDICATE ADJECTIVE

Get **your hands** *clean* before coming to the table.
I got **the computer screen** *dirty*.

OBJECT + INFINITIVE

I got **the kids** *to clean up their room*.
We finally got **the truck** *to start*.

OBJECT + PRESENT PARTICIPLE

I got **the kids** *cleaning up their room*.
It got **me** *thinking about a new solution*.

OBJECT + PAST PARTICIPLE

I finally got **my computer** *fixed*.
We got **our house** *painted*.

get _____ *arrive at*

ADVERB OF PLACE TO/FROM

Our parents got **home** early.
We can get **to the office** in 15 minutes.

get _____ *travel*

ADVERB OF PLACE TO/FROM

Did you get **to Paris** last summer?
I got **as far as Chicago**.

get _____ *cause to move*

OBJECT + ADVERB OF PLACE TO/FROM

Can you get **me** *to the airport* in 30 minutes?
I got **the car** *out of the garage*.

get _____ *be affected/infected by*

OBJECT

I got **the hiccups** just before I went on stage.
Can you get **the flu** from a flu shot?

NOTE: For the following two meanings, *get* is used only in the present perfect tense.

get _____ *have, possess*

OBJECT

I've got **a terrible cold**.
I've only got **about $20** on me.

get _____ *must*

INFINITIVE

I've got **to go now**.
He has got **to be more careful**.

(**PHRASAL VERBS**)

get across/back/down/in/out/up/etc.
move in a specified direction

The police ordered the crowd to get back.
She opened the car door and told him to get in.

get _SEP_ **in/out**/etc. *take/bring in a
specified direction*

Did you get the firewood in?
He got the cheese and crackers out.

get around/out *become known*

The news got around that they were divorced.

get around _____ *avoid*

He got around the problem by installing new software.

get away with _____ *do without
being punished*

The company got away with selling pirated software.

get back to _____ *respond to*

I must get back to Anthony tomorrow.

get behind (on _____ **)** *be late making
payments (on [something])*

Lots of people have gotten behind on their mortgages.

get by (on/with _____ **)** *manage to
survive/do (with [something])*

Amos gets by on $750 a month.
Our neighbors get by with just one car.

get in/into _____ *be admitted to*

Our son got into nursing school.

get out of _____ *avoid,
escape*

Harold got out of doing dishes four nights in a row.

get over _____ *recover from*

Pat got over the flu in three days.

get up *rise*

It's 7 o'clock—time to get up.
Please get up and get me a fork.

get _____ **up** *cause to rise*

Mom got us up before dawn.

I give   we give
you give   you give
he/she/it gives   they give

• *He gives 10% of his income to charity.*

I am giving   we are giving
you are giving   you are giving
he/she/it is giving   they are giving

• *I'm giving up on it.*

PAST

I gave   we gave
you gave   you gave
he/she/it gave   they gave

• *The company gave me a car to use.*

PAST PROGRESSIVE

I was giving   we were giving
you were giving   you were giving
he/she/it was giving   they were giving

• *We were giving a party that evening.*

PRESENT PERFECT ... have | has given
PAST PERFECT   ... had given

FUTURE   ... will give
FUTURE PROGRESSIVE ... will be giving
FUTURE PERFECT   ... will have given

PAST PASSIVE

I was given   we were given
you were given   you were given
he/she/it was given   they were given

• *All of the employees were given entry cards.*

(**COMPLEMENTS**)

give *make a gift/donation*

How much can you give?
They always give generously to the homeless shelter.

give *yield, collapse*

For the deadlock to be broken, something has to give.
The floor might give if we put that much weight on it.

give _____ *make a gift of, donate*
   INDIRECT OBJECT + DIRECT OBJECT

Terry gave *Dan* **a new computer**.
Spanky gave *Alfalfa* **the high sign**.

   to PARAPHRASE

Terry gave **a new computer** *to Dan*.
Spanky gave **the high sign** *to Alfalfa*.

give _____ *convey physically*
   OBJECT

She gave **a little smile** at the news.

   INDIRECT OBJECT + DIRECT OBJECT

Leo gave *the president* **a copy of the report**.
She gave *the boys* **a dirty look**.

   to PARAPHRASE

Leo gave **a copy of the report** *to the president*.
She gave **a dirty look** *to the boys*.

give _____ *provide*
   OBJECT

Soy-based inks give **good results**.

   INDIRECT OBJECT + DIRECT OBJECT

Give *me* **a chance to prove myself**.
This gives *gays and lesbians* **the right to marry**.
The boss gave *his cousin* **a job**.

   to PARAPHRASE

The boss gave **a job** *to his cousin*.

give _____ *host*
   OBJECT

We will give **the reception** in his honor.

   INDIRECT OBJECT + DIRECT OBJECT

I gave *my parents* **a surprise party**.
We gave *the seniors* **a graduation party**.

   for PARAPHRASE

I gave **a surprise party** *for my parents*.
We gave **a graduation party** *for the seniors*.

   PASSIVE

A graduation party was given for the seniors.
The seniors were given a graduation party.

give _____ *present*
   OBJECT

The senator is giving **a speech** on TV.
He gave **a good argument** against the proposal.

give _____ *perform*
   OBJECT

The symphony gave **a concert** last night.
The band gave **a free concert** to benefit AIDS victims.

give _____ *cause to have*
   INDIRECT OBJECT + DIRECT OBJECT

Loud music gives *me* **a headache**.

give _____ *pay*
   OBJECT

Michelle gave **$125** for her outfit.

give _____ *administer*
   INDIRECT OBJECT + DIRECT OBJECT

Freddie gave *the guard* **a punch in the mouth**.
Darla's mom gave *her* **some cough syrup**.

   to PARAPHRASE

Darla's mom gave **some cough syrup** *to her*.

give _____ *cause*
   OBJECT + INFINITIVE

You gave **me *to understand that you would support us***.
He gave **Jackson *to believe that the problem was solved***.

give _____ *sentence to*
   INDIRECT OBJECT + DIRECT OBJECT

The judge gave *the criminal* **30 days in jail**.

give _____ *sacrifice*
   OBJECT + *for* OBJECT

"It is sweet and right to give **your life** *for your country*."
   [HORACE]

give _____ *devote*
   OBJECT + *to* OBJECT

Marvin gave **his whole life** *to the cause of justice*.

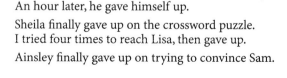

give _SEP_ away *betray*

A club member gave away our
   secret meeting place.

give _SEP_ back *return*

You'll have to give the engagement ring back.

give in (to _____) *surrender*
(to [someone/something])

After arguing for two hours, our opponents gave in.
Senator Blather gave in to pressure from his colleagues.

give it to _____ *scold, punish*

My boss really gave it to me when I walked in late.

give off _____ *release, emit*

The compost is giving off an earthy smell.
The laptop gives off a lot of heat.

give out *come to an end*

The settlers' food gave out after three weeks.

give out *wear out, stop operating*

After 203,000 miles, our 1979 Oldsmobile finally gave out.

give _SEP_ out *distribute*

C.J. gave out the president's itinerary.

give _SEP_ out *make known*

Don't give out your cell phone number.

give out _____ *produce*

This old furnace gives out a lot of heat.

give _SEP_ up *stop, cease*

Mom and Dad gave up smoking at the same time.

give _SEP_ up *surrender, yield*

Within an hour, the gunman gave up two hostages.
An hour later, he gave himself up.

give up (on _____) *admit failure*
(with [something])

Sheila finally gave up on the crossword puzzle.
I tried four times to reach Lisa, then gave up.

give up (on _____) *stop trying ([to do])*

Ainsley finally gave up on trying to convince Sam.

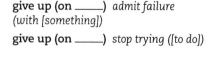

PRESENT

I go	we go
you go	you go
he/she/it goes	they go

  • *He goes to all their home games.*

PRESENT PROGRESSIVE

I am going	we are going
you are going	you are going
he/she/it is going	they are going

  • *I'm going now.*

PAST

I went	we went
you went	you went
he/she/it went	they went

  • *We never went to Spain.*

PAST PROGRESSIVE

I was going	we were going
you were going	you were going
he/she/it was going	they were going

  • *The party was going very well.*

PRESENT PERFECT	… have | has gone
PAST PERFECT	… had gone

FUTURE	… will go
FUTURE PROGRESSIVE	… will be going
FUTURE PERFECT	… will have gone

PAST PASSIVE

Go is never used in the passive voice. *Gone* in sentences like *He is gone* is a past participle functioning as an adjective.

(**COMPLEMENTS**)

go *depart, leave*	Please go.
	I'm going as soon as I can get packed.
	The seasons come and go.
go *function*	The engine won't go.
go *become worse, fail*	I think my hearing is going.
	For most athletes, the knees are the first thing to go.
go *be eliminated/discarded*	I'm afraid that Smith will have to go.
go *be worded, sung*	The song goes like this … la la di la la, la la di da.
go _____ *travel*	
ADVERB OF PLACE TO/FROM	I'm going **to Dallas** tomorrow.
	We are going **to lunch** now.
	Where do they go on vacation?
go _____ *proceed, move*	
ADVERB OF MANNER	The car in the left lane is going **too slow**.
	I'm going **as fast as I can.**
go _____ *extend, lead*	
ADVERB OF PLACE TO/FROM	Route 66 originally went **from Chicago to Los Angeles.**
	Delta goes **everywhere in the Southeast.**
	That door goes **to the kitchen.**
go _____ *pass*	
ADVERB OF MANNER	The evening went **too quickly.**
go _____ *progress*	
ADVERB OF MANNER	The meeting is going **well.**
	How is it going?
go _____ *be, become, turn out*	
PREDICATE ADJECTIVE	The soldiers went **hungry** for days.
	I think the cheese has gone **bad.**
	How many banks have gone **bankrupt**?
	My e-mails to her have all gone **unanswered.**
go _____ *attend*	
to OBJECT	Dad went **to college** on the G.I. Bill.
	Sidney went **to Harvard Law School.**
	Our family goes **to church** on Sunday.
	Let's go **to a movie** tonight.

go _____ *engage in [a sport/leisure activity]*
PRESENT PARTICIPLE

We plan to go **skiing** in Idaho.
They went **dancing** last night.

go _____ *do [something inadvisable]* [USED ONLY IN THE NEGATIVE; INFORMAL]
PRESENT PARTICIPLE

Don't go **telling everyone about it**.
We won't go **running to him with all our problems**.

go _____ *belong*
ADVERB OF PLACE

Coats go **in the closet**, not **on the floor**.

go _____ *be sent*
to OBJECT

The proposal went by e-mail **to all department heads**.

go _____ *be given/sold*
to OBJECT

The prize goes **to the lady in the blue sweater**.
The antique lamp goes **to bidder No. 17**.

(PHRASAL VERBS)

go back/down/in/out/up/etc. *move in a specified direction*	He went back to check the furnace. Ed went out to watch the sunset.
go against _____ *oppose, be contrary to*	She'll go against the incumbent in the fall election. Dispensing birth control pills goes against his conscience.
go along with _____ *agree with*	The president went along with his staff on the issue.
go away *end*	My headache went away before lunch.
go back to _____ *date back to*	The New Year's Eve custom goes back to Druid times.
go back to _____ *resume*	It's four in the morning—go back to sleep.
go by _____ *be known as*	His real name is Meredith, but he goes by Snuffy.
go down *decrease*	The swelling has slowly gone down. The temperature went down 18 degrees in one hour.
go down *stop functioning*	Cable service went down at 9:36 this morning.
go for _____ *be attracted by*	She goes for men with beards.
go for _____ *do [an activity]*	Let's go for a swim.
go for _____ *sell for [an amount]*	How much did the dining room set go for?
go into _____ *begin a career in*	Steve went into electronics, and Stuart went into medicine.
go off *explode, fire*	The gun went off accidentally.
go off *take place, happen*	The surprise party went off as planned.
go on *be switched on*	All of a sudden, the lights went on.
go on *happen*	What went on at yesterday's meeting? What's going on?
go on (_____) *continue ([doing])*	Forrest Gump just went on running. How long will the concert go on?
go out *be extinguished*	The lights went out one by one.
go through _____ *spend, consume*	We go through $5,000 a month. Our son goes through two gallons of milk a week.
go through _____ *examine*	She went through her mail during supper.
go under *fail*	A third of all small businesses go under.
go up *be built*	A new mall is going up on the edge of town.
go up *increase*	The stock market has gone up 225 points.
go with _____ *harmonize with*	This tie would go well with your blue suit. That paisley shirt doesn't go with anything.
go without _____ *manage without*	The prisoners went without food for nine days.

top 40 verb

PRESENT

I grant	we grant
you grant	you grant
he/she/it grants	they grant

- *The group grants awards to young artists.*

PRESENT PROGRESSIVE

I am granting	we are granting
you are granting	you are granting
he/she/it is granting	they are granting

- *They are granting a dozen awards this year.*

PAST

I granted	we granted
you granted	you granted
he/she/it granted	they granted

- *They granted me a leave of absence.*

PAST PROGRESSIVE

I was granting	we were granting
you were granting	you were granting
he/she/it was granting	they were granting

- *They were not granting any more loans.*

PRESENT PERFECT	... have | has granted
PAST PERFECT	... had granted

FUTURE	... will grant
FUTURE PROGRESSIVE	... will be granting
FUTURE PERFECT	... will have granted

PAST PASSIVE

I was granted	we were granted
you were granted	you were granted
he/she/it was granted	they were granted

- *Your request was granted.*

COMPLEMENTS

grant _____ *give, confer*

OBJECT	The not-for-profit granted **three scholarships** last year.
	The local government grants **home beautification awards**.
INDIRECT OBJECT + DIRECT OBJECT	Our government grants *other countries* emergency relief.
to PARAPHRASE	Our government grants **emergency relief** *to other countries*.

grant _____ *agree to allow/fulfill*

OBJECT	The fairy godmother granted **her every wish**.
	We can only grant **approved applications**.
	The judge granted **the lawyer's motion**.
INDIRECT OBJECT + DIRECT OBJECT	The president can grant *the refugees* asylum.
	They will grant *you* your freedom.
	She granted *the children* three wishes.
to PARAPHRASE	The president can grant **asylum** *to the refugees*.
	They will grant **your freedom** *to you*.
	She granted **three wishes** *to the children*.
WH-CLAUSE	The court granted **what we had requested**.
	The agency can grant **whatever amounts it wishes to**.
	The wizard will grant **whatever wish Dorothy makes**.

grant _____ *admit, assume*

INDIRECT OBJECT + DIRECT OBJECT	I granted *her* the point.
to PARAPHRASE	I granted **the point** *to her*.
THAT-CLAUSE	He granted **that I had a legitimate point**.
	I will grant **that his position is pretty solid**.
	Let's grant for the moment **that this is the case**.

grant _____ *transfer [real estate by deed]*

OBJECT	A deed grants **legal ownership of property**.
	Only a court officer can grant **a deed**.
PASSIVE	Our property was granted by the county.

EXPRESSIONS

Granted, ... *I/We admit that ...*	Granted, the conversation should not have been recorded.

PRESENT		PRESENT PROGRESSIVE	
I grind	we grind	I am grinding	we are grinding
you grind	you grind	you are grinding	you are grinding
he/she/it grinds	they grind	he/she/it is grinding	they are grinding

• *Poverty grinds everyone down.*

• *They are grinding their rusty swords and spears.*

PAST		PAST PROGRESSIVE	
I ground	we ground	I was grinding	we were grinding
you ground	you ground	you were grinding	you were grinding
he/she/it ground	they ground	he/she/it was grinding	they were grinding

• *We ground some more coffee.*

• *I was grinding my teeth in my sleep.*

PRESENT PERFECT ... have | has ground
PAST PERFECT ... had ground

FUTURE ... will grind
FUTURE PROGRESSIVE ... will be grinding
FUTURE PERFECT ... will have ground

PAST PASSIVE	
I was ground	we were ground
you were ground	you were ground
he/she/it was ground	they were ground

• *The gear teeth were ground pretty badly.*

COMPLEMENTS

grind *crush, sharpen/smooth/press by rubbing*

The wheels of justice grind slow, but
    they grind exceeding fine. [PROVERB]
The mill grinds continuously when the harvest comes in.

grind *clash/grate noisily*

The gears ground whenever I tried to shift.
His teeth were grinding loudly.
The axle wheels were grinding and squeaking.

grind _____ *crush into powder / tiny pieces*

    OBJECT

The wheel grinds **the seeds**, separating wheat from chaff.
The miller is grinding **the corn** into meal.
The heavy tanks ground **the road** to rubble.
The editorial ground **the opposition's argument** to shreds.

    PASSIVE

The corn is ground into meal.

grind _____ *sharpen/smooth by rubbing*

    OBJECT

We ground **all the edges** until they shone.
The lens maker ground **the glass** until it was perfectly smooth.

grind _____ *rub together forcefully*

    OBJECT

He grinds **his teeth** when he gets really upset.

grind _____ *press/rub with a circular motion*

    OBJECT

He ground **the black widow spider** under his heel.
They ground **the dried herbs** with their hands.

grind _____ *oppress*

    OBJECT

The tyrant ground **the colonists** with excessive taxes.

PHRASAL VERBS

grind away at _____ *work steadily on*

She ground away at her thesis.

grind SEP **down** *reduce and destroy [someone's] enthusiasm*

This job really grinds me down.

grind _____ **into** *rub into*

The workers ground dirt into the carpet.

grind on *continue, seemingly endlessly*

The Vietnam War ground on for six more years.

grind SEP **out** *produce mechanically, churn out*

The novelist grinds out a chapter a day.

grind SEP **up** *reduce to small pieces*

Bill grinds the coffee beans up very fine.

PRESENT

I grow	we grow
you grow	you grow
he/she/it grows	they grow

• *He grows wheat and barley on his land.*

PRESENT PROGRESSIVE

I am growing	we are growing
you are growing	you are growing
he/she/it is growing	they are growing

• *He is growing up.*

PAST

I grew	we grew
you grew	you grew
he/she/it grew	they grew

• *The kids grew a lot this year.*

PAST PROGRESSIVE

I was growing	we were growing
you were growing	you were growing
he/she/it was growing	they were growing

• *The passengers were growing angry at the delay.*

PRESENT PERFECT ... have | has grown
PAST PERFECT   ... had grown

FUTURE   ... will grow
FUTURE PROGRESSIVE ... will be growing
FUTURE PERFECT   ... will have grown

PAST PASSIVE

—	—
—	—
it was grown	they were grown

• *The Fair Trade coffee was grown in Mexico.*

COMPLEMENTS

grow *develop, mature*	Weeds were growing in the driveway. Many flowers won't grow in partial shade.
grow *become taller*	My, how you've grown! The kids are sure growing.
grow *become longer*	Her hair grew two inches over the summer.
grow *become bigger, expand*	Our investments have grown about eight percent a year. His reputation is growing even outside the region. The company is growing through mergers with smaller firms. The deficit has grown every year.
grow ____ *raise [plants, a crop]* OBJECT	We will grow **more corn** next year. We can grow **pansies** in the window boxes. It isn't good to grow **the same crop** in a field year after year.
WH-CLAUSE	We will grow **what sells the best.** They grow **whatever crops can tolerate the heat.**
grow ____ *cause to develop and flourish* OBJECT	We are trying to grow **the business.** The company has grown **its profits** effectively. The magazine needs to grow **its circulation.**
grow ____ *begin* INFINITIVE	I have grown **to like broccoli.** I had grown **to hate Senator Blather's speeches.**
grow ____ *become* PREDICATE ADJECTIVE	The driver grew **tired** as evening approached. Ruby grew **pale** at the sight of the snake. They grew **accustomed** to the boss's angry outbursts.

PHRASAL VERBS

grow into ____ *become big enough for*	She's grown into her sister's winter coat.
grow into ____ *develop into*	Your son has grown into a fine young man. The banking problem has grown into a major economic crisis.
grow up to be ____ *develop into*	She has grown up to be a poised and confident woman.

PRESENT

I guess	we guess
you guess	you guess
he/she/it guesses	they guess

• *I guess that we can come to the party.*

PRESENT PROGRESSIVE

I am guessing	we are guessing
you are guessing	you are guessing
he/she/it is guessing	they are guessing

• *I'm just guessing.*

PAST

I guessed	we guessed
you guessed	you guessed
he/she/it guessed	they guessed

• *I guessed wrong every time.*

PAST PROGRESSIVE

I was guessing	we were guessing
you were guessing	you were guessing
he/she/it was guessing	they were guessing

• *They were guessing that she would choose me.*

PRESENT PERFECT ... have | has guessed
PAST PERFECT ... had guessed

FUTURE ... will guess
FUTURE PROGRESSIVE ... will be guessing
FUTURE PERFECT ... will have guessed

PAST PASSIVE

I was guessed	we were guessed
you were guessed	you were guessed
he/she/it was guessed	they were guessed

• *The answer was never guessed.*

COMPLEMENTS

guess *have/state an opinion without enough information*

You don't know; you're just guessing.
You can guess as well as I can.
Go ahead—guess.

guess _____ *give an answer/solution with no certainty of being correct*

OBJECT

Can you guess **the answer?**
I can only guess **the outcome.**
Guess **my dog's name!**

OBJECT + ADVERB OF MANNER

I guessed **it** *wrong* again.
You guessed **it** *right.*

OBJECT + INFINITIVE

I guessed **Mary** *to take the prize.*
Watson didn't guess **the "opium addict"** *to be Sherlock Holmes.*
We guessed **him** *to be innocent.*

THAT-CLAUSE

She guessed **that the train would arrive in 15 minutes.**
The contractor guessed **that a new furnace would cost $3,000.**

WH-CLAUSE

You must guess **who he is.**
Guess **what time it is.**
Guess **where I'm going tomorrow.**

guess _____ *reach a correct conclusion about*

OBJECT

He guessed **the answer.**
You can probably guess **my big news.**

WH-CLAUSE

You guessed **what he wanted this time.**
Janet guessed **how many jelly beans were in the jar.**
Can you guess **how much it cost?**

guess _____ *think, suppose*

THAT-CLAUSE

I guess **(that) you're right.**
I guess **(that) I'll go straight to the party.**

EXPRESSIONS

I guess (so). *I suppose so.*
[SHOWING VAGUE AGREEMENT]

"Are you thirsty?" "I guess so."
"Will your dad be home this evening?" "I guess so."

Guess what! [CONVERSATION OPENER]

"Guess what!" "What?" "I'm going to have a baby."

PRESENT

I guide	we guide
you guide	you guide
he/she/it guides	they guide

• *He guides hikers through the park.*

PRESENT PROGRESSIVE

I am guiding	we are guiding
you are guiding	you are guiding
he/she/it is guiding	they are guiding

• *I'm guiding this trip, not you.*

PAST

I guided	we guided
you guided	you guided
he/she/it guided	they guided

• *His advice guided me through life.*

PAST PROGRESSIVE

I was guiding	we were guiding
you were guiding	you were guiding
he/she/it was guiding	they were guiding

• *The map was guiding us home.*

PRESENT PERFECT ... have | has guided
PAST PERFECT ... had guided

FUTURE ... will guide
FUTURE PROGRESSIVE ... will be guiding
FUTURE PERFECT ... will have guided

PAST PASSIVE

I was guided	we were guided
you were guided	you were guided
he/she/it was guided	they were guided

• *The ship was guided into the harbor by the pilot.*

COMPLEMENTS

guide *conduct a tour, show the way*

Who can guide better than he?
The North Star will always guide at night.

guide _____ *conduct [a tour], show the way to*

OBJECT

Ms. Brown will guide **the tour of the plant.**
Sacagawea guided **the Lewis and Clark expedition.**
The GPS guided **us** to the restaurant.
The lighthouse guided **the ship** back to harbor.

guide _____ *direct, control*

OBJECT

The score guides **the conductor** in the interpretation
  of the music.
The computer manual guided **us** through every step
  of the installation.
Software guides **the flow of electricity** in the Smart Grid.
Yoda's wisdom guided **Luke** in his struggle.

PASSIVE

The bank's actions were guided by the need to protect
  the depositors.

WH-CLAUSE

The latest research guides **what we will do.**
The environmental impact should guide **where we locate
  the new plant.**
Our income guides **how much we can spend.**

PRESENT	
I hand	we hand
you hand	you hand
he/she/it hands	they hand

• *We hand in our report every Friday.*

PRESENT PROGRESSIVE	
I am handing	we are handing
you are handing	you are handing
he/she/it is handing	they are handing

• *I'm handing the report to them now.*

PAST	
I handed	we handed
you handed	you handed
he/she/it handed	they handed

• *The waiter just handed us the menus.*

PAST PROGRESSIVE	
I was handing	we were handing
you were handing	you were handing
he/she/it was handing	they were handing

• *The hostess was handing out party favors to the kids.*

PRESENT PERFECT	… have	has handed
PAST PERFECT	… had handed

FUTURE	… will hand
FUTURE PROGRESSIVE	… will be handing
FUTURE PERFECT	… will have handed

PAST PASSIVE	
I was handed	we were handed
you were handed	you were handed
he/she/it was handed	they were handed

• *The documentation was handed to him by our lawyer.*

COMPLEMENTS

hand _____ *pass something by hand*

INDIRECT OBJECT + DIRECT OBJECT

Please hand *me* **that towel**.
Can you hand *the agent* **our tickets**?
Tarzan handed *Jane* **a banana**.

to PARAPHRASE

Please hand **that towel** *to me*.
Can you hand **our tickets** *to the agent*?
Tarzan handed **a banana** *to Jane*.

hand _____ *provide/present*

INDIRECT OBJECT + DIRECT OBJECT

The news handed *us* **a golden opportunity**.
Napoleon's delay handed *Wellington* **the battle**.
The scandal handed *Senator Blather* **the election**.
Our goalie's error handed *our opponents* **the game**.

to PARAPHRASE

The news handed **a golden opportunity** *to us*.
Napoleon's delay handed **the battle** *to Wellington*.
The scandal handed **the election** *to Senator Blather*.
Our goalie's error handed **the game** *to our opponents*.

PHRASAL VERBS

hand _SEP_ **down** *issue [an official decision]*

The judge handed down a sentence
of five to 10 years.

hand _SEP_ **down** *pass from generation to generation*

This story was handed down from mother to daughter.
The desk has been handed down through six generations.

hand _SEP_ **in** *submit [a report, assignment]*

Don't forget to hand in your essays at the end of class.

hand (_SEP_) **off** *hand off ([the football]) (to [another player])* [AMERICAN FOOTBALL]

Warner handed off to the running back.
The quarterback handed the ball off before he was
tackled.

hand _SEP_ **out** *administer*

She can hand out insults, but she can't take them.

hand _SEP_ **out** *distribute*

C.J. handed out the president's schedule to the reporters.

hand _SEP_ **over** *surrender*

Did the store clerk hand over all the money?
President Bush handed power over to President Obama.

PRESENT

I handle	we handle
you handle	you handle
he/she/it handles	they handle

• *My new car handles well.*

PRESENT PROGRESSIVE

I am handling	we are handling
you are handling	you are handling
he/she/it is handling	they are handling

• *I'm handling the fraud case.*

PAST

I handled	we handled
you handled	you handled
he/she/it handled	they handled

• *I handled this problem last week.*

PAST PROGRESSIVE

I was handling	we were handling
you were handling	you were handling
he/she/it was handling	they were handling

• *The kids were handling the baby kittens carefully.*

PRESENT PERFECT ... have | has handled
PAST PERFECT   ... had handled

FUTURE   ... will handle
FUTURE PROGRESSIVE ... will be handling
FUTURE PERFECT   ... will have handled

PAST PASSIVE

I was handled	we were handled
you were handled	you were handled
he/she/it was handled	they were handled

• *These issues were handled by our legal department.*

COMPLEMENTS

handle ＿＿＿ *function in a certain way*

ADVERB OF MANNER

His truck doesn't handle **very well at all**.
The boat's helm began to handle **sluggishly**.
Most sports cars handle **very tightly**.

handle ＿＿＿ *touch, hold, feel*

OBJECT

Please don't handle **the merchandise**.
We handled **the material** to see how soft it was.
Nobody would handle **the reptiles** at the petting zoo.

handle ＿＿＿ *take care of, manage, deal with*

OBJECT

Who is handling **the phones**?
The Major Case Squad handles **only murder cases**.
His main job is to handle **all requests to meet the senator**.
Who will handle **the problem of employee theft**?

PASSIVE

All our legal affairs are handled by their firm.

handle ＿＿＿ *endure, cope with*

OBJECT

I can't handle **the heat in Florida**.
Do you think you can handle **all the confusion**?
We couldn't handle **the cigarette smoke in the restaurant**.

WH-CLAUSE

They couldn't handle **what was happening**.
I can handle **whatever I need to**.
The soldiers could handle **whatever the enemy threw at them**.

PRESENT PARTICIPLE

He couldn't handle **working such long hours**.
The soldiers couldn't handle **being away from their families**.
The engine couldn't handle **pulling such a heavy load**.

handle ＿＿＿ *be involved in buying/selling*

OBJECT

The hardware store handles **plumbing and electrical supplies**.

handle ＿＿＿ *behave*

REFLEXIVE PRONOUN

Sam handled **himself** very well in the scandal.

EXPRESSIONS

handle ＿＿＿ **with kid gloves**
deal with very carefully

You need to handle the actor with kid gloves.

PRESENT

I hang	we hang
you hang	you hang
he/she/it hangs	they hang

- *His picture hangs in the boardroom.*

PRESENT PROGRESSIVE

I am hanging	we are hanging
you are hanging	you are hanging
he/she/it is hanging	they are hanging

- *I'm hanging around until she returns.*

PAST

I hung/hanged	we hung/hanged
you hung/hanged	you hung/hanged
he/she/it hung/hanged	they hung/hanged

- *We hung all the ornaments on the tree.*

PAST PROGRESSIVE

I was hanging	we were hanging
you were hanging	you were hanging
he/she/it was hanging	they were hanging

- *They were hanging out at Tom's house.*

PRESENT PERFECT … have | has hung/hanged
PAST PERFECT … had hung/hanged

FUTURE … will hang
FUTURE PROGRESSIVE … will be hanging
FUTURE PERFECT … will have hung/hanged

PAST PASSIVE

I was hung/hanged	we were hung/hanged
you were hung/hanged	you were hung/hanged
he/she/it was hung/hanged	they were hung/hanged

- *He was hanged in 1803.*

COMPLEMENTS

NOTE: The past tense and past participle form is *hung* for all meanings of *hang* except one: The form *hanged* is used for the meanings "be suspended by the neck until dead" and "suspend by the neck until dead."

hang *be suspended by the neck until dead*

He will hang for his crimes.
Black Bart was finally hanged.

hang _____ *be suspended, droop*

ADVERB OF PLACE

The gulls hung **above the fishing boats**.
The smoke from the forest fire hung **in the still air**.
Wet laundry hung **everywhere in the small apartment**.

ADVERB OF MANNER

The flag was hanging **limply** from the staff.
His suit hangs **a little too loosely**.
His head hung **in shame** after his arrest.

hang _____ *be prevalent*

ADVERB OF PLACE

Before the battle, tension hung **in the air**.

hang _____ *suspend/fasten without support from below, let droop*

OBJECT (+ ADVERB OF PLACE)

We've already hung **the Christmas wreath**.
We hung **our wet clothing** *on branches*.
I hung a **bird feeder** *in the oak tree.*

PASSIVE

The bridge was hung *from steel cables*.

hang _____ *exhibit [artwork]*

OBJECT

They hung **her paintings** in the main gallery.
I hung **the photograph** in the spring exhibition.

PASSIVE

His pictures have been hung at all the major art shows.

hang _____ *suspend by the neck until dead*

OBJECT

They hanged **the convict** at dawn.

PASSIVE

He was hanged for his many crimes.

PHRASAL VERBS

hang around/out *loiter, linger*   Leo hung around for Josh.
hang on *wait*   Can you hang on while I take another call?
hang on to _____ *keep*   Hang on to the baby clothes; you may need them again.
hang up *end a phone call*   I was telling her about my day when she just hung up.

PRESENT

I happen	we happen
you happen	you happen
he/she/it happens	they happen

- *It happens to be my birthday today.*

PRESENT PROGRESSIVE

—	—
—	—
it is happening	they are happening

- *It is happening all over again.*

PAST

I happened	we happened
you happened	you happened
he/she/it happened	they happened

- *I happened to be downtown on Friday.*

PAST PROGRESSIVE

—	—
—	—
it was happening	they were happening

- *Nothing was happening.*

PRESENT PERFECT ... have | has happened
PAST PERFECT   ... had happened

FUTURE   ... will happen
FUTURE PROGRESSIVE ... will be happening
FUTURE PERFECT   ... will have happened

PAST PASSIVE

Happen is never used in the passive voice.

(COMPLEMENTS)

happen *occur, take place*

Mistakes happen.
Good stuff is happening there.
What happened on this date in history?
The same thing had happened to us before.
It will happen again, you know.

happen _____ *[be/do] by chance*
    INFINITIVE

I happen **to know the combination to the lock.**
Did you happen **to see Mary on your way in?**
Do you happen **to have change for a dollar?**
We happened **to be visiting Denver at the time.**

there + *happen* + *to be* PREDICATE NOUN

There happens **to be a tool kit in my car.**
There happened **to be a police car passing by.**

it + *happen* + *to be* PREDICATE NOUN

It happens **to be trash pickup day.**
It happened **to be the third Sunday of the month.**

it + *happen* + *to be* PREDICATE ADJECTIVE

It happens **to be hot and humid here in the Midwest.**

it + *happen* + THAT-CLAUSE

It happens **that we will be out of town Saturday.**
It happened **that George went to school with him.**
It could happen **that the game will be postponed.**
It happened **that the hotel had lost our reservation.**

(PHRASAL VERBS)

happen along/by *appear, come past by chance*

We were sitting on the porch when
    a deer happened by.

happen on/upon _____ *meet/find by chance*

We happened on Luis at the baseball game.
I happened on his wallet when I was cleaning the living
    room.
My son was returning from a concert when he happened
    upon the crime scene.

happen to _____ *be done to, be the fate of*

Could something have happened to the kids?
They promised nothing would happen to me.
Pay us the money, and nothing will happen to little Jimmy.
What happened to the proposal I gave you?

PRESENT

I hate	we hate
you hate	you hate
he/she/it hates	they hate

• *He hates to be late for dinner.*

PRESENT PROGRESSIVE

Hate is rarely used in the progressive tenses.

PAST

I hated	we hated
you hated	you hated
he/she/it hated	they hated

• *I always hated driving in the snow.*

PAST PROGRESSIVE

Hate is rarely used in the progressive tenses.

PRESENT PERFECT ... have | has hated
PAST PERFECT ... had hated

FUTURE ... will hate
FUTURE PROGRESSIVE —
FUTURE PERFECT ... will have hated

PAST PASSIVE

I was hated	we were hated
you were hated	you were hated
he/she/it was hated	they were hated

• *Our dog was hated by every cat in the neighborhood.*

―(**COMPLEMENTS**)―

hate _____ *dislike very strongly*

OBJECT	The kids hate **broccoli.**
	I hate **the way my hair looks.**
	She hates **the long commute to work.**
OBJECT + PRESENT PARTICIPLE	I hate **him** *criticizing everybody's ideas.*
	The judge hates **attorneys** *filing frivolous motions.*
	The company hates **the union** *striking at the busiest time of year.*
for OBJECT + INFINITIVE	I would hate **for them** *to lose their last game.*
	We hated **for them** *to worry so much about it.*
	Mr. Jordan always hated **for meetings** *to start late.*
INFINITIVE	I hate **to interrupt,** but I need to talk to you.
	We hate **to estimate the extent of the problem** without knowing more about it.
	She hates **to throw anything away.**
(*it*) THAT-CLAUSE	I hate **(it) that the kids can't come for Christmas.**
	We hated **(it) that the candidates were unwilling to discuss the real issues.**
	I hate **(it) that the library is closed on weekends.**
WH-CLAUSE	I hate **who he has become.**
	Ben hated **what they did to his parents' house.**
	Everyone hates **how expensive gasoline is these days.**
PRESENT PARTICIPLE	My parents hate **being out so late.**
	Everyone hates **getting old.**
	Don't you hate **getting stuck at the airport?**

―(**EXPRESSIONS**)―

hate [someone's] guts *dislike [someone] intensely*	He used to be her friend, but now she hates his guts.

PRESENT		PRESENT PROGRESSIVE	
I have	we have	I am having	we are having
you have	you have	you are having	you are having
he/she/it has	they have	he/she/it is having	they are having

- *November only has 30 days.*

- *I'm having some people over.*

PAST		PAST PROGRESSIVE	
I had	we had	I was having	we were having
you had	you had	you were having	you were having
he/she/it had	they had	he/she/it was having	they were having

- *We had a really great time.*

- *We were having a lot of problems then.*

PRESENT PERFECT	... have | has had
PAST PERFECT	... had had

FUTURE	... will have
FUTURE PROGRESSIVE	... will be having
FUTURE PERFECT	... will have had

PAST PASSIVE

Have is not used in the passive voice except in idiomatic expressions.

(**COMPLEMENTS**)

NOTE: *Have* is also used as a helping verb to form the perfect tenses.

    have + PAST PARTICIPLE   She has read all six of Jane Austen's novels.

have _____ *possess, own, contain, include*

    OBJECT

         Do you have **a car**?
         I have **enough food for everyone**.
         Ted has **an interesting news item for us**.
         Do you have **a minute**?
         We have **an office in Tokyo**.
         Does the meeting room have **a projection screen**?
         The department store has **mattresses on sale**.
         A week has **seven days**.
         The knitters' club has **372 members**.

have _____ *be characterized by*

    OBJECT

         She has **red hair**.
         He has **a quick temper**.
         My car has **a tendency to stall at stop signs**.

have _____ *must*

    INFINITIVE

         I have **to be at the office by 8 o'clock**.
         We have **to stop for gas at the next exit**.
         You will have **to make up your minds soon**.

NOTE: When the information in the infinitive is clear from context, *have* + INFINITIVE is often contracted to *have* + *to*. For example, *Do you have to go now*? may be contracted to *Do you have to? Have to* is sometimes pronounced /hafta/.

have _____ *cause [to do]*

    OBJECT + BASE-FORM INFINITIVE

         I had **the kids** *put away their toys*.
         He had **me** *reprint the document*.
         We will have **the builder** *modify the deck*.

    OBJECT + PRESENT PARTICIPLE

         He had **his crew** *working on the addition*.
         The comedian really had **us** *laughing*.
         The coach had **the team** *running wind sprints*.

    OBJECT + PAST PARTICIPLE

         I had **my watch** *repaired*.
         Aunt Jenny had **her hip** *replaced* this fall.
         They had **the wedding reception** *catered*.

have _____ experience, undergo OBJECT	He had **chicken pox** when he was a child. Did you have **a good time** at the party? The Southwest had **drought conditions** for several years. They are having **an argument about visitation rights**.
have _____ keep in one's mind OBJECT	Senator Blather has **an opinion about everything**. We have **doubts about the new employee**. I have **an idea for earning extra money**.
have _____ host OBJECT	The restaurant is having **a grand opening** this Saturday.
have _____ eat, drink OBJECT	Dan is having **blackberry pie** for dessert. Tim had **a refill** on his soft drink.
have _____ be the parent(s) of OBJECT	We have **two sons and a daughter**.
have _____ study OBJECT	Terry had **three years of Spanish** in high school.
have _____ position OBJECT + ADVERB OF PLACE	Mark had **his hands** *on the steering wheel*. The graduate had **a parent** *on either side of him*.

$$\text{PHRASAL VERBS}$$

have _____ back/down/over/up/etc. *invite and host [someone] at a specified location*	We had the Smiths over for dinner.
have _____ against *have as a reason to dislike*	She has a grudge against her ex-boyfriend.
have _____ on *be operating*	She has the radio on when she's at home.
have _SEP_ on *be wearing*	He had on a turtleneck sweater and baggy trousers.
have _SEP_ out *have removed*	I had one of my upper molars out.

$$\text{EXPRESSIONS}$$

have had it *have done/endured all that one can*	I have had it with tax auditors.
have a big mouth _____ *gossip a lot, reveal secrets a lot*	Don't tell Joanie your troubles; she has a big mouth.
have a bone to pick (with _____) *have something to argue about (with [someone])*	I have a bone to pick with the editor about his changes.

**have [one's] cake and eat it too / have
it both ways** *have the advantages of
something without its disadvantages*
	Denny wants to live in the country, but he wants a
	  grocery store next door. He can't have his cake and
	  eat it too.

have it good *be rich*	The bank executive really has it good—a Mercedes, a mansion, and a vacation home in California.
have it out (with _____) *settle an argument (with [someone])*	The teacher had it out with the principal.
have it that _____ *claim/say that*	Rumor has it that Glenda is getting married.
have to do with _____ *concern, involve*	The article has to do with child labor laws.

top
40
verb

I head   we head
you head   you head
he/she/it heads   they head

• *She heads the compensation committee.*

PRESENT PROGRESSIVE

I am heading   we are heading
you are heading   you are heading
he/she/it is heading   they are heading

• *I am heading the investigation.*

PAST

I headed   we headed
you headed   you headed
he/she/it headed   they headed

• *Jones headed the list of candidates.*

PAST PROGRESSIVE

I was heading   we were heading
you were heading   you were heading
he/she/it was heading   they were heading

• *We were finally heading home.*

PRESENT PERFECT ... have | has headed
PAST PERFECT   ... had headed

FUTURE   ... will head
FUTURE PROGRESSIVE   ... will be heading
FUTURE PERFECT   ... will have headed

PAST PASSIVE

I was headed   we were headed
you were headed   you were headed
he/she/it was headed   they were headed

• *The ship was headed out to sea.*

(**COMPLEMENTS**)

head _____ *lead, be in charge of*

OBJECT

Ms. Lewis is heading **the operation**.
Who will head **the department** after she retires?

PASSIVE

The program was headed by Oliver Brown.

head _____ *be at the front/top of*

OBJECT

Clearly, she heads **the list of potential nominees**.
Who is heading **the short list**?
The Giants head **their division** again this year.

PASSIVE

The pool of applicants was headed by my mother.

head _____ *proceed/go*

ADVERB OF PLACE TO/FROM

We headed **home** after dinner.
The sheep were heading **into the south pasture**.
The fishing boats were all heading **west**.

head _____ *move (toward)*

OBJECT + ADVERB OF PLACE TO/FROM

We headed **the car** *to the curb*.
The ranchers headed **the sheep** *up to the mountains*.
They headed **the sailboat** *into the wind*.

(**PHRASAL VERBS**)

**head back/down/in/off/out/over/
up**/etc. *go in a specified direction*

Let's head down to Mexico City.
The twins headed off to college in 2006.

head after _____ *pursue*

Pierre headed after Lizbeth to apologize.

head for _____ *have as a destination*

Our family headed for the Ozarks.
Patton's army headed for Berlin.

head into _____ *begin to do*

She finished her Algebra homework and headed into Chemistry.

head SEP **off** *block, intercept*

Grant's army headed off the Confederate army at Appomattox.

PRESENT

I hear	we hear
you hear	you hear
he/she/it hears	they hear

• *He only hears what he wants to.*

PRESENT PROGRESSIVE

I am hearing	we are hearing
you are hearing	you are hearing
he/she/it is hearing	they are hearing

• *I'm not hearing anything.*

PAST

I heard	we heard
you heard	you heard
he/she/it heard	they heard

• *I heard that there was a problem.*

PAST PROGRESSIVE

I was hearing	we were hearing
you were hearing	you were hearing
he/she/it was hearing	they were hearing

• *They were hearing some surprising reports.*

PRESENT PERFECT ... have | has heard
PAST PERFECT ... had heard

FUTURE ... will hear
FUTURE PROGRESSIVE ... will be hearing
FUTURE PERFECT ... will have heard

PAST PASSIVE

I was heard	we were heard
you were heard	you were heard
he/she/it was heard	they were heard

• *All witnesses were heard in one afternoon.*

COMPLEMENTS

hear *perceive sound by ear*	She can only hear in the middle frequencies.
	Sam hears pretty well for someone his age.
hear *make out words/music*	Can everybody hear, or should I turn the radio up?
	I don't think anyone could hear while the band was playing.
hear ____ *perceive by ear*	
OBJECT	I just heard **the telephone**.
	We could hear **the surf** from our room.
	Did you just hear **something**?
PASSIVE	The dog's barking was heard by everybody in the building.
OBJECT + INFINITIVE [USED ONLY IN THE PASSIVE]	He was heard *to make threats*.
	The senator was heard *to make promises he couldn't keep*.
OBJECT + BASE-FORM INFINITIVE	I heard **him** *start the car*.
	We heard **the kids** *turn on the TV*.
	I heard **her** *play a Mozart piano concerto*.
OBJECT + PRESENT PARTICIPLE	I heard **him** *starting the car*.
	We heard **the kids** *playing in the backyard*.
	He heard **someone** *talking on the phone*.
hear ____ *be told, learn*	
OBJECT	Did you hear **the news**?
	I heard **the final score**.
	John has just heard **the results of his test**.
THAT-CLAUSE	I heard **that Jim is leaving the company**.
	Did you hear **that they are going to have a baby**?
WH-CLAUSE	Have you heard **who won the game**?
	I heard **what you said**.
hear ____ *listen to the two sides in [a court case]*	
OBJECT	The judge heard **three divorce cases** this morning.

PHRASAL VERBS

hear from ____ *receive a message from*	We heard from the Ellners last week.
hear of ____ *learn of the existence of*	I've heard of hedgehogs, but I've never seen one.
hear ____ **out** *listen to everything [someone] has to say*	Simon heard her out, but he didn't change his mind.

PRESENT

I help	we help
you help	you help
he/she/it helps	they help

• *He helps the kids with their homework.*

PRESENT PROGRESSIVE

I am helping	we are helping
you are helping	you are helping
he/she/it is helping	they are helping

• *I'm helping wherever I can.*

PAST

I helped	we helped
you helped	you helped
he/she/it helped	they helped

• *I helped as much as I could.*

PAST PROGRESSIVE

I was helping	we were helping
you were helping	you were helping
he/she/it was helping	they were helping

• *We were helping them fix dinner.*

PRESENT PERFECT ... have | has helped
PAST PERFECT ... had helped

FUTURE ... will help
FUTURE PROGRESSIVE ... will be helping
FUTURE PERFECT ... will have helped

PAST PASSIVE

I was helped	we were helped
you were helped	you were helped
he/she/it was helped	they were helped

• *The situation was helped by their timely actions.*

(**COMPLEMENTS**)

help *be of assistance/use*

He always helps if we need him.
A little extra money always helps.
The kids help around the house once in a while.

help _____ *assist, support*

OBJECT

Help **your mother** in the kitchen, will you?
The new players have really helped **the team**.
Some rain will help **the corn**.
Please help **yourself** to more coffee.

OBJECT + BASE-FORM INFINITIVE

Jerry helped **me** *get the kite off the roof*.
I will help **you** *do it*.
The guards actually helped **the prisoners** *escape*.
Can you help **me** *finish this report*?

BASE-FORM INFINITIVE

Can you help **fix it**?
He even helped **pay for it**.
Theo helped **clean out the barn**.
Help **get the dog back inside**.

help _____ *improve, give relief to*

OBJECT

The extra tutoring helped **my test scores** a lot.
Nothing would help **this food**.
A new rug would help **the living room**.
The aspirin helped **my headache**.

help _____ *avoid* [USUALLY USED IN THE NEGATIVE]

but + BASE-FORM INFINITIVE [INFORMAL]

I couldn't help **but hear what you said**.

PRESENT PARTICIPLE

I couldn't help **hearing what you said**.
They couldn't help **laughing at the situation**.
Bill can't help **making a bad situation worse**.
Romeo couldn't help **being attracted to Juliet**.

(**PHRASAL VERBS**)

help _____ **down/in/out/up**/etc. *assist in moving in a specified direction*

We helped the kitten down from the tree.
I've fallen; can you help me up?

help [someone] on/off with _____ *assist [someone] in putting on / taking off [clothing]*

She helped Gretchen on with her shoes.
Would you help me off with this sweatshirt?

hide hide | hides · hid · have hidden ☑ IRREGULAR

PRESENT

I hide	we hide
you hide	you hide
he/she/it hides	they hide

• *Our cat always hides in the closet.*

PRESENT PROGRESSIVE

I am hiding	we are hiding
you are hiding	you are hiding
he/she/it is hiding	they are hiding

• *I'm hiding from Todd.*

PAST

I hid	we hid
you hid	you hid
he/she/it hid	they hid

• *I hid a house key outside.*

PAST PROGRESSIVE

I was hiding	we were hiding
you were hiding	you were hiding
he/she/it was hiding	they were hiding

• *They were hiding the money in offshore accounts.*

PRESENT PERFECT ... have | has hidden
PAST PERFECT ... had hidden

FUTURE ... will hide
FUTURE PROGRESSIVE ... will be hiding
FUTURE PERFECT ... will have hidden

PAST PASSIVE

I was hidden	we were hidden
you were hidden	you were hidden
he/she/it was hidden	they were hidden

• *The photos were hidden in a closet.*

———————————————————————————————————(**COMPLEMENTS**)———

hide *keep oneself out of sight,*
conceal oneself

The dog hides whenever we get his cage.
The birds hide in the trees if there is a hawk nearby.
The kids were hiding behind the tree.
The thief hid in an abandoned warehouse.

hide _____ *put out of sight, conceal*
    OBJECT

The cat had hidden **her kittens** in the attic.
The burglars hid **themselves** carefully.
The old lady hid **her money** under her mattress.
He hid **the stolen property** in the basement.
Janet hid **her face** behind the newspaper.
They hid **their business losses** by altering the records.

hide _____ *keep secret*
    OBJECT
    WH-CLAUSE

I tried to hide **my confusion** by changing the subject.
The senator hid **who had actually made the campaign contribution.**
They wanted to hide **what they had done.**
Allison never hid **what she was going to do.**
We all want to hide **whatever makes us look foolish.**

hide _____ *keep from being seen*
    OBJECT
    PASSIVE

A sign hid **the entrance to his office.**
My iPod had been hidden by a stack of books.

———————————————————————————————————(**PHRASAL VERBS**)———

hide out *conceal oneself for a period*
of time

Jesse and Frank James hid out in
    Meramec Caverns.

———————————————————————————————————(**EXPRESSIONS**)———

hide [one's] head in the sand *ignore*
signs of danger

We hid our heads in the sand when Hitler
    seized control of the government.

hide [one's] light under a bushel
conceal one's talents/ideas

Share your suggestions, Donna. Don't hide your light
    under a bushel.

PRESENT

I hire	we hire
you hire	you hire
he/she/it hires	they hire

• *The firm only hires college graduates.*

PAST

I hired	we hired
you hired	you hired
he/she/it hired	they hired

• *We just hired a new IT person.*

PRESENT PERFECT ... have | has hired
PAST PERFECT ... had hired

PRESENT PROGRESSIVE

I am hiring	we are hiring
you are hiring	you are hiring
he/she/it is hiring	they are hiring

• *I am not hiring just anyone.*

PAST PROGRESSIVE

I was hiring	we were hiring
you were hiring	you were hiring
he/she/it was hiring	they were hiring

• *They were hiring staff for the new office.*

FUTURE ... will hire
FUTURE PROGRESSIVE ... will be hiring
FUTURE PERFECT ... will have hired

PAST PASSIVE

I was hired	we were hired
you were hired	you were hired
he/she/it was hired	they were hired

• *Marian was hired by a company in Texas.*

(**COMPLEMENTS**)

hire *employ someone to do a job*	The Apex Corporation is hiring now.
	Do you know anyone who is hiring?
	Nobody will hire in a recession.

hire _____ *employ to do a job, engage the services of*

OBJECT	We had to hire **a contractor**.
	He hired **his brother-in-law**.
	The hospitals are trying to hire **more skilled nurses**.
PASSIVE	My neighbor was hired for temporary work.
OBJECT + INFINITIVE	We hired **an electrician** *to wire the new ceiling fan*.
	The company hired **a salesman** *to fill in for Dolores*.
WH-CLAUSE	We can only hire **who is on the short list of applicants**.
	They will hire **whoever is the most qualified**.
	I will hire **whomever I want to**.

(**PHRASAL VERBS**)

hire _SEP_ **away** *cause [someone] to leave a job and begin a job with one's company*	They tried to hire away the top math professors at our university.
hire [oneself] out *take a job, usually temporarily*	Between campaigns, he hired himself out as a speechwriter.
	She hired herself out as a babysitter.

PRESENT

I hit	we hit
you hit	you hit
he/she/it hits	they hit

• *He always hits his target.*

PRESENT PROGRESSIVE

I am hitting	we are hitting
you are hitting	you are hitting
he/she/it is hitting	they are hitting

• *I'm hitting a lot of resistance.*

PAST

I hit	we hit
you hit	you hit
he/she/it hit	they hit

• *The storm hit us pretty hard.*

PAST PROGRESSIVE

I was hitting	we were hitting
you were hitting	you were hitting
he/she/it was hitting	they were hitting

• *Prices were hitting all-time highs.*

PRESENT PERFECT ... have | has hit
PAST PERFECT ... had hit

FUTURE ... will hit
FUTURE PROGRESSIVE ... will be hitting
FUTURE PERFECT ... will have hit

PAST PASSIVE

I was hit	we were hit
you were hit	you were hit
he/she/it was hit	they were hit

• *Our car was hit by a pickup truck.*

COMPLEMENTS

hit *deliver a blow/setback*

Depression can hit at any time.
The storm will hit sometime tomorrow morning.
The shells and bombs were hitting everywhere.

hit _____ *strike, deliver a blow to*
  OBJECT

The batter hit **the pitch** sharply.
I hit **the target** on the first shot.
The bullet hit **him** in the left shoulder.

  PASSIVE

Our oak tree was hit by lightning.

hit _____ *cause to suffer, distress*
  OBJECT

A terrible drought has hit **the entire Midwest**.
A sharp sell-off hit **the market** today.

hit _____ *activate, turn on/off*
  OBJECT

He hit **the brakes** in a panic.
Hit **the light switch**, will you?
They always want to hit **the panic button** right away.

hit _____ *reach [a level/goal]*
  OBJECT

Do you think oil will hit **$100 a barrel**?
Sales could hit **our goal of 2,000 units** this week.

  PASSIVE

A new record was hit on Wall Street today.

hit _____ *arrive/appear at*
  OBJECT

We should hit **Kansas City** around noon.
The tourists hit **all the souvenir shops**.

hit _____ *encounter*
  OBJECT

The pilot hit **a headwind** 120 miles from Singapore.
The research was going well, then we hit **a snag**.

hit _____ *become clear to*
  OBJECT

The smell of garlic hit **me** as soon as I entered the house.
The solution hit **Johanna** right after lunch.

PHRASAL VERBS

hit on/upon _____ *discover*

She hit upon the idea of extending
  Medicare to people 55 and over.

PRESENT

I hold	we hold
you hold	you hold
he/she/it holds	they hold

• *A barrel holds 55 U.S. gallons.*

PRESENT PROGRESSIVE

I am holding	we are holding
you are holding	you are holding
he/she/it is holding	they are holding

• *Come on, I'm holding the door.*

PAST

I held	we held
you held	you held
he/she/it held	they held

• *She held that position for years.*

PAST PROGRESSIVE

I was holding	we were holding
you were holding	you were holding
he/she/it was holding	they were holding

• *Susan was holding the baby.*

PRESENT PERFECT ... have | has held
PAST PERFECT ... had held

FUTURE ... will hold
FUTURE PROGRESSIVE ... will be holding
FUTURE PERFECT ... will have held

PAST PASSIVE

I was held	we were held
you were held	you were held
he/she/it was held	they were held

• *The plane was held for transfer passengers.*

COMPLEMENTS

hold *keep one's position*
So far, our defensive line is holding.
We hope the tent holds in this wind.
The beautiful weather will hold through the weekend.
Our market share is still holding.
The senator's lead in the polls has held steady.
Please hold still.
Please hold. Your call is important to us.

hold *stay together / in one piece*
I hope this rope holds.

hold ___ *grasp*
OBJECT
I held **the hammer** in my right hand.
Please hold **the ladder** while I change the lightbulb.
Hold **my hand** while we cross the street.

hold ___ *keep steady, maintain, keep control of*
OBJECT
They will hold **their prices** at the current level.
The runners held **a five-mile-per-hour pace**.
The house had held **its value** over the years.
Will you hold **the elevator** for a minute?
The framework holds **the entire structure** together.
He needs to hold **his temper** better.
How long can you hold **your breath**?
The movie completely held **my attention**.

OBJECT + PREDICATE ADJECTIVE
The senator held **his audience** *spellbound*.
The scream held **everyone** *frozen in place*.
The cables hold **the tower** *rigid*.

hold ___ *keep for later use*
OBJECT
The hotel will hold **the room** for us until 10 P.M.
Hold **my calls**.

PASSIVE
The troops were held in reserve.

hold ___ *contain, have room for*
OBJECT
The safe deposit box holds **the deed to our house**.
The tank holds **1,000 gallons**.
The auditorium can hold **400 people**.

hold _____ *consider, believe*

OBJECT + *(to be)* PREDICATE ADJECTIVE   The judge held **the defendant *(to be) blameless.***
I hold **him *(to be) fully responsible for the accident.***
"We hold **these truths *to be self-evident* …**"
[DECLARATION OF INDEPENDENCE]

THAT-CLAUSE   The court held **that citizens have a right to possess firearms.**
For years, the tobacco industry held **that cigarettes didn't cause cancer.**

hold _____ *conduct*

OBJECT   The seniors held **a bake sale** for their class trip.
We held **a seminar** for the interns.
The neighbors held **a lively conversation** on the porch.
They will hold **a special exhibit on pre-Columbian art.**
The president will hold **a press conference** on Tuesday.

hold _____ *have as one's own*

OBJECT   Amelia Earhart holds **the title of first woman to fly solo across the Atlantic Ocean.**
My wife holds **the office of County Clerk.**

hold _____ *keep in one's mind, maintain*

OBJECT   They held **the belief that the earth is flat.**
We will hold **the memory of her** in our hearts forever.

PHRASAL VERBS

hold ᴿᴱᴾ **back/down/in/out/up/etc.** *keep in a specified position*   A police barricade held the crowd back.
The auctioneer held up an antique butter churn.

hold _____ **against [someone]** *have as a reason to think poorly of [someone]*   She still holds it against him that he has never opened the door for her.

hold ˢᴱᴾ **back** *keep secret, withhold*   The juror held back the fact that he knew the defendant.
His mother was sure that he was holding something back.

hold ˢᴱᴾ **down** *have and keep [a job]*   Jake holds down two jobs and takes college classes too.

hold ˢᴱᴾ **in** *suppress*   The candidate is good at holding his emotions in.

hold off (on) _____ *delay, postpone*   She held off asking her parents for more money.

hold ˢᴱᴾ **off** *keep away, resist*   The old woman held the robber off until police arrived.

hold on *wait*   Hold on while I dry my hands.

hold on *manage to keep one's position*   Although our team was outscored in the final period, we held on and won the game.

hold ˢᴱᴾ **on** *secure*   A clasp holds the lid on.

hold out *last, endure*   How long will our food hold out?
The settlers held out until the cavalry arrived.

hold out for _____ *insist on getting*   I don't want a cookie; I'm holding out for a cupcake.
The union held out for better working conditions.

hold ˢᴱᴾ **over** *keep for more performances*   The theater held the movie over for six more weeks.

hold _____ **together** *keep united*   It was Mom who held the family together.

hold up *remain in the same condition*   This old house is holding up pretty well.
Sales of soccer balls are holding up in spite of the economy.

hold ˢᴱᴾ **up** *delay, stop*   The discovery of human remains held up construction for two weeks.

hold ˢᴱᴾ **up** *rob*   Three teenagers held the store up in broad daylight.

hold ˢᴱᴾ **up** *support*   Special bolts hold up the roof of a coal mine.

PRESENT

I honor	we honor
you honor	you honor
he/she/it honors	they honor

• *He always honors his agreements.*

PRESENT PROGRESSIVE

I am honoring	we are honoring
you are honoring	you are honoring
he/she/it is honoring	they are honoring

• *They are honoring us for our environmental work.*

PAST

I honored	we honored
you honored	you honored
he/she/it honored	they honored

• *The club honored me with an award.*

PAST PROGRESSIVE

I was honoring	we were honoring
you were honoring	you were honoring
he/she/it was honoring	they were honoring

• *The bank was honoring the letter of credit.*

PRESENT PERFECT   ... have | has honored
PAST PERFECT   ... had honored

FUTURE   ... will honor
FUTURE PROGRESSIVE   ... will be honoring
FUTURE PERFECT   ... will have honored

PAST PASSIVE

I was honored	we were honored
you were honored	you were honored
he/she/it was honored	they were honored

• *Dean Smith was honored by all of her colleagues.*

(**COMPLEMENTS**)

honor _____ *show great respect for*

OBJECT

The party honors **graduating seniors**.
"Honor **your father and your mother**." [BIBLE]
We can't honor **our soldiers** enough.
The nation honors **Presidents Washington and Lincoln**
     on Presidents' Day in February.

PASSIVE

I am greatly honored by your applause.

honor _____ *fulfill the terms of, fulfill one's commitment to pay*

OBJECT

Our country will honor **all the terms of the treaty**.
He is a person who always honors **his word**.
The company must honor **all of its bills**.

honor _____ *accept as payment*

OBJECT

Will the restaurant honor **my credit card**?

PASSIVE

A certified check will be honored at any bank.

PRESENT

I hope	we hope
you hope	you hope
he/she/it hopes	they hope

• *He hopes that he can visit sometime.*

PRESENT PROGRESSIVE

I am hoping	we are hoping
you are hoping	you are hoping
he/she/it is hoping	they are hoping

• *I'm hoping that it will snow.*

PAST

I hoped	we hoped
you hoped	you hoped
he/she/it hoped	they hoped

• *I always hoped that I could go to Italy.*

PAST PROGRESSIVE

I was hoping	we were hoping
you were hoping	you were hoping
he/she/it was hoping	they were hoping

• *We were hoping for success.*

PRESENT PERFECT … have | has hoped
PAST PERFECT   … had hoped

FUTURE   … will hope
FUTURE PROGRESSIVE … will be hoping
FUTURE PERFECT   … will have hoped

PAST PASSIVE

—	—
—	—
it was hoped	they were hoped

• *A bigger turnout was hoped for.*

COMPLEMENTS

hope _____ *desire, wish*

  for OBJECT

The kids are hoping **for snow** on Christmas Day.
We couldn't hope **for a nicer day to go to the beach.**

  THAT-CLAUSE

I hope **that everything is okay.**
We hoped **that you could join us.**
My father was hoping **that he might rest awhile.**
The players hope **that they do not have to play in the rain.**
Everyone hopes **that the market will recover.**
I hope **that I didn't offend anyone.**

hope _____ *expect, plan*

  INFINITIVE

I hope **to go Boston on Tuesday.**
The plumber hopes **to be finished in an hour.**
We hope **to see you there.**
I never hoped **to have such success with it.**
He hopes **to do better next time.**

EXPRESSIONS

hope against (all) hope *desire an improbable outcome*

The family is hoping against hope that
  their house wasn't flooded.

PRESENT	**PRESENT PROGRESSIVE**

PRESENT

I house	we house
you house	you house
he/she/it houses	they house

• *The cabinet houses his mineral collection.*

PRESENT PROGRESSIVE

I am housing	we are housing
you are housing	you are housing
he/she/it is housing	they are housing

• *I am housing two international students.*

PAST

I housed	we housed
you housed	you housed
he/she/it housed	they housed

• *They housed the flood victims in a hotel.*

PAST PROGRESSIVE

I was housing	we were housing
you were housing	you were housing
he/she/it was housing	they were housing

• *We were housing the wedding guests all over town.*

PRESENT PERFECT ... have | has housed
PAST PERFECT ... had housed

FUTURE ... will house
FUTURE PROGRESSIVE ... will be housing
FUTURE PERFECT ... will have housed

PAST PASSIVE

I was housed	we were housed
you were housed	you were housed
he/she/it was housed	they were housed

• *The refugees were temporarily housed in army tents.*

NOTE: The verb *house* ends with a /z/ sound.
The noun *house* ends with an /s/ sound.

COMPLEMENTS

house _____ give shelter/lodging to

OBJECT (+ ADVERB OF PLACE)
We offered to house **an exchange student**.
They housed **us** *in old army barracks*.
We have to house **the volunteers** *somewhere*.
Can we house **our pets** *with you*?

house _____ store

OBJECT (+ ADVERB OF PLACE)
While I was working abroad, my parents housed **my furniture**.
You must house **these papers** *somewhere dry*.

PASSIVE
His documents were housed *in various places*.

house _____ contain

OBJECT
Those buildings house **government offices**.
These rooms house **all of his photographs**.
The outbuildings house **his antique automobiles**.
These drawers house **thousands of specimens**.

PASSIVE
The printers are housed in a separate room.

PRESENT			PRESENT PROGRESSIVE	
I hurt	we hurt		I am hurting	we are hurting
you hurt	you hurt		you are hurting	you are hurting
he/she/it hurts	they hurt		he/she/it is hurting	they are hurting

 • *The scandal hurts his re-election chances.* • *The auto industry is really hurting.*

PAST			PAST PROGRESSIVE	
I hurt	we hurt		I was hurting	we were hurting
you hurt	you hurt		you were hurting	you were hurting
he/she/it hurt	they hurt		he/she/it was hurting	they were hurting

 • *I hurt my knee yesterday.* • *Lack of money was hurting our program.*

PRESENT PERFECT	… have	has hurt
PAST PERFECT	… had hurt

FUTURE	… will hurt
FUTURE PROGRESSIVE	… will be hurting
FUTURE PERFECT	… will have hurt

PAST PASSIVE

I was hurt	we were hurt
you were hurt	you were hurt
he/she/it was hurt	they were hurt

 • *He was hurt playing football.*

(COMPLEMENTS)

hurt *be a source of pain*	Mommy, my stomach hurts. My shoulder was hurting again. This injection may hurt a little. The loss of so many jobs has got to hurt.
hurt *be in a bad situation*	The entire economy is hurting.
hurt _____ *injure, cause pain/harm to* OBJECT	He hurt **his back** trying to move the refrigerator. Listening to such loud music hurts **my ears**. The new shoes are hurting **my feet**. Would it hurt **you** to wash the dishes once in a while?
PASSIVE	Her feelings were hurt by what they said.
hurt _____ *damage, harm* OBJECT	A high interest rate will hurt **car sales**. The unusually cold summer has hurt **vacation rentals**. Injuries have hurt **our team's chances**. The recession is hurting **sales**. Such negative criticism would hurt **anyone's self-image**.
PASSIVE	The dollar has been hurt by high oil prices.

PRESENT

I identify	we identify
you identify	you identify
he/she/it identifies	they identify

• *She identifies DNA sources for a lab.*

PRESENT PROGRESSIVE

I am identifying	we are identifying
you are identifying	you are identifying
he/she/it is identifying	they are identifying

• *They are identifying the plant as a new species.*

PAST

I identified	we identified
you identified	you identified
he/she/it identified	they identified

• *I identified two possible suspects.*

PAST PROGRESSIVE

I was identifying	we were identifying
you were identifying	you were identifying
he/she/it was identifying	they were identifying

• *By college, I was identifying myself as a Democrat.*

PRESENT PERFECT ... have | has identified
PAST PERFECT   ... had identified

FUTURE   ... will identify
FUTURE PROGRESSIVE ... will be identifying
FUTURE PERFECT   ... will have identified

PAST PASSIVE

I was identified	we were identified
you were identified	you were identified
he/she/it was identified	they were identified

• *He was identified by two eyewitnesses.*

COMPLEMENTS

identify _____ *establish/classify who/what [someone/something] is*

OBJECT

The police identified **the body**.
He can identify **every airplane ever made**.
Her book identifies **the causes of depression**.

PASSIVE

Fortunately, the tumor was identified at an early stage.

OBJECT + *as* PREDICATE NOUN

We identified **the flower** *as a kind of daisy*.
The poll identified **55% of likely voters** *as Democrats*.
The hospital identified **my blood type** *as AB*.

WH-CLAUSE

The police identified **who took the jewels**.
They never identified **whose body it was**.
Can you identify **what kind of car it was**?
The lab will identify **which blood type it was**.

identify _____ *be compatible, associate oneself*

with OBJECT

I always identify **with the underdog**.
Voters can identify **with her**.
I could never identify **with anybody in that movie**.

PASSIVE

Las Vegas will always be identified with gambling.

identify _____ *associate*

OBJECT + *with* OBJECT

Grandpa identifies **rock music** *with drugs and immorality*.

identify _____ *say who one is*

REFLEXIVE PRONOUN

The police asked us to identify **ourselves**.

PRESENT

I ignore	we ignore
you ignore	you ignore
he/she/it ignores	they ignore

• *He ignores what he doesn't want to hear.*

PAST

I ignored	we ignored
you ignored	you ignored
he/she/it ignored	they ignored

• *We ignored the problem far too long.*

PRESENT PERFECT	... have | has ignored
PAST PERFECT	... had ignored

PRESENT PROGRESSIVE

I am ignoring	we are ignoring
you are ignoring	you are ignoring
he/she/it is ignoring	they are ignoring

• *I am ignoring the heat as best I can.*

PAST PROGRESSIVE

I was ignoring	we were ignoring
you were ignoring	you were ignoring
he/she/it was ignoring	they were ignoring

• *They were ignoring all of our requests.*

FUTURE	... will ignore
FUTURE PROGRESSIVE	... will be ignoring
FUTURE PERFECT	... will have ignored

PAST PASSIVE

I was ignored	we were ignored
you were ignored	you were ignored
he/she/it was ignored	they were ignored

• *His early movies were ignored by the critics.*

(**COMPLEMENTS**)

ignore _____ *pay no attention to*

OBJECT	He ignored **all the overdue bills.**
	Senator Blather ignored **the reporters' questions**.
	The taxi drivers there ignore **all traffic signals.**
	The waiter ignored **us** the whole evening.
	Economists ignored **the warning signs.**
PASSIVE	My warnings were totally ignored.
WH-CLAUSE	We can never ignore **who he really is.**
	He ignored **what he had been told.**
	Should we just ignore **what happened**?

PRESENT

I illustrate	we illustrate
you illustrate	you illustrate
he/she/it illustrates	they illustrate

• *Davy illustrates his stories with crayons.*

PRESENT PROGRESSIVE

I am illustrating	we are illustrating
you are illustrating	you are illustrating
he/she/it is illustrating	they are illustrating

• *I am illustrating a graphic novel.*

PAST

I illustrated	we illustrated
you illustrated	you illustrated
he/she/it illustrated	they illustrated

• *A professional artist illustrated the book.*

PAST PROGRESSIVE

I was illustrating	we were illustrating
you were illustrating	you were illustrating
he/she/it was illustrating	they were illustrating

• *He was just illustrating his point.*

PRESENT PERFECT ... have | has illustrated
PAST PERFECT   ... had illustrated

FUTURE   ... will illustrate
FUTURE PROGRESSIVE ... will be illustrating
FUTURE PERFECT   ... will have illustrated

PAST PASSIVE

I was illustrated	we were illustrated
you were illustrated	you were illustrated
he/she/it was illustrated	they were illustrated

• *Medieval manuscripts were often beautifully illustrated.*

COMPLEMENTS

illustrate _____ *explain/decorate with pictures/diagrams*

OBJECT — Jason illustrates **children's books.**
She illustrates **wedding and birth announcements.**
The company will illustrate **any kind of promotional material.**

PASSIVE — Medical textbooks are illustrated at great expense.

illustrate _____ *show/explain with examples*

OBJECT — Good speakers always illustrate **their ideas with numerous examples.**
Henry illustrated **his concern about the economy** by showing employment data.
Preachers have always illustrated **their message** with parables.

PASSIVE — Laurie's thesis was cleverly illustrated with personal experiences.

WH-CLAUSE — Always illustrate **what you are trying to say.**
Peter illustrated **how much the project would cost** with a series of bar charts.
He illustrated **whatever point he was making** with a carefully chosen example.

PRESENT

I imagine	we imagine
you imagine	you imagine
he/she/it imagines	they imagine

• *He always imagines the worst.*

PRESENT PROGRESSIVE

I am imagining	we are imagining
you are imagining	you are imagining
he/she/it is imagining	they are imagining

• *She is always imagining things.*

PAST

I imagined	we imagined
you imagined	you imagined
he/she/it imagined	they imagined

• *I never imagined buying food online.*

PAST PROGRESSIVE

I was imagining	we were imagining
you were imagining	you were imagining
he/she/it was imagining	they were imagining

• *I was imagining everything that could go wrong.*

PRESENT PERFECT ... have | has imagined
PAST PERFECT ... had imagined

FUTURE ... will imagine
FUTURE PROGRESSIVE ... will be imagining
FUTURE PERFECT ... will have imagined

PAST PASSIVE

I was imagined	we were imagined
you were imagined	you were imagined
he/she/it was imagined	they were imagined

• *Such success was never imagined by anyone.*

―――――――――――――――――――――――――――――――――(**COMPLEMENTS**)―――

imagine _____ *suppose, picture, form an idea of*

OBJECT	Can you imagine **such a thing**? I cannot imagine **it**. You can imagine **anything you want**.
OBJECT + *as* PREDICATE NOUN	I could imagine **myself** *as a college professor*. We can't imagine **our grandparents** *as teenagers*. Can you imagine **the book** *as a movie*?
OBJECT + (*to be*) PREDICATE NOUN	I imagined **their house** *(to be) a grand mansion*. Fred imagined **himself** *(to be) quite a critic*. Everyone imagines **himself** *(to be) an honest person*.
OBJECT + (*to be*) PREDICATE ADJECTIVE	I always imagined **him** *(to be) very calm*. We never imagined **New York** *(to be) so noisy*. Larry imagines **himself** *(to be) very creative*.
OBJECT + PRESENT PARTICIPLE	I imagined **myself** *winning the lottery*. We couldn't imagine **our parents** *doing such a thing*. Thelma could imagine **Louise** *driving a truck*.
THAT-CLAUSE	I imagine **that you will want to be up early**. Who could imagine **that such a thing would happen**? An optimist always imagines **that things will get better**.
WH-CLAUSE	Just imagine **what might have happened**! I can't imagine **how much that would have cost**. Imagine **whatever you like**.
PRESENT PARTICIPLE	Can you imagine **acting like that**? I never imagined **doing so well on the test**. Who hasn't imagined **winning the lottery**?

PRESENT

I imply	we imply
you imply	you imply
he/she/it implies	they imply

· *Silence implies consent.*

PRESENT PROGRESSIVE

I am implying	we are implying
you are implying	you are implying
he/she/it is implying	they are implying

· *He is implying that he disagrees.*

PAST

I implied	we implied
you implied	you implied
he/she/it implied	they implied

· *I never implied any such thing.*

PAST PROGRESSIVE

I was implying	we were implying
you were implying	you were implying
he/she/it was implying	they were implying

· *They were implying much more than they said.*

PRESENT PERFECT ... have | has implied
PAST PERFECT   ... had implied

FUTURE   ... will imply
FUTURE PROGRESSIVE ... will be implying
FUTURE PERFECT   ... will have implied

PAST PASSIVE

—	—
—	—
it was implied	they were implied

· *It was certainly implied by what he said.*

(**COMPLEMENTS**)

imply _____ *suggest/indicate without actually saying*

OBJECT	His comments imply **a willingness to cooperate.**
	The tone of the statement implied **a relaxation of hostilities.**
	Dark clouds always imply **rain.**
	I don't think he was necessarily implying **anything.**
PASSIVE	Their cooperation was definitely implied.
THAT-CLAUSE	He implied **that they would cooperate fully.**
	The publisher has implied **that they might publish my book.**
	His knowing smile implies **that he understands you perfectly.**
	The waiter implied **that our table was needed by others.**

PRESENT		PRESENT PROGRESSIVE	
I improve	we improve	I am improving	we are improving
you improve	you improve	you are improving	you are improving
he/she/it improves	they improve	he/she/it is improving	they are improving

 • *The new road improves land values.* • *I am improving every day.*

PAST		PAST PROGRESSIVE	
I improved	we improved	I was improving	we were improving
you improved	you improved	you were improving	you were improving
he/she/it improved	they improved	he/she/it was improving	they were improving

 • *His health improved after he quit his job.* • *We were improving the kitchen little by little.*

PRESENT PERFECT ... have | has improved
PAST PERFECT ... had improved

FUTURE ... will improve
FUTURE PROGRESSIVE ... will be improving
FUTURE PERFECT ... will have improved

PAST PASSIVE

— —
— —
it was improved   they were improved

 • *The design was improved by eliminating the frills.*

(COMPLEMENTS)

improve *get better*

Paul's health is improving daily.
My knee isn't improving as quickly as I would like.
The quality of the soil was noticeably improving.
Sales figures have not improved much lately.
Our Spanish has improved since we moved to Madrid.

improve _____ *make better, increase*
OBJECT

The new antenna improved **radio reception** a lot.
My new glasses have noticeably improved **my vision**.
Urban redevelopment has improved **the city's tax base**.
Reorganization has improved **productivity** by 25%.

(PHRASAL VERBS)

improve on/upon _____
make/do better than

How could you improve on Post-it notes?
The new website improved on the navigation shortcomings
  of the old site.
Your original article has been much improved upon.

PRESENT

I include	we include
you include	you include
he/she/it includes	they include

• *The price includes all taxes.*

PAST

I included	we included
you included	you included
he/she/it included	they included

• *I included some extra brochures.*

PRESENT PERFECT ... have | has included
PAST PERFECT ... had included

PRESENT PROGRESSIVE

I am including	we are including
you are including	you are including
he/she/it is including	they are including

• *I am including everyone who wants to come.*

PAST PROGRESSIVE

I was including	we were including
you were including	you were including
he/she/it was including	they were including

• *They were including service charges on their bills.*

FUTURE ... will include
FUTURE PROGRESSIVE ... will be including
FUTURE PERFECT ... will have included

PAST PASSIVE

I was included	we were included
you were included	you were included
he/she/it was included	they were included

• *Wine was not included on the fixed-price menu.*

COMPLEMENTS

include _____ *have as part of a whole, contain* [NOT USED IN THE PROGRESSIVE TENSES]

OBJECT	The bid includes **parts and materials.**
	The nucleus includes **both protons and neutrons.**
	Their family includes **two adopted children.**
WH-CLAUSE	The treaty can only include **what both sides agree to.**

include _____ *make a part of, add*

OBJECT	Did you include **ketchup and mustard** on the shopping list?
	We have to include **all the aunts and uncles.**
	He is including **wind technology** in the nation's energy policy.
PASSIVE	A number of out-of-town friends and relatives were included on the guest list.
WH-CLAUSE	You can include **whomever you want to invite.**
	I will include **whatever else you need.**

PRESENT

I increase	we increase
you increase	you increase
he/she/it increases	they increase

• *Rainfall increases as you move east.*

PRESENT PROGRESSIVE

I am increasing	we are increasing
you are increasing	you are increasing
he/she/it is increasing	they are increasing

• *I am increasing my original estimate.*

PAST

I increased	we increased
you increased	you increased
he/she/it increased	they increased

• *His popularity increased over the years.*

PAST PROGRESSIVE

I was increasing	we were increasing
you were increasing	you were increasing
he/she/it was increasing	they were increasing

• *Costs were increasing every month.*

PRESENT PERFECT ... have | has increased
PAST PERFECT ... had increased

FUTURE ... will increase
FUTURE PROGRESSIVE ... will be increasing
FUTURE PERFECT ... will have increased

PAST PASSIVE

—	—
—	—
it was increased	they were increased

• *My salary was increased by 10%.*

COMPLEMENTS

increase *become larger/greater/faster*
Computing capacity increases every year.
New housing starts have not increased for a year.
At first, family size increases with income.
Power generation has increased 20% a year for a decade.
Population increases at a geometric rate.
The hurricane's speed is increasing as it moves away from Florida.

increase _____ *make larger/greater/faster, add to*

OBJECT
Can you increase **the power**?
Senator Blather wants to increase **his popularity**.
We should increase **the kids' allowance**.
Replacing the pipe will increase **the flow rate**.
He wanted to increase **the minimum wage** from $5.15 an hour to $7.25.
They increased **processor speed** while decreasing power consumption.

PASSIVE
Plant growth can be increased by improved fertilizers.

I indicate   we indicate
you indicate   you indicate
he/she/it indicates   they indicate

• *His temperature indicates an infection.*

PRESENT PROGRESSIVE

I am indicating   we are indicating
you are indicating   you are indicating
he/she/it is indicating   they are indicating

• *He is indicating that he will not accept the award.*

PAST

I indicated   we indicated
you indicated   you indicated
he/she/it indicated   they indicated

• *He indicated a willingness to cooperate.*

PAST PROGRESSIVE

I was indicating   we were indicating
you were indicating   you were indicating
he/she/it was indicating   they were indicating

• *Economic signs were indicating a mild recession.*

PRESENT PERFECT ... have | has indicated
PAST PERFECT ... had indicated

FUTURE ... will indicate
FUTURE PROGRESSIVE ... will be indicating
FUTURE PERFECT ... will have indicated

PAST PASSIVE

I was indicated   we were indicated
you were indicated   you were indicated
he/she/it was indicated   they were indicated

• *Prompt action was indicated.*

COMPLEMENTS

indicate _____ *point to, signify, make known*

OBJECT	The poll indicates **voter dissatisfaction**.
	The broken window indicated **an intruder**.
	Warm, wet weather usually indicates **a high-pressure system**.
	A yellow card indicates **a penalty**.
	Each blip on the screen indicates **one aircraft**.
THAT-CLAUSE	That light indicates **that the engine is overheating**.
	His hesitation indicated **that he was having doubts**.
	Their laughter indicated **that the kids were having a great time**.
	All signs indicate **that the economy will rebound**.
WH-CLAUSE	The committee never indicated **whom they would recommend**.
	The attendant indicated **where we should park**.
	A sign indicated **how much we should pay**.

indicate _____ *express*

OBJECT	He indicated **his displeasure** by frowning.
	The cat indicated **her pleasure** by purring.
	The suspect indicated **a willingness to cooperate**.
THAT-CLAUSE	I indicated **that I would be more careful**.
	The coach indicated **that he would meet us after the game**.
	We politely indicated **that we disagreed**.

indicate _____ *show/suggest the need for*

OBJECT	A system breakdown indicates **immediate action**.
	The X-rays indicate **surgery**.
	The team's poor performance indicated **a coaching change**.
PASSIVE	Intervention was clearly indicated by the circumstances.

PRESENT

I inform	we inform
you inform	you inform
he/she/it informs	they inform

- *He informs us when a deadline is near.*

PAST

I informed	we informed
you informed	you informed
he/she/it informed	they informed

- *I already informed them of the decision.*

PRESENT PERFECT ... have | has informed
PAST PERFECT ... had informed

PRESENT PROGRESSIVE

I am informing	we are informing
you are informing	you are informing
he/she/it is informing	they are informing

- *I am informing you now.*

PAST PROGRESSIVE

I was informing	we were informing
you were informing	you were informing
he/she/it was informing	they were informing

- *They were informing passengers about the delay.*

FUTURE ... will inform
FUTURE PROGRESSIVE ... will be informing
FUTURE PERFECT ... will have informed

PAST PASSIVE

I was informed	we were informed
you were informed	you were informed
he/she/it was informed	they were informed

- *We were already informed of the meeting.*

(**COMPLEMENTS**)

inform _____ *tell, give facts/information to*

OBJECT	You should inform **the staff** right away.
	When will you inform **them**?
	We can inform **all of our suppliers** by e-mail.
PASSIVE	We were informed just this morning.
OBJECT + *of* OBJECT	We informed **the members** *of the schedule change.*
	The president informed **Congress** *of weapons sales in the Mideast.*
OBJECT + THAT-CLAUSE	We informed **her** *that they were going to be late.*
	The contractor informed **Jerry** *that the tile was unavailable.*
PASSIVE	We were informed *that the class was already full.*
OBJECT + WH-CLAUSE	We informed **them** *what needed to be done.*
	I informed **them** *where the meeting would be held.*
	He informed **us** *how much the project would cost.*

inform _____ *guide, give a characteristic quality to*

OBJECT	A sense of humility informs **all his writings**.
	Research informs **our new product development**.
	Educational theories have always informed **teaching practices**.
WH-CLAUSE	The applicant's personality always informs **who we hire**.
	Conservative principles inform **what the party stands for**.
	Her own experience has always informed **what she writes about**.

(**PHRASAL VERBS**)

inform on/against _____ *give information about the criminal activity of*

Danielle informed on her boss,
  who was using questionable accounting practices.

PRESENT

I insist	we insist
you insist	you insist
he/she/it insists	they insist

• *He insists that we go ahead without him.*

PAST

I insisted	we insisted
you insisted	you insisted
he/she/it insisted	they insisted

• *I always insisted on promptness.*

PRESENT PERFECT ... have | has insisted
PAST PERFECT ... had insisted

PRESENT PROGRESSIVE

I am insisting	we are insisting
you are insisting	you are insisting
he/she/it is insisting	they are insisting

• *He is insisting on his fair share.*

PAST PROGRESSIVE

I was insisting	we were insisting
you were insisting	you were insisting
he/she/it was insisting	they were insisting

• *They were insisting that we have dinner with them.*

FUTURE ... will insist
FUTURE PROGRESSIVE ... will be insisting
FUTURE PERFECT ... will have insisted

PAST PASSIVE

—	—
—	—
it was insisted	they were insisted

• *Additional security was insisted on.*

COMPLEMENTS

insist _____ *claim forcefully*

THAT-CLAUSE

I insisted **that I had made a reservation.**
We insisted **that there had been some mistake.**
They insisted **that the roads were too icy to drive on.**

insist _____ *demand strongly*

on/upon OBJECT

He always insists **on the aisle seat.**
We insisted **on a table near the window.**
They didn't insist **on a formal bid.**
The president insists **upon integrity** among his cabinet members.

PASSIVE

A May deadline was insisted upon by the mayor.

BASE-FORM THAT-CLAUSE

I insist **that the motion be voted on.**
We insisted **that we be seated immediately.**
Fiona insists **that she be allowed to say a few words.**

on/upon PRESENT PARTICIPLE

The kids insisted **on doing it themselves.**
My parents always insist **on arriving an hour early.**
They insisted **on taking us out to dinner.**
I insist **upon speaking with your manager.**

PRESENT

I install	we install
you install	you install
he/she/it installs	they install

- *They install air conditioning systems.*

PRESENT PROGRESSIVE

I am installing	we are installing
you are installing	you are installing
he/she/it is installing	they are installing

- *She is installing the new version of the program.*

PAST

I installed	we installed
you installed	you installed
he/she/it installed	they installed

- *The church installed a new minister.*

PAST PROGRESSIVE

I was installing	we were installing
you were installing	you were installing
he/she/it was installing	they were installing

- *She was installing the garbage disposal herself.*

PRESENT PERFECT … have | has installed
PAST PERFECT … had installed

FUTURE … will install
FUTURE PROGRESSIVE … will be installing
FUTURE PERFECT … will have installed

PAST PASSIVE

I was installed	we were installed
you were installed	you were installed
he/she/it was installed	they were installed

- *He was installed as president of the historical society.*

COMPLEMENTS

install _____ be (able to be) put in position for use

ADVERB OF TIME	Our company's cable modem installs **in minutes**.
ADVERB OF PLACE	The low-flow showerhead installs **in place of the old one**.
ADVERB OF MANNER	The spam filter installs **easily on any server**.

install _____ put in a position/office with a ceremony

OBJECT	We installed **a new president** on January 20.
	The college has installed **its first African-American dean**.
OBJECT + *as* OBJECT	They installed **Michelle** *as the new secretary*.
PASSIVE	Michelle was installed *as the new secretary*.

install _____ put in place, settle

OBJECT	The cat installed **herself** on the ottoman.
	The government installed **a new colony** on the west bank of the river.

install _____ put in position for use

OBJECT	Don installed **flooring** until his knees gave out.
	We need to install **new locks** on all exterior doors.
	Casey will install **a new dishwasher** this weekend.
	My daughter installed **a new operating system** on my computer.
	Dad had installed **three different antivirus programs** on his computer.

PRESENT

I intend	we intend
you intend	you intend
he/she/it intends	they intend

• *He intends to start the meeting at eight.*

PRESENT PROGRESSIVE

I am intending	we are intending
you are intending	you are intending
he/she/it is intending	they are intending

• *I am intending for Larry to assist us.*

PAST

I intended	we intended
you intended	you intended
he/she/it intended	they intended

• *I always intended to learn Italian.*

PAST PROGRESSIVE

I was intending	we were intending
you were intending	you were intending
he/she/it was intending	they were intending

• *We were intending to go to a movie tonight.*

PRESENT PERFECT ... have | has intended
PAST PERFECT ... had intended

FUTURE ... will intend
FUTURE PROGRESSIVE ... will be intending
FUTURE PERFECT ... will have intended

PAST PASSIVE

—	—
—	—
it was intended	they were intended

• *These books were intended for children.*

(**COMPLEMENTS**)

intend _____ *plan, have in mind*

for OBJECT + INFINITIVE	I intended **for Robert** *to pick us up.*
	The captain intended **for the squad** *to hold the bridge.*
	Holmes intended **for Watson** *to solve the crime.*
INFINITIVE	I intend **to take the train to Chicago.**
	We had intended **to leave early.**
	We never intended **to stay so long.**
	What did you intend **to do about it?**

intend _____ *mean, have for the purpose/use of*

OBJECT + *as* PREDICATE NOUN	I intended **the book** *as a present.*
	He intended **the play** *as social satire.*
	We only intended **the proposal** *as a first draft.*
	They intended **it** *as a joke.*
	He intended **the remark** *as an attack on racism.*
PASSIVE	The remark was intended *as an attack on racism.*
OBJECT + *for* OBJECT	We intend **these instructions** *for beginners.*
OBJECT + *for* WH-CLAUSE	The teacher intended **the punishment** *for whoever failed to do their homework.*
for OBJECT + INFINITIVE	We intend **for these sweaters** *to be donated to disabled veterans.*

PRESENT

I interest	we interest
you interest	you interest
he/she/it interests	they interest

• *Your proposal interests me.*

PRESENT PROGRESSIVE

Interest is rarely used in the progressive tenses.

PAST

I interested	we interested
you interested	you interested
he/she/it interested	they interested

• *Her talk interested me in learning more.*

PAST PROGRESSIVE

Interest is rarely used in the progressive tenses.

PRESENT PERFECT ... have | has interested
PAST PERFECT ... had interested

FUTURE ... will interest
FUTURE PROGRESSIVE —
FUTURE PERFECT ... will have interested

PAST PASSIVE

I was interested	we were interested
you were interested	you were interested
he/she/it was interested	they were interested

• *I was really interested in what you were saying.*

───(**COMPLEMENTS**)───

interest _____ *engage the attention/involvement of*

OBJECT
Your idea has interested **all of us.**
The game will interest **the children.**
The weather interests **everyone.**

interest _____ *cause to become involved with*

OBJECT + *in* OBJECT
Can I interest **you** *in a game of checkers*?
We tried to interest **our son** *in finding his own apartment.*

OBJECT + *in* WH-CLAUSE
The writer tried to interest **them** *in what he had published.*

PASSIVE
I was interested *in what you said.*

PRESENT

I introduce	we introduce
you introduce	you introduce
he/she/it introduces	they introduce

• *He always introduces the speaker.*

PRESENT PROGRESSIVE

I am introducing	we are introducing
you are introducing	you are introducing
he/she/it is introducing	they are introducing

• *I am introducing them this afternoon.*

PAST

I introduced	we introduced
you introduced	you introduced
he/she/it introduced	they introduced

• *They introduced several new products.*

PAST PROGRESSIVE

I was introducing	we were introducing
you were introducing	you were introducing
he/she/it was introducing	they were introducing

• *We were introducing ourselves to all the visitors.*

PRESENT PERFECT ... have | has introduced
PAST PERFECT   ... had introduced

FUTURE   ... will introduce
FUTURE PROGRESSIVE   ... will be introducing
FUTURE PERFECT   ... will have introduced

PAST PASSIVE

I was introduced	we were introduced
you were introduced	you were introduced
he/she/it was introduced	they were introduced

• *The legislation was introduced last session.*

—(**COMPLEMENTS**)—

introduce _____ *present, announce*

OBJECT   Ms. Taylor will introduce **the next speaker.**
                 They are going to introduce **a new product** next week.
                 Only a member can formally introduce **a bill.**
                 The first chapter introduces **the main characters.**

PASSIVE   The speaker was introduced by Ms. Wamhoff.

introduce _____ *make acquainted*

OBJECT   I introduced **Ron and Barbara.**
                 When did you introduce **the Smiths?**
                 Let me introduce **myself** to you and your wife.
                 Our club has introduced **a number of young couples.**

PASSIVE   Ruth and I were never formally introduced.

introduce _____ *bring into use, bring for the first time*

OBJECT   The ancient Greeks introduced **writing** throughout the
                     Mediterranean world.
                 The Spanish introduced **many new diseases** to the New World.
                 Ships introduce **nonnative species of marine organisms** to ports
                     when they dock.
                 John Baskerville introduced **a method for producing smooth
                     white paper.**

PASSIVE   Insulin was introduced in the 1920s.

introduce _____ *make familiar with, bring a knowledge of [something] to*

OBJECT + to OBJECT   My mom introduced **me** *to knitting.*
                 Melvin introduced **his friends** *to archaeology.*
                 Professor Kirby introduced **his students** *to the joys of Latin poetry.*

PASSIVE   The second graders were introduced *to multiplication and division.*

introduce _____ *insert*

OBJECT + into OBJECT   Senator Blather introduced **humor** *into the debate.*
                 Scientists introduced **the modified genes** *into potato plants.*

PASSIVE   Was the virus introduced *into Japan?*

PRESENT

I invite	we invite
you invite	you invite
he/she/it invites	they invite

• *He always invites us to stay for lunch.*

PRESENT PROGRESSIVE

I am inviting	we are inviting
you are inviting	you are inviting
he/she/it is inviting	they are inviting

• *I am not inviting everyone.*

PAST

I invited	we invited
you invited	you invited
he/she/it invited	they invited

• *We invited the Flynns to dinner.*

PAST PROGRESSIVE

I was inviting	we were inviting
you were inviting	you were inviting
he/she/it was inviting	they were inviting

• *They were inviting all their old friends.*

PRESENT PERFECT ... have | has invited
PAST PERFECT ... had invited

FUTURE ... will invite
FUTURE PROGRESSIVE ... will be inviting
FUTURE PERFECT ... will have invited

PAST PASSIVE

I was invited	we were invited
you were invited	you were invited
he/she/it was invited	they were invited

• *We were invited to the reception.*

COMPLEMENTS

invite _____ ask to be one's guest(s)
  OBJECT (+ ADVERB OF PLACE TO/FROM)

We only invited **the committee members.**
We invited **them** *home.*
They invited **us** *to the concert.*
Let's invite **the Muellers** *over for dinner.*

  PASSIVE

invite _____ ask politely, request
  OBJECT + INFINITIVE

Everyone is invited *to Joe's retirement party.*

We invited **the kids' friends** *to swim in the pool.*
He invited **us** *to sit down.*
The senator invited **the reporters** *to ask questions.*

  PASSIVE

The audience was invited *to examine the displays.*

invite _____ make likely to happen
  OBJECT

Doing that just invites **trouble.**
The king's harsh policies invited **rebellion.**
The rumors will invite **financial speculation.**
The wet spring invited **a plague of mosquitoes.**

PHRASAL VERBS

invite _____ along/down/in/out/over/up/etc.
ask to be one's guest in a specified location

Let's invite the grandkids along
  on our next vacation.
The McLanes invited the Molitors over for drinks.

invite _____ out *ask on a date*

Billy Joe invited Mary Sue out for lunch.

PRESENT

I involve	we involve
you involve	you involve
he/she/it involves	they involve

• *Her music involves us completely.*

PRESENT PROGRESSIVE

I am involving	we are involving
you are involving	you are involving
he/she/it is involving	they are involving

• *I am not involving you in the project.*

PAST

I involved	we involved
you involved	you involved
he/she/it involved	they involved

• *I involved Roderick as little as possible.*

PAST PROGRESSIVE

I was involving	we were involving
you were involving	you were involving
he/she/it was involving	they were involving

• *The financial crisis was involving the banks.*

PRESENT PERFECT ... have | has involved
PAST PERFECT ... had involved

FUTURE ... will involve
FUTURE PROGRESSIVE ... will be involving
FUTURE PERFECT ... will have involved

PAST PASSIVE

I was involved	we were involved
you were involved	you were involved
he/she/it was involved	they were involved

• *We were completely involved.*

(**COMPLEMENTS**)

involve _____ *engage, occupy, affect*

OBJECT	The research involves **him** completely.
	These stupid games totally involve **the children**.
	The election has involved **the entire country**.
PASSIVE	They were all involved in the conspiracy.

involve _____ *include, entail*

OBJECT	The plan involves **a lot of risk**.
	Did the accident involve **any injuries**?
	The cancer might involve **the lymph nodes**.
PASSIVE	Some danger is involved.
PRESENT PARTICIPLE	The attack involved **making a complex flanking movement**.
	The charges involve **filing a false report**.
	The job involves **working every other weekend**.
	The play's staging will involve **flying a kite**.

involve _____ *draw into difficulty/trouble*

OBJECT + *in* OBJECT	Paying for Sonny's college involved **us** *in a lot of debt*.

PRESENT

I issue	we issue
you issue	you issue
he/she/it issues	they issue

• *The senator issues press releases nonstop.*

PRESENT PROGRESSIVE

I am issuing	we are issuing
you are issuing	you are issuing
he/she/it is issuing	they are issuing

• *I am issuing a statement shortly.*

PAST

I issued	we issued
you issued	you issued
he/she/it issued	they issued

• *The company issued new stock.*

PAST PROGRESSIVE

I was issuing	we were issuing
you were issuing	you were issuing
he/she/it was issuing	they were issuing

• *The crowd was issuing out of the stadium.*

PRESENT PERFECT … have | has issued
PAST PERFECT … had issued

FUTURE … will issue
FUTURE PROGRESSIVE … will be issuing
FUTURE PERFECT … will have issued

PAST PASSIVE

I was issued	we were issued
you were issued	you were issued
he/she/it was issued	they were issued

• *The stamps were first issued in 1945.*

COMPLEMENTS

issue _____ *send out, distribute, make available*

OBJECT
The officers were issuing **a string of frantic orders.**
The editor issued **new assignments** to all the reporters.
We need to issue **new ID cards.**
The publisher issued **a new series of foreign language textbooks.**
Senator Blather issued **an apology.**
The National Weather Service has issued **a tornado warning for our area.**

PASSIVE
The amendments to the bill were just issued.
The new Lincoln stamps were issued yesterday.

issue _____ *discharge*

OBJECT
The pipe issued **wastewater** into the lake.
The brakes were issuing **a shower of sparks.**
The volcano was issuing **clouds of toxic gases.**

issue _____ *emerge, flow out*

ADVERB OF PLACE TO/FROM
Blood issued **from the gash in his leg.**
The stream issues **out of a spring in the mountains.**
A wisp of smoke issued **from the cave.**
Additional mistakes issued **from the first error.**

issue _____ *come about as a result*

ADVERB OF PLACE TO/FROM
Nothing useful will issue **from this seminar.**

EXPRESSIONS

issue a call for _____ *request publicly*   The Red Cross issued an urgent call for blood donors.

PRESENT

I join	we join
you join	you join
he/she/it joins	they join

• *He always joins us for lunch.*

PRESENT PROGRESSIVE

I am joining	we are joining
you are joining	you are joining
he/she/it is joining	they are joining

• *I am joining an exercise class.*

PAST

I joined	we joined
you joined	you joined
he/she/it joined	they joined

• *Thompson joined the company.*

PAST PROGRESSIVE

I was joining	we were joining
you were joining	you were joining
he/she/it was joining	they were joining

• *The two companies were joining together.*

PRESENT PERFECT ... have | has joined
PAST PERFECT ... had joined

FUTURE ... will join
FUTURE PROGRESSIVE ... will be joining
FUTURE PERFECT ... will have joined

PAST PASSIVE

I was joined	we were joined
you were joined	you were joined
he/she/it was joined	they were joined

• *We were joined by several friends.*

COMPLEMENTS

join *come together*

The two rivers join farther south.
Their voices joined in perfect harmony.
I think the two segments will join nicely.
The two family lines have joined many times.

join _____ *connect, link*
     OBJECT

We joined **the pieces** with superglue.
We need to join **the two servers.**
First, join **Part A** to Part B.

     PASSIVE

The two villages are joined by a wooden bridge.

join _____ *come together with socially*
     OBJECT

We are joining **some friends** later.
Will you join **us** for lunch?

join _____ *become a member of*
     OBJECT

I would like to join **a reading group.**
They just joined our **church.**

PHRASAL VERBS

join in _____ *take part in*

Toby loosened his tie and joined
     in the fun.
Celeste would like to join in the conversation.

join up (with _____ **)** *become associated*
(with [someone/something])

Some scientists joined up with a local brewery
     and started "Science on Tap."

EXPRESSIONS

join battle *begin to fight*

The two sides joined battle at 6 A.M.

join forces *work together for a purpose*

The liberals joined forces to defeat the amendment.

join hands *hold one another's hands*

The children joined hands and sang "We Are the World."

join _____ **in marriage/matrimony**
preside over the marriage of

The minister joined the couple in marriage.

Join the club! *You're in the same*
situation that I am / we are.

You don't have money either? Join the club!

PRESENT

I judge	we judge
you judge	you judge
he/she/it judges	they judge

• *He always judges the debate contests.*

PRESENT PROGRESSIVE

I am judging	we are judging
you are judging	you are judging
he/she/it is judging	they are judging

• *I am judging the pie-eating contest.*

PAST

I judged	we judged
you judged	you judged
he/she/it judged	they judged

• *I never judged anyone unfairly.*

PAST PROGRESSIVE

I was judging	we were judging
you were judging	you were judging
he/she/it was judging	they were judging

• *They were always judging their neighbors.*

PRESENT PERFECT ... have | has judged
PAST PERFECT ... had judged

FUTURE ... will judge
FUTURE PROGRESSIVE ... will be judging
FUTURE PERFECT ... will have judged

PAST PASSIVE

I was judged	we were judged
you were judged	you were judged
he/she/it was judged	they were judged

• *They were judged innocent of the crime.*

───(**COMPLEMENTS**)───

judge *form an opinion, act as a judge*

He always judges as fairly as he can.
"Judge not, lest ye be judged." [BIBLE]
"When ye judge between people, judge ye with justice."
[KORAN]

judge ___ *hear and decide a legal case*

OBJECT

He has judged **several cases** in circuit court.
She judged **the big copyright appeal**.

judge ___ *determine, conclude*

OBJECT

How do you judge **the load capacity of a bridge**?
The experts were unable to judge **the value of the painting**.

OBJECT + (*to be*) PREDICATE NOUN

The sheriff judged **Bart** *(to be) a risk to society*.
They judged **Jim** *(to be) a skilled negotiator*.

PASSIVE

Linda's pie was judged *(to be) the best*.

OBJECT + (*to be*) PREDICATE ADJECTIVE

I judged **the watermelon** *(to be) ripe*.
We judged **the situation** *(to be) dangerous*.

OBJECT + INFINITIVE

I judged **the house** *to be in bad shape*.
I judged **the car** *to have cost around $2,000*.

THAT-CLAUSE

He judged **that the boysenberry pie was best**.
The court judged **that it could not hear the case**.

WH-CLAUSE

The committee must judge **who the best qualified person is**.
You must judge **what our best alternative is**.

WH-INFINITIVE

You must judge **what to do**.
They judged **how far to push the issue**.

judge ___ *criticize*

OBJECT

He is always judging **people**.
You can't judge **them** without knowing what happened.
He shouldn't judge **people** by how they dress.
Don't judge **me**!
My English isn't perfect, so try not to judge **me** too harshly.

judge ___ *decide the winner of [a contest]*

OBJECT

They now judge **Olympic figure skating** anonymously.
She was qualified to judge **scholastic debates**.
Three prominent citizens will judge **the local art fair**.

PRESENT

I jump	we jump
you jump	you jump
he/she/it jumps	they jump

• *He jumps at the slightest sound.*

PRESENT PROGRESSIVE

I am jumping	we are jumping
you are jumping	you are jumping
he/she/it is jumping	they are jumping

• *The kids are jumping into the pool.*

PAST

I jumped	we jumped
you jumped	you jumped
he/she/it jumped	they jumped

• *Oil prices jumped four dollars a barrel.*

PAST PROGRESSIVE

I was jumping	we were jumping
you were jumping	you were jumping
he/she/it was jumping	they were jumping

• *Prices were jumping up and down.*

PRESENT PERFECT … have | has jumped
PAST PERFECT … had jumped

FUTURE … will jump
FUTURE PROGRESSIVE … will be jumping
FUTURE PERFECT … will have jumped

PAST PASSIVE

I was jumped	we were jumped
you were jumped	you were jumped
he/she/it was jumped	they were jumped

• *My idea was jumped on by everybody.*

COMPLEMENTS

jump *spring up, leap up*	The kids were jumping with excitement.
	The survivors were jumping and waving their arms.
jump *increase sharply*	The market jumped 200 points in the first hour.
	The price of groceries jumped 17% in two years.
	The river level jumped three feet.
jump *move suddenly and quickly*	All the kids jumped in the pool at the same time.
	We jumped from rock to rock across the stream.
	I can jump on the bus and be there in 20 minutes.
	I jumped into bed right after supper.
	The cat jumped from the table onto my lap.
	The skydivers jumped from 12,000 feet.
jump *move involuntarily, jerk*	My left eye was jumping uncontrollably.
	The computer screen was jumping every few seconds.
jump *change suddenly*	He has jumped from one job to another.
jump _____ *leap over* OBJECT	He jumped **the fence** and ran across the field.
	Their new product has really jumped **the competition**.

PHRASAL VERBS

jump down/in/off/out/up/etc. *leap in a specified direction*	My friend opened the car door and said, "Jump in."
	Pookie the cat liked to jump up on the top edge of a door and meow at us.
	The players were jumping up and down along the sidelines.
jump at _____ *seize enthusiastically*	Melanie jumped at the chance to teach music.
jump in *join a conversation*	We were talking about our favorite books, and Jeremy immediately jumped in.
jump in/into/on _____ *become quickly involved in*	His assistants jumped into the problem of homelessness.
	The reporters jumped on the story about the mayor's resignation.
jump on _____ *criticize severely*	The committee jumped on his income-tax proposal.

PRESENT

I justify	we justify
you justify	you justify
he/she/it justifies	they justify

- *He always justifies himself.*

PRESENT PROGRESSIVE

I am justifying	we are justifying
you are justifying	you are justifying
he/she/it is justifying	they are justifying

- *I am not justifying my earlier remarks.*

PAST

I justified	we justified
you justified	you justified
he/she/it justified	they justified

- *He clearly justified his actions.*

PAST PROGRESSIVE

I was justifying	we were justifying
you were justifying	you were justifying
he/she/it was justifying	they were justifying

- *They were always justifying what they wanted to do.*

PRESENT PERFECT ... have | has justified
PAST PERFECT ... had justified

FUTURE ... will justify
FUTURE PROGRESSIVE ... will be justifying
FUTURE PERFECT ... will have justified

PAST PASSIVE

I am justified	we were justified
you were justified	you were justified
he/she/it was justified	they were justified

- *The manager's decision was justified.*

COMPLEMENTS

justify _____ *demonstrate to be right/fair/reasonable, give a good reason for*

OBJECT	You need to justify **your claim.**
	I can't justify **Larry's rude behavior.**
	I have to justify **my trip expenses.**
	Senator Blather tried to justify **his wild accusations against his opponent.**
PASSIVE	Her response was completely justified.
WH-CLAUSE	I can fully justify **what I did.**
	The repairman justified **how much he was charging.**
	You must justify **whatever changes you made in the contract.**
PRESENT PARTICIPLE	Nobody can justify **behaving like that.**
	I can't justify **buying a new computer.**
	We need to justify **hiring a temp.**
	How can they justify **going so far over budget**?

justify _____ *position so that the edges of [text] are straight* [TYPOGRAPHY]

OBJECT	I don't like the ragged look of this paragraph. Justify **it** left and right.

PRESENT		PRESENT PROGRESSIVE	
I keep	we keep	I am keeping	we are keeping
you keep	you keep	you are keeping	you are keeping
he/she/it keeps	they keep	he/she/it is keeping	they are keeping

- He keeps his keys in the top drawer.
- I am keeping his letters.

PAST		PAST PROGRESSIVE	
I kept	we kept	I was keeping	we were keeping
you kept	you kept	you were keeping	you were keeping
he/she/it kept	they kept	he/she/it was keeping	they were keeping

- I kept careful records of all the expenses.
- We were keeping the grandchildren for the weekend.

PRESENT PERFECT … have | has kept
PAST PERFECT … had kept

FUTURE … will keep
FUTURE PROGRESSIVE … will be keeping
FUTURE PERFECT … will have kept

PAST PASSIVE	
I was kept	we were kept
you were kept	you were kept
he/she/it was kept	they were kept

- His antique autos were kept in immaculate condition.

COMPLEMENTS

keep *remain in good condition, remain the same*

The yogurt will keep for days.
How long will meat keep in the freezer?
No secret keeps for very long.
Will the work keep until tomorrow?

keep ____ *hold in one's possession, retain*

OBJECT

We kept **all of our children's letters.**
Keep **the change.**
The quarterback kept **the ball.**

keep ____ *store*

OBJECT + ADVERB OF PLACE

We keep **all of our cash** *in a safe.*
Where do you keep **the potato chips?**
We're keeping **the extra envelopes** *in this drawer.*

keep ____ *maintain, take care of*

OBJECT

Everyone used to keep **a garden.**
Are you going to keep **your subscription to the magazine?**
You need to keep **good records.**

keep ____ *continue in an activity/position/condition*

PREDICATE ADJECTIVE

The soldiers kept **ready.**
Keep **warm!**
Amazingly, the children kept **quiet.**

PRESENT PARTICIPLE

Keep **working!**
The people behind us kept **talking throughout the concert.**
The company kept **losing money.**

keep ____ *cause to continue in an activity/position/condition*

OBJECT + ADVERB OF PLACE

Keep **your hands** *over your head!*
I kept **my eyes** *on the road.*
Kids! Keep **your hands** *to yourselves.*
The doctor kept **Alice** *in the hospital* two days longer.

OBJECT + *as* PREDICATE NOUN

The president kept **Wilson** *as ambassador to Great Britain.*
The team kept **Charlie** *as captain.*
The new company kept **Chris** *as office manager.*

keep _____ *cause to continue in an activity/position/condition* [continued]

OBJECT + PREDICATE ADJECTIVE   The soldiers kept **their weapons** *ready*.
Keep **your feet** *dry*!
Please try to keep **the room** *clean*.
The secretary kept **the file** *secret*.

OBJECT + PRESENT PARTICIPLE   The sergeant kept **the men** *digging trenches*.
Keep **them** *talking*!
He always kept **us** *laughing at his silly jokes*.

OBJECT + PAST PARTICIPLE   Keep **me** *informed* about the merger.

keep _____ *employ, have in one's service*

OBJECT   The hotel keeps **a large housekeeping staff**.

keep _____ *adhere to, fulfill*

OBJECT   John always keeps **his word**.

(**PHRASAL VERBS**)

keep away/back/down/in/off/out/etc.   Keep away from the edge
remain in a specified location   of the bluff.
My parents are coming—keep down!

keep SEP **away/back/down/in/off/out/etc.**   Can you keep the squirrels away from the corn?
cause to remain in a specified location   It's raining; keep the children in.

keep after/at _____ *nag, harass*   The teacher keeps after us about our homework.

keep at/on/up _____ *continue* [doing]   You're doing a great job. Keep at it!
Keep on writing—the paper's due tomorrow.
It kept on snowing for two days.
This report is wonderful. Keep up the good work.

keep SEP **down** *limit*   We're trying to keep our grocery bill down.

keep SEP **down** *not vomit*   When I had the flu, I couldn't keep food down.

keep ([oneself]) from _____ *prevent oneself*   I could hardly keep from laughing at his costume.
from [doing something]   I tried to keep myself from screaming at him.

keep [someone] from _____ *prevent [someone]*   His counselor kept him from using drugs.
from [doing something]

keep SEP **in/inside** *suppress*   She kept her anger inside until he left.

keep _____ **on** *continue to employ*   The boss hopes to keep all the systems analysts on.

keep _____ **on** *continue to operate*   Derek keeps the radio on all night long.

keep SEP **on** *continue to wear* [clothing]   It's cold in here; I'll keep my coat on.

keep SEP **out** *provide protection from*   This jacket should keep out the rain and wind.

keep out of _____ *not become involved in*   My sisters are arguing, and I'm keeping out of it.

keep to [oneself] *avoid being with other people*   The author keeps to himself.

keep _____ **to [oneself]** *not tell*   Be sure to keep this to yourself.

keep SEP **up** *maintain*   It's not easy for Grandpa to keep up a large house.
We have managed to keep up our family traditions.
Keep your spirits up.

keep up (with _____ **)** *stay even (with*   It's hard to keep up with our rich neighbors.
[someone/something])

PRESENT

I kill	we kill
you kill	you kill
he/she/it kills	they kill

• *He kills the engine when he brakes.*

PRESENT PROGRESSIVE

I am killing	we are killing
you are killing	you are killing
he/she/it is killing	they are killing

• *The suspense is killing me.*

PAST

I killed	we killed
you killed	you killed
he/she/it killed	they killed

• *The Senate killed the bill.*

PAST PROGRESSIVE

I was killing	we were killing
you were killing	you were killing
he/she/it was killing	they were killing

• *A fungus was killing my tomato plants.*

PRESENT PERFECT ... have | has killed
PAST PERFECT ... had killed

FUTURE ... will kill
FUTURE PROGRESSIVE ... will be killing
FUTURE PERFECT ... will have killed

PAST PASSIVE

I was killed	we were killed
you were killed	you were killed
he/she/it was killed	they were killed

• *The deer were killed by wolves.*

COMPLEMENTS

kill _____ *cause to die*

   OBJECT   Someone had killed **the night watchman**.
                       Beetles are killing **pine trees** all over the West.
   PASSIVE   The cancer can only be killed by radiation.

kill _____ *stop, shut off, put an end to*

   OBJECT   Jeff killed **the motor**.
                       Kill **the lights**, will you?
                       The scandal killed **any chance for his re-election**.
                       The company killed **the ad campaign**.
                       It might kill **the pain**.
   PASSIVE   Our competition was just killed by our new product.

kill _____ *pass [time] idly* [INFORMAL]

   OBJECT   They killed **time** looking through old magazines.
                       You have **an hour** to kill before the appointment.

kill _____ *cause extreme pain/unhappiness to* [INFORMAL]

   OBJECT   These shoes are killing **me**.
                       Turn the music down—the noise is killing **me**.
                       Working for a boss like Stanley was killing **her**.

kill _____ *entertain very well* [INFORMAL]

   OBJECT   She just killed **her audience**.

kill _____ *perform very well on* [INFORMAL]

   OBJECT   You killed **the exam**!

PHRASAL VERBS

kill for _____ *go to extremes to get*   I would kill for some frozen custard
                                           right now.

kill SEP **off** *cause the death of*   Our neighbor killed off all the dandelions in his yard.
most/all of a group   Dinosaurs were killed off 65 million years ago.

EXPRESSIONS

kill two birds with one stone   I'll kill two birds with one stone by dropping
accomplish two tasks with a single action   the package off on my way to the grocery store.

kneel

kneel | kneels · knelt · have knelt
kneel | kneels · kneeled · have kneeled

☑ IRREGULAR
☑ REGULAR

PRESENT

I kneel	we kneel
you kneel	you kneel
he/she/it kneels	they kneel

• *The priest always kneels before the altar.*

PRESENT PROGRESSIVE

I am kneeling	we are kneeling
you are kneeling	you are kneeling
he/she/it is kneeling	they are kneeling

• *He is kneeling to reach something under the bed.*

PAST

I knelt/kneeled	we knelt/kneeled
you knelt/kneeled	you knelt/kneeled
he/she/it knelt/kneeled	they knelt/kneeled

• *The clergy all knelt in prayer.*

PAST PROGRESSIVE

I was kneeling	we were kneeling
you were kneeling	you were kneeling
he/she/it was kneeling	they were kneeling

• *The soldiers were kneeling behind the wall.*

PRESENT PERFECT ... have | has knelt/kneeled
PAST PERFECT ... had knelt/kneeled

FUTURE ... will kneel
FUTURE PROGRESSIVE ... will be kneeling
FUTURE PERFECT ... will have knelt/kneeled

PAST PASSIVE

Kneel is never used in the passive voice.

COMPLEMENTS

kneel *be/rest on one's knee(s)*

Laying floor tiles kept me kneeling
    all afternoon.
The policeman was kneeling on one knee when he fired
    his pistol.

kneel *show respect/submission by being/
resting on one's knee(s)*

The king forced the rebels to kneel.
The nuns knelt before the cross.
He knelt before the king to be knighted.
They all knelt in prayer.

PHRASAL VERBS

kneel down *go down on one's knee(s)*

I knelt down to pick up the kids' toys.
We all had to kneel down to get through the low doorway.

PRESENT

I knit	we knit
you knit	you knit
he/she/it knits	they knit

• *She knits one sweater every year.*

PRESENT PROGRESSIVE

I am knitting	we are knitting
you are knitting	you are knitting
he/she/it is knitting	they are knitting

• *I am knitting a wool baby blanket.*

PAST

I knit/knitted	we knit/knitted
you knit/knitted	you knit/knitted
he/she/it knit/knitted	they knit/knitted

• *The bones knitted nicely.*

PAST PROGRESSIVE

I was knitting	we were knitting
you were knitting	you were knitting
he/she/it was knitting	they were knitting

• *He was knitting his hands together.*

PRESENT PERFECT ... have | has knit/knitted
PAST PERFECT   ... had knit/knitted

FUTURE   ... will knit
FUTURE PROGRESSIVE ... will be knitting
FUTURE PERFECT   ... will have knit/knitted

PAST PASSIVE

— —

— —

it was knit/knitted   they were knit/knitted

• *The wall hanging was knit in Scotland.*

COMPLEMENTS

knit *create fabric/clothing by interlocking loops of yarn/thread together with needles*	She knits as a full-time occupation. A lot of people knit for charity organizations. My mother knits when she watches TV.
knit *join, grow together*	The broken bone will eventually knit and become strong. Our neighborhood gradually knit into a close community.
knit ____ *create by interlocking loops of yarn/thread together with needles*	
OBJECT	I am knitting **a wool sweater** for a child in Kazakhstan. Could you knit **a pair of socks** for me?
PASSIVE	The afghan was knit by my grandmother.
knit ____ *cause to join / grow together*	
OBJECT	The tree had knitted **its roots** into a solid mass. I knit **my fingers** to form a shallow bowl. A cast may be required to knit **the broken bone** together. The major had knit **the unit** into an effective force.

PHRASAL VERBS

knit up *make a knitted item, repair by knitting*	This yarn knits up well. That scarf pattern knits up quickly. "Sleep that knits up **the ravell'd sleeve of care.**" [SHAKESPEARE]

EXPRESSIONS

knit [one's] brow(s) *wrinkle one's eyebrows*	Colin knits his brow when he's thinking.

PRESENT

I knock	we knock
you knock	you knock
he/she/it knocks	they knock

• *He always knocks before he enters.*

PRESENT PROGRESSIVE

I am knocking	we are knocking
you are knocking	you are knocking
he/she/it is knocking	they are knocking

• *I am knocking on everyone's door.*

PAST

I knocked	we knocked
you knocked	you knocked
he/she/it knocked	they knocked

• *FBI agents knocked on the hotel door.*

PAST PROGRESSIVE

I was knocking	we were knocking
you were knocking	you were knocking
he/she/it was knocking	they were knocking

• *The engine was knocking pretty badly.*

PRESENT PERFECT ... have | has knocked
PAST PERFECT ... had knocked

FUTURE ... will knock
FUTURE PROGRESSIVE ... will be knocking
FUTURE PERFECT ... will have knocked

PAST PASSIVE

I was knocked	we were knocked
you were knocked	you were knocked
he/she/it was knocked	they were knocked

• *He was knocked down by a passing motorcycle.*

COMPLEMENTS

knock *make a pounding/tapping noise*

The radiator in our room is knocking again.
The engine knocks when you go more than 45 miles an hour.
We have a woodpecker that knocks loudly every morning.

knock _____ *strike/drive*
    OBJECT + ADVERB OF PLACE

Casey knocked **the pitch** *into left field*.
I knocked **the water glass** *onto the floor*.
The explosion knocked **the soldiers** *off their feet*.
I accidentally knocked **the vase** *out of her hand*.

    PASSIVE
We were knocked *to the floor* by the earthquake.

knock _____ *criticize* [INFORMAL]
    OBJECT

Politicians are always knocking **their opponents**.
The critics really knocked **his last movie**.

knock _____ *rap with one's knuckles/fist*
    ON OBJECT

I knocked **on George's door**, but no one answered.
I knocked **on the desk** to get everyone's attention.

knock _____ *make by hitting*
    OBJECT

The carpenter knocked **a hole** in the wall.

PHRASAL VERBS

knock _SEP_ **down** *demolish*	Workers knocked down the vacant building.
knock _SEP_ **down** *hit and cause to fall*	The kids knocked the chair down as they ran past. The bully knocked him down with a single punch.
knock **off** *stop working*	We're going to knock off at 4 o'clock.
knock _SEP_ **off** *reduce the amount by*	The car dealer knocked $1,000 off the sticker price. I convinced the manager to knock off 20% from the bill.
knock _SEP_ **off/out** *make quickly*	How many afghans can you knock off in a week? Gerry can knock out 25 rolling pins in a day.
knock _SEP_ **out** *cause to stop working*	The ice storm knocked out electricity in our neighborhood.
knock _SEP_ **out** *exhaust*	Running five miles has really knocked me out.
knock _SEP_ **out** *make unconscious*	The blow to the head knocked him out.
knock [oneself] **out** *work to exhaustion*	Don't knock yourself out on this project.
knock _SEP_ **over** *surprise, shock*	The price increase knocked me over.

PRESENT

I know	we know
you know	you know
he/she/it knows	they know

• *He always knows what to say.*

PRESENT PROGRESSIVE

Know is never used in the progressive tenses.

PAST

I knew	we knew
you knew	you knew
he/she/it knew	they knew

• *I knew Ben in graduate school.*

PAST PROGRESSIVE

Know is never used in the progressive tenses.

PRESENT PERFECT … have | has known
PAST PERFECT … had known

FUTURE … will know
FUTURE PROGRESSIVE —
FUTURE PERFECT … will have known

PAST PASSIVE

I was known	we were known
you were known	you were known
he/she/it was known	they were known

• *The problem was known years ago.*

COMPLEMENTS

know *be aware / have knowledge of something*

"How old is she?" "I don't know."
"Do you think he knows?" "I am sure he doesn't know."

know _____ *be aware*

  about/of OBJECT (+ INFINITIVE)

We have known **about his cancer** for several months.
Do you know **about his refusal** *to sell the house*?
I don't know **of another doctor** *to call*.

know _____ *be aware of, realize, have information about*

  OBJECT

I know **the answer.**
Tracy knows **a lot about my personal history.**
We know **the place you mean.**

    PASSIVE

His password was known only by his wife.

  OBJECT + INFINITIVE

I know **him** *to be an honest person.*
We have known **the senator** *to give better speeches.*

    PASSIVE

The company has been known *to take big risks before.*

  THAT-CLAUSE

We knew **that it was going to be bad.**
They should have known **that we were leaving early.**
Does he know **that we are waiting?**

  WH-CLAUSE

I know **what you mean.**
Do the tourists know **where they are going?**
Do you know **why he lied to you?**
I don't know **how much it costs.**

  WH-INFINITIVE

He knows **whom to ask.**
Do you know **where to go?**
I know **how to do it.**

know _____ *have in one's memory*

  OBJECT

Most of the actors know **their lines** well.

know _____ *be acquainted/familiar with*

  OBJECT

I knew **your father** in college.
She knows **everybody in the organization.**

  OBJECT + *as* OBJECT

We knew **her** *as Liddy* when we were kids.

know _____ *recognize*

  OBJECT

I'd know **his voice** anywhere.

PRESENT

I lack	we lack
you lack	you lack
he/she/it lacks	they lack

• *He lacks the tools to do the job right.*

PRESENT PROGRESSIVE

I am lacking	we are lacking
you are lacking	you are lacking
he/she/it is lacking	they are lacking

• *The expedition is lacking both food and water.*

PAST

I lacked	we lacked
you lacked	you lacked
he/she/it lacked	they lacked

• *We lacked the necessary resources.*

PAST PROGRESSIVE

I was lacking	we were lacking
you were lacking	you were lacking
he/she/it was lacking	they were lacking

• *Up-to-the-minute information was lacking.*

PRESENT PERFECT ... have | has lacked
PAST PERFECT ... had lacked

FUTURE ... will lack
FUTURE PROGRESSIVE ... will be lacking
FUTURE PERFECT ... will have lacked

PAST PASSIVE

Lack is rarely used in the passive voice.

(COMPLEMENTS)

lack *be missing, not be enough* [USED ONLY IN THE PROGRESSIVE TENSES]

We need to make a decision, but solid information is lacking.

lack _____ *be missing, not have (enough of), need*

OBJECT

We lack **just about everything we need.**
The apartment lacks **adequate closet space.**
We never lacked **confidence in our abilities.**
The team has always lacked **a good defense.**
Is there anything **that** you lack?

for OBJECT [USUALLY NEGATIVE]

The downtown area doesn't lack **for coffee shops,** I see.
Hadley doesn't lack **for confidence,** that's for sure.

in OBJECT [USED ONLY IN THE PROGRESSIVE TENSES]

Herman is lacking **in confidence.**
My old kitchen was lacking **in storage space.**

PRESENT

I last	we last
you last	you last
he/she/it lasts	they last

  • *The concert lasts about two hours.*

PAST

I lasted	we lasted
you lasted	you lasted
he/she/it lasted	they lasted

  • *The recession lasted 18 months.*

PRESENT PERFECT … have | has lasted
PAST PERFECT … had lasted

PRESENT PROGRESSIVE

I am lasting	we are lasting
you are lasting	you are lasting
he/she/it is lasting	they are lasting

  • *The meeting is lasting longer than I expected.*

PAST PROGRESSIVE

I was lasting	we were lasting
you were lasting	you were lasting
he/she/it was lasting	they were lasting

  • *The traffic jam was lasting for hours.*

FUTURE … will last
FUTURE PROGRESSIVE … will be lasting
FUTURE PERFECT … will have lasted

PAST PASSIVE

  Last is never used in the passive voice.

COMPLEMENTS

last *continue, endure*

His Olympic record will never last.
The supplies were lasting pretty well.
Their remarkable success can't last.
The ice cream can't last in this heat.

last ＿＿＿ *continue, endure [for a specified period of time]*
    ADVERB OF TIME

All of our classes last **50 minutes**.
This far north, the sunsets seem to last **forever**.
Football games last **60 minutes**.
Marie can't last **a whole day** without ice cream.
Brick lasts **longer** than vinyl siding.
This car will last **10 years** if you take care of it.
How long can a cricket game last?

last ＿＿＿ *be available to [for a specified period of time]*
    OBJECT + ADVERB OF TIME

The water will last **you** *about two days*.
Our supplies will not last **us** *forever*.
Fifty pounds of dog food will last **them** *about a month*.
How long will the gasoline last **the convoy**?

PRESENT

I laugh	we laugh
you laugh	you laugh
he/she/it laughs	they laugh

• *She laughs a lot at my stories.*

PRESENT PROGRESSIVE

I am laughing	we are laughing
you are laughing	you are laughing
he/she/it is laughing	they are laughing

• *I'm not laughing anymore.*

PAST

I laughed	we laughed
you laughed	you laughed
he/she/it laughed	they laughed

• *I laughed so hard that my sides hurt.*

PAST PROGRESSIVE

I was laughing	we were laughing
you were laughing	you were laughing
he/she/it was laughing	they were laughing

• *He was laughing at his own mistakes.*

PRESENT PERFECT ... have | has laughed
PAST PERFECT ... had laughed

FUTURE ... will laugh
FUTURE PROGRESSIVE ... will be laughing
FUTURE PERFECT ... will have laughed

PAST PASSIVE

I was laughed	we were laughed
you were laughed	you were laughed
he/she/it was laughed	they were laughed

• *His crazy scheme was laughed at.*

COMPLEMENTS

laugh *chuckle/giggle loudly*

He is always laughing.
I am afraid that the guys will just laugh.
Go ahead, tell me. I won't laugh.
"I don't think so," John laughed.

laugh _____ *be amused by*

  at OBJECT

I laughed **at John's joke.**
We all laughed **at the skit.**

  at WH-CLAUSE

Everyone laughed **at what he said.**
The children laughed **at whatever the clown did.**

  at PRESENT PARTICIPLE

Nobody can laugh **at being stuck in an elevator.**
They laughed **at my talking with a fake British accent.**

laugh _____ *mock, make fun of*

  at OBJECT

Trixie laughed **at my predicament.**
What are you laughing **at?**
He can laugh **at himself.**

  PASSIVE

Many inventions were laughed at in the beginning.

  at WH-CLAUSE

I laughed **at how much a new house would cost.**

PHRASAL VERBS

laugh _SEP_ **off** *dismiss as silly*

They laughed off my warnings about
  snakes near the campsite.
The actress laughed off recent reports about her love life.

EXPRESSIONS

He who laughs last, laughs best/longest.
[PROVERB] *Satisfaction may be temporary; someone else may prevail and have greater satisfaction.*

Jonathan stole my girlfriend, but
  I'll get her back. He who laughs last, laughs best.

laugh all the way to the bank *make a lot of money doing something that others consider foolish*

People criticize the actress for her outrageous behavior,
  but she's laughing all the way to the bank.

laugh [one's] head off *laugh loudly and hard*

Be ready to laugh your head off when Pete's around.

laugh [oneself] silly *laugh loudly and hard*

I laugh myself silly when I read Mark Twain's sketches.

PRESENT

I lay	we lay
you lay	you lay
he/she/it lays	they lay

• *He usually lays his keys on his desk.*

PRESENT PROGRESSIVE

I am laying	we are laying
you are laying	you are laying
he/she/it is laying	they are laying

• *We are laying a new rug in the living room.*

PAST

I laid	we laid
you laid	you laid
he/she/it laid	they laid

• *He laid them somewhere else.*

PAST PROGRESSIVE

I was laying	we were laying
you were laying	you were laying
he/she/it was laying	they were laying

• *I was laying the book down when Mom called.*

PRESENT PERFECT ... have | has laid
PAST PERFECT   ... had laid

FUTURE   ... will lay
FUTURE PROGRESSIVE ... will be laying
FUTURE PERFECT   ... will have laid

PAST PASSIVE

—	—
—	—
it was laid	they were laid

• *The wet clothing was laid over bushes to dry.*

(COMPLEMENTS)

NOTE: For the differences between *lay* and *lie*, see the note in the Complements section of verb No. 290.

lay _____ *put down*
   OBJECT + ADVERB OF PLACE

I laid **the blankets** *on the foot of the bed.*
He laid **the spreadsheets** *across the table.*
I had just laid **my head** *on the pillow* when the phone rang.
Lay **them** *over there*, will you?

   PASSIVE

The presents were laid neatly *under the Christmas tree.*

lay _____ *put in position, build*
   OBJECT

Workers are laying **the foundation for a new office building.**

lay _____ *prepare*
   OBJECT

The governments laid **plans for a new world federation.**

lay _____ *attribute*
   OBJECT + *to* OBJECT

I lay **his mistake** *to youth and inexperience.*
Tanya lays **her success** *to her high school English teacher's advice.*

lay _____ *produce and push out [eggs]*
   OBJECT

The chickens were laying **eggs** normally again.
The bird had laid **a pair of eggs** in the oak tree.

(PHRASAL VERBS)

lay __SEP__ **aside/back/down/out/etc.**
put in a specified location

The student laid his book bag down.
Would you lay the pamphlets out on the table?

lay __SEP__ **aside** *abandon*

The president asked the senators to lay aside their differences.

lay __SEP__ **aside/away** *save, put away for future use*

She laid aside $100 a month for her son's college education.

lay __SEP__ **down** *impose, state clearly*

The teacher laid down the rules for playground behavior.

lay **in/up** _____ *store for future use*

There's a snowstorm coming; we should lay in plenty of food.
She laid up canned goods for the winter.

lay **into** _____ *criticize strongly*

The boss laid into the sales staff at the meeting.

lay into _____ _consume voraciously_	Did you see how Bill laid into the barbecued chicken?
lay off (_____) _stop teasing/criticizing_ [INFORMAL]	Lay off, will you!? I wish they would lay off my drag racing.
lay off _____ _stop doing/consuming_	You should lay off video games for a while. I'm laying off candy until after my next doctor's visit.
lay _SEP_ **off** _stop employing, often temporarily_	The company laid off 1,200 programmers.
lay _____ **on [someone]** _present to [someone]_	Let me lay my latest moneymaking scheme on you.
lay _____ **on [someone]** _blame [someone] for_	Don't let Bridget lay the whole crisis on you.
lay _SEP_ **on** _apply_	Parents really know how to lay on the guilt when you've done something wrong.
lay _SEP_ **out** _explain_	He laid out the campaign strategy to the senator's inner circle.
lay _SEP_ **out** _design, plan, organize_	Would you lay out the summer catalog for us?
lay out _____ _spend_	How much money did you lay out for your new computer?
lay over _make a stop during a trip_	We had to lay over at O'Hare Airport for four hours before continuing to Anchorage.
lay _____ **up** _confine, keep from normal activities_	The knee injury laid him up for two months. The mumps laid the boy up for two weeks.

(**EXPRESSIONS**)

lay a finger on _____ _touch lightly_	If he lays a finger on my computer, I'm calling the police.
lay _____ **at [someone's] door/feet** _blame [someone] for_	My supervisor laid the scheduling conflict at my door.
lay claim to _____ _state that one has a right to_	The Spanish government laid claim to the island. Prairie du Rocher lays claim to the title of the oldest continuous white settlement in Illinois.
lay down [one's] life _sacrifice one's life_	The soldier laid down his life for us and our country.
lay down the law _speak sternly_	Ned's father laid down the law about drinking and driving.
lay eyes on _____ _look at, usually for the first time_	We fell in love the first time we laid eyes on each other.
lay hold of _____ _grasp, understand_	"We must lay hold of the fact that economic laws are not made by nature. They are made by human beings." [FRANKLIN D. ROOSEVELT]
lay _SEP_ **in ruins, lay waste to** _____, **lay** _SEP_ **to waste** _destroy completely_	The Roman army laid Jerusalem in ruins in 70 A.D. The hurricane laid waste to the entire coast.
lay it on (thick) _exaggerate_	The tour guide really lays it on thick about the superiority of Wisconsin cheese.
lay it on the line _make something very clear_	Our teacher laid it on the line: Attend every class or fail the course.
lay _____ **to** _blame [something] for_	The company laid the power outage to a lightning strike.

PRESENT

I lead	we lead
you lead	you lead
he/she/it leads	they lead

• *He leads the accounting department.*

PAST

I led	we led
you led	you led
he/she/it led	they led

• *Our policy led to considerable success.*

PRESENT PERFECT ... have | has led
PAST PERFECT   ... had led

PRESENT PROGRESSIVE

I am leading	we are leading
you are leading	you are leading
he/she/it is leading	they are leading

• *He is leading the investigation.*

PAST PROGRESSIVE

I was leading	we were leading
you were leading	you were leading
he/she/it was leading	they were leading

• *We were leading until the last minute.*

FUTURE   ... will lead
FUTURE PROGRESSIVE ... will be leading
FUTURE PERFECT   ... will have led

PAST PASSIVE

I was led	we were led
you were led	you were led
he/she/it was led	they were led

• *The orchestra was led by a young German conductor.*

(COMPLEMENTS)

lead *guide*	I have never led before.
	I can't lead until I know where we are going.
	In a formal dance, it is customary for the gentleman to lead.
lead *be first/ahead (in a competition)*	The Giants are leading for the first time.
	He has led in every tournament he has played this year.
lead ___ *be ahead of, be at the head of*	
OBJECT	He leads **the league** in goals scored.
	Senator Blather will lead **the parade**.
lead ___ *be in charge of*	
OBJECT	Admiral Butler is leading **the task force**.
	She was leading **the company** at the time.
lead ___ *go [in a direction, to a place]*	
ADVERB OF PLACE	This road leads **to my Uncle's farm**.
	The path leads **back home**.
	His proposal will lead **to disaster**.
lead ___ *guide, conduct*	
OBJECT + ADVERB OF PLACE TO/FROM	A guide led **us** *to the monument*.
	He will lead **you** *wherever you want to go*.
PASSIVE	The animals were led *back inside the barn*.
lead ___ *cause, influence*	
OBJECT + INFINITIVE	The weather forecast led **them** *to cancel their trip*.
	The slow sales led **us** *to drop the entire product line*.
PASSIVE	We were led *to believe that we could get dinner here*.
lead ___ *result in*	
to OBJECT	A viral infection can lead **to pneumonia**.
	Four years of college leads **to a bachelor's degree**.
lead ___ *live, spend [time]*	
OBJECT	Our cats led **pampered lives**.

(PHRASAL VERBS)

lead ___SEP___ **away/back/down/in/on/out/** etc. *guide in a specified direction*	The police led the suspect away.
	The sergeant led the soldiers out.

PRESENT

I lean	we lean
you lean	you lean
he/she/it leans	they lean

• *His head always leans to the left.*

PRESENT PROGRESSIVE

I am leaning	we are leaning
you are leaning	you are leaning
he/she/it is leaning	they are leaning

• *I am leaning toward Senator Blather.*

PAST

I leaned	we leaned
you leaned	you leaned
he/she/it leaned	they leaned

• *I never leaned on anybody for help.*

PAST PROGRESSIVE

I was leaning	we were leaning
you were leaning	you were leaning
he/she/it was leaning	they were leaning

• *The ladder was leaning dangerously.*

PRESENT PERFECT ... have | has leaned
PAST PERFECT ... had leaned

FUTURE ... will lean
FUTURE PROGRESSIVE ... will be leaning
FUTURE PERFECT ... will have leaned

PAST PASSIVE

I was leaned	we were leaned
you were leaned	you were leaned
he/she/it was leaned	they were leaned

• *All the skis were leaned against the wall.*

COMPLEMENTS

lean *bend/tilt to one side*

The Christmas tree is leaning
  toward the fireplace.
The sailboat leaned steeply as the breeze freshened.
After the storm, the wharf was leaning and about to collapse.
The wheat was leaning in the wind.
The hikers leaned into the howling storm.

lean _____ *rest [on/against]*
ADVERB OF PLACE

He was leaning **on the rail.**
I had to lean **against the door** to close it.
He leaned **on the chair** and slowly stood up.
We leaned **on the suitcase** to get it shut.

lean _____ *favor, tend*
ADVERB OF PLACE TO/FROM

I am leaning **toward going to graduate school.**
The newspaper leans **to the left.**
Public opinion is leaning **against the government.**
Dictators can lean **either left or right.**
The citizens lean more **toward capitalism than socialism.**

PHRASAL VERBS

lean (_____) back/down/forward/off/
out/over/etc. *bend ([something]) in a
specified direction*

He leaned back and laughed.
The sheriff leaned down and picked up the gun.
The dog leaned out the window.
The dog leaned its head out the window.
The runner leaned over, gasping for breath.

lean on _____ *rely on for advice/support*

Doris is leaning on her parents for tuition.
I lean on an accountant friend of mine for investment help.

PRESENT

I leap	we leap
you leap	you leap
he/she/it leaps	they leap

• *Superman leaps tall buildings with ease.*

PRESENT PROGRESSIVE

I am leaping	we are leaping
you are leaping	you are leaping
he/she/it is leaping	they are leaping

• *The frogs are leaping all over the place.*

PAST

I leaped/leapt	we leaped/leapt
you leaped/leapt	you leaped/leapt
he/she/it leaped/leapt	they leaped/leapt

• *He leapt at every opportunity he got.*

PAST PROGRESSIVE

I was leaping	we were leaping
you were leaping	you were leaping
he/she/it was leaping	they were leaping

• *They were leaping out of the basket.*

PRESENT PERFECT ... have | has leaped/leapt
PAST PERFECT ... had leaped/leapt

FUTURE ... will leap
FUTURE PROGRESSIVE ... will be leaping
FUTURE PERFECT ... will have leaped/leapt

PAST PASSIVE

I was leaped/leapt	we were leaped/leapt
you were leaped/leapt	you were leaped/leapt
he/she/it was leaped/leapt	they were leaped/leapt

• *The wall was leaped over without any difficulty.*

COMPLEMENTS

leap *jump, spring*

He leaps whenever anybody says "Boo!"
The kids were all leaping with excitement.
Antelope were leaping across the savannah.
The fish were leaping like crazy.
Our Siamese cat leapt onto Grandmother's lap.
He hurt his leg. He can't leap.
The defensive player leapt and intercepted the ball.
The basketball player leaped and slammed the ball into the net.
I leaped as high as I could.

leap ____ *jump over*
    OBJECT

We had to leap **the ditch**.
The horses leapt **the fence** easily.
He leaped **every obstacle his opponents put in his way**.

PHRASAL VERBS

leap down/in/off/on/out/over/up/
etc. *jump in a specified direction*

The wagon slowed down, and the boys
  leaped off.
We were leaping up and down, trying to get their attention.

leap at ____ *accept eagerly*

Max leaped at the chance to be his own boss.
The club leaped at Kyle's offer to bring cupcakes.

leap out at ____ *get the*
immediate attention of

The misspelled word leaped out at the proofreader.

EXPRESSIONS

leap for joy *be extremely happy*

Tad won the spelling bee, and his parents
  leapt for joy.

leap off the page (at ____ **)** *be quickly*
noticed (by [someone])

The typographical error leaped off the page at me.
The unemployment statistics leaped off the page at her.

leap to mind *suddenly be thought of*

The author that leaps to mind is William Faulkner.

leap to [one's] feet *jump up excitedly*

The audience leapt to its feet and shouted, "Encore!"

leap to conclusions *make a hasty*
judgment without knowing the facts

Until you have read the entire article, don't leap to conclusions.

PRESENT			PRESENT PROGRESSIVE	
I learn	we learn		I am learning	we are learning
you learn	you learn		you are learning	you are learning
he/she/it learns	they learn		he/she/it is learning	they are learning

• *He always learns the hard way.* • *I am learning how to do it.*

PAST			PAST PROGRESSIVE	
I learned	we learned		I was learning	we were learning
you learned	you learned		you were learning	you were learning
he/she/it learned	they learned		he/she/it was learning	they were learning

• *I just learned what happened.* • *We were learning Italian.*

PRESENT PERFECT	... have | has learned
PAST PERFECT	... had learned

FUTURE	... will learn
FUTURE PROGRESSIVE	... will be learning
FUTURE PERFECT	... will have learned

PAST PASSIVE

— —

— —

it was learned they were learned

• *That lesson was learned at great expense.*

COMPLEMENTS

learn *gain some knowledge/skill*

I am always learning.
Nobody can learn under these circumstances.
He can learn as well as anybody else.

learn ___ *gain some knowledge/skill in*

OBJECT

I learned **English** in high school.
You need to learn **your lines** for the play.
Everyone should learn **a trade**.

PASSIVE

Carpentry can only be learned by doing it.

INFINITIVE

I eventually learned **to cook pretty well**.
He must learn **to use his time better**.
The team must learn **to work together**.

WH-CLAUSE

I quickly learned **who was really in charge**.
The students are learning **what they need to know**.
He needs to learn **where he can find the information**.

WH-INFINITIVE

I learned **whom to ask for help**.
They learned **how to deal with unexpected situations**.
He needs to learn **how to parallel park**.

learn ___ *find out, come to know*

about/of OBJECT

When did you learn **about his criminal record**?
We learned **of her death** from the newspaper.

THAT-CLAUSE

I just learned **that you have been ill**.
Everyone eventually learns **that they can't do it alone**.

learn ___ *memorize*

OBJECT

Students must learn **the Gettysburg Address** by Monday.
Learn **these 20 spelling words** by Friday.

EXPRESSIONS

learn ___ **the hard way** *learn [something]*
by (usually unpleasant) experience

Amy learned about drugs the hard way.

learn the ropes *learn how to do something*

It may take some time for the new secretary to learn
    the ropes.

learn to live with ___ *learn to adapt to*
the pain/difficulty of

Grandpa has learned to live with his arthritis.
The house has no closets, but we've learned to live with it.

PRESENT

I leave	we leave
you leave	you leave
he/she/it leaves	they leave

• *He always leaves home by eight.*

PRESENT PROGRESSIVE

I am leaving	we are leaving
you are leaving	you are leaving
he/she/it is leaving	they are leaving

• *I'm leaving the porch light on.*

PAST

I left	we left
you left	you left
he/she/it left	they left

• *I left you a little surprise.*

PAST PROGRESSIVE

I was leaving	we were leaving
you were leaving	you were leaving
he/she/it was leaving	they were leaving

• *We were just leaving the garage when they called.*

PRESENT PERFECT ... have | has left
PAST PERFECT ... had left

FUTURE ... will leave
FUTURE PROGRESSIVE ... will be leaving
FUTURE PERFECT ... will have left

PAST PASSIVE

I was left	we were left
you were left	you were left
he/she/it was left	they were left

• *Water stains were left all over the ground floor.*

COMPLEMENTS

leave *go away, depart*

We are leaving soon.
When can you leave?
I am not leaving until this is settled.

leave _____ *go away from, depart*
    OBJECT

Elvis has left **the building**.
The train will leave **the station** at 10:13 A.M.
I left **the office** early that day.

leave _____ *abandon, quit*
    OBJECT

He left **the university** in his junior year.
Ray has just left **his wife**.
I left **the law firm** some time ago.

leave _____ *cause/allow to remain behind*
    OBJECT

Red wine always leaves **a stain**.
He left **a fortune** after his death.
The surgery will leave **a little scar**.

    OBJECT + ADVERB OF PLACE

I left **my coat** *with the concierge*.
The kids left **footprints** *on the tile floor*.
She left **her purse** *on the park bench*.

    PASSIVE

Somebody's tickets were left *on the counter*.

leave _____ *cause/allow to remain/be in a certain state*
    OBJECT + PREDICATE NOUN

The accident left **him** *a broken man*.
The fire left **the building** *a ruined shell*.
The training left **the division** *a formidable fighting force*.

    OBJECT + PREDICATE ADJECTIVE

The movie left **me** *confused*.
We had to leave **the children** *alone* for a few hours.
The incident left **us** *speechless*.
Please leave **the door** *open*.
Riding a bicycle leaves **Bill** *out of breath*.

    OBJECT + PRESENT PARTICIPLE

I left **the kids** *finishing up their homework*.
The comedian left **the audience** *roaring with laughter*.
We left **the plumber** *ripping out the old sink*.
Leave **the engine** *running*.

leave _____ *deliver/provide before going away*

INDIRECT OBJECT + DIRECT OBJECT	They left *you* **a message**.
	I am leaving *the waiter* **a big tip**.
	We left *the kids* **some cookies**.
for PARAPHRASE	They left **a message** *for you*.
	I am leaving **a big tip** *for the waiter*.
	We left **some cookies** *for the kids*.

leave _____ *allow/give [someone] to do*

OBJECT + *for* OBJECT	My older sister left **the dishes** *for me*.
OBJECT + *to* OBJECT	The boss will leave **the decision** *to his assistant*.
OBJECT + *with* OBJECT	While I'm in Toronto, I'm going to leave **the project** *with you*.

leave _____ *give at one's death (often by a will)*

| OBJECT + *to* OBJECT | Grandfather left **his stamp collection** *to his granddaughter*. |
| | Mr. Plavsik left **all his money** *to charity*. |

(PHRASAL VERBS)

leave _____ **down/out/up**/etc. *allow to remain in a specified position*
Please leave the window up when you're finished in the room.

leave for _____ *depart in the direction of*
We will be leaving for the airport in 10 minutes.

leave off (_____**)** *stop temporarily*
Now, where did we leave off at yesterday's meeting?
The staff left off trying to organize a company picnic.

leave <u>SEP</u> **off/on** *not put off/on*
He left his jacket off in the classroom.
She left her coat on because it was chilly inside.

leave <u>SEP</u> **out (of** _____**)** *omit, exclude (from [something])*
Harry left out all references to World War Two.
Mrs. Crabtree left Norman out of her will.

leave <u>SEP</u> **on** *not switch off*
Leave the light on when you leave the room.

(EXPRESSIONS)

leave _____ **open** *not schedule another activity on [a day/date]*
Leave next Saturday open for the bake sale.

leave a bad taste in [one's] mouth *cause one to have a lingering bad impression*
The argument over immigration left a bad taste in my mouth.

leave no stone unturned *search everywhere, do everything possible*
The police left no stone unturned in looking for the murderer.

leave _____ **alone/be** *not disturb*
Leave me alone—I'm trying to study.
We should leave the matter be for the moment.

leave _____ **out in the cold** *not keep [someone] informed*
The rest of the staff left her out in the cold with regard to the new project.

leave (some) loose ends *not finish a project, not solve a problem*
The movie rushed the ending and left some loose ends.

be left (over) *remain*
Is there any chocolate cake left?
Some potato salad is left over from the picnic.
Half a skein of yarn is left over from my sweater project.

PRESENT

I lend	we lend
you lend	you lend
he/she/it lends	they lend

• *The bank lends money for new cars.*

PRESENT PROGRESSIVE

I am lending	we are lending
you are lending	you are lending
he/she/it is lending	they are lending

• *I am lending the truck to Anne for the weekend.*

PAST

I lent	we lent
you lent	you lent
he/she/it lent	they lent

• *The bank lent them the money.*

PAST PROGRESSIVE

I was lending	we were lending
you were lending	you were lending
he/she/it was lending	they were lending

• *The banks were not lending at that time.*

PRESENT PERFECT ... have | has lent
PAST PERFECT ... had lent

FUTURE ... will lend
FUTURE PROGRESSIVE ... will be lending
FUTURE PERFECT ... will have lent

PAST PASSIVE

I was lent	we were lent
you were lent	you were lent
he/she/it was lent	they were lent

• *The book was lent to me by a friend.*

COMPLEMENTS

lend *give money on condition of repayment (plus interest)*

Banks are not lending now.
Who can afford to lend?
Who is still lending these days?

lend ____ *allow temporary use of on condition of return/payment*

INDIRECT OBJECT + DIRECT OBJECT
I lent *Peter* **my lawnmower.**
I can lend *you* **$25.**
Could I have lent *someone* **the library book?**

to PARAPHRASE
I lent **my lawnmower** *to Peter.*
I can lend **$25** *to you.*
Could I have lent **the library book** *to someone?*

NOTE: Many speakers prefer to use the verb *loan* (rather than *lend*) when referring to money. For example, they would say "The bank will *loan* you the money" rather than "The bank will *lend* you the money." Both are grammatically correct.

lend ____ *make available to*

INDIRECT OBJECT + DIRECT OBJECT
The Red Cross lent **the flood relief effort** *its services.*

to PARAPHRASE
The Red Cross lent **its services** *to the flood relief effort.*

lend ____ *add*

OBJECT + to OBJECT
The confetti and beads lend **gaiety** *to the Mardi Gras parade.*
The bowl of fruit lends **color** *to an otherwise dull painting.*

PHRASAL VERBS

lend itself to ____ *be suitable for*
The gathering room lends itself to intimate conversation.

lend __SEP__ out *allow temporary use of on condition of return*
We lent out our copy of Jane Austen's *Pride and Prejudice.*

EXPRESSIONS

lend an/[one's] ear (to ____) *listen (to [someone])*
The president is speaking; lend an ear.
"Friends, Romans, countrymen, lend me your ears." [SHAKESPEARE]

PRESENT

I let	we let
you let	you let
he/she/it lets	they let

- *He lets us know if there is a problem.*

PAST

I let	we let
you let	you let
he/she/it let	they let

- *I let the dogs run in the backyard.*

PRESENT PERFECT ... have | has let
PAST PERFECT   ... had let

PRESENT PROGRESSIVE

I am letting	we are letting
you are letting	you are letting
he/she/it is letting	they are letting

- *The coach is letting them try again.*

PAST PROGRESSIVE

I was letting	we were letting
you were letting	you were letting
he/she/it was letting	they were letting

- *We were letting too many mistakes get through.*

FUTURE   ... will let
FUTURE PROGRESSIVE ... will be letting
FUTURE PERFECT   ... will have let

PAST PASSIVE

I was let	we were let
you were let	you were let
he/she/it was let	they were let

- *Several staff members were let go recently.*

COMPLEMENTS

let _____ *allow, permit*
   OBJECT + BASE-FORM INFINITIVE

The referee let **the game** *continue.*
Let **me** *show you around.*
We let **the kids** *watch TV for a while after dinner.*
Don't let **them** *leave without me.*
Let **me** *go!*

let's _____ [CONTRACTION OF **let us**; A WAY TO SUGGEST DOING SOMETHING]
   BASE-FORM INFINITIVE

Let's **go home now.**
Let's **find out what happened.**
Let's **not do that.**

PHRASAL VERBS

let _SEP_ by/down/in/off/on/out/through/up/etc. *allow to come/go in a specified direction*

Let the children in.
The bus stopped and let off two passengers.
Let the dog out.
Stop wrestling and let your brother up.

let _SEP_ down *disappoint*

Son, you've let your parents down again.

let _SEP_ off (easy) (with _____) *forgive/release (with [little/no punishment])*

The policeman let the boys off with a warning.
The teacher let me off easy.

let off/out _____ *release, emit*

The teakettle let off a loud whistle.

let on _____ *pretend*

Barry is letting on that he knows about the crisis.

let on _____ *admit*

Charlotte never let on that she was my sister.

let out *end*

When does the movie let out?

let up *slow down, diminish*

The rain appears to be letting up.

EXPRESSIONS

let alone _____ *not to mention, much less*

The patient can't walk, let alone run.
I don't have time to read a chapter, let alone the
   whole book.

let _____ alone/be *not disturb*

Let your sister alone. Let her be.

let _____ go *fire, lay off*

The company let four mechanics go last Friday.

let go/loose of _____ *release, stop gripping*

If we let go of the rope, we'll fall into the river.

PRESENT

I lie	we lie
you lie	you lie
he/she/it lies	they lie

• *The responsibility lies with all of us.*

PRESENT PROGRESSIVE

I am lying	we are lying
you are lying	you are lying
he/she/it is lying	they are lying

• *The cat is lying asleep on the couch.*

PAST

I lay	we lay
you lay	you lay
he/she/it lay	they lay

• *The ship lay at anchor for a week.*

PAST PROGRESSIVE

I was lying	we were lying
you were lying	you were lying
he/she/it was lying	they were lying

• *The book was lying on your desk.*

PRESENT PERFECT	... have | has lain
PAST PERFECT	... had lain

FUTURE	... will lie
FUTURE PROGRESSIVE	... will be lying
FUTURE PERFECT	... will have lain

PAST PASSIVE

Lie is never used in the passive voice.

NOTE: The irregular verb *lie* is presented here. The regular verb *lie* (*lie* | *lies · lied · have lied*) means "to say something that isn't true"; it may be used without an object (*The suspect is lying*) or with a THAT-CLAUSE (*She lied that her husband was home all evening*).

───(**COMPLEMENTS**)───

NOTE: The verbs *lie* and *lay* are often confused, in part because the past tense form of *lie* (*lay*) is the same as the present tense form of *lay*. (See verb No. 282.)

INFINITIVE	PRESENT	PAST	PAST PARTICIPLE	BASIC MEANING
lie	lie	**lay**	have lain	"be in a horizontal position"
lay	**lay**	laid	have laid	"put in a horizontal position"

The two verbs are historically related in an odd way: To *lay* means "to cause something *to lie*." In other words, *lay* always requires a direct object, while *lie* is never used with a direct object.

lie *be buried*

Here lie the bones of the city's founder.

lie _____ *be located*
  ADVERB OF PLACE

The report is lying **right in front of you.**
The town lies **in the Thames valley.**
His few hairs lay **across his bald head.**
The ocean lies **to the west.**

lie _____ *be/stay in a horizontal position*
  PREDICATE ADJECTIVE

The ocean lay **flat** as far as we could see.
The tablecloth lay **perfectly smooth.**

lie _____ *be/stay in a certain state/condition*
  PREDICATE ADJECTIVE

The cat lay **motionless,** watching the bird.
The town lay **helpless** in front of the invading army.
The nurse told him to lie **still** while she examined him.
The paintings had lain **hidden** in a barn for 50 years.

lie _____ *be, exist*
  in OBJECT
  with OBJECT

The confusion lies **in our conflicting goals.**
The problem lies **with senior management.**

lie _____ *affect*
  on OBJECT

The wrongful conviction lies heavily **on the prosecutors.**
His extramarital affair lies heavily **on his conscience.**

───(**PHRASAL VERBS**)───

lie ahead/around/back/behind/below/down/etc. *be/rest in a specified position*

She lay back and relaxed in the afternoon sun.
I'll lie down for an hour.

PRESENT

I lift	we lift
you lift	you lift
he/she/it lifts	they lift

• *His humor always lifts my spirits.*

PRESENT PROGRESSIVE

I am lifting	we are lifting
you are lifting	you are lifting
he/she/it is lifting	they are lifting

• *I'm lifting your hall pass.*

PAST

I lifted	we lifted
you lifted	you lifted
he/she/it lifted	they lifted

• *The president lifted the embargo.*

PAST PROGRESSIVE

I was lifting	we were lifting
you were lifting	you were lifting
he/she/it was lifting	they were lifting

• *The fog was finally lifting.*

PRESENT PERFECT ... have | has lifted
PAST PERFECT ... had lifted

FUTURE ... will lift
FUTURE PROGRESSIVE ... will be lifting
FUTURE PERFECT ... will have lifted

PAST PASSIVE

I was lifted	we were lifted
you were lifted	you were lifted
he/she/it was lifted	they were lifted

• *The siege of Leningrad was lifted after 872 days.*

COMPLEMENTS

lift *rise, rise and disappear*

The bank of clouds over the bay
  was lifting.
The icy mist over the frozen lake lifted slowly.
The darkness began to lift in the pre-dawn hours.
Our gloomy spirits gradually lifted.

lift ____ *raise*

OBJECT

I could hardly lift **my suitcase**.
The rescuers lifted **the fallen wall** with a crane.
The good news lifted **everyone's mood** instantly.

PASSIVE

The wounded cowboy was lifted onto the horse.

lift ____ *revoke, rescind, end*

OBJECT

The police lifted **his passport**.
The judge lifted **the restraining order**.
The governor lifted **the ban on same-sex marriage**.

PASSIVE

Censorship was only lifted after the war.
The embargo was lifted in April.

lift ____ *steal, plagiarize*

OBJECT

Someone had lifted **her purse**.
He had lifted **several paragraphs** from a magazine article.

PASSIVE

Our luggage was lifted from the room while we slept.

PHRASAL VERBS

lift _SEP_ **down/up**/etc. *move in a specified direction*

I lifted the wine glasses down from
  the cabinet.
Lift your feet up, or you'll stumble.

lift off *launch, take off* [OF SPACECRAFT]

The space shuttle lifted off at 8:54 P.M.

EXPRESSIONS

lift a finger *make an effort*
[USUALLY NEGATIVE]

Roland won't lift a finger to help around
  the house.

lift weights *exercise using* [barbells, dumbbells, etc.]

Look at Biff's biceps—he must be lifting weights.

PRESENT

I light	we light
you light	you light
he/she/it lights	they light

• *Her face lights up when she smiles.*

PRESENT PROGRESSIVE

I am lighting	we are lighting
you are lighting	you are lighting
he/she/it is lighting	they are lighting

• *I am lighting a fire.*

PAST

I lit/lighted	we lit/lighted
you lit/lighted	you lit/lighted
he/she/it lit/lighted	they lit/lighted

• *I lit the candles on the birthday cake.*

PAST PROGRESSIVE

I was lighting	we were lighting
you were lighting	you were lighting
he/she/it was lighting	they were lighting

• *Only candles were lighting the dining room.*

PRESENT PERFECT … have | has lit/lighted
PAST PERFECT … had lit/lighted

FUTURE … will light
FUTURE PROGRESSIVE … will be lighting
FUTURE PERFECT … will have lit/lighted

PAST PASSIVE

—	—
—	—
it was lit/lighted	they were lit/lighted

• *The room was lit only by the fireplace.*

COMPLEMENTS

light *catch fire*

The pile of dry leaves and twigs finally lit.
The smoldering coals lit with a whoosh.
The damp wood never lit.

light ____ *ignite, set fire to, cause to burn*

OBJECT

Sparks from the train lit **trash along the track.**
We should light **the lantern** before it gets dark.

PASSIVE

The fire was lit by an electrical short circuit in the wall.

INDIRECT OBJECT + DIRECT OBJECT

I lit *them* **a candle.**
We will light *them* **a fire.**

for PARAPHRASE

I lit **a candle** *for them.*
We will light **a fire** *for them.*

light ____ *illuminate*

OBJECT

We used torches to light **the path.**
The campfire lighted **the boys' faces.**
The golden moon lit **the southern sky.**

PASSIVE

The street was lit by the burning buildings.

light ____ *guide with a light*

OBJECT + ADVERB OF PLACE TO/FROM

We lit **the children** *to their rooms* with the lantern.
"And all our yesterdays have lighted **fools** *the way to dusty death.*" [SHAKESPEARE]

PHRASAL VERBS

light up *brighten*

The black night lit up with occasional
    flashes of lightning.
Her face lit up when she heard the news.

EXPRESSIONS

light a fire under ____ *cause to move/work faster/harder*

The coach's tirade lit a fire under his
    sluggish team.

I like   we like
you like   you like
he/she/it likes   they like

• *Everyone likes chocolate.*

PRESENT PROGRESSIVE

Like is rarely used in the progressive tenses.

PAST

I liked   we liked
you liked   you liked
he/she/it liked   they liked

• *I never liked his attitude.*

PAST PROGRESSIVE

Like is rarely used in the progressive tenses.

PRESENT PERFECT ... have | has liked
PAST PERFECT ... had liked

FUTURE ... will like
FUTURE PROGRESSIVE —
FUTURE PERFECT ... will have liked

PAST PASSIVE

I was liked   we were liked
you were liked   you were liked
he/she/it was liked   they were liked

• *She was liked by everyone.*

(COMPLEMENTS)

like _____ *enjoy, be fond of*

OBJECT
I liked **the movie** a lot.
We all liked **Venice**.
Did the kids like **their babysitter**?
I like **dogs**, and my sister likes **cats**.

OBJECT + PRESENT PARTICIPLE
I like **them** *doing their homework as soon as they get home.*
We like **our children** *living so close to us.*

INFINITIVE
They like **to go canoeing when the weather is good.**
I like **to read by the fireplace.**

WH-CLAUSE
I like **what you have done with the room.**
The committee liked **how you answered their questions.**

PRESENT PARTICIPLE
We like **living in Chicago.**
My parents like **traveling by train.**

like _____ *want, prefer*

OBJECT
We would like **some coffee**, please.
I would like **a new job**.
Would you like **red or white wine**?

OBJECT + PREDICATE ADJECTIVE
We like **our coffee** *black*, please.
My parents like **the TV** *really loud.*

OBJECT + INFINITIVE
I would like **you** *to take care of it yourself.*
Would you like **him** *to come with us*?

OBJECT + PAST PARTICIPLE
I would like **the oil** *changed every 5,000 miles.*
We would like **the wines** *uncorked now*, please.

INFINITIVE
Would you like **to go to dinner now**?
See if they would like **to join us**.
I would like **to say a few words**.

like _____ *have affection for*

OBJECT
I think Ray likes **her** too.
Mr. Rogers likes **you** just the way you are.

OBJECT + PREDICATE NOUN
Renee likes **Paul** *as a friend.*

like _____ *thrive in*

OBJECT
Pansies like **full sun**.
The blue spruce doesn't like **wet soil**.

PRESENT

I limit	we limit
you limit	you limit
he/she/it limits	they limit

- *I limit myself to two cups of coffee a day.*

PRESENT PROGRESSIVE

I am limiting	we are limiting
you are limiting	you are limiting
he/she/it is limiting	they are limiting

- *We are limiting how long the kids play video games.*

PAST

I limited	we limited
you limited	you limited
he/she/it limited	they limited

- *They limited the number of trips we take.*

PAST PROGRESSIVE

I was limiting	we were limiting
you were limiting	you were limiting
he/she/it was limiting	they were limiting

- *Charles was limiting out-of-season food.*

PRESENT PERFECT ... have | has limited
PAST PERFECT ... had limited

FUTURE ... will limit
FUTURE PROGRESSIVE ... will be limiting
FUTURE PERFECT ... will have limited

PAST PASSIVE

I was limited	we were limited
you were limited	you were limited
he/she/it was limited	they were limited

- *The power of government was limited by the Constitution.*

COMPLEMENTS

limit _____ restrict

OBJECT	We must limit **unnecessary spending.**
	The fishing industry has limited **catches of endangered species.**
	We try to limit **our use of electricity.**
	The Environmental Protection Agency has limited **mercury emissions.**
OBJECT + to OBJECT	Senator Blather will limit **his speech *to 15 minutes.***
	The company's server limits **us *to 25 e-mails a day.***
	State law limits **senators *to two terms.***
	Our cell phone plan limits **calls *to the 48 contiguous states.***
WH-CLAUSE	The high elevation limits **what plants can grow there.**
	The rescue team limited **how far they would search.**
	I should limit **how much I spend on nonessentials.**
PRESENT PARTICIPLE	Our budget limits **eating out.**
	Time limits **our taking too many side trips.**
	Company policy limits **taking spouses on business trips.**

PRESENT

I list	we list
you list	you list
he/she/it lists	they list

• *He lists himself as an Independent.*

PRESENT PROGRESSIVE

I am listing	we are listing
you are listing	you are listing
he/she/it is listing	they are listing

• *I am listing the advantages and disadvantages.*

PAST

I listed	we listed
you listed	you listed
he/she/it listed	they listed

• *I listed some of the things we need to do.*

PAST PROGRESSIVE

I was listing	we were listing
you were listing	you were listing
he/she/it was listing	they were listing

• *They were listing everything they could think of.*

PRESENT PERFECT ... have | has listed
PAST PERFECT ... had listed

FUTURE ... will list
FUTURE PROGRESSIVE ... will be listing
FUTURE PERFECT ... will have listed

PAST PASSIVE

I was listed	we were listed
you were listed	you were listed
he/she/it was listed	they were listed

• *His name was already listed.*

(**COMPLEMENTS**)

list _____ *itemize, create a series of items in written/printed form*

OBJECT
I listed **all of our supplies.**
We need to list **our expenses.**
Can you list **everyone who was present**?
List **three things that you like about the United States.**
We list **you** among the club's most valuable members.
I was listing **all the books I wanted to read**, and I ran out of paper.

PASSIVE
Is your company listed in the phone book?
Our college has been listed among the top ten engineering schools.

WH-CLAUSE
Please list **what you need.**
The participants listed **why they were taking the workshop.**
I will list **whatever times are still available.**

list _____ *place in a category*

OBJECT + *as* PREDICATE NOUN
I listed **Tom** *as a volunteer.*
They listed **the reporters** *as nonvoting observers.*

PASSIVE
The school was listed *as a private four-year college.*

OBJECT + *as* PREDICATE ADJECTIVE
The army listed **him** *as missing in action.*

list _____ *have a specified price*

for OBJECT
The car lists **for $23,995**, but we'll sell it to you for $22,500.
The book lists **for $19.95.**

PRESENT

I listen	we listen
you listen	you listen
he/she/it listens	they listen

• *He always listens to other people.*

PRESENT PROGRESSIVE

I am listening	we are listening
you are listening	you are listening
he/she/it is listening	they are listening

• *I'm listening to what you have to say.*

PAST

I listened	we listened
you listened	you listened
he/she/it listened	they listened

• *I listened long enough.*

PAST PROGRESSIVE

I was listening	we were listening
you were listening	you were listening
he/she/it was listening	they were listening

• *We were listening to the radio.*

PRESENT PERFECT … have | has listened
PAST PERFECT … had listened

FUTURE … will listen
FUTURE PROGRESSIVE … will be listening
FUTURE PERFECT … will have listened

PAST PASSIVE

I was listened	we were listened
you were listened	you were listened
he/she/it was listened	they were listened

• *Her proposal was listened to carefully.*

(**COMPLEMENTS**)

listen *pay attention to in order to hear*	Go ahead. I'm listening. Teenagers never listen. When the president speaks, the country listens. I think someone is listening.
listen ____ *hear attentively*	
to OBJECT	Just listen **to that music**! We had to listen **to their sales pitch**. I want to listen **to the news** at six.
PASSIVE	Experimental music is not listened to often.
to OBJECT + PRESENT PARTICIPLE	Listen **to the rain** *falling on the roof.* The campers listened nervously **to the wolves** *howling in the darkness.* We listened **to the kids** *playing under our window.*
to WH-CLAUSE	We will all listen **to what they propose**. I will listen **to whomever they choose as a spokesperson**. The public listens **to whatever nonsense they hear on talk radio**.
listen ____ *try to hear*	
for OBJECT	Do you know **what** to listen **for** at a congressional hearing? Listen **for the words "walrus" and "Paul."**
for OBJECT + INFINITIVE	I am listening **for the clock** *to chime.* Listen **for the owl** *to hoot.*

(**PHRASAL VERBS**)

listen in *listen to a radio broadcast*	Noam Chomsky will be interviewed on NPR tonight; I'm going to listen in.
listen in on ____ *listen to secretly*	If you heard two friends talking about you, would you listen in on them?
listen up *listen carefully*	The drill sergeant told the recruits to listen up.

(**EXPRESSIONS**)

listen to reason *accept a reasonable argument*	His lawyer recommended that he plead guilty, but he wouldn't listen to reason.

PRESENT		PRESENT PROGRESSIVE	
I live	we live	I am living	we are living
you live	you live	you are living	you are living
he/she/it lives	they live	he/she/it is living	they are living

• *They live on Chautauqua Court.*   • *He is living pretty well.*

PAST		PAST PROGRESSIVE	
I lived	we lived	I was living	we were living
you lived	you lived	you were living	you were living
he/she/it lived	they lived	he/she/it was living	they were living

• *He lived in the United States for six years.*   • *John was virtually living in his office.*

PRESENT PERFECT ... have | has lived
PAST PERFECT ... had lived

FUTURE ... will live
FUTURE PROGRESSIVE ... will be living
FUTURE PERFECT ... will have lived

PAST PASSIVE

— —
— —
it was lived   they were lived

• *His life was lived to the fullest.*

───────────────── COMPLEMENTS ─────

live *be alive, exist*	Aunt Pearl lived to be 99 years old.
	Few people live after such a terrible accident.
	King Arthur never lived.
live *have a wonderful life*	You haven't lived until you've tasted Mom's lemon meringue pie.
live _____ *subsist, survive, feed on* ADVERB OF MANNER	I can't live **that way**. The prisoners lived **under dreadful conditions**.
live _____ *reside* ADVERB OF PLACE	They live **at 3817 West Main Street**. My great-grandparents lived **on a farm**. We have never lived **outside the country**.
live _____ *experience, pass one's life in a certain way* ADVERB OF MANNER OBJECT	James Bond loves to live **dangerously**. And the prince and princess lived **happily ever after**. The actor was living **a dream**. He was living **a life of luxury**.

───────────────── PHRASAL VERBS ─────

live SEP **down** *stop being embarrassed about*	I'll never live down forgetting my wedding anniversary.
live for _____ *consider extremely important*	Betty lives for coffee.
live off (of) _____ *survive by eating*	The campers lived mostly off fruits and berries.
live off (of) _____ *depend on for food and shelter*	She lived off her parents when she was in college. They live off of the paintings that they sell.
live on *survive, continue*	The legend of the phantom funeral lives on.
live on _____ *eat, feed on*	Many poor farmers live on rice and beans. Goldfinches live on insects and seeds.
live on _____ *support oneself with* [OF PEOPLE]	Mrs. Blaine lives on Social Security and a small pension.
live through _____ *survive*	How did they live through the Great Depression?
live up to _____ *maintain, meet* [standards]	How can I live up to my parents' expectations?
live with _____ *endure, put up with*	He lived with a limp for the rest of his life.

PRESENT			PRESENT PROGRESSIVE

PRESENT

I locate   we locate
you locate   you locate
he/she/it locates   they locate

• *The agency locates missing people.*

PRESENT PROGRESSIVE

Locate is rarely used in the progressive tenses.

PAST

I located   we located
you located   you located
he/she/it located   they located

• *They located the shipwreck in 1985.*

PAST PROGRESSIVE

Locate is rarely used in the progressive tenses.

PRESENT PERFECT ... have | has located
PAST PERFECT   ... had located

FUTURE   ... will locate
FUTURE PROGRESSIVE —
FUTURE PERFECT   ... will have located

PAST PASSIVE

I was located   we were located
you were located   you were located
he/she/it was located   they were located

• *The old stadium was located at Grand and Dodier.*

(**COMPLEMENTS**)

locate _____ *find out where [someone/something] is*

OBJECT	We never located **the original deed.**
	We have to locate **the property line.**
	Have the police located **the murder weapon?**
	My parents located **a good preschool** for Thomas.
PASSIVE	The treasure was never located.
OBJECT + ADVERB OF PLACE	We eventually located **the keys** *under some papers.*
	I located **the store** *in a strip mall near the highway.*
	He located **the missing cup** *in the trash can.*
WH-CLAUSE	Historians have located **where Shakespeare's theater stood.**
	He finally located **where the smell was coming from.**
	Did you locate **whatever you were looking for?**

locate _____ *position, situate*

OBJECT + ADVERB OF PLACE	They advised us to locate **the store** *downtown.*
	You should locate **your café** *in the new business park.*
	We located **our house** *as far from the road as possible.*
PASSIVE	Our house is located *as far from the road as possible.*

locate _____ *settle, put one's home/business*

ADVERB OF PLACE	The English colonists located **on the banks of the James River.**
	The trucking company located **at the intersection of two interstate highways.**

PRESENT		PRESENT PROGRESSIVE	
I lock	we lock	I am locking	we are locking
you lock	you lock	you are locking	you are locking
he/she/it locks	they lock	he/she/it is locking	they are locking

• *My knee locks if I stand too long.*   • *I am locking all of the windows.*

PAST		PAST PROGRESSIVE	
I locked	we locked	I was locking	we were locking
you locked	you locked	you were locking	you were locking
he/she/it locked	they locked	he/she/it was locking	they were locking

• *They have just locked the gate.*   • *The left front wheel was locking.*

PRESENT PERFECT ... have | has locked   **FUTURE** ... will lock
PAST PERFECT ... had locked   **FUTURE PROGRESSIVE** ... will be locking
                                    FUTURE PERFECT ... will have locked

PAST PASSIVE

I was locked	we were locked
you were locked	you were locked
he/she/it was locked	they were locked

• *All of the doors were locked.*

COMPLEMENTS

lock *become fastened with a bolt mechanism*	The door locked with a click. The gates lock automatically. That door never locks properly.
lock *become stuck in one position*	Sometimes the car's steering wheel locks. My left elbow locks if I sit still too long. The transmission locks every time I try to shift into reverse.
lock _____ *fasten with a bolt mechanism*	
OBJECT	Please lock **the door** when you leave. You should always lock **your car doors**.
PASSIVE	The trunk was securely locked.
lock _____ *secure with a lock*	
OBJECT + ADVERB OF PLACE	I locked **the documents** *in the drawer*. We locked **the car** *in the garage*. My brother locked **me** *in a closet*.
PASSIVE	The prisoners were locked *in a cell*.
lock _____ *join together*	
OBJECT	The elks locked **horns**. As the rioters approached, the police locked **arms**. He locked **his fingers** around the steering wheel and braked hard.
PASSIVE	The bumpers were so tightly locked that we had to call a tow truck.

PHRASAL VERBS

lock _SEP_ **away/in/out**/etc. *secure with a lock in a specified location*	We locked the dogs in for the night. They locked the rest of the staff out. I locked myself out of the car.
lock up *secure a building by locking all the entrances*	I'll lock up when I leave for the night.
lock _SEP_ **up** *lock securely*	He locked his stamp collection up in a safe.
lock _SEP_ **up** *put in jail*	The police locked the suspects up.
lock _SEP_ **up** *achieve, take control of*	Our varsity team locked up first place in the conference. Senator Blather has locked up enough votes to override the president's veto.

PRESENT

I look	we look
you look	you look
he/she/it looks	they look

• *Kerry looks upset about something.*

PRESENT PROGRESSIVE

I am looking	we are looking
you are looking	you are looking
he/she/it is looking	they are looking

• *Your lawn is looking good these days.*

PAST

I looked	we looked
you looked	you looked
he/she/it looked	they looked

• *I looked for him in the barn.*

PAST PROGRESSIVE

I was looking	we were looking
you were looking	you were looking
he/she/it was looking	they were looking

• *They were looking everywhere.*

PRESENT PERFECT ... have | has looked
PAST PERFECT   ... had looked

FUTURE   ... will look
FUTURE PROGRESSIVE ... will be looking
FUTURE PERFECT   ... will have looked

PAST PASSIVE

I was looked	we were looked
you were looked	you were looked
he/she/it was looked	they were looked

• *My proposal was looked upon as brilliant.*

――――――――――――――――――――――――――――(**COMPLEMENTS**)――――

look *turn one's eyes to see something*

Don't look now!
Thanks, but I am only looking. [IN A STORE]
Whenever there is an accident, people have to stop and look.

look _____ *see, notice*

at OBJECT

Thomas doesn't look **at things** the way we do.
Uncle Theron was looking **at the family photo albums**.
What are you looking **at**?
Look **at her dress**—it's so short!

WH-CLAUSE

Look **who came to see you**!
Look **what Santa brought you**!
Look **where we are**!

look _____ *search, hunt*

ADVERB OF PLACE

Did you look **in the drawers**?
I've looked **everywhere**.
Where did you look?
You should look **online**.

for OBJECT

I'm looking **for my other sock**.
The agency was looking **for a solution to the refugee problem**.
Police are looking **for the stolen car**.

look _____ *seem, appear*

PREDICATE NOUN

The house is really looking **its age**.
You look **a total wreck**!

PREDICATE ADJECTIVE

The rug looks **old and faded**.
I thought Aunt Polly looked **pretty good**.
A recession looks **unlikely** for now.

INFINITIVE

The job looks **to be about finished**.

look _____ *expect, hope*

INFINITIVE

They are looking **to finish in first place**.
The market is looking **to rebound this quarter**.

look _____ *face [in a certain direction]*

ADVERB OF PLACE

Our vacation home looks **out over the lake**.
The cabin looks **west**.

PHRASAL VERBS

look away/back/inside/outside/etc.
look in a specified direction

There was a bad accident, and Mom
made me look away.
Open the package and look inside.

look after _____ *take care of*

Teresa looks after her 95-year-old mother.
Would you look after my children while I'm at the grocery?

look around *explore*

We entered the old fort and looked around.

look at _____ *consider*

They looked at the possibility of buying new computers.
Just look at his success in the real estate business!

look at _____ *examine*

The vet looked at Yu's pet hamster.

look at _____ *read*

I haven't looked at today's newspaper yet.

look back *think about (something in)
the past*

The old sailor spends most of his time looking back.

look down on _____ *despise, have
contempt for*

Aunt Hilda looked down on us because we were poor.
He looked down on manual labor of any kind.

look for _____ *expect*

The weatherman is looking for rain by tomorrow afternoon.

look for [someone/something] to _____
expect that [someone/something] will [do]

I look for my aunt to win the election.
We are looking for the economy to rebound within a year.

look in on _____ *visit briefly, check on*

I'll look in on Grandma when I go to the store.
The nurse looked in on the patient in Room 312.

look into _____ *investigate*

She is looking into the possibility of new office furniture.

look on *watch something happen*

Workers looked on helplessly as the boat sank in the harbor.

look on/upon _____ **as** *consider*

I've always looked on you as a friend.

look out *be careful*

Look out! The sidewalk is slippery.

look out for _____ *be cautious about*

Look out for falling rocks.

look out for _____ *be concerned about
the welfare of*

His older brother looked out for him on the playground.

look _SEP_ **over** *review, examine*

The treasurer looked over our accounts.
Patti is looking over the newspaper recipes.

look through _____ *examine the parts of*

Jim looked through the book for Civil War photos.
We looked through the desk and found nothing to keep.

look to _____ *depend on*

Donald looked to his family to help pay his medical bills.
Students look to their teachers for help.

look to _____ *think about, examine*

The playwright looks to Greek tragedies for inspiration.

look up *improve* [USED ONLY IN THE
PROGRESSIVE TENSES]

The Dow Jones average was up 126 points today;
things are looking up.

look up to _____ *admire, respect*

All the scientists looked up to Robert Oppenheimer.

look _SEP_ **up** *search for*

If you don't know a word, look it up in the dictionary.
When I'm in Buffalo, I'll look up a childhood friend of mine.

EXPRESSIONS

it looks like _____

It looks like rain.

it looks like / as if / as though _____

It looks like it will rain.
It looks as if it will rain.
It looks as though it will rain.

top 40 verb

look forward to _____
anticipate eagerly

We look forward to meeting them at the party.

look like _____ *have
the appearance of*

Dennis looks like his grandfather.
Ashley looks like a famous movie star.

PRESENT

I lose	we lose
you lose	you lose
he/she/it loses	they lose

• *My team always loses.*

PAST

I lost	we lost
you lost	you lost
he/she/it lost	they lost

• *I lost my glasses again.*

PRESENT PERFECT … have | has lost
PAST PERFECT   … had lost

PRESENT PROGRESSIVE

I am losing	we are losing
you are losing	you are losing
he/she/it is losing	they are losing

• *I am losing patience with them.*

PAST PROGRESSIVE

I was losing	we were losing
you were losing	you were losing
he/she/it was losing	they were losing

• *We were losing money on every transaction.*

FUTURE   … will lose
FUTURE PROGRESSIVE … will be losing
FUTURE PERFECT   … will have lost

PAST PASSIVE

I was lost	we were lost
you were lost	you were lost
he/she/it was lost	they were lost

• *The battle was lost in the first few minutes.*

(**COMPLEMENTS**)

lose *not win, be defeated*

The team has never lost this season.
The longer you gamble, the more certain you are to lose.
The Patriots lost by 14 points.

lose _____ *not win, be defeated in*
    OBJECT

Napoleon never lost **a battle**—except the last one.
You can win a battle, but still lose **the war**.
I lost **my bet with Sam**.

lose _____ *be deprived of*
    OBJECT

We lost **some dear friends** in the war.
He has lost **the use of his left hand**.
The senator has lost **their support**.

lose _____ *misplace, be unable to find*
    OBJECT

I lost **the key to my desk**.
The guide lost **his way** in the woods.
I lost **my place in the book**.

    PASSIVE
lose _____ *fail to keep/maintain*
    OBJECT

The mountain climbers were lost in the avalanche.

The cat is losing **its hair**.
My watch is losing **time**.
The sink has been losing **water** for days.
The boat was losing **speed**.
I lost **control of the motorcycle**.

lose _____ *get rid of*
    OBJECT
lose _____ *fail to make use of*
    OBJECT

I finally lost **some weight**.

The company lost **a great opportunity to expand**.
Don't lose **any time** getting to the bookstore.

lose _____ *cause to be deprived of*
    INDIRECT OBJECT + OBJECT

His position on immigration lost *him* **a lot of votes**.

(**PHRASAL VERBS**)

lose out (to _____ **)** *be unsuccessful*
[*in a competition (with [someone])*]

I applied for the job, but I lost out to
   a younger applicant.

PRESENT		PRESENT PROGRESSIVE	
I love	we love	I am loving	we are loving
you love	you love	you are loving	you are loving
he/she/it loves	they love	he/she/it is loving	they are loving

• *He loves living in San Francisco.*   • *I am loving this spring weather.*

PAST		PAST PROGRESSIVE	
I loved	we loved	I was loving	we were loving
you loved	you loved	you were loving	you were loving
he/she/it loved	they loved	he/she/it was loving	they were loving

• *I always loved the impressionist painters.*   • *They were loving every minute of it.*

PRESENT PERFECT	... have | has loved
PAST PERFECT	... had loved

FUTURE	... will love
FUTURE PROGRESSIVE	... will be loving
FUTURE PERFECT	... will have loved

PAST PASSIVE	
I was loved	we were loved
you were loved	you were loved
he/she/it was loved	they were loved

• *Grammar class was not always loved by everyone.*

⎛ **COMPLEMENTS** ⎞

NOTE: In the progressive tenses, the verb *love* is primarily used informally and for emphasis.

love _____ *feel romantic love for*

OBJECT
> Basil says he loves **her**, but they haven't even kissed.
> Jason and Paul have loved **each other** for years.

love _____ *like/desire very much*

OBJECT
> Don't you just love **the sunshine**?
> I love **the food in southern France**.

PASSIVE
> The professor was loved by all of his students.

OBJECT + PRESENT PARTICIPLE
> I love **John's parents** *living so close to us*.
> We love **the school** *providing after-hours care*.
> The children have loved **the beach** *being in walking distance*.

INFINITIVE
> I love **to take long walks in the fog**.
> The children love **to play in the sandbox**.
> Who wouldn't love **to go to Hawaii**?

WH-CLAUSE
> I love **what you are wearing**.
> Dogs generally love **whoever loves them**.
> I am sure we will love **whatever you are cooking**.

PRESENT PARTICIPLE
> I love **taking long walks in the fog**.
> They don't love **having to commute so far**.
> No one loves **being kept waiting for hours**.

love _____ *take pleasure in*

(*for*) OBJECT + INFINITIVE
> We would love **(for)** you *to come*.
> Jack and I would love **(for)** them *to join us*.
> They would love **(for)** you *to open the program*.

INFINITIVE
> I would love **to come to dinner with you**.
> They would love **to meet you**.
> The kids would love **to come to Jane's birthday party**.

love _____ *thrive in*

OBJECT
> Many flowering plants love **acidic soil**.
> Snails love **mild, wet weather**.
> New businesses love **word-of-mouth publicity**.

PRESENT

I maintain   we maintain
you maintain   you maintain
he/she/it maintains   they maintain
• *He maintains that he is totally innocent.*

PRESENT PROGRESSIVE

I am maintaining   we are maintaining
you are maintaining   you are maintaining
he/she/it is maintaining they are maintaining
• *I am still maintaining that old truck.*

PAST

I maintained   we maintained
you maintained   you maintained
he/she/it maintained   they maintained
• *Our stock maintained its price.*

PAST PROGRESSIVE

I was maintaining   we were maintaining
you were maintaining   you were maintaining
he/she/it was maintaining they were maintaining
• *We were maintaining a strong market position.*

PRESENT PERFECT … have | has maintained
PAST PERFECT … had maintained

FUTURE … will maintain
FUTURE PROGRESSIVE … will be maintaining
FUTURE PERFECT … will have maintained

PAST PASSIVE

I was maintained   we were maintained
you were maintained   you were maintained
he/she/it was maintained they were maintained
• *The house was maintained in excellent condition.*

COMPLEMENTS

maintain _____ *keep up, keep the same*
OBJECT
The prisoner maintained **his silence** throughout the torture.
Maintain **your speed** going downhill.
Successful companies maintain **good relationships with their customers**.
Senator Blather has maintained **his lead in the polls**.

maintain _____ *preserve, keep in good condition*
OBJECT
We spend our weekends just maintaining **our house**.
One person can't maintain **the network servers**.
WH-CLAUSE
You have to maintain **whatever you buy**.
The company will maintain **whatever you lease from them**.

maintain _____ *provide support for*
OBJECT
He is required to maintain **the children** until they are 18 years old.
The duke maintained **a household staff of 20 people**.
Rome could no longer maintain **its legions in Britain**.

maintain _____ *assert, declare as true*
OBJECT
The heirs maintained **the validity of their claim**.
The prosecutors will continue to maintain **their case**.
We have always maintained **his involvement in the crime**.
They maintain **the position that health care should be available to everyone**.
THAT-CLAUSE
He maintains **that he is completely innocent**.
President Lincoln maintained **that the war was fought to preserve the Union**.
The government maintained **that it had no involvement in the coup**.
He can't possibly maintain **that he knew nothing about it**.
WH-CLAUSE
He maintains **what he has always said**.
They will maintain **whatever benefits them**.

make _____ *force, cause*	They made **me** *do it*!
OBJECT + BASE-FORM INFINITIVE	The earthquake made **the windows** *rattle*.
	The officials made **the teams** *replay the game*.

make _____ *be used to produce*	
OBJECT	Cotton rags make **the best paper**.
PASSIVE	The sculpture was made entirely of driftwood.

make _____ *earn, succeed in achieving*	
OBJECT	You could make **a lot of money** doing that.
	We made **about 500 miles** driving today.

make _____ *amount to, total*	
OBJECT	Four quarts make **a gallon**.
	Three feet make **a yard**.

make _____ *arrive at*	
OBJECT	Glen will make **Phoenix** by tomorrow afternoon.

make _____ *be on time for*	
OBJECT	Do you think we can make **the 2 o'clock flight**?
	Three students didn't make **the deadline for submitting papers**.

(**PHRASAL VERBS**)

make away/off with _____ *steal*	The robbers made away with $3,500.
	They made off with my briefcase too.
make for _____ *go toward*	The soldier made for the nearest foxhole.
make for _____ *result in*	Good pitching and hitting make for a successful team.
make like _____ *pretend to be, imitate*	Dad made like a dinosaur and tromped around the room.
make out *succeed*	Gavin made out very well during the dot-com bubble.
make ⎵SEP⎵ **out** *distinguish, decipher*	I can barely make out the road in the snowstorm.
	The bank teller couldn't make out the signature on the check.
make ⎵SEP⎵ **out** *fill out*	Make the check out to the agency for $25.
make ⎵SEP⎵ **out** *understand*	We couldn't make out what the professor was saying.
make ⎵SEP⎵ **over** *change the appearance of*	The programmer made over his cubicle with movie posters.
make [someone] out _____ *describe [someone], usually falsely*	Dixie's parents made her out to be a perfect student.
make up *become friendly after a quarrel*	Luke and Lana finally made up after two weeks of not speaking to one another.
make up _____ *form, be the parts of*	These servers make up the backbone of our network.
	The fleet was made up of battleships, cruisers, and destroyers.
make ⎵SEP⎵ **up** *put together, prepare*	I made a pot of chili up in 30 minutes.
make ⎵SEP⎵ **up** *invent*	Gary made up a story about a dog stealing his homework.
make ⎵SEP⎵ **up** *apply cosmetics to*	The artist made her up to look like a witch.
	I have to make myself up before going out.
make ⎵SEP⎵ **up** *do [something] that one has missed*	Jan was sick and has to make up the test on Monday.
make up for _____ *compensate for*	How can I make up for the trouble I've caused you?

PRESENT

I make	we make
you make	you make
he/she/it makes	they make

- *She makes an excellent salary.*

PRESENT PROGRESSIVE

I am making	we are making
you are making	you are making
he/she/it is making	they are making

- *I'm making some coffee.*

PAST

I made	we made
you made	you made
he/she/it made	they made

- *I made lunch for my in-laws.*

PAST PROGRESSIVE

I was making	we were making
you were making	you were making
he/she/it was making	they were making

- *We were making pretty good time.*

PRESENT PERFECT ... have | has made
PAST PERFECT ... had made

FUTURE ... will make
FUTURE PROGRESSIVE ... will be making
FUTURE PERFECT ... will have made

PAST PASSIVE

I was made	we were made
you were made	you were made
he/she/it was made	they were made

- *Mistakes were made at every level.*

(**COMPLEMENTS**)

make _____ *prepare, build, create, produce*

OBJECT
I am going to make **a tuna salad.**
We made **a little shed for the bicycles.**
I made **a bookcase** out of mahogany.
My wife made **a sweater** out of merino wool.
I can make **a booklet of your favorite quotations.**
It's chilly in here; would you make **a fire?**
We're making **plans for spring break.**
The president's children make **their own beds.**
Carpenters made **a hole in the wall** for a window.

PASSIVE
His masterpiece was made in 1683.

INDIRECT OBJECT + DIRECT OBJECT
We will make *Thomas* **a Halloween costume.**
The florist made *Ruth* **a terrific centerpiece.**
His company made *us* **some custom cabinets.**

for PARAPHRASE
His company made **some custom cabinets** *for us.*

WH-CLAUSE
I can only make **what I have supplies for.**
I will make **whatever you want** for your birthday.

make _____ *do, perform*

OBJECT
Senator Blather made **a speech** at the YMCA.
Make **a left turn** at the second traffic light.

make _____ *cause to happen/exist*

OBJECT
The dog made **a terrible mess** again.
The two parties made **a deal.**

PASSIVE
Decisions have to be made quickly.

make _____ *cause to be, appoint, give a job/position to*

OBJECT + PREDICATE NOUN
He made **the company** *a household name.*
The company made **her** *vice president.*
The board made **Boyd** *the CEO.*

PASSIVE
Tom was made *a captain* in 2005.

OBJECT + PREDICATE ADJECTIVE
The new job made **Janet** *very happy.*
These paintings make the **living room**
   cheerful.
Long meetings after lunch make **me** *sleepy.*

PRESENT

I manage	we manage
you manage	you manage
he/she/it manages	they manage

• *He manages an import-export company.*

PRESENT PROGRESSIVE

I am managing	we are managing
you are managing	you are managing
he/she/it is managing	they are managing

• *I'm managing okay since the surgery.*

PAST

I managed	we managed
you managed	you managed
he/she/it managed	they managed

• *The coach managed several great teams.*

PAST PROGRESSIVE

I was managing	we were managing
you were managing	you were managing
he/she/it was managing	they were managing

• *We were just managing to break even.*

PRESENT PERFECT ... have | has managed
PAST PERFECT ... had managed

FUTURE ... will manage
FUTURE PROGRESSIVE ... will be managing
FUTURE PERFECT ... will have managed

PAST PASSIVE

I was managed	we were managed
you were managed	you were managed
he/she/it was managed	they were managed

• *The project was not managed very well.*

COMPLEMENTS

manage *cope with a stressful/difficult situation*

He is managing pretty well, under the circumstances.
The kids can't manage by themselves.
You will have to manage as best you can.

manage _____ *administer, control, regulate*

OBJECT

I will manage **the new unit**.
Everybody needs to learn how to manage **their expenses**.
This valve manages **the flow of water into the irrigation system**.

PASSIVE

Remote sensors are managed by satellite.

manage _____ *succeed in, be able to*

INFINITIVE

I finally managed **to get some sleep**.
The technician managed **to repair the server**.
Despite the awful evening, she still managed **to smile**.
He could manage **to get wet in a desert**.

PHRASAL VERBS

manage on/with _____ *be able to live/ do by using*

We can manage on $1,300 a month.
The office manages fine with just one photocopier.

PRESENT

I mark	we mark
you mark	you mark
he/she/it marks	they mark

• *The blue line marks the state boundary.*

PRESENT PROGRESSIVE

I am marking	we are marking
you are marking	you are marking
he/she/it is marking	they are marking

• *He is marking the names as they are called.*

PAST

I marked	we marked
you marked	you marked
he/she/it marked	they marked

• *I marked all the essays.*

PAST PROGRESSIVE

I was marking	we were marking
you were marking	you were marking
he/she/it was marking	they were marking

• *We were marking all the sale items.*

PRESENT PERFECT ... have | has marked
PAST PERFECT ... had marked

FUTURE ... will mark
FUTURE PROGRESSIVE ... will be marking
FUTURE PERFECT ... will have marked

PAST PASSIVE

I was marked	we were marked
you were marked	you were marked
he/she/it was marked	they were marked

• *The new rug was marked by dirty footprints.*

(**COMPLEMENTS**)

mark *become stained/dirty*

This flooring marks too easily.
The surface marks everywhere you touch it.

mark _____ *identify [something] by writing on it*

OBJECT

I marked **all the boxes that are to be shipped**.
Did you mark **all the books that the kids are taking to school**?

PASSIVE

The items on sale are marked with a green tag.

WH-CLAUSE

We marked **what we are taking with us**.
I marked **how much each item cost**.

mark _____ *identify, characterize*

OBJECT

A marble plaque marks **the house where Mozart died**.
The yellow line marks **the location of a buried gas line**.
The fever marked **a new stage in his illness**.
Gettysburg marked **the turning point of the Civil War**.

PASSIVE

The occasion was marked by a special concert.

OBJECT + *as* PREDICATE NOUN

His robe marked **him** *as a judge*.
Her clear diction marked **her** *as a professional actor*.

mark _____ *affect*

OBJECT

Being in combat marks **everyone who experiences it**.

mark _____ *grade, evaluate*

OBJECT

English teachers spend their free time marking **papers**.
We need to mark **the applicants' résumés**.

PASSIVE

The exams were marked anonymously.

(**PHRASAL VERBS**)

mark ⎯SEP⎯ **down** *lower the price of*   They marked down their pizzas by 35%.

mark ⎯SEP⎯ **down** *make a note of*   Kyle will mark down the speech's important points.

mark ⎯SEP⎯ **off** *indicate the boundaries of*   A rope marks off the staff-only area.
I marked off where we're going to put a vegetable garden.

mark ⎯SEP⎯ **up** *raise the price of*   The art dealer marks paintings up 200%.

mark ⎯SEP⎯ **up** *mar, deface*   Calvin marked up Susie's book with his crayons.
Don't touch the photographs, you will mark them up.

PRESENT

I marry	we marry
you marry	you marry
he/she/it marries	they marry

• *Many couples marry in June.*

PRESENT PROGRESSIVE

I am marrying	we are marrying
you are marrying	you are marrying
he/she/it is marrying	they are marrying

• *I am not marrying anyone!*

PAST

I married	we married
you married	you married
he/she/it married	they married

• *She just married an old friend of mine.*

PAST PROGRESSIVE

I was marrying	we were marrying
you were marrying	you were marrying
he/she/it was marrying	they were marrying

• *He was marrying for all the wrong reasons.*

PRESENT PERFECT ... have | has married
PAST PERFECT ... had married

FUTURE ... will marry
FUTURE PROGRESSIVE ... will be marrying
FUTURE PERFECT ... will have married

PAST PASSIVE

I was married	we were married
you were married	you were married
he/she/it was married	they were married

• *We were married in 2005.*

COMPLEMENTS

marry *enter into marriage*	Will they ever marry?
	We want to marry as soon as we can.
	We are not marrying anytime soon.
marry *fit together, be compatible*	The fish and wine did not marry well at all.
	The two pieces have to marry perfectly.
	The two companies will never marry successfully.
marry ___ *become the husband/wife of*	
OBJECT	John married **Marsha**.
	He asked her to marry **him**.
	Gwendolen could only marry **someone named Ernest**.
PASSIVE	He was never married.
marry ___ *join as husband and wife*	
OBJECT	My brother married **Michael and Kathy** last week.
	An ordained minister married **the happy couple**.
PASSIVE	We were married at my parents' home.
marry ___ *combine, fit together*	
OBJECT	Clint taught Dan how to marry **red wine with Italian food**.
PASSIVE	Wine and food must be married carefully.
	The two power cables were never married properly.

PHRASAL VERBS

marry above [oneself] *marry someone of a higher social class*	Jane married above herself.
marry below/beneath [oneself] *marry someone of a lower social class*	My cousin married beneath herself.
marry into ___ *become a member of by marrying someone who is a member*	Diana married into royalty.
	Wilton married into an old New England family.
marry SEP **off** *give in marriage*	The Bennets married off three daughters in one year.

EXPRESSIONS

marry money *marry a rich person*	When she finishes college, my niece wants to marry money.

PRESENT

I match	we match
you match	you match
he/she/it matches	they match

- *He matches the description.*

PRESENT PROGRESSIVE

I am matching	we are matching
you are matching	you are matching
he/she/it is matching	they are matching

- *He is not matching our expectations.*

PAST

I matched	we matched
you matched	you matched
he/she/it matched	they matched

- *I finally matched all the socks.*

PAST PROGRESSIVE

I was matching	we were matching
you were matching	you were matching
he/she/it was matching	they were matching

- *He was matching me step for step.*

PRESENT PERFECT ... have | has matched
PAST PERFECT ... had matched

FUTURE ... will match
FUTURE PROGRESSIVE ... will be matching
FUTURE PERFECT ... will have matched

PAST PASSIVE

I was matched	we were matched
you were matched	you were matched
he/she/it was matched	they were matched

- *The two teams were evenly matched.*

―――(**COMPLEMENTS**)―――

match *go well together*

The jacket and trousers do not match.
Do you think the colors will match?
The music and the occasion matched perfectly.

match ――― *go/fit well together with*
   OBJECT

The film's audio doesn't match **the video**.
His actions don't match **his words**.
The carpet matches **the drapes** perfectly.

    PASSIVE

The bedroom curtains were matched by the bedspread.

match ――― *be equal to, be as good as*
   OBJECT

The punishment must match **the crime**.
My enthusiasm matched **hers**.
I think this year's team matches **last year's**.
The price in yen doesn't match **the price in dollars**.

match ――― *succeed in equaling*
   OBJECT

I can't match **their price**.
Will they match **your offer**?
Our performance matches **expectations**.

    PASSIVE

Their bid was never matched.

    WH-CLAUSE

I can't match **what they offered you**.
They will match **whatever bid we make**.

match ――― *make/get something equal to*
   OBJECT

Can you match **this silverware pattern**?
I'd like to match **the golden oak finish of the dresser**.

match ――― *make a connection between, compare*
   OBJECT + *with* OBJECT

The pupils need to match **each animal picture**
    with its name.
The lab tries to match **each DNA sample** *with DNA*
    in its database.

PRESENT		PRESENT PROGRESSIVE	
I mean	we mean	I am meaning	we are meaning
you mean	you mean	you are meaning	you are meaning
he/she/it means	they mean	he/she/it is meaning	they are meaning

• *A warm wind means that it will rain.* • *We are meaning to go to town tomorrow.*

PAST		PAST PROGRESSIVE	
I meant	we meant	I was meaning	we were meaning
you meant	you meant	you were meaning	you were meaning
he/she/it meant	they meant	he/she/it was meaning	they were meaning

• *I always meant to try skydiving.* • *I was meaning to fix that.*

PRESENT PERFECT ... have | has meant
PAST PERFECT ... had meant

FUTURE ... will mean
FUTURE PROGRESSIVE ... will be meaning
FUTURE PERFECT ... will have meant

PAST PASSIVE	
I was meant	we were meant
you were meant	you were meant
he/she/it was meant	they were meant

• *No harm was meant.*

⎯⎯(COMPLEMENTS)⎯⎯

NOTE: The verb *mean* is used in the progressive tenses only in the sense "intend, plan."

mean ___ *signify, indicate*

OBJECT
"Aloha" means **both "hello" and "goodbye"** in Hawaiian.
A rainbow means **good luck**.
It doesn't mean **anything**.
Thanks. That meant **a lot to me**.
This means **war**!

THAT-CLAUSE
The flare means **that there has been an accident**.
The whistle means **that it is time to quit**.
A heavy snowfall means **that there will be no school**.

WH-CLAUSE
It can't mean **what I think it means**.
It means **whatever you want it to mean**.

mean ___ *intend, plan*

(*for*) OBJECT + INFINITIVE
I meant **(for) you** *to do that*.
He was meaning **(for) us** *to finish up here*.

PASSIVE
The truck was meant *to stay with the crew*.

INFINITIVE
We meant **to stop off and do some shopping**.
They didn't mean **to do anything wrong**.
I was meaning **to tell you about that**.

mean ___ *intend* [TO EXPLAIN A PREVIOUS STATEMENT]

THAT-CLAUSE
I meant **that you should wait in my office**.
He meant **that he might have made a mistake**.

⎯⎯(EXPRESSIONS)⎯⎯

mean business *be serious*
He jokes with reporters, but he means business.

mean everything / the world to ___
be very important to
Jeanine's fiancé means everything to her.
My environmental work means the world to me.

mean nothing to ___ *not be very important to*
Her criticism means nothing to me.

mean nothing to ___ *not make sense to*
This paragraph will mean nothing to the reader.

mean well *have good intentions*
Ed is a little eccentric, but he means well.

PRESENT

I measure	we measure
you measure	you measure
he/she/it measures	they measure

• *The bedroom measures 10 by 12 feet.*

PRESENT PROGRESSIVE

I am measuring	we are measuring
you are measuring	you are measuring
he/she/it is measuring	they are measuring

• *I am measuring the desk now.*

PAST

I measured	we measured
you measured	you measured
he/she/it measured	they measured

• *I already measured the rug.*

PAST PROGRESSIVE

I was measuring	we were measuring
you were measuring	you were measuring
he/she/it was measuring	they were measuring

• *They were measuring the kitchen.*

PRESENT PERFECT ... have | has measured
PAST PERFECT ... had measured

FUTURE ... will measure
FUTURE PROGRESSIVE ... will be measuring
FUTURE PERFECT ... will have measured

PAST PASSIVE

I was measured	we were measured
you were measured	you were measured
he/she/it was measured	they were measured

• *The rooms were never measured.*

(COMPLEMENTS)

measure _____ *be a certain size/amount/extent*

OBJECT

The carpet measures **9 feet by 12 feet.**
The pool measures **30 feet long.**
The material measures **45 inches wide.**

measure _____ *determine the size/amount/extent of*

OBJECT

We need to measure **the square footage.**
The pollsters measured **the extent of Senator Blather's support.**
We measured **the time it took to place an order.**
How do we measure **the value of his proposal?**
Wall Street measures **success** in monetary terms.

PASSIVE

The flow of the river is measured by the water department.

WH-CLAUSE

They measured **how far each contestant threw the discus.**
The recording engineer measured **exactly how long each segment lasted.**
We measured **how heavy the average box was.**

measure _____ *get exact portions of*

OBJECT

Before you start baking, you should measure **all the ingredients.**

measure _____ *moderate, make less strong*

OBJECT

You need to measure **your words** carefully.
Politicians always measure **their criticisms of each other.**

PASSIVE

Both criticism and blame should be measured.

(PHRASAL VERBS)

measure SEP **off** *mark the boundaries / the beginning and end of*

Andy measured off half an acre to grow tomatoes on.
Would you measure off 200 feet of kite string?

measure up *be good enough*

The candidates have been chosen; we hope they measure up.
This new brand of paper towels just doesn't measure up.

measure up to _____ *be as good as*

The coffee doesn't measure up to Oregon Trail's.
She doesn't measure up to her teacher's expectations.
The movie doesn't measure up to the book.

meet meet | meets · met · have met ☑ IRREGULAR

PRESENT

I meet	we meet
you meet	you meet
he/she/it meets	they meet

• *The stationmaster meets every train.*

PRESENT PROGRESSIVE

I am meeting	we are meeting
you are meeting	you are meeting
he/she/it is meeting	they are meeting

• *Excuse me, I am meeting someone.*

PAST

I met	we met
you met	you met
he/she/it met	they met

• *I never met your brother.*

PAST PROGRESSIVE

I was meeting	we were meeting
you were meeting	you were meeting
he/she/it was meeting	they were meeting

• *We were meeting in the conference room.*

PRESENT PERFECT ... have | has met
PAST PERFECT ... had met

FUTURE ... will meet
FUTURE PROGRESSIVE ... will be meeting
FUTURE PERFECT ... will have met

PAST PASSIVE

I was met	we were met
you were met	you were met
he/she/it was met	they were met

• *We were met at the airport by the tour guide.*

(**COMPLEMENTS**)

meet *come together for a particular purpose*	We will meet next Tuesday. "When shall we three meet again?" [SHAKESPEARE] Can we meet for lunch tomorrow? These same two teams will meet in the playoffs.
meet *be joined*	The hiking paths meet at the top of the hill.
meet *become acquainted, be introduced*	Our in-laws will meet in person for the first time. It is amazing that we never met before.
meet *come into contact*	The gates have never met properly because they sag. Their lips met tenderly. The sliding doors met with a thud.
meet _____ *come together by arrangement* OBJECT	I met **Carrie** for lunch today. I can't meet **them** until next week.
with OBJECT	You will meet **with the search committee** this afternoon.
meet _____ *become acquainted with* OBJECT	When did you first meet **your husband**? Guess **whom** I met today!
meet _____ *fulfill, satisfy, pay* OBJECT	I still have to meet **my undergraduate science requirement**. Can he meet **the deadline for the grant application**? Her organization works to meet **the needs of the homeless**. If you meet **our demands**, no one will get hurt. They might not be able to meet **their mortgage payment**.
PASSIVE	The terms of the agreement have not been met.
meet _____ *be present at the arrival of* OBJECT	Someone needs to meet **the train**. We should meet **their plane** tomorrow. Everyone will meet **the boats** when they cross the finish line.
meet _____ *encounter, experience* OBJECT	Our plans really met **an obstacle** today. My great-great-grandfather met **his death** in the Great War. The proposal met **a stone wall** in the committee hearing.

PRESENT		PRESENT PROGRESSIVE	
I mention	we mention	I am mentioning	we are mentioning
you mention	you mention	you are mentioning	you are mentioning
he/she/it mentions	they mention	he/she/it is mentioning	they are mentioning

• *He always mentions your name.*   • *I am never mentioning it again.*

PAST		PAST PROGRESSIVE	
I mentioned	we mentioned	I was mentioning	we were mentioning
you mentioned	you mentioned	you were mentioning	you were mentioning
he/she/it mentioned	they mentioned	he/she/it was mentioning	they were mentioning

• *I mentioned the problem to him.*   • *I was just mentioning that.*

PRESENT PERFECT	... have | has mentioned
PAST PERFECT	... had mentioned

FUTURE	... will mention
FUTURE PROGRESSIVE	... will be mentioning
FUTURE PERFECT	... will have mentioned

PAST PASSIVE

I was mentioned	we were mentioned
you were mentioned	you were mentioned
he/she/it was mentioned	they were mentioned

• *He was mentioned as a possible candidate.*

─────────────────────────── COMPLEMENTS ───

mention _____ *speak/write about briefly*

OBJECT	He mentioned **the problem** briefly.
	They never mentioned **anything about it.**
	He mentioned **some of his concerns.**
	The report mentioned **the possibility of tornadoes.**
PASSIVE	The issue was barely mentioned at the meeting.
OBJECT + *to* OBJECT	Somebody mentioned **it** *to me.*
	Terry mentioned **his concern** *to some of his friends.*
	She never mentioned **her trip** *to anyone.*
to OBJECT + THAT-CLAUSE	I mentioned **to him** *that we were out of eggs.*
	Harold mentioned **to Betty** *that they needed new snow tires.*
	She mentioned **to me** *that she was leaving early.*
THAT-CLAUSE	Jack mentioned **that they were going out to dinner.**
	I mentioned **that we would miss the game.**
	Did he mention **that we need to get a speaker for the conference?**
WH-CLAUSE	I mentioned **what we have been working on.**
	They never mentioned **why the project was postponed.**
	Did he mention **how much it would cost?**

mention _____ *suggest / refer to as noteworthy*

OBJECT + *as* OBJECT	They mentioned **Steve** *as a possible replacement.*
OBJECT + *for* OBJECT	Meredith mentioned **Ava** *for treasurer.*
PASSIVE	She is being mentioned *for secretary of state.*
	He was mentioned *for the vacant Senate seat.*

─────────────────────────── EXPRESSIONS ───

not to mention *and also*	I can't believe all the cooking and cleaning I have to do, not to mention the grocery shopping and laundry.

I miss · we miss
you miss · you miss
he/she/it misses · they miss

• *He misses all of his old friends.*

PRESENT PROGRESSIVE

I am missing · we are missing
you are missing · you are missing
he/she/it is missing · they are missing

• *I am missing my TV program.*

PAST

I missed · we missed
you missed · you missed
he/she/it missed · they missed

• *I never missed a class.*

PAST PROGRESSIVE

I was missing · we were missing
you were missing · you were missing
he/she/it was missing · they were missing

• *We were missing the final three pages of the report.*

PRESENT PERFECT ... have | has missed
PAST PERFECT ... had missed

FUTURE ... will miss
FUTURE PROGRESSIVE ... will be missing
FUTURE PERFECT ... will have missed

PAST PASSIVE

I was missed · we were missed
you were missed · you were missed
he/she/it was missed · they were missed

• *He was missed by everyone.*

COMPLEMENTS

NOTE: The verb *miss* is used in the progressive tenses only in the sense "be lacking."

miss *be lacking*	The veteran's right arm is missing.
	Help! All my jewelry is missing.
miss *fail to succeed*	With our pitching staff, we can't miss.
miss *fail to hit/strike*	The batter swings and misses.
	The bullet missed by inches.
miss ____ *be lacking*	
OBJECT	This computer is missing **its hard drive**.
	Our six-year-old is missing **her two front teeth**.
miss ____ *fail to hit/strike*	
OBJECT	The arrow missed **the target** by a foot.
	We just missed **a deer on the road** coming home last night.
miss ____ *fail to hear/notice/understand*	
OBJECT	I missed **his first few words**.
	We must have missed **the last turn**.
	He missed **the whole point of the presentation**.
WH-CLAUSE	I missed **what you just said**.
miss ____ *fail to attend/keep*	
OBJECT	He missed **three meetings in a row**.
	Randy missed **his doctor's appointment** yesterday.
	Rhonda missed **the application deadline**.
miss ____ *fail to reach/meet/catch/see*	
OBJECT	He went home early. You just missed **him**.
	We are going to miss **the train** if we don't hurry.
miss ____ *avoid*	
OBJECT	We really want to miss **the afternoon traffic**.
PRESENT PARTICIPLE	The bicyclist just missed **being hit by a drunk driver**.
miss ____ *feel the absence/loss of*	
OBJECT	Did you miss **me** while I was gone?
	I really miss **Cassie the cat**—she had lots of personality.
PRESENT PARTICIPLE	I don't miss **having to work so hard**.

PRESENT

I mix	we mix
you mix	you mix
he/she/it mixes	they mix

- *He only mixes what he needs.*

PRESENT PROGRESSIVE

I am mixing	we are mixing
you are mixing	you are mixing
he/she/it is mixing	they are mixing

- *She is mixing punch for the children.*

PAST

I mixed	we mixed
you mixed	you mixed
he/she/it mixed	they mixed

- *I already mixed the batter for pancakes.*

PAST PROGRESSIVE

I was mixing	we were mixing
you were mixing	you were mixing
he/she/it was mixing	they were mixing

- *He was always mixing metaphors.*

PRESENT PERFECT ... have | has mixed
PAST PERFECT ... had mixed

FUTURE ... will mix
FUTURE PROGRESSIVE ... will be mixing
FUTURE PERFECT ... will have mixed

PAST PASSIVE

I was mixed	we were mixed
you were mixed	you were mixed
he/she/it was mixed	they were mixed

- *The album was mixed in a professional recording studio.*

COMPLEMENTS

mix blend	Oil and water don't mix.
	Drinking and driving don't mix.
	We need to wait a few minutes while the dough is mixing.
mix associate, interact	They really mix well at social gatherings.
mix _____ combine, join	
OBJECT	To make concrete, you mix **sand, cement, and water**.
	The conference mixes **experts from different fields**.
	The studio can mix **eight tracks** simultaneously.
OBJECT + *with* OBJECT	The salesman mixes **business** *with pleasure*.
	Our teacher mixes **math** *with humor*.
WH-CLAUSE	I will only mix **what I can use in a few hours**.
	They mix **whatever spices will go together**.
	We mix **however much we can sell in one day**.
mix _____ make by combining [items, elements]	
OBJECT	He mixed **the final version of the CD** in just a couple of weeks.
	I'll mix **drinks** while you make the salad.
PASSIVE	All the paint was mixed at one time to keep the color uniform.
mix _____ cause to interact	
OBJECT	Their parties mix **artists and business people**.
	The training mixes **people from different social and ethnic backgrounds**.

PHRASAL VERBS

mix _SEP_ **in** stir in	Gradually mix in two cups of flour.
mix _SEP_ **up** confuse [someone/something] with [someone/something else]	She's always mixing her granddaughters up.
	The boss usually mixes up our names.
be mixed up be confused	With all these options, I'm really mixed up.
be mixed up in _____ be involved in	He got mixed up in a scheme to defraud Medicare.

I mount   we mount
you mount   you mount
he/she/it mounts   they mount
  • *The store mounts prints and photos.*

I am mounting   we are mounting
you are mounting   you are mounting
he/she/it is mounting   they are mounting
  • *Our debt is mounting day by day.*

I mounted   we mounted
you mounted   you mounted
he/she/it mounted   they mounted
  • *I never mounted a horse before.*

I was mounting   we were mounting
you were mounting   you were mounting
he/she/it was mounting   they were mounting
  • *He was mounting the stairs two steps at a time.*

... have | has mounted
... had mounted

... will mount
... will be mounting
... will have mounted

—   —
—   —
it was mounted   they were mounted
  • *The attack was mounted at six in the morning.*

COMPLEMENTS

mount *increase, rise*

The excitement is mounting.
The noise in the stadium was mounting to a fever pitch.
Our anxiety mounted as the minutes passed.
The company's debts had been mounting for months.

mount _____ *climb up/onto*
  OBJECT

We mounted **our bicycles** and rode off.
Someone was mounting **the steps** to the front door.
The conductor mounted **the podium**.

mount _____ *undertake*
  OBJECT

They are going to mount **a new ad campaign**.
Senator Blather mounted **a spirited defense of his record**.
The unhappy parents mounted **an attack on the school board**.

mount _____ *place/install*
  OBJECT

We mounted **a new light fixture** in the dining room.
They mounted **the garbage disposal** under the sink.

  PASSIVE

In the old Volkswagens, the engine was mounted in the rear.

mount _____ *arrange/fix [in a support/frame]*
  OBJECT

We mounted **the pictures** in simple black frames.
The jeweler mounted **four diamonds** in a gold setting.
The technician mounted **the slides for the biology lecture**.

  PASSIVE

Her exhibit had been beautifully mounted.

PHRASAL VERBS

mount up *get on a horse*

Once the horses are saddled,
  we'll mount up.

PRESENT

I move	we move
you move	you move
he/she/it moves	they move

  • *The new plan moves the deadline back.*

PAST

I moved	we moved
you moved	you moved
he/she/it moved	they moved

  • *They moved my desk again.*

PRESENT PERFECT ... have | has moved
PAST PERFECT   ... had moved

PRESENT PROGRESSIVE

I am moving	we are moving
you are moving	you are moving
he/she/it is moving	they are moving

  • *They are moving to Dallas next week.*

PAST PROGRESSIVE

I was moving	we were moving
you were moving	you were moving
he/she/it was moving	they were moving

  • *I was moving as fast as I could.*

FUTURE   ... will move
FUTURE PROGRESSIVE ... will be moving
FUTURE PERFECT   ... will have moved

PAST PASSIVE

I was moved	we were moved
you were moved	you were moved
he/she/it was moved	they were moved

  • *The audience was quite moved by her performance.*

COMPLEMENTS

move *change position*	They are taking your picture, so don't move.
	The policeman raised his gun and yelled, "Don't move!"
	The car is moving, and there's no driver in it!
move *change one's residence*	My family moved from Santa Monica in 1955.
move *take action*	The board decided to move quickly.
move *make progress*	The film moves slowly in the beginning.
move *be sold*	The new iPods are moving like crazy.
	Those handbags are not moving at all.
move _____ *go*	
ADVERB OF PLACE TO/FROM	Move **closer** so you can hear the speaker.
	Everyone's eyes moved **toward the person who just entered.**
	I moved **out of the hot sun.**
	Can we move **to a new topic?**
move _____ *cause to go, place*	
OBJECT (+ ADVERB OF PLACE TO/FROM)	Susanna moved **the refrigerator** by herself.
	We moved **the couch** *under the window.*
	The nurse moved **the patient** *out of the emergency room.*
	The boss moved **me** *into a new job.*
	We moved **our checking account** *to a new bank.*
PASSIVE	The refugees were moved *to a different camp.*
move _____ *sell*	
OBJECT	We are finally beginning to move **the condos.**
	They can't move **those cars** without big discounts.
move _____ *affect emotionally*	
OBJECT	Her performance totally moved **the audience.**
	The story moved **all of us.**
PASSIVE	We were deeply moved by what happened.
move _____ *cause, provide a reason for*	
OBJECT + INFINITIVE	His story moved **the jury** *to acquit him.*
	The accident moved **us** *to reconsider what*
	we were doing.
	Nothing could move **him** *to change his mind.*

move _____ *formally propose*

for OBJECT	The defense attorney moved **for dismissal of all charges.**
INFINITIVE	I moved **to adjourn the meeting until tomorrow afternoon.**
BASE-FORM THAT-CLAUSE	Mr. Chairman, I move **that the motion be tabled.**
	I move **that we accept the company's offer.**
	He moved **that the amendment be adopted.**

PHRASAL VERBS

move away/back/off/etc. *go in a specified direction*

The cop ordered us to move back.
The deer moved off in the opposite direction.

move in *go closer*

The students moved in for a closer look.

move in/out *change one's residence*

When will the new neighbors move in?
Roger and Denise moved in last summer, then moved out in April.

move in on _____ *get closer to*

The FBI is moving in on the leader of the drug cartel.

move in with _____ *take up residence with [someone]*

To save expenses, I moved in with my sister.

move into _____ *advance to*

The Grizzlies moved into first place with a win last night.

move _____ **on** *cause to go away*

The police moved the crowd on.

move on (to _____**)** *change (to [a different activity/subject])*

Congress should move on to more important issues.

move over *shift one's position slightly*

Would you move over? I need more room.

move up *become successful*

Our son is moving up in the corporate world.

move up _____ *advance in/on*

Alison has been moving up the corporate ladder.

move up to _____ *get [something] better*

Our neighbors have moved up to a hybrid car.

EXPRESSIONS

move a mile a minute *move extremely fast*

The typist's fingers were moving a mile a minute.

move into full swing / into high gear *reach the peak of activity*

The hockey season has moved into full swing.
The global warming debate has moved into high gear on Capitol Hill.

move it *start going quickly*

It's almost time for class—we'd better move it.

move _____ **to tears** *cause to cry*

The novel moved Jackie to tears.

move up in the world *become successful*

Look at Jonathan's fancy new car. He's really moved up in the world.

moved *emotionally affected*

We were moved by the president's kind gesture.

moving *causing strong emotions*

I loved the moving scene in which the boy was reunited with his parents.

PRESENT

I name	we name
you name	you name
he/she/it names	they name

• *A good reporter never names his sources.*

PRESENT PROGRESSIVE

I am naming	we are naming
you are naming	you are naming
he/she/it is naming	they are naming

• *Nobody is naming the ones responsible.*

PAST

I named	we named
you named	you named
he/she/it named	they named

• *We named our dog Scotty.*

PAST PROGRESSIVE

I was naming	we were naming
you were naming	you were naming
he/she/it was naming	they were naming

• *They were naming students to the school council.*

PRESENT PERFECT ... have | has named
PAST PERFECT   ... had named

FUTURE   ... will name
FUTURE PROGRESSIVE ... will be naming
FUTURE PERFECT   ... will have named

PAST PASSIVE

I was named	we were named
you were named	you were named
he/she/it was named	they were named

• *She was just named to a cabinet position.*

───────────────────────────────(COMPLEMENTS)───

name ＿＿＿ *give a name to*
　OBJECT (+ PREDICATE NOUN)

Have you named **your yacht** yet?
They will name **their first daughter** *Harriet*.
President Washington named **the first major ship**
　　the USS Constitution.

　PASSIVE

The atoll was named *Midway* because it was halfway
　　between North America and Asia.
I was named *Walter* after my grandfather.

name ＿＿＿ *appoint, choose*
　OBJECT + PREDICATE NOUN

The president named **her** *ambassador to India*.
We named **them** *acting chairs*.

　PASSIVE

He was named *student athlete of the year*.

　OBJECT + INFINITIVE

The court will name **him** *to oversee the election*.
The committee named **me** *to fill the vacant position*.

　PASSIVE

We were named *to administer the contract*.

name ＿＿＿ *give the name of, identify*
　OBJECT

Can you name **all the presidents**?
Name **three foods that are rich in vitamins**.

name ＿＿＿ *set, fix*
　OBJECT

Have they named **a date for the grand opening**?

───────────────────────────────(EXPRESSIONS)───

name names *identify people involved in something*

The witness in the fraud case threatened
　to name names.

name [one's] price *indicate how much one wants to buy/sell something for*

The car dealer's lot is full, so you can name your price.
　No reasonable offer will be refused.
Everyone wants the new GPS—the manufacturer can
　name his price.

PRESENT

I need	we need
you need	you need
he/she/it needs	they need

• *He needs help right away.*

PRESENT PROGRESSIVE

Need is rarely used in the progressive tenses.

PAST

I needed	we needed
you needed	you needed
he/she/it needed	they needed

• *The company needed more office space.*

PAST PROGRESSIVE

Need is rarely used in the progressive tenses.

PRESENT PERFECT ... have | has needed
PAST PERFECT ... had needed

FUTURE ... will need
FUTURE PROGRESSIVE —
FUTURE PERFECT ... will have needed

PAST PASSIVE

I was needed	we were needed
you were needed	you were needed
he/she/it was needed	they were needed

• *The rain was desperately needed.*

COMPLEMENTS

need _____ *require*

OBJECT	Man, I need **a break** now.
	The engine needs **a quart of oil**.
	I don't need **any more problems** right now.
PASSIVE	Reinforcements are needed right away.
OBJECT + (to be) PREDICATE ADJECTIVE	I need **a dictionary *(to be) handy*** when I'm reading English novels.
	Grandpa needs **the type *(to be) large and bold***.
OBJECT + INFINITIVE	I need **you *to do something for me***.
	We need **a truck *to haul all the trash away***.
PASSIVE	An editor will be needed *to write the final version*.
OBJECT + PAST PARTICIPLE	I need **something *done*** right away.
	Kyle needs **his cut *cleaned and bandaged***.
	We need **the newspapers *taken to the recycling center***.
PRESENT PARTICIPLE	My car really needs **washing**.
	He needs **convincing to do the right thing**.
	The knives need **sharpening**.

need _____ *must, should*

INFINITIVE	My car really needs **to be washed**.
	I need **to get something to eat**.
	Everybody needs **to slow down a little**.
	This letter needs **to be sent special delivery**.

PHRASAL VERBS

need _____ **back/in/out**/etc. *require to be in a specified position*	The library needs the books back in two weeks.
	I need the splinter out before I can continue.

PRESENT

I note	we note
you note	you note
he/she/it notes	they note

• *She always notes customer preferences.*

PRESENT PROGRESSIVE

I am noting	we are noting
you are noting	you are noting
he/she/it is noting	they are noting

• *I am noting it now.*

PAST

I noted	we noted
you noted	you noted
he/she/it noted	they noted

• *We noted the problem you mentioned.*

PAST PROGRESSIVE

I was noting	we were noting
you were noting	you were noting
he/she/it was noting	they were noting

• *We were noting all the discrepancies.*

PRESENT PERFECT … have | has noted
PAST PERFECT … had noted

FUTURE … will note
FUTURE PROGRESSIVE … will be noting
FUTURE PERFECT … will have noted

PAST PASSIVE

I was noted	we were noted
you were noted	you were noted
he/she/it was noted	they were noted

• *Your complaint was noted by the secretary.*

──────────────────────────────── **COMPLEMENTS** ────

note _____ *notice, observe*

OBJECT	The detective noted **the bloodstain on the rug.**
	I note **a sense of despair in your voice.**
PASSIVE	Details of Paul's odd behavior were noted by his fellow students.
THAT-CLAUSE	Did you note **that most of the new jobs pay better than average wages?**
	The guard immediately noted **that something was wrong.**
WH-CLAUSE	Did you note **who was invited to the meeting?**
	"The world will little note, nor long remember, **what we say here.**"
	[LINCOLN'S GETTYSBURG ADDRESS]
	I noted **how much more they were charging.**

note _____ *make a record of*

OBJECT	The secretary will note **all motions.**
	Please note **all students who are absent.**
	Please note **the date and time** on your reports.
	The reporter noted **the main points of the news conference.**
PASSIVE	All the extra costs must be noted and reported.
WH-CLAUSE	The detective carefully noted **what the witnesses said.**
PASSIVE	Who enters the building is always noted by the guards.

note _____ *mention*

OBJECT	The library committee chair noted **the large number of overdue books.**
	In his speech, the president noted **the upcoming summit.**
THAT-CLAUSE	The mayor noted **that the flags were at half-mast.**
	The principal noted **that school uniforms will be worn at all times.**
DIRECT QUOTATION	**"The company is financially sound,"** the accountant noted.
	The store manager noted in passing, **"We served our millionth customer yesterday."**

PRESENT

I notice	we notice
you notice	you notice
he/she/it notices	they notice

- *The guard notices everything.*

PRESENT PROGRESSIVE

I am noticing	we are noticing
you are noticing	you are noticing
he/she/it is noticing	they are noticing

- *We are noticing more squirrels in the yard.*

PAST

I noticed	we noticed
you noticed	you noticed
he/she/it noticed	they noticed

- *I noticed that the Internet was really slow.*

PAST PROGRESSIVE

I was noticing	we were noticing
you were noticing	you were noticing
he/she/it was noticing	they were noticing

- *I was just noticing your new suit.*

PRESENT PERFECT ... have | has noticed
PAST PERFECT ... had noticed

FUTURE ... will notice
FUTURE PROGRESSIVE ... will be noticing
FUTURE PERFECT ... will have noticed

PAST PASSIVE

I was noticed	we were noticed
you were noticed	you were noticed
he/she/it was noticed	they were noticed

- *Fortunately, my mistake was never noticed.*

COMPLEMENTS

notice *pay attention*

Who would ever notice?
He was too busy to notice.
Men never notice!

notice _____ *observe, become aware of*

OBJECT

Everyone noticed **her new coat.**
I noticed **an odd flickering on my computer screen.**

PASSIVE

Anne's performance was eventually noticed by the CEO.
She was first noticed in a small off-Broadway play.

OBJECT + PRESENT PARTICIPLE

I noticed **a car *turning into our driveway.***
Did you notice **him *doing anything unusual*?**

PASSIVE

The suspect was noticed *hanging around the store earlier.*

THAT-CLAUSE

I noticed **that the animals were not in their pens.**
He noticed **that the road would be closed next week.**
The doctor noticed **that my right knee was swollen.**

WH-CLAUSE

Did you notice **what time the airport shuttle comes?**
I noticed **how slippery the roads were getting.**
I didn't notice **how late it was getting.**

I observe	we observe
you observe	you observe
he/she/it observes	they observe

• *The school observes all major holidays.*

I am observing	we are observing
you are observing	you are observing
he/she/it is observing	they are observing

• *Scientists are observing animal behavior in the wild.*

I observed	we observed
you observed	you observed
he/she/it observed	they observed

• *I have observed some problems.*

I was observing	we were observing
you were observing	you were observing
he/she/it was observing	they were observing

• *The entire country was observing a minute of silence.*

PRESENT PERFECT ... have | has observed
PAST PERFECT   ... had observed

FUTURE   ... will observe
FUTURE PROGRESSIVE ... will be observing
FUTURE PERFECT   ... will have observed

I was observed	we were observed
you were observed	you were observed
he/she/it was observed	they were observed

• *The accident was observed by dozens of witnesses.*

COMPLEMENTS

observe *engage in watching*
(as opposed to participating in)

The staff can only observe.
Their job is to observe.
Will they let us observe?

observe _____ *pay careful attention to*
    OBJECT

The class observed **the debate** with interest.
The engineers observed **the re-creation of the accident**
   in slow motion.

    PASSIVE

The experimental procedure was observed by the entire staff.

observe _____ *notice, watch*
    OBJECT + BASE-FORM INFINITIVE

I did not observe **him** *actually do it.*
Did you observe **anyone** *leave the room*?
I observed **my friends** *turn green with envy.*

    OBJECT + PRESENT PARTICIPLE

I observed **him** *pacing back and forth in his office.*
We observed **the fishermen** *getting the nets ready.*

    PASSIVE

He was observed *leaving the scene of the crime.*

observe _____ *follow, be guided by*
    OBJECT

If the players don't observe **the rules**, they will be disqualified.
Does your class observe **the custom of exchanging valentines**
   on February 14?

observe _____ *celebrate, commemorate*
    OBJECT

The United States observes **Independence Day** on July 4.
We observed **a moment of silence in honor of the earthquake**
   victims.

    PASSIVE

Christmas is observed on December 25.

observe _____ *comment, remark*
    THAT-CLAUSE

The spokesperson observed **that the Senate is considering**
   a bill to reduce the speed limit.

    DIRECT QUOTATION

"A single man in possession of a good fortune," Jane Austen
   observed, **"must be in want of a wife."**

PRESENT

I obtain	we obtain
you obtain	you obtain
he/she/it obtains	they obtain

• *Commodity prices obtain everywhere.*

PRESENT PROGRESSIVE

I am obtaining	we are obtaining
you are obtaining	you are obtaining
he/she/it is obtaining	they are obtaining

• *He is obtaining some euros for our vacation.*

PAST

I obtained	we obtained
you obtained	you obtained
he/she/it obtained	they obtained

• *He obtained a law degree recently.*

PAST PROGRESSIVE

I was obtaining	we were obtaining
you were obtaining	you were obtaining
he/she/it was obtaining	they were obtaining

• *They were obtaining as much land as they could.*

PRESENT PERFECT ... have | has obtained
PAST PERFECT ... had obtained

FUTURE ... will obtain
FUTURE PROGRESSIVE ... will be obtaining
FUTURE PERFECT ... will have obtained

PAST PASSIVE

—	—
—	—
it was obtained	they were obtained

• *All of our paintings were obtained legally.*

──(COMPLEMENTS)──

obtain _____ *get, acquire*

OBJECT   It is difficult to obtain **a classic MG in good condition.**
They finally obtained **U.S. citizenship.**
You must obtain **all components** from local suppliers.

PASSIVE   An export license was obtained.

WH-CLAUSE   Very few of us obtain **what we really wish for.**
He never obtained **whatever he was looking for.**
You can only obtain **however many trucks the dealership is authorized to sell you.**

obtain _____ *be in force/use*

ADVERB OF TIME   This price will obtain **for the next few days.**
The exchange rate obtains **until the central bank changes it.**
The law obtains **until Congress changes it.**

ADVERB OF PLACE   The same price obtains **everywhere in the world.**
Standard pricing obtains **at all of our dealerships.**
The laws on torture obtain **everywhere.**

PRESENT		PRESENT PROGRESSIVE	
—	—	—	—
—	—	—	—
it occurs	they occur	it is occurring	they are occurring

• *The solstice occurs on June 20 or 21.*   • *Attacks are occurring as we speak.*

PAST		PAST PROGRESSIVE	
—	—	—	—
—	—	—	—
it occurred	they occurred	it was occurring	they were occurring

• *The same thought occurred to all of us.*   • *The epidemic was occurring everywhere.*

PRESENT PERFECT	... have | has occurred
PAST PERFECT	... had occurred

FUTURE	... will occur
FUTURE PROGRESSIVE	... will be occurring
FUTURE PERFECT	... will have occurred

PAST PASSIVE

Occur is never used in the passive voice.

──────────────────────────(COMPLEMENTS)──────

occur *happen, take place*	Bad things occur all the time.
	Accidents occur when you least expect them.
	A solar eclipse occurs when the moon passes between the sun and the earth.
	When did the meeting occur?
	Where did the assault occur?
occur *exist, be found*	A certain level of radiation occurs everywhere.
	Corruption occurs in every secretive organization.
	Flooding always occurs during the spring runoff.
occur ___ *come into [someone's] mind*	
to OBJECT	A solution just occurred **to Johanna.**
	This just occurred **to me:** Why not plug the router directly into the cable modem?
	A drawback to the plan just occurred **to the attorney.**
it + occur + to OBJECT + INFINITIVE	It never occurred **to her** *to register to vote.*
	It didn't occur **to us** *to postpone the trip.*
	Did it ever occur **to you** *to try to find a job?*
it + occur + to OBJECT + THAT-CLAUSE	It occurred **to me** *that I was running quite late.*
	It soon occurred **to everyone** *that we were completely wrong.*
	It has occurred **to us** *that we owe you an apology.*

PRESENT

I offer	we offer
you offer	you offer
he/she/it offers	they offer

• *The idea offers us a great opportunity.*

PRESENT PROGRESSIVE

I am offering	we are offering
you are offering	you are offering
he/she/it is offering	they are offering

• *I am offering a reward for finding my dog.*

PAST

I offered	we offered
you offered	you offered
he/she/it offered	they offered

• *I offered the job to Pat.*

PAST PROGRESSIVE

I was offering	we were offering
you were offering	you were offering
he/she/it was offering	they were offering

• *They were only offering the minimum wage.*

PRESENT PERFECT ... have | has offered
PAST PERFECT ... had offered

FUTURE ... will offer
FUTURE PROGRESSIVE ... will be offering
FUTURE PERFECT ... will have offered

PAST PASSIVE

I was offered	we were offered
you were offered	you were offered
he/she/it was offered	they were offered

• *I was offered a small raise.*

$\left(\text{COMPLEMENTS}\right)$

offer _____ *express, suggest*

OBJECT

May I offer **a comment or two**?
Matthew offered **two proposals** at the last meeting.
Senator Blather offered **his reasons for voting against the bill**.

offer _____ *present for [someone] to accept or refuse*

INDIRECT OBJECT + DIRECT OBJECT

They offered *us* **an interesting proposition**.
The director offered *Tom* **some useful advice**.
The guide offered *the tourists* **a special deal**.
Lucy offered *Charlie Brown* **psychiatric help** for five cents.
Charlie Brown offered *Lucy* **five cents** for psychiatric help.

to PARAPHRASE

They offered **an interesting proposition** *to us*.
The director offered **some useful advice** *to Tom*.
The guide offered **a special deal** *to the tourists*.

offer _____ *present, hand*

INDIRECT OBJECT + DIRECT OBJECT

The waiter offered *each of us* **menus**.
He offered *me* **his business card**.
Everyone offered *the couple* **their congratulations**.

to PARAPHRASE

The waiter offered **menus** *to each of us*.
He offered **his business card** *to me*.
Everyone offered **their congratulations** *to the couple*.

offer _____ *indicate that one is willing*

INFINITIVE

He offered **to drive us to the airport**.
They are offering **to buy the bonds at par**.
We offered **to replace the broken coffeepot**.

offer _____ *provide*

OBJECT (+ to OBJECT)

The job offers **an excellent health plan**.
The road offers **easy access back to the freeway**.
The city offers **many cultural opportunities** *to residents and tourists*.
Their team will not offer **much resistance** *to the new rules*.

PRESENT

I open	we open
you open	you open
he/she/it opens	they open

• *The office opens at 9 o'clock.*

PRESENT PROGRESSIVE

I am opening	we are opening
you are opening	you are opening
he/she/it is opening	they are opening

• *I am opening a new office in Cheyenne.*

PAST

I opened	we opened
you opened	you opened
he/she/it opened	they opened

• *They opened all the windows upstairs.*

PAST PROGRESSIVE

I was opening	we were opening
you were opening	you were opening
he/she/it was opening	they were opening

• *The kids were opening their presents.*

PRESENT PERFECT ... have | has opened
PAST PERFECT   ... had opened

FUTURE   ... will open
FUTURE PROGRESSIVE ... will be opening
FUTURE PERFECT   ... will have opened

PAST PASSIVE

—	—
—	—
it was opened	they were opened

• *The bids were opened last Monday at noon.*

———————————————————(**COMPLEMENTS**)———

open *become open*	His eyes slowly opened.
	His mouth opened in astonishment.
	The door suddenly opened, and in walked my mother-in-law.
	The windows in the living room won't open.
	The lilies opened in the warm summer sun.
open *start operating*	The stores open at 10 o'clock.
	New businesses are opening at the shopping mall.
open *begin*	The opera opens with a rousing chorus of happy peasants.
	You must have a pair of jacks or better to open.
open *become free of obstruction*	The tangle of trees and bushes abruptly opened in front of us.
open _____ *cause to become open*	
OBJECT	I opened **the doors to the patio**.
	The waiter opened **another bottle of wine**.
	She opened **the drawer** and took out a notebook.
	He opened **his mouth**, but said nothing.
PASSIVE	The book was opened to the last chapter.
open _____ *start the operation of*	
OBJECT	He plans to open **a coffee shop**.
	They're opening **an auto parts store** on Lebanon Avenue.
PASSIVE	The new bridge will be opened in January.
open _____ *begin*	
OBJECT	Beethoven's third piano concerto will open **the concert**.
open _____ *establish*	
OBJECT	I need to open **a checking account**.
open _____ *begin to use [a file/program]* [COMPUTERS]	
OBJECT	He opened **the spreadsheet** and began to enter data.
	I opened **Photoshop** to resize some photographs.
open _____ *lead*	
ADVERB OF PLACE TO/FROM	This door opens **onto a sun porch**.

I operate   we operate
you operate   you operate
he/she/it operates   they operate

• *The firm operates foreign subsidiaries.*

PRESENT PROGRESSIVE

I am operating   we are operating
you are operating   you are operating
he/she/it is operating   they are operating

• *The company is operating at a loss.*

PAST

I operated   we operated
you operated   you operated
he/she/it operated   they operated

• *I never operated a forklift before.*

PAST PROGRESSIVE

I was operating   we were operating
you were operating   you were operating
he/she/it was operating   they were operating

• *The surgeon was operating with a robotic device.*

PRESENT PERFECT ... have | has operated
PAST PERFECT ... had operated

FUTURE ... will operate
FUTURE PROGRESSIVE ... will be operating
FUTURE PERFECT ... will have operated

PAST PASSIVE

I was operated   we were operated
you were operated   you were operated
he/she/it was operated   they were operated

• *The controls were operated electronically.*

COMPLEMENTS

operate *function, work*	The elevator only operates during business hours. The motor operates at variable speeds. The sleeping pill operated very quickly. His network of spies has operated for years. Gangs have always operated on the fringes of society. The Seventh Fleet operates in the western Pacific. Gretchen was operating on four hours of sleep.
operate *perform surgery*	When will they operate? They couldn't operate because he still had a high temperature. The surgeon will operate as soon as she can.
operate *exert influence*	A lot of factors are operating here. Political influences always operate in making major decisions.

operate _____ *run, control the functioning of*
   OBJECT
     PASSIVE
	
	My father operated **a drill press** for 20 years.
	The device is operated by remote control.

operate _____ *direct, manage* OBJECT	 They operate **a small jewelry supply business**. Nobody can operate **a company** without accurate financial information.

operate _____ *perform surgery*
   on OBJECT
 	
     PASSIVE
	
	They will operate **on Douglas** tomorrow.
	We have to operate **on his left wrist** as soon as possible.
	Gail was operated on for appendicitis.

PRESENT

I oppose	we oppose
you oppose	you oppose
he/she/it opposes	they oppose

 • *The committee opposes the referendum.*

PRESENT PROGRESSIVE

I am opposing	we are opposing
you are opposing	you are opposing
he/she/it is opposing	they are opposing

 • *I am opposing the bill on general principle.*

PAST

I opposed	we opposed
you opposed	you opposed
he/she/it opposed	they opposed

 • *I always opposed relocating the firm.*

PAST PROGRESSIVE

I was opposing	we were opposing
you were opposing	you were opposing
he/she/it was opposing	they were opposing

 • *He was opposing the proposal because of its cost.*

PRESENT PERFECT ... have | has opposed
PAST PERFECT   ... had opposed

FUTURE   ... will oppose
FUTURE PROGRESSIVE ... will be opposing
FUTURE PERFECT   ... will have opposed

PAST PASSIVE

I was opposed	we were opposed
you were opposed	you were opposed
he/she/it was opposed	they were opposed

 • *The plan was opposed by nearly everyone.*

(COMPLEMENTS)

oppose _____ *be/argue against, disagree with*

OBJECT	Republicans generally oppose **any kind of tax increase.**
	The board will strongly oppose **the merger.**
	Lincoln opposed **slavery** from the beginning.
PASSIVE	The initiative was opposed by environmentalists.
WH-CLAUSE	I really opposed **what they were recommending.**
	They will oppose **whoever is nominated.**
	They have consistently opposed **whatever we have tried to do.**
PRESENT PARTICIPLE	I opposed **postponing the decision indefinitely.**
	He opposed **spending so much money on landscaping.**
	He never opposed **our going to France this year.**

oppose _____ *fight, act against*

OBJECT	Overwhelming forces opposed **the fleet.**
	Napoleon's 72,000 soldiers opposed **Wellington's army of 67,000** at Waterloo.
PASSIVE	The senator was opposed by a respected ex-governor.
	The mob was opposed by a handful of poorly trained soldiers.

PRESENT

I order	we order
you order	you order
he/she/it orders	they order

• *He always orders red wine with fish.*

PRESENT PROGRESSIVE

I am ordering	we are ordering
you are ordering	you are ordering
he/she/it is ordering	they are ordering

• *I am ordering you to do it.*

PAST

I ordered	we ordered
you ordered	you ordered
he/she/it ordered	they ordered

• *I ordered the replacement parts.*

PAST PROGRESSIVE

I was ordering	we were ordering
you were ordering	you were ordering
he/she/it was ordering	they were ordering

• *He was ordering takeout.*

PRESENT PERFECT … have | has ordered
PAST PERFECT … had ordered

FUTURE … will order
FUTURE PROGRESSIVE … will be ordering
FUTURE PERFECT … will have ordered

PAST PASSIVE

I was ordered	we were ordered
you were ordered	you were ordered
he/she/it was ordered	they were ordered

• *The solders were ordered to return to camp.*

— (COMPLEMENTS) —

order *request service*	Are you ready to order? We should order as soon as we can.
order _____ *command*	
OBJECT + INFINITIVE	The teacher ordered **the class** *to be silent.* The captain ordered **the troops** *to hold their fire.*
PASSIVE	I was ordered *to report on Tuesday.*
OBJECT + PAST PARTICIPLE	The officer ordered **the rioters** *arrested.* The king ordered **the duke** *placed in irons.*
PASSIVE	The fleet was ordered *held in readiness.*
BASE-FORM THAT-CLAUSE	The judge ordered **that the defendant be released.** The dean ordered **that the students be expelled.**
order _____ *request [food, merchandise]*	
OBJECT	Peter ordered **a martini**, and I ordered **a glass of wine.** We have to order **more copier paper** today.
INDIRECT OBJECT + DIRECT OBJECT	I ordered *you* **a tuna sandwich.** Peggy ordered *her husband* **a new jacket** online.
for PARAPHRASE	I ordered **a tuna sandwich** *for you.* Peggy ordered **a new jacket** *for her husband* online.
order _____ *officially direct to be done*	
OBJECT	The sergeant ordered **an inspection of the barracks.** The doctor ordered **a whole battery of tests.**
PASSIVE	A new hearing was ordered by the judge.
order _____ *arrange, organize*	
OBJECT + ADVERB OF MANNER	He always orders **his books** *alphabetically.* Some kids like to order **their toys** *in neat rows.*
PASSIVE	The letters were ordered *in careful piles on his desk.*

— (PHRASAL VERBS) —

order <u>SEP</u> **away/back/in/off/out/over/** **up/etc.** *command to go in a specified direction*	The guard ordered the student out. The general ordered up reinforcements.
order (<u>SEP</u>) **in/out** *request [food] to be* *delivered to one*	Let's order in Chinese and watch a movie. I'm tired of cooking; let's order out.

I organize   we organize
you organize   you organize
he/she/it organizes they organize

• *He always organizes the kids' games.*

I organized   we organized
you organized   you organized
he/she/it organized   they organized

• *I organized the data into a chart.*

PRESENT PERFECT ... have | has organized
PAST PERFECT   ... had organized

I am organizing   we are organizing
you are organizing   you are organizing
he/she/it is organizing they are organizing

• *I am organizing a fund-raising drive.*

I was organizing   we were organizing
you were organizing   you were organizing
he/she/it was organizing they were organizing

• *They were organizing transportation for the visitors.*

FUTURE   ... will organize
FUTURE PROGRESSIVE ... will be organizing
FUTURE PERFECT   ... will have organized

I was organized   we were organized
you were organized   you were organized
he/she/it was organized   they were organized

• *The strike was organized by an ad-hoc committee.*

COMPLEMENTS

organize *form a group*

We have to organize.
The workers are organizing.
They will never organize by themselves.

organize _____ *arrange into groups*

OBJECT

Grains of sand and silt naturally organize **themselves** by size.
For gym, we organize **the children** by age and sex.
I have to organize **my workspace** better.

PASSIVE

The memos were organized by topic.

organize _____ *make part of a group*

OBJECT

They organized **the farm workers in the Southwest**.
He will help organize **the voters in the fifth district**.

organize _____ *form, start, arrange*

OBJECT

Richard organized **a Latin club** for interested students.
I am organizing **a garden party** for my church.
We organized **Earth Day events** at local schools.
Rachel organized **an impromptu group** to perform the song.
We need to organize **a rapid response team**.
Jane helped organize **the fortieth class reunion**.

PASSIVE

The strike was organized by the union.

overcome   overcome | overcomes ·
overcame · have overcome   ☑ IRREGULAR

PRESENT			PRESENT PROGRESSIVE	
I overcome	we overcome		I am overcoming	we are overcoming
you overcome	you overcome		you are overcoming	you are overcoming
he/she/it overcomes	they overcome		he/she/it is overcoming	they are overcoming

• *He always overcomes his problems.*   • *He is overcoming a serious injury.*

PAST			PAST PROGRESSIVE	
I overcame	we overcame		I was overcoming	we were overcoming
you overcame	you overcame		you were overcoming	you were overcoming
he/she/it overcame	they overcame		he/she/it was overcoming	they were overcoming

• *She always overcame obstacles.*   • *They were gradually overcoming their opposition.*

PRESENT PERFECT	... have | has overcome
PAST PERFECT	... had overcome

FUTURE	... will overcome
FUTURE PROGRESSIVE	... will be overcoming
FUTURE PERFECT	... will have overcome

PAST PASSIVE	
I was overcome	we were overcome
you were overcome	you were overcome
he/she/it was overcome	they were overcome

• *He was overcome with emotion.*

COMPLEMENTS

overcome *prevail, fight and win*

"We shall overcome." [GOSPEL SONG]
They have finally overcome.

overcome *be strongly affected*
[USED ONLY IN THE PASSIVE]

They were overcome with emotion.
The children were overcome with excitement.
Mr. Darcy was overcome by Elizabeth's goodness.
Three firemen were overcome by smoke.

overcome _____ *prevail over, defeat, get control of*

OBJECT

The prisoners overcame **their guards**.
He overcame **all of his personal problems**.
She overcame **her addiction to cigarette smoking**.
The revised proposal overcame **the board's initial resistance**.
Mr. Knightley eventually overcomes **his concerns about Emma's foolishness**.

PASSIVE

The guards were overcome by the prisoners.

PRESENT

I owe	we owe
you owe	you owe
he/she/it owes	they owe

• *He owes a lot of money.*

PRESENT PROGRESSIVE

Owe is never used in the progressive tenses.

PAST

I owed	we owed
you owed	you owed
he/she/it owed	they owed

• *I never owed anything to anybody.*

PAST PROGRESSIVE

Owe is never used in the progressive tenses.

PRESENT PERFECT ... have | has owed
PAST PERFECT   ... had owed

FUTURE   ... will owe
FUTURE PROGRESSIVE —
FUTURE PERFECT   ... will have owed

PAST PASSIVE

I was owed	we were owed
you were owed	you were owed
he/she/it was owed	they were owed

• *We were owed a small fortune.*

───────────────(**COMPLEMENTS**)───────

owe ＿＿ *be in debt for*

OBJECT

He owes **a lot of money**.
The company owes **millions of dollars**.
He owes **a week's work**.

owe ＿＿ *be in debt to*

OBJECT

You owe **me**!
He owes **everybody in town**.
Thanks for your help. I really owe **you**.

owe ＿＿ *be obligated to pay/repay*

OBJECT

The couple owes **$6,000** in student loans.
She owes **$13,000** on her new car.
Did you owe **any income tax** last year?

INDIRECT OBJECT + DIRECT OBJECT

We owe *the bank* $200,000.

to PARAPHRASE

We owe $200,000 *to the bank*.

owe ＿＿ *be indebted to [someone] for [something]*

INDIRECT OBJECT + DIRECT OBJECT

I owe *you* **my life**.

to PARAPHRASE

I owe **my life** *to you*.

owe ＿＿ *need to [do/give]*

INDIRECT OBJECT + DIRECT OBJECT

You owe *Uncle Joe* **a letter**.
I owe *you* **an explanation**.

to PARAPHRASE

You owe **a letter** *to Uncle Joe*.
I owe **an explanation** *to you*.

it + to OBJECT + INFINITIVE

We owe it **to returning veterans** *to be sure they have jobs*.
You owe it **to yourself** *to take a vacation*.

───────────────(**EXPRESSIONS**)───────

owe [someone] a debt of gratitude
feel the need to thank [someone]

For all the hard work you have done,
   the school owes you a debt of gratitude.

owing to ＿＿ *because of*

Owing to the recent flooding, the ferry is not operating.

PRESENT

I own	we own
you own	you own
he/she/it owns	they own

• *He owns the only hotel in town.*

PRESENT PROGRESSIVE

Own is never used in the progressive tenses.

PAST

I owned	we owned
you owned	you owned
he/she/it owned	they owned

• *I owned several businesses in the 1990s.*

PAST PROGRESSIVE

Own is never used in the progressive tenses.

PRESENT PERFECT ... have | has owned
PAST PERFECT ... had owned

FUTURE ... will own
FUTURE PROGRESSIVE —
FUTURE PERFECT ... will have owned

PAST PASSIVE

I was owned	we were owned
you were owned	you were owned
he/she/it was owned	they were owned

• *The gun was owned by a man from Denver.*

COMPLEMENTS

own _____ *possess, hold as property*

OBJECT

I own **my house** outright.
Our family owns **a condo in Hawaii.**
Claude and Maude own and operate **a pizza chain in town.**
Zelda owns **a beautiful smile.**

PASSIVE

The land is owned by a corporation.

own _____ *control*

OBJECT

He is a powerful man who owns **the state legislature.**
Their offense owns **the opposing team's defense.**

own _____ *take responsibility for*

OBJECT

An honest man owns **his own mistakes.**

own _____ *acknowledge*

THAT-CLAUSE

He owns **that he was responsible for the mistake.**
They never owned **that they were in control behind the scenes.**
I owned **that I was deeply in debt.**

PHRASAL VERBS

own up to _____ *admit, confess*

The neighbor boy owned up to the vandalism.
The suspect eventually owned up to the robbery.
Marvin owned up to sneaking off to the football game.
Steve owned up to having eaten the last piece of cake.

PRESENT

I pack	we pack
you pack	you pack
he/she/it packs	they pack

• *My daughter packs her own suitcase.*

PRESENT PROGRESSIVE

I am packing	we are packing
you are packing	you are packing
he/she/it is packing	they are packing

• *I'm packing right now.*

PAST

I packed	we packed
you packed	you packed
he/she/it packed	they packed

• *I packed last night for the trip.*

PAST PROGRESSIVE

I was packing	we were packing
you were packing	you were packing
he/she/it was packing	they were packing

• *We were packing everything into boxes.*

PRESENT PERFECT   ... have | has packed
PAST PERFECT   ... had packed

FUTURE   ... will pack
FUTURE PROGRESSIVE   ... will be packing
FUTURE PERFECT   ... will have packed

PAST PASSIVE

I was packed	we were packed
you were packed	you were packed
he/she/it was packed	they were packed

• *The boxes were all packed for shipping.*

(COMPLEMENTS)

pack *put items in containers [boxes, luggage]*

We should pack as soon as possible.
I will be packing all week.

pack _____ *fill [a container]*

OBJECT

I quickly packed **my bags** and checked out.
We packed **the boxes** full of gifts.

PASSIVE

The cartons were packed at the warehouse.

pack _____ *put into a container for transport/storage*

OBJECT

Did you pack **your walking shoes?**
I forgot to pack **my toothpaste.**

PASSIVE

Apparently the brochures were never packed.

OBJECT + ADVERB OF PLACE

We packed **our camping equipment** *into the truck.*
The squirrels packed **nuts** *in their cheeks.*

pack _____ *crowd, fill to/beyond capacity*

OBJECT

Job applicants packed **the hallways.**

PASSIVE

The nightclub was packed with hundreds of people.

pack _____ *put [a large number of people] into [a place]*

OBJECT + *into* OBJECT

Organizers packed **2,700 people** *into Symphony Hall.*

PASSIVE

The passengers were packed *into three subway cars.*

pack _____ *be able to be put [somewhere] for transport*

ADVERB OF PLACE

The tent packs **into a little cube.**
The equipment packed **into a small trailer.**

pack _____ *stuff, fill*

OBJECT + *with* OBJECT

The doctor packed **the wound** *with cotton.*

PASSIVE

The medicine container was packed *with dry ice.*

(PHRASAL VERBS)

pack _SEP_ **away** *store*   Gene and Louise packed away the baby clothes.

pack _SEP_ **down** *compress, make compact*   Traffic packed the snow down on the streets.

pack _SEP_ **in** *crowd, push in*   The promoters packed people in as tightly as possible.

pack up *fill one's luggage*   We need to pack up tonight for our early-morning flight.

pack _SEP_ **up** *gather [items] for transport*   Be sure to pack up all your tools before leaving.

PRESENT

I paint	we paint
you paint	you paint
he/she/it paints	they paint

• *He paints large landscapes.*

PRESENT PROGRESSIVE

I am painting	we are painting
you are painting	you are painting
he/she/it is painting	they are painting

• *I am painting the walls green.*

PAST

I painted	we painted
you painted	you painted
he/she/it painted	they painted

• *We painted the entire second floor.*

PAST PROGRESSIVE

I was painting	we were painting
you were painting	you were painting
he/she/it was painting	they were painting

• *We were painting with an oil-based enamel.*

PRESENT PERFECT ... have | has painted
PAST PERFECT ... had painted

FUTURE ... will paint
FUTURE PROGRESSIVE ... will be painting
FUTURE PERFECT ... will have painted

PAST PASSIVE

I was painted	we were painted
you were painted	you were painted
he/she/it was painted	they were painted

• *The portrait was painted in 1860.*

(**COMPLEMENTS**)

paint *engage in painting*

I try to paint as often as I can.
They will be painting all afternoon.

paint _____ *cover [a surface/area] with paint*

OBJECT

We need to paint **the kitchen walls**.
Our neighbors will paint **their house** this summer.

PASSIVE

The deck has never been painted.

OBJECT + PREDICATE ADJECTIVE

I painted **our bedroom** *a light tan*.
You should paint **the exterior** *gray*.

PASSIVE

The porch ceiling was painted *sky blue*.

paint _____ *make a picture of with paint*

OBJECT

Gilbert Stuart painted **George Washington** many times.
Linda painted **clouds and airplanes** on Tim's bedroom walls.

PASSIVE

His ancestors were painted by Thomas Gainsborough.

INDIRECT OBJECT + DIRECT OBJECT

He painted *us a family portrait*.
She painted *them a picture of their old farm*.

for PARAPHRASE

He painted **a family portrait** *for us*.
She painted **a picture of their old farm** *for them*.

OBJECT + PRESENT PARTICIPLE

He painted **her** *laughing in the sunlight*.
She painted **the family** *working in the garden*.

PASSIVE

Gentlemen were painted *posing in front of their mansions*.

paint _____ *describe, usually in a colorful way*

OBJECT + (as) PREDICATE NOUN

The article painted **him** *(as) a complete fool*.
The newspaper painted **the administration** *(as) a disaster*.

PASSIVE

The candidate was painted *(as) a hopeless loser*.

OBJECT + *as* PREDICATE ADJECTIVE

The article painted **the flat tax proposal** *as ludicrous*.

paint _____ *apply makeup to*

OBJECT

Mindy paints **her lips** with bright red lipstick.

OBJECT + PREDICATE ADJECTIVE

She paints **her nails** *bright purple*.

(**PHRASAL VERBS**)

paint _SEP_ **out/over** *cover with paint*

She painted the dog out and replaced it with a cat.
City workers will paint over the graffiti.

PRESENT

I park	we park
you park	you park
he/she/it parks	they park

- *He parks in a garage on Locust Street.*

PRESENT PROGRESSIVE

I am parking	we are parking
you are parking	you are parking
he/she/it is parking	they are parking

- *I am parking in their garage temporarily.*

PAST

I parked	we parked
you parked	you parked
he/she/it parked	they parked

- *We parked our car on the lawn.*

PAST PROGRESSIVE

I was parking	we were parking
you were parking	you were parking
he/she/it was parking	they were parking

- *The visitors were parking on the side streets.*

PRESENT PERFECT   ... have | has parked
PAST PERFECT   ... had parked

FUTURE   ... will park
FUTURE PROGRESSIVE   ... will be parking
FUTURE PERFECT   ... will have parked

PAST PASSIVE

I was parked	we were parked
you were parked	you were parked
he/she/it was parked	they were parked

- *Cars were parked everywhere.*

COMPLEMENTS

park *engage in parking a vehicle*

He is just parking now.
I will park as soon as I can.
Many drivers park in gear so the car won't roll.

park _____ *stop [a vehicle] temporarily*

OBJECT

We parked **the car** to listen to the end of the game.
They parked **the truck** during the worst of the storm.

PASSIVE

Cars were parked along the interstate until the snowplow
came through.

park _____ *leave a vehicle [in a certain place]*

ADVERB OF PLACE

I always park **there**.
You can't park **in a handicapped space**.
He usually parks **in front of my house**.
They will park **anywhere they can find a space**.

park _____ *leave [a vehicle usually, in a certain place]*

OBJECT + ADVERB OF PLACE

I parked **the car** *in a lot behind the office*.
He always parks **his van** *on the street*.
You can park **your luggage** *in the entryway*.

PASSIVE

Their car was parked *in the neighbor's driveway*.

park _____ *settle in* [INFORMAL]

OBJECT + ADVERB OF PLACE

They parked **themselves** *on my doorstep*.
He parked **the kids** *with his mother* for the afternoon.
Bob parked **himself** *in front of the TV* and watched the game.

PRESENT

I participate	we participate
you participate	you participate
he/she/it participates	they participate

- *He participates in all group activities.*

PAST

I participated	we participated
you participated	you participated
he/she/it participated	they participated

- *I never participated in organized sports.*

PRESENT PERFECT ... have | has participated
PAST PERFECT ... had participated

PRESENT PROGRESSIVE

I am participating	we are participating
you are participating	you are participating
he/she/it is participating	they are participating

- *I am already participating in two events.*

PAST PROGRESSIVE

I was participating	we were participating
you were participating	you were participating
he/she/it was participating	they were participating

- *They were participating in planning the retreat.*

FUTURE ... will participate
FUTURE PROGRESSIVE ... will be participating
FUTURE PERFECT ... will have participated

PAST PASSIVE

—	—
—	—
it was participated	they were participated

- *The parade was participated in by the entire community.*

COMPLEMENTS

participate *take part in an event/activity*

There's a conference on global warming
  in May, and I think our company should participate.
The county fair is holding a photography contest,
  and grade-schoolers can participate.

participate _____ *take part, be involved*

in OBJECT

I couldn't participate **in the discussion**.
Everyone should participate **in citizen referendums**.
I participated **in most school activities**.

PASSIVE

Elections may be participated in by every eligible voter.

in WH-CLAUSE

Participate **in what you find most helpful**.
I couldn't participate **in what you recommended**.
I participated **in whatever activities fit my schedule**.

in PRESENT PARTICIPLE

We will participate **in planning the conference**.
I am participating **in locating the new office**.
We all participated **in cleaning up the beach**.

PRESENT

I pass	we pass
you pass	you pass
he/she/it passes	they pass

• *Time passes slowly in the mountains.*

PRESENT PROGRESSIVE

I am passing	we are passing
you are passing	you are passing
he/she/it is passing	they are passing

• *I am passing the message on to my boss.*

PAST

I passed	we passed
you passed	you passed
he/she/it passed	they passed

• *I passed my last exam.*

PAST PROGRESSIVE

I was passing	we were passing
you were passing	you were passing
he/she/it was passing	they were passing

• *The rain shower was passing.*

PRESENT PERFECT	... have | has passed
PAST PERFECT	... had passed

FUTURE	... will pass
FUTURE PROGRESSIVE	... will be passing
FUTURE PERFECT	... will have passed

PAST PASSIVE

I was passed	we were passed
you were passed	you were passed
he/she/it was passed	they were passed

• *The bill was passed by a narrow majority.*

─(COMPLEMENTS)─

pass *go by, proceed*	Slow down and let the truck pass. The day passed slowly.
pass *happen, come to an end*	The danger has passed. His moment of fame has already passed.
pass *go past each other, cross*	Our letters must have passed in the mail. The two ships passed in the night. We must have passed without seeing each other.
pass *succeed in an examination/course*	He finally passed. Do you think I will pass?
pass *be officially approved*	The bill passed without a dissenting vote.
pass *change from one state to another*	Water passes from a liquid to a gas at 100 degrees Celsius.

pass _____ *go by, move past*

ADVERB OF PLACE TO/FROM	The steamboat passed **under the bridge** at 2 o'clock. We passed **through Springfield** on our way to Chicago.
OBJECT	He passed **every vehicle on the road**. Michelle passes **our house** on her way to school. Have we already passed **the post office**?

pass _____ *succeed in [an examination/course]*

OBJECT	All the recruits passed **their physicals**. I will pass **calculus** without a problem.

pass _____ *approve officially*

OBJECT	The committee passed **all the candidates**.
PASSIVE	The motion was passed by consensus.

pass _____ *transfer*

OBJECT	Pass **the biscuits**, please.
INDIRECT OBJECT + DIRECT OBJECT	I passed *him* the envelope. Please pass *Mary* the salad. Wickenheiser passed *Pavese* the puck.
to PARAPHRASE	I passed **the envelope** *to him*. Please pass **the salad** *to Mary*. Wickenheiser passed **the puck** *to Pavese*.

pass _____ *spend, occupy [time]*

    OBJECT

             Bill and Melinda passed **the day** in meetings.
             What would you do to pass **the time on the plane**?

    OBJECT + PRESENT PARTICIPLE   The family passed **the day** *working in the garden.*

pass _____ *use illegally as money*

    OBJECT

             They were able to pass **the counterfeit bills** easily.
             Someone was passing **bad checks** at local businesses.

(PHRASAL VERBS)

pass SEP **back/down/in/over/under/**etc.
transfer in a specified direction

  Would you pass the butter back
     when you're finished?
  We passed our homework in at the beginning of class.

pass SEP **along** *relay [information]*

  Joanie always passes along the latest gossip.

pass SEP **along/on** *transfer [a price change]*

  The store passed along the price increase to its customers.

pass SEP **around/out** *distribute*

  Please pass the cookies around for me.
  The students will pass out flyers at the rally.

pass as/for _____ *be mistakenly recognized as*

  With his beard, he easily passes as an adult.
  He could pass for a professional football player.
  The magician is 55, but he could pass for 40.

pass away/on *die*

  Great-aunt Amelia passed away at the age of 83.

pass SEP **by** *ignore*

  The boss passed Lana by for promotion.
  Sometimes I feel that life has passed me by.

pass SEP **down/on** *hand down, give to a younger family member*

  Aunt Clara passed the rocking chair down to my sister.

pass _____ **off as** *succeed in presenting [oneself/something] as*

  The nurse's aide passed herself off as a doctor.
  He tried to pass the work off as his own.

pass _____ **off on** *sell as genuine to*

  He passed the fake watch off on an unsuspecting passerby.

pass on _____ *skip, not accept*

  Donald passed on the pie because he's diabetic.

pass on to _____ *move on to, change to*

  The discussion group passed on to the issue of health care.

pass out *faint, fall asleep*

  Doris passed out right in the middle of the sermon.
  John passed out after two beers.

pass SEP **over/up** *skip, not choose*

  The coach passed over Scotty and picked Lamar.
  I'll pass the main course up and go straight for dessert.

pass SEP **up** *not accept*

  Don't pass up the chance to go to college.

pass SEP **up** *go past without stopping*

  We passed up three nice restaurants and ended up
     at this dump.

(EXPRESSIONS)

pass judgment (on _____**)** *express a strong opinion (about [someone/something])*

  Don't pass judgment on the book
     until you've read it.

pass over [someone's] head *be too difficult for [someone] to understand*

  I'm afraid his lecture on black holes passed over the
     audience's head.

      pass the buck *give the responsibility for something to someone else*

  They passed the buck from one bureaucrat to the next.

      pass the hat (around) *seek donations*

  The organizers passed the hat around after the concert.

      pass the time (of day) *talk casually*

  The old men passed the time of day on a bench in front
     of the general store.

PRESENT

I pay	we pay
you pay	you pay
he/she/it pays	they pay

- *The company pays pretty good wages.*

PRESENT PROGRESSIVE

I am paying	we are paying
you are paying	you are paying
he/she/it is paying	they are paying

- *I am paying for my own health insurance.*

PAST

I paid	we paid
you paid	you paid
he/she/it paid	they paid

- *I already paid the bill.*

PAST PROGRESSIVE

I was paying	we were paying
you were paying	you were paying
he/she/it was paying	they were paying

- *They were paying him to mow the grass.*

PRESENT PERFECT	… have	has paid
PAST PERFECT	… had paid

FUTURE	… will pay
FUTURE PROGRESSIVE	… will be paying
FUTURE PERFECT	… will have paid

PAST PASSIVE

I was paid	we were paid
you were paid	you were paid
he/she/it was paid	they were paid

- *They were paid $200 for the job.*

COMPLEMENTS

pay *give money for goods/services*	The job pays pretty well. "Who's going to pay?" "I'll pay this time."
pay *be worthwhile*	Crime doesn't pay.
pay _____ *give money to [for goods / services / settlement of a bill/debt]*	
OBJECT	I paid **the plumber** today.
OBJECT + *for* OBJECT	I paid **the cashier** *for the book.*
OBJECT + INFINITIVE	We will pay **the kids** *to clean out the basement.*
PASSIVE	The firm was paid *to run a call center for us.*
OBJECT + *for* PRESENT PARTICIPLE	We will pay **the kids** *for cleaning out the basement.*
PASSIVE	The firm was paid *for running a call center for us.*
pay _____ *give money for [services / settlement of a bill/debt]*	
OBJECT	We have to pay **our car insurance** this month. Did you pay **the credit card bill**?
PASSIVE	The dentist's bill has already been paid.
pay _____ *give [a certain amount of money] for goods/services*	
OBJECT	The job pays **$30,000 a year**. He pays **$15 an hour**.
INDIRECT OBJECT + DIRECT OBJECT	He pays *his employees* **a commission**. Would you pay *me* $30 for this lamp?
to PARAPHRASE	He pays **a commission** *to his employees.*
pay _____ *be worthwhile*	
it + *pay* + INFINITIVE	It pays **to be careful**. It never pays **to be in a hurry**.

PHRASAL VERBS

pay ˢᵉᵖ **back** *return money borrowed from [someone]*	Wimpy will gladly pay you back 　on Tuesday for a hamburger today.
pay ˢᵉᵖ **back** *get even with*	We'll pay them back for stealing our tickets.
pay off *result in a profit/benefit*	Working overtime has really paid off.
pay ˢᵉᵖ **off** *settle [a debt] by paying all that is owed*	We hope to pay the car loan off in three years.

PRESENT		PRESENT PROGRESSIVE	
I perform	we perform	I am performing	we are performing
you perform	you perform	you are performing	you are performing
he/she/it performs	they perform	he/she/it is performing	they are performing

• *She performs in Los Angeles.* • *I am performing a tricky balancing act.*

PAST		PAST PROGRESSIVE	
I performed	we performed	I was performing	we were performing
you performed	you performed	you were performing	you were performing
he/she/it performed	they performed	he/she/it was performing	they were performing

• *I performed that operation once before.* • *The company was performing below expectations.*

PRESENT PERFECT	... have	has performed
PAST PERFECT	... had performed

FUTURE	... will perform
FUTURE PROGRESSIVE	... will be performing
FUTURE PERFECT	... will have performed

PAST PASSIVE

— —

— —

it was performed   they were performed

• *The play was last performed in 1989.*

COMPLEMENTS

perform *do / carry out an action/ task/function*

The violinist cannot perform because of a sprained wrist.
The candidates all performed well on the first interview.
The band will perform again at ten.

perform *do, function [in terms of success/effectiveness]*

None of my stocks is performing satisfactorily.
How is your new hybrid car performing?

perform _____ *do, carry out*

OBJECT

Jeanette has always performed **her job** well.
The veterinarian performed **two surgeries** this afternoon.
My brother performed **three wedding ceremonies** last year.
She performed **a complicated experiment for the science fair**.

perform _____ *entertain an audience by acting/singing/dancing/etc. in*

OBJECT

The kids' class is performing **a play that they wrote**.
The cast of *Saturday Night Live* performs **its comedy sketches** before a live audience.
What roles have you performed?
Penn and Teller performed **the "Sawing a Woman in Half" illusion** on television.
At the 77th Academy Awards, Beyoncé performed **three songs nominated for Best Original Song**.
My boss performed **a little dance** when he heard the good news.

PASSIVE

Shakespeare's *Henry VIII* is almost never performed.

PRESENT

I permit	we permit
you permit	you permit
he/she/it permits	they permit

· *He never permits parking on the lawn.*

PRESENT PROGRESSIVE

I am permitting	we are permitting
you are permitting	you are permitting
he/she/it is permitting	they are permitting

· *The judge is permitting the trial to proceed.*

PAST

I permitted	we permitted
you permitted	you permitted
he/she/it permitted	they permitted

· *We permitted them to watch TV tonight.*

PAST PROGRESSIVE

I was permitting	we were permitting
you were permitting	you were permitting
he/she/it was permitting	they were permitting

· *They were permitting weekend rentals for a while.*

PRESENT PERFECT ... have | has permitted
PAST PERFECT ... had permitted

FUTURE ... will permit
FUTURE PROGRESSIVE ... will be permitting
FUTURE PERFECT ... will have permitted

PAST PASSIVE

I was permitted	we were permitted
you were permitted	you were permitted
he/she/it was permitted	they were permitted

· *Smoking was permitted only in the parking lot.*

COMPLEMENTS

permit *allow, make possible*

We will eat outside if the weather permits.
If time permits, I will take questions from the audience.
We will sail back tomorrow if the winds permit.

permit _____ *allow, give permission for*

OBJECT

I will not permit **a failure on my watch**.
The court cannot permit **such an injustice**.

  PASSIVE

Such behavior is not permitted here.

OBJECT + INFINITIVE

I will permit **you** *to ask one more question*.
The law permits **18-year-olds** *to vote*.

  PASSIVE

High school students are permitted *to enroll in university classes*.

OBJECT + PRESENT PARTICIPLE

The school does not permit **freshmen** *living off campus*.
The library does not permit **books** *being copied without permission*.
Her mother does not permit **Harriet** *staying out late*.

PRESENT PARTICIPLE

Oregon doesn't permit **pumping your own gas**.
We don't permit **eating in the living room**.
Hawaii does not permit **importing snakes or other reptiles**.

PHRASAL VERBS

permit _____ **in/out/through/up**/etc.
*allow to go in a specified direction /
be in a specified position*

The teacher permitted the boys in after recess.
The doctor permitted the patient up for half an hour.

PRESENT

I persuade	we persuade
you persuade	you persuade
he/she/it persuades	they persuade

• *He persuades us with excellent arguments.*

PRESENT PROGRESSIVE

I am persuading	we are persuading
you are persuading	you are persuading
he/she/it is persuading	they are persuading

• *Donna is persuading all of us to become vegans.*

PAST

I persuaded	we persuaded
you persuaded	you persuaded
he/she/it persuaded	they persuaded

• *I persuaded him to go along with my joke.*

PAST PROGRESSIVE

I was persuading	we were persuading
you were persuading	you were persuading
he/she/it was persuading	they were persuading

• *They were persuading her to give them more dessert.*

PRESENT PERFECT ... have | has persuaded
PAST PERFECT ... had persuaded

FUTURE ... will persuade
FUTURE PROGRESSIVE ... will be persuading
FUTURE PERFECT ... will have persuaded

PAST PASSIVE

I was persuaded	we were persuaded
you were persuaded	you were persuaded
he/she/it was persuaded	they were persuaded

• *They were persuaded that it was a good investment.*

(**COMPLEMENTS**)

persuade _____ *convince [to do]*

OBJECT + INFINITIVE

The players persuaded **the coach** *to cut practice short.*
The report persuaded **a lot of people** *to sell their shares.*
I couldn't persuade **them** *to do anything.*

PASSIVE

The judge was persuaded *to allow the testimony.*

NOTE: In conversation, the infinitive following *persuade* is often left unspoken.

Okay, okay. You've persuaded me. [INSTEAD OF Okay, okay.
    You've persuaded me to go along.]
What can I do to persuade you?

persuade _____ *convince [of the truth/value of]*

OBJECT + THAT-CLAUSE

He persuaded **us** *that he was right after all.*
Roberta persuaded **the committee** *that her proposal
    deserved extra funding.*

PASSIVE

I was persuaded *that the report contained factual errors.*

PRESENT

I pick	we pick
you pick	you pick
he/she/it picks	they pick

• *He only picks the ripest fruit.*

PAST

I picked	we picked
you picked	you picked
he/she/it picked	they picked

• *They picked the best players first.*

PRESENT PERFECT	... have	has picked
PAST PERFECT	... had picked

PRESENT PROGRESSIVE

I am picking	we are picking
you are picking	you are picking
he/she/it is picking	they are picking

• *We are picking blackberries this afternoon.*

PAST PROGRESSIVE

I was picking	we were picking
you were picking	you were picking
he/she/it was picking	they were picking

• *He was picking his way across the muddy field.*

FUTURE	... will pick
FUTURE PROGRESSIVE	... will be picking
FUTURE PERFECT	... will have picked

PAST PASSIVE

I was picked	we were picked
you were picked	you were picked
he/she/it was picked	they were picked

• *We were picked to go first.*

(**COMPLEMENTS**)

pick *choose, select*

I get to pick this time.
Who will pick first?

pick _____ *choose, select*
    OBJECT

The kids picked **the programs they wanted to watch.**
I picked **the best option open to me.**
She will pick **Princeton** if she gets admitted.

    PASSIVE

Their horse was picked as the favorite.

pick _____ *pluck, remove; gather, harvest*
    OBJECT

I had to pick **lint** from my coat before leaving the house.
We need to pick **some flowers** for the party.

    PASSIVE

These strawberries were picked this morning.

(**PHRASAL VERBS**)

pick _SEP_ **apart** *criticize in detail*

Critics began to pick apart Senator
    Blather's budget proposal.

pick at _____ *take small bites of [food]*

The child had a fever and just picked at her food.

pick (away) at _____ *criticize*

The opposition party was picking away at the president's plan.

pick on _____ *tease, annoy*

Stop picking on Gary; he's doing his best.

pick _SEP_ **out** *find, single out*

How can you pick anyone out in this crowd?

pick up *resume, continue after an interruption*

The discussion picked up where it had left off.

pick up *increase, improve*

Business has picked up since Christmas.

pick _SEP_ **up** *increase*

The train is picking up speed now.
The runners picked the pace up after 20 miles.

pick _SEP_ **up** *lift*

She picked her daughter up and gave her a hug.

pick _SEP_ **up** *stop for and take along*

Would you pick us up at seven?
Don't pick up strangers along the highway.

pick _SEP_ **up** *learn easily*

I picked up Italian over the summer.

pick _SEP_ **up** *acquire, buy*

I picked some milk up on the way home.

pick _SEP_ **up** *capture, take into custody*

Police picked up the robbery suspect.

pick _SEP_ **up** *make tidy*

You must pick up your room before going out to play.

PRESENT

I place	we place
you place	you place
he/she/it places	they place

• *The team usually places in the top ten.*

PRESENT PROGRESSIVE

I am placing	we are placing
you are placing	you are placing
he/she/it is placing	they are placing

• *I am placing an ad in the newspaper.*

PAST

I placed	we placed
you placed	you placed
he/she/it placed	they placed

• *I placed the memos on your desk.*

PAST PROGRESSIVE

I was placing	we were placing
you were placing	you were placing
he/she/it was placing	they were placing

• *The kids were placing their toys on the stairs.*

PRESENT PERFECT ... have | has placed
PAST PERFECT ... had placed

FUTURE ... will place
FUTURE PROGRESSIVE ... will be placing
FUTURE PERFECT ... will have placed

PAST PASSIVE

I was placed	we were placed
you were placed	you were placed
he/she/it was placed	they were placed

• *The order was placed on December 12.*

COMPLEMENTS

place _____ *put, position*

OBJECT + ADVERB OF PLACE

I placed **the groceries** *on the counter.*
He placed **the bicycles** *in the garage.*
You shouldn't place **your money** *in an uninsured account.*
The court temporarily placed **the children** *in foster care.*
The incident placed **me** *at a distinct disadvantage.*

PASSIVE

I was placed *in an awkward position.*

place _____ *submit, arrange*

OBJECT

I am placing **an order for pizza.**
You will need to place **a call for an overseas connection.**
The new restaurant placed **a large ad in the newspaper.**
They have placed **a contract for 10 heavy trucks.**

place _____ *recall, find* [USUALLY NEGATIVE]

OBJECT

We couldn't place **him** at all.
I can't place **his name.**
He can't place **his car keys.**

place _____ *finish* [in a certain position in a competition]

ADVERB OF PLACE

We placed **third.**
The Cougars placed **behind the rest of the teams.**
They hope to place **in the top five** this year.

place _____ *rank*

OBJECT + ADVERB OF PLACE

The committee places **Geraldo** *second among the applicants.*
We place **environmental quality** *high on our list of priorities.*

PASSIVE

In the 19th century, Milton was placed *first among English writers.*

place _____ *attach* [importance/value/etc.] *to*

OBJECT + *on* OBJECT

The president places **great value** *on perseverance.*

PHRASAL VERBS

place SEP *aside/back/up/etc.*
put in a specified position

The teacher placed the essays aside
   until the weekend.
Place the books back where you found them.

place _____ **with** *get* [someone] *a job at*   The employment agency placed Wade with a law firm.

PRESENT

I plan	we plan
you plan	you plan
he/she/it plans	they plan

- *He plans to stay in Chicago.*

PRESENT PROGRESSIVE

I am planning	we are planning
you are planning	you are planning
he/she/it is planning	they are planning

- *I'm planning to take a few days off.*

PAST

I planned	we planned
you planned	you planned
he/she/it planned	they planned

- *We planned a surprise for her birthday.*

PAST PROGRESSIVE

I was planning	we were planning
you were planning	you were planning
he/she/it was planning	they were planning

- *We were planning on getting married in June.*

PRESENT PERFECT ... have | has planned
PAST PERFECT ... had planned

FUTURE ... will plan
FUTURE PROGRESSIVE ... will be planning
FUTURE PERFECT ... will have planned

PAST PASSIVE

—	—
—	—
it was planned	they were planned

- *The meeting was planned weeks in advance.*

(COMPLEMENTS)

plan _____ *decide on, make arrangements for*

OBJECT	She is planning **the fall conference.**
	The school is planning **a field trip for seniors.**
	We must plan **our strategy.**
	The prisoners had planned **their escape** for months.
PASSIVE	The senator's remarks were planned days in advance.
WH-CLAUSE	He should plan **what he is going to do.**
	We are planning **where we are going on vacation.**

plan _____ *intend, expect*

for OBJECT + INFINITIVE	He planned **for us** *to revise the contract.*
	The doctor plans **for him** *to undergo surgery Monday.*
	I had planned **for Diane** *to write the summary.*
INFINITIVE	Dave and Kathy plan **to enjoy a glass of homemade wine** in front of a blazing fire.
	How do they plan **to finish the job?**
	The company plans **to open a branch in Phoenix.**

plan _____ *depend on, expect*

on OBJECT	We were planning **on good weather for the picnic.**
	Beth is planning **on Margaret's help with the editing.**
on PRESENT PARTICIPLE	We are all planning **on attending the meeting.**
	Are you planning **on going out tonight?**
	We weren't planning **on being delayed in traffic.**

plan _____ *design*

OBJECT	An architect is planning **the new kitchen.**
	How soon can you plan **the extension?**
	He was hired to plan **the garden and reception area.**

(PHRASAL VERBS)

plan _SEP_ **out** *make complete arrangements for*

Mom and Dad planned out our entire vacation.

play _____ *act the part/role of*
    OBJECT
        She is playing **Ophelia** in *Hamlet*.

play _____ *perform music on [an instrument]*
    OBJECT
        Katie plays **the violin** beautifully.

play _____ *perform [a musical composition (by)]*
    OBJECT
        She will play **a Haydn piano sonata**.
        The symphony is playing **Beethoven** on Friday night.

play _____ *pretend to be, behave [in a certain way]*
    PREDICATE NOUN
        He always plays **the victim**.
        The reporter played **the role of a mere bystander**.
        The smuggler tried to play **a completely innocent deckhand**, but it didn't work.
    PREDICATE ADJECTIVE
        He played **dead** during the attack.
        I played **innocent**, acting like I didn't know where the noise was coming from.

(**PHRASAL VERBS**)

play along *(pretend to) cooperate*
Let's play along and see what the boss wants.

play _____ **along** *keep [someone] waiting*
The boss keeps playing us along; will we get a raise or not?

play (around) with _____ *consider, usually not seriously*
The company played around with the idea of a four-day workweek.
Mom and Dad played with moving to San Diego after the war.

play _SEP_ **down** *try to reduce the importance/likelihood/value of*
News commentators played down the probability of a recession.

play _____ **off against** *set in opposition to*
Joe played the car dealers off against each other to get the best price.

play on _____ *exploit, manipulate*
The candidate played on our desire for world peace in order to win our votes.

play _SEP_ **out** *complete*
We were behind by 12 runs but had to play the game out.
The forward played out the rest of the season with a sore hamstring.

play _____ **(straight) through** *perform all of*
Agatha played the concerto straight through.

play _SEP_ **up** *emphasize, praise*
The press release played up the politician's strong points.

play up to _____ *flatter*
Lisa is always playing up to the manager; she wants a promotion.

(**EXPRESSIONS**)

play a part/role in _____ *be influential in*
Genetics plays an important role in cancer.
Our group plays a big part in keeping politicians honest.

play ball (with _____ **)** *cooperate (with [someone])*
Will the players who used steroids play ball with the Senate subcommittee?

play _____ **by ear** *decide what to do as a situation develops*
The union will have to play it by ear with regard to future layoffs.

play (the) devil's advocate *argue against a proposal in order to test its validity*
Good journalists play devil's advocate when interviewing politicians.

play with fire *take a serious risk*
The governor is playing with fire by giving jobs to all his friends.

top
40
verb

PRESENT

I play   we play
you play   you play

PRESENT PROGRESSIVE

I am playing   we are playing
you are playing   you are playing
he/she/it is playing they are playing

• *The actor is playing the part for the first time.*

PAST PROGRESSIVE

I was playing   we were playing
you were playing   you were playing
he/she/it was playing they were playing

• *The kids were playing in the backyard.*

FUTURE   ... will play
FUTURE PROGRESSIVE ... will be playing
FUTURE PERFECT   ... will have played

we were played
you were played
red   they were played

played last night.

─────(COMPLEMENTS)─────

We promise not to play in the street.
The kids have been playing all afternoon.

The manager will let Luis play tomorrow.
Can I play, Coach?
We never play for money.

The soloist will not be able to play because of an injury.
The Beatles played at Busch Stadium on August 21, 1966.
A band was playing in the distance.

What's playing on the radio right now?
The Lord of the Rings was playing downtown.

The senator's new ad is not playing well.
Do you think my idea will play?
We thought the ad campaign would play better than
   it did.

on]
We play **softball** nearly every weekend.
The Yankees are playing **three games** at home this week.
Do you like to play **chess**?
The kids love to play **Monopoly and other board games**.

play ____ *be at [a certain position] in a game/sport*
   OBJECT

I always played **left field**, and my sister played **shortstop**.
He plays **left guard**.

play ____ *put [a player] in a game*
   OBJECT

The coach played **Felipe** in center field.

play ____ *be a member of [a sports team]*
   for OBJECT

Willie Mays played **for the Giants**.
Michael Jordan played **for the Bulls**.

play ____ *compete against* [SPORTS]
   OBJECT

The Seahawks are playing **the Rams**
   on Sunday.
Whom are we playing tomorrow?
I am playing **Ben White** in the
   semifinal match.

plead   plead | pleads · pleaded · have pleaded
                plead | pleads · pled · have pled

☑ REGULAR
☑ IRREGULAR

PRESENT

I plead	we plead
you plead	you plead
he/she/it pleads	they plead

• *The defendant pleads innocent.*

PAST

I pleaded/pled	we pleaded/pled
you pleaded/pled	you pleaded/pled
he/she/it pleaded/pled	they pleaded/pled

• *He already pled his case.*

PRESENT PERFECT ... have | has pleaded/pled
PAST PERFECT ... had pleaded/pled

PRESENT PROGRESSIVE

I am pleading	we are pleading
you are pleading	you are pleading
he/she/it is pleading	they are pleading

• *I am pleading innocent, Your Honor.*

PAST PROGRESSIVE

I was pleading	we were pleading
you were pleading	you were pleading
he/she/it was pleading	they were pleading

• *The prisoners were pleading with the guards.*

FUTURE ... will plead
FUTURE PROGRESSIVE ... will be pleading
FUTURE PERFECT ... will have pleaded/pled

PAST PASSIVE

—   —
—   —
it was pleaded/pled   they were pleaded/pled

• *The case was pled before the district court.*

COMPLEMENTS

plead *make an emotional appeal, beg*

The women and children were pleading.
Standing proudly, the men refused to plead.
The convicts were pleading on their knees.

plead _____ *present/argue [a law case, one's position]*

OBJECT

The lawyer will plead **your case.**
You shouldn't plead **your own case.**
The state's attorney will plead **the government's case.**

plead _____ *formally declare oneself [innocent/guilty] in court*

PREDICATE ADJECTIVE

He pled **guilty on all charges.**
The gang members will plead **innocent.**
How do you plead?

plead _____ *ask/beg*

for OBJECT
for OBJECT + INFINITIVE
with OBJECT (+ INFINITIVE)

INFINITIVE

The condemned man was pleading **for his life.**
We pleaded **for them** *to be careful.*
I'm pleading **with you!** Let me go to the concert.
They pleaded **with the manager** *to reconsider his decision.*
I have pleaded **with Bob** *to look for a better job.*
He pleaded **to come with us.**
The children pleaded **to get a dog.**
I pleaded **to get a bigger budget.**

plead _____ *give as an excuse*

OBJECT

THAT-CLAUSE

Tanya pleaded **ignorance of the law,** but got a ticket anyway.
The tobacco company heads pleaded **ignorance of the
    addictive properties of cigarette smoking.**
Scott pleaded **that he didn't have enough time to complete
    the assignment.**
Brandon pleaded **that he didn't see the speed limit sign.**

PRESENT

I please	we please
you please	you please
he/she/it pleases	they please

- *His behavior pleases no one.*

PRESENT PROGRESSIVE

I am pleasing	we are pleasing
you are pleasing	you are pleasing
he/she/it is pleasing	they are pleasing

- *He is pleasing everyone but himself.*

PAST

I pleased	we pleased
you pleased	you pleased
he/she/it pleased	they pleased

- *The decision pleased everyone but me.*

PAST PROGRESSIVE

I was pleasing	we were pleasing
you were pleasing	you were pleasing
he/she/it was pleasing	they were pleasing

- *They were just pleasing themselves.*

PRESENT PERFECT ... have | has pleased
PAST PERFECT ... had pleased

FUTURE ... will please
FUTURE PROGRESSIVE ... will be pleasing
FUTURE PERFECT ... will have pleased

PAST PASSIVE

I was pleased	we were pleased
you were pleased	you were pleased
he/she/it was pleased	they were pleased

- *He was pleased by the reception.*

—(**COMPLEMENTS**)—

please *give satisfaction/happiness*

He just wants to please.
We aim to please.
Ruby's Derby pie was sure to please.
Our salespeople are eager to please.

please *wish, desire*

Once dinner is over, you may do as you please.
His parents allow him to watch whatever he pleases.

please _____ *cause to be satisfied/happy*

OBJECT

The presents really pleased **the children**.
You can only please **him** by doing what he wants.
The piano recital pleased **the audience** immensely.

PASSIVE

We were pleased by what you said.

it + *please* + OBJECT + INFINITIVE

It pleased **him** *to get such good publicity.*
It pleased **everyone** *to escape from harm.*
"It has pleased **Almighty God** *to prolong our national life another year.*" [ABRAHAM LINCOLN]

PRESENT

I point	we point
you point	you point
he/she/it points	they point

• *The compass always points north.*

PRESENT PROGRESSIVE

I am pointing	we are pointing
you are pointing	you are pointing
he/she/it is pointing	they are pointing

• *He is pointing at you.*

PAST

I pointed	we pointed
you pointed	you pointed
he/she/it pointed	they pointed

• *The guide pointed out the monument.*

PAST PROGRESSIVE

I was pointing	we were pointing
you were pointing	you were pointing
he/she/it was pointing	they were pointing

• *All economic signs were pointing to a recession.*

PRESENT PERFECT ... have | has pointed
PAST PERFECT ... had pointed

FUTURE ... will point
FUTURE PROGRESSIVE ... will be pointing
FUTURE PERFECT ... will have pointed

PAST PASSIVE

I was pointed	we were pointed
you were pointed	you were pointed
he/she/it was pointed	they were pointed

• *The gun was pointed right at us.*

COMPLEMENTS

point *indicate direction by extending one's finger*

Don't point; it's not polite.
Grandma Yvette pointed with her cane.
Look! He's pointing.

point _____ *direct attention*
ADVERB OF PLACE TO/FROM

The sign pointed **up to the second floor.**
Her fingers were pointing **downward.**
He pointed **to a chair** and told me to sit down.
The site's home page points **to several helpful links.**
The children pointed **back the way they had come.**

at OBJECT

The teacher pointed **at a boy in the second row.**
The guide pointed **at a picture above the doorway.**
I pointed **at the watch in the showcase.**

point _____ *direct, aim*
OBJECT + at/to/toward OBJECT

He pointed **his finger** *at me.*
Never point **your gun** *at something* unless you mean to shoot it.
An old man pointed **me** *to the post office.*
He pointed **us** *toward the refreshment stand.*

PASSIVE

The flashlight was pointed **at a car in the ditch.**

point _____ *be oriented [in a certain direction]*
ADVERB OF PLACE TO/FROM

The altars in medieval cathedrals point **to the east.**
Our elbows point **backward,** but our knees point **forward.**
The noonday sun always points **due south.**

point _____ *indicate as a result*
to OBJECT

Everything points **to a peaceful resolution.**
The test results point **to cancer.**

PHRASAL VERBS

point _SEP_ **out** *say, mention*

The astronomer pointed out that his
conclusions were tentative.

point _SEP_ **out** *indicate, identify*

Helen pointed out the misspellings in Kristen's paper.
Can you point your grandfather out in this photograph?

point to/toward _____ *mention*

The CEO pointed to their funding of inner-city programs.

point _SEP_ **up** *emphasize*

The volcanic eruptions point up the need for volcano monitoring.

PRESENT

I possess	we possess
you possess	you possess
he/she/it possesses	they possess

• *He possesses a terrific sense of humor.*

PRESENT PROGRESSIVE

Possess is never used in the progressive tenses.

PAST

I possessed	we possessed
you possessed	you possessed
he/she/it possessed	they possessed

• *We never possessed a stereo system.*

PAST PROGRESSIVE

Possess is never used in the progressive tenses.

PRESENT PERFECT ... have | has possessed
PAST PERFECT ... had possessed

FUTURE ... will possess
FUTURE PROGRESSIVE —
FUTURE PERFECT ... will have possessed

PAST PASSIVE

I was possessed	we were possessed
you were possessed	you were possessed
he/she/it was possessed	they were possessed

• *He was possessed by a sudden desire to laugh.*

COMPLEMENTS

possess _____ *have, own*
  OBJECT

I have never possessed **any stock in that company.**
Do they possess **any firearms?**
They possessed **a large amount of cash.**
They were suspected of possessing **illegal drugs.**

possess _____ *have as a characteristic*
  OBJECT

She possesses **great natural singing ability.**
He possesses **a grumpy disposition.**
Volvos possess **a good safety record.**
The city possessed **a strong credit rating.**

possess _____ *take complete control of*
  OBJECT
  PASSIVE
  OBJECT + INFINITIVE

An uncontrollable rage possessed **him.**
He was possessed by greed.
What possessed **Donna** *to say she didn't keep a diary*?

PRESENT

I pour	we pour
you pour	you pour
he/she/it pours	they pour

• *When it rains, it pours.*

PRESENT PROGRESSIVE

I am pouring	we are pouring
you are pouring	you are pouring
he/she/it is pouring	they are pouring

• *I am pouring you some punch.*

PAST

I poured	we poured
you poured	you poured
he/she/it poured	they poured

• *I just poured the tea.*

PAST PROGRESSIVE

I was pouring	we were pouring
you were pouring	you were pouring
he/she/it was pouring	they were pouring

• *The contractor was pouring cement in the rain.*

PRESENT PERFECT ... have | has poured
PAST PERFECT ... had poured

FUTURE ... will pour
FUTURE PROGRESSIVE ... will be pouring
FUTURE PERFECT ... will have poured

PAST PASSIVE

—	—
—	—
it was poured	they were poured

• *The coffee was poured and the dessert was served.*

─────────────────────────────(**COMPLEMENTS**)───

pour *fall/flow steadily* [OF A LIQUID]

It has been pouring all night.
The milk was pouring down the baby's chin.

pour _____ *fill a glass/cup with [a liquid], serve [a liquid]*

  OBJECT

Please pour **the wine**, will you?
Don't pour **the coffee** until the guests arrive.

  INDIRECT OBJECT + DIRECT OBJECT

We poured *the children* **some lemonade**.
The hostess poured *everyone* **a glass of wine**.

  for PARAPHRASE

We poured **some lemonade** *for the children*.
The hostess poured **a glass of wine** *for everyone*.

pour _____ *dispense [a liquid]*

  OBJECT + ADVERB OF PLACE

I poured **the marinade** *over the meat*.
He poured **the water** *down the drain*.
She carefully poured **the medicine** *into the dispenser*.

  PASSIVE

The unused olive oil was poured *back into the bottle*.

pour _____ *spend, invest*

  OBJECT + *into* OBJECT

We poured **all our savings** *into a dot-com start-up*.
The government poured **billions of dollars** *into student aid*.

─────────────────────────────(**PHRASAL VERBS**)───

pour back/down/forth/in/out/through/ etc. *flow in a specified direction*

The levee collapsed, and the floodwater poured in.

pour SEP **away/back/in/out/**etc. *cause to flow in a specified direction*

Pour the milk back into the jug.

pour into / out of _____ *enter/exit in large numbers*

The candidate's supporters poured into the arena.
Fans poured out of the stadium.

pour SEP **off** *drain from the top of a container of liquid*

She poured off a little sauce before cooking.

pour [oneself] into _____ *become very involved in*

After being laid off, he poured himself into finding a new job.

pour SEP **out** *discard [a liquid]*

The milk is past its expiration date; we need to pour it out.

pour SEP **out to [someone]** *tell [one's feelings] to [someone]*

Layla poured her heart out to Eric.

PRESENT

I practice	we practice
you practice	you practice
he/she/it practices	they practice

• *He practices his Italian with a friend.*

PRESENT PROGRESSIVE

I am practicing	we are practicing
you are practicing	you are practicing
he/she/it is practicing	they are practicing

• *I'm practicing my new magic trick.*

PAST

I practiced	we practiced
you practiced	you practiced
he/she/it practiced	they practiced

• *I practiced law in Illinois and Oregon.*

PAST PROGRESSIVE

I was practicing	we were practicing
you were practicing	you were practicing
he/she/it was practicing	they were practicing

• *He was practicing medicine without a license.*

PRESENT PERFECT ... have | has practiced
PAST PERFECT ... had practied

FUTURE ... will practice
FUTURE PROGRESSIVE ... will be practicing
FUTURE PERFECT ... will have practiced

PAST PASSIVE

—	—
—	—
it was practiced	they were practiced

• *The dance routine was practiced for hours.*

(COMPLEMENTS)

practice *do something over and over to increase one's skill*

I seem to be practicing all the time.
She practices whenever she has the time.
"How do you get to Carnegie Hall?" "Practice, practice, practice."

practice _____ *do over and over to increase one's skill*

OBJECT

Philip practices **the trumpet** nearly every day.
If you don't practice **a foreign language,** you quickly forget it.

PASSIVE

Every piece was practiced until it was perfect.

WH-CLAUSE

I practiced **what I would say to my boss.**
We all practiced **what we would do in the event of an earthquake.**

WH-INFINITIVE

The apprentices were practicing **how to install ceramic tile.**

PRESENT PARTICIPLE

He needs to practice **fielding ground balls.**
The orchestra practiced **coming in together.**
Nursing students will practice **giving injections** this week.

practice _____ *do regularly*

OBJECT

All people have the right to practice **their beliefs.**
Paulette practices **yoga** daily.

PRESENT PARTICIPLE

Kids should practice **being nice to the elderly.**

practice _____ *work in* [LAW, MEDICINE]

OBJECT

He practices **law** in the state of California.
Rachel is no longer practicing **medicine.**

practice _____ *train*

on OBJECT

I don't want a surgical intern to practice **on me!**
I'm learning to tattoo. Can I practice **on you?**

(EXPRESSIONS)

Practice what you preach. [PROVERB]
Do what you advise others to do.

When my boss harassed me for being late,
I told him, "Practice what you preach."

PRESENT		PRESENT PROGRESSIVE	
I precede	we precede	I am preceding	we are preceding
you precede	you precede	you are preceding	you are preceding
he/she/it precedes	they precede	he/she/it is preceding	they are preceding

• *The national anthem precedes ballgames.* • *The police are preceding the fire trucks.*

PAST		PAST PROGRESSIVE	
I preceded	we preceded	I was preceding	we were preceding
you preceded	you preceded	you were preceding	you were preceding
he/she/it preceded	they preceded	he/she/it was preceding	they were preceding

• *Clearly, the good news preceded us.* • *The lightning was barely preceding the thunder.*

PRESENT PERFECT	... have	has preceded
PAST PERFECT	... had preceded

FUTURE	... will precede
FUTURE PROGRESSIVE	... will be preceding
FUTURE PERFECT	... will have preceded

PAST PASSIVE	
I was preceded	we were preceded
you were preceded	you were preceded
he/she/it was preceded	they were preceded

• *The program was preceded by a short introduction.*

(**COMPLEMENTS**)

precede *happen, come/go before*	Group A precedes, Group B follows.
	The professors precede, the graduates follow.
precede _____ *happen, come/go before in space/time*	
OBJECT	Wind always precedes **rain.**
	Several minor tremors preceded **the main earthquake.**
	The wail of sirens preceded **the air raid.**
	An economic collapse preceded **Roosevelt's election.**
	Who preceded **John F. Kennedy** as president?
PASSIVE	The infantry attack was preceded by an artillery barrage.
OBJECT + ADVERB OF PLACE TO/FROM	The children preceded **us** *there.*
	You should let your guests precede **you** *through the door.*
	Security forces always precede **the president** *into a building.*
PASSIVE	The boxer was preceded *into the ring* by his seconds.
precede _____ *come/go before in rank*	
OBJECT	In the army, a general precedes **a colonel,** and a colonel precedes **a major.**
	In the Roman Republic, consuls preceded **praetors.**
	In Jane Austen's time, a married daughter preceded **her unmarried sisters.**
precede _____ *introduce, preface*	
OBJECT	The professor always preceded **his lecture** with a story from his childhood.

PRESENT

I prefer	we prefer
you prefer	you prefer
he/she/it prefers	they prefer

• *He prefers white wine.*

PRESENT PROGRESSIVE

Prefer is rarely used in the progressive tenses.

PAST

I preferred	we preferred
you preferred	you preferred
he/she/it preferred	they preferred

• *I preferred traveling by train as a child.*

PAST PROGRESSIVE

Prefer is rarely used in the progressive tenses.

PRESENT PERFECT ... have | has preferred
PAST PERFECT ... had preferred

FUTURE ... will prefer
FUTURE PROGRESSIVE —
FUTURE PERFECT ... will have preferred

PAST PASSIVE

I was preferred	we were preferred
you were preferred	you were preferred
he/she/it was preferred	they were preferred

• *Jane's solution was preferred by most of us.*

(COMPLEMENTS)

prefer _____ *like better*

OBJECT	I prefer **chunky peanut butter.**
	Would you prefer **soup or salad?**
	The kids would prefer **their old babysitter.**
	Dino prefers **baseball** over football.
	Dina prefers **football** to baseball.
OBJECT + PREDICATE ADJECTIVE	I prefer **my soup** *really hot.*
	Americans prefer **their drinks** *ice-cold.*
	John prefers **his memos** *short and decisive.*
(*for*) OBJECT + INFINITIVE	Your mother would prefer (**for**) **you** *to stay home.*
	He would prefer (**for**) **the kids** *to rake the leaves.*
	They might prefer (**for**) **us** *to submit the report later.*
INFINITIVE	I would prefer **to do it myself.**
	Would you prefer **to eat in or go out?**
	Everyone would prefer **to be rich.**
(it) BASE-FORM THAT-CLAUSE	Everyone would prefer (**it**) **that he stay in school.**
	The doctor would prefer (**it**) **that you undergo the treatment.**
	The board would prefer (**it**) **that we impose a moratorium on hiring.**
PRESENT PARTICIPLE	I prefer **doing it myself.**
	Thomas really prefers **playing outside.**
	Do you prefer **watching dramas or crime shows** on TV?

prefer _____ *formally bring [a charge] in court*

OBJECT	My aunt preferred **charges against her neighbor for destroying her fence.**

PRESENT

I prepare	we prepare
you prepare	you prepare
he/she/it prepares	they prepare

• *He prepares his schedule a week ahead.*

PAST

I prepared	we prepared
you prepared	you prepared
he/she/it prepared	they prepared

• *I prepared a brief statement.*

PRESENT PROGRESSIVE

I am preparing	we are preparing
you are preparing	you are preparing
he/she/it is preparing	they are preparing

• *I am preparing to go on a short trip.*

PAST PROGRESSIVE

I was preparing	we were preparing
you were preparing	you were preparing
he/she/it was preparing	they were preparing

• *We were preparing dinner when we heard the news.*

PRESENT PERFECT ... have | has prepared
PAST PERFECT ... had prepared

FUTURE ... will prepare
FUTURE PROGRESSIVE ... will be preparing
FUTURE PERFECT ... will have prepared

PAST PASSIVE

I was prepared	we were prepared
you were prepared	you were prepared
he/she/it was prepared	they were prepared

• *The report was prepared weeks ago.*

COMPLEMENTS

prepare _____ *make ready*

OBJECT — They were in the kitchen preparing **lunch.**
Our group prepared **a position paper on the topic.**

PASSIVE — Evacuation plans were prepared in case the hurricane came ashore.

OBJECT + *for* OBJECT — Let's prepare **the car** *for driving in snow.*
Robert prepared **the float** *for the homecoming parade.*
The owner prepared **the store** *for the anniversary sale.*

PASSIVE — A brochure will be prepared *for the grand opening.*

OBJECT + INFINITIVE — The nurses prepared **me** *to be transferred.*
We prepared **them** *to hear some bad news.*
The player prepared **himself** *to be overlooked in the draft.*

PASSIVE — The soldiers were prepared *to withstand the attack.*

prepare _____ *get ready, make oneself ready*

for OBJECT — Are you preparing **for your driving test?**
We must prepare **for an economic downturn.**
The sailors were preparing **for 12 months away from their families.**

INFINITIVE — Sandra prepared **to answer the committee's questions.**
The actors are preparing **to go on stage for the second act.**
The ships should prepare **to sail at dawn tomorrow.**

PRESENT		**PRESENT PROGRESSIVE**	
I present	we present	I am presenting	we are presenting
you present	you present	you are presenting	you are presenting
he/she/it presents	they present	he/she/it is presenting	they are presenting

  • *He always presents the annual award.*   • *I am presenting my report this afternoon.*

PAST		**PAST PROGRESSIVE**	
I presented	we presented	I was presenting	we were presenting
you presented	you presented	you were presenting	you were presenting
he/she/it presented	they presented	he/she/it was presenting	they were presenting

  • *She presented a paper at the conference.*   • *The economy was presenting new challenges.*

PRESENT PERFECT ... have | has presented   **FUTURE** ... will present
PAST PERFECT   ... had presented   **FUTURE PROGRESSIVE** ... will be presenting
                                       FUTURE PERFECT ... will have presented

PAST PASSIVE

I was presented   we were presented
you were presented   you were presented
he/she/it was presented   they were presented

  • *We were presented with an unusual problem.*

NOTE: The verb *present* is stressed on the second syllable, rhyming with *event*.
The noun *present* is stressed on the first syllable.

──────────────────────(**COMPLEMENTS**)──────

present _____ *introduce*

    OBJECT   He will present **the names of the winners.**
                The speaker presented **his wife and two children** at the end of his talk.

present _____ *deliver*

    OBJECT   Diplomats must always present **their credentials.**
                 Michael presented **a talk on scientific frauds and charlatans.**
                 The architects have presented **their invoice.**

    PASSIVE   Invitations must be presented at the door.

    OBJECT + *to* OBJECT   You must present **your passport** *to the customs agent.*
                 Present **your business card** *to the receptionist.*

present _____ *display*

    OBJECT   The patient has presented **some unusual symptoms.**
                 We must present **a united front against our adversaries.**

present _____ *describe*

    OBJECT + *as* PREDICATE NOUN   He presented **himself** *as a humanitarian.*
                 They presented **the plan** *as a big opportunity for us.*

    PASSIVE   She was presented *as an old friend of the family.*

present _____ *create, offer*

    OBJECT   The economy presented **a real challenge for the new president.**
                 The meeting presented **an opportunity to get to know each other better.**
                 We hope that a suitable opportunity will present **itself** soon.

present _____ *bring before the public*

    OBJECT   The network is presenting **an hour-long special about the epidemic.**
                 The symphony will present **a concert under the stars.**

present _____ *give as a gift*

    OBJECT + *to* OBJECT   The teacher presented **a book** *to each of us.*
                 The booster club presented **a check for $500** *to the school.*

    OBJECT + *with* OBJECT   The teacher presented **each of us** *with a book.*
                 The booster club presented **the school** *with a check for $500.*

preserve preserve | preserves · preserved · have preserved ☑ REGULAR

PRESENT

I preserve	we preserve
you preserve	you preserve
he/she/it preserves	they preserve

• *John preserves every e-mail he gets.*

PRESENT PROGRESSIVE

I am preserving	we are preserving
you are preserving	you are preserving
he/she/it is preserving	they are preserving

• *I am preserving all my father's notes.*

PAST

I preserved	we preserved
you preserved	you preserved
he/she/it preserved	they preserved

• *They preserved the entire downtown area.*

PAST PROGRESSIVE

I was preserving	we were preserving
you were preserving	you were preserving
he/she/it was preserving	they were preserving

• *We were preserving the raspberries.*

PRESENT PERFECT ... have | has preserved
PAST PERFECT ... had preserved

FUTURE ... will preserve
FUTURE PROGRESSIVE ... will be preserving
FUTURE PERFECT ... will have preserved

PAST PASSIVE

—	—
—	—
it was preserved	they were preserved

• *The records were preserved for 10 years.*

───(COMPLEMENTS)───

preserve _____ *save, protect from harm/damage/destruction*

OBJECT
I have preserved **all my grandmother's letters.**
Immigrants often struggle to preserve **their native language.**
They have a grant to preserve **several endangered species.**
We must preserve **our right to life, liberty, and the pursuit of happiness.**

PASSIVE
The dinosaur bones were preserved by the museum staff.

WH-CLAUSE
We have preserved **what could be saved from the fire.**
Preserve **whatever insurance documents you have.**

preserve _____ *keep [food] from decaying by canning/freezing/etc.*

OBJECT
We preserve **all of our summer fruit.**

WH-CLAUSE
We preserve **what we grow.**

preserve _____ *maintain*

OBJECT
It is important that senior citizens preserve **their dignity.**
The movie preserves **the eerie feel of the novel.**
Despite his problems, he has preserved **his sense of humor.**
Remarkably, the town has preserved **its unique charm.**

PRESENT		PRESENT PROGRESSIVE	
I press	we press	I am pressing	we are pressing
you press	you press	you are pressing	you are pressing
he/she/it presses	they press	he/she/it is pressing	they are pressing

• *He always presses his point too hard.* • *He is pressing charges against them.*

PAST		PAST PROGRESSIVE	
I pressed	we pressed	I was pressing	we were pressing
you pressed	you pressed	you were pressing	you were pressing
he/she/it pressed	they pressed	he/she/it was pressing	they were pressing

• *We never pressed the issue.* • *They were pressing apples to make cider.*

PRESENT PERFECT ... have | has pressed
PAST PERFECT   ... had pressed

FUTURE   ... will press
FUTURE PROGRESSIVE ... will be pressing
FUTURE PERFECT   ... will have pressed

PAST PASSIVE	
I was pressed	we were pressed
you were pressed	you were pressed
he/she/it was pressed	they were pressed

• *The key was pressed too soon.*

— **COMPLEMENTS** —

press *try too hard* The coach warned the team not to press.

press _____ *push (on) with steady force*
OBJECT   I pressed **the elevator button.**
      Press **any key** to continue. [COMPUTERS]
      He pressed **my hand** to reassure me.
OBJECT + ADVERB OF PLACE TO/FROM   I pressed **my foot** *on the accelerator.*
      She pressed **the cookie dough** *into tiny balls.*
PASSIVE   We were pressed *against the wall* by the crowd.

press _____ *crowd, push closely together*
ADVERB OF PLACE TO/FROM   The crowd pressed **into the arena.**
      Reporters pressed **around the president** as he entered the room.

press _____ *make smooth/flat*
OBJECT   I need to press **my shirt.**
      The kids were pressing **flower petals.**

press _____ *squeeze*
OBJECT   Everyone in the village helped press **the grapes.**
OBJECT + *from / out of* OBJECT   They pressed **oil** *from the olives.*
      She pressed **all the juice** *out of the lemon.*

press _____ *put forward continuously and forcefully*
OBJECT   The plaintiffs were pressing **their suit.**
      We should press **the issue** in the next debate.

press _____ *urge continuously*
for OBJECT   The union is pressing **for higher wages.**
      Senator Blather was pressing **for deregulation of banks.**
OBJECT + INFINITIVE   The governor is pressing **the legislature** *to pass the bill.*
      Can you press **them** *to make a decision*?

— **PHRASAL VERBS** —

press back/forward/in/on/onward/ The mob pressed forward.
etc. *push in a specified direction*   The explorers pressed on against all odds.
press _SEP_ **back/forward/in/on/** The enemy was pressing us back.
etc. *push in a specified direction*

I prevail	we prevail
you prevail	you prevail
he/she/it prevails	they prevail

• *The stronger team usually prevails.*

I am prevailing	we are prevailing
you are prevailing	you are prevailing
he/she/it is prevailing	they are prevailing

• *Hope is prevailing over fear.*

I prevailed	we prevailed
you prevailed	you prevailed
he/she/it prevailed	they prevailed

• *Optimism about the recovery prevailed.*

I was prevailing	we were prevailing
you were prevailing	you were prevailing
he/she/it was prevailing	they were prevailing

• *Hurricane conditions were prevailing along the coast.*

PRESENT PERFECT … have | has prevailed
PAST PERFECT … had prevailed

FUTURE … will prevail
FUTURE PROGRESSIVE … will be prevailing
FUTURE PERFECT … will have prevailed

I was prevailed	we were prevailed
you were prevailed	you were prevailed
he/she/it was prevailed	they were prevailed

• *She was prevailed upon to say a few words.*

─(**COMPLEMENTS**)─

prevail *be dominant/widespread*	A sense of crisis prevails everywhere.
	Cloudy weather will prevail for the next few days.
	The New Year's Eve custom has prevailed there for nearly 300 years.
	Similar unemployment rates prevail in most states.
	Mobile homes prevail on the west side of town.
prevail *be successful, win out*	In the long run, reason must prevail.
	It was not until 1945 that the Allies prevailed.
	Our soccer team prevailed against the No. 1 team in the country.
prevail _____ *persuade, get [to do]*	
on/upon OBJECT + INFINITIVE	Can we prevail **on you** *to take notes for us*?
	The audience prevailed **upon the pianist** *to play an encore*.
	The board prevailed **upon the director** *to step aside*.
PASSIVE	I was prevailed on *to run for treasurer*.

PRESENT

I prevent	we prevent
you prevent	you prevent
he/she/it prevents	they prevent

• *My illness prevents my going to work.*

PRESENT PROGRESSIVE

I am preventing	we are preventing
you are preventing	you are preventing
he/she/it is preventing	they are preventing

• *Am I preventing you from doing your homework?*

PAST

I prevented	we prevented
you prevented	you prevented
he/she/it prevented	they prevented

• *We prevented a big mistake.*

PAST PROGRESSIVE

I was preventing	we were preventing
you were preventing	you were preventing
he/she/it was preventing	they were preventing

• *The medicines were preventing an epidemic.*

PRESENT PERFECT ... have | has prevented
PAST PERFECT   ... had prevented

FUTURE   ... will prevent
FUTURE PROGRESSIVE ... will be preventing
FUTURE PERFECT   ... will have prevented

PAST PASSIVE

I was prevented	we were prevented
you were prevented	you were prevented
he/she/it was prevented	they were prevented

• *The ship was prevented from docking.*

COMPLEMENTS

prevent _____ *stop from happening*

OBJECT

Regular exercise can prevent **major health problems.**
Only YOU can prevent **forest fires.** [ADVERTISING SLOGAN]
We are trying to prevent **further damage from the flood.**

PASSIVE

A collision was prevented by the truck driver's quick reaction.

WH-CLAUSE

We prevented **what could have been a bad mistake.**
It will prevent **whatever problems might have arisen.**

PRESENT PARTICIPLE

Lack of space prevents **our eating in the kitchen.**
Federal law prevents **building on a floodplain.**

prevent _____ *stop [from doing]*

OBJECT + *from* PRESENT PARTICIPLE

She prevented **them** *from making a really big mistake.*
Nothing could prevent **me** *from watching the game.*
An outbreak of flu prevented **the kids** *from going to school.*

PASSIVE

We were prevented *from working* by a power failure.

PRESENT

I print	we print
you print	you print
he/she/it prints	they print

• He prints everything in color.

PRESENT PROGRESSIVE

I am printing	we are printing
you are printing	you are printing
he/she/it is printing	they are printing

• The newspaper is printing a correction.

PAST

I printed	we printed
you printed	you printed
he/she/it printed	they printed

• I printed a copy of the e-mail for you.

PAST PROGRESSIVE

I was printing	we were printing
you were printing	you were printing
he/she/it was printing	they were printing

• The company was printing about 20 titles a year.

PRESENT PERFECT ... have | has printed
PAST PERFECT ... had printed

FUTURE ... will print
FUTURE PROGRESSIVE ... will be printing
FUTURE PERFECT ... will have printed

PAST PASSIVE

— —
— —
it was printed   they were printed

• The first collection of Shakespeare's plays was printed in 1623.

COMPLEMENTS

print *write in block letters*
(as opposed to cursive)

Please print.
Most forms require you to print.
I usually print, because nobody can read my handwriting.

print _____ *work/function as a printer*
    ADVERB OF MANNER

Does your copier print **in color**?
He prints **with soy-based ink**.

print _____ *produce [text/images on paper] using a printing press / photocopier / computer printer*
    OBJECT

The newspaper prints **10,000 copies** a day.
Always print **a copy of your correspondence** for the files.
The university will print **my dissertation** in July.

    PASSIVE

Art books are printed on special paper.

print _____ *publish in print, include in a publication*
    OBJECT

The journal printed **a list of Isaac Asimov's 10 favorite books**.
They printed **three of Hilary's poems** in the December issue.

print _____ *issue*
    OBJECT

The lawyers forced the magazine to print **a retraction**.
It was like a license to print **money**.
The tabloid newspaper will have to print **a formal apology**.

print _____ *press/stamp onto a surface*
    OBJECT

They can print **hundreds of millions of transistors** on
   a single microprocessor.

PHRASAL VERBS

print _SEP_ **out** *produce (a copy of)*
using a photocopier / computer printer

Would you print out six more copies
   of the report?
I need to print the drawing out in a larger size.

PRESENT			PRESENT PROGRESSIVE	

PRESENT

I proceed | we proceed
you proceed | you proceed
he/she/it proceeds | they proceed

• As the play proceeds, he becomes angrier.

PRESENT PROGRESSIVE

I am proceeding | we are proceeding
you are proceeding | you are proceeding
he/she/it is proceeding | they are proceeding

• I am proceeding as planned.

PAST

I proceeded | we proceeded
you proceeded | you proceeded
he/she/it proceeded | they proceeded

• He proceeded to tell us his life story.

PAST PROGRESSIVE

I was proceeding | we were proceeding
you were proceeding | you were proceeding
he/she/it was proceeding | they were proceeding

• The plane was proceeding to Monterey.

PRESENT PERFECT ... have | has proceeded
PAST PERFECT ... had proceeded

FUTURE ... will proceed
FUTURE PROGRESSIVE ... will be proceeding
FUTURE PERFECT ... will have proceeded

PAST PASSIVE

Proceed is never used in the passive voice.

───(COMPLEMENTS)───

proceed *go ahead, continue*

Please proceed.
The trial is proceeding smoothly.
We must proceed without delay.

proceed _____ *go on after stopping for a while*
ADVERB OF PLACE TO/FROM

After unloading, the truck proceeded **to the warehouse**.
After lunch, we proceeded **on our way**.
After clearing customs, we proceeded **to the baggage claim area**.

proceed _____ *begin and continue [to do]*
INFINITIVE

John stopped a policeman and proceeded **to tell him what had happened**.
I got the waiter's attention and proceeded **to order dinner**.
He got paid and promptly proceeded **to spend every penny**.
[USED IRONICALLY]
Aaron bought a new pair of skis and proceeded **to break his leg**.
[USED IRONICALLY]

produce produce | produces ·
produced · have produced

 REGULAR

PRESENT

I produce	we produce
you produce	you produce
he/she/it produces	they produce

• *Our firm produces cases for cell phones.*

PRESENT PROGRESSIVE

I am producing	we are producing
you are producing	you are producing
he/she/it is producing	they are producing

• *Their vineyard is producing 30 tons of grapes a year.*

PAST

I produced	we produced
you produced	you produced
he/she/it produced	they produced

• *His announcement produced a sensation.*

PAST PROGRESSIVE

I was producing	we were producing
you were producing	you were producing
he/she/it was producing	they were producing

• *They were producing 2,000 widgets an hour.*

PRESENT PERFECT ... have | has produced
PAST PERFECT ... had produced

FUTURE ... will produce
FUTURE PROGRESSIVE ... will be producing
FUTURE PERFECT ... will have produced

PAST PASSIVE

—   —
—   —
it was produced   they were produced

• *The play was first produced in 2003.*

NOTE: The verb *produce* is stressed on the second syllable, which rhymes with *loose*.
The noun *produce* is stressed on the first syllable.

COMPLEMENTS

produce *show satisfactory results*

The new ad campaign is finally producing.
Their division was eliminated because they weren't producing.

produce *bear/yield food*

Are the fruit trees producing yet?
The hens will start producing soon.
Cows stop producing during really hot weather.

produce _____ *make, create, manufacture*

OBJECT

The company produces **components** for airplanes.
Mozart produced **his compositions** at an amazing rate.
The mill produces **recycled paper** from post-consumer waste.

PASSIVE

These parts were produced at our plant in Tennessee.

WH-CLAUSE

The company will only produce **what they have orders for**.
We can produce **whatever the industry calls for**.
They will produce **however much they need to**.

produce _____ *supply* [OF A STATE, COUNTRY, REGION]

OBJECT

Oregon produces **much of the world's supply of hops**.
The Midwest produces **huge amounts of corn and wheat**.

PASSIVE

Huge amounts of corn and wheat are produced in the Midwest.

produce _____ *cause to happen/exist*

OBJECT

The announcement produced **a financial panic**.
The discovery could produce **a whole new industry**.

PASSIVE

Side effects are produced by every medicine.

produce _____ *show, make available*

OBJECT

The court ordered them to produce **the documents**.
With a smile, he produced **a bouquet of roses**.
They must produce **evidence of the drug's effectiveness**.

PASSIVE

The play was first produced on Broadway in 2001.

produce _____ *supervise the making of* [an artistic production]

OBJECT

He has produced **many successful films**.
She is producing **her newest CD** herself.
I am producing **a revival of a 1960 musical**.

☑ REGULAR

PRESENT

I promise	we promise
you promise	you promise
he/she/it promises	they promise

- *It promises to be an eventful meeting.*

PRESENT PROGRESSIVE

I am promising	we are promising
you are promising	you are promising
he/she/it is promising	they are promising

- *He is always promising to fix the gate.*

PAST

I promised	we promised
you promised	you promised
he/she/it promised	they promised

- *I promised to take the kids to the movies.*

PAST PROGRESSIVE

I was promising	we were promising
you were promising	you were promising
he/she/it was promising	they were promising

- *It was promising to be a beautiful day after all.*

PRESENT PERFECT ... have | has promised
PAST PERFECT ... had promised

FUTURE ... will promise
FUTURE PROGRESSIVE ... will be promising
FUTURE PERFECT ... will have promised

PAST PASSIVE

I was promised	we were promised
you were promised	you were promised
he/she/it was promised	they were promised

- *The job was never promised to anyone.*

COMPLEMENTS

promise _____ assure [that something will happen]

OBJECT	The weatherman promises **sunny weather all weekend.**
	The coach promised **a winning season.**
PASSIVE	Record earnings were promised by Wall Street.
OBJECT + INFINITIVE	He promised **Janet** *to have his report done tomorrow.*
	I promised **myself** *to take some time off.*
OBJECT + THAT-CLAUSE	I promised **my folks** *that I would not be late.*
	You promised **the kids** *that we would play a game with them.*
PASSIVE	We were promised *that the car would be ready today.*
INFINITIVE	I promise **to give you a call.**
	The hotel clerk promised **to forward my mail.**
	The game promises **to be a sellout.**
THAT-CLAUSE	I promised **that I would not be late.**
	The salesman promised **that we could return the rug.**
	We promise **that we will be careful.**

promise _____ pledge

INDIRECT OBJECT + DIRECT OBJECT	The coach promised *the fans* **a winning season.**
	He promised *his staff* **a bonus.**
	I never promised *the kids* **a puppy.**
to PARAPHRASE	The coach promised **a winning season** *to the fans.*
	He promised **a bonus** *to his staff.*
	I never promised **a puppy** *to the kids.*

promise _____ give a reason to expect

OBJECT	A rising barometer promises **clear weather.**
	The dark thunderclouds promised **rain.**
INFINITIVE	This promises **to be a high-scoring game.**

EXPRESSIONS

promise the moon/stars/world to _____ /   My boyfriend promised me the world.
promise _____ the moon/stars/world
make exaggerated promises to

promote promote | promotes ·
promoted · have promoted ☑ REGULAR

PRESENT

I promote	we promote
you promote	you promote
he/she/it promotes	they promote

• *The publisher promotes all his books.*

PRESENT PROGRESSIVE

I am promoting	we are promoting
you are promoting	you are promoting
he/she/it is promoting	they are promoting

• *We are promoting a new product.*

PAST

I promoted	we promoted
you promoted	you promoted
he/she/it promoted	they promoted

• *The governor promoted wind energy.*

PAST PROGRESSIVE

I was promoting	we were promoting
you were promoting	you were promoting
he/she/it was promoting	they were promoting

• *The university was promoting its science programs.*

PRESENT PERFECT ... have | has promoted
PAST PERFECT ... had promoted

FUTURE ... will promote
FUTURE PROGRESSIVE ... will be promoting
FUTURE PERFECT ... will have promoted

PAST PASSIVE

I was promoted	we were promoted
you were promoted	you were promoted
he/she/it was promoted	they were promoted

• *She was promoted to associate dean.*

COMPLEMENTS

promote _____ *raise to a higher rank/level/position*

OBJECT
The captain will promote **three soldiers from our squad.**
The teacher promoted **the entire class** to fifth grade.
Did they ever promote **Ralph**?
The candidate is promoting **his daughter** to campaign manager.

PASSIVE
Sally was just promoted.

promote _____ *encourage, actively support*

OBJECT
Senator Blather has always promoted **free enterprise.**
The art department promotes **individual creativity.**

PASSIVE
The hiring of minorities is promoted by the government.

promote _____ *give publicity to*

OBJECT
We aggressively promote **all of our new products.**
The athletic department has heavily promoted **the star of the basketball team.**

PASSIVE
Sugary breakfast cereals are constantly being promoted.

PRESENT

I propose	we propose
you propose	you propose
he/she/it proposes	they propose

• *He proposes reducing the budget by 5%.*

PRESENT PROGRESSIVE

I am proposing	we are proposing
you are proposing	you are proposing
he/she/it is proposing	they are proposing

• *I am proposing a totally new plan.*

PAST

I proposed	we proposed
you proposed	you proposed
he/she/it proposed	they proposed

• *I proposed that we adopt the motion.*

PAST PROGRESSIVE

I was proposing	we were proposing
you were proposing	you were proposing
he/she/it was proposing	they were proposing

• *We were only proposing it as a temporary measure.*

PRESENT PERFECT ... have | has proposed
PAST PERFECT ... had proposed

FUTURE ... will propose
FUTURE PROGRESSIVE ... will be proposing
FUTURE PERFECT ... will have proposed

PAST PASSIVE

I was proposed	we were proposed
you were proposed	you were proposed
he/she/it was proposed	they were proposed

• *An acceptable agreement was finally proposed.*

COMPLEMENTS

propose _____ *suggest for consideration*

OBJECT	Shelly has proposed **an exciting idea.** The dean proposed **the elimination of several programs.**
PASSIVE	The plan was proposed by someone I didn't know.
OBJECT + *as* PREDICATE NOUN	The president will propose **him** *as ambassador.* I proposed **Marty** *as a new member.* He proposed **her plan** *as an alternative strategy.*
OBJECT + INFINITIVE	He proposed **me** *to act as secretary.* I proposed **a consulting firm** *to develop our marketing plan.*
PASSIVE	Tom was proposed *to head the new branch.*
to OBJECT + BASE-FORM THAT-CLAUSE	I proposed **to them** *that we rent out the cottage.* Harry proposed **to us** *that we leave early.* Charles proposed **to him** *that he delay the press release.*
INFINITIVE	The major proposed **to attack their left flank.** I proposed **to return via Boston.** Bob proposed **to go out for pizza.**
BASE-FORM THAT-CLAUSE	Someone proposed **that he delay the staff meeting.** Who proposed **that John manage the reception?** Nobody is proposing **that we stop working on it.** We will propose **that the amendment be tabled.**
PRESENT PARTICIPLE	I proposed **taking a little break.** No one wanted to propose **our giving up.** She proposed **getting married in June.**

propose _____ *ask to marry one*

to OBJECT	Tim proposed **to Katie** on a horse-drawn carriage ride. I'll propose **to Stephanie** when I'm home on leave.

propose _____ *intend, plan*

INFINITIVE	Do you propose **to leave us here alone?** The engaged couple proposed **to honeymoon in Montreal.**

EXPRESSIONS

propose a toast *honor publicly and drink to the health/happiness of*	I propose a toast to the bride and groom. I propose a toast to the President of the United States.

PRESENT

I protect	we protect
you protect	you protect
he/she/it protects	they protect

• *Sunscreen really protects children's skin.*

PRESENT PROGRESSIVE

I am protecting	we are protecting
you are protecting	you are protecting
he/she/it is protecting	they are protecting

• *I am not protecting you any longer.*

PAST

I protected	we protected
you protected	you protected
he/she/it protected	they protected

• *The umbrella protected us from the sun.*

PAST PROGRESSIVE

I was protecting	we were protecting
you were protecting	you were protecting
he/she/it was protecting	they were protecting

• *We were protecting ourselves as best we could.*

PRESENT PERFECT ... have | has protected
PAST PERFECT ... had protected

FUTURE ... will protect
FUTURE PROGRESSIVE ... will be protecting
FUTURE PERFECT ... will have protected

PAST PASSIVE

I was protected	we were protected
you were protected	you were protected
he/she/it was protected	they were protected

• *We were protected from the strong winds by a line of trees.*

COMPLEMENTS

protect ____ *keep safe from harm/damage/loss*

OBJECT
You must protect **yourself** at all times.
The senator is careful to protect **his reputation**.
The cast protects **your arm** until the bone is healed.
He protected **his money** by investing cautiously.

PASSIVE
We were fully protected by our insurance policy.

OBJECT + *from* OBJECT
A healthy diet can help protect **us** *from heart disease*.
A barrier reef protects **the island** *from waves*.

PASSIVE
The firefighters were protected *from the flames* by special fire-resistant clothing.

OBJECT + *from* PRESENT PARTICIPLE
Only good records protected **us** *from being sued*.
The barrier protected **our car** *from colliding with oncoming traffic*.

PASSIVE
Our house was protected *from being destroyed* by the quick response of the fire department.

PRESENT		PRESENT PROGRESSIVE	
I prove	we prove	I am proving	we are proving
you prove	you prove	you are proving	you are proving
he/she/it proves	they prove	he/she/it is proving	they are proving

- *His experiment proves that we are right.*
- *Cal is proving to be a bit of a problem.*

PAST		PAST PROGRESSIVE	
I proved	we proved	I was proving	we were proving
you proved	you proved	you were proving	you were proving
he/she/it proved	they proved	he/she/it was proving	they were proving

- *It proved to be much more difficult.*
- *Francine was proving to be a great success.*

PRESENT PERFECT ... have | has proven	FUTURE ... will prove
PAST PERFECT ... had proven	FUTURE PROGRESSIVE ... will be proving
	FUTURE PERFECT ... will have proven

PAST PASSIVE

I was proven	we were proven
you were proven	you were proven
he/she/it was proven	they were proven

- *His guilt was never proven.*

━━━━━━━━━━━━━━(COMPLEMENTS)━━━━

prove ＿＿＿ *demonstrate that something is true/correct*

OBJECT	For homework, Johanna told the students to prove **the theorem.**
	I can prove **my claim.**
PASSIVE	The validity of the will was proven in court.
REFLEXIVE PRONOUN + *as* PREDICATE NOUN	Sandra has proven **herself** *as an astronaut.*
	Emily has proven **herself** *as a teacher.*
OBJECT + *(to be)* PREDICATE NOUN	The lawyer proved **the defendant** *(to be) an innocent bystander.*
	Her boyfriend's subsequent behavior proved **him** *(to be) a complete loser.*
	Placido has proved **himself** *(to be) an excellent shortstop.*
OBJECT + *(to be)* PREDICATE ADJECTIVE	Our analysis proved **the plan** *(to be) feasible.*
	Madeline has proved **herself** *(to be) fearless.*
to OBJECT + THAT-CLAUSE	He proved **to us** *that he had been right all along.*
	Can they prove **to the police** *that they were not involved in the crime?*
THAT-CLAUSE	In 1616, William Harvey proved **that blood circulates.**
	The police proved **that the driver was lying.**
WH-CLAUSE	Can they prove **who caused the accident?**
	I can prove **what I am saying.**

prove ＿＿＿ *turn out [to be]*

(to be) PREDICATE NOUN	Our guide proved **(to be) a stranger to the region.**
	Our hotel proved **(to be) a dumpy guest house.**
	Her suggestion proved **(to be) a stroke of pure genius.**
(to be) PREDICATE ADJECTIVE	The guide proved **(to be) quite unreliable.**
	Their claim proved **(to be) false.**
	Our best guess proved **(to be) totally wrong.**

PRESENT

I provide	we provide
you provide	you provide
he/she/it provides	they provide

 • *The catering service provides great food.*

PAST

I provided	we provided
you provided	you provided
he/she/it provided	they provided

 • *The barn provided shelter from the storm.*

PRESENT PERFECT … have | has provided
PAST PERFECT … had provided

PRESENT PROGRESSIVE

I am providing	we are providing
you are providing	you are providing
he/she/it is providing	they are providing

 • *He is not providing much help.*

PAST PROGRESSIVE

I was providing	we were providing
you were providing	you were providing
he/she/it was providing	they were providing

 • *The staff was providing us with a lot of information.*

FUTURE … will provide
FUTURE PROGRESSIVE … will be providing
FUTURE PERFECT … will have provided

PAST PASSIVE

I was provided	we were provided
you were provided	you were provided
he/she/it was provided	they were provided

 • *The animals were provided with food and water.*

-----(COMPLEMENTS)-----

provide _____ *supply*

OBJECT	He provided **some helpful advice.**
	They didn't provide **enough food for the group.**
PASSIVE	Complete assembly instructions were provided.
INDIRECT OBJECT + DIRECT OBJECT	The unlocked back door provided *them* **easy entry.**
	The annuity will provide *your parents* **an adequate income.**
for PARAPHRASE	The unlocked back door provided **easy entry** *for them.*
	The annuity will provide **an adequate income** *for your parents.*
OBJECT + *with* OBJECT	The book provided **us** *with the answers.*
	The weather provides **you** *with a reason to cancel the party.*

provide _____ *state*

THAT-CLAUSE	The ordinance provides **that apartments must pass inspection before they can be rented.**
	The contract provides **that any legal disputes will be tried in Sangamon County.**

-----(PHRASAL VERBS)-----

provide against _____ *prepare for*
Have you provided against flood damage if the levee breaks?

provide for _____ *allow*
The employment contract provides for two weeks of paid vacation.

provide for _____ *support*
He provides for his wife, his two children, and his aging mother.
A trust provides for their daughter's education.

PRESENT

I publish	we publish
you publish	you publish
he/she/it publishes	they publish

· *The company publishes reference works.*

PRESENT PROGRESSIVE

I am publishing	we are publishing
you are publishing	you are publishing
he/she/it is publishing	they are publishing

· *The press is publishing a special series on evolution.*

PAST

I published	we published
you published	you published
he/she/it published	they published

· *She recently published two fine essays.*

PAST PROGRESSIVE

I was publishing	we were publishing
you were publishing	you were publishing
he/she/it was publishing	they were publishing

· *The newspaper was publishing 30,000 copies a day.*

PRESENT PERFECT ... have | has published
PAST PERFECT ... had published

FUTURE ... will publish
FUTURE PROGRESSIVE ... will be publishing
FUTURE PERFECT ... will have published

PAST PASSIVE

I was published	we were published
you were published	you were published
he/she/it was published	they were published

· *The book was published by a university press.*

———(COMPLEMENTS)———

publish *have one's writing printed in a book/journal/etc.*

For many young academics, the motto is "Publish or perish."
There is great pressure on us to publish.
Do you want to publish or teach? It is hard to do both.

publish *prepare, print, and distribute books/magazines/newspapers/etc.*

The newspaper publishes daily.
How often does the magazine publish?
Some university presses can no longer afford to publish.

publish _____ *have one's writing printed in [a book/magazine/newspaper/etc.]*
OBJECT

Ross has published **his new book about climate change.**
I have published **a dozen articles in my field.**
He will publish **his study** in a linguistics journal.

publish _____ *prepare, print, and distribute [books/magazines/newspapers/etc. or parts thereof]*
OBJECT

The press only publishes **art books.**
University presses have an obligation to publish **scholarly works.**
The newspaper will publish **a story about homelessness in America.**

PASSIVE

Many of Shakespeare's plays were first published in pirated editions.

publish _____ *make known*
OBJECT

The drug company should publish **the study's findings.**

──(PHRASAL VERBS)──

pull away/back/down/in/out/over/up/etc. *move in a specified direction*

The van pulled away slowly.
We're lost. Let's pull over and look at a map.

pull ___SEP___ **along/aside/away/down/over/ under/up**/etc. *cause to move in a specified direction*

She pulled the child aside and told him to behave.
Can you pull the kids away from the TV?
Pull the shade down, please.
The cop pulled my brother over for speeding.
The secretary pulled up a chair and sat down.
Pull the weeds up, but leave the flowers.

pull ahead *take the lead*

The Brazilian runner pulled ahead at the 12-mile marker.

pull ___SEP___ **apart** *find fault with*

The accountants pulled apart my proposed budget.

pull ___SEP___ **apart** *affect emotionally very strongly*

The divorce was pulling my cousin apart.

pull away *increase one's lead*

The racehorse pulled away in the backstretch and won easily.

pull ___SEP___ **down** *reduce*

Higher unemployment pulled stock prices down.

pull ___SEP___ **down** *make sad/depressed*

The owner's death pulled the whole team down.

pull down/in ___ *earn*

The stockbroker was pulling down $200,000 a year.

pull for ___ *hope for the success of*

Most of the crowd was pulling for the underdog.

pull ___SEP___ **in** *attract*

Blackstone's magic show pulled in huge audiences.

pull ___SEP___ **in** *capture, take into custody*

Police pulled two of the suspects in last night.

pull in/up *arrive by car*

Grandma and Grandpa just pulled in.

pull ___SEP___ **off** *perform successfully*

The James Brothers pulled off the perfect bank robbery.

pull ___SEP___ **on/off** *put on / take off [clothing]*

He pulled the sweater on over his head.
They pulled their muddy uniforms off after the game.

pull out (of ___ **)** *withdraw/retreat (from [something])*

The general decided to pull out before his army was surrounded.
The other company pulled out of the merger at the last minute.

pull ___SEP___ **out** *produce*

Mom pulled out her checkbook and wrote me a check for $400.

pull through *survive, recover from illness/ difficulty*

Scott has a nasty head injury, but he'll pull through.

pull ___SEP___ **together** *gather and organize*

The editor pulled together a team of reporters to investigate bribery at City Hall.
Would you pull the latest cost-of-living data together?

pull up *come to a stop*

A truck is pulling up in front of our house.

pull up *move forward*

A police car pulled up beside me.

──(EXPRESSIONS)──

pull a stunt/trick on ___ *fool, deceive*

Grandpa was always pulling tricks on us kids.

pull out all the stops *use all available resources, hold nothing back*

When the polls showed the candidate losing, his campaign pulled out all the stops.

pull (some) strings *use one's influence*

My sister pulled some strings and got me a job at her company.

pull [someone's] leg *fool, trick [someone]*

He's not serious; he's just pulling your leg.

pull the plug on ___ *stop, put an end to*

Investors pulled the plug on our latest venture.

PRESENT

I pull	we pull
you pull	you pull
he/she/it pulls	they pull

- *The steering wheel pulls to the right.*

PRESENT PROGRESSIVE

I am pulling	we are pulling
you are pulling	you are pulling
he/she/it is pulling	they are pulling

- *The tide is pulling the boat out to sea.*

PAST

I pulled	we pulled
you pulled	you pulled
he/she/it pulled	they pulled

- *Matt pulled his kayak into the water.*

PAST PROGRESSIVE

I was pulling	we were pulling
you were pulling	you were pulling
he/she/it was pulling	they were pulling

- *He was pulling nails out of the recycled boards.*

PRESENT PERFECT ... have | has pulled
PAST PERFECT ... had pulled

FUTURE ... will pull
FUTURE PROGRESSIVE ... will be pulling
FUTURE PERFECT ... will have pulled

PAST PASSIVE

I was pulled	we were pulled
you were pulled	you were pulled
he/she/it was pulled	they were pulled

- *The posts were pulled upright.*

COMPLEMENTS

pull *drag/tug/tow something*

We will all pull on the count of three.
The horses were pulling as hard as they could.
I couldn't keep pulling much longer.

pull ___ *drag, tug, tow*
   OBJECT

The tractor was pulling **a big agricultural sprayer.**
I don't think my car can pull **such a heavy trailer.**
Will you pull **me** in the wagon?

   PASSIVE

The barges were being pulled by a towboat.

pull ___ *move*
   ADVERB OF PLACE TO/FROM

We pulled **into the parking lot.**
The car pulled **to the side of the road.**
The ship slowly pulled **out to sea.**

pull ___ *cause to move*
   OBJECT + ADVERB OF PLACE TO/FROM

The pilot pulled **the plane** *into the hangar.*
The brakes pull **the car** *to the right.*
Pull **your chair** *closer.*

   PASSIVE

All heavy trucks were pulled *to the side* by the police.

pull ___ *drag toward one*
   OBJECT + ADVERB OF PLACE TO/FROM

I pulled **the children** *onto my lap.*
I pulled **the book** *closer to me.*
He pulled **the coins** *into a heap in front of him.*

pull ___ *remove*
   OBJECT

We pulled **weeds** all afternoon.
The dentist pulled **her wisdom teeth.**
The manager pulled **the pitcher** after four innings.

   OBJECT + ADVERB OF PLACE TO/FROM

The robber pulled **a gun** *from his jacket.*
I can't pull **the cork** *out of the wine bottle.*

pull ___ *injure by stretching*
   OBJECT

The athlete pulled **a muscle** during his
   morning sprints.

top
40
verb

purchase purchase | purchases · purchased · have purchased ☑ REGULAR

PRESENT

I purchase	we purchase
you purchase	you purchase
he/she/it purchases	they purchase

• *He purchases old furniture to refinish.*

PRESENT PROGRESSIVE

I am purchasing	we are purchasing
you are purchasing	you are purchasing
he/she/it is purchasing	they are purchasing

• *I am only purchasing useful items this Christmas.*

PAST

I purchased	we purchased
you purchased	you purchased
he/she/it purchased	they purchased

• *We purchased presents for the children.*

PAST PROGRESSIVE

I was purchasing	we were purchasing
you were purchasing	you were purchasing
he/she/it was purchasing	they were purchasing

• *We were purchasing some drapes for the living room.*

PRESENT PERFECT ... have | has purchased
PAST PERFECT ... had purchased

FUTURE ... will purchase
FUTURE PROGRESSIVE ... will be purchasing
FUTURE PERFECT ... will have purchased

PAST PASSIVE

—	—
—	—
it was purchased	they were purchased

• *The items were purchased with a credit card.*

───(COMPLEMENTS)───

purchase _____ *buy*

OBJECT
He purchased **everything we would need for the picnic.**
We have never purchased **anything** at that store.
We could purchase **the refrigerator** on an installment plan.

PASSIVE
Supplies are purchased by the office manager.

WH-CLAUSE
You should only purchase **what you need right away.**
We will only purchase **what is on sale.**
He can purchase **whatever he wants to.**

purchase _____ *acquire/achieve by sacrifice*

OBJECT
The army purchased **its victory** at a very high price.

PASSIVE
Our goal was purchased at great expense.
The fortress was purchased by the sacrifice of many brave men.

PRESENT

I pursue	we pursue
you pursue	you pursue
he/she/it pursues	they pursue

• *He pursues moderation in all things.*

PRESENT PROGRESSIVE

I am pursuing	we are pursuing
you are pursuing	you are pursuing
he/she/it is pursuing	they are pursuing

• *I am pursuing a career in electronics.*

PAST

I pursued	we pursued
you pursued	you pursued
he/she/it pursued	they pursued

• *The company pursued a number of options.*

PAST PROGRESSIVE

I was pursuing	we were pursuing
you were pursuing	you were pursuing
he/she/it was pursuing	they were pursuing

• *We were pursuing an impossible goal.*

PRESENT PERFECT ... have | has pursued
PAST PERFECT   ... had pursued

FUTURE   ... will pursue
FUTURE PROGRESSIVE ... will be pursuing
FUTURE PERFECT   ... will have pursued

PAST PASSIVE

I was pursued	we were pursued
you were pursued	you were pursued
he/she/it was pursued	they were pursued

• *The stolen vehicle was pursued by several police cars.*

COMPLEMENTS

pursue _____ *chase/follow in order to catch/attack*

OBJECT   The hunters pursued **the elk** all day.
Grant's army pursued **Lee's remaining forces** westward.
A good salesman pursues **anyone who expresses the slightest interest in his product.**

PASSIVE   The suspect is being pursued by the police.

pursue _____ *continue to work to achieve*

OBJECT   Barbara is pursuing **a master's degree.**
Becky is pursuing **a career in architecture.**
We all must pursue **our own dreams.**
Sam pursues **knowledge** for its own sake.

PASSIVE   An appeal to a higher court was pursued.

pursue _____ *carry further, continue*

OBJECT   The teacher won't pursue **the matter.**
Can we pursue **this discussion** after lunch?

pursue _____ *engage in, practice*

OBJECT   I pursue **letterpress printing** as a hobby.
Melanie pursues **music**, and Kathy pursues **gardening**.

PRESENT

I push	we push
you push	you push
he/she/it pushes	they push

• *He always pushes things too far.*

PRESENT PROGRESSIVE

I am pushing	we are pushing
you are pushing	you are pushing
he/she/it is pushing	they are pushing

• *The company is pushing its new insurance product.*

PAST

I pushed	we pushed
you pushed	you pushed
he/she/it pushed	they pushed

• *I already pushed the elevator button.*

PAST PROGRESSIVE

I was pushing	we were pushing
you were pushing	you were pushing
he/she/it was pushing	they were pushing

• *I was pushing the bike because it had a flat tire.*

PRESENT PERFECT ... have | has pushed
PAST PERFECT ... had pushed

FUTURE ... will push
FUTURE PROGRESSIVE ... will be pushing
FUTURE PERFECT ... will have pushed

PAST PASSIVE

I was pushed	we were pushed
you were pushed	you were pushed
he/she/it was pushed	they were pushed

• *The table was pushed against the wall.*

COMPLEMENTS

push *shove, crowd forward*

Stop pushing!
I hate it when people push.

push *press (against) something*

Nothing happens when I push.
Push and hold for a few seconds.

push _____ *cause to move ahead of one*
   OBJECT

Can you push **the stroller**?

push _____ *press (against)*
   OBJECT

Don't push **the red button**!

push _____ *move with force*
   ADVERB OF PLACE TO/FROM

The crowd pushed **through the door**.
The army was pushing **south**.
He pushed **past the security guards**.

push _____ *cause to move with force*
   OBJECT + ADVERB OF PLACE TO/FROM

The nurse pushed **the needle** *into my arm*.
We had to push **the car** *off the road*.

push _____ *promote, advocate*
   OBJECT

The company was pushing **its new allergy drug**.
The Democrats were pushing **their defense policy**.

push _____ *put pressure on*
   OBJECT
     PASSIVE
   OBJECT + INFINITIVE
     PASSIVE

The coach was pushing **his players**.
We were being pushed too hard.
We pushed **them** *to make a decision as soon as possible*.
The sales force was being pushed *to sell more*.

PHRASAL VERBS

push SEP **along/aside/away/back/down/in/out/**etc. *cause to move with force in a specified direction*

Maria pushed the baby carriage along.
Gwen pushed her plate away and left the table.
I couldn't push the lid down.

push off *leave, go away*

It's midnight—time to push off.

push on *continue moving*

They hadn't eaten in days, and still they pushed on.

push SEP **through** *succeed in accomplishing* We finally managed to push the proposal through.

PRESENT

I put	we put
you put	you put
he/she/it puts	they put

• *He always puts his car in the garage.*

PAST

I put	we put
you put	you put
he/she/it put	they put

• *I put the package on his desk.*

PRESENT PERFECT … have | has put
PAST PERFECT … had put

PRESENT PROGRESSIVE

I am putting	we are putting
you are putting	you are putting
he/she/it is putting	they are putting

• *I am putting the dishes into the dishwasher.*

PAST PROGRESSIVE

I was putting	we were putting
you were putting	you were putting
he/she/it was putting	they were putting

• *The kids were putting peanut butter on their fruit.*

FUTURE … will put
FUTURE PROGRESSIVE … will be putting
FUTURE PERFECT … will have put

PAST PASSIVE

I was put	we were put
you were put	you were put
he/she/it was put	they were put

• *The documents were put into the safe.*

───(COMPLEMENTS)───

put ——— *place, set*

   OBJECT + ADVERB OF PLACE

I always put **my keys** *on the dresser.*
We put **the new rug** *in the living room.*
The guards put **a barricade** *across the road.*
She put **her hand** *under the kitten* to lift it.
Terry put **her knitting** *aside* and picked up a book.
The clerk put **a price of $49.99** *on the dress.*
The coach put **pressure** *on the team.*

   PASSIVE

The picture was put *above the fireplace.*

put ——— *insert*

   OBJECT + ADVERB OF PLACE TO/FROM

I put **the key** *into the lock* and turned it.
We put **the note** *under his door.*
The telephone company will put **a new satellite** *into orbit.*
You will need to put **your car** *into the garage.*

   PASSIVE

The suitcases were put *into the closet.*

put ——— *cause to be in a certain condition/state*

   OBJECT + ADVERB OF MANNER

His lectures put **me** *to sleep* sometimes.
The CEO's decision put **3,000 people** *out of work.*
Don't put **yourself** *in danger.*
He always puts **me** *in a good mood.*
I'd like to put **the old lawn mower** *to good use.*

put ——— *express, say*

   OBJECT + ADVERB OF MANNER

I thought he put **it** *very well.*
You will need to put **your ideas** *in a simpler form.*
I put **my comments** *in writing.*

   PASSIVE

His complaints were put *rather rudely,* I thought.

put _SEP_ across *communicate successfully*	He managed to put across the complexity of the plan.
put _SEP_ aside *save*	We put aside the income tax refund for our retirement.
put _SEP_ away *store*	We need to put away the good silverware. Would you put the ketchup away, please?
put _SEP_ away *eat/drink a lot of*	Steve can really put away the potato chips.
put _SEP_ down *overcome with force, suppress*	The government put down a rebellion in the provinces.
put _SEP_ down *write down*	It's important to put everything down on paper.
put _SEP_ down *include on a list*	The campaign volunteer put me down as a "maybe."
put _SEP_ down *find fault with, insult*	She put him down in front of all their friends.
put _SEP_ down *pay as the first installment*	You can put 10% down and pay the rest in 90 days.
put forth ____ *grow* [PLANTS]	The daffodils are putting forth their blooms early.
put _SEP_ forth/forward *propose, suggest*	She put forward her plan to save endangered species.
put _SEP_ in *add*	Could you put in a paragraph about offshore drilling?
put _SEP_ in *install*	We put in more shelves for our books.
put in for ____ *formally request*	The defendant put in for a change of venue. Drake put in for the vacant Senate seat.
put _SEP_ off *repel*	Bubba's vulgar language really puts me off.
put _SEP_ off *postpone*	We'll have to put the meeting off until next week.
put on ____ *pretend*	Ron put on his fake French accent, and we all laughed.
put ____ on *deceive [someone]*	Don't believe him; he's just putting you on.
put _SEP_ on *dress in [clothing]*	Will I need to put my coat on?
put _SEP_ on *add*	Uncle Nelson has put on quite a bit of weight.
put _SEP_ on *present [entertainment]*	The senior class put on a musical.
put _SEP_ on *apply [cosmetics]*	She puts lipstick on in the morning and after lunch.
put _SEP_ on *start [something] playing/ working*	We put on some rock music for Dad. Mom put a pot of coffee on for us.
put _SEP_ out *extinguish*	The campers put the fire out with water from the pond.
put _SEP_ out *publish, issue*	They put out 40 titles a year. The Beatles put "The White Album" out in 1968.
put out ____ *generate a lot of*	Your laptop puts out a lot of heat.
put _SEP_ out *make unconscious*	The anesthesia will put you out, and you won't remember the surgery.
put _SEP_ through *succeed in doing*	The new CEO put the merger through.
put ____ through *pay for [someone's] attendance at*	Laurie put herself through law school at Georgetown.
put _SEP_ up *give lodging to*	We can put your parents up for one night. The airline put the stranded passengers up at a hotel.
put _SEP_ up *offer*	Our neighbors put their house up for sale.
put _SEP_ up *provide*	John put up $2,000 for the new playground.
put _SEP_ up *build*	They put up a new drugstore in just four months.
put _SEP_ up *nominate*	They put Renni up for a three-year term.
put up with ____ *tolerate*	Martha couldn't put up with the noise anymore.
put upon ____ *take advantage of*	I don't like to be put upon by my friends.

PRESENT

I question	we question
you question	you question
he/she/it questions	they question

• *The committee questions our estimates.*

PRESENT PROGRESSIVE

I am questioning	we are questioning
you are questioning	you are questioning
he/she/it is questioning	they are questioning

• *The detective is questioning the suspect now.*

PAST

I questioned	we questioned
you questioned	you questioned
he/she/it questioned	they questioned

• *Nobody questioned his good intentions.*

PAST PROGRESSIVE

I was questioning	we were questioning
you were questioning	you were questioning
he/she/it was questioning	they were questioning

• *The auditor was questioning our travel expenses.*

PRESENT PERFECT ... have | has questioned
PAST PERFECT ... had questioned

FUTURE ... will question
FUTURE PROGRESSIVE ... will be questioning
FUTURE PERFECT ... will have questioned

PAST PASSIVE

I was questioned	we were questioned
you were questioned	you were questioned
he/she/it was questioned	they were questioned

• *He was questioned about the accident.*

(**COMPLEMENTS**)

question _____ *request information from, ask*

OBJECT	The police were questioning **everyone**.
	Whom will they question next?
PASSIVE	The whole family was questioned.
OBJECT + *about* OBJECT	A policeman questioned **them** *about the accident.*
	The whole office questioned **me** *about the memo.*
PASSIVE	We were questioned *about Alice's dinner party.*
OBJECT + *about* WH-CLAUSE	I questioned **the kids** *about who had started the fight.*
	The reporter questioned **us** *about what had happened.*
	Parents always question **teenagers** *about where they are going.*
OBJECT + *on* OBJECT	He questioned **me** *on the difference between banks and credit unions.*
	The students questioned **the professor** *on the uses of science and technology.*
PASSIVE	The expert witness was questioned *on the validity of DNA testing.*

question _____ *doubt, object to*

OBJECT	The press questioned **Senator Blather's vague explanation**.
	The detective questioned **the suspect's alibi**.
PASSIVE	Brent's honesty was never questioned.
WH-CLAUSE	I really question **what they are doing**.
	Didn't you question **why Bobbie got in so late?**
	We need to question **how much all of this is going to cost**.
PRESENT PARTICIPLE	I question **spending any more money than we have to**.
	The chair questioned **taking any more time on this issue**.
	Everyone questioned **John's behaving so strangely at the party**.

PRESENT

I quit	we quit
you quit	you quit
he/she/it quits	they quit

• *He usually quits around 5 o'clock.*

PRESENT PROGRESSIVE

I am quitting	we are quitting
you are quitting	you are quitting
he/she/it is quitting	they are quitting

• *I am quitting next week.*

PAST

I quit	we quit
you quit	you quit
he/she/it quit	they quit

• *I quit my job last year.*

PAST PROGRESSIVE

I was quitting	we were quitting
you were quitting	you were quitting
he/she/it was quitting	they were quitting

• *He was quitting because he needed a full-time job.*

PRESENT PERFECT ... have | has quit
PAST PERFECT ... had quit

FUTURE ... will quit
FUTURE PROGRESSIVE ... will be quitting
FUTURE PERFECT ... will have quit

PAST PASSIVE

Quit is never used in the passive voice.

COMPLEMENTS

quit *stop functioning*

My cell phone just quit.
The engine quits if you give it too much gas.
His poor old heart finally quit.

quit *stop working at the end of a work period*

When do they quit for the day?
I am getting tired. How soon can we quit?
We can't quit until the next shift comes in.

quit *resign from a job*

That's it. I quit!
How many people quit in the course of a month?
We are moving to a new town, so I will have to quit.

quit *admit defeat, give up*

You beat me again. I quit.
No matter how bad things look, we will never quit.
They quit before the game was half over.

quit _____ *voluntarily stop doing [a job, school, activity]*

OBJECT

I am going to quit **my job** at the end of the year.
Tom quit **the police force** and went to law school.
Mike quit **college** to join the Marines.
He quit **the team** because he injured his knee.

WH-CLAUSE

You need to quit **what you are doing** and get a better job.
Quit **whatever you are doing** and listen to this!

PRESENT PARTICIPLE

I have to quit **smoking so much**.
The company is going to quit **paying overtime**.
He can't quit **worrying about what is going to happen**.

quit _____ *leave, move away from*

OBJECT

They quit **the suburbs** and moved into the city.

PHRASAL VERBS

quit on _____ *leave one's job without warning [someone]*

The carpenters quit on us in the middle of the renovation.

quit on _____ *stop functioning while [someone] is using it*

The lawn mower quits on me when I get into the tall grass.
The furnace quit on us again.

PRESENT

I quote	we quote
you quote	you quote
he/she/it quotes	they quote

• *Margo quotes Jane Austen all the time.*

PRESENT PROGRESSIVE

I am quoting	we are quoting
you are quoting	you are quoting
he/she/it is quoting	they are quoting

• *I am quoting you; is that okay?*

PAST

I quoted	we quoted
you quoted	you quoted
he/she/it quoted	they quoted

• *He quoted a price that was too high.*

PAST PROGRESSIVE

I was quoting	we were quoting
you were quoting	you were quoting
he/she/it was quoting	they were quoting

• *He was quoting something he heard on the radio.*

PRESENT PERFECT ... have | has quoted
PAST PERFECT ... had quoted

FUTURE ... will quote
FUTURE PROGRESSIVE ... will be quoting
FUTURE PERFECT ... will have quoted

PAST PASSIVE

I was quoted	we were quoted
you were quoted	you were quoted
he/she/it was quoted	they were quoted

• *You were quoted in the newspaper yesterday.*

(**COMPLEMENTS**)

quote *repeat another's words/writing*
Don't blame me; I was only quoting.
You shouldn't quote without citing the original source.
Why quote when you can write your own original material?

quote _____ *repeat / closely paraphrase another's words/writing*

OBJECT
The reporter was quoting **a government official.**
Can I quote **you** on that?
You're quoting **Jane Austen** quite a lot in this book.
Gregory likes to quote **Hamlet.** [THE CHARACTER]
To quote **Hamlet:** "To be or not to be, that is the question."

PASSIVE
Shakespeare is probably quoted more often than any other writer.

from OBJECT
Gregory likes to quote from *Hamlet.* [THE PLAY]
Omar quotes from **the Talmud** a lot.
Manuel quotes from *Don Quijote.*

quote _____ *draw on or make allusions to previous work*

OBJECT
The film quotes **1930s gangster movies.**
The fourth movement quotes **themes from the opening movement.**

PASSIVE
Classical references are often quoted in Renaissance literature.

quote _____ *make one's opinion/feelings public*

OBJECT + *as* PRESENT PARTICIPLE
They quoted **the CEO** *as rejecting the contract offer.*

PASSIVE
The president was quoted *as having no regrets.*
Senator Blather was quoted *as doubting the validity of global warming.*

quote _____ *give [the price of]*

INDIRECT OBJECT + DIRECT OBJECT
He quoted *me* **a good price.**
United Airlines quoted *us* **a fare of $360.**
The lawn service quoted *Judy* **a price of $60 an hour.**

to PARAPHRASE
He quoted **a good price** *to me.*
United quoted **a fare of $360** *to us.*
The lawn service quoted **a price of $60 an hour** *to Judy.*

PRESENT

I raise	we raise
you raise	you raise
he/she/it raises	they raise

 • *He raises money for nonprofit groups.*

PRESENT PROGRESSIVE

I am raising	we are raising
you are raising	you are raising
he/she/it is raising	they are raising

 • *The campaign is raising awareness of breast cancer.*

PAST

I raised	we raised
you raised	you raised
he/she/it raised	they raised

 • *My family raised cotton in Central Valley.*

PAST PROGRESSIVE

I was raising	we were raising
you were raising	you were raising
he/she/it was raising	they were raising

 • *They were raising the anchor just as we boarded.*

PRESENT PERFECT	... have	has raised
PAST PERFECT	... had raised

FUTURE	... will raise
FUTURE PROGRESSIVE	... will be raising
FUTURE PERFECT	... will have raised

PAST PASSIVE

I was raised	we were raised
you were raised	you were raised
he/she/it was raised	they were raised

 • *The bid on the painting was raised to $10,000.*

⟨ **COMPLEMENTS** ⟩

raise _____ *lift, move to a higher position/level*

OBJECT	I raised **my hand** to get the teacher's attention.
	The crane raised **the air conditioning unit** to the roof.
	A car raised **a cloud of dust** along the lane.
PASSIVE	The boats were all being raised off the sand by the tide.

raise _____ *increase the amount/strength of*

OBJECT	The news raised **everyone's hopes**.
	The Fed announced that it would raise **the interest rate**.
	We will have to raise **our offer**.
	The boss raised **my salary** $75 a week.
	The meeting raised **our hopes for a quick settlement**.
PASSIVE	The noise was raised to an unbearable level.

raise _____ *cause to grow [plants, animals]*

OBJECT	Their farm raises **barley and lentils**.
	Everyone used to raise **a few chickens**.

raise _____ *bring up [children]*

OBJECT	We raised **three children** in that house.
	Grandma raised **her family** single-handedly.
OBJECT + INFINITIVE	"I didn't raise **my boy** *to be a soldier.*" [1915 ANTIWAR SONG]
PASSIVE	Children were raised *to respect their elders.*
	Our children weren't raised *to act like that.*

raise _____ *amass, collect [money, resources]*

OBJECT	The company has to raise **more capital**.
	We raised **money** for the hurricane victims.
	The rebels are raising **an army** in the mountains.

raise _____ *bring up [an issue/topic for consideration]*

OBJECT	He raised **a number of objections to the bill**.
	You raise **a good point**.
PASSIVE	The issue was raised earlier.

raise _____ *cause to happen/exist*

OBJECT	His bad jokes raised **a few groans from the audience**.

PRESENT

I range	we range
you range	you range
he/she/it ranges	they range

- *His territory ranges across California.*

PRESENT PROGRESSIVE

I am ranging	we are ranging
you are ranging	you are ranging
he/she/it is ranging	they are ranging

- *The wolves are ranging farther into the valley.*

PAST

I ranged	we ranged
you ranged	you ranged
he/she/it ranged	they ranged

- *The children ranged widely in age.*

PAST PROGRESSIVE

I was ranging	we were ranging
you were ranging	you were ranging
he/she/it was ranging	they were ranging

- *The scouts were ranging deep into enemy territory.*

PRESENT PERFECT ... have | has ranged
PAST PERFECT ... had ranged

FUTURE   ... will range
FUTURE PROGRESSIVE ... will be ranging
FUTURE PERFECT   ... will have ranged

PAST PASSIVE

Range is never used in the passive voice.

――――――――――――――――――――――――――――――――(COMPLEMENTS)―――――

range _____ *vary [between two limits], extend*

ADVERB OF TIME	The Age of Discovery ranges **from the late 15th to the early 17th centuries.**
	The children range **from six to nine in age.**
ADVERB OF PLACE	The area we service ranges **from the Atlantic Ocean to the Mississippi River.**
	Our archaeological work ranged **across the entire Southwest.**
ADVERB OF MANNER	The rugs range **from inexpensive cotton ones to pricey handwoven wool ones.**
	The Thai dishes ranged **from very spicy to extremely spicy.**
	The wedding caterer's menu ranged **from mostaccioli and fried chicken to chateaubriand and pan-seared halibut.**
	The cost ranges **between two and three hundred dollars.**

range _____ *scan, wander*

ADVERB OF PLACE TO/FROM	His eyes ranged **around the room.**
	Her glance ranged **from face to face.**

range _____ *live in*

OBJECT	The sawfish ranged **the Atlantic Ocean from New York to Brazil.**
ADVERB OF PLACE	In 1850, 50 million bison ranged **over the North American prairie.**

PRESENT

I reach	we reach
you reach	you reach
he/she/it reaches	they reach

• *His show reaches its intended audience.*

PRESENT PROGRESSIVE

I am reaching	we are reaching
you are reaching	you are reaching
he/she/it is reaching	they are reaching

• *We are reaching our limit.*

PAST

I reached	we reached
you reached	you reached
he/she/it reached	they reached

• *The train reached St. Louis around 2:45.*

PAST PROGRESSIVE

I was reaching	we were reaching
you were reaching	you were reaching
he/she/it was reaching	they were reaching

• *I was reaching for the salt.*

PRESENT PERFECT ... have | has reached
PAST PERFECT ... had reached

FUTURE ... will reach
FUTURE PROGRESSIVE ... will be reaching
FUTURE PERFECT ... will have reached

PAST PASSIVE

I was reached	we were reached
you were reached	you were reached
he/she/it was reached	they were reached

• *He was reached by phone this morning.*

COMPLEMENTS

reach *stretch one's hand to grasp something*

How far can you reach?
I am reaching as far as I can, but I still can't get it.

reach ____ *stretch one's hand to grasp*

OBJECT

The little boy could barely reach **the door handle**.
Can you reach **the phone** for me?
I can't reach **the books on the top shelf**.

for OBJECT

Peter and Gisela reached **for the milk jug** at the same time.
Clint reached in his pocket **for his keys**.

INDIRECT OBJECT + DIRECT OBJECT

Reach *me* **my glasses**, please.
Can you reach *me* **the phone**?

for PARAPHRASE

Reach **my glasses** *for me*, please.
Can you reach **the phone** *for me*?

ADVERB OF PLACE TO/FROM

I reached **down** and picked up my shoes.
He reached **into the drawer** and took out a knife.
Alison reached **under her seat** and pulled out a package.

reach ____ *arrive at*

OBJECT

We should reach **Phoenix** soon.
The news didn't reach **us** until yesterday.
I reached **the finish line** totally exhausted.
The negotiators finally reached **an agreement** last night.

reach ____ *extend/develop/increase to*

OBJECT

The tide had reached **its highest point**.
The extension cord won't reach **the desk**.
Our broadcast signal reaches **the entire metropolitan area**.
We can vote when we reach **18 years of age**.
It will reach **68 degrees** tomorrow.
Unemployment reached **its peak in 1933**.
Our Smart Car can reach **30 miles per hour** in 6.5 seconds.
The teacher's patience had finally reached **its limit**.

reach ____ *get in touch with, contact*

OBJECT

Were you able to reach **Samuel**?

reach ____ *affect, influence*

OBJECT

Successful authors reach **their readers' hearts**.

PRESENT

I read	we read
you read	you read
he/she/it reads	they read

• *He never reads his e-mail.*

PRESENT PROGRESSIVE

I am reading	we are reading
you are reading	you are reading
he/she/it is reading	they are reading

• *Be quiet! I'm reading.*

PAST

I read	we read
you read	you read
he/she/it read	they read

• *She read nothing but short stories.*

PAST PROGRESSIVE

I was reading	we were reading
you were reading	you were reading
he/she/it was reading	they were reading

• *I was just reading your note.*

PRESENT PERFECT ... have | has read
PAST PERFECT ... had read

FUTURE ... will read
FUTURE PROGRESSIVE ... will be reading
FUTURE PERFECT ... will have read

PAST PASSIVE

—	—
—	—
it was read	they were read

• *The transcript was read aloud in court.*

NOTE: The present form of *read* rhymes with *seed*; the past forms of *read* rhyme with *bed*.

COMPLEMENTS

read *understand writing/printing*	Can any of the children read yet?
read *look at and understand the content of printed material*	I love to read. I always read on the airplane.
read _____ *speak [written/printed/on-screen words] aloud*	
ADVERB OF MANNER	She reads **beautifully**. DJ reads **with a different voice for each character**. He reads **too softly for everyone to hear**.
OBJECT	Thank you. You read **that** beautifully. Paul read **the memo** in a perfect imitation of the boss's voice.
INDIRECT OBJECT + DIRECT OBJECT	Can you read *me* a story? The teacher reads *the class* a book for the last 15 minutes.
to PARAPHRASE	Can you read **a story** *to me*? The teacher reads **a book** *to the class* for the last 15 minutes.
PASSIVE	We were read a story every night.
read _____ *decode and get information from [a set of letters/numbers/symbols]*	
OBJECT	I can't read **her handwriting**. He taught himself to read **Old Icelandic**. The gas man came to read **the meter** this morning. Yvonne can't read **music**, but she plays beautifully. Will my computer be able to read **this file**?
read _____ *look at and understand the content of [written/printed/on-screen material]*	
OBJECT	I read **the newspaper** every morning at breakfast. He read **your e-mail** and will get back to you.
PASSIVE	*Julius Caesar* was read in every tenth-grade classroom.
WH-CLAUSE	I read **what you said about me**. You need to read **what is in the fine print** very carefully. He will read **whatever he can get his hands on**.

read _____ *learn from printed/on-screen material*

THAT-CLAUSE

I read **that the company may be up for sale.**
The coach read **that we are favored to win.**
We read **that the parade may be cancelled.**

read _____ *learn/interpret the meaning of*

OBJECT

I couldn't read **her face** at all.
He is very good at reading **people's body language.**
Economists don't always read **inflationary signals** correctly.
Diplomatic experts read **the implications of every government action.**

OBJECT + *as* OBJECT

I read **his note** *as an apology.*
Everyone read **his press release** *as an announcement of his candidacy.*

read _____ *measure and show*

OBJECT

The speedometer reads **55 miles per hour.**
The thermometer reads **32 degrees Celsius.**

read _____ *state*

DIRECT QUOTATION

The sign reads, **"No shirt, no shoes, no service."**

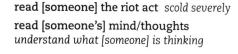

PHRASAL VERBS

read _____ **in/into** *infer [additional ideas/messages] from reading*

What did you read into Senator Blather's remarks?

read SEP **off** *read aloud [a list]*

The teacher read off the names of students who had won awards.

read SEP **over/through** *read completely*

Would you read over my paper before I turn it in?

read up on _____ *study/learn by reading*

We have to read up on the current drug laws before the conference next week.

EXPRESSIONS

read between the lines *understand the intended but not explicit meaning of something said/written*

She is good at reading between the lines of politicians' speeches.

read lips *determine the words that someone is saying by watching him/her speak*

When talking to someone who reads lips, you should talk normally.

Read my lips. *Believe what I am about to tell you.*

"Read my lips: No new taxes." [PRESIDENT GEORGE H.W. BUSH]

read [someone] his/her rights *state [someone's] legal rights to [someone who has been arrested]*

The arresting officer read the suspect his rights.

read [someone] like a book *understand [someone] well*

His calm manner doesn't fool me; I can read him like a book.

read [someone] the riot act *scold severely*

When Ed came home late, his father read him the riot act.

read [someone's] mind/thoughts *understand what [someone] is thinking*

How did you know I wanted pizza for dinner? You must have read my mind.

PRESENT	
I realize	we realize
you realize	you realize
he/she/it realizes	they realize

• *He now realizes that he made a mistake.*

PRESENT PROGRESSIVE	
I am realizing	we are realizing
you are realizing	you are realizing
he/she/it is realizing	they are realizing

• *Toni is realizing her potential as a platform diver.*

PAST	
I realized	we realized
you realized	you realized
he/she/it realized	they realized

• *I realized how much it was going to cost.*

PAST PROGRESSIVE	
I was realizing	we were realizing
you were realizing	you were realizing
he/she/it was realizing	they were realizing

• *We were just realizing how much is at stake.*

PRESENT PERFECT ... have | has realized
PAST PERFECT ... had realized

FUTURE ... will realize
FUTURE PROGRESSIVE ... will be realizing
FUTURE PERFECT ... will have realized

PAST PASSIVE	
—	—
—	—
it was realized	they were realized

• *His worst fears were realized.*

-(**COMPLEMENTS**)-

realize _____ *understand completely*

OBJECT
I finally realized **my anxiety** for what it was.
Eventually they realized **the magnitude of the problem.**

PASSIVE
The full extent of the problem was never realized.

THAT-CLAUSE
I realized **that we were totally lost.**
No one had realized **that the car had a flat tire.**
Do you realize **that we are leaving in two days?**

WH-CLAUSE
He finally realized **who I was.**
Everyone realized **what was involved.**
I realize **how strange my proposal sounds.**

realize _____ *make real, achieve*

OBJECT
We were realizing **our dream vacation.**
Good coaching helps players realize **their full potential.**

PASSIVE
Our goal was never realized.

realize _____ *earn*

OBJECT
How soon can the business realize **a profit?**
We realized **$200,000** from the sale of the property.

PASSIVE
The sum of $240 was realized from the senior class car wash.

PRESENT

I recall	we recall
you recall	you recall
he/she/it recalls	they recall

• *The incident recalls a similar one in 2001.*

PRESENT PROGRESSIVE

I am recalling	we are recalling
you are recalling	you are recalling
he/she/it is recalling	they are recalling

• *We are recalling troops from the war zone.*

PAST

I recalled	we recalled
you recalled	you recalled
he/she/it recalled	they recalled

• *I finally recalled his name.*

PAST PROGRESSIVE

I was recalling	we were recalling
you were recalling	you were recalling
he/she/it was recalling	they were recalling

• *The company was recalling all packaged spinach.*

PRESENT PERFECT ... have | has recalled
PAST PERFECT ... had recalled

FUTURE ... will recall
FUTURE PROGRESSIVE ... will be recalling
FUTURE PERFECT ... will have recalled

PAST PASSIVE

I was recalled	we were recalled
you were recalled	you were recalled
he/she/it was recalled	they were recalled

• *The ambassador was recalled in protest.*

COMPLEMENTS

recall _____ *remember*

OBJECT	I can recall **the accident** like it was yesterday. He couldn't recall **the combination to his locker**.
PASSIVE	Many early memories are easily recalled.
OBJECT + PRESENT PARTICIPLE	Everyone recalled **Senator Blather** *promising to cut taxes*. I certainly recall **Kathi** *ordering a taxi for 9 A.M.*
THAT-CLAUSE	He recalled **that he had to go to another meeting.** I recall **that you were pretty upset about it.** Fortunately, Betty recalled **that we had already ordered the replacement part.**
WH-CLAUSE	He just recalled **who she is.** I can't recall **what I was about to say.** Can you recall **how much they charged us last year?**
WH-INFINITIVE	He couldn't recall **whom to ask for.** Do you recall **where to go next?** I am trying to recall **how to set my alarm clock.**
PRESENT PARTICIPLE	Tom recalled **meeting them once before.** He recalled **leaving his passport at the hotel.** I dimly recall **hearing something about it.**

recall _____ *bring to mind*

OBJECT	What happened to him recalls **some similar events in my own life.** Every pirate movie recalls **Stevenson's** *Treasure Island*. Let us recall **the words of our Founding Fathers.** The fourth movement recalls **themes from the first movement.**

recall _____ *order the return of*

OBJECT	India recalled **the ambassador** to demonstrate its concern over the incident. Meat processors are recalling **ground beef** again.
PASSIVE	Food products containing nuts are frequently recalled.

PRESENT

I receive	we receive
you receive	you receive
he/she/it receives	they receive

• *He receives a monthly pension check.*

PRESENT PROGRESSIVE

I am receiving	we are receiving
you are receiving	you are receiving
he/she/it is receiving	they are receiving

• *I am receiving a mixed message here.*

PAST

I received	we received
you received	you received
he/she/it received	they received

• *I just received the package in the mail.*

PAST PROGRESSIVE

I was receiving	we were receiving
you were receiving	you were receiving
he/she/it was receiving	they were receiving

• *We were receiving a dozen inquiries a day.*

PRESENT PERFECT ... have | has received
PAST PERFECT   ... had received

FUTURE   ... will receive
FUTURE PROGRESSIVE ... will be receiving
FUTURE PERFECT   ... will have received

PAST PASSIVE

I was received	we were received
you were received	you were received
he/she/it was received	they were received

• *The visitors were received with open arms.*

———(COMPLEMENTS)———

receive _____ *get/take [what has been given/sent]*

OBJECT
The kids received **birthday presents** from their grandparents.
Every struggling business wants to receive **a tax cut.**
I typically receive **$20 an hour.**
I received **your shipment of 20,000 widgets** today.

PASSIVE
Your letter was received yesterday.

receive _____ *formally greet/welcome*

OBJECT
The wedding party received **the guests** in the church hall.
The company only receives **visitors** during working hours.

PASSIVE
We were received with great hospitality.

receive _____ *experience, be given*

OBJECT
The play received **a standing ovation.**
He received **a suspended sentence.**
The senator's statement received **a lot of press coverage.**
I only received **minor cuts and scrapes** in the accident.
The Gulf Coast received **the full force of the hurricane.**
Maude received **a liver transplant.**

OBJECT + THAT-CLAUSE
The office received **the news** *that one of our deliverymen had been robbed.*
He received **the feeling** *that they were not getting along very well.*
I received **the distinct impression** *that they were hostile to the idea.*

receive _____ *get [a radio/television signal]*

OBJECT
We can only receive **AM radio** where we live.

PRESENT

I recognize	we recognize
you recognize	you recognize
he/she/it recognizes	they recognize

• *Everyone recognizes the problem.*

PRESENT PROGRESSIVE

Recognize is rarely used in the progressive tenses.

PAST

I recognized	we recognized
you recognized	you recognized
he/she/it recognized	they recognized

• *We recognized what she meant.*

PAST PROGRESSIVE

Recognize is rarely used in the progressive tenses.

PRESENT PERFECT ... have | has recognized
PAST PERFECT ... had recognized

FUTURE ... will recognize
FUTURE PROGRESSIVE —
FUTURE PERFECT ... will have recognized

PAST PASSIVE

I was recognized	we were recognized
you were recognized	you were recognized
he/she/it was recognized	they were recognized

• *The suspect was recognized by a neighbor.*

(**COMPLEMENTS**)

recognize _____ *identify [someone/something previously known]*

OBJECT
I hardly recognized **him** with his mustache.
You may not recognize **me** after all these years.
I didn't even recognize **our old house** when I saw it.

recognize _____ *identify on the basis of some characteristic*

OBJECT
Most doctors today wouldn't recognize **a case of scurvy** if they saw one.
The software can recognize **virtually any type font.**

PASSIVE
The scar was recognized by the murder victim's sister.

OBJECT + AS PREDICATE NOUN
Jack recognized **the language** *as Catalan.*
Apparently, the guards had not recognized **the man** *as a threat.*

OBJECT + INFINITIVE
I recognized **him** *to be a friend of my brother's.*
We finally recognized **the bird** *to be a kind of parrot.*

WH-CLAUSE
Don't you recognize **who she is?**
I quickly recognized **what the problem was.**
I didn't recognize **where we were.**

recognize _____ *publicly give special notice to*

OBJECT
We would like to recognize **all members of the armed forces.**

PASSIVE
Would Ms. Smith please stand and be recognized?

recognize _____ *formally authorize to speak*

OBJECT
The chair recognizes **Mr. Peabody.**
"The chair recognizes **the distinguished gentleman from California.**" [FORMAL LANGUAGE OF THE U.S. HOUSE OF REPRESENTATIVES]

recognize _____ *acknowledge the existence/validity/legality of*

OBJECT
I recognize **the problems you face.**
Everyone recognizes **Bob's many qualifications for the job.**

PASSIVE
Dual citizenship is not recognized in some countries.

THAT-CLAUSE
We recognize **that you have a legitimate claim.**
Everyone recognized **that the problem had gotten out of hand.**

PRESENT

I recommend	we recommend
you recommend	you recommend
he/she/it recommends	they recommend

• *The chef recommends the grilled trout.*

PRESENT PROGRESSIVE

I am recommending	we are recommending
you are recommending	you are recommending
he/she/it is recommending	they are recommending

• *I am recommending her for the job.*

PAST

I recommended	we recommended
you recommended	you recommended
he/she/it recommended	they recommended

• *She recommended that we eat lunch here.*

PAST PROGRESSIVE

I was recommending	we were recommending
you were recommending	you were recommending
he/she/it was recommending	they were recommending

• *Her doctor was recommending antibiotics.*

PRESENT PERFECT ... have | has recommended
PAST PERFECT ... had recommended

FUTURE ... will recommend
FUTURE PROGRESSIVE ... will be recommending
FUTURE PERFECT ... will have recommended

PAST PASSIVE

I was recommended	we were recommended
you were recommended	you were recommended
he/she/it was recommended	they were recommended

• *The play was highly recommended.*

COMPLEMENTS

recommend _____ *suggest favorably / as advice*

OBJECT	Can you recommend **a plumber**?
	The architect recommends **a granite countertop**.
PASSIVE	Term life insurance is recommended for young couples.
to OBJECT + BASE-FORM THAT-CLAUSE	I will recommend **to Bob** *that he look for a better job*.
	She recommended **to her parents** *that they travel while they still can*.
	The agent recommended **to Jayne** *that she take the train instead of flying*.
BASE-FORM THAT-CLAUSE	The committee recommended **that he be hired**.
	The doctor recommends **that I be seen by a specialist**.
	Alex is recommending **that he stay home today**.
PRESENT PARTICIPLE	He recommended **our staying overnight in Monterey**.
	Would anybody recommend **doing that**?
	They recommend **setting the thermostat at 65 degrees**.

PRESENT

I record	we record
you record	you record
he/she/it records	they record

• *The device records blood pressure.*

PRESENT PROGRESSIVE

I am recording	we are recording
you are recording	you are recording
he/she/it is recording	they are recording

• *I am recording every word of the speech.*

PAST

I recorded	we recorded
you recorded	you recorded
he/she/it recorded	they recorded

• *I recorded all of our expenses.*

PAST PROGRESSIVE

I was recording	we were recording
you were recording	you were recording
he/she/it was recording	they were recording

• *The band was recording in the 1950s.*

PRESENT PERFECT ... have | has recorded
PAST PERFECT ... had recorded

FUTURE ... will record
FUTURE PROGRESSIVE ... will be recording
FUTURE PERFECT ... will have recorded

PAST PASSIVE

I was recorded	we were recorded
you were recorded	you were recorded
he/she/it was recorded	they were recorded

• *Our telephone conversation was recorded.*

NOTE: The verb *record* is stressed on the second syllable, which rhymes with *board*.
The noun *record* is stressed on the first syllable.

(**COMPLEMENTS**)

record *make an audio or visual recording*
Are we recording now?
The band first recorded in 1985.

record _____ *make an audio or visual recording of*

OBJECT
She is recording **her first album.**
The studio is recording **all of his songs.**

PASSIVE
All of her stage performances have been recorded.
All 911 calls are recorded.

record _____ *write down for later use*

OBJECT
We need to record **all of our appointments.**
The doctor asked him to record **everything he eats.**
The coroner recorded **a verdict of accidental death.**

PASSIVE
The minutes of all our meetings are recorded.

THAT-CLAUSE
The committee recorded **that it could not reach a decision.**
His notes recorded **that there had been an earthquake that day.**

WH-CLAUSE
The police recorded **who went in and out of the building.**
I carefully recorded **what our expenses were.**
Did you record **how long it took?**

record _____ *achieve*

OBJECT
Our team recorded **its first victory of the season.**

record _____ *measure and show*

OBJECT
The thermometer recorded **a high of 103** today.
Electrocardiography records **the heart's electrical signals.**

PRESENT		PRESENT PROGRESSIVE	
I reduce	we reduce	I am reducing	we are reducing
you reduce	you reduce	you are reducing	you are reducing
he/she/it reduces	they reduce	he/she/it is reducing	they are reducing

• *The software reduces background noise.*   • *We are reducing our fixed costs.*

PAST		PAST PROGRESSIVE	
I reduced	we reduced	I was reducing	we were reducing
you reduced	you reduced	you were reducing	you were reducing
he/she/it reduced	they reduced	he/she/it was reducing	they were reducing

• *The government reduced the speed limit.*   • *The storm was reducing visibility.*

PRESENT PERFECT	… have | has reduced
PAST PERFECT	… had reduced

FUTURE	… will reduce
FUTURE PROGRESSIVE	… will be reducing
FUTURE PERFECT	… will have reduced

PAST PASSIVE	
I was reduced	we were reduced
you were reduced	you were reduced
he/she/it was reduced	they were reduced

• *Their wages were reduced by 10%.*

(COMPLEMENTS)

reduce *lose weight*   After Christmas, everyone is trying to reduce.

reduce _____ *make less/smaller*

OBJECT
> We used mufflers to reduce **the noise.**
> I have reduced **my waist** by two inches.
> The stimulus program should reduce **unemployment** by 3.5 million people.
> The company reduced **my work hours.**
> Erosion is reducing **the thickness of the topsoil.**
> She reduced **her dress size** from 18 to 14.
> Before serving, reduce **the sauce** until it is thick and glossy.

PASSIVE
> The swelling had been reduced by 50%.

reduce _____ *change the state/condition of (usually smaller/lower/weaker/poorer)*

OBJECT + *to* OBJECT
> The storm reduced **the town** *to rubble.*
> The news reduced **us** *to stunned silence.*
> Hyperinflation had reduced **the currency** *to play money.*
> Termites were reducing **the table** *to a pile of dust.*
> The transportation department reduced **the highway** *to one lane.*
> The prosecutor reduced **the charge** *to a misdemeanor.*

PASSIVE
> The populations of entire communities were reduced *to beggars.*

OBJECT + *to* PRESENT PARTICIPLE
> The foreclosure reduced **the family** *to living out of their car.*

reduce _____ *simplify*

OBJECT + *to* OBJECT
> Good teachers can reduce **complex ideas** *to their basic elements.*
> He reduced **the whole process** *to three simple steps.*

PASSIVE
> Wedding planning can't be reduced *to a list of do's and don'ts.*

PRESENT

I refer	we refer
you refer	you refer
he/she/it refers	they refer

• *He never refers to notes when he speaks.*

PRESENT PROGRESSIVE

I am referring	we are referring
you are referring	you are referring
he/she/it is referring	they are referring

• *I know what you are referring to.*

PAST

I referred	we referred
you referred	you referred
he/she/it referred	they referred

• *She referred me to the research librarian.*

PAST PROGRESSIVE

I was referring	we were referring
you were referring	you were referring
he/she/it was referring	they were referring

• *Perhaps you were referring to something else.*

PRESENT PERFECT ... have | has referred
PAST PERFECT ... had referred

FUTURE ... will refer
FUTURE PROGRESSIVE ... will be referring
FUTURE PERFECT ... will have referred

PAST PASSIVE

I was referred	we were referred
you were referred	you were referred
he/she/it was referred	they were referred

• *I was referred to a specialist.*

COMPLEMENTS

NOTE: The verb *refer* is always used with *to*.

refer _____ *mention, speak of*

to OBJECT
He is always referring **to his famous friends.**
Are you referring **to me?**
The title of the movie refers **to a term from classical Greek rhetoric.**

to OBJECT + AS PREDICATE NOUN
They refer **to their pets** *as their children.*
The general referred **to his own soldiers** *as rabble.*

PASSIVE
New York is referred to *as the Big Apple.*

refer _____ *go for help/information/etc.*

to OBJECT
Applicants may refer **to the company's policy manual.**
Students should refer **to the map on page 354.**
The carpenters referred **to the architect's blueprints.**

refer _____ *tell/direct to go for help/information/etc.*

OBJECT + to OBJECT
John referred **them** *to his lawyer.*
The instructions refer **you** *to the company's website.*

PASSIVE
Alice was referred *to yet another office.*

refer _____ *direct*

OBJECT + to OBJECT
We must refer **this matter** *to the whole committee.*

refer _____ *concern, be about*

to OBJECT
This paragraph refers **to the use of solar energy for heating and cooling.**
His remark refers **to his son's graduation five years before.**

PHRASAL VERBS

refer _____ **back** *return*
The court referred the case back to the prosecutor's office.
I referred the complaint back to Customer Service.

PRESENT		PRESENT PROGRESSIVE	
I reflect	we reflect	I am reflecting	we are reflecting
you reflect	you reflect	you are reflecting	you are reflecting
he/she/it reflects	they reflect	he/she/it is reflecting	they are reflecting

    • *The mirror reflects the sun into the box.*   • *That light is reflecting right in my face.*

PAST		PAST PROGRESSIVE	
I reflected	we reflected	I was reflecting	we were reflecting
you reflected	you reflected	you were reflecting	you were reflecting
he/she/it reflected	they reflected	he/she/it was reflecting	they were reflecting

    • *I reflected on what my wife had just said.*   • *He was reflecting on the problem.*

PRESENT PERFECT   … have | has reflected   FUTURE   … will reflect
PAST PERFECT   … had reflected   FUTURE PROGRESSIVE   … will be reflecting
                                         FUTURE PERFECT   … will have reflected

PAST PASSIVE

I was reflected	we were reflected
you were reflected	you were reflected
he/she/it was reflected	they were reflected

    • *The car was reflected in the mirror.*

(**COMPLEMENTS**)

reflect _____ *throw back energy [light, sound, heat]*

   ADVERB OF PLACE TO/FROM   The sun was reflecting **into my eyes.**
                                   The sound reflects **off the walls.**
                                   An amazing amount of heat was reflecting **from the building.**

   OBJECT + ADVERB OF PLACE TO/FROM   The sun reflects **light** *off the water.*
                                   The walls reflected **the sound** *all around the square.*
                                   The building reflects **the heat** *into the courtyard.*

reflect _____ *throw back the image of*

   OBJECT   The still pond reflected **the trees** in the moonlight.
                                   The mirror didn't reflect **the face of Count Dracula, who was**
                                         standing right in front of it.

   PASSIVE   The statue was reflected in the wading pool.

reflect _____ *be the same as*

   OBJECT   His feelings seemed to reflect **my own.**
                                   The review certainly reflected **my feelings about the play.**
                                   The Dow generally reflects **the market as a whole.**

reflect _____ *bring [credit/discredit] as a result*

   ADVERB OF MANNER + *on* OBJECT   His behavior reflected **badly** *on the school.*
                                   The incident reflects **poorly** *on his judgment.*
                                   Their actions reflect **well** *on the entire division.*

   OBJECT + *on* OBJECT   This award reflects **credit** *on our whole organization.*

reflect _____ *think seriously*

   on OBJECT   He reflected **on the misery he had caused his family.**

   THAT-CLAUSE   He reflected **that things had turned out surprisingly well.**
                                   I reflected **that I had jumped to conclusions.**
                                   Guy reflected **that he should have been more careful.**

   on WH-CLAUSE   He reflected **on what had just happened.**
                                   We were reflecting **on how it had all started.**
                                   I reflected **on how much he had learned.**

PRESENT

I refuse	we refuse
you refuse	you refuse
he/she/it refuses	they refuse

• *He refuses to admit his mistakes.*

PAST

I refused	we refused
you refused	you refused
he/she/it refused	they refused

• *The car refused to start.*

PRESENT PERFECT ... have | has refused
PAST PERFECT ... had refused

PRESENT PROGRESSIVE

I am refusing	we are refusing
you are refusing	you are refusing
he/she/it is refusing	they are refusing

• *She is refusing to get involved.*

PAST PROGRESSIVE

I was refusing	we were refusing
you were refusing	you were refusing
he/she/it was refusing	they were refusing

• *They were refusing to cooperate.*

FUTURE ... will refuse
FUTURE PROGRESSIVE ... will be refusing
FUTURE PERFECT ... will have refused

PAST PASSIVE

I was refused	we were refused
you were refused	you were refused
he/she/it was refused	they were refused

• *Our offer was flatly refused.*

NOTE: The verb *refuse* is stressed on the second syllable and rhymes with *accuse*. The noun *refuse* is stressed on the first syllable.

──────────────────────────── COMPLEMENTS ────

refuse *not accept something*

I am sure they will refuse.
If I were in their shoes, I would refuse too.
It is too late to refuse now.

refuse _____ *reject, not accept*
OBJECT

We decided to refuse **the offer**.
I steadfastly refused **the dessert menu**.

PASSIVE

All offers of help were politely refused.

refuse _____ *not allow*
INDIRECT OBJECT + DIRECT OBJECT

The theater refused *them* admission because they were
only 15 years old.
I refused *her* the satisfaction of seeing me upset.
The restaurant refused *them* a table without a reservation.

refuse _____ *say that one is unwilling*
INFINITIVE

He refused **to talk to us**.
They refused **to be drawn into the controversy**.

refuse _____ *fail*
INFINITIVE

This door refuses **to stay closed**.
My computer absolutely refuses **to talk to my printer**.

PRESENT

I regard	we regard
you regard	you regard
he/she/it regards	they regard

• *He regards the situation with optimism.*

PRESENT PROGRESSIVE

Regard is rarely used in the progressive tenses.

PAST

I regarded	we regarded
you regarded	you regarded
he/she/it regarded	they regarded

• *I regarded the strange food suspiciously.*

PAST PROGRESSIVE

Regard is rarely used in the progressive tenses.

PRESENT PERFECT ... have | has regarded
PAST PERFECT ... had regarded

FUTURE ... will regard
FUTURE PROGRESSIVE —
FUTURE PERFECT ... will have regarded

PAST PASSIVE

I was regarded	we were regarded
you were regarded	you were regarded
he/she/it was regarded	they were regarded

• *He was regarded as a potential leader.*

(**COMPLEMENTS**)

regard ____ *look at, consider*

OBJECT + ADVERB OF MANNER	I regarded **my empty wallet** *sadly.*
	The hikers regarded **the rope bridge** *with apprehension.*
	Rob regarded **the senator's campaign** *with disdain.*
PASSIVE	The economic downturn is regarded *with great concern.*
OBJECT + *as* PREDICATE NOUN	She regarded **Barbara** *as a second daughter.*
	The company regards **Nebraska** *as its test market.*
	I have always regarded **him** *as something of a lightweight.*
PASSIVE	Arizona has always been regarded *as our winter home.*
OBJECT + *as* PREDICATE ADJECTIVE	The agency regards **the safety of children** *as paramount.*
	The prosecutor regarded **the governor's actions** *as fraudulent.*
PASSIVE	His last novel is regarded *as foolishly sentimental.*
WH-CLAUSE + ADVERB OF MANNER	I regarded **where he had parked his car** *with disbelief.*
	We regarded **how much we had earned** *with amazement.*
PASSIVE	What we had accomplished was regarded *with satisfaction.*

regard ____ *concern, be about*

OBJECT	This letter regards **your mining company's intention to blast off the top of Black Mountain.**

PRESENT

I register	we register
you register	you register
he/she/it registers	they register

• *He always registers as an Independent.*

PRESENT PROGRESSIVE

I am registering	we are registering
you are registering	you are registering
he/she/it is registering	they are registering

• *I am registering to vote this afternoon.*

PAST

I registered	we registered
you registered	you registered
he/she/it registered	they registered

• *I registered my purchases with Customs.*

PAST PROGRESSIVE

I was registering	we were registering
you were registering	you were registering
he/she/it was registering	they were registering

• *We were registering about 20 participants an hour.*

PRESENT PERFECT ... have | has registered
PAST PERFECT ... had registered

FUTURE ... will register
FUTURE PROGRESSIVE ... will be registering
FUTURE PERFECT ... will have registered

PAST PASSIVE

I was registered	we were registered
you were registered	you were registered
he/she/it was registered	they were registered

• *My complaint was duly registered.*

COMPLEMENTS

register *enroll oneself in an activity / school*

Every participant has to register at the front desk.
The students will be registering all this week.
When can we register?

register *be recognized*

The importance of what she said didn't register until later.
His remark didn't register with me at all.

register *measure and show a reading* [OF INSTRUMENTS]

The dial didn't register at all.
Such a small earth tremor won't register.

register _____ *enroll oneself*
  INFINITIVE

He registered **to vote** in 1945.
I registered **to join the debate club**.
Ten thousand people registered **to run in this year's marathon**.

register _____ *enroll on a list*
  OBJECT

We registered **the boat** with the Coast Guard.
Our precinct usually registers **several hundred new voters**.
You must register **all documents**.
The bride registered **her gift list** with Neiman Marcus.

  PASSIVE

Two thousand incoming freshmen were registered this year.

register _____ *give notice of, express*
  OBJECT

I would like to register **a complaint**.
He certainly registered **his opposition**.
We registered **our support of the bill** publicly.
Her face registered **complete surprise**.

register _____ *achieve*
  OBJECT

Our team registered **its first win in two weeks**.
Rob's company will register **one million dollars in sales** this year.

register _____ *measure and show*
  OBJECT

The thermometer registers **54 degrees**.
The rain gauge registered **1.3 inches**.

PRESENT

I reject	we reject
you reject	you reject
he/she/it rejects	they reject

• *He rejects all offers of help.*

PRESENT PROGRESSIVE

I am rejecting	we are rejecting
you are rejecting	you are rejecting
he/she/it is rejecting	they are rejecting

• *We are rejecting your application.*

PAST

I rejected	we rejected
you rejected	you rejected
he/she/it rejected	they rejected

• *We rejected their proposal.*

PAST PROGRESSIVE

I was rejecting	we were rejecting
you were rejecting	you were rejecting
he/she/it was rejecting	they were rejecting

• *He was rejecting all solid food.*

PRESENT PERFECT ... have | has rejected
PAST PERFECT ... had rejected

FUTURE ... will reject
FUTURE PROGRESSIVE ... will be rejecting
FUTURE PERFECT ... will have rejected

PAST PASSIVE

I was rejected	we were rejected
you were rejected	you were rejected
he/she/it was rejected	they were rejected

• *No reasonable offer was rejected.*

(**COMPLEMENTS**)

reject _____ *not accept, refuse to believe / use / agree to*

OBJECT	We rejected **all the bids.**
	The union rejected **the first offer the company made.**
	Harvard might reject **my application.**
	He rejects **the idea that HIV causes AIDS.**
	The publisher has rejected **all three of my manuscripts.**
PASSIVE	The first draft of our proposal was rejected.
	Organ transplants are sometimes rejected by the recipient's immune system.
WH-CLAUSE	The committee will reject **whomever the president nominates.**
	They rejected **whatever we proposed.**
	Smith always rejects **whichever proposal is the most expensive.**

reject _____ *refuse to love / care for*

OBJECT	The mother bird rejected **all the chicks.**
PASSIVE	Bobby was just rejected by his girlfriend.
	Nobody likes being rejected.

PRESENT		PRESENT PROGRESSIVE	
I relate	we relate	I am relating	we are relating
you relate	you relate	you are relating	you are relating
he/she/it relates	they relate	he/she/it is relating	they are relating

• *Your son relates well to other children.*   • *He is relating global warming to rainfall patterns.*

PAST		PAST PROGRESSIVE	
I related	we related	I was relating	we were relating
you related	you related	you were relating	you were relating
he/she/it related	they related	he/she/it was relating	they were relating

• *I related the story as best I could.*   • *My boyfriend was relating all his troubles.*

PRESENT PERFECT ... have | has related
PAST PERFECT ... had related

FUTURE ... will relate
FUTURE PROGRESSIVE ... will be relating
FUTURE PERFECT ... will have related

PAST PASSIVE	
I was related	we were related
you were related	you were related
he/she/it was related	they were related

• *Stories of Eudora Welty's childhood were related in her memoir.*

─(**COMPLEMENTS**)─

relate *feel a bond with people /*
a performance

Shy people have a hard time relating.
The new kid is relating surprisingly well.
Some people liked the music, but I just couldn't relate.

relate _____ *feel a bond with, interact with*
to OBJECT

The kids really relate **to Uncle Charlie.**
Philip never did relate **to his music teacher.**
The audience related **to her performance of the Mendelssohn violin concerto.**

relate _____ *tell about, give an account of*
OBJECT

He related **the events leading up to the strike.**
The movie related **the lives of a family in New England.**

PASSIVE

The entire story of his summer vacation was related in agonizing detail.

relate _____ *concern, be about*
to OBJECT

The legislation relates **to interstate commerce.**
Your suggestion does not relate **to the issue.**

to PRESENT PARTICIPLE

My proposal relates **to reducing copying expenses.**
The article relates **to making foreign travel easier.**

relate _____ *connect, link, associate*
OBJECT + to/and/with OBJECT

The study related **road accidents** *to cell phone use.*
Florence Nightingale related **hospital sanitation** *and mortality rates.*
Studies have related **lung cancer** *with smoking.*

be related _____ *be connected/linked* [USED ONLY IN THE PASSIVE]
to OBJECT

Earthquakes are related to tectonic plate movements.
Levels of vitamin D are related to sunshine.
The company's success is related to the economy.

be related _____ *be connected by blood or marriage* [USED ONLY IN THE PASSIVE]
to OBJECT

I am related to Perry on my mother's side.
He is related to my cousin.
Whom she is related to?

PRESENT

I release	we release
you release	you release
he/she/it releases	they release

• He releases the fish that he catches.

PAST

I released	we released
you released	you released
he/she/it released	they released

• He released the information to the press.

PRESENT PERFECT ... have | has released
PAST PERFECT ... had released

PRESENT PROGRESSIVE

I am releasing	we are releasing
you are releasing	you are releasing
he/she/it is releasing	they are releasing

• Watch out—I'm releasing the brake.

PAST PROGRESSIVE

I was releasing	we were releasing
you were releasing	you were releasing
he/she/it was releasing	they were releasing

• The chemical plant was releasing sulfur dioxide.

FUTURE ... will release
FUTURE PROGRESSIVE ... will be releasing
FUTURE PERFECT ... will have released

PAST PASSIVE

I was released	we were released
you were released	you were released
he/she/it was released	they were released

• The movie was released in 2002.

(**COMPLEMENTS**)

release *allow something to return to its normal position*

Flex your muscles, then release.
Push the button down, then release.

release *allow something to escape*

Hold your breath, then release.

release _____ *set free, allow to escape*
   OBJECT

I released **the butterflies that I had captured.**
The children released **the balloons.**
The judge released **the three suspects** without bail.

   PASSIVE

The fumes were released harmlessly into the air.

release _____ *free from obligation*
   OBJECT

The candidate released **her delegates** to vote for whomever
   they chose.
The king released **the duke** from his oath.

   PASSIVE

Our inheritance was finally released from escrow.

release _____ *make available*
   OBJECT

The senator released **his tax returns** to the press.
The campaign will release **its list of donors** tomorrow.
The administration wouldn't release **the names of the
   prisoners.**

PRESENT		PRESENT PROGRESSIVE	
I relieve	we relieve	I am relieving	we are relieving
you relieve	you relieve	you are relieving	you are relieving
he/she/it relieves	they relieve	he/she/it is relieving	they are relieving

• *Aspirin usually relieves my headache.* • *Captain Picard is relieving him next month.*

PAST		PAST PROGRESSIVE	
I relieved	we relieved	I was relieving	we were relieving
you relieved	you relieved	you were relieving	you were relieving
he/she/it relieved	they relieved	he/she/it was relieving	they were relieving

• *The good news relieved all our worries.* • *The medication was finally relieving my congestion.*

PRESENT PERFECT ... have | has relieved
PAST PERFECT ... had relieved

FUTURE ... will relieve
FUTURE PROGRESSIVE ... will be relieving
FUTURE PERFECT ... will have relieved

PAST PASSIVE	
I was relieved	we were relieved
you were relieved	you were relieved
he/she/it was relieved	they were relieved

• *The guard was relieved at midnight.*

(COMPLEMENTS)

relieve _____ *reduce, get rid of*

OBJECT
I need something to relieve **the itching**.
Exercise helps relieve **stress**.
Another lane would relieve **the traffic congestion**.
Eating locally grown food would relieve **pressure on the environment**.

PASSIVE
Our anxiety was relieved by the doctor's reassuring words.

relieve _____ *release from responsibility*

OBJECT + *of* OBJECT
The agreement relieved **the defendant** *of liability in the matter*.
The Air Force relieved **the colonel** *of his command*.
Her employer relieved **her** *of all management responsibilities*.

relieve _____ *release from duty/work by replacing*

OBJECT
You must relieve **the sentries** every two hours.
Franklin relieved **Motte** in the ninth inning.
Col. Wright relieved **Col. Franks** in a formal retirement ceremony.

PASSIVE
The drivers must be relieved periodically.

relieve _____ *make more pleasant*

OBJECT
Only the children's laughter relieved **the gloomy family dinner**.
Shakespeare usually relieves **his tragedies** with comic interludes.

PASSIVE
His dark paintings are relieved only by tiny threads of color.

relieve _____ *bring help to*

OBJECT
The agency rushed to relieve **the flooded city**.
We hired temps to relieve **the store** during the Christmas rush.

PASSIVE
Leningrad was relieved after 872 days of fighting.

relieve _____ *urinate*

REFLEXIVE PRONOUN
Where can I relieve **myself**?
Call the nurse if you need to relieve **yourself**.
The patient may have difficulty relieving **himself** for a few days.

NOTE: The use of *relieve* in this sense is acceptable in a clinical setting.

PRESENT		PRESENT PROGRESSIVE	
I remain	we remain	I am remaining	we are remaining
you remain	you remain	you are remaining	you are remaining
he/she/it remains	they remain	he/she/it is remaining	they are remaining

• *The problem still remains to be dealt with.* • *I am remaining here in the shade.*

PAST		PAST PROGRESSIVE	
I remained	we remained	I was remaining	we were remaining
you remained	you remained	you were remaining	you were remaining
he/she/it remained	they remained	he/she/it was remaining	they were remaining

• *We remained inside until the rain stopped.* • *Two soldiers were remaining behind.*

PRESENT PERFECT ... have | has remained
PAST PERFECT   ... had remained

FUTURE   ... will remain
FUTURE PROGRESSIVE ... will be remaining
FUTURE PERFECT   ... will have remained

PAST PASSIVE

Remain is never used in the passive voice.

(COMPLEMENTS)

remain *stay, linger*
> The teacher asked me to remain after class.
> I can only remain for a few seconds.

remain *continue to exist, be left*
> After the fire, only the chimney and foundation remained.
> The snow remained for weeks.
> The bad smell from the fire remained for days.
> Only three slices of cake remain.

remain _____ *continue to be*

ADVERB OF PLACE
> Please remain **here**.
> Please remain **in the car**.
> Please remain **where you are**.

PREDICATE NOUN
> The platoon still remained **an effective fighting unit**.
> Paul remained **sheriff** for years.
> Storms remained **a major threat to shipping**.

PREDICATE ADJECTIVE
> Fortunately, the guards had remained **alert**.
> I couldn't remain **awake** during the long drive.
> Despite the accident, we all remained **friendly** with each other.

remain _____ *be left [to deal with / do]*

INFINITIVE
> Nothing remains **to be done**.
> A thorough cleaning remained **to be done**.
> The full extent of the damage remains **to be seen**.

(PHRASAL VERBS)

remain ahead/behind/down/under/up/etc. *stay in a specified position*
> Our hockey team remained ahead
>   after two periods.
> The player remained down for several minutes.

remain up *stay awake and out of bed*
> The kids were allowed to remain up on Christmas Eve.

remember remember | remembers · remembered · have remembered ☑ REGULAR

PRESENT

I remember	we remember
you remember	you remember
he/she/it remembers	they remember

• *He never remembers to turn off the light.*

PRESENT PROGRESSIVE

I am remembering	we are remembering
you are remembering	you are remembering
he/she/it is remembering	they are remembering

• *I am not remembering anything these days.*

PAST

I remembered	we remembered
you remembered	you remembered
he/she/it remembered	they remembered

• *I remembered what I was going to do.*

PAST PROGRESSIVE

I was remembering	we were remembering
you were remembering	you were remembering
he/she/it was remembering	they were remembering

• *We were just remembering something he said.*

PRESENT PERFECT ... have | has remembered
PAST PERFECT ... had remembered

FUTURE ... will remember
FUTURE PROGRESSIVE ... will be remembering
FUTURE PERFECT ... will have remembered

PAST PASSIVE

I was remembered	we were remembered
you were remembered	you were remembered
he/she/it was remembered	they were remembered

• *He was remembered with great fondness.*

COMPLEMENTS

remember *recall something*

I am trying to remember.
Sorry, I can't remember.

remember _____ *recall, think about again*

OBJECT

I finally remembered **his name**.
Do you remember **the day we met**?

PASSIVE

The accident will be remembered for a long time.

THAT-CLAUSE

I remembered **that I had an appointment at 10 o'clock**.
We remembered just in time **that the train was running on a holiday schedule**.

NOTE: The imperative of *remember* with THAT-CLAUSES is also used to emphasize the importance of something, in the sense "don't forget."

Please remember **that the meeting time has been changed**.
Remember **that your homework must be finished before you can watch TV**.
You must remember **that this information is confidential**.

WH-CLAUSE

Sure, I remember **who you are**.
Everybody remembers **what happened next**.
I couldn't remember **where I was supposed to go next**.

WH-INFINITIVE

John tried to remember **what to do in case of fire**.
Sam couldn't remember **where to put the commas**.
I hope the children remember **how to behave**.

PRESENT PARTICIPLE

I distinctly remember **putting the keys on the desk**.
Do you remember **getting a call from a Mr. Rex**?
He doesn't remember **locking the door**.

remember _____ *do [what one intends to / should do]*

INFINITIVE

I finally remembered **to mail the letter in my pocket**.
Did you remember **to set the alarm system**?
The kids never remember **to hang up their coats**.

remember _____ *think about respectfully*

OBJECT

Let us remember **those who have died that we might be free**.

remember _____ *give a gift/card to*

OBJECT

Grandmother always remembers **me** on my birthday.
Ruby remembered **us** on our anniversary.

PRESENT

I remind	we remind
you remind	you remind
he/she/it reminds	they remind

• *She reminds me of my mother.*

PRESENT PROGRESSIVE

I am reminding	we are reminding
you are reminding	you are reminding
he/she/it is reminding	they are reminding

• *I am reminding everyone to turn in their time sheets.*

PAST

I reminded	we reminded
you reminded	you reminded
he/she/it reminded	they reminded

• *He reminded us to keep the door locked.*

PAST PROGRESSIVE

I was reminding	we were reminding
you were reminding	you were reminding
he/she/it was reminding	they were reminding

• *He was reminding the tour group where to meet.*

PRESENT PERFECT … have | has reminded
PAST PERFECT … had reminded

FUTURE … will remind
FUTURE PROGRESSIVE … will be reminding
FUTURE PERFECT … will have reminded

PAST PASSIVE

I was reminded	we were reminded
you were reminded	you were reminded
he/she/it was reminded	they were reminded

• *I was reminded that we must finish by 4 o'clock.*

COMPLEMENTS

remind _____ *cause to remember / think of*

OBJECT + *of* OBJECT	My secretary reminded **me** *of the luncheon date.*
	The coach reminded **his players** *of the early curfew.*
	His hearty laugh reminded **us** *of his father.*
	Those limestone bluffs remind **me** *of my childhood.*
PASSIVE	They were reminded *of the time Randy broke his arm.*
OBJECT + INFINITIVE	We reminded **the boys** *to set their alarms.*
	Please remind **me** *to call Mr. Ross.*
PASSIVE	The passengers were reminded *to pick up their customs declarations.*
OBJECT + THAT-CLAUSE	We reminded **the guests** *that breakfast was at eight.*
	Remind **the staff** *that they need to replace their ID cards.*
PASSIVE	They were reminded *that smoking is not permitted anywhere in the building.*
OBJECT + WH-CLAUSE	I reminded **Charles** *what he needed to bring to the meeting.*
	He reminded **us** *where we would have to park.*
PASSIVE	We were all reminded *how much we missed her.*
OBJECT + WH-INFINITIVE	Remind **us** *what to do.*
	Cary reminded **the participants** *where to get the handouts.*
PASSIVE	The students were reminded *how to fill out the forms.*

PRESENT

I remove	we remove
you remove	you remove
he/she/it removes	they remove

• *Acetone removes fingernail polish.*

PAST

I removed	we removed
you removed	you removed
he/she/it removed	they removed

• *We removed our hats and went inside.*

PRESENT PERFECT	... have	has removed
PAST PERFECT	... had removed

PRESENT PROGRESSIVE

I am removing	we are removing
you are removing	you are removing
he/she/it is removing	they are removing

• *The nurse is removing the bandages now.*

PAST PROGRESSIVE

I was removing	we were removing
you were removing	you were removing
he/she/it was removing	they were removing

• *The children were removing their jackets.*

FUTURE	... will remove
FUTURE PROGRESSIVE	... will be removing
FUTURE PERFECT	... will have removed

PAST PASSIVE

I was removed	we were removed
you were removed	you were removed
he/she/it was removed	they were removed

• *Ground beef products were removed from stores in seven states.*

───(**COMPLEMENTS**)───

remove _____ *take away, eliminate*

OBJECT

First, we need to remove **all the rust.**
Remove **the lids** and mix the paint.
The surgeon decided to remove **the tumor.**
The editor removed **three chapters of the book.**
Congress voted to remove **the sanctions.**

PASSIVE

Nothing can be removed from the scene of the crime.

remove _____ *dismiss [from a position/office]*

OBJECT

The committee members voted to remove **the chair.**

PASSIVE

The governor of Illinois was removed from office in 2009.

remove _____ *take off [clothing, etc.]*

OBJECT

Please remove **your outer garments.**
I removed **my muddy boots** and went inside.
He removed **his watch and glasses** and dove into the pool.

PRESENT

I repeat	we repeat
you repeat	you repeat
he/she/it repeats	they repeat

- *He repeats what he's read in the paper.*

PRESENT PROGRESSIVE

I am repeating	we are repeating
you are repeating	you are repeating
he/she/it is repeating	they are repeating

- *The speaker is repeating himself.*

PAST

I repeated	we repeated
you repeated	you repeated
he/she/it repeated	they repeated

- *He repeated that we would have to leave.*

PAST PROGRESSIVE

I was repeating	we were repeating
you were repeating	you were repeating
he/she/it was repeating	they were repeating

- *They were repeating the course.*

PRESENT PERFECT ... have | has repeated
PAST PERFECT ... had repeated

FUTURE ... will repeat
FUTURE PROGRESSIVE ... will be repeating
FUTURE PERFECT ... will have repeated

PAST PASSIVE

—	—
—	—
it was repeated	they were repeated

- *The announcement was repeated several times.*

COMPLEMENTS

repeat *happen again, do something again*

The noise repeats at regular intervals.
The theme repeats in the third movement.
Do you think the champions can repeat?
Repeat after me: "On my honor I will do my best...."
The shawl's lace pattern repeats every 16 rows.

repeat _____ *say again*

OBJECT

The teacher repeated **the question.**
Please repeat **the oath** after me.
Nick repeated **the secret** to Nora.

PASSIVE

The storm warning was repeated every 10 minutes.

THAT-CLAUSE

The waiter repeated **that the tip was not included.**
The weatherman repeated **that there would be a severe winter storm.**
I had to repeat several times **that their party was too loud.**

WH-CLAUSE

Please repeat **what you just said.**
I can't repeat **what I heard.**
The parrot will repeat **whatever you say.**

repeat _____ *do/perform again*

OBJECT

The band kept repeating **the only tunes they knew.**
The hackers repeated **their attack on the server.**

PASSIVE

The program is repeated every few months.

WH-CLAUSE

Other scientists must be able to repeat **what you did.**
We don't need to repeat **whatever mistakes they made.**
Young children always repeat **whatever their parents do.**

repeat _____ *say/do [something] again*

REFLEXIVE PRONOUN

You should be careful not to repeat **yourself.**
History seldom repeats **itself** exactly the same way.

PRESENT

I replace	we replace
you replace	you replace
he/she/it replaces	they replace

• *He never replaces burned-out lightbulbs.*

PRESENT PROGRESSIVE

I am replacing	we are replacing
you are replacing	you are replacing
he/she/it is replacing	they are replacing

• *The company is replacing the strikers.*

PAST

I replaced	we replaced
you replaced	you replaced
he/she/it replaced	they replaced

• *I finally replaced my old truck.*

PAST PROGRESSIVE

I was replacing	we were replacing
you were replacing	you were replacing
he/she/it was replacing	they were replacing

• *They were replacing the old badges.*

PRESENT PERFECT ... have | has replaced
PAST PERFECT   ... had replaced

FUTURE   ... will replace
FUTURE PROGRESSIVE ... will be replacing
FUTURE PERFECT   ... will have replaced

PAST PASSIVE

I was replaced	we were replaced
you were replaced	you were replaced
he/she/it was replaced	they were replaced

• *The faulty printer was replaced.*

─────────────────────────────(**COMPLEMENTS**)─────

replace _____ *take the place of*

OBJECT	Sunshine soon replaced **the dreary fog.**
	Nobody can replace **Roberta.**
	Johnson will replace **Smith** at quarterback in the second half.
	Smiles soon replaced **the tears on the kids' faces.**
PASSIVE	Will translators be replaced by robots?

replace _____ *put [someone/something new] in the place of*

OBJECT (+ *with* OBJECT)	We must replace **the clutch** before the car breaks down somewhere.
	Oboe players must replace **their reeds** frequently.
	Her doctor said it was necessary to replace **her right knee joint.**
	The company replaced **all its computers** at once.
	The board is going to replace **the entire management team.**
	The gardener replaced **the roses** *with more heat-resistant varieties.*
	We should replace **our incandescent bulbs** *with compact florescents.*
	They replaced **their standard copier paper** *with a brighter white paper.*
WH-CLAUSE	We replaced **what we thought caused the problem.**
	They are going to replace **whoever can't meet the quota.**
	Find and replace **whatever is broken.**

replace _____ *take the place of*

OBJECT	High-definition TVs have almost entirely replaced **conventional ones.**
	Automatic transmissions began to replace **manual transmissions** in the 1950s.

replace _____ *put back where it belongs*

OBJECT + ADVERB OF PLACE	I carefully replaced **the vase** *on the shelf.*
	He replaced **the blanket** *on the bed.*
PASSIVE	The pictures were all replaced *in the album.*

PRESENT

I reply	we reply
you reply	you reply
he/she/it replies	they reply

· *He always replies promptly.*

PRESENT PROGRESSIVE

I am replying	we are replying
you are replying	you are replying
he/she/it is replying	they are replying

· *I am replying to her e-mail right now.*

PAST

I replied	we replied
you replied	you replied
he/she/it replied	they replied

· *I replied to him yesterday.*

PAST PROGRESSIVE

I was replying	we were replying
you were replying	you were replying
he/she/it was replying	they were replying

· *We were replying as soon as we could.*

PRESENT PERFECT ... have | has replied
PAST PERFECT ... had replied

FUTURE ... will reply
FUTURE PROGRESSIVE ... will be replying
FUTURE PERFECT ... will have replied

PAST PASSIVE

I was replied	we were replied
you were replied	you were replied
he/she/it was replied	they were replied

· *His comments were never replied to.*

COMPLEMENTS

reply *answer, respond*

I never got around to replying.
There is no point in writing because he never replies.
How soon can you reply?

reply *respond to an action with a similar action*

Their artillery shelled us, and we promptly replied.
They sued us, so naturally we replied by countersuing.
Their country expelled our diplomats, so we replied the same way.

reply ⸺ *answer, respond*

to OBJECT

I will reply **to him** as soon as I can.
He never replied **to our e-mail**.
Whom did she reply **to**?

PASSIVE

Our letters were not replied to.

to OBJECT + THAT-CLAUSE

I replied **to Don** *that the meeting time was fine.*
The receptionist replied **to us** *that an agent would call back later.*
Ralph replied **to Frank** *that they should get together sometime.*

THAT-CLAUSE

I replied **that we would be glad to meet with them.**
Shirley replied **that she could meet us in Chicago.**
Did they reply **that it would be okay?**

DIRECT QUOTATION

"**No**," Arthur replied, "**I'm not leaving until tomorrow.**"

PRESENT

I report	we report
you report	you report
he/she/it reports	they report

• *She reports business news on CNN.*

PRESENT PROGRESSIVE

I am reporting	we are reporting
you are reporting	you are reporting
he/she/it is reporting	they are reporting

• *We are reporting the incident to the police.*

PAST

I reported	we reported
you reported	you reported
he/she/it reported	they reported

• *The school reported record enrollment.*

PAST PROGRESSIVE

I was reporting	we were reporting
you were reporting	you were reporting
he/she/it was reporting	they were reporting

• *The radio was reporting record snowfalls.*

PRESENT PERFECT ... have | has reported
PAST PERFECT ... had reported

FUTURE ... will report
FUTURE PROGRESSIVE ... will be reporting
FUTURE PERFECT ... will have reported

PAST PASSIVE

I was reported	we were reported
you were reported	you were reported
he/she/it was reported	they were reported

• *The governor was reported to be involved in bribery.*

COMPLEMENTS

report _____ *tell about, give an account of; announce; tell [someone in authority] about [an accident/crime/etc.]*

OBJECT	The police reported **an accident on Route 9.**
	The mayor reported **an unexpected drop in city revenues.**
PASSIVE	All schoolyard accidents must be reported to the principal.
on OBJECT	As a society writer, I report **on the lives of famous people.**
	Jack reported **on the need to make Horse Creek flood proof.**
OBJECT + *to* OBJECT	My neighbor reported **an attempted burglary** *to the police.*
	Gayle reported **the shoplifting** *to the store manager.*
	Senator Blather reported **his achievements** *to a skeptical audience.*
OBJECT + PREDICATE ADJECTIVE	The captain reported **the soldiers** *ready for duty.*
	The doctor reported **the patient** *strong enough to go home.*
PASSIVE	He was reported *unhappy with the settlement.*
OBJECT + INFINITIVE	The captain reported **the soldiers** *to be ready.*
PASSIVE	He was reported *to be the nominee.*
	The company was reported *to be going public.*
OBJECT + PRESENT PARTICIPLE	The paper reported **him** *working in Denver.*
	The teacher reported **Johnny** *misbehaving in class.*
PASSIVE	The escaped convict was reported *hiding in a barn.*
OBJECT + PAST PARTICIPLE	Henry reported **his flight** *cancelled due to mechanical problems.*
PASSIVE	The boat was reported *sunk in the storm.*
	The car was reported *stolen.*
(*to* OBJECT +) THAT-CLAUSE	The coach reported **that two players had been suspended.**
	The treasurer reported *to the board* that revenues were down.
WH-CLAUSE	The watchman reported **what he had seen.**
	The radio reported **which areas were likely to flood.**
PRESENT PARTICIPLE	The patient reports **feeling dizzy when he stands up.**

PHRASAL VERBS

report for _____ *appear / be present for the purpose of*

The recruits reported for duty at 6 A.M.
Managers must report for work an hour early.

report to _____ *appear / be present at*

Report to your commander—on the double.
New employees should report to the Human Resources department.

PRESENT

I represent	we represent
you represent	you represent
he/she/it represents	they represent

• *John represents a nonprofit organization.*

PRESENT PROGRESSIVE

I am representing	we are representing
you are representing	you are representing
he/she/it is representing	they are representing

• *He is representing them in court.*

PAST

I represented	we represented
you represented	you represented
he/she/it represented	they represented

• *The idea represented a bold approach.*

PAST PROGRESSIVE

I was representing	we were representing
you were representing	you were representing
he/she/it was representing	they were representing

• *I was representing our company at the trade show.*

PRESENT PERFECT ... have | has represented
PAST PERFECT ... had represented

FUTURE ... will represent
FUTURE PROGRESSIVE ... will be representing
FUTURE PERFECT ... will have represented

PAST PASSIVE

I was represented	we were represented
you were represented	you were represented
he/she/it was represented	they were represented

• *Our district was represented by Ms. Santos for 14 years.*

(COMPLEMENTS)

represent _____ *be an official agent for*

OBJECT	He represents **Italy** in international trade negotiations.
	She is representing **a company in Dallas.**
	He represents **the fifth congressional district in Oregon.**
	They will represent **the United States** in figure skating at the next Winter Olympics.
PASSIVE	We were represented at the trial by Browne and Forbes.

NOTE: For the following two meanings, *represent* is not used in the progressive tenses.

represent _____ *constitute, make up*

OBJECT	Her sales represent **half of the company's total.**
	The dessert alone represented **475 calories.**

represent _____ *portray, stand for, signify*

OBJECT	The picture represents **a storm at sea.**
	The scale is a symbol that represents **justice.**
	The availability of the land represents **a real opportunity for us.**
	The sample represents **a typical population.**
	She represents **all that is best about our country.**
	The schwa represents **the unstressed "uh" sound in English words.**
PASSIVE	Terrorist strongholds are represented by the green areas on the map.
OBJECT + *as* PREDICATE NOUN	The lawyer represented **our client** *as a greedy crook.*
	The agent represented **the screenplay** *as a surefire hit.*
PASSIVE	The merger was represented *as our last hope.*
OBJECT + *as* PREDICATE ADJECTIVE	I represented **the proposal** *as risky and costly.*
	The salesman represented **the car** *as almost new.*
PASSIVE	The hotel was represented *as highly desirable.*

PRESENT

I require	we require
you require	you require
he/she/it requires	they require

• *This paint requires extra drying time.*

PRESENT PROGRESSIVE

I am requiring	we are requiring
you are requiring	you are requiring
he/she/it is requiring	they are requiring

• *They are requiring a photo ID now.*

PAST

I required	we required
you required	you required
he/she/it required	they required

• *The rental agency required a deposit.*

PAST PROGRESSIVE

I was requiring	we were requiring
you were requiring	you were requiring
he/she/it was requiring	they were requiring

• *We were requiring registration in advance.*

PRESENT PERFECT ... have | has required
PAST PERFECT ... had required

FUTURE ... will require
FUTURE PROGRESSIVE ... will be requiring
FUTURE PERFECT ... will have required

PAST PASSIVE

I was required	we were required
you were required	you were required
he/she/it was required	they were required

• *He was required to appear in traffic court.*

───(**COMPLEMENTS**)───

require _____ *need*

OBJECT	The project requires **a larger budget.**
	The soup requires **more seasoning.**
	The patient is going to require **surgery.**
	Organic certification requires **avoidance of most synthetic fertilizers and pesticides.**
PASSIVE	Some assembly is required.
PRESENT PARTICIPLE	The floors require **finishing.**
	The food requires **microwaving for five minutes on high.**
	The plants require **watering every other day.**

require _____ *order, demand, make necessary*

OBJECT	The company requires **drug tests** of all applicants.
	This job requires **the ability to multitask.**
OBJECT + INFINITIVE	The government requires **us** *to file form 990-N annually.*
	The airline requires **you** *to stay over Saturday night.*
	The building code requires **public buildings** *to have automatic sprinkler systems.*
PASSIVE	You are required *to have a valid driver's license for this job.*
BASE-FORM THAT-CLAUSE	The law requires **that he be informed of his rights.**
	The committee requires **that each candidate have a current résumé.**
	The court required **that the children be placed in foster care.**

PRESENT

I respond	we respond
you respond	you respond
he/she/it responds	they respond

• *The dog always responds when he's called.*

PRESENT PROGRESSIVE

I am responding	we are responding
you are responding	you are responding
he/she/it is responding	they are responding

• *The patient is not responding, Doctor.*

PAST

I responded	we responded
you responded	you responded
he/she/it responded	they responded

• *The firemen responded to the fire quickly.*

PAST PROGRESSIVE

I was responding	we were responding
you were responding	you were responding
he/she/it was responding	they were responding

• *They were finally responding to the problem.*

PRESENT PERFECT ... have | has responded
PAST PERFECT ... had responded

FUTURE ... will respond
FUTURE PROGRESSIVE ... will be responding
FUTURE PERFECT ... will have responded

PAST PASSIVE

I was responded	we were responded
you were responded	you were responded
he/she/it was responded	they were responded

• *Our complaint was never responded to.*

COMPLEMENTS

respond *reply, answer*	There is no need to respond.
	They will respond if they want to.
	Jim responded without enthusiasm.
	Marty responded by quoting their own words back to them.
respond *show a reaction*	The accident victim wasn't responding.
respond _____ *say/do in answer, react*	
to OBJECT	I need to respond **to his letter.**
	You must respond **to their complaint** in writing.
	The police responded **to the emergency** within minutes.
PASSIVE	The newspaper editorial must be responded to promptly.
to WH-CLAUSE	I responded immediately **to what had happened.**
	We will respond with a press release **to whatever claim they make.**
	The fleet will respond **to whatever move the enemy makes.**
(to OBJECT +) THAT-CLAUSE	They responded **that they would be delighted to come.**
	Carl responded *to her* **that she should come to his house instead.**
	I responded *to the group* **that our plans had changed.**
DIRECT QUOTATION	The tour guide responded, **"Sorry, there is no restroom on this bus."**
respond _____ *react favorably*	
to OBJECT	The infection was finally responding **to antibiotics.**
	Will the cancer respond **to chemotherapy?**

PRESENT

I rest	we rest
you rest	you rest
he/she/it rests	they rest

• *He always rests his arm on the table.*

PRESENT PROGRESSIVE

I am resting	we are resting
you are resting	you are resting
he/she/it is resting	they are resting

• *Not now! I'm resting.*

PAST

I rested	we rested
you rested	you rested
he/she/it rested	they rested

• *The children rested under the tree.*

PAST PROGRESSIVE

I was resting	we were resting
you were resting	you were resting
he/she/it was resting	they were resting

• *We were resting when the call came.*

PRESENT PERFECT ... have | has rested
PAST PERFECT ... had rested

FUTURE ... will rest
FUTURE PROGRESSIVE ... will be resting
FUTURE PERFECT ... will have rested

PAST PASSIVE

I was rested	we were rested
you were rested	you were rested
he/she/it was rested	they were rested

• *The horses were rested for two days.*

COMPLEMENTS

rest *relax, stop working, stop an activity*	Let's take a break. I need to rest. We can rest when we get done. "Let us cross over the river, and rest under the shade of the trees." [GENERAL STONEWALL JACKSON'S LAST WORDS] Darla couldn't rest until she learned who her father was.
rest *stay unchanged, be still*	Just let it rest! And there the matter rests.
rest _____ *support, lay, lean* OBJECT + ADVERB OF PLACE	He rested **his elbows** *on the table*. I lightly rested **my hand** *on his shoulder* to warn him. Jeff rested **his hands** briefly *on the wall*, and then he vaulted over.
rest _____ *be supported, lie, be fixed* ADVERB OF PLACE	My arm rested **on the wheel**, ready to turn it in an instant. His hand was resting **on the gun in his holster**. His arm rested **on her shoulder**. Her eyes rested briefly **on my face**. The shovel rested **against the tree**.
rest _____ *cause to relax / be inactive* OBJECT	I have to rest **my eyes** after working on the computer. The coach will probably rest **some of the best players** in the second half. I should rest **my legs** before we start hiking again.
PASSIVE	The fields are rested every other year.

PHRASAL VERBS

rest in/on/upon _____ *be based on*	His success rests in his ability to delegate.
rest on/upon _____ *depend on*	The team's fate rests on its All-American point guard.
rest up for _____ *relax before exertion*	The runner needs to rest up for the marathon.
rest up from _____ *relax after exertion*	She needs to rest up from the 17-hour flight.
rest with _____ *be the responsibility of*	The success of the class reunion rests with its organizers.

PRESENT

—   —

—   —

it results   they result
- *Rickets results from a lack of vitamin D.*

PAST

—   —

—   —

it resulted   they resulted
- *Deregulation resulted in disaster.*

PRESENT PERFECT ... have | has resulted
PAST PERFECT   ... had resulted

PRESENT PROGRESSIVE

—   —

—   —

it is resulting   they are resulting
- *The decision is resulting in a lot of grief.*

PAST PROGRESSIVE

—   —

—   —

it was resulting   they were resulting
- *His thoughtless action was resulting in hard feelings.*

FUTURE   ... will result
FUTURE PROGRESSIVE ... will be resulting
FUTURE PERFECT   ... will have resulted

PAST PASSIVE

Result is never used in the passive voice.

───(**COMPLEMENTS**)───

result ___ *cause to happen*
    in OBJECT

Haste always results **in confusion.**
The storm resulted **in a massive power failure.**
The committee's rash actions resulted **in a lawsuit.**

result ___ *be caused by*
    from OBJECT

Our failure resulted **from inadequate planning.**
The team's success resulted **from its ability to recruit good players.**
The increase in shipping rates results **from the high cost of insurance.**
A lot of our health problems result **from too much stress in our lives.**

PRESENT

I retain	we retain
you retain	you retain
he/she/it retains	they retain

• *Grandpa retains his sense of humor.*

PRESENT PROGRESSIVE

I am retaining	we are retaining
you are retaining	you are retaining
he/she/it is retaining	they are retaining

• *The company is retaining its high-value employees.*

PAST

I retained	we retained
you retained	you retained
he/she/it retained	they retained

• *The dam retained all of the floodwaters.*

PAST PROGRESSIVE

I was retaining	we were retaining
you were retaining	you were retaining
he/she/it was retaining	they were retaining

• *I was retaining fluid and gaining weight.*

PRESENT PERFECT ... have | has retained
PAST PERFECT ... had retained

FUTURE ... will retain
FUTURE PROGRESSIVE ... will be retaining
FUTURE PERFECT ... will have retained

PAST PASSIVE

I was retained	we were retained
you were retained	you were retained
he/she/it was retained	they were retained

• *Mary was retained as counsel in the case.*

COMPLEMENTS

retain _____ *keep, hold*

OBJECT — Fortunately, our house has retained **its value**.
It is hard to retain **a foreign language** unless you use it.
We seem to retain **our childhood memories** all our lives.
Glass cookware retains **heat** better than metal.
Democrats retained **their majority in the Senate**.
Terry retained **her birth surname** when she married.
The country must retain **its young scientists**.

PASSIVE — Capital letters are retained, as in the original document.

retain _____ *hire by payment of a fee*

OBJECT — You need to retain **a good lawyer**.
The hotel has always retained **an excellent staff**.
We will have to retain **someone to look after the house while we are away**.

PASSIVE — The services of an independent auditor have been retained.

OBJECT + *as* OBJECT — They retained **Ms. Locke** *as a consultant*.
The restaurant retained **her** *as executive chef*.

PASSIVE — I was retained *as an assistant to the treasurer*.

retain _____ *remember, keep in mind*

OBJECT — Nine-year-old David John retains **everything he reads**.

PRESENT

I retire	we retire
you retire	you retire
he/she/it retires	they retire

- *He retires next January.*

PRESENT PROGRESSIVE

I am retiring	we are retiring
you are retiring	you are retiring
he/she/it is retiring	they are retiring

- *I am retiring next year.*

PAST

I retired	we retired
you retired	you retired
he/she/it retired	they retired

- *The ladies retired to the drawing room.*

PAST PROGRESSIVE

I was retiring	we were retiring
you were retiring	you were retiring
he/she/it was retiring	they were retiring

- *The attackers were retiring into the woods.*

PRESENT PERFECT ... have | has retired
PAST PERFECT   ... had retired

FUTURE   ... will retire
FUTURE PROGRESSIVE ... will be retiring
FUTURE PERFECT   ... will have retired

PAST PASSIVE

I was retired	we were retired
you were retired	you were retired
he/she/it was retired	they were retired

- *The mortgage was retired in 1995.*

(**COMPLEMENTS**)

retire *quit working permanently*	He couldn't wait to retire.
	When will you retire?
	I won't retire for at least 10 years.
	Judy and Rich will eventually retire to their cabin in Virginia.
retire *give up one's career/profession*	The team's quarterback had to retire because of knee injuries.
	Dancers often retire from the stage in their thirties.
	Four senators retired, and three others lost re-election.
	Many actors retire because they can't get enough jobs to support themselves full-time.
retire *go to bed*	My parents usually retire around eleven.
	We can't retire until the kids get back home.
	When do you normally retire?
retire *withdraw, retreat*	In times of stress, Mr. Bennet retired to his library.
	The actors retired in confusion after the stage set collapsed.
	The committee has retired into the conference room.
	The troops retired from the battlefield.
retire ____ *remove from a position/office*	
OBJECT	The law retires **judges** when they reach age 75.
	The Pentagon retired **three generals** yesterday.
PASSIVE	He was involuntarily retired by the new administration.
retire ____ *remove from use/production*	
OBJECT	It's time to retire **this old baseball glove**.
	The U.S. government is retiring **its fleet of gas guzzlers**.
	The company will retire **its cosmetics line** next fall.
retire ____ *pay off [a debt]*	
OBJECT	The company retired **the bonds** ten years early.
	You should retire **your mortgage** as soon as possible.
PASSIVE	Older notes and debts are usually retired first.

PRESENT

I return	we return
you return	you return
he/she/it returns	they return

    • *He returns to Los Angeles next week.*

PRESENT PROGRESSIVE

I am returning	we are returning
you are returning	you are returning
he/she/it is returning	they are returning

    • *I am returning your call.*

PAST

I returned	we returned
you returned	you returned
he/she/it returned	they returned

    • *I returned the book to the library yesterday.*

PAST PROGRESSIVE

I was returning	we were returning
you were returning	you were returning
he/she/it was returning	they were returning

    • *We were returning home when the car broke down.*

PRESENT PERFECT ... have | has returned
PAST PERFECT ... had returned

FUTURE ... will return
FUTURE PROGRESSIVE ... will be returning
FUTURE PERFECT ... will have returned

PAST PASSIVE

I was returned	we were returned
you were returned	you were returned
he/she/it was returned	they were returned

    • *The letter was returned by the post office.*

―――――――――――――――――――――――――――――――― (**COMPLEMENTS**)――――

return *go/come back*

The visitors will return after lunch.
"I came through and I shall return."
     [GENERAL DOUGLAS MACARTHUR]
The rains have finally returned.
Her good humor quickly returned.
My appetite has returned.

return _____ *go/come back*
ADVERB OF PLACE TO/FROM

When will our neighbors return **from vacation?**
He will return **to his country** in the fall.
Shouldn't they return **home?**
Johanna and Tim just returned **from Vietnam.**
Larry returned **to work** two weeks after surgery.
She gradually returned **to full health.**
After the interruption, I returned **to my book.**

return _____ *send/give/carry/put back*
OBJECT (+ ADVERB OF PLACE TO/FROM)

Nikki returned **the skirt** for a larger size.
Fill out this form and return **it** *to this address.*
Return **visitor passes** *here* when you are ready to leave.
My son returned **the ladder** *to the garage.*
Harrison returned **the opening kickoff** *to the 40-yard line.*
Voters returned **the governor** *to office.*

PASSIVE   Keys must be returned *to the front desk.*

return _____ *respond to in the same way*
OBJECT

She returned **his kiss.**
We will return **your hospitality** as soon as we can.

return _____ *yield, produce*
OBJECT

The bonds will return **10% a year.**
We hope to return **a profit** in our second year.
Our investment didn't return **a penny.**

return _____ *send something back in a certain condition*
OBJECT + PAST PARTICIPLE

The post office returned **the package** *marked "undeliverable."*
She returned **his letter** *unopened.*

PASSIVE   His manuscript was returned *unread.*

PRESENT		PRESENT PROGRESSIVE	
I reveal	we reveal	I am revealing	we are revealing
you reveal	you reveal	you are revealing	you are revealing
he/she/it reveals	they reveal	he/she/it is revealing	they are revealing

• *He never reveals what he is going to do.*   • *I am not revealing any secrets.*

PAST		PAST PROGRESSIVE	
I revealed	we revealed	I was revealing	we were revealing
you revealed	you revealed	you were revealing	you were revealing
he/she/it revealed	they revealed	he/she/it was revealing	they were revealing

• *Jane's letter revealed some terrible news.*   • *The CEO was revealing his master plan to the board.*

PRESENT PERFECT	... have | has revealed
PAST PERFECT	... had revealed

FUTURE	... will reveal
FUTURE PROGRESSIVE	... will be revealing
FUTURE PERFECT	... will have revealed

PAST PASSIVE	
I was revealed	we were revealed
you were revealed	you were revealed
he/she/it was revealed	they were revealed

• *The information was revealed at a press conference.*

                (**COMPLEMENTS**)

reveal _____ *show / make known [what was unknown/secret]*

OBJECT	John revealed **the new budget** at the meeting.
	The lawyers will not reveal **the contents of the will**.
	His book revealed **previously classified information about the war**.
	The report reveals **her role in health care reform**.
PASSIVE	The president's nominee will be revealed at a press conference today.
OBJECT + INFINITIVE	The evidence revealed **her** *to have been murdered*.
	The audit revealed **the company** *to be running at a loss*.
	Harold revealed **their decision** *to have been a mistake*.
(to OBJECT +) THAT-CLAUSE	The museum revealed **that the artifacts had been improperly obtained**.
	He revealed *to the employees* **that the company would be sold**.
	Marsha revealed *to her friends* **that she had been secretly married to John**.
WH-CLAUSE	The police will not reveal **whom they suspect**.
	I can't reveal **what was decided**.
	He never revealed **why he did it**.

PRESENT

I rid	we rid
you rid	you rid
he/she/it rids	they rid

• *The cat rids the barn of mice.*

PAST

I rid	we rid
you rid	you rid
he/she/it rid	they rid

• *They rid themselves of all their coats.*

PRESENT PERFECT … have | has rid
PAST PERFECT … had rid

PRESENT PROGRESSIVE

I am ridding	we are ridding
you are ridding	you are ridding
he/she/it is ridding	they are ridding

• *The store is ridding itself of unsold merchandise.*

PAST PROGRESSIVE

I was ridding	we were ridding
you were ridding	you were ridding
he/she/it was ridding	they were ridding

• *I was ridding myself of all my junk.*

FUTURE … will rid
FUTURE PROGRESSIVE … will be ridding
FUTURE PERFECT … will have rid

PAST PASSIVE

I was rid	we were rid
you were rid	you were rid
he/she/it was rid	they were rid

• *We were finally rid of unwanted visitors.*

─────────────────────────────────────── (**COMPLEMENTS**)───

rid _____ *free from [someone/something not wanted]*

OBJECT + *of* OBJECT   They hoped to rid **the world** *of nuclear weapons.*
I can't rid **myself** *of this miserable cold.*
You must rid **yourself** *of all debt.*
They were trying to rid **the field** *of all noxious weeds.*
The alderman wants to rid **the city** *of one-way streets.*
The sheriff is trying to rid **the county** *of drug dealers.*
"Will no one rid **me** *of this troublesome priest?*" [HENRY II,
LEADING TO THE MURDER OF THOMAS BECKET IN 1170]

PASSIVE   The tent was rid *of all mosquitoes.*

PRESENT

I ride	we ride
you ride	you ride
he/she/it rides	they ride

• *He rides the bus to work every day.*

PRESENT PROGRESSIVE

I am riding	we are riding
you are riding	you are riding
he/she/it is riding	they are riding

• *Our hopes are riding on the new government.*

PAST

I rode	we rode
you rode	you rode
he/she/it rode	they rode

• *I rode my bicycle to the store yesterday.*

PAST PROGRESSIVE

I was riding	we were riding
you were riding	you were riding
he/she/it was riding	they were riding

• *He was riding in the first race.*

PRESENT PERFECT	... have | has ridden
PAST PERFECT	... had ridden

FUTURE	... will ride
FUTURE PROGRESSIVE	... will be riding
FUTURE PERFECT	... will have ridden

PAST PASSIVE

—	—
—	—
it was ridden	they were ridden

• *That horse was last ridden a week ago.*

───────────────────────(COMPLEMENTS)───────────

ride *sit on a horse/bicycle/motorcycle/ etc. and make it move along*

Do you know how to ride?
She rides quite well.
You never forget how to ride.
The cowboys rode 70 miles the first day.

ride *move along in a vehicle*

He never rides when he can walk.
I rode to work that day.
They rode in a school bus to the meeting.

ride _____ *sit on and make move along*
   OBJECT

The kids were riding **their bicycles** in the park.
We rented horses and rode **them** all afternoon.

ride _____ *move along in/on*
   OBJECT

We rode **the train** when we were in Germany.
I usually ride **the bus** to work.
They rode **every ride** at Disneyland.

ride _____ *be carried along on/by*
   OBJECT

The surfers were riding **the waves**.
Investors rode **the boom in housing** for 20 years.
The TV networks were still riding **the fad of reality TV**.

ride _____ *tease, nag*
   OBJECT

The girls are constantly riding **each other** about music.
I had better get back to work. The boss is really riding **us**.

───────────────────────(PHRASAL VERBS)───────────

ride away/down/off/out/up/etc.
move along in a specified direction

Marvin stopped by to talk, then rode off.
We rode out to the ferry landing this morning.

ride on _____ *depend on*

The company's reputation is riding on these negotiations.
All his hopes are riding on being promoted to news anchor.

ride _SEP_ **out** *survive in safety*

We rode the storm out in the basement.
Can our company ride out these perilous economic times?

ride up *move upward out of place*

His jeans rode up as he jogged across the parking lot.

PRESENT		PRESENT PROGRESSIVE	
I ring	we ring	I am ringing	we are ringing
you ring	you ring	you are ringing	you are ringing
he/she/it rings	they ring	he/she/it is ringing	they are ringing

• *The bell rings on the quarter hour.* • *Your alarm clock is ringing.*

PAST		PAST PROGRESSIVE	
I rang	we rang	I was ringing	we were ringing
you rang	you rang	you were ringing	you were ringing
he/she/it rang	they rang	he/she/it was ringing	they were ringing

• *The phone rang as I was doing dishes.* • *The phone was ringing all morning.*

PRESENT PERFECT	... have | has rung
PAST PERFECT	... had rung

FUTURE	... will ring
FUTURE PROGRESSIVE	... will be ringing
FUTURE PERFECT	... will have rung

PAST PASSIVE	
I was rung	we were rung
you were rung	you were rung
he/she/it was rung	they were rung

• *The church bell was rung every Sunday for years.*

NOTE: The irregular verb *ring* is presented here. The regular verb *ring* (*ring* | *rings* · *ringed* · *ringed*) means "surround, form a circle around," as in *Cypress trees ring the lake.*

COMPLEMENTS

ring *make the sound of a bell*	All of the church bells were ringing.
	Good wine glasses will ring if you tap them.
ring *call for service by telephone/bell*	If you need help, just ring.
	We rang, but nobody came.
	Please ring for service.
ring *fill a place with sound*	The sound of cannons rang through the air.
ring *be filled with sound*	The halls rang with laughter as the students left for the holiday.
	After the explosion, my ears rang for half an hour.
ring _____ *cause [a bell/alarm] to sound*	
OBJECT	I knocked and rang **the doorbell.**
	It takes a lot of practice to ring **the big church bells.**
PASSIVE	The bells are always rung on Easter.
ring _____ *seem to be*	
PREDICATE ADJECTIVE	The immigrant's story rings **true.**
	Harry's apology rang **hollow.**

PHRASAL VERBS

ring out *sound clearly and loudly*	Three shots rang out in the crisp autumn air.
ring SEP up *record the price of [something] on a cash register*	The cashier rang up the cauliflower at $1.99 a head.

EXPRESSIONS

ring a bell *seem familiar*	You're right—that name rings a bell.
ring in the new (year), ring out the old *celebrate the beginning of the new year*	We ring in the new year by watching the ball drop at New York's Times Square.
ring off the hook *ring constantly*	I got nothing done this morning—the phone was ringing off the hook.

PRESENT

I rise	we rise
you rise	you rise
he/she/it rises	they rise

  • *The land slowly rises toward the hills.*

PRESENT PROGRESSIVE

I am rising	we are rising
you are rising	you are rising
he/she/it is rising	they are rising

  • *His temperature is still rising.*

PAST

I rose	we rose
you rose	you rose
he/she/it rose	they rose

  • *The river rose until the banks overflowed.*

PAST PROGRESSIVE

I was rising	we were rising
you were rising	you were rising
he/she/it was rising	they were rising

  • *Prices were steadily rising.*

PRESENT PERFECT ... have | has risen
PAST PERFECT   ... had risen

FUTURE   ... will rise
FUTURE PROGRESSIVE ... will be rising
FUTURE PERFECT   ... will have risen

PAST PASSIVE

Risen is never used in the passive voice.

COMPLEMENTS

rise *go to a higher level*

The tide will be rising until four.
The moon was just rising above the trees.
A loud cheer rose from the spectators.
White smoke was rising from the chimney.
The Beatles rose to fame overnight.
Carly rose to be CEO of a Fortune 500 company.
He rose from office boy to company director.

rise *stand/get up*

All rise! [COMMAND ISSUED WHEN A JUDGE ENTERS
     A COURTROOM]
He rose from the couch and turned off the TV.
We usually rise before dawn.

rise *become greater/higher/stronger*

As we start going downhill, our speed will rise rapidly.
The Roman Empire rose and fell.
Stock prices rose two percent today.
My income has not risen as much as inflation has.
During the concert, the noise rose to unbearable levels.
The hills steadily rose as we drove northward.
The bread dough was rising quickly.
His voice rose to a pitiful squeak.
Gas prices have been rising lately.
The wind rose to near gale force.

PHRASAL VERBS

rise above _____ *ignore [a bad situation]*

The legislators rose above their
  petty disagreements and passed an excellent bill.

rise up (against _____ **)** *rebel/revolt*
(against [someone/something])

The colonists rose up against George III and his army.

EXPRESSIONS

rise and shine *get out of bed and be
energetic*

Rise and shine! We've got a big day
ahead of us.

rise to the occasion *succeed in dealing
with a difficult situation*

The president rose to the occasion and delivered
a forceful, inspiring speech.

PRESENT

I roll	we roll
you roll	you roll
he/she/it rolls	they roll

• *Sometimes the ball rolls into the gutter.*

PRESENT PROGRESSIVE

I am rolling	we are rolling
you are rolling	you are rolling
he/she/it is rolling	they are rolling

• *The ship is rolling pretty badly.*

PAST

I rolled	we rolled
you rolled	you rolled
he/she/it rolled	they rolled

• *I rolled the wheelbarrow out of the garage.*

PAST PROGRESSIVE

I was rolling	we were rolling
you were rolling	you were rolling
he/she/it was rolling	they were rolling

• *The waves were rolling onto the beach.*

PRESENT PERFECT ... have | has rolled
PAST PERFECT ... had rolled

FUTURE ... will roll
FUTURE PROGRESSIVE ... will be rolling
FUTURE PERFECT ... will have rolled

PAST PASSIVE

—	—
—	—
it was rolled	they were rolled

• *The dough was rolled out until it was quite thin.*

COMPLEMENTS

roll *move on wheels*	Look out—the car is rolling!
roll *move by turning over and over*	The kittens rolled all over the bed. The ball rolled down the driveway and into the street. Her necklace broke and the beads rolled across the floor.
roll *move/rock back and forth*	The plane was rolling uncontrollably. The ship was rolling in a most uncomfortable way.
roll ____ *move on wheels/rollers* OBJECT + ADVERB OF PLACE TO/FROM PASSIVE	We rolled **the car** *down the driveway*. I rolled **the grocery cart** *to the checkout*. The patient was rolled *into Radiology*.
roll ____ *turn over and over* OBJECT + ADVERB OF PLACE TO/FROM	We rolled **the logs** *down the hill*. The kids rolled **the ball** *back and forth*.
roll ____ *form into a ball/tube* OBJECT + ADVERB OF PLACE TO/FROM	He rolled **the cookie dough** *into balls*. She rolled **the rugs** *into tight cylinders*.

PHRASAL VERBS

roll about/away/back/by/down/in/off/out/ over/up/etc. *move in a specified direction*	A late-model Porsche just rolled by. The puppy rolled over.
roll _SEP_ **away/back/in/out/up**/etc. *cause to move in a specified direction*	The trash men rolled the barrels away. Roll the windows up; it's windy.
roll around *happen, arrive*	When fall rolls around, we'll get out our winter clothing.
roll _SEP_ **back** *reduce*	The drugstore rolled back prices on vitamins.
roll by *move past*	The years roll by.
roll _SEP_ **out** *introduce*	The company rolled out its latest allergy drug.
roll _SEP_ **out** *flatten*	Mom was rolling out the pie dough.

PRESENT

I rule	we rule
you rule	you rule
he/she/it rules	they rule

• *The court rules in favor of the defendant.*

PRESENT PROGRESSIVE

I am ruling	we are ruling
you are ruling	you are ruling
he/she/it is ruling	they are ruling

• *We are ruling in the defendant's favor.*

PAST

I ruled	we ruled
you ruled	you ruled
he/she/it ruled	they ruled

• *Henry VIII ruled from 1509 to 1547.*

PAST PROGRESSIVE

I was ruling	we were ruling
you were ruling	you were ruling
he/she/it was ruling	they were ruling

• *Fear was ruling everyone's life.*

PRESENT PERFECT ... have | has ruled
PAST PERFECT   ... had ruled

FUTURE   ... will rule
FUTURE PROGRESSIVE ... will be ruling
FUTURE PERFECT   ... will have ruled

PAST PASSIVE

I was ruled	we were ruled
you were ruled	you were ruled
he/she/it was ruled	they were ruled

• *The law was eventually ruled unconstitutional.*

───(**COMPLEMENTS**)───

rule *make an official decision*	When will the judge rule? The judge ruled against admitting new evidence.
rule *prevail, govern*	During the conflict, chaos ruled. When the financial markets are fluctuating wildly, caution rules. In the long run, the law of supply and demand always rules.

rule _____ *decide officially*

OBJECT + (to be) PREDICATE NOUN	The referee ruled **the personal foul *(to be) a flagrant one.*** The judge ruled **the crime *(to be) a misdemeanor.***
OBJECT + (to be) PREDICATE ADJECTIVE	The court ruled **us *(to be) legally responsible for the accident.*** The judge ruled **the defendant *(to be) innocent.*** The judge ruled **the driver of the van *(to be) guilty.***
THAT-CLAUSE	The court ruled **that the defendant was guilty.** The judge ruled **that the motion was out of order.** The committee ruled **that Henry was due overtime pay.**
BASE-FORM THAT-CLAUSE	The court ruled **that the defendant be sentenced to five years in the state penitentiary.** The judge ruled **that he be released without charges.** He ruled **that the company be charged with tax evasion.**

rule _____ *govern, have power/control over*

OBJECT	Elizabeth I ruled **England, Ireland, and Wales.** During the Napoleonic era, England ruled **the oceans.** Fear of the plague ruled **the city.**
PASSIVE	Our day-to-day lives are ruled by convention and habit.
WH-CLAUSE	The king ruled **who could and could not become a noble.** The referee ruled **which team would be considered the visitors.** Our budget rules **how much we can afford to spend.**

───(**PHRASAL VERBS**)───

rule _SEP_ **out** *eliminate from consideration*	We ruled three applicants out because they didn't have a college degree. Senator Blather isn't ruling out running for president. The legislators wouldn't rule out a tax increase on cigarettes.

run _____ _perform_ OBJECT	Can you run **some errands** for me? The doctor will need to run **some tests**.
run _____ _cost_ [INFORMAL] (INDIRECT OBJECT +) DIRECT OBJECT	The shipping will run **$8.95**. The trip will run *you* about **$500**.
run _____ _publish_ OBJECT	The newspaper ran **a series of articles on homeless people**. Our company ran **an ad** in the July issue.
run _____ _be [at a certain level]_ PREDICATE ADJECTIVE	The store is running **low** on toilet paper. We ran **late** getting to the theater.

―――――――――――――――――――――――――――――――(**PHRASAL VERBS**)―――

run across _____ _come upon by chance_	We ran across our cousins at the farmers' market. We ran across old photos of Great-grandfather.
run against _____ _be a candidate opposing_	Senator Blather ran against gun control. She ran against another alderman in the primary.
run along _go away_	Why don't you kids run along? Be back here in two hours.
run (around) with _____ _socialize with_	Tara runs around with her friends from high school.
run _____ **by/past** _seek advice about / approval for [something] from_	Sam ran the speech by Toby.
run _SEP_ **down** _drain all the power from_	Stop trying to start the car; you're running the battery down.
run _SEP_ **down** _criticize_	Brandi ran down the rest of the group.
run for _____ _be a candidate for_	The governor is running for a fourth term.
run _____ **for** _support [someone] as a candidate for_	The party ran an unknown businessman for mayor.
run into _____ _collide with_	My sister ran into a deer on the highway.
run into _____ _meet by chance_	Janey ran into Hulga at the grocery store.
run _SEP_ **off** _print, make copies of_	I ran off several extra sets for you.
run on _____ _use for power_	Our hybrid car runs on gasoline and an NiMH battery.
run on _continue without stopping_	The presentation of awards ran on forever.
run out _come to an end, be used up_	Time is running out, and I still have four questions to answer. Our supply of helium ran out—no more balloons!
run out of _____ _use up_	Mom finally ran out of patience with us kids. They ran out of popcorn before the second show.
run over _overflow_	Quick! The bathtub is running over.
run over _____ _knock down while driving_	Her friend ran over a skunk.
run over _____ _exceed a limit_	The class was supposed to last an hour, but it ran over.
run _SEP_ **over** _bring [something]_	Would you run the latest proposal over to my office?
run through _____ _use up_	Shane ran through his inheritance in a year.
run to _____ _amount to_	The grocery bill runs to $123.44. Homer's *Odyssey* runs to more than 12,000 lines.
run _SEP_ **up** _accumulate [debt]_	George ran up a sizable tab at the luxury hotel.
run _SEP_ **up** _cause to increase_	Technology gains ran stock prices up. The Cobras ran up a big lead, then benched their starters.
run up against _____ _encounter_	He finally ran up against a problem he couldn't solve.

PRESENT

I run	we run
you run	you run
he/she/it runs	they run

- *The road runs west to the river.*

PAST

I ran	we ran
you ran	you ran
he/she/it ran	they ran

- *The children ran through the door.*

PRESENT PERFECT ... have | has run
PAST PERFECT   ... had run

PRESENT PROGRESSIVE

I am running	we are running
you are running	you are running
he/she/it is running	they are running

- *He is running in the Boston Marathon.*

PAST PROGRESSIVE

I was running	we were running
you were running	you were running
he/she/it was running	they were running

- *The program was running a little late.*

FUTURE   ... will run
FUTURE PROGRESSIVE ... will be running
FUTURE PERFECT   ... will have run

PAST PASSIVE

I was run	we were run
you were run	you were run
he/she/it was run	they were run

- *The store was run by Harry and his children.*

COMPLEMENTS

run *go by moving one's legs faster than in walking*	The kids never stop running. I try to run two miles every day. The tiger has escaped! Run!
run *flow* [OF LIQUIDS]	The Missouri River runs into the Mississippi River at St. Louis. The paint was too thin. It was running down the wall in streaks.
run *spread, move freely*	A murmur ran through the crowd. A light breeze ran through the tall grass.
run *operate, be in use/action*	The train runs three times a day. The engine is not running very smoothly. The network servers are not running.
run _____ *operate* OBJECT	Do you know how to run **this printing press**? She can run **any equipment in the woodworking shop**.
run _____ *manage* OBJECT	He runs **the local supermarket**. The church runs **a preschool program**.
run _____ *go* ADVERB OF PLACE TO/FROM	I need to run **to the bank**. We've got to run **home** for something. The ferry runs **from Modoc to Ste. Genevieve and back**.
run _____ *transport* OBJECT + ADVERB OF PLACE TO/FROM	Can you run **me** *back to the office*? I will run **you** *over to the station*.
run _____ *continue, extend* ADVERB OF TIME	The festival runs **for four weeks in June**. The fiscal year runs **from July 1 to June 30**. The literature class runs **every quarter**.
ADVERB OF PLACE TO/FROM	This path runs **up the bluff to the reservoir**.
run _____ *cause to continue/extend* OBJECT + ADVERB OF PLACE TO/FROM	We ran **electrical conduit** *under the floor*. The logging company ran **a gravel road** *out to the camp*.

PRESENT

I rush	we rush
you rush	you rush
he/she/it rushes	they rush

• *He rushes into situations without thinking.*

PRESENT PROGRESSIVE

I am rushing	we are rushing
you are rushing	you are rushing
he/she/it is rushing	they are rushing

• *We are rushing your order.*

PAST

I rushed	we rushed
you rushed	you rushed
he/she/it rushed	they rushed

• *We rushed the shipment.*

PAST PROGRESSIVE

I was rushing	we were rushing
you were rushing	you were rushing
he/she/it was rushing	they were rushing

• *I was rushing to get everything done.*

PRESENT PERFECT ... have | has rushed
PAST PERFECT ... had rushed

FUTURE ... will rush
FUTURE PROGRESSIVE ... will be rushing
FUTURE PERFECT ... will have rushed

PAST PASSIVE

I was rushed	we were rushed
you were rushed	you were rushed
he/she/it was rushed	they were rushed

• *I was rushed to the hospital in an ambulance.*

COMPLEMENTS

rush *move/act quickly, hurry*

Take your time; don't rush.
We are late, so we will have to rush.

rush _____ *move quickly, hurry*
ADVERB OF PLACE TO/FROM

I rushed **after the taxi.**
Firefighters rushed **to the scene of the warehouse fire.**
Water was rushing **down the street.**
The wind was rushing **through my hair.**
The young couple rushed **into marriage.**

rush _____ *do/make quickly*
OBJECT

The printer rushed **the invitations,** and the date was wrong.
Don't rush **the job.** Make it perfect.

rush _____ *cause/force to act quickly*
OBJECT

I don't want to rush **you,** but the store is about to close.
I hate salesmen who try to rush **me.**

PASSIVE

He wasn't rushed by the manager.

rush _____ *deliver/send quickly*
OBJECT + ADVERB OF PLACE TO/FROM

They rushed **the patient** *to the emergency room.*
The Red Cross rushed **workers** *to the flooded area.*

INDIRECT OBJECT + DIRECT OBJECT

Can you rush *me* **six copies of the book**?
We will rush *you* **the contract** overnight.

to PARAPHRASE

Can you rush **six copies of the book** *to me*?
We will rush **the contract** *to you* overnight.

rush _____ *attack suddenly*
OBJECT

Santa Anna's army rushed **the Alamo.**
Longstreet's infantry rushed **the center of the Union line.**

PHRASAL VERBS

rush around/down/in/off/out/up/etc.
move quickly in a specified direction

Volunteers rushed around making
  everyone comfortable.

rush SEP **down/in**/etc. *move [someone/ something] quickly in a specified direction*

Hospitals rushed medical supplies in.

PRESENT

I satisfy	we satisfy
you satisfy	you satisfy
he/she/it satisfies	they satisfy

- *His qualifications satisfy our criteria.*

PAST

I satisfied	we satisfied
you satisfied	you satisfied
he/she/it satisfied	they satisfied

- *Her answers satisfied the examiners.*

PRESENT PERFECT ... have | has satisfied
PAST PERFECT ... had satisfied

PRESENT PROGRESSIVE

I am satisfying	we are satisfying
you are satisfying	you are satisfying
he/she/it is satisfying	they are satisfying

- *He is not satisfying any of the critics.*

PAST PROGRESSIVE

I was satisfying	we were satisfying
you were satisfying	you were satisfying
he/she/it was satisfying	they were satisfying

- *She was only satisfying her curiosity.*

FUTURE ... will satisfy
FUTURE PROGRESSIVE ... will be satisfying
FUTURE PERFECT ... will have satisfied

PAST PASSIVE

I was satisfied	we were satisfied
you were satisfied	you were satisfied
he/she/it was satisfied	they were satisfied

- *They were satisfied with his explanation.*

COMPLEMENTS

satisfy _____ *meet the needs/wishes/expectations of*

OBJECT

His work satisfied **the client**.
Was that enough food to satisfy **your hunger**?
The design satisfied **all the requirements**.
Only the Nobel Prize will satisfy **him**.
This cell phone has satisfied **all my expectations**.
The actor satisfied **the director** with his portrayal of Sinbad.

NOTE: *Satisfy is one of the few verbs that uses* with *(instead of* by*) to introduce the passive agent.*

PASSIVE

The committee was satisfied with his work.

satisfy _____ *convince*

OBJECT + THAT-CLAUSE

I satisfied **myself** *that we were on the right track*.
Joan satisfied **us** *that Harold could do the job well*.
We have to satisfy **the press** *that the senator had no conflict of interest*.

PASSIVE

Everybody was satisfied *that he was telling the truth*.

EXPRESSIONS

satisfy a/[one's] debt
pay off a debt

The prisoner has satisfied his debt to society.

I save	we save
you save	you save
he/she/it saves	they save

• *He saves money by riding a bike to work.*

I am saving	we are saving
you are saving	you are saving
he/she/it is saving	they are saving

• *I am saving cardboard for recycling.*

I saved	we saved
you saved	you saved
he/she/it saved	they saved

• *I saved my store receipt.*

I was saving	we were saving
you were saving	you were saving
he/she/it was saving	they were saving

• *We were saving as much as we could.*

PRESENT PERFECT ... have | has saved
PAST PERFECT ... had saved

FUTURE ... will save
FUTURE PROGRESSIVE ... will be saving
FUTURE PERFECT ... will have saved

PAST PASSIVE
I was saved	we were saved
you were saved	you were saved
he/she/it was saved	they were saved

• *The money was saved for just that purpose.*

(COMPLEMENTS)

save _____ *rescue/keep from harm/danger*

OBJECT

The farmers were trying to save **their animals** from the flood.
We want to save **the old train station.**

PASSIVE

The passengers were saved by the prompt action of the crew.

WH-CLAUSE

They could only save **what they could carry.**
We will save **whatever we can.**

save _____ *keep/store for future use*

OBJECT (+ *for* OBJECT)

Save **the file** before you turn off the computer.
I am saving **room** *for dessert.*
We are saving **our money** *for a down payment on a house.*
We need to save **some time after the presentation** *for discussion.*

PASSIVE

The champagne is being saved *for a special occasion.*

INDIRECT OBJECT + DIRECT OBJECT

We saved *you* **some dinner.**
Save *me* **a seat,** will you?

for PARAPHRASE

We saved **some dinner** *for you.*
Save **a seat** *for me,* will you?

save _____ *keep from being wasted/lost*

OBJECT

We saved **money** by fixing the dishwasher ourselves.
You can save **time** with these shortcuts.

save _____ *avoid/reduce [expense / use of resources]*

(*on*) OBJECT

Carpooling saves **(on) transportation costs.**
Turning the computers off saves **(on) electricity.**
The new freeway will save **(on) commuting time.**

INDIRECT OBJECT + DIRECT OBJECT

It will save *us* **a lot of trouble.**
The plan will save *the company* **a fortune in electric bills.**
Online deposit saves *me* **a trip to the bank.**

for PARAPHRASE

It will save **a lot of trouble** *for us.*
The plan will save **a fortune in electric bills** *for the company.*

(OBJECT + *from*) PRESENT PARTICIPLE

The compact florescents save **replacing bulbs every month.**
The new trail saves *me from* **having to walk through town.**
My parking permit saves *me from* **having to park on the street.**

PRESENT

I saw	we saw
you saw	you saw
he/she/it saws	they saw

• *He saws plywood with a special blade.*

PRESENT PROGRESSIVE

I am sawing	we are sawing
you are sawing	you are sawing
he/she/it is sawing	they are sawing

• *I am sawing fence posts.*

PAST

I sawed	we sawed
you sawed	you sawed
he/she/it sawed	they sawed

• *I sawed the board in half.*

PAST PROGRESSIVE

I was sawing	we were sawing
you were sawing	you were sawing
he/she/it was sawing	they were sawing

• *He was sawing as fast as he could.*

PRESENT PERFECT ... have | has sawed/sawn
PAST PERFECT ... had sawed/sawn

FUTURE ... will saw
FUTURE PROGRESSIVE ... will be sawing
FUTURE PERFECT ... will have sawed/sawn

PAST PASSIVE

—	—
—	—
it was sawed/sawn	they were sawed/sawn

• *The beams were sawn nearly through.*

COMPLEMENTS

saw *cut using a saw*

We have been sawing all afternoon.
I will have to saw at an angle.
Look out for nails when you saw.
The new blade saws smoothly.

saw *be cut using a saw*

These pine two-by-fours saw very easily.

saw *use a sawing motion*

Holmes was sawing on his violin.
When he jumped off the cliff, his arms sawed up and down.

saw _____ *cut/shape using a saw*
OBJECT

We are sawing **oak planks** for flooring.
I will saw **the sheets of fiberglass** with a special blade.
John sawed **the boards** into two-foot lengths.
They have sawn **a lot of timber** this week.
We were sawing **jigsaw puzzles** out of masonite.

PASSIVE

The lumber had been sawn against the grain.

PHRASAL VERBS

saw at _____ *cut back and forth using a knife/bar/etc.*

The prisoner was sawing at the window bars with a table knife.

saw _SEP_ **down** *cut down*

The lumberjacks sawed the entire woods down.

saw _SEP_ **off** *cut off*

She sawed off the branches that she could reach.

saw _SEP_ **up** *cut into pieces*

Gerry sawed the board up into seven pieces of equal length.

PRESENT

I say	we say
you say	you say
he/she/it says	they say

- *He always says that he is too busy.*

PRESENT PROGRESSIVE

I am saying	we are saying
you are saying	you are saying
he/she/it is saying	they are saying

- *I am not saying anything.*

PAST

I said	we said
you said	you said
he/she/it said	they said

- *She said something I couldn't understand.*

PAST PROGRESSIVE

I was saying	we were saying
you were saying	you were saying
he/she/it was saying	they were saying

- *We were saying that it wouldn't be a problem.*

PRESENT PERFECT ... have | has said
PAST PERFECT ... had said

FUTURE ... will say
FUTURE PROGRESSIVE ... will be saying
FUTURE PERFECT ... will have said

PAST PASSIVE

I was said	we were said
you were said	you were said
he/she/it was said	they were said

- *They were said to be in the oil business.*

COMPLEMENTS

say _____ *speak, put into words, express*

OBJECT	He said **the right answer.**
	The teacher said **"hello" in Latin.**
	They said **nothing about it.**
	Would you say **your name** again, slowly?
PASSIVE	His name was said, but I didn't catch it.
INFINITIVE	He said **to go ahead without him.**
	The tour guide says **to be back on the bus in 15 minutes.**
	The recipe said **to use only the egg whites.**
	Her note said **to leave the back door unlocked.**
THAT-CLAUSE	They said **that they would come back later.**
	The law says **that everyone is presumed to be innocent.**
	He said **that we should expect snow.**
WH-CLAUSE	He never said **what he meant to do about the problem.**
	Did he say **when they were coming?**
WH-INFINITIVE	The instructions say **how to attach the handlebars.**
DIRECT QUOTATION	**"Good morning,"** she said. **"We're glad you're here."**

say _____ *show, indicate*

OBJECT	The clock says **2:15.**
	His expression said **it all.**
(to OBJECT +) THAT-CLAUSE	The tone of his voice says **that he's disappointed.**
	My instinct says *to me* **that we should really be cautious.**
WH-CLAUSE	Their veto says **what they think about the proposal.**

be said _____ *be commonly reported* [USED ONLY IN THE PASSIVE]

INFINITIVE	She was said to be one of the best lawyers around.
	He is said to take forever to make up his mind.

EXPRESSIONS

have _____ **to say for yourself** *be able to say in one's favor/defense*

The defendant had nothing to say for himself.
What do you have to say for yourself, young man?

say the word *give a signal*

When I say the word, jump out and shout "Happy Birthday!"

say yes/no (to _____ **)** *agree/disagree (with [someone/something])*

Sarah said yes to Lucas when he proposed to her.
Just say no to drugs.

PRESENT

I search	we search
you search	you search
he/she/it searches	they search

- *The guard always searches my briefcase.*

PRESENT PROGRESSIVE

I am searching	we are searching
you are searching	you are searching
he/she/it is searching	they are searching

- *We are searching everywhere for a stapler.*

PAST

I searched	we searched
you searched	you searched
he/she/it searched	they searched

- *The police searched the house thoroughly.*

PAST PROGRESSIVE

I was searching	we were searching
you were searching	you were searching
he/she/it was searching	they were searching

- *They were searching the Internet for the information.*

PRESENT PERFECT ... have | has searched
PAST PERFECT ... had searched

FUTURE ... will search
FUTURE PROGRESSIVE ... will be searching
FUTURE PERFECT ... will have searched

PAST PASSIVE

I was searched	we were searched
you were searched	you were searched
he/she/it was searched	they were searched

- *He was searched before he was allowed to enter.*

COMPLEMENTS

search *try to find something by looking*

Should we start searching?
We need to keep searching until we find it.
How long did the volunteers search?

search _____ *try to find by looking*

for OBJECT

What are the auditors searching **for?**
The teacher is searching **for the missing tests.**
The police are searching **for clues.**

search _____ *try to find [something] by examining carefully*

ADVERB OF PLACE

They searched **in the woods.**
I searched **everywhere** but never found my keys.
We still have to search **in the attic and garage.**

OBJECT

They were searching **everybody who entered the building.**
Did they search **the car?**
They only searched **backpacks and handbags.**

PASSIVE

All of the suitcases have been searched.

OBJECT + *for* OBJECT

You can search **the Web *for population statistics.***
The FBI searched **his house *for illegal drugs.***
Would you search **the living room *for the TV remote*?**
I searched **the report *for evidence of wrongdoing.***

PASSIVE

The house was searched *for illegal drugs.*

PHRASAL VERBS

search after _____ *seek / look for*
[something abstract]

The philosopher is searching after the truth.

search out _____ *look for and find*

Donna searched out the data that Josh required.

search through _____ *try to find*
something by examining the contents of

I searched through the archives.
They even searched through my dirty laundry.

EXPRESSIONS

search high and low for _____
try to find by looking carefully in every
possible place

We searched high and low for the
  missing photos.

see _____ *meet with, visit*	
OBJECT	I will see **the reporters** at 2 o'clock.
	Guess **whom** I saw today?
	Would you stop by and see **Aunt Tillie**?
PASSIVE	You will be seen by the next available doctor.
see _____ *seek advice/information/help from*	
OBJECT	You should see **a doctor** about that rash.
	Steve saw **a cancer specialist** today.
	Alexander is seeing **his thesis advisor** on Tuesday.
see _____ *find out*	
WH-CLAUSE	See **who's at the door**, please.
	Kari will see **what the congressman wants**.
see _____ *have a romantic relationship with* [USED ONLY IN THE PROGRESSIVE TENSES]	
OBJECT	Paul is seeing **a friend of mine**.
	She is finally seeing **someone that we all like**.
	Are you seeing **anyone**?
see _____ *accompany*	
OBJECT + ADVERB OF PLACE TO/FROM	Louise saw **her guests** *to the door*.
	Jake saw **Mallory** *home from the party*.
see _____ *consider*	
OBJECT + *as* PREDICATE NOUN	They saw **Laura** *as a threat*.
	I see **this** *as a golden opportunity*.
OBJECT + *as* PREDICATE ADJECTIVE	We see **her** *as inexperienced and unreliable*.
	The manager saw **his staff** *as eager and energetic*.
	Traders will see **the economic picture** *as unstable*.
see _____ *make sure*	
(to it) THAT-CLAUSE	See **(to it) that the lights are turned off before you leave**.
	We asked the janitor to see **(to it) that the boxes are removed from the hallway**.
see _____ *experience*	
OBJECT	My hometown has seen **lots of changes**.
	The price of milk has seen **a large increase**.

(PHRASAL VERBS)

see _____ **back/down/in/out/up**/etc. *accompany in a specified direction*	May I see you back to your office? The receptionist will see you out.
see about _____ *take care of*	My secretary will see about ordering new carpet.
see in *look inside*	The neighbors can see in if the drapes are open.
see _____ **off** *accompany [to a place of departure]*	I'll see you off at the train station.
see out *look outside*	The windows were papered over so we couldn't see out.
see through *look through something*	The windshield is so dirty I can't see through.
see through _____ *understand the deception in*	His wife finally saw through all his lies.
see ⸻SEP⸻ **through** *bring to completion*	Glenda saw the project through.
see ⸻SEP⸻ **through** *help in a difficult time*	An extra $100 a week will see us through.
see to _____ *take care of*	Would you see to the lizard in the kitchen?

PRESENT

I see	we see
you see	you see
he/she/it sees	they see

• *He sees a physical therapist once a week.*

PRESENT PROGRESSIVE

I am seeing	we are seeing
you are seeing	you are seeing
he/she/it is seeing	they are seeing

• *I am seeing them at 10 o'clock.*

PAST

I saw	we saw
you saw	you saw
he/she/it saw	they saw

• *I saw Marian yesterday.*

PAST PROGRESSIVE

I was seeing	we were seeing
you were seeing	you were seeing
he/she/it was seeing	they were seeing

• *We were seeing some friends last night.*

PRESENT PERFECT ... have | has seen
PAST PERFECT   ... had seen

FUTURE   ... will see
FUTURE PROGRESSIVE ... will be seeing
FUTURE PERFECT   ... will have seen

PAST PASSIVE

I was seen	we were seen
you were seen	you were seen
he/she/it was seen	they were seen

• *The suspect was last seen fleeing the crime scene.*

COMPLEMENTS

see *understand [something previously said]*	Oh, I see! [USUALLY SPOKEN EMPHATICALLY]
see *acknowledge [something previously said]*	I see. [USUALLY SPOKEN IN A LEVEL OR FALLING TONE]
see *use the sense of sight*	You won't be able to see temporarily.
	Ray can't see anymore.

see _____ *observe with one's eyes*

OBJECT	I saw **Tom** at the grocery store.
	We saw **the documentary** on TV last night.
	What do you see?
PASSIVE	The star is best seen through a high-powered telescope.
OBJECT + BASE-FORM INFINITIVE	Sam saw **the wind** *rip the roof off the house.*
	Nobody saw **the suspect** *break into the house.*
OBJECT + PRESENT PARTICIPLE	We saw **Charles** *walking to school.*
	I'm sorry. I didn't see **you** *standing there.*
PASSIVE	Mary was seen *talking to Brett.*
OBJECT + PAST PARTICIPLE	Someone must have seen **the car** *stolen.*
	We saw **the bridge** *swept away in the flood.*
THAT-CLAUSE	I see **that you bought a new car.**
	We saw in the paper **that your son is getting married.**
EMPHATIC PARAPHRASE	**You bought a new car,** I see.
WH-CLAUSE	I saw **what they are making for dinner.**
	Did anybody see **where the kids went**?

see _____ *understand*

OBJECT	I see **your point.**
	Nobody saw **the magnitude of the risk.**
	We all see **the attractions of living in a big city.**
OBJECT + INFINITIVE	He is widely seen *to be qualified.*
[USED ONLY IN THE PASSIVE]	The judge was seen *to favor the prosecution.*
THAT-CLAUSE	I see **that we are in big trouble.**
	Our lawyer saw **that they were on shaky legal ground.**
WH-CLAUSE	I see **what we should do.**
	Nobody saw **how risky the plan was.**

PRESENT		PRESENT PROGRESSIVE	
I seek	we seek	I am seeking	we are seeking
you seek	you seek	you are seeking	you are seeking
he/she/it seeks	they seek	he/she/it is seeking	they are seeking

- *France seeks to establish trade relations.* ・ *We are only seeking the truth.*

PAST		PAST PROGRESSIVE	
I sought	we sought	I was seeking	we were seeking
you sought	you sought	you were seeking	you were seeking
he/she/it sought	they sought	he/she/it was seeking	they were seeking

- *The hikers sought a safe place to camp.* ・ *The birds were seeking suitable nesting places.*

PRESENT PERFECT ... have | has sought
PAST PERFECT ... had sought

FUTURE ... will seek
FUTURE PROGRESSIVE ... will be seeking
FUTURE PERFECT ... will have sought

PAST PASSIVE	
I was sought	we were sought
you were sought	you were sought
he/she/it was sought	they were sought

- *Voting rights were sought by women's groups for decades.*

COMPLEMENTS

seek _____ *look for*
    OBJECT
Ruby was seeking **a good place for the family reunion.**
Seek **shelter** immediately when you hear the tornado siren.
We sought **anybody who could answer our questions.**

      PASSIVE
A suspect in the killing is being sought by the police.

seek _____ *ask for*
    OBJECT
You need to seek **professional advice.**
I am seeking **information about cell phones.**
We should seek **help on this problem.**

      PASSIVE
Technical information on wind farms is being sought.

seek _____ *try, attempt*
    INFINITIVE
We sought **to find a better solution to the problem.**
They are seeking **to replace their old computers.**
We never sought **to cause any problems.**
The company has always sought **to have excellent customer relations.**

seek _____ *try to get/achieve*
    OBJECT
The plaintiff is seeking **damages of $2 million.**
He sought **revenge for his brother's murder.**
She sought **perfection in everything she did.**

PHRASAL VERBS

seek _SEP_ **out** *look for and find*
The candidate sought out the best pollsters in the country.

EXPRESSIONS

Seek and ye shall find. *If you look hard enough for something, you will find it.* [BIBLE]

The farmers' market has every kind of vegetable and fruit you can think of. Just seek and ye shall find.

PRESENT

I seem	we seem
you seem	you seem
he/she/it seems	they seem

• *It seems to be a good idea.*

PRESENT PROGRESSIVE

Seem is rarely used in the progressive tenses.

PAST

I seemed	we seemed
you seemed	you seemed
he/she/it seemed	they seemed

• *John seemed upset about something.*

PAST PROGRESSIVE

Seem is rarely used in the progressive tenses.

PRESENT PERFECT ... have | has seemed
PAST PERFECT   ... had seemed

FUTURE   ... will seem
FUTURE PROGRESSIVE —
FUTURE PERFECT   ... will have seemed

PAST PASSIVE

Seem is never used in the passive voice.

─────────────────────────────────(COMPLEMENTS)───

seem _____ *give the impression of being, appear*

(to be) PREDICATE NOUN	The message seems (**to be**) **a plea for help.**
	Harry seems (**to be**) **a very likeable young man.**
	San Francisco seems (**to be**) **a very civilized city.**
	It seemed (**to be**) **a good idea** at the time.
(to be) PREDICATE ADJECTIVE	Teenagers seem (**to be**) **hungry** all the time.
	They seem (**to be**) **unhappy** with our suggestion.
	Allen seemed (**to be**) **very professional** in his approach.

NOTE: The following uses of *seem* make the following clause less definite, direct, or confrontational.

seem _____ *appear, in the opinion of the speaker/writer*

INFINITIVE	I seem **to remember telling you to clean up that mess.**
	He seemed **to think we were rude to him.**
	Dorothy seemed **to dislike her new slippers.**
	A groundhog seems **to have dug a burrow in the river bank.**

seem _____ *appear, in the opinion of the person addressed* [USED ONLY IN QUESTIONS]

WH + *seem* + INFINITIVE	**Who** seemed *to be the most seriously injured*?
	What seems *to be the problem here*?
	What seemed *to cause the landslide*?
	Whatever seems *to be the matter*?

seem _____ *appear to be true*

it + *seem* + THAT-CLAUSE	It seemed **that we had made a big mistake.**
	It seems **that they might cancel the flight.**
	It may seem **that I have changed my mind.**
it + *seem* + as if / as though / like CLAUSE	It seems **as if you were right after all.**
	It seems **as though her ideas are the ones that worked the best.**
	It seems **like he didn't like her anymore.**

seem _____ *appear to exist*

there + *seem* + to be PREDICATE NOUN	There seems **to be a problem with the bill.**
	There seems **to be some misunderstanding.**
	There seemed **to be some confusion about the recommendation.**

PRESENT

I select	we select
you select	you select
he/she/it selects	they select

• *He always selects the best one for himself.*

PRESENT PROGRESSIVE

I am selecting	we are selecting
you are selecting	you are selecting
he/she/it is selecting	they are selecting

• *He is selecting decorations for the Christmas tree.*

PAST

I selected	we selected
you selected	you selected
he/she/it selected	they selected

• *Our daughter finally selected a college.*

PAST PROGRESSIVE

I was selecting	we were selecting
you were selecting	you were selecting
he/she/it was selecting	they were selecting

• *We were selecting a place for our vacation.*

PRESENT PERFECT ... have | has selected
PAST PERFECT ... had selected

FUTURE ... will select
FUTURE PROGRESSIVE ... will be selecting
FUTURE PERFECT ... will have selected

PAST PASSIVE

I was selected	we were selected
you were selected	you were selected
he/she/it was selected	they were selected

• *We were selected to be in the final round.*

COMPLEMENTS

select _____ *choose, pick out*

OBJECT	Please select **one of the following options.**
	The committee finally selected **its new chairperson.**
	Which wine did you select?
	Select **the words you want to delete** by highlighting them.
	Click on "File," then select **"Save."**
	She selected **three jackets** for her husband.
	Teams always selected **me** last.
PASSIVE	The cast for the play has already been selected.
from OBJECT	Shoppers can select **from a range of colors.**
	Students selected **from a long list of activities.**
	The bride and groom can select **from seven reception dinner menus.**
OBJECT + *as* PREDICATE NOUN	They selected **Lloyd** *as the best person for the job.*
	We selected **the Marriott** *as the convention site.*
	What did you select *as its name?*
PASSIVE	Southwest was selected *as the official airline.*
OBJECT + INFINITIVE	We selected **you** *to make the presentation.*
	They selected **Tony's restaurant** *to cater the dinner.*
	The magazine selected **our school** *to be featured in the article.*
PASSIVE	Sarah Greene was selected *to be the main speaker.*

PRESENT

I sell	we sell
you sell	you sell
he/she/it sells	they sell

• *Our store sells sports equipment.*

PRESENT PROGRESSIVE

I am selling	we are selling
you are selling	you are selling
he/she/it is selling	they are selling

• *These gadgets are selling like crazy.*

PAST

I sold	we sold
you sold	you sold
he/she/it sold	they sold

• *We sold the desk on craigslist.*

PAST PROGRESSIVE

I was selling	we were selling
you were selling	you were selling
he/she/it was selling	they were selling

• *We were selling children's clothing at half price.*

PRESENT PERFECT … have | has sold
PAST PERFECT … had sold

FUTURE … will sell
FUTURE PROGRESSIVE … will be selling
FUTURE PERFECT … will have sold

PAST PASSIVE

I was sold	we were sold
you were sold	you were sold
he/she/it was sold	they were sold

• *That house was sold last week.*

(**COMPLEMENTS**)

sell *be a successful product/idea*

I think that his new CD will really sell.
His proposal will never sell.

sell ____ *exchange for money*

OBJECT

I want to sell **my old computer**.
He finally sold **his jewelry business**.
Should we sell **the rocking chair** or give it away?

OBJECT + *for* OBJECT

She sold **the lamp** *for $10*.
How much did you sell **the table** *for*?

INDIRECT OBJECT + DIRECT OBJECT

We sold *them* **some lawn furniture**.
Jay sold *the dealer* **his coin collection**.

to PARAPHRASE

We sold **some lawn furniture** *to them*.
Jay sold **his coin collection** *to the dealer*.

OBJECT + WH-CLAUSE

He sold **us** *just what we had in mind*.
We sell **people** *whatever kind of car they want*.

sell ____ *be given in exchange [for money]*

for OBJECT

The Picasso painting sold **for $104 million**.
The antique rolling pin sold **for $25**.

sell ____ *offer for purchase*

OBJECT

The hardware store sells **electrical and plumbing supplies**.
Our group is selling **raffle tickets**.
They sell **fish sandwiches** on Friday.

PASSIVE

Gym memberships are sold by the month.

OBJECT + *for* OBJECT

The boutique is selling **scarves** *for as little as $7*.

sell ____ *be offered for purchase*

for OBJECT

Milk is selling **for $3.50 a gallon**.

sell ____ *successfully promote*

OBJECT

John really knows how to sell **his vision for the company**.

(**PHRASAL VERBS**)

sell _SEP_ **off** *liquidate*

We sold off our clothing division two years ago.

sell out of ____ *sell all of*

We sold out of French Roast coffee yesterday.
We are sold out of chocolate ice cream.

PRESENT

I send	we send
you send	you send
he/she/it sends	they send

- *The firm sends letters by registered mail.*

PRESENT PROGRESSIVE

I am sending	we are sending
you are sending	you are sending
he/she/it is sending	they are sending

- *I am sending you an e-mail.*

PAST

I sent	we sent
you sent	you sent
he/she/it sent	they sent

- *They sent us a nice note.*

PAST PROGRESSIVE

I was sending	we were sending
you were sending	you were sending
he/she/it was sending	they were sending

- *They were sending their children to a private school.*

PRESENT PERFECT ... have | has sent
PAST PERFECT ... had sent

FUTURE ... will send
FUTURE PROGRESSIVE ... will be sending
FUTURE PERFECT ... will have sent

PAST PASSIVE

I was sent	we were sent
you were sent	you were sent
he/she/it was sent	they were sent

- *The letter was sent to the wrong address.*

COMPLEMENTS

send _____ *mail, dispatch*

OBJECT — They forgot to send **the letter**.
We will send **a car** to pick them up.

send _____ *cause to go / be carried*

OBJECT + ADVERB OF PLACE TO/FROM — We sent **our luggage** *on ahead*.
I sent **the children** *to bed* early.
The wizard sent **Dorothy** *back to Kansas*.
The accident sent **a cloud of dust** *into the air*.

PASSIVE — The package was sent *to the wrong office*.
INDIRECT OBJECT + DIRECT OBJECT — Send *me* **your ideas**.
We sent *them* **a wedding present**.
to PARAPHRASE — Send **your ideas** *to me*.
We sent **a wedding present** *to them*.

PHRASAL VERBS

send _SEP_ **away/back/by/down/in/out/ over**/etc. *cause to go in a specified direction* — The publisher sent my manuscript back unread.
You may send the ambassador in now.

send (away/back/down/off/out/up) for _____ *summon, request* — Send for the school nurse immediately.
Abby sent away for extra copies of the report.
Let's send out for pizza.

send _SEP_ **in** *submit* — Please send your application in by December 31.

send _____ **in for** *put [someone] into a contest as a replacement for* — The coach sent Hopkins in for Busam.

send _SEP_ **off** *mail* — We sent off a present to our granddaughter.

send _SEP_ **off** *cause to go away* — Send the children off so that we can talk privately.

send _SEP_ **off** *say farewell to [someone leaving on a trip]* — The town sent the soldiers off with a parade.

send _SEP_ **out** *issue, distribute* — The company sent a press release out this morning.

send _____ **out for** *cause [someone] to go on an errand to get* — I sent Billie out for some more ice cream.

send _SEP_ **up/down** *cause to go up/down* — Good economic news sent the stock market up.

PRESENT

I separate	we separate
you separate	you separate
he/she/it separates	they separate

- *The path separates at the top of the hill.*

PRESENT PROGRESSIVE

I am separating	we are separating
you are separating	you are separating
he/she/it is separating	they are separating

- *Her parents are separating.*

PAST

I separated	we separated
you separated	you separated
he/she/it separated	they separated

- *Brian separated the yolks and egg whites.*

PAST PROGRESSIVE

I was separating	we were separating
you were separating	you were separating
he/she/it was separating	they were separating

- *The searchers were separating to cover more ground.*

PRESENT PERFECT ... have | has separated
PAST PERFECT ... had separated

FUTURE ... will separate
FUTURE PROGRESSIVE ... will be separating
FUTURE PERFECT ... will have separated

PAST PASSIVE

I was separated	we were separated
you were separated	you were separated
he/she/it was separated	they were separated

- *The groups were separated by age and ability.*

COMPLEMENTS

separate *move/go/break apart*	Tell the girls to separate and mix with the guests.
	The train tracks separate in the next town.
	Orange juice will separate if you leave it too long.
	We separated at the airport but agreed to meet later for dinner.
	The first stage of the rocket didn't separate properly.
separate *stop living together*	The Johnstons are separating after 10 years of marriage.
separate _____ *cause to move/be apart, divide, be between*	
OBJECT	The police separated **the two gangs**.
	A high wooden fence separated **the two yards**.
	The teacher separated **the class** into four groups.
	Please separate **the invoices** into folders by month.
PASSIVE	John and Mary were separated by mutual agreement.
	A lot of families were separated during the war.
OBJECT + *from* OBJECT	We must separate **fact** *from fiction*.
	Separate **the bruised pears** *from the others*.
	How do you separate **your private life** *from your public life*?
	The dairy separates **the milk** *from the cream*.

PHRASAL VERBS

separate __SEP__ out (from / out of _____) *remove (from [something])*	Separate out the milk jugs from the rest of the recycled plastic.
	Electrolysis separates hydrogen out of water.

EXPRESSIONS

separate the men from the boys *show who is competent and who is not*	The current economy will really separate the men from the boys.
separate the wheat from the chaff *set what is valuable apart from what is worthless*	When it comes to books, our book club tries to separate the wheat from the chaff.

PRESENT

I serve	we serve
you serve	you serve
he/she/it serves	they serve

• *The laser printer serves the whole office.*

PAST

I served	we served
you served	you served
he/she/it served	they served

• *Grandpa served in the Navy.*

PRESENT PERFECT ... have | has served
PAST PERFECT ... had served

PRESENT PROGRESSIVE

I am serving	we are serving
you are serving	you are serving
he/she/it is serving	they are serving

• *We are serving the guests coffee on the deck.*

PAST PROGRESSIVE

I was serving	we were serving
you were serving	you were serving
he/she/it was serving	they were serving

• *The waiter was serving another couple.*

FUTURE ... will serve
FUTURE PROGRESSIVE ... will be serving
FUTURE PERFECT ... will have served

PAST PASSIVE

I was served	we were served
you were served	you were served
he/she/it was served	they were served

• *Sorry, lunch was served at noon.*

(**COMPLEMENTS**)

serve *perform a duty/service/obligation*	He has served for many years. Everyone has a need to serve.
serve *provide food/drink*	We will start serving at five. We will have to hire someone to serve.
serve *hit a ball over a net to begin play*	The visiting team always serves first.

serve _____ *perform [a duty, service, obligation] to/for*

OBJECT	He has served **his country** for many years. How can we serve **our customers** better? One grocery store serves **the whole town**. The power company serves **Arizona and southern California**. He is serving **a three-year term in the state penitentiary**.
as OBJECT	Marilyn served **as church administrator** for 31 years.
OBJECT + *as* OBJECT	Mycroft Holmes served **his brother** *as a crime consultant*.
on OBJECT	I served **on a committee to eliminate waste in government**.

serve _____ *provide food/drink to/for*

OBJECT	The restaurant cannot serve **minors** in the lounge. We are not able to serve **large tour groups**. The recipe serves **six**.

serve _____ *provide [food/drink]*

OBJECT	The restaurant serves **Mandarin food**. The school serves **waffles** on the weekend.
PASSIVE	Dinner is served.
INDIRECT OBJECT + DIRECT OBJECT	They served *the whole group* **lasagna**. The cooks served *the grateful soldiers* **a hot meal**.
to PARAPHRASE	They served **lasagna** *to the whole group*. The cooks served **a hot meal** *to the grateful soldiers*.

serve _____ *hit [a ball over a net] to begin play*

OBJECT + ADVERB OF PLACE TO/FROM	Meyers serves **the ball** *to Larsen*.

serve _____ *function, be used*

as OBJECT	Our school serves **as a model of racial harmony**.
INFINITIVE	Sweating serves **to regulate body temperature**. The severe penalty serves **to discourage other cheaters**.

PRESENT

I set	we set
you set	you set
he/she/it sets	they set

  • *The auctioneer sets a minimum bid.*

PRESENT PROGRESSIVE

I am setting	we are setting
you are setting	you are setting
he/she/it is setting	they are setting

  • *I am setting the alarm for 6 A.M.*

PAST

I set	we set
you set	you set
he/she/it set	they set

  • *I set my chair next to the window.*

PAST PROGRESSIVE

I was setting	we were setting
you were setting	you were setting
he/she/it was setting	they were setting

  • *We were setting a new direction for the company.*

PRESENT PERFECT ... have | has set
PAST PERFECT ... had set

FUTURE ... will set
FUTURE PROGRESSIVE ... will be setting
FUTURE PERFECT ... will have set

PAST PASSIVE

I was set	we were set
you were set	you were set
he/she/it was set	they were set

  • *The couch was set in front of the TV screen.*

───(**COMPLEMENTS**)───

set *sink below the horizon*	The sun will set at 6:43 tonight. The moon was just setting below the trees in the west. Orion was setting behind the snowy hills.
set *become solid/rigid*	The chocolate mousse never set properly. The cement in the patio was setting nicely. Be careful. The glue sets in just a few seconds.
set ____ *put, lay* OBJECT + ADVERB OF PLACE	The hunters set **their guns** *against the fence.* I set **my foot** *on the bottom rung of the ladder.* She set **the novel** *in postwar Canada.*
PASSIVE	The house was set *well back from the road.* The movie was set *in Los Angeles.* The album had been set *on a shelf in the living room.*
set ____ *arrange, adjust* OBJECT	The doctor set **my dislocated shoulder.** I have set **the clock** for daylight saving time. I set **the volume on the radio** way too high. Last winter, we set **the thermostat** at 62 degrees.
PASSIVE	His face was set in a permanent scowl.
set ____ *establish, fix* OBJECT	The track team set **a record for the 400-meter relay.** The Hunt brothers tried to set **the price of silver.** Sarah and Lucas have set **the date of their wedding.** Graham sets **a good example for the other children.** We set **a fund-raising goal of $200.** The real estate agent set **the price of our house** at $235,000.

set ____ *cause to be in a certain state/condition*
   OBJECT + PREDICATE ADJECTIVE
	Lincoln set **the slaves** *free.*
	Grandpa always set **the dogs** *loose* after
	  breakfast.

OBJECT + *to* PRESENT PARTICIPLE	The speech set **us** *to thinking about harnessing* *the sun's energy.*

PHRASAL VERBS

set _SEP_ aside/down/forward/out/ up/etc. *put in a specified position*
> The logician set the problem aside and went to lunch.
> Our neighbors set scraps out for our dog.

set about _____ *begin*
> The Scouts set about repairing the holes in the tent.

set _____ against *cause to disagree with*
> His budget policies set the president against Congress.

set _____ apart *make distinctive*
> His honesty and sense of justice set him apart.

set _SEP_ aside *keep apart*
> We set aside $200 a month for the kids' education.

set _SEP_ aside *reject, nullify*
> They set their differences aside and became close friends.
> Congress set the issue aside for the time being.
> The Supreme Court set aside the appellate court ruling.

set _SEP_ back *delay*
> The bad economy will set back our plans to expand.
> The president's order set genetic research back six years.

set _SEP_ back *cost [someone]* [INFORMAL]
> How much did the new lawn tractor set you back?

set _SEP_ down *put in writing*
> The secretary has set down what was said at the executive meeting.

set _____ down to *blame [something] on*
> The boss set Hank's mistake down to inexperience and naiveté.

set _SEP_ forth *announce, make known*
> The church set forth its principles of equality and inclusion.

set in *begin*
> Decay has already set in.
> With all the political commercials on TV, voter fatigue has set in.

set off/out *depart, start out*
> Three hundred pioneers set off from St. Joseph, Missouri.
> Refugees set out in overcrowded boats for the mainland.

set _SEP_ off *make distinctive*
> The designer set the title off from the text below.

set _SEP_ off *cause to be very emotional*
> Be careful not to set Dolores off; she's already angry.

set _SEP_ off *trigger, cause to make a noise*
> My husband set the metal detector off with his belt buckle.

set _SEP_ off *cause to explode*
> Quarrymen set off 150 pounds of dynamite.

set on/upon _____ *attack*
> The citizens set upon the soldiers and beat them badly.

set _SEP_ out *display*
> The store sets out its Christmas items right after Halloween.

set _SEP_ out *plant*
> Don't set your tomatoes out before the last frost.

set to _____ *begin*
> Farmers set to plugging the hole in the dike.
> Engineers set to work on the project.

set _____ to *order to*
> My parents set me to vacuuming the dining room.

set _SEP_ up *arrange*
> Let's set a meeting up with the committee chairpersons.

set _SEP_ up *build, erect*
> Gerry set up a miniature railroad in the living room.

set _SEP_ up *found, establish*
> Our group set up a web-based discussion forum.

set _SEP_ up *prepare for use*
> She set her mom's computer up to do e-mail.

set _SEP_ up *raise to power / a higher position / etc.*
> Adolf Hitler set himself up as dictator.

set _SEP_ up *make [someone] the target of a joke/deception*
> They set me up on April Fool's Day, and I fell for it.

set _SEP_ up with *arrange a date for [someone] with*
> Would you set me up with your roommate?

PRESENT

I settle	we settle
you settle	you settle
he/she/it settles	they settle

• *He always settles his bills promptly.*

PAST

I settled	we settled
you settled	you settled
he/she/it settled	they settled

• *They finally settled their argument.*

PRESENT PERFECT ... have | has settled
PAST PERFECT   ... had settled

PRESENT PROGRESSIVE

I am settling	we are settling
you are settling	you are settling
he/she/it is settling	they are settling

• *We are settling a dispute between family members.*

PAST PROGRESSIVE

I was settling	we were settling
you were settling	you were settling
he/she/it was settling	they were settling

• *The dust was settling over the furniture.*

FUTURE   ... will settle
FUTURE PROGRESSIVE ... will be settling
FUTURE PERFECT   ... will have settled

PAST PASSIVE

I was settled	we were settled
you were settled	you were settled
he/she/it was settled	they were settled

• *New Zealand was first settled by Polynesians.*

COMPLEMENTS

settle *come to an agreement*	The two sides will never settle.
	The judge asked them to settle before the case came to trial.
settle *sink gradually*	Wait until the tea leaves settle before you pour.
	The house has settled about two inches.
	We couldn't drive until the dust settled.
settle _____ *come to an agreement/decision [on]*	
OBJECT	Will you settle **a bet** for us?
PASSIVE	The suit was settled out of court.
on OBJECT	Did she ever settle **on a wedding dress**?
settle _____ *pay [a debt, bill]*	
OBJECT	You must settle **your hotel bill** before you leave.
settle _____ *cause to sink gradually*	
OBJECT	A rain shower settled **the dust**.
settle _____ *make calm*	
OBJECT	Ginger ale will settle **your stomach**.
settle _____ *put in a comfortable position*	
OBJECT + ADVERB OF PLACE	Michael settled **himself** *behind the wheel* and started the car.
	The nurse settled **Mrs. Reems** *in her bed*.
settle _____ *establish a home/colony*	
ADVERB OF PLACE	We eventually settled **near Portland**.
	The Greeks settled **all along the Mediterranean coast**.
settle _____ *establish a colony in*	
OBJECT	English Puritans settled **New England**.
settle _____ *come to rest*	
ADVERB OF PLACE	Pookie finally settled **on my lap**.
	Her arthritis settled **in her knees**.

PHRASAL VERBS

settle down	*calm down*	The teacher told the rowdy kids to settle down.
settle down	*establish a home*	Adam eventually settled down in south St. Louis.
settle for _____	*accept*	I'd like $50 for the bike, but I'll settle for $40.

PRESENT

I shake	we shake
you shake	you shake
he/she/it shakes	they shake

• *The windows shake when it's windy.*

PRESENT PROGRESSIVE

I am shaking	we are shaking
you are shaking	you are shaking
he/she/it is shaking	they are shaking

• *My hands are shaking.*

PAST

I shook	we shook
you shook	you shook
he/she/it shook	they shook

• *I shook the umbrella before I closed it.*

PAST PROGRESSIVE

I was shaking	we were shaking
you were shaking	you were shaking
he/she/it was shaking	they were shaking

• *He was shaking his head in disbelief.*

PRESENT PERFECT ... have | has shaken
PAST PERFECT ... had shaken

FUTURE ... will shake
FUTURE PROGRESSIVE ... will be shaking
FUTURE PERFECT ... will have shaken

PAST PASSIVE

I was shaken	we were shaken
you were shaken	you were shaken
he/she/it was shaken	they were shaken

• *Everyone was badly shaken by the earthquake.*

(**COMPLEMENTS**)

shake *tremble, vibrate*
His voice shakes whenever he gets excited.
The floor shakes whenever a train goes by.
My legs were beginning to shake from the strain of lifting the box.

shake _____ *cause to move quickly up and down / back and forth / from side to side*
OBJECT
The cat is shaking **its toy mouse** furiously.
I shook **David** by the shoulder to wake him up.
I shook **my head** vigorously, trying to get him to stop talking.
We shook **the rugs** and put them back on the floor.
They shook **hands** and smiled for the camera.
Shake **the dressing** well before using.

shake _____ *shock, surprise, upset*
OBJECT
The news about the accident shook **us all** badly.
The sudden increase in oil prices shook **the financial markets**.
Her daughter's death shook **her religious faith**.
PASSIVE
She was visibly shaken when she returned.

(**PHRASAL VERBS**)

shake _SEP_ **down/off/out/up**/etc.
cause to move quickly in a specified direction
The gardener shook the apples down.
Tip Top stood up and shook the dust off.

shake _SEP_ **down** *get money from by using threats*
The politician shook down corporations for campaign
  contributions.

shake _SEP_ **off** *get away from*
The car thief was unable to shake the police off.

shake _SEP_ **off** *get rid of*
It took me a week to shake off a cold.

shake _SEP_ **out** *clean by shaking*
We put fresh sheets on the bed and shook out the blankets.

shake _SEP_ **out** *straighten by shaking*
Lydia shook the shirts out before hanging them up.

shake _SEP_ **up** *mix by shaking*
I shook the salad dressing up before opening the bottle.

shake _SEP_ **up** *change greatly*
The new department head shook up the staff with a round
  of hiring and firing.

PRESENT		PRESENT PROGRESSIVE	
I share	we share	I am sharing	we are sharing
you share	you share	you are sharing	you are sharing
he/she/it shares	they share	he/she/it is sharing	they are sharing

• *Thomas always shares his toys.*   • *Brandon isn't sharing!*

PAST		PAST PROGRESSIVE	
I shared	we shared	I was sharing	we were sharing
you shared	you shared	you were sharing	you were sharing
he/she/it shared	they shared	he/she/it was sharing	they were sharing

• *We shared a cubicle when we were interns.*   • *We were sharing a cab to the airport.*

PRESENT PERFECT ... have | has shared
PAST PERFECT ... had shared

FUTURE ... will share
FUTURE PROGRESSIVE ... will be sharing
FUTURE PERFECT ... will have shared

PAST PASSIVE	
—	—
—	—
it was shared	they were shared

• *The profits and expenses were shared equally.*

COMPLEMENTS

share *divide something into parts for the use of two or more people*

Mommy! They aren't sharing!
We would be happy to share; we have more than enough.
Some kids have a hard time learning to share.
All members of the group must share equally.

share _____ *divide into parts for the use of two or more people, have/use together*

OBJECT
Let's share **a dessert.**
Barb and I often share **a bottle of wine** at dinner.
Can I share **this box of donuts** with you?
We shared **an apartment** in Pittsburgh.

PASSIVE
The costs must be shared by all participants equally.

WH-CLAUSE
We will share **what resources we have.**
You can't share **what you don't have.**
Investors will share **whatever profits the company makes.**

share _____ *participate*

in OBJECT
The whole class shared **in the gift for the teacher.**
All of us share **in my brother's happiness.**

share _____ *have in common*

OBJECT
Tim and Johanna share **a love for old movies.**
We don't share **their enthusiasm for home-roasted coffee.**

PASSIVE
A dislike of snakes and spiders is shared by most cultures.

share _____ *tell, express*

OBJECT
The boss shared **a story from his childhood.**
Please share **your ideas** with us.
The widow was unable to share **her feelings** with the
  support group.

PRESENT

I shave	we shave
you shave	you shave
he/she/it shaves	they shave

• *He shaves every morning.*

PRESENT PROGRESSIVE

I am shaving	we are shaving
you are shaving	you are shaving
he/she/it is shaving	they are shaving

• *Can you get the phone? I'm shaving.*

PAST

I shaved	we shaved
you shaved	you shaved
he/she/it shaved	they shaved

• *We shaved some soap to get thin flakes.*

PAST PROGRESSIVE

I was shaving	we were shaving
you were shaving	you were shaving
he/she/it was shaving	they were shaving

• *He was shaving by the time he was 16.*

PRESENT PERFECT ... have | has shaved
PAST PERFECT ... had shaved

FUTURE ... will shave
FUTURE PROGRESSIVE ... will be shaving
FUTURE PERFECT ... will have shaved

PAST PASSIVE

I was shaved	we were shaved
you were shaved	you were shaved
he/she/it was shaved	they were shaved

• *His head was shaved every few days.*

COMPLEMENTS

shave *cut off one's beard*

I need to shave.
Richard Nixon had such a heavy beard that he shaved twice a day.
When was the last time you shaved?

shave _____ *cut off the hair of with a razor*

OBJECT
Before the surgery, a nurse shaved **my back**.
Most women shave **their legs**.
Competitive swimmers shave **their whole bodies**.

PASSIVE
Before the makeup could be applied, his head was shaven.

shave _____ *cut a thin slice from*

OBJECT
We shaved **dark chocolate** to get chocolate curls.
Shave **the cheese** as thin as you can.

PASSIVE
Thin slices of prosciutto were shaved for the appetizers.

shave _____ *reduce slightly*

OBJECT
We have to shave **our prices** to remain competitive.
The factory shaved **costs** by turning the heat down five degrees.
The store shaved **ten cents** off the regular price.
The injury shaved **the odds of our winning**.

PASSIVE
A few seconds were shaved from the old record.

PHRASAL VERBS

shave SEP **off** *cut [from]*

He shaved off a little sliver from the edge
of the table with a plane.

PRESENT

I shed	we shed
you shed	you shed
he/she/it sheds	they shed

• *The tree sheds its leaves all over the patio.*

PRESENT PROGRESSIVE

I am shedding	we are shedding
you are shedding	you are shedding
he/she/it is shedding	they are shedding

• *They are shedding their distrust of modern ways.*

PAST

I shed	we shed
you shed	you shed
he/she/it shed	they shed

• *The dogs shed all over my black sweater.*

PAST PROGRESSIVE

I was shedding	we were shedding
you were shedding	you were shedding
he/she/it was shedding	they were shedding

• *The animals were shedding as the days grew longer.*

PRESENT PERFECT ... have | has shed
PAST PERFECT ... had shed

FUTURE ... will shed
FUTURE PROGRESSIVE ... will be shedding
FUTURE PERFECT ... will have shed

PAST PASSIVE

I was shed	we were shed
you were shed	you were shed
he/she/it was shed	they were shed

• *Our coats were shed as soon as we stepped onto the plane.*

COMPLEMENTS

shed *cast off / lose fur/skin/leaves naturally*

My dog sheds in the spring and autumn.
Most reptiles shed whenever they get too big for their old skin.
Most trees in temperate latitudes shed annually.

shed _____ *cast off / lose [fur/skin/leaves] naturally*

OBJECT

Most long-haired dogs shed **a lot of fur** in the spring.
All snakes shed **their skins**.
Most shade trees shed **their leaves**.

PASSIVE

Cat hair had been shed all over the rug.

shed _____ *take off, get rid of*

OBJECT

The kids shed **their clothes** and put on their bathing suits.
I hope to shed **about ten pounds** this year.
Many people never shed **their fear of public speaking**.
You will have to shed **some of your low-performing stocks**.

PASSIVE

Their fear of foreign travel has never really been shed.

shed _____ *cause to flow/drain/slough off*

OBJECT

My new jacket sheds **water** pretty well.
Our tent didn't seem to shed **a drop of water**.
The roof is steep enough to shed **snow**.

shed _____ *let flow*

OBJECT

We shed **many tears** over her death.
The soldier shed **a lot of blood** before a tourniquet was applied.

EXPRESSIONS

shed crocodile tears *pretend that one is crying*

The banks were shedding crocodile tears
for depositors who lost money.

PRESENT		PRESENT PROGRESSIVE	
I shift	we shift	I am shifting	we are shifting
you shift	you shift	you are shifting	you are shifting
he/she/it shifts	they shift	he/she/it is shifting	they are shifting

• *He always shifts the blame to you.*   • *Be careful—the load is shifting.*

PAST		PAST PROGRESSIVE	
I shifted	we shifted	I was shifting	we were shifting
you shifted	you shifted	you were shifting	you were shifting
he/she/it shifted	they shifted	he/she/it was shifting	they were shifting

• *The mayor shifted uneasily in his chair.*   • *The campaign was shifting its advertising strategy.*

PRESENT PERFECT ... have | has shifted
PAST PERFECT ... had shifted

FUTURE ... will shift
FUTURE PROGRESSIVE ... will be shifting
FUTURE PERFECT ... will have shifted

PAST PASSIVE	
I was shifted	we were shifted
you were shifted	you were shifted
he/she/it was shifted	they were shifted

• *The balance of power was shifted by recent events.*

(**COMPLEMENTS**)

shift *change position*

The house has shifted a bit on its foundation.
The audience shifted uneasily during the angry exchange.
The wind is shifting.
Ken's eyes shifted from the café to the bank.
Can you shift a little so I can get by?
Political beliefs have definitely shifted.
Consumer preferences are constantly shifting.

shift ——— *move, change*

OBJECT

Learning to shift **your balance** correctly is the key to skiing.
They want to shift **the date of the conference**.
Shift **the boxes** so we can get the car out of the garage.
They were really trying to shift **the blame**.
Let's shift **the discussion** back to economic policy.
Young people shift **their music preferences** almost weekly.
Advertising tries to shift **consumer brand loyalty**.
It is nearly impossible to shift **a person's basic temperament**.
She shifted **her gaze** to the watercolor by Édouard Manet.

PASSIVE

The guns were shifted to cover the port better.
The cargo was shifted to keep the boat balanced.
Political allegiances have been shifted by the economic downturn.

PRESENT

I shine	we shine
you shine	you shine
he/she/it shines	they shine

- *The sun always shines in Arizona.*

PRESENT PROGRESSIVE

I am shining	we are shining
you are shining	you are shining
he/she/it is shining	they are shining

- *A light is shining in the window.*

PAST

I shone/shined	we shone/shined
you shone/shined	you shone/shined
he/she/it shone/shined	they shone/shined

- *He shined the light right into our eyes.*

PAST PROGRESSIVE

I was shining	we were shining
you were shining	you were shining
he/she/it was shining	they were shining

- *Their eyes were shining with excitement.*

PRESENT PERFECT ... have | has shone/shined
PAST PERFECT ... had shone/shined

FUTURE ... will shine
FUTURE PROGRESSIVE ... will be shining
FUTURE PERFECT ... will have shone/shined

PAST PASSIVE

—	—
—	—
it was shone/shined	they were shone/shined

- *My shoes were shined and my suit was pressed.*

(**COMPLEMENTS**)

NOTE: The irregular form *shone* is used both with and without an object, except in the sense "make bright by polishing"; the regular form *shined* is used only with an object.

shine *give off / reflect light, be bright*	The stars were shining brightly. The jewels shone in the display case. The sun, reflecting from the glass building, shone in our eyes. Their swords and spears shone in the moonlight. The princess's hair shone like gold. The lighthouse shone through the mist, guiding us to port.
shine *have a bright appearance*	Fred's face was shining with joy as he ran to meet Rosemary.
shine *do very well*	Melissa shines in social studies.
shine _____ *cause to give off light* OBJECT + ADVERB OF PLACE TO/FROM	The guide shined **his flashlight** *into the back of the tomb*. The policeman is shining **his headlights** *on the abandoned car*. The newspaper shined **light** *on corruption at City Hall*.
PASSIVE	Bright lights were shone *on the prisoners' faces* all night long.
shine _____ *make bright by polishing* OBJECT	The jeweler shined **the gem** until it sparkled. I shined **my shoes** carefully before the interview.

(**PHRASAL VERBS**)

shine down/in/out/up/etc. *give off light in a specified direction*	The sun shone down on us as we walked along the beach.
shine _____ **down/in/out/up**/etc. *cause to give off light in a specified direction*	Shine the flashlight up a little higher.
shine through *be clearly shown*	Her personality really shines through in her photography.

PRESENT

I shoot	we shoot
you shoot	you shoot
he/she/it shoots	they shoot

• *MacInnis shoots and scores!*

PRESENT PROGRESSIVE

I am shooting	we are shooting
you are shooting	you are shooting
he/she/it is shooting	they are shooting

• *The basketball team is shooting from the perimeter.*

PAST

I shot	we shot
you shot	you shot
he/she/it shot	they shot

• *They shot several deer this fall.*

PAST PROGRESSIVE

I was shooting	we were shooting
you were shooting	you were shooting
he/she/it was shooting	they were shooting

• *They were shooting the scene in our neighborhood.*

PRESENT PERFECT ... have | has shot
PAST PERFECT ... had shot

FUTURE ... will shoot
FUTURE PROGRESSIVE ... will be shooting
FUTURE PERFECT ... will have shot

PAST PASSIVE

I was shot	we were shot
you were shot	you were shot
he/she/it was shot	they were shot

• *Up in the Air was shot in St. Louis.*

COMPLEMENTS

shoot *fire a weapon*	The police were ordered to shoot if necessary. I picked up the bow and shot.
shoot *hit/kick/throw/strike a ball/puck toward a goal*	James shoots from the baseline. [BASKETBALL] Beckham shoots from just outside the penalty area. [SOCCER] Pronger shoots under the goalie's glove. [HOCKEY]
shoot *make a photograph/film*	Just point the camera and shoot. The crew is shooting in Las Vegas.
shoot _____ *fire [a gun]* OBJECT	Can you shoot **a rifle**? Revelers shot **pistols** into the air on New Year's Eve.

shoot _____ *strike with a bullet/arrow*
   OBJECT
     PASSIVE
     WH-CLAUSE
	An unknown assailant shot **three people**.
	We were shooting **tin cans** behind the barn.
	Somebody has been shot.
	You can only shoot **what is in season**.
	Shoot **whatever moves**.

shoot _____ *photograph, film*
   OBJECT
     PASSIVE
	We want to shoot **the boats in the harbor**.
	They were shooting **a video of the parade**.
	The dream sequence was shot in black and white.

shoot _____ *move very quickly* ADVERB OF PLACE TO/FROM	The car shot **through the intersection**. Our boat shot **under the bridge**. The song shot **straight to the top of the charts**.

PHRASAL VERBS

shoot away/down/in/off/out/ over/up/etc. *move very quickly in a specified direction*	The motorcycle shot away when the light turned green.
shoot for _____ *have as a goal*	Eli is shooting for a Ph.D. in environmental sciences.
shoot up *grow quickly*	The daffodils shot up overnight. Yu-chan is really shooting up.

PRESENT

I shout	we shout
you shout	you shout
he/she/it shouts	they shout

• *He shouts when he's angry.*

PRESENT PROGRESSIVE

I am shouting	we are shouting
you are shouting	you are shouting
he/she/it is shouting	they are shouting

• *She is shouting into her cell phone.*

PAST

I shouted	we shouted
you shouted	you shouted
he/she/it shouted	they shouted

• *He shouted at the referees.*

PAST PROGRESSIVE

I was shouting	we were shouting
you were shouting	you were shouting
he/she/it was shouting	they were shouting

• *They were shouting as loud as they could.*

PRESENT PERFECT ... have | has shouted
PAST PERFECT ... had shouted

FUTURE ... will shout
FUTURE PROGRESSIVE ... will be shouting
FUTURE PERFECT ... will have shouted

PAST PASSIVE

I was shouted	we were shouted
you were shouted	you were shouted
he/she/it was shouted	they were shouted

• *Alarms were sounded and warnings were shouted.*

COMPLEMENTS

shout *cry out loudly*

The kids are always shouting.
Don't shout! I can hear you just fine.
We had to shout above the noise of the engines.
The kids shouted with delight when Santa appeared.
Devon shouted in pain when the nurse gave him a shot.

shout _____ *say very loudly*

OBJECT

They were shouting **the news.**
Someone in the crowd was shouting **my name.**

PASSIVE

Instructions on how to unlock the door were shouted
    through the window.

THAT-CLAUSE

I shouted **that I had won the race.**
Marian shouted **that she was in the garden.**
The conductor shouted **that the train was about to leave.**

shout _____ *signal unmistakably*

OBJECT

Her clothes shouted "**money.**"
Our accent and clothing shout "**tourists.**"
The patient's pale skin and unresponsiveness shouted "**shock.**"

PHRASAL VERBS

shout _SEP_ **down** *prevent from speaking by shouting*

Protesters shouted the speaker down.

PHRASAL VERBS

show _SEP_ **around/away/down/in/out/ up/etc.** _lead/guide in a specified direction_	Sam was showing the White House visitors around. A guide showed us down to the cafeteria.
show _SEP_ **off** _display, exhibit_	The bride-to-be showed off her wedding gown.
show off _do something to attract attention_	Ronny was always showing off in front of the girls.
show up _arrive_	Ozzie showed up just in time for dinner.
show up _appear_	The Republican ratings show up as the red line on your screen.
show up _be easily seen_	His thinning hair really shows up in this photo.
show _SEP_ **up** _outmatch, humble_	Fred showed everybody up at the math contest.

EXPRESSIONS

show [one's] face _make an appearance_	I wonder if Todd will show his face at the party tonight.
show [one's] hand _reveal one's intentions_	He never showed his hand while discussing free trade.
show [one's] teeth _act in a threatening manner_	Boyd showed his teeth whenever someone criticized his girlfriend.
show signs of _____ _give indications of_	The patient shows signs of bipolar disorder. The student is showing signs of fatigue.
show [someone] the ropes _show [someone] how to do something_	Don't worry; the secretary who's retiring will show you the ropes.
show [one's] true colors _show what one is really like_	The boss showed his true colors when he laughed about firing three employees right before Christmas.

PRESENT

I show	we show
you show	you show
he/she/it shows	they show

• *The picture shows a vase of sunflowers.*

PRESENT PROGRESSIVE

I am showing	we are showing
you are showing	you are showing
he/she/it is showing	they are showing

• *I am showing some friends around the garden.*

PAST

I showed	we showed
you showed	you showed
he/she/it showed	they showed

• *He showed no emotion as he spoke.*

PAST PROGRESSIVE

I was showing	we were showing
you were showing	you were showing
he/she/it was showing	they were showing

• *The movie was showing at a theater downtown.*

PRESENT PERFECT ... have | has shown
PAST PERFECT ... had shown

FUTURE ... will show
FUTURE PROGRESSIVE ... will be showing
FUTURE PERFECT ... will have shown

PAST PASSIVE

I was shown	we were shown
you were shown	you were shown
he/she/it was shown	they were shown

• *The theory was shown to be seriously flawed.*

───(COMPLEMENTS)───

show *be visible/present/presented/ displayed*	The house's age is obviously showing. The buds are just beginning to show. Nothing showed on the X-rays. The wine stain doesn't show. Our visitors never showed. When is the movie showing? He never lets his feelings show.
show ____ *lead, guide* OBJECT + ADVERB OF PLACE TO/FROM	May I show **you** *to your seats*, ladies? The receptionist will show **us** *to the conference room*.
show ____ *display* OBJECT	You must show **your ID card** before you can enter. The car showed **signs of having been in an accident.**
PASSIVE	Her paintings have been shown all over the world.
INDIRECT OBJECT + DIRECT OBJECT	Show *me* **the money.** The realtor showed *some prospective buyers* **the house.** They always showed *their employees* **real consideration.**
to PARAPHRASE	Show **the money** *to me*. The realtor showed **the house** *to some prospective buyers*. They always showed **real consideration** *to their employees*.
show ____ *demonstrate* OBJECT + INFINITIVE	John showed **himself** *to be an excellent landscaper.* The plans showed **the home** *to be smaller than we had been told.*
PASSIVE	The results were shown *to be faked.*
(OBJECT +) THAT-CLAUSE	The concert will show **that Louise has made enormous progress.** We showed *them* **that we were fully prepared to do the job.**
(OBJECT +) WH-CLAUSE	The results showed **just what we had expected.** Janet showed *me* **how much we could save on insurance.**
(OBJECT +) WH-INFINITIVE	The chart showed **how much to invest.** The manual shows *you* **what to do.** Lou will show *them* **where to park.**

PRESENT		PRESENT PROGRESSIVE	
I shrink	we shrink	I am shrinking	we are shrinking
you shrink	you shrink	you are shrinking	you are shrinking
he/she/it shrinks	they shrink	he/she/it is shrinking	they are shrinking

- *Wool shrinks if washed in hot water.*
- *Our margin of error is shrinking.*

PAST		PAST PROGRESSIVE	
I shrank	we shrank	I was shrinking	we were shrinking
you shrank	you shrank	you were shrinking	you were shrinking
he/she/it shrank	they shrank	he/she/it was shrinking	they were shrinking

- *The architect shrank the house by a third.*
- *The laundry was always shrinking my shirts.*

PRESENT PERFECT	... have | has shrunk
PAST PERFECT	... had shrunk

FUTURE	... will shrink
FUTURE PROGRESSIVE	... will be shrinking
FUTURE PERFECT	... will have shrunk

PAST PASSIVE

I was shrunk	we were shrunk
you were shrunk	you were shrunk
he/she/it was shrunk	they were shrunk

- *The deficit was shrunk significantly in the third quarter.*

───────────────(**COMPLEMENTS**)───

shrink *become smaller*

Hot metal shrinks as it cools.
Our budget is shrinking by the minute.
Average take-home pay has shrunk over the last five years.
Arctic sea ice is shrinking more every summer.
My waist has shrunk a bit, thanks to my diet.

shrink ___ *cause to become smaller*

OBJECT

He shrank **the wool sweaters** by using water that was too hot.
We waterproofed the wet barrels by shrinking **them** in the sun.
We are trying to shrink **our inventory of unsold goods**.

PASSIVE

Our profits have been shrunk by rising costs.

shrink ___ *try to avoid*

from OBJECT

Most actors don't shrink **from the limelight**.
The president does not shrink **from his role as commander-in-chief**.

from PRESENT PARTICIPLE

Reggie won't shrink **from telling the truth on the witness stand**.
Scientists don't shrink **from examining all the data**.

───────────────(**PHRASAL VERBS**)───

shrink away/back (from ___)
draw back (from [someone/something]), as in fear

The children shrank away from the homeless man.
The cats shrank back at the sight of the dogs.

I shut	we shut
you shut	you shut
he/she/it shuts	they shut

- *Sandy shuts the store by 8 P.M.*

PRESENT PROGRESSIVE

I am shutting	we are shutting
you are shutting	you are shutting
he/she/it is shutting	they are shutting

- *Hurry! The ushers are shutting the doors.*

PAST

I shut	we shut
you shut	you shut
he/she/it shut	they shut

- *He shut himself in his office.*

PAST PROGRESSIVE

I was shutting	we were shutting
you were shutting	you were shutting
he/she/it was shutting	they were shutting

- *The highway patrol was shutting the roads.*

PRESENT PERFECT ... have | has shut
PAST PERFECT   ... had shut

FUTURE   ... will shut
FUTURE PROGRESSIVE ... will be shutting
FUTURE PERFECT   ... will have shut

PAST PASSIVE

I was shut	we were shut
you were shut	you were shut
he/she/it was shut	they were shut

- *The gates were shut by the guard.*

COMPLEMENTS

shut *close*

The door is shutting behind him.
The gate shut with a loud crash.
My eyes slowly shut and I fell asleep.
The lid shut on my fingers.
We heard the trap shut with a snap.
All government offices shut at five.

shut ____ *cause to close*

OBJECT

I shut **the windows** and drew the curtains.
President Roosevelt shut **all the banks** temporarily to prevent
    failures.
He shut **the book** and returned it to the shelf.
The Navy is going to shut **the entire shipyard**.
Once inside, I shut **the umbrella**.

PASSIVE

The entrance was shut after the last worker arrived.

shut ____ *confine, pen*

OBJECT + ADVERB OF PLACE

We always shut **the animals *in the barn*** at night.
The blockade shut **the enemy fleet *inside the port***.

PASSIVE

The prisoners were shut *inside a makeshift jail*.

PHRASAL VERBS

shut _SEP_ **down** *close permanently*

Producers shut the play down after
    only 10 performances.
The car manufacturer shut down three automotive plants.

shut _SEP_ **in** *surround, enclose*

The cowboys shut the cattle in.

shut off *stop operating*

The motor shut off 15 minutes ago.

shut _SEP_ **off** *turn off*

They shut off the gas before leaving on vacation.

shut _SEP_ **off** *stop movement into and out of*

Police shut the street off during the standoff.
Authorities shut off the downtown area because of a bomb threat.

shut _SEP_ **out** *exclude*

The manager shut us out of the decision making.

shut up *stop talking* [INFORMAL]

Would you shut up and listen to me?

shut _SEP_ **up** *lock up*

Guards shut the prisoners up in their cells.

PRESENT

I sign	we sign
you sign	you sign
he/she/it signs	they sign

• *The sheriff signs all the release forms.*

PRESENT PROGRESSIVE

I am signing	we are signing
you are signing	you are signing
he/she/it is signing	they are signing

• *We are signing the contract tomorrow.*

PAST

I signed	we signed
you signed	you signed
he/she/it signed	they signed

• *The governor signed the bill yesterday.*

PAST PROGRESSIVE

I was signing	we were signing
you were signing	you were signing
he/she/it was signing	they were signing

• *She was signing books for the entire class.*

PRESENT PERFECT ... have | has signed
PAST PERFECT ... had signed

FUTURE ... will sign
FUTURE PROGRESSIVE ... will be signing
FUTURE PERFECT ... will have signed

PAST PASSIVE

I was signed	we were signed
you were signed	you were signed
he/she/it was signed	they were signed

• *The Treaty of Versailles was signed on June 28, 1919.*

COMPLEMENTS

sign *write one's name*	Where should I sign? Sign here, please.
sign *formally agree to the terms of a contract/agreement*	The players for next season have all signed. All participating countries must sign.
sign *communicate in sign language*	Do you know how to sign? She has been hired to sign at the convention. The hospital needs people who can sign.
sign ⎯⎯ *write one's name on*	
OBJECT	Be sure to sign and date **the document**. The president himself signed **the note**. The actress was signing **autographs** for her fans.
PASSIVE	The get-well card had been signed by everyone in the office.
sign ⎯⎯ *formally accept the terms of [a contract, an agreement]*	
OBJECT	The union finally signed **the new contract**. The government never actually signed **the trade agreement**.
PASSIVE	The copyright agreement was signed by all parties.
sign ⎯⎯ *hire with a contract*	
OBJECT	The team's management signed **all of its veteran players**. The city signed **the company** to provide trash collection.
PASSIVE	Our conductor was signed for another three seasons.

PHRASAL VERBS

sign in/out *indicate one's arrival/ departure by recording one's name*	Members must sign in between 8 and 9 A.M. Be sure to sign out as you leave.
sign off on ⎯⎯ *formally agree to by signing*	The president signed off on the proposed labor policies.
sign on/off *begin/stop broadcasting*	The disc jockey signed on at 6 A.M. When do you sign off tonight?
sign on/up *join by signing*	The entire committee signed on for another two-year term. Dozens of people signed up for the Great Books series.
sign _SEP_ **up** *record an agreement with [someone] to join*	The company signed up 22 software engineers at the job fair. We hope to sign up 50 volunteers for Habitat for Humanity.

PRESENT

I sing	we sing
you sing	you sing
he/she/it sings	they sing

• *He sings in the church choir.*

PRESENT PROGRESSIVE

I am singing	we are singing
you are singing	you are singing
he/she/it is singing	they are singing

• *The birds are singing in the trees.*

PAST

I sang	we sang
you sang	you sang
he/she/it sang	they sang

• *She sang several songs by Bellini.*

PAST PROGRESSIVE

I was singing	we were singing
you were singing	you were singing
he/she/it was singing	they were singing

• *The group was singing around the campfire.*

PRESENT PERFECT ... have | has sung
PAST PERFECT ... had sung

FUTURE ... will sing
FUTURE PROGRESSIVE ... will be singing
FUTURE PERFECT ... will have sung

PAST PASSIVE

—	—
—	—
it was sung	they were sung

• *The opera was sung in English.*

COMPLEMENTS

sing *make musical sounds with one's voice*	Do you like to sing? Everybody can learn to sing. She sings beautifully. Jeff sang at his and Susan's wedding. The birds are already singing by 5:30.
sing *make musical sounds, hum, buzz, whistle*	The engine's vibration was making some metal part sing. The telephone wires were singing in the wind. The teakettle began to sing.
sing ____ *perform [a piece of vocal music]*	
OBJECT	The choir sang **several traditional Christmas carols**. The Beatles sang **their own compositions**. Herbie sang **1960s hits** at the class reunion.
PASSIVE	The national anthem is sung before every baseball game.

PHRASAL VERBS

sing along *sing together*	Everyone at the party sang along with the music.

EXPRESSIONS

sing a different tune *have changed one's opinion*	He used to favor the death penalty; now he's singing a different tune.
sing [someone's] praises *say good things about [someone]*	Your English teacher is singing your praises.
sing the praises of ____ *say good things about [someone/something]*	The whole office is singing the praises of the new copier.
sing ____ **to sleep** *put to sleep by singing*	The babysitter was able to sing the baby to sleep.

PRESENT

I sink	we sink
you sink	you sink
he/she/it sinks	they sink

• *Productivity sinks in the summer.*

PRESENT PROGRESSIVE

I am sinking	we are sinking
you are sinking	you are sinking
he/she/it is sinking	they are sinking

• *Oil production is gradually sinking.*

PAST

I sank	we sank
you sank	you sank
he/she/it sank	they sank

• *The stock market sank again today.*

PAST PROGRESSIVE

I was sinking	we were sinking
you were sinking	you were sinking
he/she/it was sinking	they were sinking

• *Our spirits were sinking by the minute.*

PRESENT PERFECT ... have | has sunk
PAST PERFECT ... had sunk

FUTURE ... will sink
FUTURE PROGRESSIVE ... will be sinking
FUTURE PERFECT ... will have sunk

PAST PASSIVE

I was sunk	we were sunk
you were sunk	you were sunk
he/she/it was sunk	they were sunk

• *The boat was sunk in 50 feet of water.*

(**COMPLEMENTS**)

sink *go below the surface*	The ship sank in less than an hour. My boots were sinking in the soft mud. The wheels sank into the snowdrift.
sink *go down gradually*	The hot air balloon was sinking to the earth. Tired and hungry, the travelers sank to their knees. The sun was sinking in the west. The temperature sank as night fell. Senator Blather's poll numbers were steadily sinking. The value of our portfolio has sunk by 20%.
sink *become weaker*	My heart sank when I heard the bad news. The patient in Room 413 is sinking rapidly, Doctor.
sink _____ *cause to go below the surface*	
OBJECT	An explosion in the engine room sank **the fishing boat**. I sank **a shovel** into the wet ground.
PASSIVE	The barges were sunk by the storm.
OBJECT + ADVERB OF PLACE TO/FROM	We sank **the screws *into the wood***. The ship sank **its anchor *into the sandy bottom of the bay***. The dog sank **its teeth *into my leg***.
PASSIVE	The steel supports were sunk *in five feet of concrete*.
sink _____ *go gradually [into a certain state/condition]*	
into OBJECT	The family sank **into poverty**. The once-proud company sank **into oblivion**. His widow and orphans sank **into despair**.
sink _____ *ruin*	
OBJECT	These awful rumors could sink **the company**. The defeat sank **all our hopes for the championship**.
PASSIVE	The plans for expansion were sunk by the economic downturn.

(**PHRASAL VERBS**)

sink back *lean back and relax*	After work, I poured a drink and sank back on the sofa.
sink in *be understood*	Has Trina's desperate situation sunk in yet? The teacher's explanation will sink in eventually.

PRESENT

I sit	we sit
you sit	you sit
he/she/it sits	they sit

• *The cat always sits by the window.*

PRESENT PROGRESSIVE

I am sitting	we are sitting
you are sitting	you are sitting
he/she/it is sitting	they are sitting

• *I'm just sitting here, waiting for somebody.*

PAST

I sat	we sat
you sat	you sat
he/she/it sat	they sat

• *We sat on a park bench in the sun.*

PAST PROGRESSIVE

I was sitting	we were sitting
you were sitting	you were sitting
he/she/it was sitting	they were sitting

• *We were sitting by the fireplace.*

PRESENT PERFECT ... have | has sat
PAST PERFECT ... had sat

FUTURE ... will sit
FUTURE PROGRESSIVE ... will be sitting
FUTURE PERFECT ... will have sat

PAST PASSIVE

Sit is rarely used in the passive voice.

(**COMPLEMENTS**)

sit *be seated*	Never stand when you can sit.
	The plane can't take off until you sit and fasten your seat belt.
	I can't sit very long before my legs start to hurt.
	We trained the dog to sit on command.
sit *be in session, meet* [OF A GOVERNMENTAL BODY]	By law, the Supreme Court sits on the first Monday in October.
	The budget committee is sitting this afternoon.
	The state legislature does not normally sit during the summer.
sit ____ *be seated/located* ADVERB OF PLACE	I sat **next to him** at dinner.
	The flock of birds sat **on a telephone wire**.
	We are sitting **on the runway**, waiting to take off.
	The statue sits **in the center of the town square**.
	When I got to the office, a new computer was sitting **on my desk**.
	My briefcase was sitting **by the chair**, right where I had left it.
sit ____ *have enough seats for* OBJECT	Our dining room table sits **eight**.

(**PHRASAL VERBS**)

sit around *spend time idly*	We're just sitting around listening to music.
sit back *relax*	We sat back and enjoyed the show.
sit back/by *not be involved*	I refuse to sit back and do nothing when people's lives are in danger.
sit SEP down *cause to be in a sitting position*	Momma sat us kids down and told us that Grandma had died.
sit in for ____ *replace*	The sports editor sat in for the regular news anchor last night.
sit in (on ____) *attend ([an event])*	The board meeting is tomorrow morning, and I'd like to sit in.
	Would it be okay if I sat in on your Language and Culture class?
sit on ____ *be a member of*	She sat on the jury that convicted my neighbor.
	Senator Blather sits on the Committee on Appropriations.
sit on ____ *delay in revealing*	The reporter is sitting on a story about the president's health.
sit SEP out *not participate in*	I'm going to sit this dance out.
sit through ____ *attend all of*	Do we have to sit through another boring lecture?
sit up *sit upright*	Sit up! Slouching is bad for your posture.
sit up *not go to bed*	Kristen sat up knitting half the night.
sit up *become suddenly alert*	Cassie sat up suddenly and looked at the door.

PRESENT

I sleep	we sleep
you sleep	you sleep
he/she/it sleeps	they sleep

- *He usually sleeps seven hours a night.*

PRESENT PROGRESSIVE

I am sleeping	we are sleeping
you are sleeping	you are sleeping
he/she/it is sleeping	they are sleeping

- *I am not sleeping very well lately.*

PAST

I slept	we slept
you slept	you slept
he/she/it slept	they slept

- *The kids slept in a tent in the backyard.*

PAST PROGRESSIVE

I was sleeping	we were sleeping
you were sleeping	you were sleeping
he/she/it was sleeping	they were sleeping

- *Our guests were sleeping in the downstairs bedroom.*

PRESENT PERFECT ... have | has slept
PAST PERFECT ... had slept

FUTURE ... will sleep
FUTURE PROGRESSIVE ... will be sleeping
FUTURE PERFECT ... will have slept

PAST PASSIVE

Sleep is never used in the passive voice.

―――(**COMPLEMENTS**)―――

sleep *not be awake*	We all need to sleep.
	I slept through the storm.
	He only slept a few hours last night.
	Be quiet; the baby is sleeping.
sleep *be inactive*	New York never sleeps.
	The surveillance system never sleeps.
	The security force never sleeps.
sleep ――― *take as a place for sleeping*	
ADVERB OF PLACE	The children sleep **in their own bedrooms**.
	We usually sleep **at a motel** when we visit my grandparents.
	When we go camping, we sleep **in an ultralight tent**.
	If I get home late, I sleep **downstairs** so I don't wake anybody.
sleep ――― *provide sleeping accommodations for*	
OBJECT	The suite sleeps **four adults** comfortably.
	The studio apartments only sleep **two people**.
	The lodge will be able to sleep **our entire family**.

―――(**PHRASAL VERBS**)―――

sleep in *sleep after one's normal time to rise*	Sorry, I slept in this morning. What's for lunch?
sleep SEP **off** *recover from while sleeping*	Sherri drank too much at the party and had to sleep it off.
sleep on ――― *delay a decision on*	I'll sleep on the matter and give you an answer tomorrow.
sleep through ――― *be asleep and unaware of*	Our neighbors slept through the thunderstorm.

―――(**EXPRESSIONS**)―――

sleep a wink *sleep briefly* [USUALLY NEGATIVE]	I didn't sleep a wink last night.
sleep like a baby/log *sleep long and well*	I played two hours of tennis last evening and slept like a log.

PRESENT

I slide	we slide
you slide	you slide
he/she/it slides	they slide

• *The glass door slides easily now.*

PRESENT PROGRESSIVE

I am sliding	we are sliding
you are sliding	you are sliding
he/she/it is sliding	they are sliding

• *Look out! The car is sliding.*

PAST

I slid	we slid
you slid	you slid
he/she/it slid	they slid

• *The car slid into the ditch.*

PAST PROGRESSIVE

I was sliding	we were sliding
you were sliding	you were sliding
he/she/it was sliding	they were sliding

• *The kids were sliding down Prosser Hill.*

PRESENT PERFECT ... have | has slid
PAST PERFECT ... had slid

FUTURE ... will slide
FUTURE PROGRESSIVE ... will be sliding
FUTURE PERFECT ... will have slid

PAST PASSIVE

I was slid	we were slid
you were slid	you were slid
he/she/it was slid	they were slid

• *The logs were slid down the hill.*

(**COMPLEMENTS**)

slide *slip, shift, drop*

Hang on to me—I'm sliding.
The bag of groceries slid from my hand.
Make sure the load doesn't slide.

slide *gradually become worse*

His reputation is beginning to slide.
Our once-strong financial position was sliding.

slide _____ *move/glide smoothly over a surface*
  ADVERB OF PLACE TO/FROM

The car slid **into a snowbank**.
I slid **behind the wheel**.
The canoes slid **into the water**.
The truck in front of us was sliding **all over the road**.
The drawer slides **on side-mounted tracks**.

slide _____ *gradually go/move [into a worse condition]*
  ADVERB OF PLACE TO/FROM

The patient was sliding **into a coma**.
The company gradually slid **into mediocrity**.
The quality of dental care was sliding **downhill**.
The temperature slid **into the twenties** overnight.

slide _____ *put/push/move smoothly*
  OBJECT + ADVERB OF PLACE TO/FROM

She slid the **keys** *into her purse*.
I slid **my hands** gently *under the kitten* and lifted it up.
Just slide **your paper** *under my office door*.

  PASSIVE

The refrigerator was slid *into place*.

  INDIRECT OBJECT + DIRECT OBJECT

The suspect slid *the detective* his driver's license.
The cook slid *me* a bowl of soup.

  to PARAPHRASE

The suspect slid **his driver's license** *to the detective*.
The cook slid **a bowl of soup** *to me*.

(**PHRASAL VERBS**)

slide around/back/down/off/out/under/up/etc. *slide in a specified direction*

We slid back down several times.
Her shawl slid off.
The window easily slides up and down.

slide SEP **around/back/down/in/off/out/up**/etc. *cause to slide in a specified direction*

The goalie slid the puck back to a defenseman.
The locksmith can't slide the bolt in and out.
The roofer lost his balance and slid off.

slip _____ *go/move [from one state/condition to another]*
ADVERB OF PLACE TO/FROM   The patient was slipping **in and out of consciousness**.

slip _____ *gradually go/move [into a worse condition]*
ADVERB OF PLACE TO/FROM   The company's profits were slipping **to record lows**.
                                         The riots were slipping **into total chaos**.

PHRASAL VERBS

slip away/back/by/down/in/out/past/   Time is slipping away.
under/up/etc. *go without being noticed /*   We slipped away when they turned their backs.
shift in a specified direction   Their anniversary slipped by without our remembering it.
                                             My glasses slipped down again.
                                             The key slipped out and fell on the floor.
                                             Hilary and DJ slipped off to spend time in Caliban's.

slip SEP away/back/by/down/in/out/   The dock worker slipped the rope back on the pulley.
past/under/up/etc. *cause to slide/shift*   The carpenter slipped the bolt in and out.
in a specified direction

slip into / out of _____ *put on / take off* Gloria slipped into jeans and a sweatshirt.
[clothing]   Nate slipped out of his pajamas and into the shower.

slip SEP on/off *put on / take off [clothing]* Bridget slipped a jacket on.
                                                Greg slipped his sweater off.

slip out *be said in error*   I didn't mean to say it; the words just slipped out.

EXPRESSIONS

let it slip *reveal something, usually*   The press secretary let it slip that the
unintentionally   president would travel to the Mideast soon.

slip between/through the cracks   Veterans' benefits slipped between the cracks in the
be neglected/forgotten   military budget.
                                             These proposals will slip through the cracks if we don't
                                                write them down.

slip one over on _____ *fool, deceive*   Debbie slipped one over on her boss and didn't get caught.

slip [someone's] mind *be forgotten by*   This afternoon's meeting completely slipped my mind.
[someone]

slip through [someone's] fingers *avoid*   The bank robbers slipped through our fingers again.
capture by / elude [someone]   She almost figured out the problem, but the solution
                                                slipped through her fingers.

PRESENT

I slip	we slip
you slip	you slip
he/she/it slips	they slip

• *The transmission slips when in reverse.*

PRESENT PROGRESSIVE

I am slipping	we are slipping
you are slipping	you are slipping
he/she/it is slipping	they are slipping

• *The candidate's approval ratings are slipping.*

PAST

I slipped	we slipped
you slipped	you slipped
he/she/it slipped	they slipped

• *I slipped on the ice.*

PAST PROGRESSIVE

I was slipping	we were slipping
you were slipping	you were slipping
he/she/it was slipping	they were slipping

• *The wheels were slipping on the icy road.*

PRESENT PERFECT ... have | has slipped
PAST PERFECT   ... had slipped

FUTURE   ... will slip
FUTURE PROGRESSIVE ... will be slipping
FUTURE PERFECT   ... will have slipped

PAST PASSIVE

I was slipped	we were slipped
you were slipped	you were slipped
he/she/it was slipped	they were slipped

• *The usher was slipped a few dollars and we got really good seats.*

COMPLEMENTS

slip *lose traction / one's grip, fall accidentally*	Tom slipped and fell off the ladder.
	He slipped and fell to his hands and knees.
	The rear tires slipped and the car slid off the road.
	The rope slipped and the load crashed to the floor.
	The gears are slipping badly.
slip *make a mistake*	Her boss slipped and told her she was getting a raise.
slip *gradually become worse*	Grandpa's memory is really slipping.
	Our control over events was slipping.
	The senator's ability to shape the story was slipping.
slip _____ *slide, shift, drop*	
ADVERB OF PLACE TO/FROM	The book slipped **from her hand**.
	She slipped **on the icy sidewalk**.
	The wrench was constantly slipping **off the bolt**.
	Events were slipping **out of our grasp**.
slip _____ *go without being noticed*	
ADVERB OF PLACE TO/FROM	We slipped **out of the noisy room**.
slip _____ *slide, put/push/move smoothly (often unobtrusively)*	
OBJECT + ADVERB OF PLACE TO/FROM	I slipped **the gun** *into my pocket*.
	He slipped **the ring** *onto her finger*.
PASSIVE	A letter had been slipped *under my door*.
INDIRECT OBJECT + DIRECT OBJECT	I slipped *the cab driver* a ten-dollar bill.
	My mother always slips *her grandchildren* little treats.
	The senator slipped *the reporters* some information.
to PARAPHRASE	I slipped **a ten-dollar bill** *to the cab driver*.
	My mother always slips **little treats** *to her grandchildren*.
	The senator slipped **some information** *to the reporters*.
slip _____ *be released/freed from*	
OBJECT	The ship slipped **its mooring** and set sail.
	The hounds slipped **their leashes** and raced ahead.
	"Cry 'Havoc,' and let slip **the dogs of war**."
	[SHAKESPEARE]

PRESENT

I smile	we smile
you smile	you smile
he/she/it smiles	they smile

• *He always smiles when he sees us.*

PRESENT PROGRESSIVE

I am smiling	we are smiling
you are smiling	you are smiling
he/she/it is smiling	they are smiling

• *He is always smiling.*

PAST

I smiled	we smiled
you smiled	you smiled
he/she/it smiled	they smiled

• *I smiled as pleasantly as I could.*

PAST PROGRESSIVE

I was smiling	we were smiling
you were smiling	you were smiling
he/she/it was smiling	they were smiling

• *Everybody was smiling when they returned.*

PRESENT PERFECT ... have | has smiled
PAST PERFECT ... had smiled

FUTURE ... will smile
FUTURE PROGRESSIVE ... will be smiling
FUTURE PERFECT ... will have smiled

PAST PASSIVE

Smile is rarely used in the passive voice.

───────────────(COMPLEMENTS)───────────────

smile *make the corners of one's mouth turn up to show amusement/happiness/pleasure*

Keep smiling!
Babies smile when people smile at them.
Americans automatically smile when they meet someone.
Can you smile for the camera?

smile ⎯⎯⎯ *convey with a smile*
   OBJECT

The queen smiled **her appreciation for the gift**.
The boss smiled **his approval**.

smile ⎯⎯⎯ *give [a smile of a certain type]*
   OBJECT

The little girl smiled **a bashful little smile**.
The villain in old movies always smiled **a sneering leer**.
I smiled **a self-conscious, stupid grin** when my name
   was called.

───────────────(PHRASAL VERBS)───────────────

smile on ⎯⎯⎯ *be favorable to*

Fortune smiles on the brave. [PROVERB]
Fate smiled on Napoleon at Austerlitz.

PRESENT

I sneak	we sneak
you sneak	you sneak
he/she/it sneaks	they sneak

• *He sneaks a candy bar at bedtime.*

PRESENT PROGRESSIVE

I am sneaking	we are sneaking
you are sneaking	you are sneaking
he/she/it is sneaking	they are sneaking

• *The prisoners are sneaking past the guards.*

PAST

I sneaked	we sneaked
you sneaked	you sneaked
he/she/it sneaked	they sneaked

• *We sneaked out of the meeting early.*

PAST PROGRESSIVE

I was sneaking	we were sneaking
you were sneaking	you were sneaking
he/she/it was sneaking	they were sneaking

• *I was sneaking a quick snack in the kitchen.*

PRESENT PERFECT ... have | has sneaked
PAST PERFECT ... had sneaked

FUTURE ... will sneak
FUTURE PROGRESSIVE ... will be sneaking
FUTURE PERFECT ... will have sneaked

PAST PASSIVE

I was sneaked	we were sneaked
you were sneaked	you were sneaked
he/she/it was sneaked	they were sneaked

• *Food was sneaked out of the cafeteria.*

─────────────────────────── **COMPLEMENTS** ───

sneak _____ *move quietly and secretly in order not to be noticed*

ADVERB OF PLACE TO/FROM

They were trying to sneak **into the game.**
We had to sneak **back into the dorms** after curfew.
Apparently, the prisoners had sneaked **over the wall.**
Someone had sneaked **into the coffee room** and eaten all the donuts.

sneak _____ *take/bring quietly and secretly in order not to be noticed*

OBJECT + ADVERB OF PLACE TO/FROM

I sneaked **a recorder** *into the meeting.*
The kids had sneaked **some cookies** *out of the kitchen.*
They had sneaked **some friends** *into the hotel pool.*

PASSIVE

Something had been sneaked *out of the secure area.*

─────────────────────────── **PHRASAL VERBS** ───

sneak along/around/away/in/out/ up/etc. *sneak in a specified direction*

Nobody likes people who sneak around.
The kids sneaked away with a bag of candy.

sneak _____ **along/away/in/out/ up**/etc. *sneak [someone/something] in a specified direction*

I wasn't invited, but my friends sneaked me in.

sneak up on _____ *approach quietly and secretly*

We sneaked up on Dad while he was working the crossword puzzle.
Sandy sneaked up on me and tapped me on the shoulder.

PRESENT		PRESENT PROGRESSIVE	
I solve	we solve	I am solving	we are solving
you solve	you solve	you are solving	you are solving
he/she/it solves	they solve	he/she/it is solving	they are solving

• *Sherlock always solves the mystery.*

• *The police are solving about half their cases.*

PAST		PAST PROGRESSIVE	
I solved	we solved	I was solving	we were solving
you solved	you solved	you were solving	you were solving
he/she/it solved	they solved	he/she/it was solving	they were solving

• *I finally solved the equation.*

• *My students were solving 90% of the math problems.*

PRESENT PERFECT ... have | has solved
PAST PERFECT ... had solved

FUTURE ... will solve
FUTURE PROGRESSIVE ... will be solving
FUTURE PERFECT ... will have solved

PAST PASSIVE

—   —

—   —

it was solved   they were solved

• *The murder case was solved.*

─────────────────────────────(COMPLEMENTS)───

solve _____ *find the answer to [a mystery, problem, puzzle]*

OBJECT
In books, the detective always solves **the crime.**
My students haven't learned to solve **quadratic equations** yet.
No one has solved **the mystery of inflation.**
She can solve the **Rubik's Cube** in three minutes.
Oedipus solved **the riddle of the Sphinx.**
We finally solved **Tim's crossword puzzle in yesterday's** *New York Times.*
Many mathematicians have tried to solve **Goldbach's conjecture.**
Which problem were you trying to solve?

PASSIVE
A good puzzle can only be solved by several people working together.

PRESENT

I sound	we sound
you sound	you sound
he/she/it sounds	they sound

  • *An alarm sounds when the door opens.*

PRESENT PROGRESSIVE

I am sounding	we are sounding
you are sounding	you are sounding
he/she/it is sounding	they are sounding

  • *His voice is sounding hoarse.*

PAST

I sounded	we sounded
you sounded	you sounded
he/she/it sounded	they sounded

  • *He sounded pretty worried about it.*

PAST PROGRESSIVE

I was sounding	we were sounding
you were sounding	you were sounding
he/she/it was sounding	they were sounding

  • *The news was sounding pretty bad.*

PRESENT PERFECT ... have | has sounded
PAST PERFECT   ... had sounded

FUTURE   ... will sound
FUTURE PROGRESSIVE ... will be sounding
FUTURE PERFECT ... will have sounded

PAST PASSIVE

—	—
—	—
it was sounded	they were sounded

  • *A bell was sounded at the start of the final lap.*

(COMPLEMENTS)

sound *make a noise*	The bell sounds every 15 minutes. My alarm sounds like the crack of doom. The buzzer sounded before he shot the ball. Behind them in the forest, a horn was sounding.
sound _____ *make a noise by blowing on/into* OBJECT	The huntsmen sounded **the horn** to call the hounds. Sound **the car horn** to tell them to open the garage door. The truck sounded **its horn** to warn the car in front of it.
PASSIVE	The trumpets were sounded and the procession began.
sound _____ *give an audible signal/warning* OBJECT	The captain sounds **three blasts** when the ship leaves the dock. The bell sounds **the hour.** The whistle sounds **the shift change at the factory.**
sound _____ *seem, appear* (like) PREDICATE NOUN	Donna sounded **(like) a perfect fit for the job.** It sounded **(like) a reasonable idea to us.** His proposal sounded **(like) a huge gamble.**
PREDICATE ADJECTIVE	Harry sounds **a little strange.** The violin sounded **off-key to me.** It doesn't sound **right** that it should take so long to fix the car. His story sounded **improbable.**
it + *sound* + *as if / as though / like* CLAUSE	It sounds **as if Vince wants to come to the party.** It sounds **as though we'll have to leave tomorrow.** It sounded **like Beth had lost her purse again.**

(PHRASAL VERBS)

sound off *complain, often loudly*	Citizens were sounding off about traffic congestion on Mulberry Street.

PRESENT

I speak	we speak
you speak	you speak
he/she/it speaks	they speak

 • *He speaks really well.*

PRESENT PROGRESSIVE

I am speaking	we are speaking
you are speaking	you are speaking
he/she/it is speaking	they are speaking

 • *I am speaking at the luncheon this afternoon.*

PAST

I spoke	we spoke
you spoke	you spoke
he/she/it spoke	they spoke

 • *They spoke about website design.*

PAST PROGRESSIVE

I was speaking	we were speaking
you were speaking	you were speaking
he/she/it was speaking	they were speaking

 • *They were speaking French at the time.*

PRESENT PERFECT ... have | has spoken
PAST PERFECT ... had spoken

FUTURE ... will speak
FUTURE PROGRESSIVE ... will be speaking
FUTURE PERFECT ... will have spoken

PAST PASSIVE

—	—
—	—
it was spoken	they were spoken

 • *English was spoken everywhere they traveled.*

(COMPLEMENTS)

speak *talk, say words*	Are you hurt? Can you speak? Most children start speaking before their second birthday. He was so upset he couldn't speak.
speak *have a conversation*	They need to find a place where they can speak privately. They were speaking in whispers. After their argument, they weren't speaking for months.
speak *make a public presentation*	Everybody at the conference wants to hear her speak. It takes a lot of practice to speak in public. I am not used to speaking without notes.
speak _____ *say, express* OBJECT	They are speaking **the truth about what happened**. He spoke **gentle words of wisdom**.
speak _____ *have a conversation with* to OBJECT	We spoke **to the police** about the break-in. Have you spoken **to your mother**? May I speak **to Mr. Huntleigh**?
speak _____ *talk in [a specific language]* OBJECT PASSIVE	She can speak **German and Dutch** pretty well. **How many languages** do you speak? Both English and French were spoken at the conference.

(PHRASAL VERBS)

speak for _____ *say something on behalf of*	I am speaking only for myself. The candidate spoke for lowering taxes. "I speak for the trees, for the trees have no tongues." [DR. SEUSS]
speak for _____ *ask for*	I'd like to speak for the last slice of cheesecake. The last copy of the book is already spoken for.
speak of _____ *speak about*	Grandpa spoke of hardships during the Great Depression.
speak out *express one's opinion*	Thomas speaks out at every meeting he attends.
speak up *speak more loudly*	Speak up! We can't hear you in the back row.
speak up for _____ *speak in support of*	She always speaks up for military families.

I speed   we speed
you speed   you speed
he/she/it speeds   they speed

- *He speeds when he gets on the freeway.*

PRESENT PROGRESSIVE

I am speeding   we are speeding
you are speeding   you are speeding
he/she/it is speeding   they are speeding

- *She is already speeding away.*

PAST

I sped   we sped
you sped   you sped
he/she/it sped   they sped

- *The sailboat sped before the wind.*

PAST PROGRESSIVE

I was speeding   we were speeding
you were speeding   you were speeding
he/she/it was speeding   they were speeding

- *We got pulled over because we were speeding.*

PRESENT PERFECT ... have | has sped	
PAST PERFECT ... had sped	

FUTURE ... will speed
FUTURE PROGRESSIVE ... will be speeding
FUTURE PERFECT ... will have sped

PAST PASSIVE

Speed is rarely used in the passive voice.

(**COMPLEMENTS**)

speed *go/move fast*	The dogs sped across the roadway. The skiers sped down the slope toward the lodge. The horses are speeding around the final turn. The rescuers were speeding to the scene of the accident.
speed *drive faster than the legal limit*	If you speed, you could lose your driver's license. He was speeding in a construction zone and had to pay a huge fine.
speed ____ *cause to go/move faster* OBJECT	We changed the rules to speed **the approval process**. Some men will try anything to speed **hair growth**. Trying to speed **an entrenched bureaucracy** is next to impossible.

(**PHRASAL VERBS**)

speed along/away/down/over/past/ up/etc. *go fast in a specified direction*	An ambulance sped past with its siren blaring. Teens were speeding up and down Main Street.
speed ____ **along/away/down/over/ past/up**/etc. *cause to go faster in a specified direction*	The manager tried to speed the process along. The delivery service sped the package over.
speed up *go/move faster*	Ricky sped up when he saw the police car. We tend to speed up going downhill.
speed _SEP_ **up** *cause to go/move faster*	We really need to speed up the production line.

PRESENT

I spend	we spend
you spend	you spend
he/she/it spends	they spend

• *He spends too much when he eats out.*

PRESENT PROGRESSIVE

I am spending	we are spending
you are spending	you are spending
he/she/it is spending	they are spending

• *We are spending too much time on this project.*

PAST

I spent	we spent
you spent	you spent
he/she/it spent	they spent

• *We spent some time with my parents.*

PAST PROGRESSIVE

I was spending	we were spending
you were spending	you were spending
he/she/it was spending	they were spending

• *We were spending a week in Phoenix.*

PRESENT PERFECT ... have | has spent
PAST PERFECT ... had spent

FUTURE ... will spend
FUTURE PROGRESSIVE ... will be spending
FUTURE PERFECT ... will have spent

PAST PASSIVE

I was spent	we were spent
you were spent	you were spent
he/she/it was spent	they were spent

• *A fortune was spent trying to fix the problem.*

〔 **COMPLEMENTS** 〕

spend *pay out money*

They just love to spend.
We can't keep spending at this rate.
They spend and spend until they are broke.

spend _____ *pay [money]*

OBJECT

We will spend **a lot** fixing our roof.
They spend **over half their income** on housing.
You have to spend **money** to make money.

PASSIVE

The insurance settlement had already been spent.

spend _____ *be occupied for [a period of time]*

OBJECT + ADVERB OF PLACE

I will spend **all of next week** *in Chicago*.
The kids spent **half the summer** *at camp*.

OBJECT + PRESENT PARTICIPLE

We spent **all week** *working on the budget*.
A horse spends **three hours a day** *sleeping*.

PASSIVE

Last weekend was spent *cleaning out the garage*.

spend _____ *exhaust, use up*

OBJECT

The storm finally spent **itself** during the night.
General Lee had already spent **all his reserves**.

PASSIVE

Your talent would be better spent writing textbooks.

PRESENT

I spill	we spill
you spill	you spill
he/she/it spills	they spill

• *The coffee spills if you fill the cup too full.*

PRESENT PROGRESSIVE

I am spilling	we are spilling
you are spilling	you are spilling
he/she/it is spilling	they are spilling

• *Look out—you're spilling your drink.*

PAST

I spilled	we spilled
you spilled	you spilled
he/she/it spilled	they spilled

• *I spilled tea on my sweater.*

PAST PROGRESSIVE

I was spilling	we were spilling
you were spilling	you were spilling
he/she/it was spilling	they were spilling

• *The water in the tub was spilling over the top.*

PRESENT PERFECT ... have | has spilled
PAST PERFECT   ... had spilled

FUTURE   ... will spill
FUTURE PROGRESSIVE ... will be spilling
FUTURE PERFECT   ... will have spilled

PAST PASSIVE

—	—
—	—
it was spilled	they were spilled

• *Some of the soup was spilled, so I cleaned it up.*

NOTE: The past form *spilled* may also be spelled *spilt*.

COMPLEMENTS

spill *flow over the edge of a container*

Careful! The milk is spilling.
The water was spilling over the dam in a great torrent.
Blood spilt from the soldier's abdominal wound.
Tears spilled from my mother's eyes.
The tools were spilling out of the chest.

spill ____ *be emptied [onto a surface]*
    ADVERB OF PLACE TO/FROM

The sugar spilled **all over the tablecloth**.
The pencils and books spilled **across the desk**.
The concertgoers spilled **onto the street**.
The kids' toys spilled **onto the playroom floor**.

spill ____ *cause to flow over / run out*
    OBJECT

Careful! You're spilling **the wine**.
The tanker spilled **diesel oil** into the harbor.

      PASSIVE

Gasoline had been spilled down the side of our car.

spill ____ *cause to be emptied [onto a surface]*
    OBJECT + ADVERB OF PLACE TO/FROM

I spilled **rice *all over the kitchen floor***.
I spilled **the contents of the suitcase *across the bed***.

      PASSIVE

Wreckage from the airplane crash had been spilled
over several miles.

PHRASAL VERBS

spill over *overflow*

The teakettle boiled and spilled over.
The revolt in Boston spilled over into the countryside.

EXPRESSIONS

spill the beans *reveal a secret/surprise*

The producers won't spill the beans
on who will star in the film.

PRESENT

I spin	we spin
you spin	you spin
he/she/it spins	they spin

- *The disk spins at a high speed.*

PRESENT PROGRESSIVE

I am spinning	we are spinning
you are spinning	you are spinning
he/she/it is spinning	they are spinning

- *The senator's office is spinning the story.*

PAST

I spun	we spun
you spun	you spun
he/she/it spun	they spun

- *I spun the wool to make yarn.*

PAST PROGRESSIVE

I was spinning	we were spinning
you were spinning	you were spinning
he/she/it was spinning	they were spinning

- *Our wheels were spinning on the ice.*

PRESENT PERFECT ... have | has spun
PAST PERFECT ... had spun

FUTURE ... will spin
FUTURE PROGRESSIVE ... will be spinning
FUTURE PERFECT ... will have spun

PAST PASSIVE

I was spun	we were spun
you were spun	you were spun
he/she/it was spun	they were spun

- *The bets were placed and the roulette wheel was spun.*

COMPLEMENTS

spin *whirl around quickly*	The altimeter was spinning fast. The dryer is still spinning. Your wheels will spin in this slush. The earth spins on a 23.4-degree axis. The policeman spun when he heard the shot.
spin *seem to be whirling around quickly, as if to make someone dizzy*	I have to sit down; my head is spinning. The news was enough to make your head spin.
spin _____ *cause to whirl around quickly*	
OBJECT	I spun **the propeller** to get the engine started. The drivers were spinning **their wheels** in the soft ground. I showed the kids how to spin **their new top**. The server spun **the ball** so that it bounced at an odd angle.
PASSIVE	The wheel was spun by the next contestant.
spin _____ *draw out and twist into yarn*	
OBJECT	My daughter spins **wool fleece** into yarn.
PASSIVE	The cashmere yarn had been spun by hand.
spin _____ *make a web* [OF SPIDERS]	
OBJECT	Spiders had spun **webs** in every corner.
spin _____ *interpret in a way favorable to oneself*	
OBJECT	The aides were busily spinning **the election results**. He was trying to spin **the news** to minimize the damage.
PASSIVE	The story was spun until it was unrecognizable.

PHRASAL VERBS

spin away/off/out/etc. *spin in a specified direction*	The Frisbee is spinning away into the air.
spin SEP **away/off/out**/etc. *cause to spin in a specified direction*	He spun himself away from the computer.
spin off *separate and fly away from something that is spinning*	The fan blade may spin off if you don't tighten it.
spin SEP **off** *create a separate company from part of an existing one*	The chemical company spun off its herbicide division.

PRESENT

I spit · we spit
you spit · you spit
he/she/it spits · they spit

• *Our cat spits when she sees a dog.*

PRESENT PROGRESSIVE

I am spitting · we are spitting
you are spitting · you are spitting
he/she/it is spitting · they are spitting

• *The victim is spitting blood.*

PAST

I spit/spat · we spit/spat
you spit/spat · you spit/spat
he/she/it spit/spat · they spit/spat

• *He coughed and spit into his handkerchief.*

PAST PROGRESSIVE

I was spitting · we were spitting
you were spitting · you were spitting
he/she/it was spitting · they were spitting

• *They were spitting watermelon seeds.*

PRESENT PERFECT ... have | has spit/spat
PAST PERFECT ... had spit/spat

FUTURE ... will spit
FUTURE PROGRESSIVE ... will be spitting
FUTURE PERFECT ... will have spit/spat

PAST PASSIVE

I was spit/spat · we were spit/spat
you were spit/spat · you were spit/spat
he/she/it was spit/spat · they were spit/spat

• *The words were spat in utter contempt.*

(COMPLEMENTS)

spit *force something [often, saliva] from one's mouth*

Rinse out your mouth and spit, please.
People who chew tobacco have to spit constantly.
I have such a bad taste in my mouth that I'm spitting all the time.

spit *be very angry*

He was spitting angrily.
The defendant was spitting with sudden rage.

spit *rain/snow lightly*

It's spitting outside; you'd better wear a raincoat.

spit _____ *force from one's mouth*
  OBJECT

The diner spit **a chicken bone** across the table.
Aaron accidentally spit **a mouthful of soda** all over the floor.

spit _____ *throw out [liquid, fire]*
  OBJECT

The engine was spitting **oil**.
The pan was so hot that it spit **cooking oil** on my hand.
The bonfire was spitting **sparks** high into the night air.

spit _____ *say/express angrily*
  OBJECT

The man spit **abuse** at the crowd.
He spat **an oath** and slammed the door.
The man spat **an incoherent warning** at the children.

PRESENT

I split	we split
you split	you split
he/she/it splits	they split

• *Pine always splits along the grain.*

PRESENT PROGRESSIVE

I am splitting	we are splitting
you are splitting	you are splitting
he/she/it is splitting	they are splitting

• *The couple next door is splitting.*

PAST

I split	we split
you split	you split
he/she/it split	they split

• *We split the cost equally.*

PAST PROGRESSIVE

I was splitting	we were splitting
you were splitting	you were splitting
he/she/it was splitting	they were splitting

• *I was splitting enough wood to last all winter.*

PRESENT PERFECT ... have | has split
PAST PERFECT ... had split

FUTURE ... will split
FUTURE PROGRESSIVE ... will be splitting
FUTURE PERFECT ... will have split

PAST PASSIVE

I was split	we were split
you were split	you were split
he/she/it was split	they were split

• *The prize was split among the winning contestants.*

―――――――――――――――――――――――――(**COMPLEMENTS**)―――

split *separate/divide into parts*

My lips were splitting from the sun.
The ice was heaving and splitting.
The trail splits at the top of the ridge.
The class split into three groups.

split *end a marriage/relationship*

My cousin and his wife are splitting after five years.
Jayne got into a fight with her boyfriend and they decided to split.
Do you think they will split after what happened?
This issue could cause the Republican Party to split.

split _____ *cause to separate/divide into parts*

OBJECT

We split the **logs** for firewood.
Would you split **the English muffins** and toast them?
They split **the searchers** into small groups so they could cover more ground.

PASSIVE

Diamonds are still split by hand.
The atom was first split in 1932.

split _____ *share/divide among participants*

OBJECT

We need to split **the workload** more fairly.
Investors will split **the profits** in proportion to the size of their investment.
Rhonda split **a pizza** with Stan.
If we get the winning ticket, we will split **the prize** equally.

PASSIVE

Overtime hours must be split among all workers.

WH-CLAUSE

The group split **what they had earned**.
We will split **whatever we win**.
They decided to split **however much money they get**.

―――――――――――――――――――――――――(**PHRASAL VERBS**)―――

split _SEP_ up (into _____) *divide (into [groups, etc.])*

He split the class up into three groups according to height.

split _SEP_ off *separate*

The forum moderator split the topic off from the main thread.

split off (from _____) *separate (from [someone/something])*

Icebergs are splitting off from glaciers at an alarming rate.

PRESENT

I spoil	we spoil
you spoil	you spoil
he/she/it spoils	they spoil

• *He spoils the party for everyone else.*

PAST

I spoiled	we spoiled
you spoiled	you spoiled
he/she/it spoiled	they spoiled

• *The food spoiled due to a power outage.*

PRESENT PERFECT ... have | has spoiled
PAST PERFECT   ... had spoiled

PRESENT PROGRESSIVE

I am spoiling	we are spoiling
you are spoiling	you are spoiling
he/she/it is spoiling	they are spoiling

• *I can do it myself. You're spoiling me!*

PAST PROGRESSIVE

I was spoiling	we were spoiling
you were spoiling	you were spoiling
he/she/it was spoiling	they were spoiling

• *The potato salad was spoiling in the hot sun.*

FUTURE ... will spoil
FUTURE PROGRESSIVE ... will be spoiling
FUTURE PERFECT ... will have spoiled

PAST PASSIVE

I was spoiled	we were spoiled
you were spoiled	you were spoiled
he/she/it was spoiled	they were spoiled

• *The children were hopelessly spoiled by their parents.*

NOTE: The past form *spoiled* may also be spelled *spoilt*.

━━━━━━━━━━━━━━━━━━━━━━━━━━━━━━━━━━━(**COMPLEMENTS**)━━━

spoil *rot, become inedible/undrinkable* — The food will spoil unless we refrigerate it right away.
We had lunch in the shade so the egg salad wouldn't spoil.
The wine had spoiled because of bad corks.

spoil ___ *ruin, make useless/worthless*

OBJECT — A tacky housing development completely spoiled **the view.**
Too many cooks spoil **the broth.** [PROVERB]
Their desserts are spoiling **my diet.**
The scandal could spoil **the senator's chances for re-election.**

PASSIVE — The wedding was nearly spoiled by those obnoxious photographers.

WH-CLAUSE — Jefferson could spoil **what his father has built.**
The hotel totally spoiled **whatever beauty the beach had.**
The poor publicity spoiled **whatever chance the movie had.**

spoil ___ *raise with too little discipline*

OBJECT — Martha, you are spoiling **that child!**
They have spoiled **their dogs.** They are completely out of control.

spoil ___ *treat very well*

OBJECT — Uncle Bill spoils **his nieces and nephews** on their birthdays.
She spoiled **me** with a gift card from the local bakery.

PASSIVE — Children are often spoiled by their grandparents.

PRESENT

I spread	we spread
you spread	you spread
he/she/it spreads	they spread

• *He spreads peanut butter on his bagels.*

PRESENT PROGRESSIVE

I am spreading	we are spreading
you are spreading	you are spreading
he/she/it is spreading	they are spreading

• *The city is spreading into the valley.*

PAST

I spread	we spread
you spread	you spread
he/she/it spread	they spread

• *We spread a blanket on the grass.*

PAST PROGRESSIVE

I was spreading	we were spreading
you were spreading	you were spreading
he/she/it was spreading	they were spreading

• *They were spreading rumors about the senator.*

PRESENT PERFECT ... have | has spread
PAST PERFECT ... had spread

FUTURE ... will spread
FUTURE PROGRESSIVE ... will be spreading
FUTURE PERFECT ... will have spread

PAST PASSIVE

I was spread	we were spread
you were spread	you were spread
he/she/it was spread	they were spread

• *The seeds were spread by a mechanical applicator.*

COMPLEMENTS

spread *move/extend outward*

Bad news spreads like wildfire.
The floodwater was spreading by the minute.
Violence is spreading in much of the world.

spread ___ *extend [over/to an area]*
ADVERB OF PLACE TO/FROM

The ripples spread **across the pond.**
Elm disease has spread **through the upper Midwest.**
The impact of deflation spread **throughout the economy.**
The city is spreading **in all directions.**
The forest fire spread **to several hilltop villages.**

spread ___ *cause to move/expand outward*
OBJECT

He is always spreading **rumors.**
The senator hopes to spread **the blame for the mistake.**

PASSIVE

Malaria is spread by one type of mosquito.

spread ___ *open/stretch out*
OBJECT

The bird spread **its wings.**

spread ___ *distribute*
OBJECT + ADVERB OF PLACE TO/FROM

He spread **the map** *across the hood of the car.*
Spread **the jam** *on every corner of the bread.*
The eruption spread **dust** *over hundreds of square miles.*
They spread **the payments** *over five years.*

PASSIVE

Protective cloths had been spread *across the floor.*

PHRASAL VERBS

spread _SEP_ **around** *publicize*

They spread the news around that
  her campaign staff had been fired.

spread out *scatter*

The rescuers spread out to search the mountainside.

EXPRESSIONS

spread it on thick *exaggerate praise/blame*

The car salesman was really spreading
  it on thick.

spread [oneself] too thin *do too many things at once*

Between work and volunteer activities, Emma has spread
  herself too thin.

PRESENT

I spring	we spring
you spring	you spring
he/she/it springs	they spring

• *He springs out of bed in the morning.*

PRESENT PROGRESSIVE

I am springing	we are springing
you are springing	you are springing
he/she/it is springing	they are springing

• *Crocuses are springing up everywhere.*

PAST

I sprang	we sprang
you sprang	you sprang
he/she/it sprang	they sprang

• *The door sprang open.*

PAST PROGRESSIVE

I was springing	we were springing
you were springing	you were springing
he/she/it was springing	they were springing

• *Dolphins were springing out of the water.*

PRESENT PERFECT ... have | has sprung
PAST PERFECT ... had sprung

FUTURE ... will spring
FUTURE PROGRESSIVE ... will be springing
FUTURE PERFECT ... will have sprung

PAST PASSIVE

I was sprung	we were sprung
you were sprung	you were sprung
he/she/it was sprung	they were sprung

• *The trap was sprung by a raccoon.*

COMPLEMENTS

spring ——— *jump/move suddenly*
   ADVERB OF PLACE TO/FROM

I sprang **out of my chair** and ran to the door.
The soldiers sprang **up** when the captain came into the room.
We sprang **to the ropes** before the boat could pull away.
The car sprang **forward**, nearly hitting us.
The car door sprung **open** and Fred jumped out.

spring ——— *suddenly appear*
   ADVERB OF PLACE TO/FROM

A dog suddenly sprang **out of the fog.**
Jack sprang **out the front door** and greeted us warmly.
The robbers sprang **out of nowhere.**
Tears sprang **from his eyes.**
A cry sprang **from her throat.**

spring ——— *cause to snap shut*
   OBJECT

An opossum sprang **the trap.**

PHRASAL VERBS

spring for ——— *pay for*

I'll spring for a new coat for you.

spring up *begin, be started*

A wonderful friendship sprang up between us.
A new fast-food restaurant sprang up on the corner.

spring up *begin to grow*

Flowers and weeds are springing up in the garden.

EXPRESSIONS

spring a leak *begin to leak*

Our boat sprang a leak in the middle of the lake.

spring into action *become suddenly active*

After Amber read his letter, she sprang into action.

spring to mind *be thought of*

Which president springs to mind when I say "father of our country"?

stand _____ *tolerate, endure* [USUALLY USED IN QUESTIONS OR NEGATIVE STATEMENTS]

OBJECT	How do you stand **the pressure**?
	I can't stand **the suspense**.
	No one can stand **his superior attitude**.
PRESENT PARTICIPLE	How can you stand **listening to that nonsense**?
	Wine grapes can't stand **being in poorly drained soil**.
	I can't stand **not knowing what happened**.

stand _____ *be of a specified height*

| OBJECT | Tim stands **six foot four**. |
| | The horse stands **15 hands at the withers**. |

PHRASAL VERBS

stand apart/aside/back/off/etc. *stand in a specified position*
Max stood aside and let the medics by.
We stood back so that we wouldn't get hurt.

stand around *loiter, be idle*
The teenagers stood around with their hands in their pockets.

stand at _____ *be at a specified amount/ number*
The bid stands at $250.
Our team's record stands at 11–4.

stand by *be near and ready if needed*
He asked me to stand by in case his car wouldn't start.

stand by *stand near but not involve oneself*
Three people stood by and watched the robbery take place.

stand by _____ *support, defend*
She stood by her husband throughout his illness.

stand for _____ *represent*
"U.S.A." stands for "United States of America."

stand for _____ *tolerate* [USUALLY NEGATIVE]
We won't stand for your nonsense any longer.

stand in for _____ *take the place of, act for*
Would you stand in for me at next Tuesday's meeting?

stand out *be distinctive*
Because of his height, Don really stands out in a crowd.

stand over _____ *keep close watch on*
I can't get any work done if you're standing over me.

stand up *prove to be true/good*
This idea won't stand up under scrutiny.

stand SEP **up** *fail to keep a date with*
Lori stood him up again.

stand up for _____ *support, defend*
When Nancy was criticized, her coach stood up for her.
My parents always stood up for immigrants' rights.

stand up to _____ *resist, refuse to be treated badly by*
The candidate stood up to the lies on talk radio.

EXPRESSIONS

stand a chance (of _____ **)** *have a chance of*
Does your team stand a chance of winning?

stand corrected *admit that one is wrong*
I stand corrected; there are two *m*'s in *recommend*.

stand head and shoulders above _____ *be far superior to*
Their book stood head and shoulders above the competition.

stand in [someone's] way *oppose/obstruct [someone]*
She beat every candidate who stood in her way to the nomination.

stand on [one's] own two feet *be independent, not need anyone's help*
Son, it's time for you to get your own apartment and stand on your own two feet.

stand [one's] ground *maintain one's position while being attacked*
The politician stood his ground in spite of accusations by the opposition party.

stand still for _____ *tolerate* [USUALLY NEGATIVE]
Senator Blather won't stand still for criticism of his immigration policy.

stand to reason *be sensible/reasonable*
It stands to reason that interest rates are low in a recession.

top 40 verb

PRESENT			PRESENT PROGRESSIVE	
I stand	we stand		I am standing	we are standing
you stand	you stand		you are standing	you are standing
he/she/it stands	they stand		he/she/it is standing	they are standing

• *The treasurer stands by the CEO.*   • *I am standing in the checkout lane.*

PAST			PAST PROGRESSIVE	
I stood	we stood		I was standing	we were standing
you stood	you stood		you were standing	you were standing
he/she/it stood	they stood		he/she/it was standing	they were standing

• *We all stood for the national anthem.*   • *We were standing for hours at the reception.*

PRESENT PERFECT ... have | has stood   **FUTURE**   ... will stand
PAST PERFECT   ... had stood   **FUTURE PROGRESSIVE** ... will be standing
                                                FUTURE PERFECT   ... will have stood

PAST PASSIVE	
I was stood	we were stood
you were stood	you were stood
he/she/it was stood	they were stood

• *The pictures were all stood along the wall.*

───────────────────────────────────(COMPLEMENTS)───

stand *be/get in an upright position*
Please stand.
Everyone stood when the funeral procession went by.
By the end of the game, we were all standing and cheering.

stand *remain undisturbed*
[OF FOOD, LIQUID]
Let the tea leaves stand for a few minutes.
The custard needs to stand until it is at room temperature.
The mixture should stand until all the liquid is absorbed.

stand *remain as is*
The committee's original recommendation stands.
The judge let the lower court's ruling stand.
That tradition has stood since the school began.

stand _____ *cause to be in an upright position*
OBJECT + ADVERB OF PLACE
She stood **the dolls** *against the dresser*.
The librarian stood **the books** *on the shelf*.
Stand **the children** *in front of a mirror*.
Stand **the rugs** *in the corner*, please.
We stood **the flagstaff** *in a big pot*.

PASSIVE
The palm plants were stood *along the garden wall*.

stand _____ *be located*
ADVERB OF PLACE
The church stands **at the corner of Waterman and
    Kingshighway.**
A rake and hoe stood **against the fence.**
The train is standing **at the station.**
He was standing **just outside the door**, waiting for us.
The town stands **on a little hill overlooking the bay.**

stand _____ *step to and remain [in a certain place]*
ADVERB OF PLACE
Stand **over there**, please.
I stood **to the side** and let them pass.
We all stood **on the grass** so that the
    ambulance could get by.

stand _____ *be [in a certain condition]*
PREDICATE ADJECTIVE
He stood **firm in his opposition to the plan.**
I stand **ready to help.**
The house stood **empty** for many years.

PRESENT

I stare	we stare
you stare	you stare
he/she/it stares	they stare

• *He stares whenever someone talks to him.*

PRESENT PROGRESSIVE

I am staring	we are staring
you are staring	you are staring
he/she/it is staring	they are staring

• *You are staring off into space again.*

PAST

I stared	we stared
you stared	you stared
he/she/it stared	they stared

• *I stared in disbelief at the television.*

PAST PROGRESSIVE

I was staring	we were staring
you were staring	you were staring
he/she/it was staring	they were staring

• *Everyone was staring at his ridiculous costume.*

PRESENT PERFECT ... have | has stared
PAST PERFECT ... had stared

FUTURE ... will stare
FUTURE PROGRESSIVE ... will be staring
FUTURE PERFECT ... will have stared

PAST PASSIVE

I was stared	we were stared
you were stared	you were stared
he/she/it was stared	they were stared

• *We were stared at by the other hotel guests.*

COMPLEMENTS

stare *look steadily with one's eyes open, often in awe/fear/stupidity/surprise*

The dead soldiers lay there, staring with empty eyes.
I just stood there, staring in astonishment.
The news stunned Robert. He stared with his mouth open and his face blank.

stare _____ *look steadily with one's eyes open*

at OBJECT

I stared **at my broken cell phone** in dismay.
We stared **at the unexpected results**.
The kids stared **at the broken window** in amazement.

    PASSIVE

We were always stared at when we held our knifes and forks in the American style.

at WH-CLAUSE

They stared **at what they had done**.
The kids were staring **at what Uncle Matt had brought them**.
People were staring **at whoever had just come in**.

PHRASAL VERBS

stare _SEP_ **down** *stare at another person until he/she looks away*

The batter stared the umpire down after the called third strike.

stare out *gaze outward*

The farmer stared out across his fields of wheat.

EXPRESSIONS

stare _____ **in the face** *be obvious to [someone]*

His keys were staring him in the face the whole time.

stare (off) into space *look straight ahead without seeing anything in particular*

After the indictment, he stared off into space and sighed.

PRESENT

I start	we start
you start	you start
he/she/it starts	they start

• *The meeting starts promptly at nine.*

PRESENT PROGRESSIVE

I am starting	we are starting
you are starting	you are starting
he/she/it is starting	they are starting

• *We are starting now.*

PAST

I started	we started
you started	you started
he/she/it started	they started

• *They started a restaurant near Portland.*

PAST PROGRESSIVE

I was starting	we were starting
you were starting	you were starting
he/she/it was starting	they were starting

• *The snow was starting to build up on the roofs.*

PRESENT PERFECT ... have | has started
PAST PERFECT ... had started

FUTURE ... will start
FUTURE PROGRESSIVE ... will be starting
FUTURE PERFECT ... will have started

PAST PASSIVE

I was started	we were started
you were started	you were started
he/she/it was started	they were started

• *The fire was started by campers.*

COMPLEMENTS

start *begin*	Hurry up! The program is starting. Go ahead and start without me. My English class starts at 8:30 A.M. The desert starts just beyond the coastal range.
start *begin operating*	The engine started with a roar. Our car doesn't start easily on cold mornings.
start *move/jump/jerk suddenly in alarm/surprise*	The horses start at any unusual sound or movement. He is so upset that he starts at the slightest noise. We never know what will cause the baby to start.
start _____ *begin* OBJECT	Harry will start **kindergarten** in the fall. I started **my new job** this week.
PASSIVE	The restoration of the old train station was started today.
INFINITIVE	It started **to rain** this morning. I started **to vacuum the living room rug.** We started **to read the newspaper.**
PRESENT PARTICIPLE	It started **raining** this morning. I started **vacuuming the living room rug.** We started **reading the newspaper.**
start _____ *cause to happen/operate* OBJECT	I started **the car** and pulled back onto the highway.
PASSIVE	Apparently, the fire was started by lightning.
OBJECT + PRESENT PARTICIPLE	The incident started **me *thinking about what happened.*** The tax incentives started **them *considering using solar power.***
start _____ *originate, establish* OBJECT	Steven started **the argument.** We started **our business** in 1977.

PHRASAL VERBS

start off/out *begin [an action, trip]*	The Lewis and Clark Expedition started off in August 1803. We started out walking, then we began to run. Rick started out as a pitcher, but now he's an outfielder.

PRESENT		PRESENT PROGRESSIVE	
I state	we state	I am stating	we are stating
you state	you state	you are stating	you are stating
he/she/it states	they state	he/she/it is stating	they are stating

• *He always states the obvious.*   • *I am stating what I believe to be the truth.*

PAST		PAST PROGRESSIVE	
I stated	we stated	I was stating	we were stating
you stated	you stated	you were stating	you were stating
he/she/it stated	they stated	he/she/it was stating	they were stating

• *She stated that we needed to delay our trip.*   • *They were stating their side of the argument.*

PRESENT PERFECT	… have | has stated
PAST PERFECT	… had stated

FUTURE	… will state
FUTURE PROGRESSIVE	… will be stating
FUTURE PERFECT	… will have stated

PAST PASSIVE

—   —
—   —
it was stated   they were stated

• *The facts were stated in a clear and simple manner.*

—————————————————————————————————— (**COMPLEMENTS**)——

state _____ *report, express in a definite and formal manner*

OBJECT	Everyone stated **their opinions about what we should do.**
	Just state **the facts**, please.
	I stated **our options** as I saw them.
	The teacher stated **the classroom rules** on the first day of school.
	The secretary stated **the time and date of the next meeting.**
PASSIVE	Her recommendations were stated in no uncertain terms.
(*to* OBJECT +) THAT-CLAUSE	He stated **that his car had been stolen.**
	The report will state **that driving deaths have declined by 15% this year.**
	I can confidently state **that my client is completely innocent.**
	I stated *to the salesmen* that we could not pay their expenses.
	We stated *to the driver* that we had to return to the hotel.
	The aide stated *to us* that we would need to come back the next day.
WH-CLAUSE	The reporter won't state **who gave her the information.**
	You should only state **what you are absolutely sure about.**
	Please state **where you live.**

—————————————————————————————————————— (**EXPRESSIONS**)——

state the obvious *express*
what people already know

The treasurer stated the obvious: The company
   will lose money this year.

PRESENT		PRESENT PROGRESSIVE	
I stay	we stay	I am staying	we are staying
you stay	you stay	you are staying	you are staying
he/she/it stays	they stay	he/she/it is staying	they are staying

• *He stays with friends when he's in town.*   • *I am staying at the Hilton.*

PAST		PAST PROGRESSIVE	
I stayed	we stayed	I was staying	we were staying
you stayed	you stayed	you were staying	you were staying
he/she/it stayed	they stayed	he/she/it was staying	they were staying

• *Charlotte stayed remarkably calm.*   • *Were the kittens staying warm?*

PRESENT PERFECT ... have | has stayed
PAST PERFECT   ... had stayed

FUTURE   ... will stay
FUTURE PROGRESSIVE ... will be staying
FUTURE PERFECT   ... will have stayed

PAST PASSIVE

—   —
—   —
it was stayed   they were stayed

• *The court's decision was stayed.*

━━━━━━━━━━━━━━━━━━━━━━━━━━━━━━━━━━━━━(**COMPLEMENTS**)━━━

stay *remain in a place*

Can you stay for minute?
Please stay; I want to ask you something.
I'd like to stay and talk, but I'm in a hurry.
"'What is truth?' said jesting Pilate, and would not stay
  for an answer." [FRANCIS BACON]

stay _____ *remain [in a place]*
  ADVERB OF PLACE

I stay **at home** when it rains.
Can you stay **on the phone** while I take another call?

stay _____ *live for a while, usually as a guest*
  ADVERB OF PLACE

We are going to stay a few days **with my sister and her family**.
I am just staying **there** for the weekend.
We can't stay **where we are** for more than a week.

stay _____ *remain [in a certain state/condition]*
  PREDICATE NOUN

They stayed **good friends** all their lives.
He stayed **a bachelor** for as long as I knew him.
I stayed **a private** the whole time I was in the army.

  PREDICATE ADJECTIVE

Stay **calm**—everything is going to be all right.
The cuttings need to stay **damp** until they are planted.
The deer stayed **perfectly motionless** until we made a noise.

stay _____ *stop/delay [a formal action]*
  OBJECT

The judge issued an order to stay **the execution**.
The chair can stay **any committee action**.

  PASSIVE

The sentence was stayed by court order.

━━━━━━━━━━━━━━━━━━━━━━━━━━━━━━━━━━━━(**PHRASAL VERBS**)━━━

**stay away/back/behind/down/in/
out/etc.** *remain in a specified position*

He asked the children to stay away
  while he finished working on the speech.

stay off _____ *avoid*

Thank goodness our children stayed off drugs.

stay on *remain at a job*

Marilyn said she would stay on until we hire a replacement.

stay out *remain away from home*

Allison stayed out all night partying.

stay out of _____ *not involve oneself in*

You should stay out of their argument.

stay up *remain out of bed*

The kids are going to stay up and watch a movie.

PRESENT

I steal	we steal
you steal	you steal
he/she/it steals	they steal

• *Our dog steals food from the cats' dishes.*

PRESENT PROGRESSIVE

I am stealing	we are stealing
you are stealing	you are stealing
he/she/it is stealing	they are stealing

• *I am stealing an idea from you—okay?*

PAST

I stole	we stole
you stole	you stole
he/she/it stole	they stole

• *Someone stole my wallet at the gym.*

PAST PROGRESSIVE

I was stealing	we were stealing
you were stealing	you were stealing
he/she/it was stealing	they were stealing

• *They were stealing into the kitchen for cookies.*

PRESENT PERFECT ... have | has stolen
PAST PERFECT ... had stolen

FUTURE ... will steal
FUTURE PROGRESSIVE ... will be stealing
FUTURE PERFECT ... will have stolen

PAST PASSIVE

I was stolen	we were stolen
you were stolen	you were stolen
he/she/it was stolen	they were stolen

• *The car was stolen right out of the garage.*

COMPLEMENTS

steal *take something that doesn't belong to one without paying for it / without permission*

"Thou shalt not steal." [BIBLE]
Fagin forced the children to steal.
Even though he was starving, Oliver refused to steal.

steal _____ *take without paying for / without permission*

OBJECT

Somebody stole **my son's bicycle.**
He claimed that they had stolen **his idea.**

PASSIVE

iPods are stolen out of backpacks every day.

steal _____ *take/borrow while acknowledging the fact* [OFTEN USED HUMOROUSLY]

OBJECT

Can I steal **your husband** for a few minutes?
I need to steal **a few minutes of your time.**
Can I steal **your chair?**

steal _____ *move quietly/secretly*

ADVERB OF PLACE TO/FROM

The thieves stole **into the garage** and took some tools.
We stole **into the boss's office** for a surprise birthday party.
The cavalry stole **behind Union lines** and attacked
  from the rear.

steal _____ *get/win in a tricky manner*

OBJECT

Sam felt that Bob had stolen **Martha's affections.**

steal _____ *take secretly and slyly*

OBJECT

He managed to steal **a look at the classified documents.**
I stole **a kiss** when we had driven for a mile.

PHRASAL VERBS

steal away/down/in/out/up/etc. *move quietly/secretly in a specified direction*

My aunt stole away and cried.

EXPRESSIONS

steal [someone's] thunder *say/do what [someone else] intended to say/do, thereby lessening his/her impact*

Her opponent stole her thunder by
  appearing on TV an hour before she did.

steal the show *receive more attention than anyone else at an event*

A young tap dancer named Dulé Hill stole the show.

PRESENT

I step	we step
you step	you step
he/she/it steps	they step

• *He steps aside so other people can pass.*

PRESENT PROGRESSIVE

I am stepping	we are stepping
you are stepping	you are stepping
he/she/it is stepping	they are stepping

• *Everyone is stepping over the broken glass.*

PAST

I stepped	we stepped
you stepped	you stepped
he/she/it stepped	they stepped

• *He stepped back from the curb.*

PAST PROGRESSIVE

I was stepping	we were stepping
you were stepping	you were stepping
he/she/it was stepping	they were stepping

• *The hikers were stepping from stone to stone.*

PRESENT PERFECT	... have | has stepped
PAST PERFECT	... had stepped

FUTURE	... will step
FUTURE PROGRESSIVE	... will be stepping
FUTURE PERFECT	... will have stepped

PAST PASSIVE

Step is rarely used in the passive voice.

─────────────────────────────(COMPLEMENTS)───

step _____ walk a short distance	
ADVERB OF PLACE TO/FROM	Jason stepped **out of the garage** and used his cell phone.
	I had to step **around the large dog sleeping in the middle of the path.**
	We stepped **down from the deck.**
	Please step **over here.**
	Could you step **into my office** for a minute?
	Please step **out of the boat**, sir.

─────────────────────────────(PHRASAL VERBS)───

step aside/away/back/down/in/off/ out/over/past/under/etc. *walk in a* *specified direction*	Would you all please step back? We stepped out for a breath of fresh air.
step aside/down *leave one's job*	The senior forward stepped aside for a talented freshman. Our club's secretary stepped down after six years on the job.
step forward *offer information*	A stranger stepped forward and identified the robber.
step in *become involved*	Do you think the president will step in to settle the dispute?
step ___SEP___ off *measure by taking steps*	The appraiser stepped off all the rooms in the house.
step ___SEP___ up *increase*	The club has stepped up pressure on members who haven't paid their dues. The factory stepped production up when war was declared.

─────────────────────────────(EXPRESSIONS)───

step on it / step on the gas *hurry up*	We'll have to step on it if we want to be on time.
step on [someone's] toes *offend* [someone]	I don't want to step on anyone's toes, but this report has lots of misspellings.
step out of line *misbehave*	Steve stepped out of line and got scolded by Sister Mary.

PRESENT

I stick	we stick
you stick	you stick
he/she/it sticks	they stick

• *The store sticks labels on fruit.*

PRESENT PROGRESSIVE

I am sticking	we are sticking
you are sticking	you are sticking
he/she/it is sticking	they are sticking

• *The glue isn't sticking very well.*

PAST

I stuck	we stuck
you stuck	you stuck
he/she/it stuck	they stuck

• *A nurse stuck a bandage on Lynda's knee.*

PAST PROGRESSIVE

I was sticking	we were sticking
you were sticking	you were sticking
he/she/it was sticking	they were sticking

• *My shoes were sticking to the floor.*

PRESENT PERFECT … have | has stuck
PAST PERFECT … had stuck

FUTURE … will stick
FUTURE PROGRESSIVE … will be sticking
FUTURE PERFECT … will have stuck

PAST PASSIVE

I was stuck	we were stuck
you were stuck	you were stuck
he/she/it was stuck	they were stuck

• *A note was stuck on my door while I was gone.*

COMPLEMENTS

stick *remain fixed in place*

The drawer is still sticking.
Our wheels stuck in the soft earth.
I'm afraid the proposal is stuck in committee.
The transmission has stuck in first gear.
If you throw enough dirt at somebody, some of it will stick.
Snow was sticking on the ground.
Our pants were sticking to the plastic seats.

stick _____ *attach, fasten, fix*
  OBJECT + ADVERB OF PLACE

We stuck **a patch** *on the tire*.
I stuck **some pictures** *on the wall*.
They stuck **the interns** *in a dingy basement office*.

  PASSIVE

He was stuck *in a dead-end job*.

stick _____ *poke, pierce, thrust*
  OBJECT + ADVERB OF PLACE

The nurse stuck **a thermometer** *in his mouth*.
The cowboy stuck **a cigarette** *behind his ear*.
The little boy stuck **a pin** *into the balloon*.
The workers stuck **their hands** *in their pockets*.

  PASSIVE

Political signs had been stuck *on the lawn*.

PHRASAL VERBS

stick down/in/out/up/etc. *extend in a specified position*

My toes were sticking out from under the quilt.
The lid was sticking up on the jewelry box.

stick SEP **away/back/down/in/on/ out/up/**etc. *thrust/attach in a specified location*

Margaret stuck the report back in the drawer.
I'll stick the stamps on at the post office.
He stuck his tongue out at the teacher.

stick around *remain nearby*

I asked Barb to stick around until I started my car.

stick by _____ *remain loyal to*

Sara stuck by him through thick and thin.

stick out *be distinctive*

That lime green shirt of his really sticks out.

stick SEP **out** *endure*

Bob quit his new job after a week; he couldn't stick it out.

stick to _____ *adhere to*

Everyone should stick to the point being discussed.

stick SEP **up** *rob*

Two masked men stuck up a gas station last night.

stick up for _____ *defend*

Mom always stuck up for us kids.

PRESENT

I sting	we sting
you sting	you sting
he/she/it stings	they sting

• *That antiseptic really stings.*

PRESENT PROGRESSIVE

I am stinging	we are stinging
you are stinging	you are stinging
he/she/it is stinging	they are stinging

• *My hands are still stinging.*

PAST

I stung	we stung
you stung	you stung
he/she/it stung	they stung

• *The smoke from the grill stung our eyes.*

PAST PROGRESSIVE

I was stinging	we were stinging
you were stinging	you were stinging
he/she/it was stinging	they were stinging

• *Sweat bees were stinging everyone at the picnic.*

PRESENT PERFECT ... have | has stung
PAST PERFECT ... had stung

FUTURE ... will sting
FUTURE PROGRESSIVE ... will be stinging
FUTURE PERFECT ... will have stung

PAST PASSIVE

I was stung	we were stung
you were stung	you were stung
he/she/it was stung	they were stung

• *The swimmers were stung by jellyfish.*

COMPLEMENTS

sting *hurt by pricking/piercing the skin*

Wasps will sting if you get too close
  to their nest.
Careful—those plants sting if you even brush them.
The insects sting when the wind dies down.

sting *feel a sharp tingling/burning pain*

My skin is stinging.
Our throats were stinging from the exhaust.
My hands stung from the vibrations.

sting *cause emotional pain*

His criticisms stung at first.
Malicious gossip stings terribly.
Man, what he said really stings!

sting _____ *cause a sharp tingling/burning pain to*

OBJECT

A bee just stung **me**.
The medicine stung **my throat**.
The sunblock stung **my eyes**.
The cold stung **my ears and hands**.

PASSIVE

The kids who were playing in the sandbox were stung
  by ants.

sting _____ *cause emotional pain to*

OBJECT

Unjust criticism stings **a writer**.
Being ridiculed would sting **anyone**.

PASSIVE

I was stung by her malicious attack.
We were stung by how quickly they reacted.

stink   stink | stinks · stank · have stunk
stink | stinks · stunk · have stunk

☑ IRREGULAR
☑ IRREGULAR

PRESENT

I stink	we stink
you stink	you stink
he/she/it stinks	they stink

• *The barn really stinks.*

PRESENT PROGRESSIVE

I am stinking	we are stinking
you are stinking	you are stinking
he/she/it is stinking	they are stinking

• *The durian is stinking and I can't take it on the bus.*

PAST

I stank/stunk	we stank/stunk
you stank/stunk	you stank/stunk
he/she/it stank/stunk	they stank/stunk

• *The whole economic situation stank.*

PAST PROGRESSIVE

I was stinking	we were stinking
you were stinking	you were stinking
he/she/it was stinking	they were stinking

• *The dead skunk was stinking to high heaven.*

PRESENT PERFECT ... have | has stunk
PAST PERFECT   ... had stunk

FUTURE   ... will stink
FUTURE PROGRESSIVE ... will be stinking
FUTURE PERFECT   ... will have stunk

PAST PASSIVE

Stink is never used in the passive voice.

───────────────────────────────(**COMPLEMENTS**)───

stink *give off a strong, unpleasant smell*	The alley stank like an open sewer. When tissue swells and stinks, it may be a sign of gangrene. His breath stank from cheap tobacco. You need to take out the garbage before it starts to stink.
stink *be worthless / very bad*	The movie stinks. No one liked it. The proposed merger stinks and will probably end up in court. I think the plan stinks and should be junked. The company's reputation stinks because of what they did.

───────────────────────────────(**PHRASAL VERBS**)───

stink _SEP_ **up** *fill with a strong, unpleasant smell*	Will hamsters stink up the house?

───────────────────────────────(**EXPRESSIONS**)───

stink up the joint/place *perform very badly*	Our team really stunk up the joint tonight.
stink to high heaven *give off an extremely unpleasant smell*	When broccoli goes bad, it stinks to high heaven.

PRESENT

I stop	we stop
you stop	you stop
he/she/it stops	they stop

· *The train stops there for 10 minutes.*

PRESENT PROGRESSIVE

I am stopping	we are stopping
you are stopping	you are stopping
he/she/it is stopping	they are stopping

· *We are stopping for lunch.*

PAST

I stopped	we stopped
you stopped	you stopped
he/she/it stopped	they stopped

· *My watch just stopped.*

PAST PROGRESSIVE

I was stopping	we were stopping
you were stopping	you were stopping
he/she/it was stopping	they were stopping

· *The police were stopping all traffic on the Interstate.*

PRESENT PERFECT ... have | has stopped
PAST PERFECT   ... had stopped

FUTURE   ... will stop
FUTURE PROGRESSIVE   ... will be stopping
FUTURE PERFECT   ... will have stopped

PAST PASSIVE

I was stopped	we were stopped
you were stopped	you were stopped
he/she/it was stopped	they were stopped

· *The game was stopped by the referee.*

(COMPLEMENTS)

stop *halt*	The rain has stopped.
	The train stopped between stations.
	We stopped to stretch our legs and take a few pictures.
	The laughing stopped abruptly.
stop *cease functioning*	The engine stops whenever I step on the gas.
	My watched has stopped. What time is it?
stop _____ *cause to halt*	
OBJECT	Stop **the car**!
	The drugs should stop **the infection**.
	The opposition will try to stop **the bill's passage**.
	Don't try to stop **me**.
	The bank stopped **payment on the check**.
PASSIVE	The attack must be stopped.
OBJECT + (*from*) PRESENT PARTICIPLE	I can't stop **you** *(from) going ahead with your plan.*
	We must stop **him** *(from) hurting himself.*
PASSIVE	Luckily, he was stopped *(from) investing in the crazy scheme.*
WH-CLAUSE	The guard will stop **whoever tries to enter after hours**.
	The plastic will stop **whatever water leaks through the roof**.
PRESENT PARTICIPLE	The children stopped **giggling** and began to listen.
	I couldn't stop **laughing at what he had said**.
	The factory stopped **producing that model last year**.
stop _____ *pause*	
INFINITIVE	Has he stopped **to think how many people depend on him**?
	Mario doesn't stop **to consider the effect on the environment**.

(PHRASAL VERBS)

stop by/in/off *visit briefly, often on one's way to another place*	Senator Blather stopped by my office on his way to Capitol Hill.
	Aunt Luella stopped in for a few minutes this morning.
stop over *stay at a place before continuing a trip*	We usually stop over in Memphis on our way to New Orleans.
stop _SEP_ **up** *plug, clog*	The plumber stopped the leak up with putty.
	The kitchen sink drain is stopped up.

PRESENT

I stress	we stress
you stress	you stress
he/she/it stresses	they stress

• *The company always stresses safety.*

PRESENT PROGRESSIVE

I am stressing	we are stressing
you are stressing	you are stressing
he/she/it is stressing	they are stressing

• *You are stressing yourself needlessly.*

PAST

I stressed	we stressed
you stressed	you stressed
he/she/it stressed	they stressed

• *I stressed that papers were due by Friday.*

PAST PROGRESSIVE

I was stressing	we were stressing
you were stressing	you were stressing
he/she/it was stressing	they were stressing

• *The schools were stressing math skills.*

PRESENT PERFECT ... have | has stressed
PAST PERFECT   ... had stressed

FUTURE   ... will stress
FUTURE PROGRESSIVE ... will be stressing
FUTURE PERFECT ... will have stressed

PAST PASSIVE

I was stressed	we were stressed
you were stressed	you were stressed
he/she/it was stressed	they were stressed

• *The importance of exercise was stressed in health class.*

──────────────────────────────────(**COMPLEMENTS**)───

stress *become extremely tense/anxious*	You shouldn't stress like this. It's not good for you.
	It's okay. No one is stressing.
stress ___ *emphasize*	
OBJECT	I can't stress enough **the need to be accurate in your work.**
	The doctor stressed **the importance of taking your medication.**
	The actor stressed **every word in his farewell speech.**
	Stress **the second syllable of "record"** when it's used as a verb.
PASSIVE	Keeping costs under control was always stressed.
THAT-CLAUSE	Please stress **that we expect quite cold weather on the trip.**
	I stressed **that the kids really need to be patient during dinner.**
	We stressed **that we haven't got much time.**
WH-CLAUSE	He stressed **what he wanted us to accomplish.**
	Politicians always stress **how patriotic they are.**
	I can't stress enough **how much this means to us.**
stress ___ *strain, put physical/emotional pressure on*	
OBJECT	Weight lifting can really stress **your knee joints.**
	The unusually heavy snow has stressed **the roof trusses.**
PASSIVE	Our communication system has been stressed to the point of collapse.
	Everyone has been stressed by money concerns.

PRESENT

I stretch	we stretch
you stretch	you stretch
he/she/it stretches	they stretch

 • *He always stretches before he runs.*

PRESENT PROGRESSIVE

I am stretching	we are stretching
you are stretching	you are stretching
he/she/it is stretching	they are stretching

 • *The sweater is stretching out of shape.*

PAST

I stretched	we stretched
you stretched	you stretched
he/she/it stretched	they stretched

 • *The cat stretched in front of the fireplace.*

PAST PROGRESSIVE

I was stretching	we were stretching
you were stretching	you were stretching
he/she/it was stretching	they were stretching

 • *We were already stretching the budget.*

PRESENT PERFECT ... have | has stretched
PAST PERFECT   ... had stretched

FUTURE   ... will stretch
FUTURE PROGRESSIVE ... will be stretching
FUTURE PERFECT   ... will have stretched

PAST PASSIVE

I was stretched	we were stretched
you were stretched	you were stretched
he/she/it was stretched	they were stretched

 • *The canvas was stretched over the wooden frame.*

(**COMPLEMENTS**)

stretch *extend, become larger*	My sweater stretched in the laundry.
	These pants are stretching badly.
	Will this material stretch?
stretch *warm up one's muscles*	You need to stretch before exercising.
	If you don't stretch, you can pull a muscle.
stretch *extend one's limbs*	The cat was stretching in the sun.
	I couldn't stretch enough to reach the top shelf.

stretch _____ *cause to extend, cause to become larger/longer*

OBJECT	I stretched **the sweater** over my head and went out for a walk.
	The Scouts stretched **the rope** between two trees.
	We stretched **the canvas** over the frame.
PASSIVE	The rubber band was stretched until it nearly broke.

stretch _____ *extend [one's limbs]*

OBJECT (+ ADVERB OF PLACE TO/FROM)	The student yawned and stretched **his arms and legs**.
	Melanie stretched **her arms** *toward the puppies*.

stretch _____ *extend the length/amount of*

OBJECT	The bank has stretched **their payments** over a longer period.
	I stretched **the main dish** by adding more noodles.
	They decided to stretch **their vacation** a few more days.
PASSIVE	Our finances were already stretched to the limit.

stretch _____ *extend/spread*

ADVERB OF PLACE TO/FROM	Their ranch stretches **for fifty miles**.
	The military base has stretched **into the desert**.
	The long hours of the night stretched **before me**.

(**PHRASAL VERBS**)

stretch down/out/up *extend one's limbs in a specified direction*	Can you stretch down and touch your toes?
	Anne stretched out on the living room floor.
stretch out *be prolonged*	How long will this concert stretch out?
stretch SEP **out** *prolong*	My boss stretches staff meetings out forever.

PRESENT

I stride	we stride
you stride	you stride
he/she/it strides	they stride

• *He strides in like he is on a mission.*

PAST

I strode	we strode
you strode	you strode
he/she/it strode	they strode

• *The cowboys strode into the town square.*

PRESENT PERFECT ... have | has stridden
PAST PERFECT ... had stridden

PRESENT PROGRESSIVE

I am striding	we are striding
you are striding	you are striding
he/she/it is striding	they are striding

• *The horses are striding along at a fast clip now.*

PAST PROGRESSIVE

I was striding	we were striding
you were striding	you were striding
he/she/it was striding	they were striding

• *They were striding as though they were on parade.*

FUTURE ... will stride
FUTURE PROGRESSIVE ... will be striding
FUTURE PERFECT ... will have stridden

PAST PASSIVE

Stride is never used in the passive voice.

COMPLEMENTS

stride *walk with long steps*

He doesn't walk, he strides.
The boys were pretending to stride like soldiers.
He was striding so fast that he was almost running.

stride _____ *walk briskly*
ADVERB OF PLACE TO/FROM

He strode **across the room** in two quick steps and jerked open the door.
They strode angrily **down the street and into the mayor's office**.
The delegation strode **past us**, grim faced, not looking to the left or right.

PHRASAL VERBS

stride along/away/down/in/out/up/etc. *stride in a specified direction*

He was striding along, muttering to himself.
Leon glared at the boss, then strode away.
The captain strode up and shook my hand.

PRESENT

I strike	we strike
you strike	you strike
he/she/it strikes	they strike

- *The idea strikes us as promising.*

PRESENT PROGRESSIVE

I am striking	we are striking
you are striking	you are striking
he/she/it is striking	they are striking

- *The flu is striking everyone.*

PAST

I struck	we struck
you struck	you struck
he/she/it struck	they struck

- *She struck her foot on a chair.*

PAST PROGRESSIVE

I was striking	we were striking
you were striking	you were striking
he/she/it was striking	they were striking

- *The union was striking at midnight.*

PRESENT PERFECT ... have | has struck
PAST PERFECT ... had struck

FUTURE ... will strike
FUTURE PROGRESSIVE ... will be striking
FUTURE PERFECT ... will have struck

PAST PASSIVE

I was struck	we were struck
you were struck	you were struck
he/she/it was struck	they were struck

- *He was suddenly struck by a brilliant idea.*

COMPLEMENTS

strike *attack, cause sudden damage/injury*

An earthquake struck this morning
  in northern California.
Disaster struck when the ferry capsized in heavy seas.
The killer has struck again.
Many snakes hiss before they strike.

strike *refuse to work until one's demands are met*

The maintenance workers voted to strike.
We will strike if our demands are not met.
They are striking for better health benefits.

strike _____ *hit forcefully*

  OBJECT

A falling tree limb struck **me** on the shoulder.
The van struck **several parked cars**.
He struck **the ball** with his head.
Sunshine struck **the mirror**, temporarily blinding me.

  PASSIVE

The Pinkston family was struck by tragedy today.
We were all struck by the coincidence.

strike _____ *occur to*

  OBJECT

A great idea just struck **me**.
The solution to the problem struck **him**.

  it + strike + OBJECT *+* THAT-CLAUSE

It struck **us** *that our problem had been solved.*
It strikes **me** *that you are taking an unnecessary risk.*
It struck **everyone** *that it was getting very late.*

OBJECT *+ as* PREDICATE NOUN

NOTE: The predicate noun refers to the subject, not the object.

He struck **her** *as an honest man.*
The attack struck **the policeman** *as a suicide bombing.*
The proposal struck **us** *as an idiotic idea.*

OBJECT *+ as* PREDICATE ADJECTIVE

NOTE: The predicate adjective refers to the subject, not the object.

Thomas struck **her** *as nice but a little*
  strange.
The proposal struck **me** *as promising.*
Their children struck **us** *as well-behaved.*

strike _____ *reach/achieve [an agreement, compromise]*

OBJECT	The two sides finally struck **a deal**. You must strike **the right balance between compassion and assertiveness**.
PASSIVE	A compromise on the budget was finally struck.

(PHRASAL VERBS)

strike back/down/out *attack in a specified direction*
  The hero struck back with his mighty sword.

strike SEP **back/down/out** *hit in a specified direction*
  Roger struck Steve down with a blow to the head.

strike SEP **down** *invalidate [a law]*
  The Supreme Court struck down the gay marriage ban as unconstitutional.

strike SEP **off** *remove*
  The secretary struck off the names of those who hadn't paid dues.

strike off/out (for _____ **)** *set out (to [someplace])*
  Thousands struck out for California in search of gold.

strike on _____ *realize suddenly*
  The author struck on the idea of setting the novel in colonial America.

strike out *fail*
  Brandy struck out trying to convince the boss to give her a raise.

strike SEP **up** *begin*
  Ben struck up a conversation with the receptionist.
  Sadie and Sally struck up a friendship at school.

(EXPRESSIONS)

strike a balance (between _____ **)** *compromise (between [two things])*
  She manages to strike a balance between her work and her family.

strike a bargain/deal *reach agreement*
  The union and the company struck a bargain at the eleventh hour.

strike a chord (with _____ **)** *sound familiar to [someone]*
  Those words strike a chord with me; what song are they from?

strike a happy medium *find a satisfactory compromise*
  She speaks French and I speak English, so we struck a happy medium and watched a French film with English subtitles.

strike a nerve *cause a strong negative reaction*
  Your insensitive comment about immigration really struck a nerve.

strike _____ **funny** *seem humorous/odd to*
  It strikes me funny that they dropped charges against the politician.

strike home *make sense*
  His advice to save for a rainy day really strikes home.

strike it rich *become suddenly wealthy*
  They struck it rich in the real estate business.

strike [one, two, … twelve / midnight] [OF A CLOCK] *indicate the hour by a certain number of sounds*
  The clock struck one, and the mouse ran down. [NURSERY RHYME]

strike pay dirt *become suddenly successful*
  The Mars rover has struck pay dirt: It has discovered evidence of water on the planet.

strike [someone's] fancy *appeal to [someone]*
  Miss Elizabeth Bennet struck Mr. Darcy's fancy.

strike while the iron is hot *do something while one has the opportunity*
  The economy is booming, and the board recommends that the company strike while the iron is hot.

top 40 verb

I string · we string
you string · you string
he/she/it strings · they string
• *He strings Christmas lights in the trees.*

PRESENT PROGRESSIVE
I am stringing · we are stringing
you are stringing · you are stringing
he/she/it is stringing · they are stringing
• *The kids are stringing beads.*

PAST
I strung · we strung
you strung · you strung
he/she/it strung · they strung
• *I strung the bows for the children.*

PAST PROGRESSIVE
I was stringing · we were stringing
you were stringing · you were stringing
he/she/it was stringing · they were stringing
• *We were stringing shells for a wall hanging.*

PRESENT PERFECT ... have | has strung
PAST PERFECT ... had strung

FUTURE ... will string
FUTURE PROGRESSIVE ... will be stringing
FUTURE PERFECT ... will have strung

PAST PASSIVE
I was strung · we were strung
you were strung · you were strung
he/she/it was strung · they were strung
• *My tennis racket was strung too tight.*

COMPLEMENTS

string _____ hang/stretch [in a line]
  OBJECT
We used to string **popcorn and cranberries** on our Christmas tree.
The fishermen strung **lines** in the channel.
The decorating committee wanted to string **lanterns** in the hall.
  PASSIVE
A trip wire had been strung across the path.

string _____ thread (on a line/cord)
  OBJECT
Kids love to string **different shapes of uncooked pasta**.
When we catch fish, we string **them** on a line.
  PASSIVE
The beads were strung to make simple necklaces.

string _____ put strings on [a racket, bow, musical instrument]
  OBJECT
You can't string **a tennis racket** by hand.
It takes a great deal of strength to string **a powerful bow**.
  PASSIVE
The instruments were all strung by a professional musician.

PHRASAL VERBS

string _SEP_ along keep [someone] hoping for romance / a reward
Jenny strung Reggie along for several months before telling him to get lost.
He strings employees along by promising raises that they never get.

string _SEP_ out prolong
The professor was stringing out his lecture on quantum gravity.

string _SEP_ up hang by the neck
An angry mob strung the cattle thieves up in the town square.

strive

strive | strives · strove · have striven
strive | strives · strived · have strived

☑ IRREGULAR
☑ REGULAR

PRESENT

I strive	we strive
you strive	you strive
he/she/it strives	they strive

• *He strives to do his very best.*

PAST

I strove	we strove
you strove	you strove
he/she/it strove	they strove

• *We strove to get the job finished on time.*

PRESENT PERFECT ... have | has striven
PAST PERFECT ... had striven

PRESENT PROGRESSIVE

I am striving	we are striving
you are striving	you are striving
he/she/it is striving	they are striving

• *He is striving to succeed.*

PAST PROGRESSIVE

I was striving	we were striving
you were striving	you were striving
he/she/it was striving	they were striving

• *Everyone was striving to beat the deadline.*

FUTURE ... will strive
FUTURE PROGRESSIVE ... will be striving
FUTURE PERFECT ... will have striven

PAST PASSIVE

Strive is never used in the passive voice.

───────────(COMPLEMENTS)───────────

strive _____ *make a great effort, try very hard*

INFINITIVE

You must always strive **to improve yourself.**
We always strove **to get the kids to school on time.**
Successful companies constantly strive **to make their products better.**
If you don't strive **to succeed,** you will surely fail in the long run.
The whole team was striving **to be the best in the league.**

strive _____ *fight, struggle*

for OBJECT
against OBJECT

We strive **for peace and freedom.**
The activists are striving **against poverty and injustice.**

PRESENT

I study	we study
you study	you study
he/she/it studies	they study

• *He studies two hours every morning.*

PRESENT PROGRESSIVE

I am studying	we are studying
you are studying	you are studying
he/she/it is studying	they are studying

• *Don't bother her now—she's studying.*

PAST

I studied	we studied
you studied	you studied
he/she/it studied	they studied

• *I studied Latin and Classical Greek.*

PAST PROGRESSIVE

I was studying	we were studying
you were studying	you were studying
he/she/it was studying	they were studying

• *The class was studying the Civil War.*

PRESENT PERFECT ... have | has studied
PAST PERFECT ... had studied

FUTURE ... will study
FUTURE PROGRESSIVE ... will be studying
FUTURE PERFECT ... will have studied

PAST PASSIVE

I was studied	we were studied
you were studied	you were studied
he/she/it was studied	they were studied

• *The proposal was studied from every angle.*

COMPLEMENTS

study *spend time learning*

It seems like all I do is study.
He really needs to study harder.
I can't study when it's so noisy.
Nobody likes to study all the time.

study _____ *spend time learning in preparation*
for OBJECT

Laurie is studying **for her midterm exams.**
John is studying **for his driver's test.**

study _____ *take one or more courses in*
OBJECT

I plan to study **Chinese** next year.
He hopes to study **geology** when he gets to college.
She is studying **voice and piano** at the conservatory.

PASSIVE

Latin is still studied in some high schools.

study _____ *thoroughly investigate*
OBJECT

I have been studying **the railroad timetable**, and I still don't
     understand it.
The police have been studying **the suspect's movements** that day.
The reporter studied **his notes** before answering.

PASSIVE

The grant applications were carefully studied.

study _____ *visually examine carefully*
OBJECT

The school board studied **the architect's drawings.**
The dermatologist studied **every inch of my face and hands.**
He anxiously studied **the faces of the passengers.**

PASSIVE

The plans for the new house were studied and debated endlessly.

PHRASAL VERBS

study up on _____ *learn a lot*
about in a short time

We need to study up on when to plant
     tomatoes.
You need to study up on French culture before your trip to Paris.

PRESENT

I submit	we submit
you submit	you submit
he/she/it submits	they submit

 • *He submits his dissertation this semester.*

PRESENT PROGRESSIVE

I am submitting	we are submitting
you are submitting	you are submitting
he/she/it is submitting	they are submitting

 • *I am submitting my resignation on Friday.*

PAST

I submitted	we submitted
you submitted	you submitted
he/she/it submitted	they submitted

 • *I submitted the additional evidence.*

PAST PROGRESSIVE

I was submitting	we were submitting
you were submitting	you were submitting
he/she/it was submitting	they were submitting

 • *We were submitting ourselves to additional costs.*

PRESENT PERFECT	... have | has submitted
PAST PERFECT	... had submitted

FUTURE	... will submit
FUTURE PROGRESSIVE	... will be submitting
FUTURE PERFECT	... will have submitted

PAST PASSIVE

—	—
—	—
it was submitted	they were submitted

 • *The paperwork was submitted in March.*

———(COMPLEMENTS)———

submit *surrender, yield*

The opposition will not submit without a fight.
Without reinforcements, the castle will have to submit.
The employers got a court order that forced the strikers to submit.

submit _____ *subject [to a process/treatment]*

OBJECT + to OBJECT

We submitted **the bone fragment** *to DNA testing*.
I submitted **myself** *to a body search*.
The parties submitted **the issue** *to binding arbitration*.

submit _____ *formally present [a document]*

OBJECT

You have to submit **your application** three weeks in advance.
I will submit **my grant proposal** next week.
He is going to submit **his resignation** tomorrow.
The defense lawyer was allowed to submit **additional evidence**.

PASSIVE

The request must be submitted in writing.

submit _____ *formally present/argue*

THAT-CLAUSE

Mr. Smith submits **that he is totally innocent of all charges**.
In the indictment, they submit **that you left the scene of the accident**.
In his testimony, Dr. Brown will submit **that the defendant is not
   competent to stand trial**.

PRESENT

I succeed	we succeed
you succeed	you succeed
he/she/it succeeds	they succeed

• *That magic trick always succeeds.*

PRESENT PROGRESSIVE

I am succeeding	we are succeeding
you are succeeding	you are succeeding
he/she/it is succeeding	they are succeeding

• *We are succeeding pretty well with the fund-raiser.*

PAST

I succeeded	we succeeded
you succeeded	you succeeded
he/she/it succeeded	they succeeded

• *He succeeded in ending the war.*

PAST PROGRESSIVE

I was succeeding	we were succeeding
you were succeeding	you were succeeding
he/she/it was succeeding	they were succeeding

• *The new ad campaign was finally succeeding.*

PRESENT PERFECT ... have | has succeeded
PAST PERFECT ... had succeeded

FUTURE ... will succeed
FUTURE PROGRESSIVE ... will be succeeding
FUTURE PERFECT ... will have succeeded

PAST PASSIVE

I was succeeded	we were succeeded
you were succeeded	you were succeeded
he/she/it was succeeded	they were succeeded

• *Henry VIII was succeeded by his son Edward.*

COMPLEMENTS

succeed *perform/happen as planned/desired*

You can't succeed unless you try.
The pilot test succeeded beyond our expectations.
They succeeded more by luck than design.
Jerry succeeded as a trial lawyer.
It seemed that Barry succeeded at nearly everything he tried.
Nicole succeeded in her role as Virginia Woolf.

succeed _____ *achieve [a goal]*
   in PRESENT PARTICIPLE

They succeeded **in getting the contract.**
I hope to succeed **in finding the right job.**
We have succeeded **in recruiting an excellent staff.**

succeed _____ *follow [into a job/office]*
   OBJECT

John Adams succeeded **George Washington** in 1797.
Roger will succeed **his father** as head of the company.

   PASSIVE

Roberta was succeeded by Terry as chair of the committee.

suffer  suffer | suffers · suffered · have suffered   ☑ REGULAR

PRESENT		PRESENT PROGRESSIVE	
I suffer	we suffer	I am suffering	we are suffering
you suffer	you suffer	you are suffering	you are suffering
he/she/it suffers	they suffer	he/she/it is suffering	they are suffering

• *His family suffers when he works late.*   • *She is suffering from severe headaches.*

PAST		PAST PROGRESSIVE	
I suffered	we suffered	I was suffering	we were suffering
you suffered	you suffered	you were suffering	you were suffering
he/she/it suffered	they suffered	he/she/it was suffering	they were suffering

• *We suffered a major setback yesterday.*   • *I was suffering a terrible cold at the time.*

PRESENT PERFECT ... have | has suffered
PAST PERFECT ... had suffered

FUTURE ... will suffer
FUTURE PROGRESSIVE ... will be suffering
FUTURE PERFECT ... will have suffered

PAST PASSIVE

— —
— —
it was suffered they were suffered

• *Severe losses were suffered in the attack.*

___

COMPLEMENTS

suffer *feel physical/emotional pain/loss*

In war, it is always the civilians who suffer.
The economic downturn has caused many people to suffer.
Too many patients were suffering unnecessarily.

suffer *become worse*

Our profit margin has suffered since the merger.
The kids' grades suffered because we moved so often.
Concerns about mad cow disease have caused beef prices to suffer.

suffer _____ *experience, undergo* [pain/loss/damage/unpleasantness]

OBJECT

She has suffered **migraine headaches** all her life.
We expect to suffer **a small loss** this quarter.
Mom suffered **a stroke** when she was 70.
The team suffered **two losses** on its recent road trip.
The police department suffered **a total breakdown in its communication system.**
We suffered **a setback** on our way to financial independence.

PASSIVE

Only minor injuries were suffered in the accident.

from OBJECT

Our team suffers **from too many mental errors.**
Nancy has suffered **from arthritis for decades.**
The wounded soldier was suffering **from shock.**

suffer _____ *tolerate* [USUALLY NEGATIVE]

OBJECT

The country will not suffer **such an attack** without retaliation.
Senator Blather won't suffer **criticism.**

___

EXPRESSIONS

suffer fools gladly *tolerate stupidity in others*

Our professor does not suffer fools gladly.

PRESENT

I suggest	we suggest
you suggest	you suggest
he/she/it suggests	they suggest

· *He suggests that we come back after lunch.*

PRESENT PROGRESSIVE

I am suggesting	we are suggesting
you are suggesting	you are suggesting
he/she/it is suggesting	they are suggesting

· *I am suggesting that we take a break.*

PAST

I suggested	we suggested
you suggested	you suggested
he/she/it suggested	they suggested

· *I suggested lunch at a Mexican restaurant.*

PAST PROGRESSIVE

I was suggesting	we were suggesting
you were suggesting	you were suggesting
he/she/it was suggesting	they were suggesting

· *The dark clouds were suggesting a storm.*

PRESENT PERFECT ... have | has suggested
PAST PERFECT ... had suggested

FUTURE ... will suggest
FUTURE PROGRESSIVE ... will be suggesting
FUTURE PERFECT ... will have suggested

PAST PASSIVE

I was suggested	we were suggested
you were suggested	you were suggested
he/she/it was suggested	they were suggested

· *The idea was suggested in April.*

COMPLEMENTS

suggest _____ *recommend, mention for consideration*

OBJECT
The waiter suggested **the salmon.**
I suggested **a gift certificate** for her birthday.
The designer suggests **a different typeface** for the text.

PASSIVE
Several candidates were suggested and discussed.

(*to* OBJECT +) BASE-FORM THAT-CLAUSE
No one is suggesting **that we give up.**
I suggested *to my son* **that we have pancakes for breakfast.**
The committee suggested *to the board* **that Susan be named president.**
The senator suggested *to his staff* **that they ignore all questions from the press.**

WH-CLAUSE
I suggested **whom they might contact in Madrid.**
Can you suggest **where we should go next?**
The guidebook suggested **how much we should expect to pay for a hotel there.**

WH-INFINITIVE
The people at the next table suggested **what to order.**
Some friends suggested **where to stay.**
Tony suggested **how to proceed next.**

PRESENT PARTICIPLE
Jan suggested **renting some movies for the kids.**
The consultant suggested **reducing our overhead costs.**
I suggested **just redoing the kitchen and leaving everything else alone.**

suggest _____ *bring to mind as similar/connected to*

OBJECT
The perfume is designed to suggest **a tropical forest.**
Her paintings suggest **the work of Georgia O'Keeffe.**
The crime suggests **a revenge killing.**

suggest _____ *imply, say indirectly*

THAT-CLAUSE
Nick is suggesting **that the package was never delivered.**
A recent study suggests **that red wine may make your heart healthier.**
Are you suggesting **that no one wants me at the party?**

PRESENT

I supply	we supply
you supply	you supply
he/she/it supplies	they supply

• *The farm supplies vegetables to restaurants.*

PRESENT PROGRESSIVE

I am supplying	we are supplying
you are supplying	you are supplying
he/she/it is supplying	they are supplying

• *We are supplying most of the manpower.*

PAST

I supplied	we supplied
you supplied	you supplied
he/she/it supplied	they supplied

• *Wikipedia supplied most of the answers.*

PAST PROGRESSIVE

I was supplying	we were supplying
you were supplying	you were supplying
he/she/it was supplying	they were supplying

• *The publicity committee was supplying the brochures.*

PRESENT PERFECT ... have | has supplied
PAST PERFECT ... had supplied

FUTURE ... will supply
FUTURE PROGRESSIVE ... will be supplying
FUTURE PERFECT ... will have supplied

PAST PASSIVE

I was supplied	we were supplied
you were supplied	you were supplied
he/she/it was supplied	they were supplied

• *Lunch was supplied by a local caterer.*

──(**COMPLEMENTS**)──

supply _____ *furnish, provide*

OBJECT

Ralph's Pretty Good Grocery will supply **everything for your picnics.**
Robbery seemed to supply **the motive for the break-in.**
The union will supply **extra workers** if they are needed.
Sunshine does not always supply **an adequate amount of vitamin D.**

PASSIVE

About half of our power is supplied by wind and solar.

supply _____ *take care of the needs of*

INDIRECT OBJECT + DIRECT OBJECT

The Ordnance Corps supplies *the troops* **ammunition.**
I supplied *them* **the information they wanted.**
His firm supplies *our company* **technical support.**

to PARAPHRASE

The Ordnance Corps supplies **ammunition** *to the troops.*
I supplied **the information they wanted** *to them.*
His firm supplies **technical support** *to our company.*

OBJECT + *with* OBJECT

The Ordnance Corps supplies **the troops** *with ammunition.*
I supplied **them** *with the information they wanted.*
His firm supplies **our company** *with technical support.*

OBJECT + (*with*) WH-CLAUSE

He supplied **the children** (*with*) *whatever art supplies they needed.*
She supplies **the manager** (*with*) *whatever reports he requests.*

PRESENT

I support	we support
you support	you support
he/she/it supports	they support

- *The senator supports the bill.*

PRESENT PROGRESSIVE

I am supporting	we are supporting
you are supporting	you are supporting
he/she/it is supporting	they are supporting

- *Whom are you supporting in the election?*

PAST

I supported	we supported
you supported	you supported
he/she/it supported	they supported

- *Dad supported his family on $400 a week.*

PAST PROGRESSIVE

I was supporting	we were supporting
you were supporting	you were supporting
he/she/it was supporting	they were supporting

- *The fans were supporting the underdogs.*

PRESENT PERFECT ... have | has supported
PAST PERFECT ... had supported

FUTURE ... will support
FUTURE PROGRESSIVE ... will be supporting
FUTURE PERFECT ... will have supported

PAST PASSIVE

I was supported	we were supported
you were supported	you were supported
he/she/it was supported	they were supported

- *The bridge was supported by two huge piers.*

COMPLEMENTS

support _____ *carry (the weight of), hold up*

OBJECT	Two rotting wooden posts supported **the sagging porch**.
	His knees can't support **his weight** anymore.
PASSIVE	The wounded soldier was supported by his comrades.

support _____ *advocate, approve of, agree with*

OBJECT	Senator Blather supports **farm subsidies and fully funded crop insurance**.
	Our organization has supported **civil rights legislation** for decades.
	We support **Jack Eberhardt** for commissioner.
WH-CLAUSE	I can't support **what you are doing**.
	The senator will support **whomever his party nominates**.
PRESENT PARTICIPLE	The government has supported **growing corn for ethanol**.
	We supported **Jane's starting her own business**.
	I supported **his going to school out of state**.

support _____ *provide a living for*

OBJECT	People cannot support **a family** on the minimum wage.
PASSIVE	Doris has always been supported by her family.

support _____ *sustain*

OBJECT	The island could no longer support **vegetation** after the volcano erupted.
PRESENT PARTICIPLE	The company cannot support **carrying such a high level of debt**.

support _____ *help to prove*

OBJECT	The new research supports **our hypothesis**.
	A recent study supports **the value of using alternative energy sources**.

support _____ *be compatible with*

OBJECT	Will the new computer support **all of our old applications**?
WH-CLAUSE	The computer will support **whatever programs you need to run**.
PRESENT PARTICIPLE	The operating system supports **having 256 windows open at the same time**.

PRESENT

I suppose	we suppose
you suppose	you suppose
he/she/it supposes	they suppose

• *He supposes that the worst will happen.*

PRESENT PROGRESSIVE

I am supposing	we are supposing
you are supposing	you are supposing
he/she/it is supposing	they are supposing

• *We are supposing that you can get the job done right.*

PAST

I supposed	we supposed
you supposed	you supposed
he/she/it supposed	they supposed

• *I supposed him to be a visitor.*

PAST PROGRESSIVE

I was supposing	we were supposing
you were supposing	you were supposing
he/she/it was supposing	they were supposing

• *I was supposing that we might not make the flight.*

PRESENT PERFECT ... have | has supposed
PAST PERFECT ... had supposed

FUTURE ... will suppose
FUTURE PROGRESSIVE ... will be supposing
FUTURE PERFECT ... will have supposed

PAST PASSIVE

I was supposed	we were supposed
you were supposed	you were supposed
he/she/it was supposed	they were supposed

• *He was supposed to be at the airport.*

(**COMPLEMENTS**)

suppose *make assumptions*

Don't suppose so much.
He is only supposing.

suppose ＿＿＿ *think of as true/possible without really knowing*

OBJECT
> The defense is supposing **facts that are not in the evidence.**
> His idea supposes **a long chain of unlikely events.**
> Some interpretations of quantum mechanics suppose
>   **the existence of parallel universes.**

OBJECT + (to be) PREDICATE NOUN
> Quinn supposed **them** *(to be)* **loyal supporters.**
> The agent supposed **the house** *(to be)* **a rental property.**
> The coach supposed **the other team** *(to be)* **a weak opponent.**

OBJECT + (to be) PREDICATE ADJECTIVE
> I supposed **the strange man** *(to be)* **delusional.**
> Everyone supposed **the house** *(to be)* **mortgaged to the hilt.**
> We supposed **the children** *(to be)* **ready for bed.**

OBJECT + INFINITIVE
> Everyone supposed **the family** *to have a fortune.*

PASSIVE
> Children were supposed *to know how to behave.*
> Until the 19th century, diseases were supposed *to be caused*
>   *by an imbalance of humours.*

it + be supposed + INFINITIVE
> It's supposed **to rain today and tomorrow.**

THAT-CLAUSE
> Suppose **that you are right.** What would you do next?
> Let's suppose **that money is no object.**
> Suppose **that you were in my shoes.**

suppose ＿＿＿ *guess, believe*

THAT-CLAUSE
> I suppose **that the accident happened sometime during**
>   **the night.**
> Do you suppose **that the flight was delayed?**
> I suppose **that it is time to quit.**

be supposed ＿＿＿ *be expected/obliged/allowed* [USED ONLY IN THE PASSIVE]

INFINITIVE
> I am supposed to give you this message.
> The children are not supposed to go to the park alone.
> We are supposed to meet someone at the airport.

I surprise	we surprise
you surprise	you surprise
he/she/it surprises	they surprise

• *He surprises us with his bizarre ideas.*

I am surprising	we are surprising
you are surprising	you are surprising
he/she/it is surprising	they are surprising

• *They are surprising him with a new workbench.*

I surprised	we surprised
you surprised	you surprised
he/she/it surprised	they surprised

• *I surprised Mary when I came home early.*

I was surprising	we were surprising
you were surprising	you were surprising
he/she/it was surprising	they were surprising

• *He was surprising her with symphony tickets.*

... have | has surprised
... had surprised

... will surprise
... will be surprising
... will have surprised

I was surprised	we were surprised
you were surprised	you were surprised
he/she/it was surprised	they were surprised

• *Everyone was surprised by Bill's early retirement.*

COMPLEMENTS

surprise _____ *cause mild astonishment/shock to*

OBJECT — The announcement surprised **everyone**.
The children surprised **us** with a trip to Hawaii.
We surprised **some deer** when we were walking in the woods.

PASSIVE — Was anybody surprised by what happened?

surprise _____ *attack/encounter suddenly/unexpectedly* [NOT USED IN THE PROGRESSIVE TENSES]

OBJECT — The Japanese Navy surprised **the U.S. fleet at Pearl Harbor**.
The security guard surprised **the shoplifter**.
Mom surprised **us** in the middle of a video game.

PASSIVE — Union forces were surprised by Stonewall Jackson's corps
at Chancellorsville.

OBJECT + PRESENT PARTICIPLE — The police surprised **them** *stealing scrap metal*.
The principal surprised **some students** *smoking in the gym*.
We surprised **the dogs** *sleeping on the couch again*.

PRESENT

I surround	we surround
you surround	you surround
he/she/it surrounds	they surround

- *The garden surrounds the house.*

PRESENT PROGRESSIVE

I am surrounding	we are surrounding
you are surrounding	you are surrounding
he/she/it is surrounding	they are surrounding

- *The police are surrounding the building.*

PAST

I surrounded	we surrounded
you surrounded	you surrounded
he/she/it surrounded	they surrounded

- *A fence surrounded the original factory.*

PAST PROGRESSIVE

I was surrounding	we were surrounding
you were surrounding	you were surrounding
he/she/it was surrounding	they were surrounding

- *The floodwater was surrounding the hill.*

PRESENT PERFECT … have | has surrounded
PAST PERFECT … had surrounded

FUTURE … will surround
FUTURE PROGRESSIVE … will be surrounding
FUTURE PERFECT … will have surrounded

PAST PASSIVE

I was surrounded	we were surrounded
you were surrounded	you were surrounded
he/she/it was surrounded	they were surrounded

- *I was surrounded by noise.*

COMPLEMENTS

surround _____ *form a circle/ring around, enclose, envelop*

OBJECT A ring of forts completely surrounded **the city**.
The children surrounded **us**, asking endless questions.
The empty prairie surrounded **our camp** from horizon to horizon.

PASSIVE The village was completely surrounded by high mountains.
The rock star was surrounded by screaming fans.

surround _____ *dominate the environment of*

OBJECT Controversy surrounded **everything he did**.
A cloud of suspicion surrounded **the courtroom**.
Confusion and uncertainty surrounded **them** like fog.

PASSIVE He felt that he was surrounded by fools.

PRESENT

I survive	we survive
you survive	you survive
he/she/it survives	they survive

• *He survives one crisis after another.*

PRESENT PROGRESSIVE

I am surviving	we are surviving
you are surviving	you are surviving
he/she/it is surviving	they are surviving

• *I am only surviving day to day.*

PAST

I survived	we survived
you survived	you survived
he/she/it survived	they survived

• *The bank barely survived the Depression.*

PAST PROGRESSIVE

I was surviving	we were surviving
you were surviving	you were surviving
he/she/it was surviving	they were surviving

• *The army was surviving on half rations.*

PRESENT PERFECT   ... have | has survived
PAST PERFECT   ... had survived

FUTURE   ... will survive
FUTURE PROGRESSIVE ... will be surviving
FUTURE PERFECT   ... will have survived

PAST PASSIVE

I was survived	we were survived
you were survived	you were survived
he/she/it was survived	they were survived

• *He was survived by a daughter and two grandchildren.*

⟨ **COMPLEMENTS** ⟩

survive *continue to live/exist*

Against all odds, the baby survived.
The shipwrecked crew clung to the raft, hoping to survive.
People can survive under the most adverse conditions.
Very few fossils from that period survive.
The old French custom survives today.

survive *continue to live/exist*
[USED HUMOROUSLY/IRONICALLY]

Oh, I think we might survive after all.
I'm sure the kids will survive.
The economy will probably survive despite our best efforts
   to ruin it.

survive _____ *continue to live/exist in spite of*

OBJECT

The duke survived **the assassination attempt.**
His family survived **a terrible ordeal in the earthquake.**
Senator Blather survived **a political scandal involving illegal
   campaign contributions.**

PASSIVE

The fire was survived by two children.

survive _____ *live longer than [a close relative]*

OBJECT

He survived **his wife** by only two months.
Private Ryan survived **his three brothers.**
Donald survived **his son** by eight years.

PASSIVE

He is survived by his wife and three children.
Mrs. Brown is survived by her lovely daughter.

PRESENT

I suspect	we suspect
you suspect	you suspect
he/she/it suspects	they suspect

• *He suspects that a circuit malfunctioned.*

PRESENT PROGRESSIVE

Suspect is rarely used in the progressive tenses.

PAST

I suspected	we suspected
you suspected	you suspected
he/she/it suspected	they suspected

• *The doctor suspected a low-grade infection.*

PAST PROGRESSIVE

Suspect is rarely used in the progressive tenses.

PRESENT PERFECT ... have | has suspected	
PAST PERFECT ... had suspected	

FUTURE	... will suspect
FUTURE PROGRESSIVE —	
FUTURE PERFECT	... will have suspected

PAST PASSIVE

I was suspected	we were suspected
you were suspected	you were suspected
he/she/it was suspected	they were suspected

• *A gas leak was suspected as the cause of the explosion.*

NOTE: The verb *suspect* is stressed on the second syllable, like *inspect*.
The noun *suspect* is stressed on the first syllable.

(COMPLEMENTS)

suspect _____ *believe to be guilty of / the fault of*

OBJECT	The police suspect **a local gang.**
	You have no reason to suspect **him.**
	The garage mechanic suspects **the car's oxygen sensor.**
PASSIVE	A faulty power supply is suspected.
OBJECT + *of* OBJECT	No one would suspect **her** *of drug abuse.*
	The cops suspect **him** *of murder.*
OBJECT + INFINITIVE	I suspected **John** *to be the cause of the delay.*
	Doctors suspect **inflammation** *to increase the risk of heart attacks.*
	George suspected **Donald** *to have leaked the memo to the press.*
OBJECT + *of* PRESENT PARTICIPLE	We suspect **a neighbor** *of trampling our flower bed.*
	Who would suspect **Grandma** *of hiding candy around her house*?

suspect _____ *consider likely/true*

OBJECT	Researchers suspect **a link between diabetes and Alzheimer's disease.**
	The investigator suspected **fraud.**
THAT-CLAUSE	I suspect **that you are right.**
	We suspected **that the builder was overcharging us.**
	The doctor suspected **that Kathy might have torn the cartilage in her knee.**
	No one could have suspected **that the loans were so risky.**

PRESENT		PRESENT PROGRESSIVE	
I swear	we swear	I am swearing	we are swearing
you swear	you swear	you are swearing	you are swearing
he/she/it swears	they swear	he/she/it is swearing	they are swearing

• *He swears that he knew nothing about it.*
              • *They are swearing that they are innocent.*

PAST		PAST PROGRESSIVE	
I swore	we swore	I was swearing	we were swearing
you swore	you swore	you were swearing	you were swearing
he/she/it swore	they swore	he/she/it was swearing	they were swearing

• *The witness swore to tell the truth.*
              • *The soldiers were swearing and yelling at us.*

PRESENT PERFECT	... have | has sworn
PAST PERFECT	... had sworn

FUTURE	... will swear
FUTURE PROGRESSIVE	... will be swearing
FUTURE PERFECT	... will have sworn

PAST PASSIVE

I was sworn	we were sworn
you were sworn	you were sworn
he/she/it was sworn	they were sworn

• *The appropriate oaths were sworn during the ceremony.*

(COMPLEMENTS)

swear *use offensive language, usually in anger*	He swore under his breath.
	Please don't swear around the children.
	It was enough to make one swear!
swear _____ *promise, vow, pledge, state very seriously*	
OBJECT	He swore **the oath of office.**
	I swore **a solemn promise.**
	Peter swore **his undying love to Héloïse.**
	The nobles all swore **their allegiance to the king.**
PASSIVE	The oath was sworn and witnessed.
INFINITIVE	I swear **to do it.**
	Criminals always swear **to never commit another crime.**
	He swears **to mend the error of his ways.**
	"I swear **to tell the truth, the whole truth, and nothing but the truth.**" [COMMON COURTROOM OATH]
THAT-CLAUSE	I swear **that we were not the cause of the accident.**
	The defendant swore **that he only shot in self-defense.**
	The kids all swore **that they didn't let the dog out.**
	"I do solemnly swear **that I will faithfully execute the office of President of the United States....**" [OATH OF OFFICE]

(PHRASAL VERBS)

swear at _____ *curse at*	He swore at me when I told him to leave the room.
swear by _____ *have great faith in*	Trudy swears by yoga.
swear _SEP_ **in** *administer an oath to*	The Chief Justice of the Supreme Court swears in the President of the United States.
	The witness was sworn in by the bailiff.
swear off _____ *promise to quit*	Randi has sworn off dieting.

(EXPRESSIONS)

swear _____ **to secrecy** *cause to promise not to repeat a secret*	Annette swore me to secrecy about her background.
swear to it *be absolutely certain about something* [USUALLY NEGATIVE]	I wouldn't swear to it, but I think Elvis is still alive.

PRESENT

I sweat	we sweat
you sweat	you sweat
he/she/it sweats	they sweat

• He sweats heavily when he exercises.

PRESENT PROGRESSIVE

I am sweating	we are sweating
you are sweating	you are sweating
he/she/it is sweating	they are sweating

• I am really sweating tomorrow's exam.

PAST

I sweated	we sweated
you sweated	you sweated
he/she/it sweated	they sweated

• They sweated so much they felt faint.

PAST PROGRESSIVE

I was sweating	we were sweating
you were sweating	you were sweating
he/she/it was sweating	they were sweating

• We were all sweating by the time we finished.

PRESENT PERFECT   ... have | has sweated/sweat
PAST PERFECT   ... had sweated/sweat

FUTURE   ... will sweat
FUTURE PROGRESSIVE   ... will be sweating
FUTURE PERFECT   ... will have sweated/sweat

PAST PASSIVE

I was sweated	we were sweated
you were sweated	you were sweated
he/she/it was sweated	they were sweated

• The wrestlers were sweated until they got down to 190 pounds.

COMPLEMENTS

sweat *perspire*	Everyone in the hot office was sweating like crazy.
	I always sweat when I work out.
	He sweats so much that he has to change his clothes after lunch.
sweat *form drops of water on its surface*	The bottles of water began to sweat.
	The plaster walls were actually sweating in the humid air.
	The cheese is sweating and needs to be refrigerated.
sweat *be worried/nervous*	The police let him sweat overnight.
	Don't sweat. Everything will be okay.
	They are going to make him sweat until he tells what happened.
sweat _____ *cause to perspire through exertion*	
OBJECT	The coach wants to sweat **the football players** at every practice.
	The training session had sweat **everybody**.
PASSIVE	The horses were sweat by the trainers and then allowed to slowly cool off.
sweat _____ *be worried/nervous about*	
OBJECT	Noel was sweating **the job interview**.
	Everyone sweats **the final exam**.
over OBJECT	Maureen sweated **over her English literature grade**.
	Ruth was sweating **over the upcoming conference in Montreal**.
sweat _____ *work very hard on*	
over OBJECT	The candidate sweated **over the wording of his acceptance speech**.
	Jeffrey sweated all day **over his essay**.

PHRASAL VERBS

sweat _SEP_ **off** *lose [an amount of weight] by exercising*	Angie sweated off 22 pounds in two months.

EXPRESSIONS

sweat blood *work very hard*	She was willing to sweat blood for a spot on the Olympic team.
sweat bullets *be extremely worried/nervous*	Poor Leroy was sweating bullets outside the principal's office.

PRESENT

I sweep	we sweep
you sweep	you sweep
he/she/it sweeps	they sweep

• *He sweeps the leaves into the gutter.*

PAST

I swept	we swept
you swept	you swept
he/she/it swept	they swept

• *The Giants swept the three-game series.*

PRESENT PERFECT … have | has swept
PAST PERFECT … had swept

PRESENT PROGRESSIVE

I am sweeping	we are sweeping
you are sweeping	you are sweeping
he/she/it is sweeping	they are sweeping

• *She is sweeping the front porch.*

PAST PROGRESSIVE

I was sweeping	we were sweeping
you were sweeping	you were sweeping
he/she/it was sweeping	they were sweeping

• *The incoming tide was sweeping across the bay.*

FUTURE … will sweep
FUTURE PROGRESSIVE … will be sweeping
FUTURE PERFECT … will have swept

PAST PASSIVE

I was swept	we were swept
you were swept	you were swept
he/she/it was swept	they were swept

• *The room was swept this morning.*

COMPLEMENTS

sweep _____ *clean with a broom/brush*

OBJECT
You need to sweep **the kitchen floor.**
I'll sweep **the carpet** in the entryway.

PASSIVE
The garage has already been swept.

sweep _____ *clear away*

OBJECT + ADVERB OF PLACE TO/FROM
The archaeologist carefully swept **dirt** *from the bones.*
The waiter swept **the crumbs** *onto a tray.*

PASSIVE
The trash had been swept *into a pile in the corner.*

sweep _____ *carry along in a continuous motion*

OBJECT + ADVERB OF PLACE TO/FROM
The cook swept **a greasy cloth** *over the lunch counter.*
The current swept **the boat** *onto the rocks.*
The mud slide swept **the house** *off its foundation.*

PASSIVE
We were swept *out to sea* by the offshore winds.

sweep _____ *pass over in a continuous motion*

OBJECT
The guard's eyes swept **the room.**
The politician's glance swept **the crowd.**

sweep _____ *move quickly*

ADVERB OF PLACE TO/FROM
The rumor swept **through the crowd.**
A gust of rain swept **down the empty street.**

sweep _____ *search*

OBJECT
The volunteers swept **the woods,** looking for the lost children.
Technicians swept **the office** for hidden electronic devices.

PASSIVE
The crime scene has already been swept.

sweep _____ *win all that can be won in*

OBJECT
Our party swept **the fall election.**

PHRASAL VERBS

sweep along/down/in/off/out/past/up/etc. *sweep in a specified direction*
The queen swept in with all her attendants.
The motorcade swept past.

sweep SEP **along/aside/away/back/in/off/out/past/up**/etc. *sweep [something] in a specified direction*
The Russian revolution swept the old system away overnight.
His election swept in a host of governmental reforms.
The tornado swept up everything in its path.

swell

swell | swells · swelled · have swelled
swell | swells · swelled · have swollen

☑ REGULAR
☑ IRREGULAR

PRESENT

I swell	we swell
you swell	you swell
he/she/it swells	they swell

• *My ankles swell if I stand too long.*

PRESENT PROGRESSIVE

I am swelling	we are swelling
you are swelling	you are swelling
he/she/it is swelling	they are swelling

• *The wood is swelling from all the moisture.*

PAST

I swelled	we swelled
you swelled	you swelled
he/she/it swelled	they swelled

• *The sails swelled in the wind.*

PAST PROGRESSIVE

I was swelling	we were swelling
you were swelling	you were swelling
he/she/it was swelling	they were swelling

• *Naturally, her parents were swelling with pride.*

PRESENT PERFECT ... have | has swelled
PAST PERFECT ... had swelled

FUTURE ... will swell
FUTURE PROGRESSIVE ... will be swelling
FUTURE PERFECT ... will have swelled

PAST PASSIVE

I was swollen	we were swollen
you were swollen	you were swollen
he/she/it was swollen	they were swollen

• *The river was swollen by weeks of rain.*

COMPLEMENTS

swell *become larger/stronger, expand*

My hands swelled from the heat.
The crowd in front of the gate was swelling by the minute.
The orchestra music was swelling and the lights dimmed.
The balloon swelled and began to lift.

swell ___ *cause to become larger/stronger, cause to expand*

OBJECT

The snowmelt had swollen **all the lakes**.
The bad news swelled **the rumors about layoffs**.
The pump quickly swelled **the balloons** to full size.

PASSIVE

My lymph nodes were swollen.

swell ___ *become filled [with an emotion]*

with OBJECT

Ebenezer's heart swelled **with the Christmas spirit**.
Tiny Tim swelled **with gratitude**.
The cyclist was swelling **with confidence** after winning
the Tour de France.

PRESENT

I swim	we swim
you swim	you swim
he/she/it swims	they swim

• *He swims three times a week.*

PRESENT PROGRESSIVE

I am swimming	we are swimming
you are swimming	you are swimming
he/she/it is swimming	they are swimming

• *The kids are swimming in the pool.*

PAST

I swam	we swam
you swam	you swam
he/she/it swam	they swam

• *I swam competitively in college.*

PAST PROGRESSIVE

I was swimming	we were swimming
you were swimming	you were swimming
he/she/it was swimming	they were swimming

• *My head was swimming from her perfume.*

PRESENT PERFECT ... have | has swum
PAST PERFECT ... had swum

FUTURE ... will swim
FUTURE PROGRESSIVE ... will be swimming
FUTURE PERFECT ... will have swum

PAST PASSIVE

—	—
—	—
it was swum	they were swum

• *The English Channel was first swum in 1875.*

───────────────────────────────── **COMPLEMENTS**

swim *travel through water by moving one's arms and legs*	Look at me! I'm swimming. Do you know how to swim? I could swim before I could ride a bicycle.
swim *be dizzy*	The cocktails make my head swim. After the accident, my head swam and my ears rang. They gave me so many different directions that my head was swimming.
swim ____ *travel through water by moving one's arms and legs* ADVERB OF PLACE TO/FROM	Let's swim **out to the reef.** The fish swam **into the net.** We had swum **clear across the lake.** The kids like to swim **under the dock.**
swim ____ *cross by swimming* OBJECT	Salmon can swim **most of the Columbia River.** A few people have swum **the Strait of Messina.** The kids are trying to swim **the length of the pool** under water.
swim ____ *seem to be whirling* ADVERB OF PLACE	After he drank the punch, the room swam **before his eyes.**
swim ____ *be completely covered with* [USED ONLY IN THE PROGRESSIVE TENSES] ADVERB OF PLACE	The lettuce was practically swimming **in salad dressing.**

───────────────────────────────── **PHRASAL VERBS**

swim along/around/away/in/off/out/ up/etc. *swim in a specified direction*	The kids were swimming around in the pond. After we fed the dolphins, they swam off.

───────────────────────────────── **EXPRESSIONS**

sink or swim *fail or succeed*	Donna has a new job, and we are wondering if she will sink or swim.
swim against the current/tide *act in a way opposite to others*	I swam against the tide in high school—and often got punished for it.

PRESENT	
I swing	we swing
you swing	you swing
he/she/it swings	they swing

• *Watch out—the door swings toward you.*

PRESENT PROGRESSIVE	
I am swinging	we are swinging
you are swinging	you are swinging
he/she/it is swinging	they are swinging

• *You are swinging the bat too late.*

PAST	
I swung	we swung
you swung	you swung
he/she/it swung	they swung

• *He swung his racket and missed.*

PAST PROGRESSIVE	
I was swinging	we were swinging
you were swinging	you were swinging
he/she/it was swinging	they were swinging

• *The kids were swinging on vines.*

PRESENT PERFECT ... have | has swung
PAST PERFECT ... had swung

FUTURE ... will swing
FUTURE PROGRESSIVE ... will be swinging
FUTURE PERFECT ... will have swung

PAST PASSIVE	
I was swung	we were swung
you were swung	you were swung
he/she/it was swung	they were swung

• *The heavy beam was swung into place.*

COMPLEMENTS

swing *sway/rock back and forth*	The gate was swinging in the wind.
	The earthquake caused the chandeliers to swing.
	The dancers were swinging in time to the music.
swing *change suddenly*	The storm winds swung crazily from one direction to another.
	His moods were swinging more and more wildly.
	Opinion polls were swinging all over the map.
swing *strike at something in a sweeping motion*	The batter swings and misses.
	The tired boxers were swinging wildly.
	A good golfer swings with his hips, not just with his arms.
swing ____ *move ([something]) in a sweeping motion*	
ADVERB OF PLACE TO/FROM	The cowboy swung **into the saddle.**
	The children swung **onto the wagon.**
	I swung **into the driver's seat.**
OBJECT	He swung **the bat** and drove the ball into left field.
	The player swung **a punch** when the referee wasn't looking.
	He swung **the golf club** and topped the ball.
OBJECT + ADVERB OF PLACE TO/FROM	I swung **my leg** *over the top rail* and jumped.
	Larry swung **his suitcase** *onto the bed.*
	She swung **her arm** *around my shoulder.*
	The kids swung **the rope** *over a limb.*
swing ____ *influence decisively*	
OBJECT	The senator thought his ad could swing **the election.**
	We hoped to swing **enough undecided voters** to win.

PHRASAL VERBS

swing around/down/in/off/out/etc. *swing in a specified direction*	The cowboy swung down from the saddle.
	The path swings off to the right at the top of the hill.
swing SEP **around/down/in/off/out/**etc. *swing [something] in a specified direction*	The knight swung his sword around, and everyone stepped back.
swing by/over *visit briefly*	Susan will swing by if she has a chance.
swing by/over ____ *visit briefly*	I'll swing by Grandma's on the way to the store.
	Can you swing over to the drugstore and buy some aspirin?

PRESENT

I take	we take
you take	you take
he/she/it takes	they take

- *He always takes the bus to work.*

PRESENT PROGRESSIVE

I am taking	we are taking
you are taking	you are taking
he/she/it is taking	they are taking

- *He is taking a long time.*

PAST

I took	we took
you took	you took
he/she/it took	they took

- *Someone took the last cup of coffee.*

PAST PROGRESSIVE

I was taking	we were taking
you were taking	you were taking
he/she/it was taking	they were taking

- *We were taking the bus to New York.*

PRESENT PERFECT ... have | has taken
PAST PERFECT ... had taken

FUTURE ... will take
FUTURE PROGRESSIVE ... will be taking
FUTURE PERFECT ... will have taken

PAST PASSIVE

I was taken	we were taken
you were taken	you were taken
he/she/it was taken	they were taken

- *All of the seats were already taken.*

(**COMPLEMENTS**)

take _____ grasp, take possession of
OBJECT
PASSIVE

He took **his daughter's hand**.
Our ID cards were taken by the police.

take _____ get, obtain
OBJECT

Frank took **a job at the radio station**.
Gerry took **a jar of olives** from the refrigerator.

take _____ carry, transport
OBJECT

You should always take **your passport** when you travel.
Take **an umbrella** in case it rains.
Can you take **the kids** with you?
I usually take **my lunch**.

OBJECT + ADVERB OF PLACE TO/FROM

Would you take **these books** *to the library*?
Amos took **the package** *to the post office*.
This bus takes **riders** *to the stadium*.

take _____ bring, lead
OBJECT + ADVERB OF PLACE TO/FROM

Bill is taking **Fran** *to the dance*.
This path takes **you** *to the top of Buttimer Hill*.

take _____ travel by [a vehicle, route]
OBJECT (+ ADVERB OF PLACE TO/FROM)

We can take **the elevator or the stairs**—you choose.
My parents once took **the Queen Mary**.
Let's take **the scenic route**.
We took **Route 66** *from Chicago to Los Angeles*.
The kids took **a shortcut** *through the woods*.
They took **the bus** *home*.

take _____ move to [a position]
OBJECT

Gentlemen, please take **your seats**.
The two teams are taking **the field**.

take _____ engage in [an activity]
OBJECT

Let's take **a 10-minute break**.
Thomas always takes **an afternoon nap**.
We took **a nice walk in the park**.
Bill took **a class in income tax preparation**.

top 40 verb

take _____ *eat, drink, swallow* OBJECT	I'll take **a black coffee and two donuts**, please. I took **an aspirin** for my headache.
take _____ *capture, win* OBJECT	After a brief fight, the soldiers took **the fort**. The Cardinals took **three out of four games** from the Mets.
take _____ *subscribe to, rent* OBJECT	They take **several newspapers and magazines**. We took **an apartment in the city**.
take _____ *steal* OBJECT	Somebody took **my wallet**. People often take **newspapers** without paying for them.
take _____ *require, use up* OBJECT + INFINITIVE	It took **a long time** *to repair the leak*. It takes **$50** *to fill the truck with gas*. They took **two days** *to drive to Dallas*. It takes **a lot of courage** *to go skydiving*.
take _____ *endure, suffer* OBJECT	Football players take **a lot of physical punishment**. I can't take **this heat and humidity**.
take _____ *photograph* OBJECT	Uncle Cecil took **pictures** during the family reunion.
take _____ *interpret* OBJECT + ADVERB OF MANNER	She took **my joke** *seriously*.

─────────────────────────────────(**PHRASAL VERBS**)───

take _SEP_ along/aside/away/down/in/ out/up/etc. *bring/carry/lead/transport in a specified direction*	Grandmother took us along to the store. The elevator takes you down to the parking garage.
take _SEP_ down *write down, record*	The officer took down his address and phone number.
take _SEP_ down *dismantle*	Volunteers took the political signs down after the election.
take _____ for *mistake for*	Betty took me for my older brother.
take in _____ *attend, visit*	We could eat at Lombardo's and take in a movie. Today we'll take in the zoo and the art museum.
take _SEP_ in *give shelter to*	My husband takes in stray cats from the neighborhood.
take off *leave, depart*	Our plane will take off at 3:05 P.M.
take off *become very active/successful*	Sales of used cars have taken off like a rocket.
take _SEP_ off *remove [clothing, etc.]*	The players took off their helmets.
take _SEP_ off *deduct*	The dealer took 50% off because the table was scratched.
take _SEP_ on *hire*	My company took 30 new employees on in March.
take _SEP_ on *undertake*	Sorry, I just can't take on another project.
take _SEP_ out *remove*	The surgeon took Dad's gallbladder out.
take _SEP_ over *begin managing*	A recent college graduate took over the programming department.
take to _____ *become fond of*	Khalil has really taken to calligraphy. Susan has taken to Leonard in a big way.
take up _____ *fill, occupy*	Your printing presses are taking up the whole basement! Meetings took up the governor's entire afternoon.
take _SEP_ up *become interested in*	Stephanie has taken up knitting.

top 40 verb

PRESENT

I talk	we talk
you talk	you talk
he/she/it talks	they talk

• *He talks when he should be listening.*

PRESENT PROGRESSIVE

I am talking	we are talking
you are talking	you are talking
he/she/it is talking	they are talking

• *Can you turn the TV down? We're talking.*

PAST

I talked	we talked
you talked	you talked
he/she/it talked	they talked

• *They talked for the first time in years.*

PAST PROGRESSIVE

I was talking	we were talking
you were talking	you were talking
he/she/it was talking	they were talking

• *They were talking on the phone.*

PRESENT PERFECT ... have | has talked
PAST PERFECT ... had talked

FUTURE ... will talk
FUTURE PROGRESSIVE ... will be talking
FUTURE PERFECT ... will have talked

PAST PASSIVE

I was talked	we were talked
you were talked	you were talked
he/she/it was talked	they were talked

• *The problem was talked over before the committee met.*

COMPLEMENTS

talk *say words, speak*	After his stroke, he couldn't talk. When do children first learn to talk? The ability to talk is uniquely human.
talk *converse*	We have to talk. My kids spend all their time talking on their cell phones.
talk *gossip*	The whole school was talking. Be careful, or you will have people talking.
talk *reveal secret/confidential information*	I don't believe he would ever talk. We can't afford to let him talk.
talk _____ *use [a particular language] in speaking* (in) OBJECT	The waiters are talking in **Italian**. They were talking **a language I did not know**.
talk _____ *discuss* OBJECT	Let's talk **business**.
talk _____ *communicate the significance of* [USED ONLY IN THE PROGRESSIVE TENSES] OBJECT	They were talking **big money**. He was talking **a major crisis** in the near future. I am talking **big losses** here.
talk _____ *convince [to do / not to do]* OBJECT + *into* PRESENT PARTICIPLE OBJECT + *out of* PRESENT PARTICIPLE	The staff talked **Sam *into running for Congress***. Dad talked **me *out of enlisting in the Army***.

PHRASAL VERBS

talk [someone] down _____ *convince [someone] to sell for [less money]*	She talked the salesman down $1,700.
talk ˢᵉᵖ **out/over/through** *discuss fully*	The engineers talked the difficulties over. You need to talk this through with your teacher.
talk [someone] through _____ *explain the steps of to [someone]*	The receptionist talked me through the application form.
talk ˢᵉᵖ **up** *promote*	She is talking up her plan to help families pay for college.

PRESENT

I teach	we teach
you teach	you teach
he/she/it teaches	they teach

• *He teaches computer science.*

PRESENT PROGRESSIVE

I am teaching	we are teaching
you are teaching	you are teaching
he/she/it is teaching	they are teaching

• *I am teaching Introduction to Physics again.*

PAST

I taught	we taught
you taught	you taught
he/she/it taught	they taught

• *I taught in Spain for a year.*

PAST PROGRESSIVE

I was teaching	we were teaching
you were teaching	you were teaching
he/she/it was teaching	they were teaching

• *They were teaching him to play baseball.*

PRESENT PERFECT ... have | has taught
PAST PERFECT ... had taught

FUTURE ... will teach
FUTURE PROGRESSIVE ... will be teaching
FUTURE PERFECT ... will have taught

PAST PASSIVE

I was taught	we were taught
you were taught	you were taught
he/she/it was taught	they were taught

• *English was taught beginning in the earliest grades.*

(**COMPLEMENTS**)

teach *instruct professionally*

I have been teaching for ten years.
Her sister teaches at Osaka University.
I would like to teach.

teach ____ *provide training/instruction in [a skill, topic]*

OBJECT

He teaches **martial arts**.
I would like to teach **English**.
Experience teaches **moderation in all things**.

INDIRECT OBJECT + DIRECT OBJECT

She taught *them* **the names of the constellations**.
He taught *first-year students* **world history**.
I taught *myself* **the basics of geometry**.

to PARAPHRASE

She taught **the names of the constellations** *to them*.
He taught **world history** *to first-year students*.
I taught **the basics of geometry** *to myself*.

teach ____ *provide training/instruction to*

OBJECT

Kathy teaches **seventh graders**.
She only teaches **graduate students**.
He teaches **management trainees**.

OBJECT + INFINITIVE

I taught **the kids** *to drive*.
The army taught **them** *to be disciplined*.

PASSIVE

We were taught *to think for ourselves*.

(OBJECT +) WH-INFINITIVE

Their religion teaches **how to act**.
The class teaches *students* **how to write a resume**.
The book taught *investors* **what to look for in a stock**.

teach ____ *provide [a particular philosophy/knowledge] to*

(OBJECT +) THAT-CLAUSE

History teaches **that the pen is mightier than the sword**.
My parents taught *us* **that hard work never hurt anyone**.
The instructor taught *the class* **that a 60-40 mixture of stocks and bonds is best**.

(**EXPRESSIONS**)

teach ____ a lesson *show [someone] the correct way to behave*

His mother taught him a lesson on the value of money by making him work for his allowance.

PRESENT		PRESENT PROGRESSIVE	
I tear	we tear	I am tearing	we are tearing
you tear	you tear	you are tearing	you are tearing
he/she/it tears	they tear	he/she/it is tearing	they are tearing

• *He tears stamps off envelopes.*   • *Be careful—you're tearing your shirt.*

PAST		PAST PROGRESSIVE	
I tore	we tore	I was tearing	we were tearing
you tore	you tore	you were tearing	you were tearing
he/she/it tore	they tore	he/she/it was tearing	they were tearing

• *The ligament tore with a "popping" sound.*   • *The kids were tearing into the chocolate brownies.*

PRESENT PERFECT	... have | has torn	FUTURE	... will tear
PAST PERFECT	... had torn	FUTURE PROGRESSIVE	... will be tearing
		FUTURE PERFECT	... will have torn

PAST PASSIVE	
I was torn	we were torn
you were torn	you were torn
he/she/it was torn	they were torn

• *A huge hole was torn in the building by the explosion.*

NOTE: The irregular verb *tear*, which rhymes with *care*, is presented here.
The regular verb *tear*, which rhymes with *deer*, means "to cry."

(COMPLEMENTS)

tear *rip, come apart*
Darn it! My new jeans are tearing.
The canvas will tear if there is a high wind.

tear _____ *cause to rip / come apart*
OBJECT
I tore **the envelope** trying to open it.
A big gust of wind tore **our only sail**.
PASSIVE
The documents had been torn in shipping.

tear _____ *make/punch [a hole, opening] in*
OBJECT
The artillery fire tore **a huge gap** in our right flank.
PASSIVE
A hole was torn in his shield by a spear.

tear _____ *move with force/speed*
ADVERB OF PLACE TO/FROM
The kids tore **out of the room**.
The horses tore **around the last curve**.

tear _____ *damage [a muscle, ligament] by overstretching*
OBJECT
Dirk tore **his rotator cuff** playing tennis.
Soccer players often tear **muscles in their knees**.
PASSIVE
His shoulder was torn lifting weights.

tear _____ *damage greatly* [USED ONLY IN THE PASSIVE]
OBJECT
The country was torn by war and famine.

(PHRASAL VERBS)

tear around/away/down/off/out/etc.
move with force/speed in a specified direction
The limousine tore away from the curb.
The neighbor's dog always tears out after moving cars.

tear _SEP_ **apart/away/down/off/out/up/**
etc. *pull in a specified direction*
Tear the coupons apart and organize them.
Carpenters tore up the old carpet.

tear into _____ *begin to do/eat/etc. forcefully*
Jackie is tearing into remodeling the kitchen.
The girls really tore into the peanut butter.

tear into _____ *scold severely*
The boss tore into an employee who was late.

tear _SEP_ **up** *reject*
The manager tore up the singer's contract and offered
    her 10 times the money.

PRESENT

I tell	we tell
you tell	you tell
he/she/it tells	they tell

• *He tells people what they want to hear.*

PRESENT PROGRESSIVE

I am telling	we are telling
you are telling	you are telling
he/she/it is telling	they are telling

• *I'm telling the whole world that I love you.*

PAST

I told	we told
you told	you told
he/she/it told	they told

• *I told the truth.*

PAST PROGRESSIVE

I was telling	we were telling
you were telling	you were telling
he/she/it was telling	they were telling

• *We were just telling them what happened.*

PRESENT PERFECT … have | has told
PAST PERFECT … had told

FUTURE … will tell
FUTURE PROGRESSIVE … will be telling
FUTURE PERFECT … will have told

PAST PASSIVE

I was told	we were told
you were told	you were told
he/she/it was told	they were told

• *The children were told that they could stay up late.*

(**COMPLEMENTS**)

tell *reveal secret/confidential information*	Please don't tell. I will never tell.
tell *have a definite effect*	The long hours are beginning to tell. The constant battering by the artillery was starting to tell.
tell *know the outcome/result* [USED IN QUESTIONS AND NEGATIVE SENTENCES]	Who can tell? I certainly can't tell.
tell ____ *put into words, express*	
OBJECT	I told **the truth,** but he was telling **a flat-out lie.** He told **a story about growing up in Greece.**
INDIRECT OBJECT + DIRECT OBJECT	I told *the kids* **a ghost story.** Who wants to tell *them* **the bad news?**
to PARAPHRASE	I told **a ghost story** *to the kids.* Who wants to tell **the bad news** *to them?*
tell ____ *inform*	
OBJECT + THAT-CLAUSE	We need to tell **them** *that the trip has been canceled.* I told **everyone** *that we were engaged.*
PASSIVE	The press had been told *that the senator was ill.*
OBJECT + WH-CLAUSE	The consultant told **us** *what we should do.* I told **them** *how much it would cost.*
OBJECT + WH-INFINITIVE	The taxi driver told **us** *where to go.*
PASSIVE	The staff was told *what to expect.*
tell ____ *order, command*	
OBJECT + INFINITIVE	I told **her** *to return the book as soon as she could.*
PASSIVE	They had been told *to stay inside during the storm.*
tell ____ *recognize, determine with certainty* [USUALLY WITH *can* OR *could*]	
THAT-CLAUSE	I couldn't tell **that anything had happened.** Can you tell **that we remodeled the kitchen?**
WH-CLAUSE	Can you tell **who it is?** I can't tell **what went wrong.**

(**PHRASAL VERBS**)

tell _SEP_ **off** *scold, criticize*	She told my brother off for not keeping his room clean.

PRESENT

I tend	we tend
you tend	you tend
he/she/it tends	they tend

- *John tends to worry about everything.*

PRESENT PROGRESSIVE

I am tending	we are tending
you are tending	you are tending
he/she/it is tending	they are tending

- *We are tending to eat out less often.*

PAST

I tended	we tended
you tended	you tended
he/she/it tended	they tended

- *He tended to get jumpy if he ate chocolate.*

PAST PROGRESSIVE

I was tending	we were tending
you were tending	you were tending
he/she/it was tending	they were tending

- *They were tending west along the river.*

PRESENT PERFECT ... have | has tended
PAST PERFECT ... had tended

FUTURE ... will tend
FUTURE PROGRESSIVE ... will be tending
FUTURE PERFECT ... will have tended

PAST PASSIVE

Tend is never used in the passive voice.

COMPLEMENTS

tend _____ *be likely*

  INFINITIVE

We all tend **to favor our dominant hand**.
He tends **to get rattled** when he has to speak in public.
That jacket always tends **to ride up in back**.
I tend **to get a headache** if I work at the computer too long.
Most right-handed golfers tend **to pull the ball to the right**.
We tend not **to trust politicians**.

tend _____ *go/move in a certain way*

  ADVERB OF PLACE TO/FROM

The river tends **southward** as it crosses the plain.
Richard tends **toward an urban lifestyle**.
Valerie's taste tends **toward avant-garde**.

PRESENT

I test	we test
you test	you test
he/she/it tests	they test

• *The school tests every incoming student.*

PRESENT PROGRESSIVE

I am testing	we are testing
you are testing	you are testing
he/she/it is testing	they are testing

• *We are testing the latest software.*

PAST

I tested	we tested
you tested	you tested
he/she/it tested	they tested

• *I tested the antenna's reception.*

PAST PROGRESSIVE

I was testing	we were testing
you were testing	you were testing
he/she/it was testing	they were testing

• *The vet was testing the cattle for mad cow disease.*

PRESENT PERFECT ... have | has tested
PAST PERFECT ... had tested

FUTURE ... will test
FUTURE PROGRESSIVE ... will be testing
FUTURE PERFECT ... will have tested

PAST PASSIVE

I was tested	we were tested
you were tested	you were tested
he/she/it was tested	they were tested

• *My patience was severely tested by his rambling phone calls.*

COMPLEMENTS

test *administer examinations*
I will be testing all afternoon.
How often do we need to test?

test _____ *check the quality/suitability/performance/condition of*

OBJECT
They tested **the paint** for traces of lead.
You should always test **the temperature of the water in the kids' bath**.
The state tests **each fourth, eighth, and twelfth grader**.
The doctor tested **my reflexes**.
I tested **the brakes** before we started down the mountain.
We tested **all drug addicts** for HIV infection.

PASSIVE
Every qualifying runner will be tested for drugs.

test _____ *put under extreme stress*

OBJECT
Carol would test **the patience of a saint**.
Such behavior would test **any marriage**.
The series of defeats severely tested **the army's resolve**.

PASSIVE
Even his good nature was tested by their rudeness.

EXPRESSIONS

test the water(s) *determine the level of support/approval for a new product/ plan/proposal*
We were testing the water with an online version of the dictionary.
Senator Blather is testing the waters for a possible presidential bid.

PRESENT

I thank	we thank
you thank	you thank
he/she/it thanks	they thank

• *The senator always thanks the voters.*

PRESENT PROGRESSIVE

I am thanking	we are thanking
you are thanking	you are thanking
he/she/it is thanking	they are thanking

• *They are thanking all the volunteers.*

PAST

I thanked	we thanked
you thanked	you thanked
he/she/it thanked	they thanked

• *I thanked them again for helping us.*

PAST PROGRESSIVE

I was thanking	we were thanking
you were thanking	you were thanking
he/she/it was thanking	they were thanking

• *We were thanking the sponsors.*

PRESENT PERFECT ... have | has thanked
PAST PERFECT ... had thanked

FUTURE ... will thank
FUTURE PROGRESSIVE ... will be thanking
FUTURE PERFECT ... will have thanked

PAST PASSIVE

I was thanked	we were thanked
you were thanked	you were thanked
he/she/it was thanked	they were thanked

• *We were thanked for the flowers we sent.*

(**COMPLEMENTS**)

thank _____ *express gratitude to*

OBJECT (+ *for* OBJECT)
 Please thank **them** on behalf of all of us.
 I would like to thank **you** *for all your help*.
 We thanked **our friends** *for all their work*.
 Whom should we thank *for the lovely gift*?
 I have **my teachers** to thank *for my success*.

PASSIVE
 Our hosts must be properly thanked.

OBJECT (+ *for* PRESENT PARTICIPLE)
 The president thanked **us** *for volunteering our time*.

PASSIVE
 The group will be thanked *for donating time and money to the project*.

WH-CLAUSE
 I would like to thank **whoever arranged the meeting**.
 They thanked **whoever could take a minute to talk to them**.
 We will thank **whomever you got to help my parents**.

thank _____ *blame* [USED IRONICALLY]

OBJECT (+ *for* OBJECT)
 Look at this mess! I guess I can thank **you**, kids.
 We have **Greg** to thank *for the mix-up*.
 You can thank **my parents** *for choosing a Bambi party theme*.

(**EXPRESSIONS**)

thank [one's] lucky stars *be grateful for one's luck*
 Gretchen should thank her lucky stars.

thank God/goodness/heaven(s) *I/we are grateful*
 Thank goodness I had an extra computer battery.
 Thank heavens that winter is over.

PRESENT

I think	we think
you think	you think
he/she/it thinks	they think

• *He thinks that the movie begins at 7:45.*

PRESENT PROGRESSIVE

I am thinking	we are thinking
you are thinking	you are thinking
he/she/it is thinking	they are thinking

• *Don't rush me—I'm thinking.*

PAST

I thought	we thought
you thought	you thought
he/she/it thought	they thought

• *I thought long and hard about it.*

PAST PROGRESSIVE

I was thinking	we were thinking
you were thinking	you were thinking
he/she/it was thinking	they were thinking

• *They were thinking that the worst had happened.*

PRESENT PERFECT ... have | has thought
PAST PERFECT ... had thought

FUTURE ... will think
FUTURE PROGRESSIVE ... will be thinking
FUTURE PERFECT ... will have thought

PAST PASSIVE

I was thought	we were thought
you were thought	you were thought
he/she/it was thought	they were thought

• *The accident was thought to have been caused by pilot error.*

COMPLEMENTS

think *use one's mind, reason*
Think twice before you do anything.
"I think, therefore I am." [RENÉ DESCARTES]

think _____ *believe, expect*
THAT-CLAUSE
I thought **that dinner was good, but a little too heavy.**
Do they think **that the flight will leave on time?**

think _____ *consider, judge*
OBJECT + *(to be)* PREDICATE NOUN
The reviewer thought **the book *(to be) a bit of a dud*.**
The public thought **Clark *(to be) a dashing hero*.**
  PASSIVE
At first, Truman was thought ***(to be) a failed president*.**
OBJECT + *(to be)* PREDICATE ADJECTIVE
Everyone thought **Thomas *(to be) promising*.**
They thought **the idea *(to be) ready to present to the board*.**
  PASSIVE
The car was thought ***(to be) quite overpriced*.**
OBJECT + INFINITIVE
I thought **him *to have more sense than that*.**
  PASSIVE
He was thought ***to own several Renoirs*.**

think _____ *remember* [USED IN QUESTIONS AND NEGATIVE SENTENCES, OFTEN WITH *can* OR *could*]
of OBJECT
I can't think **of the girl's name.**
INFINITIVE
Did you think **to lock the back door?**
Who thought **to bring some insect repellent?**
WH-CLAUSE
We couldn't think **what his name was.**
I couldn't think **where we were supposed to meet the group.**
WH-INFINITIVE
I couldn't think **what to say.**
Aunt Polly couldn't think **where to turn next.**

think _____ *contemplate, consider*
of/about OBJECT
The board was thinking **of Rex for secretary.**
She thinks **about him** all the time.
of/about PRESENT PARTICIPLE
Anne was thinking **of asking Wentworth to the concert.**
We were thinking **about ordering Chinese for dinner.**

PHRASAL VERBS

think _SEP_ **over** *consider carefully*
I need to think your proposal over before making a decision.

think _SEP_ **up** *invent, plan*
We thought up a better way to manage inventory.
They thought up a clever way to trick Bartholomew and Jacob.

PRESENT

I threaten	we threaten
you threaten	you threaten
he/she/it threatens	they threaten

• *He threatens to quit about once a week.*

PRESENT PROGRESSIVE

I am threatening	we are threatening
you are threatening	you are threatening
he/she/it is threatening	they are threatening

• *The union is threatening to strike.*

PAST

I threatened	we threatened
you threatened	you threatened
he/she/it threatened	they threatened

• *He threatened us with extra homework.*

PAST PROGRESSIVE

I was threatening	we were threatening
you were threatening	you were threatening
he/she/it was threatening	they were threatening

• *He was threatening a lawsuit.*

PRESENT PERFECT ... have | has threatened
PAST PERFECT ... had threatened

FUTURE ... will threaten
FUTURE PROGRESSIVE ... will be threatening
FUTURE PERFECT ... will have threatened

PAST PASSIVE

I was threatened	we were threatened
you were threatened	you were threatened
he/she/it was threatened	they were threatened

• *Our plans were threatened by the economic downturn.*

────────────────────────────(**COMPLEMENTS**)───

threaten _____ *state one's intention to harm/punish / perform a harmful/punitive act*

OBJECT	The gang threatened **the shop owners.** The pirates were threatening **the shippers.**
PASSIVE	The students were threatened by the vice principal.
(OBJECT +) THAT-CLAUSE	The police threatened **that they would use tear gas.** The sergeant threatened *the recruits* **that they would do guard duty.** The treasurer threatened *the company* **that he would not approve the loan.**
OBJECT + *with* OBJECT	The sergeant threatened **the recruits** *with guard duty.* The principal threatened **the students** *with suspension.*
OBJECT + *with* PRESENT PARTICIPLE	We threatened **the kids** *with unplugging the TV.*
INFINITIVE	The outraged patient threatened **to sue the hospital.** I threatened **to take my business elsewhere.** The renters threatened **to stop paying the landlord** unless the leaks were repaired.

threaten _____ *endanger*

OBJECT	The weather was threatening **our plans for a picnic.** The broken finger threatened **his career as a pianist.** The recession threatened **the entire economy.**
PASSIVE	His health had been threatened by years of smoking.

threaten _____ *seem likely [to cause harm]*

INFINITIVE	The virus threatened **to spread to other villages.** The storm threatened **to cut off the only road across the mountains.** The freeze threatened **to ruin the peach crop.**

throw _____ *put suddenly [in a place, condition]*
   OBJECT + *into* OBJECT

The sheriff threw **the suspects *into jail***.
His remarks threw **the audience *into hysteria***.

PHRASAL VERBS

throw ^SEP^ **around/aside/back/down/ in/off/out/up**/etc. *toss/hurl in a specified direction*

The players were throwing a Frisbee around.
Would you throw the ball back?
He threw his head back and laughed.
He threw his book bag down.

throw ^SEP^ **around** *spend [money] freely*

He throws money around like it grows on trees.

throw ^SEP^ **away** *discard, get rid of*

Don't throw the lamp away; I'm going to fix it.

throw ^SEP^ **in** *interject*

Jan threw in the idea of working at a soup kitchen.

throw ^SEP^ **in** *add as an extra*

They will throw in a medium pizza for free.

throw ^SEP^ **off** *mislead, fool*

His foreign accent threw the police off.

throw ^SEP^ **on** *put on in haste*

I'll throw on a jacket and be ready to go.

throw ^SEP^ **out** *discard, get rid of*

We won't throw the plastic out; we'll recycle it instead.

throw ^SEP^ **out** *expel*

The teacher threw him out for using profanity.

throw ^SEP^ **out** *reject*

The judge will throw the convict's testimony out.

throw ^SEP^ **out** *offer*

Dave is always throwing out suggestions.

throw ^SEP^ **together** *put together in haste*

We can throw together some pasta for supper.
Our engineering department can throw a scale model together in a week.

throw **up** *vomit*

He threw up on the way home from the ballpark.

throw ^SEP^ **up** *build quickly*

A developer threw up a flimsy apartment building on the corner.

EXPRESSIONS

throw _____ **a curve** *surprise [someone]*

The company threw us a curve by switching medical insurance plans.

throw **a fit/tantrum** *display anger*

Johnny throws a fit when I ask him to wash his hands.

throw **[a lot of / some] light on** _____ *clarify, give details about*

Scientists threw some light on the human genome.

throw **cold water on** _____ *discourage*

The committee threw cold water on our ideas for reducing waste.

throw _____ **for a loop** *shock/confuse [someone]*

The program glitch threw the programmers for a loop.

throw **good money after bad** *waste even more money on something*

Frank threw good money after bad by buying 100 more shares of the worthless stock.

throw **in the sponge/towel** *quit, give up*

The firm is throwing in the towel after losing its three biggest customers.

throw **[one's] hands up** *quit in despair*

After losing eight straight Solitaire games, Dad threw his hands up and decided to read the newspaper.

throw **[one's] weight around** *use one's power excessively*

Mid-level managers love to throw their weight around when the boss is gone.

throw **[oneself] into** _____ *involve oneself in [something] eagerly*

Paul threw himself into basketweaving.

throw **the book at** _____ *charge [someone] with as many crimes as possible*

The district attorney threw the book at the alleged child molester.

PRESENT

I throw	we throw
you throw	you throw
he/she/it throws	they throw

• *He throws great parties.*

PRESENT PROGRESSIVE

I am throwing	we are throwing
you are throwing	you are throwing
he/she/it is throwing	they are throwing

• *I am throwing an informal reception for them.*

PAST

I threw	we threw
you threw	you threw
he/she/it threw	they threw

• *I threw another log on the fire.*

PAST PROGRESSIVE

I was throwing	we were throwing
you were throwing	you were throwing
he/she/it was throwing	they were throwing

• *He was throwing rocks into the pond.*

PRESENT PERFECT ... have | has thrown
PAST PERFECT ... had thrown

FUTURE ... will throw
FUTURE PROGRESSIVE ... will be throwing
FUTURE PERFECT ... will have thrown

PAST PASSIVE

I was thrown	we were thrown
you were thrown	you were thrown
he/she/it was thrown	they were thrown

• *A rope was thrown to the people in the canoe.*

COMPLEMENTS

throw toss/hurl a projectile

He doesn't throw with much force.
I couldn't throw because I had injured my shoulder.
If you want to play baseball, you have to learn how to throw.

throw _____ toss, hurl

OBJECT

Kids love to throw **rocks**.
The mob started throwing **bricks**.
The pitcher could throw **the ball** sidearm.

OBJECT + ADVERB OF PLACE TO/FROM

My sister threw **her coat** *on the sofa*.
Josh threw **the report** *on my desk*.

throw _____ propel suddenly and forcefully

OBJECT + ADVERB OF PLACE TO/FROM

The explosion threw **me** *to the ground*.
Someone threw **a chair** *against the wall*.
The cook threw **the pizza dough** *high into the air*.

PASSIVE

The driver was thrown *into the ditch*.

throw _____ direct, cast

OBJECT + ADVERB OF PLACE TO/FROM

The actor threw **a dirty look** *at the people talking in the front row*.
The lantern threw **light** *around the barn*.

PASSIVE

All of our resources were thrown *into the project*.

throw _____ toss, give

INDIRECT OBJECT + DIRECT OBJECT

He threw *the dog* a bone.
Throw *me* that notebook, will you?

to PARAPHRASE

He threw **a bone** *to the dog*.
Throw **that notebook** *to me*, will you?

throw _____ host [an event]

OBJECT

The church threw **a potluck dinner**.

INDIRECT OBJECT + DIRECT OBJECT

We threw *my sister* an engagement party.
They are going to throw *us* a going-away party.

for PARAPHRASE

We threw **an engagement party** *for my sister*.
They are going to throw **a going-away party** *for us*.

PRESENT

I thrust	we thrust
you thrust	you thrust
he/she/it thrusts	they thrust

• *He thrusts the note in his pocket and sighs.*

PRESENT PROGRESSIVE

I am thrusting	we are thrusting
you are thrusting	you are thrusting
he/she/it is thrusting	they are thrusting

• *Someone is always thrusting a petition at you.*

PAST

I thrust	we thrust
you thrust	you thrust
he/she/it thrust	they thrust

• *I thrust through the crowd frantically.*

PAST PROGRESSIVE

I was thrusting	we were thrusting
you were thrusting	you were thrusting
he/she/it was thrusting	they were thrusting

• *A rodent was thrusting through the undergrowth.*

PRESENT PERFECT ... have | has thrust
PAST PERFECT ... had thrust

FUTURE ... will thrust
FUTURE PROGRESSIVE ... will be thrusting
FUTURE PERFECT ... will have thrust

PAST PASSIVE

I was thrust	we were thrust
you were thrust	you were thrust
he/she/it was thrust	they were thrust

• *A gun was thrust into my hand.*

COMPLEMENTS

thrust _____ *push forward suddenly*

OBJECT + ADVERB OF PLACE TO/FROM

The soldier thrust **a sword** *through his shield.*
Batman thrust **his elbow** *into the villain's stomach.*
The host thrust **the children** *into the limelight.*

PASSIVE

My head was thrust *into a barrel of water.*
Fame had been thrust *on her* at an early age.

thrust _____ *move forward forcefully*

ADVERB OF PLACE TO/FROM

A tugboat was thrusting **through the waves.**
Her scream thrust **through the still night air.**

thrust _____ *jut, extend out*

ADVERB OF PLACE TO/FROM

A long wharf thrust **into the river.**
A diving board thrust **over the water.**

PHRASAL VERBS

thrust back/down/in/out/up/etc.
move forcefully in a specified direction

The boy's tongue thrust out as he
   sighted down the barrel.
Daffodils were thrusting up on the first warm day of spring.

thrust SEP **aside/away/back/down/
in/out/up/**etc. *push suddenly in a
specified direction*

The police thrust the protesters aside.
He opened his briefcase and thrust the report in.

PRESENT	
I tie	we tie
you tie	you tie
he/she/it ties	they tie

• *A hospital gown ties in the back.*

PRESENT PROGRESSIVE	
I am tying	we are tying
you are tying	you are tying
he/she/it is tying	they are tying

• *We are tying bows for the Christmas tree.*

PAST	
I tied	we tied
you tied	you tied
he/she/it tied	they tied

• *I tied my shoelaces before going out.*

PAST PROGRESSIVE	
I was tying	we were tying
you were tying	you were tying
he/she/it was tying	they were tying

• *They were tying the load so it wouldn't move.*

PRESENT PERFECT … have | has tied
PAST PERFECT   … had tied

FUTURE   … will tie
FUTURE PROGRESSIVE … will be tying
FUTURE PERFECT   … will have tied

PAST PASSIVE	
I was tied	we were tied
you were tied	you were tied
he/she/it was tied	they were tied

• *The deaths were tied to a faulty space heater.*

―――――――――――――――(**COMPLEMENTS**)―――

tie *be fastened by string/cord/rope/etc.*	The apron ties in front.
	These shoes don't tie; they fasten with Velcro.
tie *have the same score/rank*	At this point, the best we could do is tie.
	We want to win, not just tie.
	Mary Kay tied with Jill for first place.
	Mary Kay and Jill tied for first place.
tie _____ *fasten/bind/fix with string/cord/rope/etc.*	
OBJECT	Grayson just learned to tie **his own shoes.**
	Can you help me tie **this package?**
PASSIVE	The old box was tied with heavy twine.
OBJECT + ADVERB OF PLACE	They tied **his hands** *behind him.*
	We tied **the dresser** *on the back of the truck.*
	The kids tied **the wagon** *to the bicycle.*
PASSIVE	The volleyball net was tied *between two trees.*
tie _____ *form [into a knot/bow]*	
OBJECT	He tied **a perfect square knot.**
	The kids were tying **ribbons.**
	Can you tie **a bowtie?**
tie _____ *connect, relate*	
OBJECT + to OBJECT	Experts tie **many cancer deaths** *to secondhand smoke.*
PASSIVE	All currencies are tied *to the U.S. dollar.*
	Our economic future is tied *to the global market.*

―――――――――――――――(**PHRASAL VERBS**)―――

tie _SEP_ **down/in/off/together/up**/etc. *fasten/bind/fix in a specified position*	The campers tied the tent down.
	The robbers tied up all of the hostages.
tie _SEP_ **down/up** *limit the freedom of, cause to be busy, block*	The new puppy tied them down on weekends.
	I am tied down all day tomorrow.
	Meetings will tie me up all morning.
	The boss will be tied up until 4 P.M.
	We were tied up in rush-hour traffic.
tie in (with _____) *be related/connected (to [something])*	Your story ties in with what the police already know.

PRESENT

I touch	we touch
you touch	you touch
he/she/it touches	they touch

• *This problem touches everyone.*

PRESENT PROGRESSIVE

I am touching	we are touching
you are touching	you are touching
he/she/it is touching	they are touching

• *The tree branches are touching the roof.*

PAST

I touched	we touched
you touched	you touched
he/she/it touched	they touched

• *He touched a button and the door closed.*

PAST PROGRESSIVE

I was touching	we were touching
you were touching	you were touching
he/she/it was touching	they were touching

• *The hem of her skirt was touching the ground.*

PRESENT PERFECT ... have | has touched
PAST PERFECT ... had touched

FUTURE ... will touch
FUTURE PROGRESSIVE ... will be touching
FUTURE PERFECT ... will have touched

PAST PASSIVE

I was touched	we were touched
you were touched	you were touched
he/she/it was touched	they were touched

• *Everyone was touched by her performance.*

COMPLEMENTS

touch *come into contact*
The two boats touched with a bump.
The wires must have touched, causing a short circuit.
Their hands touched briefly.

touch _____ *place one's hand / body part on*
OBJECT
He touched **Jerry's shoulder** and whispered something in his ear.
He was so tall he could reach up and touch **the ceiling**.
Don't touch **the wet paint on the cabinet**.
My knees were touching **the back of the seat in front of me**.

touch _____ *consume, handle, disturb* [OFTEN NEGATIVE]
OBJECT
I haven't touched **a drink** in years.
You have hardly touched **your dinner**.
She told her little sister not to touch **her stuff**.
No contractor would touch **that job**.
We haven't touched **a penny of our retirement fund**.
Don't touch **a single paper on my desk**.

PASSIVE
Gang members can't be touched by the police.

touch _____ *make physical contact with* [OF INANIMATE OBJECTS]
OBJECT
A downed electrical wire touched **the automobile** and sparked.
Don't let the flag touch **the ground**.

touch _____ *affect*
OBJECT
His music really touches **me**.
The recession has touched **every business in the county**.

PASSIVE
They were touched by his loyalty.

PHRASAL VERBS

touch down *land* [OF A PLANE]
Our flight will touch down in
   Cincinnati at 8:05 P.M.

touch off _____ *cause, ignite*
Bad banking practices touched off a financial crisis.
A spark from an electric motor touched off the explosion.

touch _SEP_ **up** *improve the appearance of*
We need to touch up the paint on this table.

touch (up)on _____ *mention briefly*
The speaker barely touched on the need for stricter regulations.

PRESENT

I train	we train
you train	you train
he/she/it trains	they train

• *He trains at least three times a week.*

PRESENT PROGRESSIVE

I am training	we are training
you are training	you are training
he/she/it is training	they are training

• *I am training to run my first marathon.*

PAST

I trained	we trained
you trained	you trained
he/she/it trained	they trained

• *Ralph trained his staff really well.*

PAST PROGRESSIVE

I was training	we were training
you were training	you were training
he/she/it was training	they were training

• *We were training in the old gym.*

PRESENT PERFECT ... have | has trained
PAST PERFECT   ... had trained

FUTURE   ... will train
FUTURE PROGRESSIVE ... will be training
FUTURE PERFECT   ... will have trained

PAST PASSIVE

I was trained	we were trained
you were trained	you were trained
he/she/it was trained	they were trained

• *The dogs were trained to assist handicapped people.*

───────────────────────────── COMPLEMENTS ─────

train *prepare for a profession/job*

My doctor trained at Johns Hopkins
    School of Medicine.
The football players train all summer.
Even superior athletes must train.
If you want to get better, you have to train harder.

train _____ *teach, coach*

  OBJECT

I train **dogs**.
The camp trains **track and field athletes**.
The school specializes in training **young singers**.

  OBJECT + in/on OBJECT

Her tutor trained **her** *in the art of public speaking.*
I trained **my dad** *on the computer.*

  OBJECT + INFINITIVE

The circus trains **animals** *to do tricks.*
The class will train **dogs** *to obey a set of commands.*

    PASSIVE

When Amber was a puppy, she was trained *to stay off*
    the street.

  OBJECT + WH-INFINITIVE

I trained **my children** *where to go to get help if they needed it.*
The Coast Guard trains **people** *how to use their boats safely.*

    PASSIVE

The dogs were never trained *how to search for drugs.*

train _____ *rear, develop the character of*

  OBJECT + INFINITIVE

We trained **our daughters** *to be nice.*
The school trains **its students** *to respect authority.*

───────────────────────────── EXPRESSIONS ─────

train [one's] sights on _____ *focus on*

The candidate trained his sights on his
    opponent.
Blanche trained her sights on getting a college scholarship.

PRESENT

I travel	we travel
you travel	you travel
he/she/it travels	they travel

• *Anne travels a lot in her current job.*

PRESENT PROGRESSIVE

I am traveling	we are traveling
you are traveling	you are traveling
he/she/it is traveling	they are traveling

• *I am traveling all week.*

PAST

I traveled	we traveled
you traveled	you traveled
he/she/it traveled	they traveled

• *We traveled to Cambodia and Vietnam.*

PAST PROGRESSIVE

I was traveling	we were traveling
you were traveling	you were traveling
he/she/it was traveling	they were traveling

• *They were traveling when they got the news.*

PRESENT PERFECT ... have | has traveled
PAST PERFECT ... had traveled

FUTURE ... will travel
FUTURE PROGRESSIVE ... will be traveling
FUTURE PERFECT ... will have traveled

PAST PASSIVE

—	—
—	—
it was traveled	they were traveled

• *The old road was traveled by a lot of people.*

COMPLEMENTS

travel *make a trip/journey*

> When we retire, we want to travel.
> They travel every chance they get.

travel _____ *make a trip/journey*
   ADVERB OF PLACE TO/FROM
   (+ ADVERB OF TIME)

> The boat travels **from Athens to Genoa.**
> The convoy traveled **from Washington to San Francisco.**
> We plan to travel **to Southeast Asia** *this winter.*
> They will travel **home** *after Christmas.*

   ADVERB OF MANNER

> My boss always travels **first-class.**
> Vivian has learned to travel **like a pro.**

travel _____ *make a trip/journey in/on/through*
   OBJECT

> We always travel **the back roads,** if we have a choice.
> My parents have traveled **the length of the Amalfi Coast.**

   PASSIVE

> The Australian outback is rarely traveled by tourists.

travel _____ *move through time/space*
   ADVERB OF PLACE TO/FROM

> The pain traveled **across his chest and down his left arm.**

   ADVERB OF MANNER

> Light waves travel **faster than sound waves.**

travel _____ *be transported*
   ADVERB OF MANNER

> Many local wines travel **poorly.**
> The coal is traveling **by barge** on the Mississippi River.

travel _____ *spread, be passed*
   ADVERB OF MANNER

> The news of General Lee's surrender traveled **slowly.**
> Rumors travel **at lightning speed.**

PHRASAL VERBS

travel along/around/down/over/
up/etc. *travel in a specified direction*

> We traveled around in search of
> historic sites.
> The tour group traveled down to Lisbon.

PRESENT

I treat	we treat
you treat	you treat
he/she/it treats	they treat

- *He treats his employees very well.*

PRESENT PROGRESSIVE

I am treating	we are treating
you are treating	you are treating
he/she/it is treating	they are treating

- *I am treating everyone to an ice cream cone.*

PAST

I treated	we treated
you treated	you treated
he/she/it treated	they treated

- *I treated my sore finger as best I could.*

PAST PROGRESSIVE

I was treating	we were treating
you were treating	you were treating
he/she/it was treating	they were treating

- *The medical staff was treating a gunshot wound.*

PRESENT PERFECT ... have | has treated
PAST PERFECT ... had treated

FUTURE ... will treat
FUTURE PROGRESSIVE ... will be treating
FUTURE PERFECT ... will have treated

PAST PASSIVE

I was treated	we were treated
you were treated	you were treated
he/she/it was treated	they were treated

- *The most seriously injured patients were treated first.*

(COMPLEMENTS)

treat *pay for someone's food/ entertainment*	Put your money away! I'm treating. He never treats, even when it's his turn. Grandparents love to treat.
treat _____ *pay for / provide [the food/entertainment] of, reward*	
OBJECT	He treated **the whole office.** The coach treated **the team** after every game.
PASSIVE	Children with birthdays were always treated by their classmates.
OBJECT + to OBJECT	My best friend treated **me** *to some sushi.* Can I treat **you** *to lunch?* The teacher treated **us** *to chocolate chip cookies.* Jane treated **herself** *to a day at the spa.*
treat _____ *act toward, deal with*	
OBJECT + ADVERB OF MANNER	The children treated **their pets** *gently.* Most cultures treat **visitors** *with great respect.* The staff treated **the information** *very seriously.*
PASSIVE	The civilians were treated *quite roughly* by the soldiers.
treat _____ *try to cure/heal*	
OBJECT	By law, emergency rooms must treat **all persons requiring care.** A nurse treated **my burned hand.**
PASSIVE	Unusual skin rashes should be treated by a dermatologist.
treat _____ *discuss in writing*	
OBJECT (+ ADVERB OF MANNER)	Her book treats **the period from August to October 1914.** His book treats **the issue of global warming** *with seriousness and urgency.*
PASSIVE	Health care reform was treated *very superficially* in that article.
treat _____ *add a cleaning/preserving substance to*	
OBJECT (+ with OBJECT)	Dave treats **his deck** every other year. We treat **the deck** every spring *with a waterproof sealant.* Treat **the ketchup stain** *with warm soapy water.*
PASSIVE	The swimming pool water is treated *with chlorine.*

PRESENT		PRESENT PROGRESSIVE	
I trust	we trust	I am trusting	we are trusting
you trust	you trust	you are trusting	you are trusting
he/she/it trusts	they trust	he/she/it is trusting	they are trusting

• *John trusts people more than he should.* • *I am trusting you to do a good job.*

PAST		PAST PROGRESSIVE	
I trusted	we trusted	I was trusting	we were trusting
you trusted	you trusted	you were trusting	you were trusting
he/she/it trusted	they trusted	he/she/it was trusting	they were trusting

• *Everyone trusted Bernard.* • *At the time, no one was trusting anybody else.*

PRESENT PERFECT ... have | has trusted
PAST PERFECT ... had trusted

FUTURE ... will trust
FUTURE PROGRESSIVE ... will be trusting
FUTURE PERFECT ... will have trusted

PAST PASSIVE	
I was trusted	we were trusted
you were trusted	you were trusted
he/she/it was trusted	they were trusted

• *Successful Civil War generals were trusted by their soldiers.*

─────(COMPLEMENTS)─────

trust *believe in someone's/something's truth/reliability/ability*

Trust, but verify. [RUSSIAN PROVERB]
Dishonest people take advantage of the human tendency to trust.
Abused children have to learn to trust again.

trust _____ *believe in the truth/reliability/ability of*

OBJECT
We all trusted **their assessment of the project's risk.**
Children inherently trust **their parents.**

 PASSIVE
Gold is trusted when paper currencies fail.

 in OBJECT
The general is trusting **in his infantry.**
Vineyard owners were trusting **in the weather.**

 WH-CLAUSE
Trust **what you see with your own eyes,** not **what you hear.**
You can't always trust **what brokers tell you.**
You can trust **whomever they recommend.**

trust _____ *depend/rely on*

OBJECT + INFINITIVE
We trust **you** *to deliver the message.*
You can always trust **people** *to act in their own self-interest.*

 PASSIVE
Can you be trusted *to babysit your little brother this afternoon?*

trust _____ *hope, expect* [AS A POLITE FORM OF IMPLIED QUESTION, USUALLY WITH RISING INTONATION]

THAT-CLAUSE
I trust **that you had pleasant trip.**
We trust **that everything will turn out all right.**
I trust **that the children are well.**
I trust **that your parents and all your sisters are well.**

trust _____ *put in the care of, allow to use*

OBJECT + *with* OBJECT
She trusted **the hotel manager** *with her jewelry.*
I don't trust **Grandpa** *with the car* anymore.

PRESENT

I try	we try
you try	you try
he/she/it tries	they try

• *He always tries to do his best.*

PRESENT PROGRESSIVE

I am trying	we are trying
you are trying	you are trying
he/she/it is trying	they are trying

• *I'm trying to finish the report.*

PAST

I tried	we tried
you tried	you tried
he/she/it tried	they tried

• *I tried to call them earlier.*

PAST PROGRESSIVE

I was trying	we were trying
you were trying	you were trying
he/she/it was trying	they were trying

• *We were trying to exchange our tickets.*

PRESENT PERFECT … have | has tried
PAST PERFECT … had tried

FUTURE … will try
FUTURE PROGRESSIVE … will be trying
FUTURE PERFECT … will have tried

PAST PASSIVE

I was tried	we were tried
you were tried	you were tried
he/she/it was tried	they were tried

• *The Dover case was tried in U.S. District Court.*

COMPLEMENTS

NOTE: When the verb *try* is used in the past tense in the sense "attempt," it implies that the attempt did not succeed.

try *attempt / make an effort to do something*

He tried really hard.
"If at first you don't succeed, try, try again. Then quit."
　　[COMEDIAN W.C. FIELDS]

try ____ *attempt, make an effort*

INFINITIVE

I tried **to call you last night**.
We will try **to see them** when we are in Los Angeles.
He tried **to talk them out of it**.

PRESENT PARTICIPLE

I tried **calling you last night**.
We will have to try **borrowing the keys from the janitor**.
They tried **fixing the porch light**.

try ____ *attempt to use, test*

OBJECT

I tried **his number**, but no one answered.
We tried **the engine** again, and this time it worked.
Try **the door** to see if it's unlocked.
You should try **the white wine**. You'll like it.

PASSIVE

Everything we could think of had already been tried.

try ____ *conduct [a trial]*

OBJECT

Justice Brown tried **the case**.
The Illinois Appellate Court tried **the appeal**.

PASSIVE

The case was tried by a three-person judicial panel.

try ____ *put on trial*

OBJECT

The court first tried **Mr. Coleman** in 2005.

PASSIVE

The suspect was tried and convicted.

PHRASAL VERBS

try _SEP_ **on** *put on [clothing] to see how it looks and fits*

Hilary tried on seven pairs of shoes
　　before she found a pair she liked.
Try this dress on; the color will look good on you.

try out for ____ *compete for a position/role*

Elizabeth tried out for the marching band.
Elton tried out for the role of Macbeth.

turn _____ *change in condition/color/form*	
OBJECT + *into* OBJECT	When will they turn **the book** *into a movie*? The genie turned **Cotton** *into a monkey*.
PASSIVE	Cinderella's coach was turned *into a pumpkin* at midnight.
PREDICATE ADJECTIVE	Eventually, of course, his luck turned **bad**. The milk turned **sour** when the refrigeration failed. Charles turned **pale** and swallowed hard. Oak leaves turn **yellow and orange** in the fall.

PHRASAL VERBS

turn aside/around/away/back/ down/in/off/out/over/up/etc. *turn in a specified direction*	We should turn around now because it is getting dark. Everyone turned away when my brother entered the room. She turned the card over so she could write on the back.
turn _SEP_ **aside/around/away/back/ down/out/up**/etc. *turn [someone/ something] in a specified direction*	Security guards turned the protesters away. The secretary turned the box over.
turn against _____ *defy, stop supporting*	The politician turned against the voters who elected him.
turn [someone] against _____ *cause [someone] to defy / stop supporting*	The 1939 Stalin-Hitler pact turned him against totalitarianism of any kind.
turn _SEP_ **down** *decrease the quantity/ volume of*	You should turn the heat down when you're not at home. Will someone turn the radio down? I'm on the phone.
turn _SEP_ **down** *reject*	We turned down Jack's offer to drive. Every publisher turned his manuscript down—except one!
turn in *go to bed* [INFORMAL]	I think I'll turn in early tonight.
turn _SEP_ **in** *submit, hand over*	Turn in your homework at the beginning of class.
turn _SEP_ **off** *shut/switch off*	The sink is full; turn off the water. Turn the lights off when you leave.
turn _SEP_ **off** *make [someone] bored/ annoyed* [INFORMAL]	Her constant criticism really turns us off.
turn on _____ *attack*	The lion turned on the zoo handler.
turn _SEP_ **on** *switch on*	Turn the heat on; it's cold in here.
turn _SEP_ **on** *make [someone] happy/ excited* [INFORMAL]	Reggae music really turns me on.
turn out *develop, transpire, end*	"How did your weekend turn out?" "It turned out fine." She turned out to be his long-lost sister.
turn out (for _____ **)** *attend ([an event])*	More than four hundred people turned out for Randy Pausch's last lecture.
turn _SEP_ **out** *switch off*	Turn out the lights; the party's over.
turn _SEP_ **out** *produce*	The school turns out very talented musicians. The factory will turn out 1,000 wind turbines a month.
turn _SEP_ **over** *hand over*	The guard told us to turn over our wallets and belts.
turn to _____ *begin work on*	The staff turned to organizing the packages for delivery.
turn to _____ *ask for help*	The flood victims turned to the government for shelter.
turn up *arrive*	Aunt Edith finally turned up at suppertime.
turn up *appear, be found*	Did your other sock ever turn up?
turn _SEP_ **up** *increase the quantity/volume of*	You could turn the heat up if you're cold. Would you please turn up the music?
turn _SEP_ **up** *discover*	The reporter turned up evidence of fraud.

PRESENT

I turn	we turn
you turn	you turn
he/she/it turns	they turn

- *The road turns south at the river.*

PRESENT PROGRESSIVE

I am turning	we are turning
you are turning	you are turning
he/she/it is turning	they are turning

- *We are turning here.*

PAST

I turned	we turned
you turned	you turned
he/she/it turned	they turned

- *He turned pale when he heard the results.*

PAST PROGRESSIVE

I was turning	we were turning
you were turning	you were turning
he/she/it was turning	they were turning

- *The leaves were just turning when we were there.*

PRESENT PERFECT ... have | has turned
PAST PERFECT   ... had turned

FUTURE   ... will turn
FUTURE PROGRESSIVE ... will be turning
FUTURE PERFECT ... will have turned

PAST PASSIVE

I was turned	we were turned
you were turned	you were turned
he/she/it was turned	they were turned

- *The boat was turned south into the bay.*

—(**COMPLEMENTS**)—

turn *rotate, revolve, move around an axis*

The big wheel slowly began to turn.
His head turned when I called his name.
I turned so I could slip through the narrow opening.

turn *change direction*

The tide will turn at dusk.
The senator could feel public opinion beginning to turn.
General Blake could sense that the battle was turning.

turn _____ *cause to rotate/revolve*

OBJECT

The helmsman turned **the wheel**.
I turned **my head** to see who was calling my name.

PASSIVE

The millstone is turned by a waterwheel.

turn _____ *change direction/position*

ADVERB OF PLACE TO/FROM

The car turned **into the last driveway on the left**.
Turn **left** at the next corner.
The sailboat turned **downstream**.
The crowd all turned **toward the new speaker**.
The birds turned **into the wind**.

turn _____ *cause to change direction*

OBJECT + ADVERB OF PLACE TO/FROM
PASSIVE

The captain turned **the boat** *into the wind*.
The water was turned *into the canal*.

turn _____ *cause the other side of to be visible*

OBJECT

I turned **the pages on the calendar**.
He turned **the page** and began to read.

turn _____ *change the setting of*

OBJECT + to OBJECT

He turned **the TV** *to the Weather Channel*.
Turn **the oven** *to 350 degrees* after 15 minutes.

turn _____ *perform by moving in a circle*

OBJECT

Little Leslie can turn **a somersault**.
The cheerleaders turned **cartwheels** on the gym floor.

turn _____ *reach, pass*

OBJECT

Juan's brother turned **18** yesterday.
My car's odometer just turned **12,000 miles**.

PRESENT

I understand	we understand
you understand	you understand
he/she/it understands	they understand

• *He understands the situation perfectly.*

PRESENT PROGRESSIVE

I am understanding	we are understanding
you are understanding	you are understanding
he/she/it is understanding	they are understanding

• *We are understanding each other better now.*

PAST

I understood	we understood
you understood	you understood
he/she/it understood	they understood

• *They understood only a few words.*

PAST PROGRESSIVE

I was understanding	we were understanding
you were understanding	you were understanding
he/she/it was understanding	they were understanding

• *They weren't understanding his Italian very well.*

PRESENT PERFECT ... have | has understood
PAST PERFECT ... had understood

FUTURE ... will understand
FUTURE PROGRESSIVE ... will be understanding
FUTURE PERFECT ... will have understood

PAST PASSIVE

I was understood	we were understood
you were understood	you were understood
he/she/it was understood	they were understood

• *The tour guide was easily understood.*

(COMPLEMENTS)

understand *know the meaning of something*

Do you understand?
He is too young to understand.

understand _____ *comprehend, know the meaning of*

OBJECT
The doctor understood **the nature of the patient's symptoms.**
Do you understand **this equation**?
Nobody could understand **the cockney slang used in the movie.**

PASSIVE
The assembly instructions must not have been understood.

WH-CLAUSE
I understood **what he was trying to say.**
Did you understand **where we were going?**
We need to understand **how much this is going to cost.**

WH-INFINITIVE
Do you understand **whom to call if you have a problem?**
I understand **what to do.**
Do you understand **where to pick up your passengers?**

understand _____ *know what makes [something] work/happen*

OBJECT
It takes students a long time to really understand **evolution.**
Does anyone understand **the stock market?**
Almost no one understands **credit and default swaps.**

PASSIVE
The role of washing hands to control disease was not understood at the time.

WH-CLAUSE
Do you understand **what drives the global economy?**
Even third graders understand **why the sun seems to rise in the east and set in the west.**

understand _____ *know and be sympathetic to the feelings/attitudes of*

OBJECT
My boyfriend doesn't understand **me.**
I don't think the director understood **Lady Macbeth** very well.
Older people never understand **the younger generation.**

understand _____ *get the idea/notion* [OFTEN AS A POLITE FORM OF IMPLIED QUESTION]

OBJECT + INFINITIVE
I understand **you** *to be a student at Santa Cruz.*
We understand **them** *to be having lunch with us.*
I understand **the apartment** *to be available.*

THAT-CLAUSE
I understand **that you are applying for a job with us.**
We understand **that the flight may be delayed.**
It is understood **that the parents will have joint custody.**

PRESENT

I unite	we unite
you unite	you unite
he/she/it unites	they unite

• *The treaty unites the two warring factions.*

PRESENT PROGRESSIVE

I am uniting	we are uniting
you are uniting	you are uniting
he/she/it is uniting	they are uniting

• *The denominations are uniting to form a new church.*

PAST

I united	we united
you united	you united
he/she/it united	they united

• *Italy united under Victor Emmanuel II.*

PAST PROGRESSIVE

I was uniting	we were uniting
you were uniting	you were uniting
he/she/it was uniting	they were uniting

• *Rebel forces were uniting under a single leader.*

PRESENT PERFECT ... have | has united
PAST PERFECT ... had united

FUTURE ... will unite
FUTURE PROGRESSIVE ... will be uniting
FUTURE PERFECT ... will have united

PAST PASSIVE

I was united	we were united
you were united	you were united
he/she/it was united	they were united

• *Farmers were united in opposition to the proposed regulations.*

─(**COMPLEMENTS**)─

unite *join together for a common purpose*

Many small rural school districts
  have been forced to unite.
He called on the party to unite.
"Workers of the world, unite." [KARL MARX AND
  FRIEDRICH ENGELS]
The divided enemy forces were unable to unite.
The community unites in the spring to celebrate Earth Day.
The country united against the threats to its citizens.
Cells unite to form tissues.

unite _____ *combine, join/put together to make one*

OBJECT

Einstein tried to unite **electromagnetism and gravity**
  in a unified field theory.
He was able to unite **theory and practice** in his work.

PASSIVE

Charlotte and John were united in marriage on March 23.
Scotland and England were united in 1707 to form the
  Kingdom of Great Britain.

PRESENT

I uphold	we uphold
you uphold	you uphold
he/she/it upholds	they uphold

• *The firm upholds its tradition of service.*

PRESENT PROGRESSIVE

I am upholding	we are upholding
you are upholding	you are upholding
he/she/it is upholding	they are upholding

• *The Marine Corps is upholding centuries of tradition.*

PAST

I upheld	we upheld
you upheld	you upheld
he/she/it upheld	they upheld

• *The court upheld the lower court ruling.*

PAST PROGRESSIVE

I was upholding	we were upholding
you were upholding	you were upholding
he/she/it was upholding	they were upholding

• *We were upholding our end of the bargain.*

PRESENT PERFECT ... have | has upheld
PAST PERFECT ... had upheld

FUTURE ... will uphold
FUTURE PROGRESSIVE ... will be upholding
FUTURE PERFECT ... will have upheld

PAST PASSIVE

—	—
—	—
it was upheld	they were upheld

• *The ruling was upheld by the appellate court.*

COMPLEMENTS

uphold _____ *confirm/support [a decision, opinion]*

   OBJECT   The courts will usually uphold **lower court rulings** unless there
                is a demonstrable error of fact or law.
                The whole committee upheld **the ruling of the subcommittee.**
                The Supreme Court upheld **the plaintiff** in *Brown v. Board of Education.*

   PASSIVE   The decision was upheld unanimously by the appeals court.

uphold _____ *maintain [a custom, practice]*

   OBJECT   John upheld **the family tradition** by joining the Navy.
                Sadly, the school has not been able to uphold **its superior image.**
                The new CEO vowed to uphold **the company's reputation for fiscal**
                responsibility.

   PASSIVE   The honor of the Corps had been upheld.

PRESENT

I upset	we upset
you upset	you upset
he/she/it upsets	they upset

- *The new development upsets all our plans.*

PRESENT PROGRESSIVE

I am upsetting	we are upsetting
you are upsetting	you are upsetting
he/she/it is upsetting	they are upsetting

- *I'm sorry that I'm upsetting you.*

PAST

I upset	we upset
you upset	you upset
he/she/it upset	they upset

- *The president's decision upset the voters.*

PAST PROGRESSIVE

I was upsetting	we were upsetting
you were upsetting	you were upsetting
he/she/it was upsetting	they were upsetting

- *The weather was upsetting all of our arrangements.*

PRESENT PERFECT ... have | has upset
PAST PERFECT   ... had upset

FUTURE   ... will upset
FUTURE PROGRESSIVE ... will be upsetting
FUTURE PERFECT   ... will have upset

PAST PASSIVE

I was upset	we were upset
you were upset	you were upset
he/she/it was upset	they were upset

- *Naturally, we were quite upset by what happened.*

COMPLEMENTS

upset _____ *knock over*

OBJECT
The dogs upset **some potted plants** on the patio.
The waiter upset **a bottle of wine** as he was clearing the table.

PASSIVE
A whole gallon of paint had been upset.

upset _____ *cause to be disturbed/worried/unhappy*

OBJECT
The hotel clerk's rudeness really upset **us**.
Thunderstorms upset **the dogs** terribly.
Spicy food always upsets **my stomach**.
He delights in upsetting **the administrators**.

PASSIVE
The parents were upset at the news of the school's closure.

upset _____ *disturb the order/working of*

OBJECT
The kids are really good at upsetting **my daily routine**.
The rain upset **our plans for a trip to the beach**.
Global warming is upsetting **many delicate ecosystems**.
The collapse of the credit market has upset **the normal balance of supply and demand for housing**.

PASSIVE
The orderly transfer of power was totally upset by the prince's unexpected death.

upset _____ *win a surprising victory over*

OBJECT
The Jets upset **the Colts** in Superbowl III.
Harry Truman upset **Thomas Dewey** in the 1948 presidential election.

EXPRESSIONS

upset the apple cart *ruin something*   Grady upset the apple cart by telling
Louise about the surprise party.

PRESENT		PRESENT PROGRESSIVE	
I urge	we urge	I am urging	we are urging
you urge	you urge	you are urging	you are urging
he/she/it urges	they urge	he/she/it is urging	they are urging

• She urges us to read Jane Austen's novels.　• The mayor is urging everyone to remain calm.

PAST		PAST PROGRESSIVE	
I urged	we urged	I was urging	we were urging
you urged	you urged	you were urging	you were urging
he/she/it urged	they urged	he/she/it was urging	they were urging

• We urged them to come for dinner.　• The police were urging drivers to stay off the roads.

PRESENT PERFECT ... have | has urged
PAST PERFECT ... had urged

FUTURE ... will urge
FUTURE PROGRESSIVE ... will be urging
FUTURE PERFECT ... will have urged

PAST PASSIVE	
I was urged	we were urged
you were urged	you were urged
he/she/it was urged	they were urged

• A thorough investigation was urged by the committee.

COMPLEMENTS

urge _____ *recommend, advocate strongly*

OBJECT
Our financial advisor urged **patience**.
The captain urged **a dawn attack on the enemy's right flank**.

PASSIVE
Parental discretion is strongly urged.

OBJECT + INFINITIVE
The doctor urged **my mom** *to see a specialist*.
The lawyers urged **the judge** *to give the defendant a new trial*.

BASE-FORM THAT-CLAUSE
The doctor urged **that my mom see a specialist**.
The lawyers urged **that the judge give the defendant a new trial**.

urge _____ *encourage*

OBJECT + INFINITIVE
I urged **them** *to speak up about what had happened*.
He urged **us** *to keep our options open at this point*.
My parents urged **my sister** *to move closer to them*.
The speakers urged **the city council** *to provide better snow removal*.

PASSIVE
The driver was repeatedly urged *to slow down*.

urge _____ *encourage/force to move*

OBJECT + ADVERB OF PLACE TO/FROM
We urged **the children** *inside*.
The coach urged **the players** *onto the field*.
The police urged **the crowd** *away from the accident*.

PASSIVE
The passengers were urged *to the rear of the bus*.

PHRASAL VERBS

urge _SEP_ **away/back**/etc. *encourage to move in a specified direction*
The ushers urged the spectators back.

urge _SEP_ **on** *encourage*
The candidate urged her supporters on by viciously attacking her opponent.
The lieutenant urged his troops on through the rain.

PRESENT

I use	we use
you use	you use
he/she/it uses	they use

• *She uses a taxi to go to the airport.*

PRESENT PROGRESSIVE

I am using	we are using
you are using	you are using
he/she/it is using	they are using

• *No one is using this chair.*

PAST

I used	we used
you used	you used
he/she/it used	they used

• *I used the elevator instead of the stairs.*

PAST PROGRESSIVE

I was using	we were using
you were using	you were using
he/she/it was using	they were using

• *They were using too much salt on their food.*

PRESENT PERFECT   ... have | has used
PAST PERFECT   ... had used

FUTURE   ... will use
FUTURE PROGRESSIVE   ... will be using
FUTURE PERFECT   ... will have used

PAST PASSIVE

I was used	we were used
you were used	you were used
he/she/it was used	they were used

• *A computer was used to map the best route.*

NOTE: The verb *use* ends in a /z/ sound, rhyming with *lose*.
The noun *use* ends in an /s/ sound, rhyming with *goose*.

─────────────────────────(**COMPLEMENTS**)───

use _____ *employ, put into service*

OBJECT	I can use **a stick shift**. Do you know how to use **chopsticks**?
PASSIVE	The printer can't be used until we get a new ink cartridge.
OBJECT + ADVERB OF MANNER	Use **your troops** *well* and they will not fail you. You can finish it if you use **your time** *carefully*.
PASSIVE	The paint remover should be used *with extreme caution*.
OBJECT + INFINITIVE	We used **an architect** *to remodel the kitchen*. I used **my shoulder** *to push open the heavy gate*.
PASSIVE	The National Guard was used *to help clear the roads*.

use _____ *exploit, treat badly*

OBJECT	He's using **us** to get a promotion. It's obvious now: He used **family connections** to get the job.
PASSIVE	We were being used.

use _____ *consume, exhaust the supply of*

OBJECT	Don't use **all the hot water**—save some for me. We used **all the spaghetti sauce** at lunch.
PASSIVE	All of the allocated funds have been used.

use _____ *need* [WITH *can* OR *could*]

OBJECT	These walls could use **a fresh coat of paint**.

used to _____ *did at an earlier time* [HELPING VERB INTRODUCING AN HABITUAL ACTION/STATE IN THE PAST]

BASE-FORM INFINITIVE	I used to **live in Chicago**. We used to **have a little cabin on the lake**. She used to **play the viola professionally**.

be/get used to _____ *be/get accustomed to / familiar with*

OBJECT	You will get used to **David's strange sense of humor**. I am not used to **daylight saving time** yet.
PRESENT PARTICIPLE	I will never get used to **driving on the left side of the road**. We are used to **getting up pretty early**. The animals are not used to **having strangers around**.

PRESENT

I vary	we vary
you vary	you vary
he/she/it varies	they vary

• *Seafood prices vary from day to day.*

PRESENT PROGRESSIVE

I am varying	we are varying
you are varying	you are varying
he/she/it is varying	they are varying

• *I am varying my exercise routine.*

PAST

I varied	we varied
you varied	you varied
he/she/it varied	they varied

• *The temperature never varied.*

PAST PROGRESSIVE

I was varying	we were varying
you were varying	you were varying
he/she/it was varying	they were varying

• *We were varying our diet as much as we could.*

PRESENT PERFECT ... have | has varied
PAST PERFECT ... had varied

FUTURE ... will vary
FUTURE PROGRESSIVE ... will be varying
FUTURE PERFECT ... will have varied

PAST PASSIVE

—	—
—	—
it was varied	they were varied

• *The courier's route was varied for greater security.*

———————————————————————————————————⟨ **COMPLEMENTS** ⟩———

vary *change, differ in size/amount/degree*

At the equator, the length of day
  varies only slightly.
Your mileage may vary.
The terms of the contracts can vary quite a lot.
The amount of rainfall varies enormously from year to year.
Opinions vary about the impact of global warming.
The nutritional value of fruits and vegetables varies
  according to climate and soil conditions.

vary _____ *change to be less uniform/predictable*

OBJECT

The conductor never varied **the tempo**, making the piece
  sound too mechanical.
Don't vary **the format of the reports** without a good reason.
He never varied **his comedy act**, and it eventually failed.
You should vary **your reading**; all those romance novels
  can't be good for you.

PASSIVE

The activities at camp were always varied, so we never
  got bored.

PRESENT	
I view	we view
you view	you view
he/she/it views	they view

• *He always views the parade with his son.*

PRESENT PROGRESSIVE	
I am viewing	we are viewing
you are viewing	you are viewing
he/she/it is viewing	they are viewing

• *They are viewing the gardens.*

PAST	
I viewed	we viewed
you viewed	you viewed
he/she/it viewed	they viewed

• *The inspector viewed the office wiring.*

PAST PROGRESSIVE	
I was viewing	we were viewing
you were viewing	you were viewing
he/she/it was viewing	they were viewing

• *Detectives were viewing a surveillance video.*

PRESENT PERFECT	… have | has viewed
PAST PERFECT	… had viewed

FUTURE	… will view
FUTURE PROGRESSIVE	… will be viewing
FUTURE PERFECT	… will have viewed

PAST PASSIVE	
I was viewed	we were viewed
you were viewed	you were viewed
he/she/it was viewed	they were viewed

• *The new rules were not viewed favorably by the staff.*

──(COMPLEMENTS)──

view ＿＿＿ *examine, inspect*

OBJECT
> The owner of the building viewed **the water damage**.
> The governor viewed **the flood damage** from a helicopter.

view ＿＿＿ *look at carefully*

OBJECT
> People from all over the world come to view **the fall foliage in New England**.
> Whenever there is an automobile accident, drivers slow down to view **the wreck**.
> We got up in the middle of the night to view **the northern lights**.

PASSIVE
> The exhibit was viewed by nearly 100,000 visitors.
> Our website is viewed by 4,000 people a day.

WH-CLAUSE
> They wanted to view **what was left of the shipwreck**.
> Our tour group hopes to view **where the first atomic device was detonated in the New Mexico desert**.

view ＿＿＿ *consider, regard*

OBJECT + ADVERB OF MANNER
> Most politicians viewed **Senator Blather** *with utter contempt*.
> The farmers viewed **the restrictions on the use of pesticides** *with conflicting emotions*.

PASSIVE
> The proposal was viewed *with alarm*.

OBJECT + *as* PREDICATE NOUN
> The committee views **smoking** *as a health and ethics issue*.
> Brutus viewed **Caesar** *as a threat to republican rule*.

OBJECT + *as* PREDICATE ADJECTIVE
> Experts view **the economic downturn** *as temporary*.
> The opposition viewed **the proposal** *as shortsighted*.

view ＿＿＿ *watch [a movie, TV program]*

OBJECT
> Forty percent of children viewed **the first episode**.

PASSIVE
> The Nixon-Kennedy debate was viewed by more than 66 million people.

PRESENT

I visit	we visit
you visit	you visit
he/she/it visits	they visit

• *He visits our office when he's in town.*

PRESENT PROGRESSIVE

I am visiting	we are visiting
you are visiting	you are visiting
he/she/it is visiting	they are visiting

• *She is visiting her grandmother.*

PAST

I visited	we visited
you visited	you visited
he/she/it visited	they visited

• *They visited some old friends in Dallas.*

PAST PROGRESSIVE

I was visiting	we were visiting
you were visiting	you were visiting
he/she/it was visiting	they were visiting

• *We were visiting someone in the neighborhood.*

PRESENT PERFECT ... have | has visited
PAST PERFECT ... had visited

FUTURE ... will visit
FUTURE PROGRESSIVE ... will be visiting
FUTURE PERFECT ... will have visited

PAST PASSIVE

I was visited	we were visited
you were visited	you were visited
he/she/it was visited	they were visited

• *We were visited by the Bennets recently.*

COMPLEMENTS

visit *talk briefly with each other*

They visited during the intermission.
We visited for a few minutes at the grocery store.
We don't often get a chance to visit without being interrupted
by the children.

visit _____ *talk briefly*

with OBJECT

I visited **with Brian** during the afternoon break.
She visits **with her niece** on the phone every morning.

visit _____ *come/go to see socially*

OBJECT

We visit **Kevin and Janet** whenever we can.
No one ever visits **them.**

PASSIVE

My parents were visited by some old college friends this weekend.

visit _____ *go to [a place] as a tourist*

OBJECT

We visited **the Lake District** for a few days.
I'd like to visit **the ruins of the Roman Forum.**
Everyone who visits **Australia** wants to go again.

PASSIVE

Hawaii is visited by millions of tourists every year.

visit _____ *go to [a place] for a certain reason*

OBJECT

The cargo ship visits **every major trading port in the
Mediterranean.**
We visited **the clinic** to get Thomas a flu shot.
Ten thousand customers a day visit **our website.**
A food inspector visits **the restaurant** periodically.

PASSIVE

Every nursing home is visited by state inspectors at least twice a year.

PRESENT

I vote	we vote
you vote	you vote
he/she/it votes	they vote

• *He always votes early in the day.*

PAST

I voted	we voted
you voted	you voted
he/she/it voted	they voted

• *I voted by mail this year.*

PRESENT PERFECT ... have | has voted
PAST PERFECT   ... had voted

PRESENT PROGRESSIVE

I am voting	we are voting
you are voting	you are voting
he/she/it is voting	they are voting

• *I am not voting in this election.*

PAST PROGRESSIVE

I was voting	we were voting
you were voting	you were voting
he/she/it was voting	they were voting

• *People were voting in record numbers.*

FUTURE   ... will vote
FUTURE PROGRESSIVE   ... will be voting
FUTURE PERFECT   ... will have voted

PAST PASSIVE

I was voted	we were voted
you were voted	you were voted
he/she/it was voted	they were voted

• *He was voted the new chair of the committee.*

COMPLEMENTS

vote *cast a ballot*

Let's vote.
Are you registered to vote?
I have already voted.
"Vote early and vote often." [A CHICAGO MAYOR]

vote _____ *indicate [a choice] by ballot / other expression of choice*

OBJECT

He always votes **Republican**.
A "yellow dog Democrat" is a voter who would vote **Democratic** even if the candidate were a yellow dog.
Congress voted **stricter limits on campaign contributions**.

PASSIVE

A straight party ticket is not voted as often as it used to be.

against OBJECT

Our representative is voting **against the free trade proposal**.

for OBJECT

The school board voted **for new social studies textbooks**.
Whom will you vote **for** in the mayoral election?

OBJECT + (*to be*) PREDICATE NOUN

The public voted **our restaurant (to be) the best in town**.
The House voted **Nancy (to be) the next speaker**.

PASSIVE

In college, he was voted **(to be) the most likely to succeed**.

INFINITIVE

They voted **to go on strike**.
The kids voted **to have pizza tonight**.
The board voted **to fire the CEO**.

PHRASAL VERBS

vote <u>SEP</u> **down** *defeat, reject*

The Senate voted the amendment down.

vote <u>SEP</u> **in** *elect*

They voted him in by 348 votes.

vote <u>SEP</u> **out** *defeat*

My brother wants to vote all the incumbents out.

EXPRESSIONS

vote with [one's] feet *indicate dissatisfaction by leaving a business without purchasing anything*

The restaurant didn't have vegetarian options, so we voted with our feet.

vote with [one's] wallet/pocketbook *decide on the basis of one's financial interest*

I voted with my wallet and bought the product online: free shipping and no sales tax.

PRESENT

I wait	we wait
you wait	you wait
he/she/it waits	they wait

• *He waits to hear what everyone else says.*

PRESENT PROGRESSIVE

I am waiting	we are waiting
you are waiting	you are waiting
he/she/it is waiting	they are waiting

• *We are waiting for a taxi.*

PAST

I waited	we waited
you waited	you waited
he/she/it waited	they waited

• *I waited at the station for you.*

PAST PROGRESSIVE

I was waiting	we were waiting
you were waiting	you were waiting
he/she/it was waiting	they were waiting

• *They were waiting to speak to someone.*

PRESENT PERFECT ... have | has waited
PAST PERFECT ... had waited

FUTURE ... will wait
FUTURE PROGRESSIVE ... will be waiting
FUTURE PERFECT ... will have waited

PAST PASSIVE

I was waited	we were waited
you were waited	you were waited
he/she/it was waited	they were waited

• *We were finally waited on.*

COMPLEMENTS

wait *stay in a place or do nothing until a certain event occurs*	Come on! We can't wait forever. Hurry up—the Nelsons are waiting. I can't stand waiting like this.
wait *be delayed until later*	The report will have to wait until tomorrow. The job can't wait; do it now.

wait _____ *stay [in a place], remain ready*

ADVERB OF TIME	I can only wait **until 3 o'clock**. Wait **until the light turns green**. Wait **10 minutes** before removing the cake from the pan.
ADVERB OF PLACE	Please wait **here**. A limo will be waiting **at the station**. Please tell our guests to wait **in the garden**. **Where** do you want us to wait?
for OBJECT	We're waiting **for Hilary and DJ**, and then we'll go to Gullifty's.
for OBJECT + INFINITIVE	The driver was waiting **for the rain *to stop***.
INFINITIVE	They are waiting **to take the elevator**. Are you waiting **to use the copier**?

wait _____ *delay* [USUALLY NEGATIVE]

INFINITIVE	I can't wait **to meet them**. Don't wait **to get started**.

PHRASAL VERBS

wait on _____ *serve/assist* *[a customer]*	Have you been waited on yet, sir? I'm waiting on customers in the automotive department. It takes forever to get waited on here.
wait ˢᴱᴾ **out** *defeat by waiting*	The company waited him out, and he eventually signed the contract.
wait up *delay going to bed*	Don't wait up for us; we won't be home until midnight.

EXPRESSIONS

wait on _____ **hand and foot** *serve [someone] extremely well*	She waits on him hand and foot—how awful!

☑	REGULAR
☑	IRREGULAR
☑	REGULAR

wake | wakes · waked · have waked
wake | wakes · woke · have woken
waken | wakens · wakened · have wakened

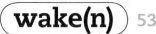 536

PRESENT

I wake	we wake
you wake	you wake
he/she/it wakes	they wake

- *He usually wakes at seven.*

PRESENT PROGRESSIVE

I am waking	we are waking
you are waking	you are waking
he/she/it is waking	they are waking

- *He's waking the neighborhood with his lawn mower.*

PAST

I woke	we woke
you woke	you woke
he/she/it woke	they woke

- *I woke just before the alarm went off.*

PAST PROGRESSIVE

I was waking	we were waking
you were waking	you were waking
he/she/it was waking	they were waking

- *The birds were always waking us at dawn.*

PRESENT PERFECT ... have | has woken/waked
PAST PERFECT ... had woken/waked

FUTURE ... will wake
FUTURE PROGRESSIVE ... will be waking
FUTURE PERFECT ... will have woken/waked

PAST PASSIVE

I was woken	we were woken
you were woken	you were woken
he/she/it was woken	they were woken

- *We were woken in the middle of the night by a dog barking.*

COMPLEMENTS

NOTE: *Wake* and *waken* have the same meanings and the same general uses. They are similar to *awake/awaken* (verb No. 49), with this difference: *Wake* is used with *up* (*Jane woke up at 7 o'clock*), but *awake, awaken,* and *waken* are not.

wake *quit sleeping*	We need to be quiet because the children wake so easily. The patient began wakening from the anesthetic. In the springtime, I wake long before I need to get up.
wake ___ *arouse from sleeping*	
OBJECT	Wake **the children** at eight if they are not up already. Don't wake **me** unless it is an emergency. His snoring would wake **the dead**.
PASSIVE	I was woken by the sound of dripping water.
WH-CLAUSE	The thunderstorm woke **whoever was sleeping**.
wake ___ *stir up*	
OBJECT	Spring woke **the slumbering land**. The injustice woke **a feeling of outrage in the entire community**. His good fortune wakened **feelings of envy in the little village**.

PHRASAL VERBS

wake up *become aware of what is happening*	I hope he wakes up before it's too late. Fritz woke up after the heart attack and started exercising and eating right.
wake _SEP_ **up** *cause to become aware of what is happening*	The advisor woke the mayor up to the danger of rising water. This report will wake citizens up to the importance of alternative energy sources.

EXPRESSIONS

wake up and smell the coffee *become aware of what is happening*	The world has changed, and we must wake up and smell the coffee.

PRESENT

I walk	we walk
you walk	you walk
he/she/it walks	they walk

• *He always walks to work.*

PRESENT PROGRESSIVE

I am walking	we are walking
you are walking	you are walking
he/she/it is walking	they are walking

• *We are walking to the store for ice cream.*

PAST

I walked	we walked
you walked	you walked
he/she/it walked	they walked

• *We walked about three miles this morning.*

PAST PROGRESSIVE

I was walking	we were walking
you were walking	you were walking
he/she/it was walking	they were walking

• *They were walking the kids to school.*

PRESENT PERFECT ... have | has walked
PAST PERFECT ... had walked

FUTURE ... will walk
FUTURE PROGRESSIVE ... will be walking
FUTURE PERFECT ... will have walked

PAST PASSIVE

I was walked	we were walked
you were walked	you were walked
he/she/it was walked	they were walked

• *The horses were walked after they were ridden.*

COMPLEMENTS

walk *move on foot at a normal speed*

After I broke my hip, I couldn't walk for months.
Children first start walking at about the age of one year.

walk *abandon/withdraw from negotiations* [INFORMAL]

If we don't get a better offer, we'll walk.
The merger talks are not succeeding; I think the other company is going to walk.

walk *be released from jail, escape prosecution for a crime* [INFORMAL]

If the police can't find more evidence, he will walk.
He's going to walk after just two months in jail.

walk _____ *go on foot*
ADVERB OF PLACE TO/FROM

They walked **to the barn.**
We walked **home** after the movie.
I don't like the suburbs; you can't walk **anywhere.**

walk _____ *move in/on/over/through on foot*
OBJECT

I've walked **this street** every morning for years.
We walked **two miles,** then turned around.

walk _____ *exercise [an animal]*
OBJECT
PASSIVE

You will have to walk **the dogs** twice a day.
Have the horses been walked?

walk _____ *push [a bicycle, motorcycle] on foot*
OBJECT

He had to walk **his mountain bike** back to the car.
She walked **her bike** while talking to us.

walk _____ *go with / guide on foot*
OBJECT + ADVERB OF PLACE TO/FROM

PASSIVE

The usher walks **the wedding guests** *to their seats.*
I need to walk **my mother** *home.*
Prisoners must be walked *to the gate* by a guard.

PHRASAL VERBS

walk around/back/forth/in/off/out/over/ etc. *walk in a specified direction*

Guess who walked in just now.
Pam screamed at me, then walked off.

walk _____ **around/back/over/**etc. *take/ deliver on foot*

Matt walked Emily back to her dorm room.
Would you walk this package over to the post office?

walk in on _____ *interrupt by entering a room*

He walked in on a meeting of the board of directors.

walk out on _____ *leave, abandon*

We're nearly finished; you can't walk out on us now.

PRESENT

I want	we want
you want	you want
he/she/it wants	they want

• *He wants to know if you are free for lunch.*

PRESENT PROGRESSIVE

I am wanting	we are wanting
you are wanting	you are wanting
he/she/it is wanting	they are wanting

• *He is wanting to go to Paris next summer.*

PAST

I wanted	we wanted
you wanted	you wanted
he/she/it wanted	they wanted

• *The kids wanted pizza for lunch.*

PAST PROGRESSIVE

I was wanting	we were wanting
you were wanting	you were wanting
he/she/it was wanting	they were wanting

• *We were wanting to go out for dinner tonight.*

PRESENT PERFECT ... have | has wanted
PAST PERFECT ... had wanted

FUTURE ... will want
FUTURE PROGRESSIVE ... will be wanting
FUTURE PERFECT ... will have wanted

PAST PASSIVE

I was wanted	we were wanted
you were wanted	you were wanted
he/she/it was wanted	they were wanted

• *The murderer was wanted by the FBI.*

COMPLEMENTS

want _____ *need, wish, desire*

OBJECT	Our daughter wants **her own cell phone.**
	Do you want **fries** with that?
	We want **a driver who knows the area.**
OBJECT + ADVERB OF PLACE	We want **a table** *by the window.*
	Security wants **a guard** *at every entrance.*
	The decorator wants **a rug** *in the entryway.*
OBJECT + INFINITIVE	The doctor wants **you** *to take it easy for a while.*
	I just want **them** *to leave us alone.*
	We want **a cab** *to take us to the airport at four.*
OBJECT + PRESENT PARTICIPLE	The boss wants **them** *working on the landscaping project.*
	I don't want **you** *staying out too late.*
	He doesn't want **anybody** *finding out about our plans.*
OBJECT + PAST PARTICIPLE	I want **the job** *finished by noon.*
	The sheriff wants **him** *placed under arrest.*
	We want **lunch** *served in the conference room.*
INFINITIVE	The kids want **to go home soon.**
	I want **to set the record straight.**
	Does anyone want **to take notes?**
WH-CLAUSE	We all want **what is best for you.**
	He wants **whoever left the message for him.**
	I want **whatever she's having.**

want _____ *desire to capture*

OBJECT	The police want **him** for armed robbery.
PASSIVE	He is wanted by the police in three states.

PHRASAL VERBS

want down/in/out/up/etc. *desire to be in a specified position*	The baby's squirming; he wants down.
	I think the cat wants in.
want out *desire to be freed of a responsibility*	The hours are too long, the work is too hard, and I want out.

PRESENT

I warn	we warn
you warn	you warn
he/she/it warns	they warn

• *The sign warns people to stay away.*

PRESENT PROGRESSIVE

I am warning	we are warning
you are warning	you are warning
he/she/it is warning	they are warning

• *I am warning you.*

PAST

I warned	we warned
you warned	you warned
he/she/it warned	they warned

• *I warned them to be careful.*

PAST PROGRESSIVE

I was warning	we were warning
you were warning	you were warning
he/she/it was warning	they were warning

• *The police were warning drivers to stay off the roads.*

PRESENT PERFECT ... have | has warned
PAST PERFECT ... had warned

FUTURE ... will warn
FUTURE PROGRESSIVE ... will be warning
FUTURE PERFECT ... will have warned

PAST PASSIVE

I was warned	we were warned
you were warned	you were warned
he/she/it was warned	they were warned

• *We were warned about hitchhikers along prison property.*

COMPLEMENTS

warn _____ caution, alert, inform [about a danger, threat]

OBJECT	We warned **the hikers,** but they paid no attention.
	I am warning **you:** Don't do it.
PASSIVE	All of the race participants have been warned.
OBJECT + *about/of* OBJECT	The company warned **doctors** *about a vaccine shortage.*
	Gerry warned **her students** *about plagiarism.*
	Spies warned **the government** *of a terrorist plot.*
OBJECT + INFINITIVE	The guide warned **us** *to watch out for pickpockets.*
	I warned **the children** *to stay on the paths.*
	Police warned **the crowd** *not to enter the building.*
	Mom warned **us** *not to eat too much before swimming.*
PASSIVE	We had been warned *to drink only bottled water.*
OBJECT + THAT-CLAUSE	We warned **them** *that it could snow.*
	The Coast Guard warned **boaters** *that the winds in the channel would be dangerous.*
PASSIVE	Everyone was warned *that there was a risk of cholera in the area.*
OBJECT + WH-INFINITIVE	He warned **us** *what to expect.*
	The guidebook warned **us** *which places to stay away from.*
PASSIVE	The visitors were warned *what topics to avoid.*

warn _____ issue a general caution

THAT-CLAUSE	The Surgeon General has warned **that smoking is dangerous to your health.**
	The sign warned **that violators would be prosecuted.**

PHRASAL VERBS

warn __SEP__ **off** tell [someone] to keep out   The farmer warned the hunters off as soon as they got out of their truck.

PRESENT

I wash	we wash
you wash	you wash
he/she/it washes	they wash

- *He washes his car every weekend.*

PRESENT PROGRESSIVE

I am washing	we are washing
you are washing	you are washing
he/she/it is washing	they are washing

- *The kids are washing the dog in the backyard.*

PAST

I washed	we washed
you washed	you washed
he/she/it washed	they washed

- *I washed and dressed the wound.*

PAST PROGRESSIVE

I was washing	we were washing
you were washing	you were washing
he/she/it was washing	they were washing

- *We were washing dishes when we heard the news.*

PRESENT PERFECT ... have | has washed
PAST PERFECT ... had washed

FUTURE ... will wash
FUTURE PROGRESSIVE ... will be washing
FUTURE PERFECT ... will have washed

PAST PASSIVE

I was washed	we were washed
you were washed	you were washed
he/she/it was washed	they were washed

- *The clothes were washed in hot water.*

COMPLEMENTS

wash *clean/bathe oneself*

Go back and wash!
How often does he wash?
Be sure to wash behind your ears.
I can't wash; there isn't any water.

wash ____ *clean with a liquid and (usually) a cleansing agent*

OBJECT

I washed and dried **my hands**.
We need to wash **the curtains**.
I washed **five loads of laundry** after our camping trip.
Use a baking soda solution to wash **the chrome**.

PASSIVE

The metal is first washed in an acid bath.

wash ____ *splash, sweep, flow*

ADVERB OF PLACE TO/FROM

The waves were washing **over the dock**.
Water was washing **along the deck of the ship**.
Tears washed **down her face**.

wash ____ *carry away by the action of water*

OBJECT + ADVERB OF PLACE TO/FROM

The tide had washed **our little boat** *back onto the beach*.
The storm had washed **debris** *across the road*.

PASSIVE

Sand and mud had been washed *onto our patio*.

PHRASAL VERBS

wash away/down/in/off/out/up/etc. *be carried in a specified direction by the action of water*

The Gummersheimer home washed
away in the floodwater.
A dead whale washed up on the Oregon coast.

wash SEP **away** *remove by the action of water*

The incoming tide washed away the sandcastle we had built.
The bridge was washed out at Maeystown.

wash SEP **away/off/out** *clean [dirt, etc.] from*

Pam washed off the patio chairs.

wash SEP **away/out** *ruin*

Her injury washed away any chance of winning the match.

wash SEP **down** *take a drink in order to help swallow [food]*

She washed the cookies down with a glass of milk.

wash SEP **up** *exhaust, finish*

With the drug conviction, Bubba is all washed up as a player.

I watch	we watch
you watch	you watch
he/she/it watches	they watch

• *He only watches sports on TV.*

PRESENT PROGRESSIVE

I am watching	we are watching
you are watching	you are watching
he/she/it is watching	they are watching

• *He is really watching his weight.*

PAST

I watched	we watched
you watched	you watched
he/she/it watched	they watched

• *We watched our daughter's soccer game.*

PAST PROGRESSIVE

I was watching	we were watching
you were watching	you were watching
he/she/it was watching	they were watching

• *They were watching our house for us.*

PRESENT PERFECT ... have | has watched
PAST PERFECT ... had watched

FUTURE ... will watch
FUTURE PROGRESSIVE ... will be watching
FUTURE PERFECT ... will have watched

PAST PASSIVE

I was watched	we were watched
you were watched	you were watched
he/she/it was watched	they were watched

• *The program was watched by millions of people.*

COMPLEMENTS

watch *look at something carefully*

The movie was too scary for me to watch.
I don't know what happened; I wasn't watching.

watch _____ *look at, observe*

OBJECT

Everybody watched **the folk dancers.**
Does anybody like to watch **his home movies?**
It felt like somebody was watching **us.**

PASSIVE

The game will be watched by all our friends.

OBJECT + BASE-FORM INFINITIVE

They watched **the car in front of them** *slide off the icy road.*
The fans watched **their team** *lose its third game in a row.*

OBJECT + PRESENT PARTICIPLE

We all watched **the men** *working on the power line.*
The children watched **the seaplanes** *landing on the water.*
We watched **the bluebirds** *building their nests.*

WH-CLAUSE

Watch **what happens next.**
I wasn't watching **which key he used to open the door.**

watch _____ *monitor, pay careful attention to*

OBJECT

I am really trying to watch **my weight.**
A financial advisor will watch **your portfolio balance.**
The government is watching **the situation in Iran** closely.

WH-CLAUSE

Watch **what you are doing!**
Watch **where you are driving.**
You need to watch **how much you are spending on
   nonessentials.**

watch _____ *take care of, protect*

OBJECT

Grandma watched **the children** while I was at the store.
Watch **my purse** for me, will you?

PHRASAL VERBS

watch for _____ *look for [someone/
   something that one expects to see]*

We can watch for Doris from the window.
Astronomers were watching for planets in other solar systems.

watch out *be careful*

Watch out! There's a snake!

watch out for / over _____ *protect,
take care of*

The teachers were watching out for the pupils.
Our Great Pyrenees dog was watching over the sheep.

PRESENT

I wear	we wear
you wear	you wear
he/she/it wears	they wear

• He always wears a coat and tie.

PRESENT PROGRESSIVE

I am wearing	we are wearing
you are wearing	you are wearing
he/she/it is wearing	they are wearing

• I am wearing a skirt and sweater to the concert.

PAST

I wore	we wore
you wore	you wore
he/she/it wore	they wore

• She wore her little black dress to the party.

PAST PROGRESSIVE

I was wearing	we were wearing
you were wearing	you were wearing
he/she/it was wearing	they were wearing

• What were they wearing?

PRESENT PERFECT ... have | has worn
PAST PERFECT ... had worn

FUTURE ... will wear
FUTURE PROGRESSIVE ... will be wearing
FUTURE PERFECT ... will have worn

PAST PASSIVE

I was worn	we were worn
you were worn	you were worn
he/she/it was worn	they were worn

• In those days, white was never worn after Labor Day.

COMPLEMENTS

wear remain in good condition after much use
That fabric won't wear very well.
The carpet in the hall will wear for years.

wear _____ have/carry on one's body
OBJECT
The kids wear **jeans** most of the time.
Politicians felt it necessary to wear **flag pins**.
Men are required to wear **ties** when meeting with clients.
Mary wears **bifocals** now.
PASSIVE
Casual clothing is worn nearly everywhere.
WH-CLAUSE
The tribe only wore **what they themselves produced**.
I give up; wear **whatever you want to**.

wear _____ have [a certain hairstyle]
OBJECT + ADVERB OF MANNER
She wore **her hair** *off the shoulder*.
He wore **his hair** *in a ponytail*.
PASSIVE
Her hair was worn *in a huge Afro*.

wear _____ have [a certain facial expression]
OBJECT
He was wearing **a silly grin** when he made the announcement.
His face wears **a permanent scowl**.
Why are you wearing **such a sad face**?

wear _____ damage/erode gradually, usually by friction
OBJECT
Wagon wheels wore **ruts** along the Oregon Trail.
The Mississippi River wore **a new channel** east of Kaskaskia.
PASSIVE
A path had been worn through the forest.

PHRASAL VERBS

wear SEP **down** make weak/tired
The 12-hour days are wearing the staff down.

wear off go away gradually
The effects of the painkiller wore off after a few hours.

wear on continue, pass
The meeting wore on into the early hours of the morning.
It got more cloudy as the day wore on.

wear out become exhausted/useless
The tires have worn out on my pickup truck.

wear SEP **out** use until exhausted
Our son has worn out his winter coat.

wear SEP **out** exhaust, tire out
Shopping all day with his wife wore him out.

weave

weave | weaves · wove · have woven
weave | weaves · weaved · have weaved

☑ IRREGULAR
☑ REGULAR

PRESENT

I weave	we weave
you weave	you weave
he/she/it weaves	they weave

• *She weaves baskets from birch bark.*

PRESENT PROGRESSIVE

I am weaving	we are weaving
you are weaving	you are weaving
he/she/it is weaving	they are weaving

• *The children are weaving simple placemats.*

PAST

I wove	we wove
you wove	you wove
he/she/it wove	they wove

• *The spider wove a web across the doorway.*

PAST PROGRESSIVE

I was weaving	we were weaving
you were weaving	you were weaving
he/she/it was weaving	they were weaving

• *They were weaving a wool rug.*

PRESENT PERFECT ... have | has woven
PAST PERFECT ... had woven

FUTURE ... will weave
FUTURE PROGRESSIVE ... will be weaving
FUTURE PERFECT ... will have woven

PAST PASSIVE

—	—
—	—
it was woven	they were woven

• *These wall hangings were woven by hand.*

COMPLEMENTS

NOTE: The regular past form *weaved* is used only in the sense "move in and out / side to side"; *wove* and *woven* are used in all other senses.

weave *pass threads/strips/etc. over and under one another to form something*

They are teaching the students how to weave.
Children learn by watching their mothers weave.
In some cultures, only men weave.

weave *move in and out / side to side*

A red SUV weaved through the bridge traffic.

weave _____ *pass [threads/strips/etc.] over and under one another [to form something]*

OBJECT

They wove **palm fronds** to make a thatched roof.
I wove **my fingers** to make a step for her.
We wove **the reeds** into a simple boat.

weave _____ *form by passing threads/strips/etc. over and under one another*

OBJECT

The mill wove **beautiful linen tablecloths.**
Every society on earth has woven **some kind of basket.**
The women wove **a crown from flowers they had picked.**

PASSIVE

A crude filter was woven from plant stalks.

weave _____ *combine to make a whole*

OBJECT

A good story weaves **a number of plot lines.**
The poem weaves **the themes of love and loss**
in 19th-century England.

weave _____ *make by combining into a whole*

OBJECT

"Oh! what **a tangled web** we weave
When first we practice to deceive." [SIR WALTER SCOTT]

PASSIVE

Wagner's operas are woven from many musical themes.

weave _____ *form [a web] [OF A SPIDER]*

OBJECT

A spider wove **a beautiful web** between those two trees.

PRESENT

I wed	we wed
you wed	you wed
he/she/it weds	they wed

• *His opera weds two different traditions.*

PRESENT PROGRESSIVE

I am wedding	we are wedding
you are wedding	you are wedding
he/she/it is wedding	they are wedding

• *The composer is wedding folk and rock music.*

PAST

I wed	we wed
you wed	you wed
he/she/it wed	they wed

• *They wed as soon as they graduated.*

PAST PROGRESSIVE

I was wedding	we were wedding
you were wedding	you were wedding
he/she/it was wedding	they were wedding

• *He was wedding the design to other brochures.*

PRESENT PERFECT ... have | has wed
PAST PERFECT ... had wed

FUTURE ... will wed
FUTURE PROGRESSIVE ... will be wedding
FUTURE PERFECT ... will have wed/wedded

PAST PASSIVE

I was wed	we were wed
you were wed	you were wed
he/she/it was wed	they were wed

• *The couple was wed by her family's minister.*

COMPLEMENTS

wed *marry*

When did they wed?
John and Marcia wed after a tumultuous engagement.
My parents wed in Hawaii when Dad was in the Navy.

wed _____ *marry*
　OBJECT

She wed **her childhood sweetheart.**
Whom did she finally wed?
My father wed **my mother** in 1982.

wed _____ *perform the marriage ceremony for*
　OBJECT

I have wed **hundreds of people** over the years.
Reverend Gerry wed **your parents.**

　PASSIVE

They were wed in the garden, if I remember correctly.

wed _____ *unite, join closely*
　OBJECT

Fusion cuisine weds **cooking styles from all over the world.**
The building weds **Spanish and modernist styles.**
His art weds **realism and postmodernism.**

PRESENT

I weep	we weep
you weep	you weep
he/she/it weeps	they weep

• *He always weeps at weddings.*

PRESENT PROGRESSIVE

I am weeping	we are weeping
you are weeping	you are weeping
he/she/it is weeping	they are weeping

• *She is weeping uncontrollably.*

PAST

I wept	we wept
you wept	you wept
he/she/it wept	they wept

• *They wept when they heard the news.*

PAST PROGRESSIVE

I was weeping	we were weeping
you were weeping	you were weeping
he/she/it was weeping	they were weeping

• *The children were all weeping.*

PRESENT PERFECT	… have | has wept
PAST PERFECT	… had wept

FUTURE	… will weep
FUTURE PROGRESSIVE	… will be weeping
FUTURE PERFECT	… will have wept

PAST PASSIVE

—	—
—	—
it was wept	they were wept

• *No tears were wept for him.*

(**COMPLEMENTS**)

weep *shed tears, cry*	You have to take time to weep.
	The whole family was weeping during the service.
	She wept every time she thought of the accident.
weep *give off drops of liquid*	The walls were weeping in the humid air.
	Aloe plants weep if you cut them.
	The damp air weeps when it comes into contact with the cold metal.
weep _____ *shed [tears]*	
OBJECT	Weep **no tears** for me.
	He wept **bitter tears** for what he had done.
PASSIVE	Endless tears were wept over such a senseless death.

PRESENT

I wet	we wet
you wet	you wet
he/she/it wets	they wet

• *She always wets her lips before she speaks.*

PRESENT PROGRESSIVE

I am wetting	we are wetting
you are wetting	you are wetting
he/she/it is wetting	they are wetting

• *She is wetting her hair to keep it from blowing.*

PAST

I wet/wetted	we wet/wetted
you wet/wetted	you wet/wetted
he/she/it wet/wetted	they wet/wetted

• *He wet his fingers before taking the ball.*

PAST PROGRESSIVE

I was wetting	we were wetting
you were wetting	you were wetting
he/she/it was wetting	they were wetting

• *They were wetting the canvas to make the tent cooler.*

PRESENT PERFECT ... have | has wet/wetted
PAST PERFECT ... had wet/wetted

FUTURE ... will wet
FUTURE PROGRESSIVE ... will be wetting
FUTURE PERFECT ... will have wet

PAST PASSIVE

—	—
—	—
it was wet/wetted	they were wet/wetted

• *Once the insulation was wetted by the storm, it was useless.*

(COMPLEMENTS)

wet _____ *moisten, dampen*

OBJECT
The barber always wets **my hair** before he cuts it.
You should wet **the cork** before putting it back in the bottle.
Lightly wet **the metal** with oil so the engine won't smoke.

PASSIVE
The oily pavement had been wet by the mist, making it slippery.

wet _____ *urinate in/on*

OBJECT
The baby always wets **his diaper** at the most inconvenient time.
We will need to change his pajamas; he wet **them** again.
One of the kids wet **the bed**.

(PHRASAL VERBS)

wet _SEP_ **down** *put water on*
After every game, they wet the infield down.

(EXPRESSIONS)

wet [one's] whistle *take a drink*
Thirsty? Here's some lemonade for you
to wet your whistle.

PRESENT

I win	we win
you win	you win
he/she/it wins	they win

- *He wins most card games he plays.*

PRESENT PROGRESSIVE

I am winning	we are winning
you are winning	you are winning
he/she/it is winning	they are winning

- *We're winning!*

PAST

I won	we won
you won	you won
he/she/it won	they won

- *I won first place in the math contest.*

PAST PROGRESSIVE

I was winning	we were winning
you were winning	you were winning
he/she/it was winning	they were winning

- *They were winning most of their games.*

PRESENT PERFECT	... have	has won
PAST PERFECT	... had won

FUTURE	... will win
FUTURE PROGRESSIVE	... will be winning
FUTURE PERFECT	... will have won

PAST PASSIVE

I was won	we were won
you were won	you were won
he/she/it was won	they were won

- *The election was won by superior organization.*

COMPLEMENTS

win *be victorious in a contest/competition*

I never win.
They could win if they played their very best.
Who's winning?

win ___ *be victorious in [a contest, competition]*

OBJECT

Alice and Albert won **the dance competition**.
Barack Obama won **the 2008 presidential election**.
Heather always wins **the argument**.

PASSIVE

The game was won in the last minute.

win ___ *receive as the result of a contest/conflict/bet*

OBJECT

We won **a week's vacation in Hawaii**.
After bitter fighting, they finally won **the fortress**.
They hope to win **the Rose Bowl** this year.
I almost won **the jackpot in last week's Lotto**.

INDIRECT OBJECT + DIRECT OBJECT

You could win *yourself* a prize.
The victory won *us* **a little more time**.
Excellent coaching won *them* **the championship**.

for PARAPHRASE

You could win **a prize** *for yourself*.
The victory won **a little more time** *for us*.
Excellent coaching won **the championship** *for them*.

win ___ *gain [affection, support, admiration, etc.]*

OBJECT

Ministers have to win **a congregation's respect**.
The comedian won **the audience's applause**.
Their goal was to win **the hearts and minds of the people**.
Faint heart never won **fair lady**. [PROVERB]

PHRASAL VERBS

win out *be finally victorious*

It took six months, but our proposal
won out.

win ___SEP___ **over** *convert, persuade*

The president won congressional leaders over to his point
of view.

PRESENT		PRESENT PROGRESSIVE	
I wind	we wind	I am winding	we are winding
you wind	you wind	you are winding	you are winding
he/she/it winds	they wind	he/she/it is winding	they are winding

• *The path winds across the hills for miles.*   • *The press conference is winding down.*

PAST		PAST PROGRESSIVE	
I wound	we wound	I was winding	we were winding
you wound	you wound	you were winding	you were winding
he/she/it wound	they wound	he/she/it was winding	they were winding

• *She wound the cloth around her head.*   • *She was winding the clock with a key.*

PRESENT PERFECT ... have | has wound
PAST PERFECT ... had wound

FUTURE ... will wind
FUTURE PROGRESSIVE ... will be winding
FUTURE PERFECT ... will have wound

PAST PASSIVE

I was wound	we were wound
you were wound	you were wound
he/she/it was wound	they were wound

• *The rope was wound around a tree trunk.*

NOTE: The verb *wind*, which rhymes with *kind*, is presented here; its irregular past form *wound* rhymes with *sound*. The regular verb *wind*, which rhymes with *sinned* and means "to make out of breath," is rarely used.

COMPLEMENTS

wind _____ coil, move in twists and turns

ADVERB OF PLACE TO/FROM

We wound **in and out through the trees.**
The path wound **around the hill.**
Vines wound **around the old oak tree.**
The river winds **through a maze of canyons.**
The wire wound **across the ceiling and out the window.**

wind _____ wrap, cover by circling

OBJECT + ADVERB OF PLACE TO/FROM

To make an electromagnet, wind **wire *around an iron core*.**
He wound **his shirt *over his fist*** and broke the window.
I wound **the rope *around my waist*** and began to climb down.
She wound **her arms *around her daughter*** and consoled her.

PASSIVE

Her long hair had been wound *into a coil on her head*.

wind _____ tighten the spring of

OBJECT

Did you remember to wind **the clock?**
Wind **the top** and put it on the floor.

PASSIVE

In old cars, the starter was wound by hand.

wind _____ wrap around a center/core

OBJECT + ADVERB OF PLACE TO/FROM

We wound **the videotape *to where the game started*.**
She is winding **the yarn *into a center-pull ball*.**

PASSIVE

The film had been wound *to the end of the reel*.

PHRASAL VERBS

wind along/around/down/up/etc.
twist in a specified direction

The creek winds along for several miles.

wind down *come slowly to an end*

The party was winding down by midnight.

wind down *relax*

Mike was beginning to wind down after a hectic day at work.

wind up *end*

The conference is scheduled to wind up at noon.
The acrobat wound up in the hospital with a broken leg.
They wound up living in Paris for the rest of their lives.

wind __SEP__ up *bring to an end*

Let's wind this meeting up, okay?

PRESENT		PRESENT PROGRESSIVE	
I wish	we wish	I am wishing	we are wishing
you wish	you wish	you are wishing	you are wishing
he/she/it wishes	they wish	he/she/it is wishing	they are wishing

• *He wishes to be alone for a while.*   • *You are wishing for too much.*

PAST		PAST PROGRESSIVE	
I wished	we wished	I was wishing	we were wishing
you wished	you wished	you were wishing	you were wishing
he/she/it wished	they wished	he/she/it was wishing	they were wishing

• *I wished that I had done it differently.*   • *We were all wishing for better weather.*

PRESENT PERFECT … have | has wished
PAST PERFECT … had wished

FUTURE … will wish
FUTURE PROGRESSIVE … will be wishing
FUTURE PERFECT … will have wished

PAST PASSIVE	
I was wished	we were wished
you were wished	you were wished
he/she/it was wished	they were wished

• *I was wished a happy birthday by everyone.*

COMPLEMENTS

wish *long for / desire something*   Dorothy closed her eyes and wished.
Don't wish, act!

wish ＿＿ *desire/want [something that cannot or probably will not happen]*

THAT-CLAUSE   I wish **that I were more prepared.**
We wished **that the rain would stop before we got to Pittsburgh.**
Little Bo Peep wished **that she had taken better care of her sheep.**
Stymie wished **that Cotton was a monkey.**
I wish **that I were a rich man.**

wish ＿＿ *have/express a desire*

OBJECT + to be PREDICATE NOUN   We all wished **the play** *to be a smash hit.*
I wished **the winter** *to be a mild one.*

OBJECT + to be PREDICATE ADJECTIVE   I just wished **the project** *to be ready on time.*
We all wished **the young couple** *to be happy.*
They wished **the evaluation** *to be favorable.*

INDIRECT OBJECT + DIRECT OBJECT   We wished *him* a pleasant flight.
Everyone wished *the graduates* successful careers.
The doctor wished *his patient* a swift recovery.

for OBJECT   He was wishing **for a quick response from the company.**
What are you wishing **for?**
They wished **for more time to complete the project.**

(*for*) OBJECT + INFINITIVE   I didn't wish **(for)** them *to go to so much trouble.*
Do you wish **(for)** the caterer *to prepare a new menu*?
We wished **(for)** a taxi *to be here at seven.*

INFINITIVE   She wishes **to say a few words.**
They wish **to make a reservation for dinner.**
We wish **to apologize for being so late.**

PHRASAL VERBS

wish ＿＿ **on** [someone] *want [something bad] to happen to [someone]* [USUALLY NEGATIVE]   I wouldn't wish cancer on my worst enemy.

PRESENT

I wonder	we wonder
you wonder	you wonder
he/she/it wonders	they wonder

• *He wonders if you would like to join us.*

PRESENT PROGRESSIVE

I am wondering	we are wondering
you are wondering	you are wondering
he/she/it is wondering	they are wondering

• *We're wondering whether it is going to rain.*

PAST

I wondered	we wondered
you wondered	you wondered
he/she/it wondered	they wondered

• *I wondered what had happened to you.*

PAST PROGRESSIVE

I was wondering	we were wondering
you were wondering	you were wondering
he/she/it was wondering	they were wondering

• *They were wondering whom to call in an emergency.*

PRESENT PERFECT … have | has wondered
PAST PERFECT … had wondered

FUTURE … will wonder
FUTURE PROGRESSIVE … will be wondering
FUTURE PERFECT … will have wondered

PAST PASSIVE

—	—
—	—
it was wondered	they were wondered

• *His unexpected success was much wondered at.*

COMPLEMENTS

wonder _____ *want / be curious to know*

about OBJECT

We were wondering **about the price of gas.**
Did you wonder **about the car's safety features?**
The boss was wondering **about Elaine's ability to do the job.**

WH-CLAUSE

I wonder **who she is.**
Everyone wondered **what went wrong.**
John is wondering **where he left his car keys.**
I wonder **why she never answered my e-mail.**
We wondered **how much it was going to cost.**

WH-INFINITIVE

My parents were wondering **what to do while the grandkids were at school.**
Janet was wondering **when to break the news.**
I wondered **how to respond to such an awkward question.**

if/whether CLAUSE

I wonder **if we can afford a new car.**
I wonder **if Holly is coming home for Christmas.**
I wonder **whether we will arrive on time.**

if/whether CLAUSE [USED TO INTRODUCE A POLITE QUESTION]

I wonder **if you would like to have dinner with me.**
I wonder **if that was a good idea.**
I wonder **whether we would be more comfortable indoors.**
I wonder **whether we should call.**

wonder _____ *be surprised, marvel*

at OBJECT

We wondered **at his reluctance to attend the meeting.**
Others wondered **at Arianna's conversion to liberalism.**

THAT-CLAUSE

I don't wonder **that he would be so upset.**
We didn't wonder **that it was such a big deal for them.**
Do you wonder **that they canceled their vacation?**
I don't wonder **that she would feel that way.**

work _____ *cause to function at/near capacity*
    OBJECT

The coach really worked **the defense** today.
We worked **the pump** as hard as we could, getting all the water out of the basement.
During an emergency, your job is to work **the phones**.

work _____ *knead, massage, cause to move by manipulation*
    OBJECT

Work **the clay and water** until it is a smooth paste.
The dentist worked **the tooth** back and forth to loosen it.
I worked **my calf muscle** until it stopped cramping.

─────────────────────────────────────── (**PHRASAL VERBS**)

work around _____ *avoid [a problem, situation] without eliminating it*

We can work around your busy schedule.

work at/on _____ *try to do [something] better*

The linebacker needs to work at running backward.
Jimmy needs to work on his spelling.

work away *continue to work hard*

Carl worked away at the translation for years.

work _SEP_ **down** *reduce*

Dad worked his weight down to 190.
She worked the debt down to $500.

work for _____ *work as a replacement for*

I'm working for Janey this week; she's on vacation.

work _SEP_ **in** *make time available for*

We can work you in to see the doctor at 3:45.

work _SEP_ **in** *include, put in*

The author worked in a reference to her cat.

work _SEP_ **off** *get rid of through effort*

She worked off the last of her student loans.
Mike worked off 20 pounds in three months.

work on _____ *have the desired effect on*

This drug doesn't work on all allergy sufferers.

work on _____ *try to persuade*

I'll work on Eli to attend the conference.

work on _____ *be engaged in producing*

The designer is working on a new website.

work on _____ *tinker with, repair*

Artie is working on his old Ford truck.

work out *exercise*

Don works out at the gym three days a week.

work out *happen, develop*

How did the job interview work out?

work _SEP_ **out** *develop, agree on*

They worked out a plan to repay the loan.

work out to _____ *amount to*

The bill works out to $8.53 for each of us.

work _SEP_ **up** *excite, arouse*
[OFTEN PASSIVE]

Don't work yourself up over nothing.
The speaker got the crowd all worked up.

work _SEP_ **up** *stimulate, develop*

Go grocery shopping if you want to work up an appetite.
Will Lennie work up the courage to ask Barbara out?

work _SEP_ **up** *prepare, often quickly*

Donna, can you work up the unemployment figures?

work up to _____ *advance to, reach*

My son worked up to assistant manager in two years.

─────────────────────────────────────── (**EXPRESSIONS**)

work [one's] way along/into/out of/over/through/up/etc. _____ *move/proceed in a specified direction*

The mountaineer worked his way along the cliff's edge.
Jimmy worked his way up to DC-9 captain.

work it/things out *solve one's problems*

We hope that the young couple can work things out.

work like a beaver/dog/horse *work very hard*

Gordon works like a horse, even on weekends.

work like a charm *function perfectly*

The new page layout software works like a charm.

work [one's] fingers to the bone *work very hard*

She's working her fingers to the bone so her children have enough to eat.

top
40
verb

PRESENT

I work	we work
you work	you work
he/she/it works	they work

- *He works at home one day a week.*

PRESENT PROGRESSIVE

I am working	we are working
you are working	you are working
he/she/it is working	they are working

- *I'm working late tonight.*

PAST

I worked	we worked
you worked	you worked
he/she/it worked	they worked

- *The phone worked the last time I used it.*

PAST PROGRESSIVE

I was working	we were working
you were working	you were working
he/she/it was working	they were working

- *He was working the night shift.*

PRESENT PERFECT ... have | has worked
PAST PERFECT   ... had worked

FUTURE   ... will work
FUTURE PROGRESSIVE ... will be working
FUTURE PERFECT   ... will have worked

PAST PASSIVE

I was worked	we were worked
you were worked	you were worked
he/she/it was worked	they were worked

- *The dough was worked until it was smooth and elastic.*

(**COMPLEMENTS**)

work *labor, toil*	Don't bother us—we're working.
work *function properly* [OF A MACHINE]	The printer was finally working. Cell phones won't work here in the valley. I couldn't get the snow blower to work this morning. Are the lights working?
work *succeed* [OF A PLAN, STRATEGY]	The new marketing campaign seems to have worked. Our redesigned kitchen works really well. His get-rich-quick schemes never work.
work ____ *labor, toil, have [a job]*	
ADVERB OF TIME	My boyfriend works **from nine to five**. **How many hours** do you work in an average week?
ADVERB OF PLACE	Christopher works **in book publishing**. Jean is still working **at a lawyer's office**. I worked **on a farm** when I was younger.
ADVERB OF MANNER	They have been working **pretty hard**. The sculptor works **in wood and metal**.
OBJECT	She works **two jobs** to make ends meet. Joe and Frank were working **the day shift** out of homicide.
as OBJECT	Danny worked **as a waiter** in college. Frederic was working **as a type designer**.
work ____ *operate [a machine]*	
OBJECT	I couldn't use his car because I can't work **a stick shift**. Do you know how to work **an abacus**? Can you work **this DVD player**? The warehouse job involves working **a forklift**.
work ____ *solve [a puzzle, problem]*	
OBJECT	I couldn't work **my daughter's algebra problems**. Do you like to work **crossword puzzles**? Tim works **Sudoku puzzles** during his lunch hour.

PRESENT

I worry	we worry
you worry	you worry
he/she/it worries	they worry

• *He worries too much.*

PRESENT PROGRESSIVE

I am worrying	we are worrying
you are worrying	you are worrying
he/she/it is worrying	they are worrying

• *If you aren't worrying, you aren't paying attention.*

PAST

I worried	we worried
you worried	you worried
he/she/it worried	they worried

• *We worried that we were late for the movie.*

PAST PROGRESSIVE

I was worrying	we were worrying
you were worrying	you were worrying
he/she/it was worrying	they were worrying

• *We were worrying because you didn't call.*

PRESENT PERFECT ... have | has worried
PAST PERFECT ... had worried

FUTURE ... will worry
FUTURE PROGRESSIVE ... will be worrying
FUTURE PERFECT ... will have worried

PAST PASSIVE

I was worried	we were worried
you were worried	you were worried
he/she/it was worried	they were worried

• *I was worried by his odd response.*

―――――――――――――――――――――――――――(**COMPLEMENTS**)――

worry *be anxious/concerned*

There is good reason to worry.
I never worry.
"Don't Worry, Be Happy." [BOBBY MCFERRIN SONG]

worry _____ *cause to be anxious/concerned*

OBJECT

The financial news is worrying **everyone**.
Please don't worry **your mother** now.
The approaching storm front worried **all of us**.

PASSIVE

The doctor was worried by his patient's high fever.

worry _____ *be anxious/concerned*

about OBJECT

Floyd worries **about his retirement fund**.
They are worried **about the neighbor's pit bull**.
We were worried **about roof damage after the storm**.

about PRESENT PARTICIPLE

She worries **about having colon cancer**.
He's always worried **about doing the right thing**.
We are worried **about being able to afford health care**.

THAT-CLAUSE

I worry **that we have overcommitted ourselves**.
Nobody worries **that they have too much money**.
She's worried **that their horses aren't getting enough exercise**.

PRESENT

I wrap	we wrap
you wrap	you wrap
he/she/it wraps	they wrap

- *He always wraps gifts on Christmas Eve.*

PRESENT PROGRESSIVE

I am wrapping	we are wrapping
you are wrapping	you are wrapping
he/she/it is wrapping	they are wrapping

- *We are wrapping presents in the spare bedroom.*

PAST

I wrapped	we wrapped
you wrapped	you wrapped
he/she/it wrapped	they wrapped

- *I wrapped duct tape around the pipe.*

PAST PROGRESSIVE

I was wrapping	we were wrapping
you were wrapping	you were wrapping
he/she/it was wrapping	they were wrapping

- *They were wrapping the children in blankets.*

PRESENT PERFECT ... have | has wrapped
PAST PERFECT ... had wrapped

FUTURE ... will wrap
FUTURE PROGRESSIVE ... will be wrapping
FUTURE PERFECT ... will have wrapped

PAST PASSIVE

I was wrapped	we were wrapped
you were wrapped	you were wrapped
he/she/it was wrapped	they were wrapped

- *His swollen ankle was tightly wrapped.*

COMPLEMENTS

wrap *cover something by winding/folding material around it*

Don't wrap so tight; the paper is tearing.
We can wrap after the kids go to bed.

wrap _____ *cover by winding/folding material around it*

OBJECT

We need to wrap **all of the wine glasses**.
I'll wrap **the baby** while you get the car.
I wrapped **my sore wrist** as well as I could.

PASSIVE

The letters had been neatly wrapped in a lacy pink handkerchief.

PHRASAL VERBS

wrap around _____ *go around*

The line of ticket holders went down the street and wrapped around the corner.

wrap SEP **up** *complete, finalize*

The director has wrapped up the shooting of his latest film.
They don't know when they can wrap the job up.

wrap [someone] up in _____ *engross/ absorb [someone] in*

Angela is wrapped up in a detective novel.
He got wrapped up in his design project and missed dinner.

EXPRESSIONS

wrap [one's]/the [vehicle] around _____ *drive into, usually at high speed*

Derek wrapped his SUV around a tree.

wrap [someone] around [one's] (little) finger *have total control over*

Delilah had Samson wrapped around her finger.
His granddaughter can wrap him around her little finger.

PRESENT

I write	we write
you write	you write
he/she/it writes	they write

• *He never writes anymore.*

PRESENT PROGRESSIVE

I am writing	we are writing
you are writing	you are writing
he/she/it is writing	they are writing

• *I am writing as fast as I can.*

PAST

I wrote	we wrote
you wrote	you wrote
he/she/it wrote	they wrote

• *Jane Austen wrote* Emma *before 1816.*

PAST PROGRESSIVE

I was writing	we were writing
you were writing	you were writing
he/she/it was writing	they were writing

• *He was writing a letter to Georgiana.*

PRESENT PERFECT … have | has written
PAST PERFECT … had written

FUTURE … will write
FUTURE PROGRESSIVE … will be writing
FUTURE PERFECT … will have written

PAST PASSIVE

I was written	we were written
you were written	you were written
he/she/it was written	they were written

• *The letter was written to a family friend.*

COMPLEMENTS

write *form letters/words with a pen/pencil/etc.*	His arthritis made it hard for him to write. Please write neatly.
write *compose and send a letter*	The kids promised to write from camp as soon as they could. People don't write nearly as much as they used to.
write _____ *compose and send [a letter]*	
OBJECT	John and Abigail Adams wrote **each other** frequently.
INDIRECT OBJECT + DIRECT OBJECT	John wrote *Marcia* **a touching letter**.
to PARAPHRASE	John wrote **a touching letter** *to Marcia*.
write _____ *compose [a text, work]*	
OBJECT	Donizetti apparently wrote *The Elixir of Love* in three weeks. Mark Twain wrote **hilariously funny letters to the editor.**
write _____ *put in writing*	
OBJECT	I wrote **a check for $40.** The doctor wrote **a prescription for an antibiotic.** Please write **your name and address** in the space provided.
write _____ *express/communicate in written form*	
(OBJECT +) THAT-CLAUSE	Darwin wrote **that species evolve over the course of generations through natural selection.** He wrote *me* **that they might move back to California.**
(OBJECT +) WH-CLAUSE	She wrote **how the product should be introduced.** Teddy wrote *his parents* **what he thought of the camp food.**
DIRECT QUOTATION	**"There was never a good war,"** wrote Benjamin Franklin, **"or a bad peace."**

PHRASAL VERBS

write SEP **down** *make a note/record of*	The secretary wrote down everything she said.
write SEP **off** *give up on, cancel*	The bank wrote off the $8,000 loan.
write SEP **off** *consider lost, hopeless, etc.*	The hotel manager wrote off the missing towels. Many fans write the Cubs off before September.
write SEP **off** *deduct from one's taxes*	We wrote the computer off as an itemized deduction.
write SEP **out** *spell out [a number, abbreviation]*	Write out "621" as "six hundred twenty-one."